ENGLAND
THE FOOTBALL FACTS

ENGLAND
THE FOOTBALL FACTS

DEAN HAYES

Michael O'Mara Books Limited

First published in Great Britain in 2006 by
Michael O'Mara Books Limited
9 Lion Yard
Tremadoc Road
London SW4 7NQ

A CIP catalogue record for this book is available from the British Library

ISBN (10 digit): 1-84317-188-0
ISBN (13 digit): 978-1-84317-188-1

1 3 5 7 9 10 8 6 4 2

www.mombooks.com

Designed and typeset by E-Type
Plates section designed by Design 23

Printed and bound in England by Clays Ltd, St Ives plc

Photograph Acknowledgements

Getty Images – 1 (*above left*), 7 (*above*), 8 (*below*), 10 (*above left* and *below left*),
15 (*below right*); S&G/Empics/Alpha – 2 (*above*), 4 (*above*), 5 (*both*), 6 (*above*),
12 (*below*); Barnaby's Picture Library/Empics – 4 (*below*); PA/Empics – 9 (*above right*);
Neal Simpson/Empics – 9 (*below right*); Peter Robinson/Empics – 10 (*below right*),
11 (*above left*); 12 (*above*), 13 (*above*); Phil O'Brien/Empics – 11 (*above right*); Michael
Stephens/PA/Empics – 11 (*below left*); John Stillwell/PA/Empics – 11 (*below right*);
Daniel Motz/Empics – 13 (*below*); Roberto Pfeil/AP/Empics – 14 (*above*); Adam
Butler/PA/Empics – 14 (*below left*); Matthew Ashton/Empics – 15 (*above*); Mike
Egerton/Empics – 16 (*above left*); Tony Marshall – 16 (*above right*); Simon
Bellis/Empics – 16 (*below left*).

The photographs on pages 1 (*below right*), 2 (*below left*), 3 (*all*), 6 (*below left* and *below
right*), 7 (*below left* and *below right*), 8 (*above*), 9 (*above left* and *below left*) and 10 (*above
right*) are provided by the author, courtesy of the *Lancashire Evening Post*.

Author's note

Every effort has been made by the author and editor to ensure the
accuracy of each fact and statistic in this book. In the unfortunate event
of any errors, however, I offer sincere apologies in advance.

CONTENTS

INTRODUCTION

England: The Football Facts is a unique work of reference about the English national football team, providing an in-depth history of all aspects of the national game.

It features full details of every England player since 1872, including date of birth, position, clubs played for, appearances and goals scored; complete match-by-match records from 1872 to the present day with full teams plus clubs, results and goalscorers; a history of the England team through the years; England's managers appraised from the early selection committee through to Sven-Göran Eriksson; famous featured match reports from the archives and Home International, European Championship and World Cup record sections; and interspersed throughout the text is a selection of fascinating facts and trivia.

Who could possibly have imagined that when the first England side ran on to the field against Scotland at the West of Scotland Cricket Club at Hamilton Crescent, in Glasgow on 30 November 1872, they were setting the scene for the world's largest spectator sport? Now, 134 years later, the mother country of the world's greatest game may no longer enjoy total supremacy, but England continues to be the side that every country is desperate to beat.

From the early clashes against the Scots to the titanic battles with Germany and the devastating defeats against the United States and Hungary in the 1950s, through the highs and lows of thirteen World Cup campaigns, there has never been a dull moment in England's colourful history.

As a proud supporter of England's heritage, and its current standing as one of the leading football teams in the world, I hope that all England football fans will find my book, illustrated with many rare pictures, not only a veritable mine of information but also an indispensable work of reference.

Dean Hayes, March 2006

1 A HISTORY OF THE ENGLAND TEAM

Charles W. Alcock, the Football Association's first Secretary, can be credited as the father of the England national team, for it was his 1870 letter to *The Sportsman* newspaper – in which he invited men from England and Scotland to represent their countries at football – that sparked off a series of matches between Englishmen and Scotsmen. Initially, all these games were played in England, with players drawn from residents of the home country. However, two years after Alcock's original correspondence, it was decided that a true test of the two nations' footballing ability could only be gauged if the Scots drew their players from north of the border.

Thus, on 30 November 1872, the world's first full international football match was played at the west of Scotland's cricket ground at Partick in Glasgow. The inaugural result was a disappointing goalless draw – a scoreline repeated only twice since then (in April 1970 and May 1987) in all matches between England and Scotland.

The fixture soon became an annual event with home advantage alternating between the two sides every other year. Of the first ten matches played, England only managed to win two, and it was because of this dismal early record that the Corinthians Football Club was later developed.

Concerned at the national team's form, the FA's Honorary Secretary 'Pa' Jackson created the Corinthians in October 1882 to draw the best talent from the public schools and universities in an effort to improve the country's standing. The members of the Corinthians, which was not a competitive side, provided more than fifty players for England.

Wales, and later Ireland, joined the football family and soon began arranging annual matches against their English and Scottish brethren. Ireland's first match against England in Belfast in February 1882 saw the biggest result achieved by England's full international side, 13–0, with debutant Oliver Vaughton scoring five times.

With the four nations playing each other on a regular basis, the first Home International Championship series was instigated in 1884 with Scotland the first winners. In all, there have been eighty-eight completed annual series, during which England were outright winners on thirty-four occasions. The last was played in 1984 with Northern Ireland becoming the final British champions.

Even in the early days, the England v Scotland game was regarded as the all-important one to win. The matches against the other two home countries were almost taken as trials for the 'auld enemy' encounter. Indeed, the seriousness of the Wales and Ireland confrontations can be gauged by the fact that in 1890, 1891 and 1892, England played both nations on the same day – obviously fielding two completely different teams.

English football in its early years was undoubtedly the preserve of the amateur, as the England side consisted of players from the public schools and the Oxbridge universities. However, the organizers were also aware of football as a commercial concern and, in particular, the value of the paying spectator. England's home matches were played at venues all over the country and it was not beyond the selectors to choose a particular player or two just to provide an extra draw for the local crowds. For example, when England played Ireland at Molineux in March 1891, Rose and Brodie of Wolverhampton Wanderers made appearances, and similarly, two years later at Stoke, when England faced Wales, Clare and Schofield of the host club both pulled on the white shirt of England.

Britain was the creator of modern-day football, and as a result the belief was that the nation was the best in the world or at least that England and Scotland alternated as world leaders. However, the game was developing throughout the world, and in Paris, in May 1904, FIFA – Fédération Internationale de Football Association – was formed. The English FA was not a great supporter of the new organization and decided not to attend meetings until two years later.

In 1908, the year they won the gold medal in the London Olympics, England met their first non-British opposition at full international level when they embarked on a tour of Eastern Europe. The tourists played four matches, during which they thrashed Austria twice, 6–1 and 11–1, and Hungary 7–0 before letting up against Bohemia by scoring a mere four goals. On this occasion, therefore, foreign opposition had done nothing to dent the belief that England were the best in the world. In fact, it wasn't until November 1923 that England first failed to win an international against a foreign team, when Belgium held them to a 2–2 draw in Antwerp, and their first ever defeat didn't occur until May 1929, when, in spite of the presence of the great Raich Carter, the side lost 4–3 to Spain in Madrid.

England's first ever match at Wembley Stadium took place on 12 April 1924, when they drew 1–1 against Scotland, the only country welcomed there before the Second World War. Argentina were the first foreign opposition to meet England at Wembley in May 1951, with Austria visiting six months later, and Wales and Belgium appearing the following year. Northern Ireland were not invited until 1955.

With football beginning to develop into an international game, in 1930 FIFA staged the first World Cup tournament in Uruguay, albeit without England and the other home nations. In 1920, the British Football Associations had withdrawn from FIFA because they refused to play Austria, Germany and Hungary or any neutral allies from the First World War who played against these three countries. The FA officially returned to the fold four years later, yet during the period of absence, England still played internationals against Belgium, France and Sweden.

The 1930s did bring some memorable matches, though not all for the right reasons, as with the 'Battle of Highbury' in 1934. This match saw an England team featuring seven Arsenal players beat World Champions Italy by a 3–2 margin – but not without a good deal of bad feeling. Equally, the game in Germany in May 1938 will be remembered more for the infamous Hitler salute the England team were to give before the game than for the 6–3 winning score-line enjoyed by the visitors.

After the Second World War, Walter Winterbottom was appointed England's first team manager and coach. His responsibility was to prepare the players for the matches; he had no control over their respective selection except in an advisory capacity, for since 1872 the England national side had been chosen by a committee.

The post-war era saw England carry all before them, buoyed by a huge upsurge of interest in the game at home. New arrivals like Tom Finney and Wilf Mannion joined a handful of seasoned professionals anxious to make up for lost time. In September 1946, the selection panel put their trust in youth for the first post-war international against Northern Ireland at Windsor Park, a match England won 7–2. Two months later, Tommy Lawton was among the goals as Holland took on England at Huddersfield's Leeds Road ground. The Dutch scored twice but conceded eight with Lawton netting four times. Buoyed by 1947 victories against Portugal (10–0) and Belgium (5–2), England were keen to challenge the best the world had to offer.

In May 1948, the defeat of Italy in Turin by a 4–0 margin appeared as significant as the Battle of Highbury in throwing down a gauntlet to the world. But the following year the team would face a rude awakening against the Republic of Ireland, when, at Goodison Park, the visitors recorded a 2–0 win, thus destroying England's proud record of never having lost against continental (i.e. non-Home Country) opposition.

Having qualified for the 1950 World Cup Finals through the Home International Championships, England made their first visit to South America, bound for Brazil, where the finals were being staged. Unfortunately, the team approached the tournament with a ridiculous air of complacency. Drawn in Pool II, they were placed against Chile, considered part-time also-rans; the United States, no-hopers in everyone's eyes; and Spain, the only side that the England team considered decent.

On 25 June, England played their first match against Chile in Rio de Janeiro, which they won 2–0 with goals from Stan Mortensen and Wilf Mannion. Four days later, in Belo Horizonte, England met the United States in front of a 20,000 crowd. Though Walter Winterbottom had been keen to select Stanley Matthews, the Selection Committee rejected his request. England dominated the match and should have scored the hatful of goals expected of them, but in the 38th minute it was Joe Gaetajns, the Haiti-born forward, who headed past Bert Williams to score the only goal of the game. Not surprisingly, the shock result reverberated around the football world. Four changes were made for the game against Spain on 2 July, which was a match that England had to win to qualify for the quarter-finals. On this occasion, however, it was not to be, and another 1–0 defeat sent them crashing out of the tournament.

Their performance at the 1950 World Cup was considered an aberration to England. They had gone out to Brazil as one of the tournament favourites, but had returned home shamefaced. Despite this major setback, though, their confident attitude remained unchanged and they proceeded as before until one day in November 1953, when an England side including players of the calibre of Alf Ramsey, Stanley Matthews, Stan Mortensen and Billy Wright was comprehensively taken apart during a football masterclass by the 'Magical Magyars'. Hungary – comprising such players as Czibor, Grosics, Hidegkuti, Kocsis and Puskas – beat England 6–3, their first ever Wembley defeat. To emphasize the point, six months later in Budapest, in England's last game before the 1954 World Cup Finals, the same Hungarian side mesmerized their visitors with a devastating performance resulting in a 7–1 win. Clearly England had no claims to be the best in the world any more.

The 1954 World Cup pooled England, Belgium, Switzerland (the hosts) and Italy together. England and Italy were both seeded, and as such would not face each other, but rather the two non-seeded countries in their group matches, namely Belgium and Switzerland. In the opening game against Belgium, England led 3–1 with quarter of an hour remaining, but allowed the Belgians to pull two goals back to send the game into extra time. With the final score at four goals apiece, it was a defensive disaster. To aggravate the situation, England's last four matches against foreign opposition had seen them concede eighteen goals. Fortunately, England dealt with Switzerland simply enough with a 2–0 win. They finished top of Group IV to earn a quarter-final tie against Uruguay, the 1930 World Cup winners, who had already demolished Scotland 7–0. Birmingham's Gil Merrick, who had been the man in goal during the nightmare matches against the Hungarians, was at fault for two of the goals that ended England's World Cup hopes – the South Americans, who later lost their semi-final and finished in fourth place, beat England 4–2.

A sixteen-game unbeaten run over two years from November 1955 steadied the ship, only for the loss of three key Manchester United men – Roger Byrne, Tommy Taylor and Duncan Edwards – in the February 1958 Munich air crash to cause further anxiety in the England camp.

Thus, the four matches England played in April and May in the run-up to the 1958 World Cup saw a new-look team beat Scotland 4–0 and Portugal 2–1, lose to Yugoslavia 5–0 and draw 1–1 with the Soviet Union. Their last opponents were one of three teams in their World Cup group along with Austria and Brazil.

The first match in Gothenburg against the Soviet Union found England with a two-goal deficit until Derek Kevan and Tom Finney with a penalty levelled the scores. The second match against Brazil saw the defence hold firm but the forwards failed to score, and the game, ended goalless. Another draw, this time 2–2 with Austria in the third group game, forced England into a quarter-final play-off match with the Soviets. Once again England were unable to progress any further, thanks, on this occasion, to the great goalkeeping display of Lev Yashin. In fact it was Yashin's opposite number, Colin McDonald, who was responsible for the only goal of the game. He threw the ball to the Soviets, who set up Ilyin to score.

Manager Walter Winterbottom could not really be held responsible for England's lack of success, since the autonomy he had sought would never be forthcoming until his successor took over. The far-sighted Winterbottom proposed a policy of developing a young team that would play together, mature together and be ready within a four-year cycle. Unfortunately, an attempt to start this in 1959 with a team of mostly under-21s, including Jimmy Greaves and Brian Clough, was abandoned at his colleagues' insistence after a 3–2 defeat at home to Sweden in October, and so it was 'back to the old regime'.

Winterbottom approached his fourth – and last – World Cup in the hope that things would no longer blight the national side's bid for glory. For the tournament in Chile in 1962, England qualified to join Argentina, Bulgaria and Hungary in their pool. Hungary once again recorded victory over England, except this time by the less formidable score of 2–1. In the match against Argentina, England played better and won 3–1, and for the last game in the group they competed in a miserable goalless draw with Bulgaria. England reached the quarter-finals on goal average and were rewarded with a match against a Brazilian side that included greats such as Garrincha and Vava. The defending world champions deservedly beat a rather lacklustre England 3–1. After the tournament, Winterbottom resigned, the England side never having been close to fulfilling the home-spun belief that the nation's football was the best in the world.

Winterbottom's successor was Alf Ramsey, who was chosen because of his domestic success with unfashionable Ipswich Town, a team he had led to the League Championship a season after winning the Second Division title.

In October 1962, Ramsey's first match in charge was a European Nations Cup first-round, first-leg tie at home to France. It was England's first appearance in the competition and they drew 1–1, but crashed out of the competition four months later when the second leg was played in Paris – France winning 5–2.

With England having been designated hosts for the 1966 World Cup Finals, Ramsey had three years to build a quality squad. He used his time well, putting together a team that quickly began producing a sequence of impressive results – in fact, only four of the next forty-two games would see England defeated.

For World Cup '66, things seemed to bode well for England. Having been placed in a pool that included Uruguay, Mexico and France, the home team were scheduled to play all their first-round matches at Wembley.

The tournament began with a dull goalless draw between the hosts and Uruguay, but things improved when England recorded an expected 2–0 victory over Mexico. The same scoreline was attained against France, though less convincingly. In the quarter-final against Argentina, the South American side felt that everything was against them and resorted to using vicious tactics in an effort to stop England from playing their game. The Argentinian captain Antonio Rattin led the way in fouling at every opportunity and hurling verbal abuse at the host nation. Inevitably, he was sent off and England won with a single Geoff Hurst goal. Ramsey dubbed the Argentines 'animals'. The semi-finals paired up England with a Portugal side that featured the talented Eusebio, and a superb game followed which gave credit to both English and Portuguese football. England won 2–1 with two cracking goals from Bobby Charlton.

The 1966 World Cup Final – England v West Germany – has gone down in history as one of the greatest ever played: the early German lead through Haller after thirteen minutes; Hurst's equalizer six minutes later, which kept the teams level for most of the game; Martin Peters scoring what most England fans hoped would be the winning goal thirteen minutes from time; the dramatic, last-minute equalizer from Weber, which sent the match into extra time, which led to England's controversial third goal and later Hurst's hat-trick. England were World Champions. Gordon Banks, George Cohen, Ray Wilson, Nobby Stiles, Jack Charlton, Bobby Moore, Alan Ball, Geoff Hurst, Bobby Charlton, Roger Hunt and Martin Peters became national and international heroes.

The following season saw England successfully begin qualification for the European Nations Cup through the Home International Championships, although Scotland's 3–2 win at Wembley in April 1967 brought a nineteen-match unbeaten run to an end. Alf Ramsey led England to the quarter-finals, where a 3–1 aggregate victory over Spain booked them a ticket to Italy and a semi-final clash with Yugoslavia. For the first time during his England reign, Ramsey experienced disaster. In an ugly game, for which England were as much to blame as the Yugoslav opposition, Alan Mullery became England's first full international ever to be sent off, and the team's remaining ten men lost 1–0.

A 2–0 win against the Soviet Union was poor consolation for a team that still rightly considered itself the world's best. Indeed nineteen games between that third-place play-off and the next World Cup Finals (for which England, as holders, qualified automatically) would see England lose only once, and that in Rio de Janeiro in Brazil.

Before the squad even reached Mexico to defend their world crown at the 1970 World Cup, a cloud hung over their challenge, as Bobby Moore was held by Colombian authorities on suspicion of stealing a bracelet. The England captain was innocent of any crime, and it was widely believed that he had been framed in an attempt to jeopardize England's chances of retaining their World Cup title. Indeed, there was open hostility towards the England squad on their arrival in Mexico.

England had a rough ride in their first game against Romania, but fortunately won through with a Geoff Hurst goal. A sleepless night before the encounter with Brazil did not augur well as Mexican and Brazilian fans chanted outside the squad's hotel. Brazil did indeed win the encounter 1–0, but the match is best remembered for Gordon Banks's spectacular save from Pele's header. Fortunately, the England team went on to qualify for the quarter-finals after beating Czechoslovakia 1–0, no doubt aided by the fact that the Czechs had been having problems with disruptive internal disputes and had lost all of their games.

The quarter-final against West Germany was a disconcerting affair, however, particularly as England had lost the services of Gordon Banks – diagnosed with a mystery illness – before the match had even begun.

The champions started marvellously and had established a 2–0 lead early in the second half, making their chances of progressing to the semi-finals far more realistic. Despite the Germans pulling a goal back through Franz Beckenbauer, Ramsey decided to take off Bobby Charlton and Martin Peters, to rest them for the next round, but the Germans duly equalized with just eight minutes remaining and the game went into extra time. West Germany took full advantage and a Gerd Müller goal put them through to the semi-finals. Although Ramsey had clearly made a tactical mistake, it was Banks's replacement Peter Bonetti who was held personally responsible for the unfortunate defeat.

Ramsey's reign was not over despite this setback and he would lead England into another European Championship – where once again it was the Germans, now inspired by a new Beckenbauer in Günther Netzer, who ended England's hopes at the quarter-final stage in April 1972.

In the event it was England's failure to qualify for the next World Cup that signalled the end of an era. One October 1973 night at Wembley, Polish goalkeeper Jan Tomaszewski – dubbed a 'clown' by manager-turned-TV-pundit Brian Clough – defied England single-handedly to secure the all-important 1–1 draw. Norman Hunter, Bobby Moore's replacement, proved all too fallible, slipping at the wrong moment to allow little Grzegorz Lato to free scorer Jan Domarski.

Ramsey, the World Cup winner, had failed to create a second winning team and paid the price. Nevertheless, his was the most successful spell in the England national team's history with 69 wins, 27 draws and just 17 defeats from his 113 games. Little wonder the FA softened their blow with 'deep appreciation for all Sir Alf has accomplished and the debt owed to him by English football for his loyalty, dedication and integrity'.

Joe Mercer acted as caretaker-manager for seven games during the European tour that summer, before being succeeded by Don Revie, three times Manager of the Year thanks to his achievements with Leeds United. With the Yorkshire team, Revie had almost patented the 1–0 win, and he had also been downright unco-operative under Ramsey's reign as regards releasing his club players for international duty.

The Revie era had few highlights – Malcolm Macdonald's five goals against Cyprus in the European Championship qualifying game, and the emphatic 5–1 win over Scotland, both in 1975 – and it ended in controversial circumstances. In the summer of 1977, England were on tour in South America and Revie was supposed to be away in Finland, watching the Finns in preparation for the World Cup qualifier in the autumn. Instead, he had been secretly negotiating a coaching contract with the United Arab Emirates national side. An exclusive *Daily Mail* story revealed Revie's resignation to the world and a very surprised FA.

Revie's replacement was West Ham United manager Ron Greenwood, who, unlike both Ramsey and Revie, had not been an England international player. Greenwood took England to the European Championship Finals in Italy in the summer of 1980, though defeat by the host nation confined them to an early exit. In May 1981, Greenwood endured a shock World Cup qualifying defeat at the hands of Switzerland – it was later revealed that the England manager had quit on the plane home, only to reconsider in the face of 'player power'. Fortunately, he was to bounce back to winning ways a month later, when he masterminded England's first ever victory in Budapest's Nep Stadium; belated revenge for the defeats against Hungary in the 1950s, perhaps?

So England had managed to scrape through to the 1982 finals in Spain, and in their opening match against France, which they won 3–1, Bryan Robson scored after just 27 seconds – the fastest ever World Cup goal. The England team beat Czechoslovakia 2–0 in the next game to secure their second-phase place and a single Trevor Francis goal guaranteed a win over Kuwait to give England maximum points.

As group winners, England joined West Germany and Spain in their second-phase group. Sadly, England were disappointing with just two goalless draws. Kevin Keegan, who was brought on for the last quarter of the game against Spain, certainly rued a missed opportunity with an easy header in front of goal that went wide.

On Greenwood's departure, the role of England manager was once again vacant, and it was time for the Ipswich Town manager, Bobby Robson, to step into the breach. Though he failed in his first task of qualifying for the 1984 European Championships, he did succeed in taking England to the 1986 World Cup Finals. Along the way, in June 1984 his team inflicted a 2–0 defeat on Brazil in their Maracanã Stadium, with Watford's young winger John Barnes cementing his place in the national team for years to come with a fine individual goal.

England started badly in Mexico '86, losing 1–0 to Portugal, and, to make matters worse, in the second game against Morocco captain Bryan Robson dislocated his suspect shoulder and Ray Wilkins was sent off; the ten remaining men hung on for a goalless draw. In the final group game against Poland, however, England redeemed themselves thanks to a Gary Lineker hat-trick, and recorded a vital 3–0 win.

In the first round of the knockout phase, England beat Paraguay 3–0 to reach the quarter-finals, where they faced the skill and guile of Argentina, and it was here that England's World Cup challenge came to an end. Two goals from Diego Maradona put the England team out: the first was the result of the now infamous 'Hand of God' incident; the second probably the greatest goal ever seen on a world stage. Argentina won 2–1, but Gary Lineker, who netted England's goal, will probably never forget how close he was to reaching the John Barnes cross in the final minutes, which could have taken the game into extra time.

On 9 September 1987, Neil Webb came off the bench to replace Glenn Hoddle in a friendly match against West Germany. In doing so, Webb's Düsseldorf debut registered him as England's 1,000th full international footballer.

The England team then flattered to deceive, qualifying with ease for the 1988 European Championships, but then losing all three games they played in the German-staged finals. The Republic of Ireland, Holland and USSR all beat

Robson's side by a single goal, and, though the victory by the Irish was bemoaned by the press due to the presence of World Cup '66 hero Jack Charlton as Eire manager, it should perhaps be pointed out that the other two sides were the eventual finalists.

Despite a mauling from the critics, Bobby Robson survived to justify the FA's faith in him and take England to the 1990 World Cup Finals in Italy. Five games, two of them with extra time attached, saw them end a barren spell as England made it into the World Cup semi-finals – their best performance since the Wembley win. As in 1966 and 1970, their opponents were West Germany. The tie was decided on penalties – never a really satisfactory way of producing a result and, for England, certainly a less effective one. Stuart Pearce and Chris Waddle proved unable to convert and a campaign that had seen victories over Egypt, Belgium and Cameroon, as well as draws with the Republic of Ireland and Holland, ended on a decidedly low note. England subsequently lost 2–1 to Italy in the third-place play-off. They did, however, go home with a trophy – the Fair Play trophy – awarded for incurring the fewest cautions and fouls. Also, their shining star of the tournament, Paul Gascoigne, whose tears after incurring a booking that would have ruled him out of taking part in the final match, became the image of the campaign.

Bobby Robson bowed out with dignity after the World Cup, to be replaced by Aston Villa manager Graham Taylor. Few games were won convincingly during his time in charge, but a hard-fought 1–1 draw in Poland took England to the 1992 European Championship Finals, a tournament chiefly remembered for the England manager's decision to have captain Gary Lineker substituted when he stood just one goal short of Bobby Charlton's record tally of forty-nine and had already announced his decision to retire after the tournament. It was a petty decision that undoubtedly cost Taylor much public sympathy, but in truth, England were wholly unconvincing.

England failed to qualify for the 1994 World Cup Finals in America, and the match against Holland in April 1993, which signalled Taylor's demise, was one of the more public humiliations any manager had ever undergone, thanks in no small part to his wearing a microphone while being filmed by a TV documentary team. The programme that resulted made riveting viewing, but did little for Taylor or the job he would shortly vacate.

In 1994 he was replaced by the charismatic Terry Venables, who was pointedly given the title of 'coach'. Terry Venables had, it was implied, been selected for his ability as a tactician and man-manager, likely to bring success to the national team, rather than representing a figurehead for English football. His first dozen games brought steady rather than spectacular progress, but since qualification for the 1996 European Championships was assured as hosts, the forecast was optimistic. However, Venables's shock decision to quit after the Finals rather than take England forward to the 1998 World Cup in France was announced six months before the tournament. It represented a blow to the game and underlined the media pressures that had brought down Graham Taylor before him.

For reasons best known to themselves, the FA had taken the national squad to China and Hong Kong for pre-championship friendlies in May. After the last match, some of the players had gone for a night out and had been photographed with their shirts torn and drinking copious amounts of alcohol. Furthermore, on the flight home, two TV sets were broken and the players were accused of vandalism. The uproar and media frenzy went on for days, and when England only drew 1–1 with Switzerland in their opening game, the tabloids went into overdrive. However, in their next game, England beat Scotland 2–0, with David Seaman saving a Gary McAllister penalty and Paul Gascoigne scoring a virtuoso goal. England's final group opponents were Holland, one of the pre-tournament favourites, but they were beaten 4–1 with Shearer and Sheringham each scoring twice.

In the quarter-finals, England then defeated Spain, Seaman again saving brilliantly, this time from Miguel Nadal in the penalty shoot-out. The semi-final saw England paired with Germany and at the final whistle the score was 1–1. The first eight minutes of extra time were some of the most extraordinary ever witnessed in a football match. Anderton hit the post, Seaman saved spectacularly from Andreas Moller, the referee disallowed a Stefan Kuntz 'goal' and Gascoigne was a toe away from scoring. The drama heightened as the dreaded nightmare of penalties dawned – Gareth Southgate missed and Moller scored his and Germany were through 6–5.

Venables's departure was followed by the appointment of Glenn Hoddle. After weeks of hype, England qualified for the 1998 World Cup finals in France, courtesy of a goalless draw against Italy in Rome. The match was marred by scenes of violence on the terraces and this was carried over to the finals themselves, when English football hooligans fought a running battle with Marseille police and rival supporters on the eve of the first match against Tunisia. Fortunately, England made a solid start on the pitch, with goals by Shearer and Scholes helping them beat Tunisia 2–0.

They then lost 2–1 to Romania after Petrescu pounced on Graeme Le Saux's 90th-minute slip, but the team rekindled the fire and moved into the second round with an exciting 2–0 win over Colombia. Sadly, though, England's World Cup adventure ended in heroic failure at St Etienne, after they were beaten on penalties by Argentina. The match had begun badly for England when, within five minutes of the start, Gabriel Batistuta had scored from a penalty. But when Michael Owen was fouled in the penalty box, Shearer also converted from the spot to draw level. The Liverpool striker then brought the house down with a spectacular solo run and finish only for Javier Zanetti to replay on the stroke of half-time. Reduced to ten men for 73 minutes after David Beckham's dismissal, England held out for a 2–2 draw after extra time. With the score in the penalty shoot-out at 4–3 to the South Americans, David Batty, on as a substitute, saw his spot kick saved by Carlos Roa. A record TV home audience of 28 million watched Hoddle's team fail after a match laced with high drama.

In February 1999, following the publication of his baffling views on the disabled, which dominated the front pages of virtually every national newspaper, Glenn Hoddle's contract was terminated by the FA.

After Howard Wilkinson stepped in for just a single game as caretaker-boss, Kevin Keegan agreed to take over the reins. Despite some poor showings, England gained a place in the 2000 European Championship play-offs against Scotland, thanks to Sweden's defeat of Norway, and beat the Scots 2–1 on aggregate to reach the finals. After a 3–2 defeat by Portugal, Alan Shearer's stunning header in Charleroi ended thirty-four years of hurt as England beat Germany in a competitive fixture for the first time since the 1966 World Cup. Unfortunately, England's Euro 2000 hopes were short-lived. Needing only a draw against Romania, at 2–2 Phil Neville conceded an 89th-minute penalty to give Romania a 3–2 win.

Later that year, in October, Keegan stunned England by quitting as national coach following England's 1–0 home defeat at the hands of Germany in a World Cup qualifier, the last game to be played at Wembley before work on the new stadium began. Howard Wilkinson and Peter Taylor each took charge for a match until the FA appointed Sven-Göran Eriksson as England's new manager in January 2001.

England made a bright start under Eriksson, beating Spain 3–0 at Villa Park and then securing World Cup qualifying victories over Finland, Albania and Greece. On 1 September 2001, an historic Michael Owen hat-trick helped England devastate Germany with a 5–1 victory in Munich. The victory was the first in a World Cup qualifier on German soil and England's first success there since 1965. The following month, with England trailing 2–1 to Greece on the brink of full-time, in the final seconds of the game the inspirational David Beckham sent a trademark 25-yard free kick into the net, dramatically securing England's World Cup Finals spot.

The England team started the 2002 tournament with an unconvincing 1–1 draw against Sweden, but five days later, David Beckham wiped out four years of misery with a penalty winner against Argentina. A goalless draw against Nigeria assured Eriksson's men of a place in the last sixteen, where they faced Denmark. After a number of defensive errors, England beat the Danes 3–0, only to lose 2–1 to Brazil in the quarter-finals, this after Michael Owen had given England the lead.

England's Euro 2004 campaign witnessed the emergence of a talented teenage striker, Wayne Rooney. However, disgraceful crowd scenes marred England's Rooney-inspired feisty 2–0 win over Turkey at Sunderland's Stadium of Light in April 2003, and almost resulted in England having to play their next qualifier behind closed doors. Results continued to go England's way, however, leaving them needing a point in Turkey to qualify for the finals. Despite Beckham's penalty miss, and a tunnel bust-up at half-time, England survived a searching examination of their character to qualify for Portugal by virtue of a goalless draw.

In the first match of Euro 2004, the national side seemed to be on course to beating tournament favourites France after Frank Lampard had given them a 1–0 lead. The goal tally could also have increased to two, but David Beckham's penalty was saved by Fabien Barthez. However, a shock free kick and penalty from Zinedine Zidane in injury time meant that Eriksson's team had to accept a damning defeat. Four days later, England bounced back to beat Switzerland 3–0 with Wayne Rooney scoring twice. At 18 years and 236 days, Rooney became the youngest marksman ever to play in the European Championship finals.

In the next match Rooney's domination continued, netting another brace as England beat Croatia 4–2 to reach the quarter-finals, where they faced a tough encounter with hosts Portugal. A match packed with incident saw Rooney limp off the pitch in the first half and referee Urs Meier disallow a Sol Campbell goal with the score at 1–1, just a minute before the full-time whistle was blown. The game ended all-square at 2–2 after extra time, but England exited the competition in traditional manner – on penalties.

Despite a lack of polished performances in the 2006 World Cup qualifiers, including the embarrassing 1–0 defeat by Northern Ireland in Belfast in September 2005, England managed to qualify for the finals in Germany, finishing top of their group after a 2–1 victory over Poland in their last qualifying game.

Sven-Göran Eriksson's biggest test lies ahead of him in summer 2006. Under his leadership in the last two major international tournaments, England have only reached the quarter-final stage and his tactics have come under scrutiny. Despite this, the FA have consistently backed him to the hilt throughout his reign – will they be proved right in Germany?

2 ENGLAND'S PLAYERS

1. William John Maynard
Goalkeeper/Forward
Born   Camberwell, 18 March 1853
Died   2 September 1921
Clubs   1st Surrey Rifles; Wanderers; Surrey
Caps   2   Result
        30 Nov 1872 v Scotland   0–0
        4 Mar 1876 v Scotland   0–3

2. Ernest Harwood Greenhalgh
Fullback
Born   Mansfield, 15 November 1849
Clubs   Notts County
Caps   2   Result
        30 Nov 1872 v Scotland   0–0
        8 Mar 1873 v Scotland   4–2

3. Reginald de Courtney Welch
Fullback/Goalkeeper
Born   Kensington, 16 January 1851
Died   4 June 1939
Clubs   Old Harrovians; Harrow Chequers; Wanderers;
        Remnants; Middlesex
Caps   2   Result
        30 Nov 1872 v Scotland   0–0
        7 Mar 1874 v Scotland   1–2

4. Frederick Brunning Maddison
Fullback/Forward
Born   Oxford, 20 June 1850
Died   25 September 1907
Clubs   Oxford University; Wanderers; Crystal Palace
Caps   1   Result
        30 Nov 1872 v Scotland   0–0

5. Robert Barker
Forward
Born   Wouldham, Kent, 19 June 1847
Died   11 November 1915
Clubs   Hertfordshire Rangers; Middlesex; Kent
Caps   1   Result
        30 Nov 1872 v Scotland   0–0

6. John Brockbank
Forward
Born   Whitehaven, 22 August 1848
Died   29 January 1904
Clubs   Cambridge University; London
Caps   1   Result
        30 Nov 1872 v Scotland   0–0

7. John Charles Clegg
Forward
Born   Sheffield, 15 June 1850
Died   26 June 1937
Clubs   Sheffield Wednesday; Sheffield FC
Caps   1   Result
        30 Nov 1872 v Scotland   0–0

8. Arnold Kirke Smith
Forward
Born   Ecclesfield, 23 April 1850
Died   8 October 1927
Clubs   Oxford University; Sheffield FC; Sheffield FA
Caps   1   Result
        30 Nov 1872 v Scotland   0–0

9. Cuthbert John Ottaway
Forward
Born   Dover, 20 July 1850
Died   2 April 1878
Clubs   Oxford University; Old Etonians
Caps   2   Result
        30 Nov 1872 v Scotland   0–0
        7 Mar 1874 v Scotland   1–2

10. Charles John Chenery
Forward
Born   Lambourn, Berks, 1 January 1850
Clubs   Crystal Palace; Barnes; Wanderers; Surrey; London
Caps   3   Result   Goals
        30 Nov 1872 v Scotland   0–0
        8 Mar 1873 v Scotland   4–2   1
        7 Mar 1874 v Scotland   1–2

11. Charles John Morice
Forward
Born   Kensington, 27 May 1850
Died   17 June 1932
Clubs   Harrow Chequers; Barnes FC
Caps   1   Result
        30 Nov 1872 v Scotland   0–0

12. Alexander Morten
Goalkeeper
Born   Middlesex, 16 June 1832
Died   24 February 1900
Clubs   Crystal Palace; Wanderers; Middlesex; London
Caps   1   Result
        8 Mar 1873 v Scotland   4–2

13. Leonard Sidgwick Howell
Fullback/Halfback
Born   Dulwich, 6 August 1848
Died   7 September 1895
Clubs   Wanderers; Surrey
Caps   1   Result
        8 Mar 1873 v Scotland   4–2

14. Alfred George Goodwyn
Fullback/Halfback
Born   India, 2 October 1850
Died   14 March 1874
Clubs   Royal Military Academy, Woolwich; Royal Engineers
Caps   1   Result
        8 Mar 1873 v Scotland   4–2

15. Robert Walpole Sealy Vidal
Forward
Born   Cornborough, 3 September 1853
Died   5 November 1914
Clubs   Oxford University; Wanderers; Old Westminsters
Caps   1   Result
        8 Mar 1873 v Scotland   4–2

16. Pelham George Von Donop
Forward
Born   Southsea, 28 April 1851
Died   7 November 1921
Clubs   Royal Military Academy, Woolwich; Royal Engineers
Caps   2   Result
        8 Mar 1873 v Scotland   4–2
        6 Mar 1875 v Scotland   2–2

17. William Edwin Clegg
Halfback
Born	Sheffield, 21 April 1852	
Died	22 August 1932	
Clubs	Sheffield Wednesday; Sheffield FC; Perseverance; Sheffield Albion; Norfolk FC; Sheffield FA	
Caps	2	*Result*
	8 Mar 1873 v Scotland	4–2
	18 Jan 1879 v Wales	2–1

18. Alexander George Bonsor
Forward
Born	London, 1850		
Died	17 August 1907		
Clubs	Old Etonians; Wanderers; Surrey		
Caps	2	*Result*	*Goals*
	8 Mar 1873 v Scotland	4–2	1
	6 Mar 1875 v Scotland	2–2	

19. Rt. Hon. William Kenyon-Slaney
Forward
Born	Rajkot, India, 24 August 1847		
Died	24 April 1908		
Clubs	Oxford University; Old Etonians; Wanderers		
Caps	1	*Result*	*Goals*
	8 Mar 1873 v Scotland	4–2	2

20. George Hubert Hugh Heron
Forward
Born	Uxbridge, 30 January 1852	
Died	5 June 1914	
Clubs	Uxbridge; Wanderers; Swifts; Middlesex	
Caps	5	*Result*
	8 Mar 1873 v Scotland	4–2
	7 Mar 1874 v Scotland	1–2
	6 Mar 1875 v Scotland	2–2
	4 Mar 1876 v Scotland	0–3
	2 Mar 1878 v Scotland	2–7

21. Robert Andrew Muter Macindoe Ogilvie
Fullback
Born	London, October 1852	
Died	7 March 1938	
Clubs	Upton Park; Clapham Rovers	
Caps	1	*Result*
	7 Mar 1874 v Scotland	1–2

22. Alfred Hugh Stratford
Fullback
Born	Kensington, 5 September 1853	
Died	2 May 1914	
Clubs	Old Malvernians; Wanderers; Swifts; Middlesex	
Caps	1	*Result*
	7 Mar 1874 v Scotland	1–2

23. Francis Hornby Birley
Halfback
Born	Chorley, 14 March 1850	
Died	1 August 1910	
Clubs	Oxford University; Wanderers; Middlesex	
Caps	2	*Result*
	7 Mar 1874 v Scotland	1–2
	6 Mar 1875 v Scotland	2–2

24. Charles Henry Reynolds Wollaston
Forward
Born	Felpham, 31 July 1849		
Died	22 June 1926		
Clubs	Oxford University; Lancing Old Boys; Clapham Rovers; Wanderers; Middlesex		
Caps	4	*Result*	*Goals*
	7 Mar 1874 v Scotland	1–2	
	6 Mar 1875 v Scotland	2–2	1
	3 Mar 1877 v Scotland	1–3	
	13 Mar 1880 v Scotland	4–5	

25. Robert Kennett Kingsford
Forward
Born	Sydenham, 23 December 1849		
Died	14 October 1895		
Clubs	Old Marlburians; Wanderers; Crystal Palace; Surrey		
Caps	1	*Result*	*Goals*
	7 Mar 1874 v Scotland	1–2	1

26. John Hawley Edwards
Forward
Born	Shrewsbury, 20 January 1850	
Died	14 January 1893	
Clubs	Shropshire Wanderers; Wanderers; Shrewsbury FC	
Caps	1	*Result*
	7 Mar 1874 v Scotland	1–2

27. John Robert Blayney Owen
Forward
Born	Reading, 4 March 1848	
Died	13 June 1921	
Clubs	Oxford University; Sheffield FC; Sheffield FA; Maldon FC; Nottinghamshire; Essex	
Caps	1	*Result*
	7 Mar 1874 v Scotland	1–2

28. William Henry Carr
Goalkeeper
Born	Sheffield, 15 November 1848	
Died	22 February 1924	
Clubs	Walkley; Owlerton; Sheffield Wednesday; Sheffield FA	
Caps	1	*Result*
	6 Mar 1875 v Scotland	2–2

29. Edward Brownlow Haygarth
Fullback
Born	Cirencester, 26 April 1854	
Died	14 April 1915	
Clubs	Wanderers; Swifts; Reading; Berkshire	
Caps	1	*Result*
	6 Mar 1875 v Scotland	2–2

30. William Stepney Rawson
Halfback
Born	Cape Town, 14 October 1854	
Died	4 November 1932	
Clubs	Oxford University; Old Westminsters; Wanderers	
Caps	2	*Result*
	6 Mar 1875 v Scotland	2–2
	3 Mar 1877 v Scotland	1–3

31. Charles William Alcock
Forward
Born	Sunderland, 2 December 1842		
Died	26 February 1907		
Clubs	Wanderers; Surrey		
Caps	1	*Result*	*Goals*
	6 Mar 1875 v Scotland	2–2	1

⚽ **DID YOU KNOW...?**

W. E. Clegg had been chosen to play for England against Wales at The Oval in January 1879, but as a solicitor he was engaged in preparing evidence for the trial of the infamous Charlie Peace and had to work late on the case. He was unable to leave Sheffield for London on the night before the match and the next morning his train was delayed by heavy snow, so when he finally arrived at the ground the match had been in progress for twenty minutes.

32. Herbert Edward Rawson
Forward
Born Port Louis, Mauritius, 3 September 1852
Died 18 October 1924
Clubs Royal Engineers; Royal Military Academy, Woolwich; Kent

Caps	1	*Result*
	6 Mar 1875 v Scotland	2–2

33. Richard Lyon Geaves
Wing forward
Born Mexico, 6 May 1854
Died 21 March 1935
Clubs Cambridge University; Clapham Rovers; Old Harrovians

Caps	1	*Result*
	6 Mar 1875 v Scotland	2–2

34. Arthur Henry Savage
Goalkeeper
Born Sydney, Australia, 18 October 1850
Died 15 August 1905
Clubs Crystal Palace; Surrey

Caps	1	*Result*
	4 Mar 1876 v Scotland	0–3

35. Frederick Thomas Green
Halfback
Born Winchester, 21 June 1851
Died 6 July 1928
Clubs Oxford University; Wanderers; Middlesex

Caps	1	*Result*
	4 Mar 1876 v Scotland	0–3

36. Edgar Field
Fullback
Born Wallingford, 29 July 1854
Died 11 January 1934
Clubs Reading; Clapham Rovers; Berkshire; Buckinghamshire

Caps	2	*Result*
	4 Mar 1876 v Scotland	0–3
	26 Mar 1881 v Scotland	1–6

37. Ernest Henry Bambridge
Forward
Born Windsor, 16 May 1848
Died 16 October 1917
Clubs Swifts; Windsor Home Park; East Sheen; Corinthians; Berkshire

Caps	1	*Result*
	4 Mar 1876 v Scotland	0–3

38. Beaumont Griffith Jarrett
Halfback
Born London, 18 July 1855
Died 11 April 1905
Clubs Cambridge University; Old Harrovians; Grantham FC

Caps	3	*Result*
	4 Mar 1876 v Scotland	0–3
	3 Mar 1877 v Scotland	1–3
	2 Mar 1878 v Scotland	2–7

39. Arthur William Cursham
Outside right
Born Wilford, 14 March 1853
Died 24 December 1884
Clubs Nottingham Law Club; Notts County; Sheffield FC

Caps	6	*Result*	*Goals*
	4 Mar 1876 v Scotland	0–3	
	3 Mar 1877 v Scotland	1–3	
	2 Mar 1878 v Scotland	2–7	1
	18 Jan 1879 v Wales	2–1	
	3 Feb 1883 v Wales	5–0	1
	10 Mar 1883 v Scotland	2–3	

40. Charles Francis William Heron
Forward
Born Uxbridge, 16 May 1853
Died 23 October 1914
Clubs Uxbridge; Swifts; Wanderers; Windsor

Caps	1	*Result*
	4 Mar 1876 v Scotland	0–3

41. Charles Eastlake Smith
Forward
Born Colombo, Sri Lanka, 28 July 1850
Died 10 January 1917
Clubs Crystal Palace; Wanderers; Surrey

Caps	1	*Result*
	4 Mar 1876 v Scotland	0–3

42. Walter Scott Buchanan
Forward
Born Hornsey, 1 June 1855
Died 11 November 1926
Clubs Clapham Rovers; Barnes; Surrey

Caps	1	*Result*
	4 Mar 1876 v Scotland	0–3

43. Morton Peto Betts
Fullback/Forward
Born London, 30 August 1847
Died 19 April 1914
Clubs Old Harrovians; Wanderers; Kent

Caps	1	*Result*
	3 Mar 1877 v Scotland	1–3

44. William Lindsay
Fullback/Forward
Born India, 3 August 1847
Died 15 February 1923
Clubs Old Wykehamists; Wanderers; Surrey

Caps	1	*Result*
	3 Mar 1877 v Scotland	1–3

45. Lindsay Bury
Fullback
Born Withington, 9 July 1857
Died 30 October 1935
Clubs Cambridge University; Old Etonians

Caps	2	*Result*
	3 Mar 1877 v Scotland	1–3
	18 Jan 1879 v Wales	2–1

46. Hon. Alfred Lyttelton
Forward
Born Westminster, 7 February 1857
Died 5 July 1913
Clubs Cambridge University; Old Etonians; Hagley FC

Caps	1	*Result*	*Goals*
	3 Mar 1877 v Scotland	1–3	1

47. Cecil Vernon Wingfield-Stratford
Forward
Born West Malling, 7 October 1853
Died 5 February 1939
Clubs Royal Military Academy, Woolwich; Royal Engineers; Kent

Caps	1	*Result*
	3 Mar 1877 v Scotland	1–3

48. John Bain
Forward
Born Bothwell, 15 July 1854
Died 7 August 1929
Clubs Oxford University

Caps	1	*Result*
	3 Mar 1877 v Scotland	1–3

49. William Mosforth
Outside left
Born Sheffield, 25 April 1858
Died 11 July 1929
Clubs Hallam; Heeley; Providence; Ecclesfield; Sheffield Wednesday; Sheffield Albion; Sheffield Utd

Caps	9	Result	Goals
	3 Mar 1877 v Scotland	1–3	
	2 Mar 1878 v Scotland	2–7	
	18 Jan 1879 v Wales	2–1	
	5 Apr 1879 v Scotland	5–4	1
	13 Mar 1880 v Scotland	4–5	1
	15 Mar 1880 v Wales	3–2	
	26 Feb 1881 v Wales	0–1	
	11 Mar 1882 v Scotland	1–5	
	13 Mar 1882 v Wales	3–5	1

50. Conrad Warner
Goalkeeper
Born Cripplegate, London, 19 April 1852
Died 10 April 1890
Clubs Upton Park; London; Middlesex

Caps	1	Result
	2 Mar 1878 v Scotland	2–7

51. Hon. Edward Lyttelton
Fullback
Born Westminster, 23 July 1855
Died 26 January 1942
Clubs Cambridge University; Old Etonians; Hagley FC

Caps	1	Result
	2 Mar 1878 v Scotland	2–7

52. John Hunter
Halfback
Born Sheffield, 18 February 1852
Died 13 April 1903
Clubs Sheffield Heeley; Providence; Sheffield Wednesday; Sheffield Albion; Blackburn Olympic; Blackburn Rovers

Caps	7	Result
	2 Mar 1878 v Scotland	2–7
	13 Mar 1880 v Scotland	4–5
	15 Mar 1880 v Wales	3–2
	26 Feb 1881 v Wales	0–1
	26 Mar 1881 v Scotland	1–6
	11 Mar 1882 v Scotland	1–5
	13 Mar 1882 v Wales	3–5

53. Norman Coles Bailey
Halfback
Born Streatham, 23 July 1857
Died 13 January 1923
Clubs Old Westminsters; Clapham Rovers; Wanderers; Swifts; Corinthians; Surrey; London

Caps	19	Result	Goals
	2 Mar 1878 v Scotland	2–7	
	18 Jan 1879 v Wales	2–1	
	5 Apr 1879 v Scotland	5–4	1
	13 Mar 1880 v Scotland	4–5	
	26 Mar 1881 v Scotland	1–6	
	11 Mar 1882 v Scotland	1–5	
	13 Mar 1882 v Wales	3–5	
	3 Feb 1883 v Wales	5–0	
	10 Mar 1883 v Scotland	2–3	
	25 Feb 1884 v Ireland	8–1	
	15 Mar 1884 v Scotland	0–1	
	17 Mar 1884 v Wales	4–0	1
	28 Feb 1885 v Ireland	4–0	
	14 Mar 1885 v Wales	1–1	
	21 Mar 1885 v Scotland	1–1	
	29 Mar 1886 v Wales	3–1	
	31 Mar 1886 v Scotland	1–1	
	26 Feb 1887 v Wales	4–0	
	19 Mar 1887 v Scotland	2–3	

54. Percy Fairclough
Forward
Born Mile End, London, 1 February 1858
Died 22 June 1947
Clubs Old Foresters; Corinthians; Essex; London

Caps	1	Result
	2 Mar 1878 v Scotland	2–7

55. Henry Wace
Forward
Born Shrewsbury, 21 September 1853
Died 5 November 1947
Clubs Cambridge University; Wanderers; Clapham Rovers; Shropshire Wanderers

Caps	3	Result
	2 Mar 1878 v Scotland	2–7
	18 Jan 1879 v Wales	2–1
	5 Apr 1879 v Scotland	5–4

56. John George Wylie
Forward
Born Shrewsbury, 20 June 1854
Died 30 July 1924
Clubs Wanderers; Sheffield FC; Sheffield FA

Caps	1	Result	Goals
	2 Mar 1878 v Scotland	2–7	1

⚽ DID YOU KNOW...?

William Kenyon-Slaney, who played just one match against Scotland in March 1873, was the first England international to be born overseas – he was born in India.

57. Rupert Darnley Anderson
Goalkeeper
Born Liverpool, 29 April 1859
Died 23 December 1944
Clubs Cambridge University; Old Etonians

Caps	1	Result
	18 Jan 1879 v Wales	2–1

58. Claude William Wilson
Fullback
Born Banbury, 9 September 1858
Died 7 June 1881
Clubs Oxford University; Old Brightonians; Sussex

Caps	2	Result
	18 Jan 1879 v Wales	2–1
	26 Mar 1881 v Scotland	1–6

59. Edward Hagarty Parry
Forward
Born Toronto, Canada, 24 April 1855
Died 19 July 1931
Clubs Oxford University; Old Carthusians; Swifts; Remnants; Stoke Poges; Windsor; Berks & Bucks FA

Caps	3	Result	Goals
	18 Jan 1879 v Wales	2–1	
	11 Mar 1882 v Scotland	1–5	
	13 Mar 1882 v Wales	3–5	1

60. Thomas Heathcote Sorby
Forward
Born Sheffield, 16 February 1856
Died 13 December 1930
Clubs Thursday Wanderers; Sheffield FC; Sheffield FA

Caps	1	Result	Goals
	18 Jan 1879 v Wales	2–1	1

61. Herbert Whitfeld
Forward
Born Lewes, 15 November 1858
Died 6 May 1909
Clubs Cambridge University; Old Etonians

Caps	1	Result	Goals
	18 Jan 1879 v Wales	2–1	1

62. Reginald Halsey Birkett
Goalkeeper
Born London, 28 March 1849
Died 30 June 1898
Clubs Lancing Old Boys; Clapham Rovers; Surrey

Caps	1	Result
	5 Apr 1879 v Scotland	5–4

63. Harold Morse
Fullback
Born Birmingham, 4 March 1860
Clubs Notts County; Notts Rangers

Caps	1	Result
	5 Apr 1879 v Scotland	5–4

64. Edward Christian
Fullback
Born Malvern, 14 September 1858
Died 3 April 1934
Clubs Cambridge University; Old Etonians

Caps	1	Result
	5 Apr 1879 v Scotland	5–4

65. James Frederick McLeod Prinsep
Halfback
Born India, 27 July 1861
Died 22 November 1895
Clubs Old Carthusians; Clapham Rovers; Surrey

Caps	1	Result
	5 Apr 1879 v Scotland	5–4

66. Arnold Frank Hills
Forward
Born Lambeth, 12 March 1857
Died 7 March 1927
Clubs Oxford University; Old Harrovians

Caps	1	Result
	5 Apr 1879 v Scotland	5–4

67. Arthur Copeland Goodyer
Winger
Born Stamford, 25 April 1854
Died 8 January 1932
Clubs Nottingham Forest

Caps	1	Result	Goals
	5 Apr 1879 v Scotland	5–4	1

68. Francis John Sparks
Forward
Born Billericay, 4 July 1855
Died 13 February 1934
Clubs Upton Park; Hertfordshire Rangers; Clapham Rovers; Essex; London

Caps	3	Result	Goals
	5 Apr 1879 v Scotland	5–4	
	13 Mar 1880 v Scotland	4–5	1
	15 Mar 1880 v Wales	3–2	2

69. Edward Charles Bambridge
Outside left
Born Windsor, 30 July 1858
Died 8 November 1935
Clubs Windsor Home Park; Upton Park; Clapham Rovers; Swifts; Corinthians; Surrey; Berkshire; London

Caps	18	Result	Goals
	5 Apr 1879 v Scotland	5–4	2
	13 Mar 1880 v Scotland	4–5	2
	26 Mar 1881 v Scotland	1–6	1
	18 Feb 1882 v Ireland	13–0	1
	11 Mar 1882 v Scotland	1–5	
	13 Mar 1882 v Wales	3–5	
	3 Feb 1883 v Wales	5–0	1
	25 Feb 1884 v Ireland	8–1	2
	15 Mar 1884 v Scotland	0–1	
	17 Mar 1884 v Wales	4–0	
	28 Feb 1885 v Ireland	4–0	1
	14 Mar 1885 v Wales	1–1	
	21 Mar 1885 v Scotland	1–1	1
	29 Mar 1886 v Wales	3–1	1
	31 Mar 1886 v Scotland	1–1	
	5 Feb 1887 v Ireland	7–0	
	26 Feb 1887 v Wales	4–0	
	19 Mar 1887 v Scotland	2–3	

70. Harry Albemarle Swepstone
Goalkeeper
Born Stepney, 12 October 1859
Died 7 May 1907
Clubs Clapton Orient; Pilgrims; Ramblers; Swifts; Corinthians; Essex; London

Caps	6	Result
	13 Mar 1880 v Scotland	4–5
	11 Mar 1882 v Scotland	1–5
	13 Mar 1882 v Wales	3–5
	3 Feb 1883 v Wales	5–0
	24 Feb 1883 v Ireland	7–0
	10 Mar 1883 v Scotland	2–3

71. Thomas Brindle
Left back
Born Darwen, 28 July 1861
Died 15 April 1905
Clubs Darwen; Blackburn Olympic

Caps	2	Result	Goals
	13 Mar 1880 v Scotland	4–5	
	15 Mar 1880 v Wales	3–2	1

72. Edwin Luntley
Right back
Born Croydon, 31 August 1857
Died 1 August 1921
Clubs Nottingham Castle FC; Nottingham Forest

Caps	2	Result
	13 Mar 1880 v Scotland	4–5
	15 Mar 1880 v Wales	3–2

73. Segal Richard Bastard
Wing forward
Born Bow, London, 25 January 1854
Died 20 March 1921
Clubs Upton Park; Corinthians; Essex

Caps	1	Result
	13 Mar 1880 v Scotland	4–5

74. Sam Weller Widdowson
Centre forward
Born Hucknall Torkard, 16 April 1851
Died 9 May 1927
Clubs Nottingham Forest

Caps	1	Result
	13 Mar 1880 v Scotland	4–5

75. John Sands
Goalkeeper
Born Nottingham, 4 March 1859
Died 29 February 1924
Clubs Nottingham Forest

Caps	1	Result
	15 Mar 1880 v Wales	3–2

76. Frederick William Hargreaves
Halfback
Born Blackburn, 16 August 1858
Died 5 April 1897
Clubs Blackburn Rovers; Lancashire

Caps	3	Result
	15 Mar 1880 v Wales	3–2
	26 Feb 1881 v Wales	0–1
	18 Feb 1882 v Ireland	13–0

77. Thomas Marshall
Outside right
Born Withnell, 12 September 1858
Died 29 April 1917
Clubs Darwen; Blackburn Olympic

Caps	2	Result
	15 Mar 1880 v Wales	3–2
	26 Feb 1881 v Wales	0–1

78. Clement Mitchell
Centre forward
Born Cambridge, 20 February 1862
Died 6 October 1937
Clubs Upton Park; Corinthians; Essex; London

Caps	5	Result	Goals
	15 Mar 1880 v Wales	3–2	
	26 Mar 1881 v Scotland	1–6	
	3 Feb 1883 v Wales	5–0	3
	10 Mar 1883 v Scotland	2–3	1
	14 Mar 1885 v Wales	1–1	1

79. Henry Alfred Cursham
Forward
Born Wilford, 27 November 1859
Died 6 August 1941
Clubs Notts County; Corinthians; Grantham FC; Thursday Wanderers

Caps	8	Result	Goals
	15 Mar 1880 v Wales	3–2	
	18 Feb 1882 v Ireland	13–0	1
	11 Mar 1882 v Scotland	1–5	
	13 Mar 1882 v Wales	3–5	1
	3 Feb 1883 v Wales	5–0	
	24 Feb 1883 v Ireland	7–0	
	10 Mar 1883 v Scotland	2–3	
	25 Feb 1884 v Ireland	8–1	3

80. Edward Johnson
Forward
Born Stoke-on-Trent, 11 March 1860
Died 30 June 1901
Clubs Saltley College; Stoke; Birmingham FA; Staffordshire FA

Caps	2	Result	Goals
	15 Mar 1880 v Wales	3–2	
	25 Feb 1884 v Ireland	8–1	2

81. John Purvis Hawtrey
Goalkeeper
Born Eton, 19 July 1850
Died 17 August 1925
Clubs Old Etonians; Remnants; London; Berkshire; Buckinghamshire

Caps	2	Result
	26 Feb 1881 v Wales	0–1
	26 Mar 1881 v Scotland	1–6

82. Arthur Harvey
Fullback
Clubs Wednesbury Strollers; Staffordshire

Caps	1	Result
	26 Feb 1881 v Wales	0–1

83. Arthur Leopold Bambridge
Fullback/Halfback
Born Windsor, 16 June 1861
Died 27 November 1923

Clubs Upton Park; Swifts; Clapham Rovers; Corinthians; Berkshire

Caps	3	Result	Goals
	26 Feb 1881 v Wales	0–1	
	3 Feb 1883 v Wales	5–0	
	25 Feb 1884 v Ireland	8–1	1

84. Thurston 'Tot' Rostron
Forward
Born Darwen, 21 April 1863
Died 3 July 1891
Clubs Helmshore FC; Old Wanderers; Darwen; Great Lever; Blackburn Rovers; Lancashire

Caps	2	Result
	26 Feb 1881 v Wales	0–1
	26 Mar 1881 v Scotland	1–6

85. James Brown
Centre forward
Born Blackburn, 31 July 1862
Died 4 July 1922
Clubs Blackburn Rovers

Caps	5	Result	Goals
	26 Feb 1881 v Wales	0–1	
	18 Feb 1882 v Ireland	13–0	2
	28 Feb 1885 v Ireland	4–0	1
	14 Mar 1885 v Wales	1–1	
	21 Mar 1885 v Scotland	1–1	

86. George Tait
Centre forward
Born Birmingham, 16 June 1859
Died 15 November 1882
Clubs Birmingham Excelsior

Caps	1	Result
	26 Feb 1881 v Wales	0–1

87. John Hargreaves
Winger
Born Blackburn, 13 December 1860
Died 13 January 1903
Clubs Blackburn Rovers; Lancashire

Caps	2	Result
	26 Feb 1881 v Wales	0–1
	26 Mar 1881 v Scotland	1–6

88. George Henry Holden
Outside right
Born West Bromwich, 6 October 1859
Died 2 October 1924
Clubs Wednesbury Old Park; Wednesbury St James; Wednesbury Old Athletic; West Bromwich Albion; Derby Midland

Caps	4	Result
	26 Mar 1881 v Scotland	1–6
	25 Feb 1884 v Ireland	8–1
	15 Mar 1884 v Scotland	0–1
	17 Mar 1884 v Wales	4–0

89. Reginald Herbert Macaulay
Forward
Born Hodnet, 24 August 1858
Died 15 December 1937
Clubs Cambridge University; Old Etonians

Caps	1	Result
	26 Mar 1881 v Scotland	1–6

90. John Frederick Peel Rawlinson
Goalkeeper
Born New Alresford, 21 December 1860
Died 14 January 1926
Clubs Cambridge University; Old Etonians; Corinthians

Caps	1	Result
	18 Feb 1882 v Ireland	13–0

91. Alfred Thomas Carrick Dobson
Right back
Born   Basford, 11 October 1859
Died   22 October 1932
Clubs Notts County; Corinthians

Caps	4	*Result*
	18 Feb 1882 v Ireland	13–0
	25 Feb 1884 v Ireland	8–1
	15 Mar 1884 v Scotland	0–1
	17 Mar 1884 v Wales	4–0

92. Doctor Haydock Greenwood
Fullback
Born   Blackburn, 31 October 1860
Died   3 November 1851
Clubs Blackburn Rovers; Corinthians

Caps	2	*Result*
	18 Feb 1882 v Ireland	13–0
	11 Mar 1882 v Scotland	1–5

93. Robert Stuart King
Halfback
Born   Leigh-on-Sea, 4 April 1862
Died   4 March 1950
Clubs Oxford University; Upton Park; Grimsby Town

Caps	1	*Result*
	18 Feb 1882 v Ireland	13–0

94. Horace Hutton Barnet
Forward
Born   Kensington, 23 September 1855
Died   29 March 1941
Clubs Royal Engineers; Corinthians

Caps	1	*Result*
	18 Feb 1882 v Ireland	13–0

95. Arthur Brown
Inside right
Born   Birmingham, 22 May 1859
Died   1 July 1909
Clubs Florence FC; Aston Unity; Aston Villa; Birmingham St George; Birmingham Excelsior

Caps	3	*Result*	*Goals*
	18 Feb 1882 v Ireland	13–0	4
	11 Mar 1882 v Scotland	1–5	
	13 Mar 1882 v Wales	3–5	

96. Oliver Howard Vaughton
Inside left
Born   Aston, 9 January 1861
Died   6 January 1937
Clubs Waterloo FC; Birmingham FC; Wednesbury Strollers; Aston Villa

Caps	5	*Result*	*Goals*
	18 Feb 1882 v Ireland	13–0	5
	11 Mar 1882 v Scotland	1–5	1
	13 Mar 1882 v Wales	3–5	
	15 Mar 1884 v Scotland	0–1	
	17 Mar 1884 v Wales	4–0	

97. Alfred Jones
Fullback
Born   Walsall, 16 January 1861
Clubs Walsall Town Swifts; Great Lever; Aston Villa

Caps	3	*Result*
	11 Mar 1882 v Scotland	1–5
	13 Mar 1882 v Wales	3–5
	10 Mar 1883 v Scotland	2–3

98. Percival Chase Parr
Goalkeeper/Centre forward
Born   Widmore, 2 December 1859
Died   3 September 1912
Clubs Oxford University; West Kent; Kent

Caps	1	*Result*
	13 Mar 1882 v Wales	3–5

---

99. Percy John de Paravicini
Fullback
Born   Kensington, 15 July 1862
Died   11 October 1921
Clubs Cambridge University; Old Etonians; Windsor; Corinthians; Berks & Bucks FA

Caps	3	*Result*
	3 Feb 1883 v Wales	5–0
	24 Feb 1883 v Ireland	7–0
	10 Mar 1883 v Scotland	2–3

100. Bruce Bremner Russell
Left back
Born   Kensington, 25 August 1859
Died   13 May 1942
Clubs Royal Military Academy, Woolwich; Royal Engineers

Caps	1	*Result*
	3 Feb 1883 v Wales	5–0

101. Stuart Macrae
Halfback
Born   Isle of Bute, 20 January 1856
Died   27 January 1927
Clubs Notts County; Corinthians; Newark FC

Caps	5	*Result*
	3 Feb 1883 v Wales	5–0
	24 Feb 1883 v Ireland	7–0
	10 Mar 1883 v Scotland	2–3
	25 Feb 1884 v Ireland	8–1
	15 Mar 1884 v Scotland	0–1

102. Harry Chester Goodhart
Forward
Born   Wimbledon, 17 July 1858
Died   21 April 1895
Clubs Cambridge University; Old Etonians

Caps	3	*Result*
	3 Feb 1883 v Wales	5–0
	24 Feb 1883 v Ireland	7–0
	10 Mar 1883 v Scotland	2–3

103. Henry Thomas Moore
Fullback
Born   Nottingham, 27 June 1861
Died   24 September 1939
Clubs Notts County

Caps	2	*Result*
	24 Feb 1883 v Ireland	7–0
	14 Mar 1885 v Wales	1–1

104. John Hudson
Halfback
Born   Sheffield, 12 June 1860
Died   14 November 1941
Clubs Sheffield Heeley; Sheffield FC; Sheffield Wednesday; Blackburn Olympic; Sheffield Utd

Caps	1	*Result*
	24 Feb 1883 v Ireland	7–0

105. Oliver Whateley
Inside forward
Born Birmingham, 30 June 1862
Died 12 October 1926
Clubs Gladstone Unity; Aston Villa

Caps	2	Result	Goals
	24 Feb 1883 v Ireland	7–0	2
	10 Mar 1883 v Scotland	2–3	

106. Francis William Pawson
Forward
Born Sheffield, 6 April 1861
Died 4 July 1921
Clubs Cambridge University; Swifts; Sheffield FC; Casuals; Corinthians; Surrey

Caps	2	Result	Goals
	24 Feb 1883 v Ireland	7–0	1
	28 Feb 1885 v Ireland	4–0	

107. Arthur Tempest Blakiston Dunn
Centre forward
Born Whitby, 12 August 1860
Died 20 February 1902
Clubs Cambridge University; Old Etonians; Granta; Corinthians; Cambridgeshire; Norfolk

Caps	4	Result	Goals
	24 Feb 1883 v Ireland	7–0	2
	25 Feb 1884 v Ireland	8–1	
	5 Mar 1892 v Wales	2–0	
	2 Apr 1892 v Scotland	4–1	

108. William Nevill Cobbold
Forward
Born Long Melford, 4 February 1863
Died 8 April 1922
Clubs Cambridge University; Corinthians

Caps	9	Result	Goals
	24 Feb 1883 v Ireland	7–0	2
	10 Mar 1883 v Scotland	2–3	1
	28 Feb 1885 v Ireland	4–0	
	21 Mar 1885 v Scotland	1–1	
	29 Mar 1886 v Wales	3–1	
	31 Mar 1886 v Scotland	1–1	
	5 Feb 1887 v Ireland	7–0	2
	26 Feb 1887 v Wales	4–0	2
	19 Mar 1887 v Scotland	2–3	

109. William Crispin Rose
Goalkeeper
Born St Pancras, London, 4 March 1861
Died 4 February 1937
Clubs Small Heath; Swifts; Preston North End; Stoke; Wolverhampton Wanderers; Loughborough Town

Caps	5	Result
	25 Feb 1884 v Ireland	8–1
	15 Mar 1884 v Scotland	0–1
	17 Mar 1884 v Wales	4–0
	13 Mar 1886 v Ireland	6–1
	7 Mar 1891 v Ireland	6–1

110. Joseph Beverley
Fullback
Born Blackburn, 12 November 1856
Died 21 May 1897
Clubs Black Star FC; Blackburn Olympic; Blackburn Rovers

Caps	3	Result
	25 Feb 1884 v Ireland	8–1
	15 Mar 1884 v Scotland	0–1
	17 Mar 1884 v Wales	4–0

111. Charles Plumpton Wilson
Wing half
Born Roydon, 12 May 1859
Died 9 March 1938
Clubs Cambridge University; Hendon; Casuals; Corinthians

Caps	2	Result
	15 Mar 1884 v Scotland	0–1
	17 Mar 1884 v Wales	4–0

112. William Bromley-Davenport
Centre forward
Born London, 21 January 1862
Died 6 February 1949
Clubs Oxford University; Old Etonians

Caps	2	Result	Goals
	15 Mar 1884 v Scotland	0–1	
	17 Mar 1884 v Wales	4–0	2

113. William Gunn
Outside left
Born Nottingham, 4 December 1858
Died 29 January 1921
Clubs Nottingham Forest; Notts County

Caps	2	Result	Goals
	15 Mar 1884 v Scotland	0–1	
	17 Mar 1884 v Wales	4–0	1

114. James Henry Forrest
Left half
Born Blackburn, 24 June 1864
Died 30 December 1925
Clubs Imperial Utd; Witton FC; King's Own FC; Blackburn Rovers; Darwen

Caps	11	Result
	17 Mar 1884 v Wales	4–0
	28 Feb 1885 v Ireland	4–0
	14 Mar 1885 v Wales	1–1
	21 Mar 1885 v Scotland	1–1
	29 Mar 1886 v Wales	3–1
	31 Mar 1886 v Scotland	1–1
	5 Feb 1887 v Ireland	7–0
	26 Feb 1887 v Wales	4–0
	19 Mar 1887 v Scotland	2–3
	13 Apr 1889 v Scotland	2–3
	15 Mar 1890 v Ireland	9–1

115. William John Herbert Arthur
Goalkeeper
Born Blackburn, 14 February 1863
Died 27 November 1930
Clubs Lower Bank Academy; King's Own FC; Blackburn Rovers; Southport Central

Caps	7	Result
	28 Feb 1885 v Ireland	4–0
	14 Mar 1885 v Wales	1–1
	21 Mar 1885 v Scotland	1–1
	29 Mar 1886 v Wales	3–1
	31 Mar 1886 v Scotland	1–1
	5 Feb 1887 v Ireland	7–0
	26 Feb 1887 v Wales	4–0

116. Percy Melmoth Walters
Left back
Born Ewell, 30 September 1863
Died 6 October 1936
Clubs Oxford University; Old Carthusians; Corinthians; East Sheen; Epsom; Surrey

Caps	13	Result
	28 Feb 1885 v Ireland	4–0
	21 Mar 1885 v Scotland	1–1
	13 Mar 1886 v Ireland	6–1
	29 Mar 1886 v Wales	3–1
	31 Mar 1886 v Scotland	1–1
	26 Feb 1887 v Wales	4–0
	19 Mar 1887 v Scotland	2–3
	17 Mar 1888 v Scotland	5–0
	31 Mar 1888 v Ireland	5–1
	23 Feb 1889 v Wales	4–1
	13 Apr 1889 v Scotland	2–3
	15 Mar 1890 v Wales	3–1
	5 Apr 1890 v Scotland	1–1

117. Arthur Melmoth Walters
Right back
Born   Ewell, 26 January 1865
Died   2 May 1941
Clubs   Cambridge University; Old Carthusians;
        Corinthians; East Sheen; Surrey

Caps	9	Result
	28 Feb 1885 v Ireland	4–0
	21 Mar 1885 v Scotland	1–1
	31 Mar 1886 v Scotland	1–1
	26 Feb 1887 v Wales	4–0
	19 Mar 1887 v Scotland	2–3
	23 Feb 1889 v Wales	4–1
	13 Apr 1889 v Scotland	2–3
	15 Mar 1890 v Wales	3–1
	5 Apr 1890 v Scotland	1–1

118. Joseph Morris Lofthouse
Outside right
Born   Witton, 14 April 1865
Died   10 June 1919
Clubs   King's Own FC; Blackburn Rovers; Accrington;
        Darwen; Walsall

Caps	7	Result	Goals
	28 Feb 1885 v Ireland	4–0	1
	14 Mar 1885 v Wales	1–1	
	21 Mar 1885 v Scotland	1–1	
	26 Feb 1887 v Wales	4–0	
	19 Mar 1887 v Scotland	2–3	
	2 Mar 1889 v Ireland	6–1	1
	15 Mar 1890 v Ireland	9–1	1

119. Benjamin Ward Spilsbury
Winger
Born   Findern, 1 August 1864
Died   15 August 1938
Clubs   Cambridge University; Corinthians; Derby County

Caps	3	Result	Goals
	28 Feb 1885 v Ireland	4–0	1
	13 Mar 1886 v Ireland	6–1	4
	31 Mar 1886 v Scotland	1–1	

120. James Thomas Ward
Fullback
Born   Blackburn, 28 March 1865
Clubs   Little Harwood; Blackburn Olympic; Blackburn
        Rovers

Caps	1	Result
	14 Mar 1885 v Wales	1–1

121. James Kenyon 'Kenny' Davenport
Inside right
Born   Bolton, 23 March 1862
Died   27 September 1908
Clubs   Gilnow Rangers; Bolton Wanderers; Southport
        Central; Lancashire

Caps	2	Result	Goals
	14 Mar 1885 v Wales	1–1	
	15 Mar 1890 v Ireland	9–1	2

122. John Auger Dixon
Outside left
Born   Grantham, 27 May 1861
Died   8 June 1931
Clubs   Notts County; Corinthians

Caps	1	Result
	14 Mar 1885 v Wales	1–1

123. Andrew Amos
Halfback
Born   Southwark, 20 September 1863
Died   2 October 1931
Clubs   Cambridge University; Corinthians; Old
        Carthusians; Hitchin Town; Hertfordshire

Caps	2	Result
	21 Mar 1885 v Scotland	1–1
	29 Mar 1886 v Wales	3–1

124. Thomas Danks
Inside right
Born   Nottingham, 30 May 1863
Died   27 April 1908
Clubs   Nottingham Forest; Notts County; Burslem Port
        Vale

Caps	1	Result
	21 Mar 1885 v Scotland	1–1

125. Richard Baugh
Right back
Born   Wolverhampton, 14 February 1864
Died   14 August 1929
Clubs   Rose Villa; Wolverhampton Rangers; Stafford Road;
        Wolverhampton Wanderers; Walsall

Caps	2	Result
	13 Mar 1886 v Ireland	6–1
	15 Mar 1890 v Ireland	9–1

126. George Shutt
Centre half
Born   Stoke-on-Trent, 20 June 1861
Died   6 August 1936
Clubs   Stoke

Caps	1	Result
	13 Mar 1886 v Ireland	6–1

127. Ralph Tyndall Squire
Fullback/Halfback
Born   Marylebone, London, 10 September 1863
Died   22 August 1944
Clubs   Cambridge University; Old Westminsters;
        Corinthians; Clapham Rovers; London

Caps	3	Result
	13 Mar 1886 v Ireland	6–1
	29 Mar 1886 v Wales	3–1
	31 Mar 1886 v Scotland	1–1

128. Charles Frederick Dobson
Halfback
Born   Basford, 9 September 1862
Died   18 May 1939
Clubs   Notts County; Corinthians

Caps	1	Result
	13 Mar 1886 v Ireland	6–1

129. John Edward Leighton
Outside left
Born   Nottingham, 26 March 1865
Died   15 April 1944
Clubs   Nottingham Forest; Corinthians

Caps	1	Result
	13 Mar 1886 v Ireland	6–1

130. Frederick Dewhurst
Inside left
Born   Preston, 16 December 1863
Died   21 April 1895
Clubs   Preston North End; Corinthians

Caps	9	Result	Goals
	13 Mar 1886 v Ireland	6–1	1
	29 Mar 1886 v Wales	3–1	1
	5 Feb 1887 v Ireland	7–0	2
	26 Feb 1887 v Wales	4–0	
	19 Mar 1887 v Scotland	2–3	1
	4 Feb 1888 v Wales	5–1	2
	17 Mar 1888 v Scotland	5–0	2
	31 Mar 1888 v Ireland	5–1	1
	23 Feb 1889 v Wales	4–1	1

131. Tinsley Lindley
Centre forward

Born	Nottingham, 27 October 1865	
Died	31 March 1940	
Clubs	Cambridge University; Nottingham Forest; Corinthians; Casuals; Notts County; Crusaders; Swifts; Preston North End	

Caps	13	Result	Goals
	13 Mar 1886 v Ireland	6–1	1
	29 Mar 1886 v Wales	3–1	1
	31 Mar 1886 v Scotland	1–1	1
	5 Feb 1887 v Ireland	7–0	3
	26 Feb 1887 v Wales	4–0	2
	19 Mar 1887 v Scotland	2–3	1
	4 Feb 1888 v Wales	5–1	1
	17 Mar 1888 v Scotland	5–0	1
	31 Mar 1888 v Ireland	5–1	1
	13 Apr 1889 v Scotland	2–3	
	15 Mar 1890 v Wales	3–1	1
	5 Apr 1890 v Scotland	1–1	
	7 Mar 1891 v Ireland	6–1	2

132. Thelwell Mather Pike
Winger

Born	Andover, 17 November 1866
Died	21 July 1957
Clubs	Cambridge University; Crusaders; Old Malvernians; Brentwood Swifts; Thanet Wanderers; Corinthians

Caps	1	Result
	13 Mar 1886 v Ireland	6–1

133. George Brann
Outside right/Inside right

Born	Eastbourne, 23 April 1865
Died	14 June 1954
Clubs	Swifts; Slough FC; Corinthians

Caps	3	Result
	29 Mar 1886 v Wales	3–1
	31 Mar 1886 v Scotland	1–1
	7 Mar 1891 v Wales	4–1

134. Robert Henry Howarth
Right back

Born	Preston, 20 June 1865
Died	20 August 1938
Clubs	Preston North End; Everton

Caps	5	Result
	5 Feb 1887 v Ireland	7–0
	4 Feb 1888 v Wales	5–1
	17 Mar 1888 v Scotland	5–0
	6 Apr 1891 v Scotland	2–1
	1 Mar 1894 v Ireland	2–2

135. Charles Mason
Left back

Born	Wolverhampton, 1 April 1863
Died	3 February 1941
Clubs	Wolverhampton Wanderers

Caps	3	Result
	5 Feb 1887 v Ireland	7–0
	4 Feb 1888 v Wales	5–1
	15 Mar 1890 v Ireland	9–1

136. George Haworth
Right half/Centre half

Born	Accrington, 17 October 1864
Clubs	Christ Church FC; Accrington; Blackburn Rovers

Caps	5	Result
	5 Feb 1887 v Ireland	7–0
	26 Feb 1887 v Wales	4–0
	19 Mar 1887 v Scotland	2–3
	17 Mar 1888 v Scotland	5–0
	5 Apr 1890 v Scotland	1–1

137. Edward Brayshaw
Right back

Born	Kirkstall, Leeds, 20 June 1863
Died	20 November 1908
Clubs	Walkley All Saints; Sheffield Wednesday; Grimsby Town

Caps	1	Result
	5 Feb 1887 v Ireland	7–0

138. James Sayer
Outside right

Born	Mexborough, 11 November 1862
Died	1 February 1922
Clubs	Mexborough FC; Sheffield Heeley; Sheffield Wednesday; Stoke

Caps	1	Result
	5 Feb 1887 v Ireland	7–0

139. Robert John Roberts
Goalkeeper

Born	West Bromwich, 25 April 1859
Died	28 October 1929
Clubs	West Bromwich Albion; Sunderland Albion; Aston Villa

Caps	3	Result
	19 Mar 1887 v Scotland	2–3
	31 Mar 1888 v Ireland	5–1
	15 Mar 1890 v Ireland	9–1

140. William Robert Moon
Goalkeeper

Born	Maida Vale, 27 June 1868
Died	9 January 1943
Clubs	Old Westminsters; Corinthians, London

Caps	7	Result
	4 Feb 1888 v Wales	5–1
	17 Mar 1888 v Scotland	5–0
	23 Feb 1889 v Wales	4–1
	13 Apr 1889 v Scotland	2–3
	15 Mar 1890 v Wales	3–1
	5 Apr 1890 v Scotland	1–1
	6 Apr 1891 v Scotland	2–1

141. Frank Etheridge Saunders
Centre half/Wing half

Born	Brighton, 26 August 1864
Died	14 May 1905
Clubs	Cambridge University; Swifts; Corinthians; St Thomas's Hospital; Sussex

Caps	1	Result
	4 Feb 1888 v Wales	5–1

142. Henry Allen
Centre half

Born	Walsall, 19 January 1866
Died	23 February 1895
Clubs	Walsall Swifts; Wolverhampton Wanderers

Caps	5	Result
	4 Feb 1888 v Wales	5–1
	17 Mar 1888 v Scotland	5–0
	31 Mar 1888 v Ireland	5–1
	13 Apr 1889 v Scotland	2–3
	5 Apr 1890 v Scotland	1–1

143. Charles Henry Holden-White
Left half

Born	London, 23 October 1869
Died	14 July 1948
Clubs	Clapham Rovers; Corinthians; Swifts

Caps	2	Result
	4 Feb 1888 v Wales	5–1
	17 Mar 1888 v Scotland	5–0

144. George 'Spry' Woodhall
Winger

Born	West Bromwich, 5 September 1863
Died	29 September 1924
Clubs	West Bromwich All Saints; Churchfield Foresters; West Bromwich Albion; Wolverhampton Wanderers; Berwick Rangers; Oldbury Town

Caps	2	Result	Goals
	4 Feb 1888 v Wales	5–1	1
	17 Mar 1888 v Scotland	5–0	

145. John Goodall
Inside right/Centre forward

Born	Westminster, London, 19 June 1863		
Died	20 May 1942		
Clubs	Kilmarnock Athletic; Great Lever; Preston North End; Derby County; New Brighton Tower; Glossop; Watford; Maerdy		

Caps	14	Result	Goals
	4 Feb 1888 v Wales	5–1	1
	17 Mar 1888 v Scotland	5–0	1
	23 Feb 1889 v Wales	4–1	1
	13 Apr 1889 v Scotland	2–3	
	7 Mar 1891 v Wales	4–1	1
	6 Apr 1891 v Scotland	2–1	1
	2 Apr 1892 v Scotland	4–1	2
	13 Mar 1893 v Wales	6–0	1
	7 Apr 1894 v Scotland	2–2	1
	9 Mar 1895 v Ireland	9–0	2
	6 Apr 1895 v Scotland	3–0	
	16 Mar 1896 v Wales	9–1	1
	4 Apr 1896 v Scotland	1–2	
	28 Mar 1898 v Wales	3–0	

146. Dennis Hodgetts
Inside left/Outside left

Born	Birmingham, 28 November 1863
Died	26 March 1945
Clubs	Birmingham St George's; Great Lever; Aston Villa; Small Heath

Caps	6	Result	Goals
	4 Feb 1888 v Wales	5–1	
	17 Mar 1888 v Scotland	5–0	1
	31 Mar 1888 v Ireland	5–1	
	5 Mar 1892 v Ireland	2–0	
	2 Apr 1892 v Scotland	4–1	
	1 Mar 1894 v Ireland	2–2	

147. Albert James Aldridge
Fullback

Born	Walsall, 13 April 1864
Died	May 1891
Clubs	Walsall Swifts; West Bromwich Albion; Aston Villa

Caps	2	Result
	31 Mar 1888 v Ireland	5–1
	2 Mar 1889 v Ireland	6–1

148. Robert Holmes
Fullback

Born	Preston, 23 June 1867
Died	17 November 1955
Clubs	Preston Olympic; Preston North End

Caps	7	Result
	31 Mar 1888 v Ireland	5–1
	6 Apr 1891 v Scotland	2–1
	2 Apr 1892 v Scotland	4–1
	13 Mar 1893 v Wales	6–0
	1 Apr 1893 v Scotland	5–2
	1 Mar 1894 v Ireland	2–2
	9 Mar 1895 v Ireland	9–0

149. Charles Shelton
Left half

Born	Nottingham, 22 January 1864
Died	27 January 1899
Clubs	Notts Rangers; Notts County

Caps	1	Result
	31 Mar 1888 v Ireland	5–1

150. William Isaiah Bassett
Outside right

Born	West Bromwich, 27 January 1869
Died	8 April 1937
Clubs	Oak Villa; Old Church FC; West Bromwich Strollers; West Bromwich Albion

Caps	16	Result	Goals
	31 Mar 1888 v Ireland	5–1	
	23 Feb 1889 v Wales	4–1	1
	13 Apr 1889 v Scotland	2–3	1
	15 Mar 1890 v Wales	3–1	
	5 Apr 1890 v Scotland	1–1	
	7 Mar 1891 v Ireland	6–1	1
	6 Apr 1891 v Scotland	2–1	
	2 Apr 1892 v Scotland	4–1	
	13 Mar 1893 v Wales	6–0	1
	1 Apr 1893 v Scotland	5–2	
	7 Apr 1894 v Scotland	2–2	
	9 Mar 1895 v Ireland	9–0	1
	6 Apr 1895 v Scotland	3–0	
	7 Mar 1896 v Ireland	2–0	
	16 Mar 1896 v Wales	9–1	1
	4 Apr 1896 v Scotland	1–2	1

151. Albert Allen
Inside left

Born	Aston, 25 April 1867
Died	13 October 1899
Clubs	Aston Villa

Caps	1	Result	Goals
	31 Mar 1888 v Ireland	5–1	3

152. Albert Thomas Fletcher
Right half

Born	Wolverhampton, 4 June 1867
Died	27 July 1940
Clubs	Willenhall Pickwick; Wolverhampton Wanderers

Caps	2	Result
	23 Feb 1889 v Wales	4–1
	15 Mar 1890 v Wales	3–1

153. Arthur Lowder
Left half

Born	Wolverhampton, 4 May 1863
Died	4 January 1926
Clubs	Wolverhampton Wanderers

Caps	1	Result
	23 Feb 1889 v Wales	4–1

154. William Betts
Centre half

Born	Sheffield, 18 June 1864
Died	8 August 1941
Clubs	Sheffield Wednesday; Lockwood Bros.

Caps	1	Result
	23 Feb 1889 v Wales	4–1

155. John Southworth
Centre forward

Born	Blackburn, 22 December 1866
Died	16 October 1956
Clubs	Blackburn Olympic; Blackburn Rovers; Everton

Caps	3	Result	Goals
	23 Feb 1889 v Wales	4–1	1
	7 Mar 1891 v Wales	4–1	1
	2 Apr 1892 v Scotland	4–1	1

156. William Townley
Outside left

Born	Blackburn, 14 February 1866
Died	30 May 1950
Clubs	Blackburn Olympic; Blackburn Rovers; Stockton; Darwen; Manchester City

Caps	2	Result	Goals
	23 Feb 1889 v Wales	4–1	
	15 Mar 1890 v Ireland	9–1	2

157. William Rowley
Goalkeeper

Born	Hanley, 28 July 1865
Died	1939
Clubs	Hanley Orion; Burslem Port Vale; Stoke; Staffordshire

Caps	2	Result
	2 Mar 1889 v Ireland	6–1
	5 Mar 1892 v Ireland	2–0

158. Thomas Clare
Right back
Born   Congleton, 21 August 1865
Died   27 December 1929
Clubs   Talke FC; Goldenhill Wanderers; Stoke;
        Staffordshire

Caps	4	Result
	2 Mar 1889 v Ireland	6–1
	5 Mar 1892 v Ireland	2–0
	13 Mar 1893 v Wales	6–0
	7 Apr 1894 v Scotland	2–2

159. Charles Wreford-Brown
Centre half
Born   Clifton, Bristol, 9 October 1866
Died   26 November 1951
Clubs   Oxford University; Corinthians; Old Carthusians;
        Casuals; London

Caps	4	Result
	2 Mar 1889 v Ireland	6–1
	12 Mar 1894 v Wales	5–1
	18 Mar 1895 v Wales	1–1
	2 Apr 1898 v Scotland	3–1

160. David Weir
Forward
Born   Aldershot, 4 November 1863
Died   11 November 1933
Clubs   Maybole FC; Glasgow Thistle; Halliwell; Bolton
        Wanderers; Ardwick

Caps	2	Result	Goals
	2 Mar 1889 v Ireland	6–1	1
	13 Apr 1889 v Scotland	2–3	1

161. Alfred Shelton
Left half
Born   Nottingham, 11 September 1865
Died   24 July 1923
Clubs   Notts Rangers; Notts County; Loughborough Town;
        Heanor Town

Caps	6	Result
	2 Mar 1889 v Ireland	6–1
	15 Mar 1890 v Wales	3–1
	5 Apr 1890 v Scotland	1–1
	7 Mar 1891 v Wales	4–1
	6 Apr 1891 v Scotland	2–1
	2 Apr 1892 v Scotland	4–1

162. Frank Ernest Burton
Inside right
Born   Nottingham, 18 March 1865
Died   10 February 1948
Clubs   Notts County; Nottingham Forest

Caps	1	Result
	2 Mar 1889 v Ireland	6–1

163. John Brant Brodie
Centre forward
Born   Wightwick, 22 September 1862
Died   16 February 1925
Clubs   Wolverhampton Wanderers

Caps	3	Result	Goals
	2 Mar 1889 v Ireland	6–1	1
	13 Apr 1889 v Scotland	2–3	
	7 Mar 1891 v Ireland	6–1	

164. Henry Butler Daft
Outside left
Born   Radcliffe-on-Trent, 5 April 1866
Died   12 January 1945
Clubs   Notts County; Nottingham Forest; Newark;
        Corinthians; Nottinghamshire

Caps	5	Result	Goals
	2 Mar 1889 v Ireland	6–1	
	15 Mar 1890 v Wales	3–1	
	5 Apr 1890 v Scotland	1–1	1
	7 Mar 1891 v Ireland	6–1	1
	5 Mar 1892 v Ireland	2–0	2

165. John Yates
Outside left
Born   Blackburn, 2 December 1861
Died   1 June 1917
Clubs   Accrington; Blackburn Olympic; Burnley; Lancashire

Caps	1	Result	Goals
	2 Mar 1889 v Ireland	6–1	3

166. Henry Edward Denison Hammond
Right half
Born   Priston, near Bath, 26 November 1866
Died   16 June 1910
Clubs   Oxford University; Lancing Old Boys; Corinthians

Caps	1	Result
	13 Apr 1889 v Scotland	2–3

167. John Holt
Centre half
Born   Church, 10 April 1865
Clubs   King's Own FC; Blackpool St John's; Church; Bootle;
        Everton; Reading

Caps	10	Result
	15 Mar 1890 v Wales	3–1
	7 Mar 1891 v Wales	4–1
	6 Apr 1891 v Scotland	2–1
	5 Mar 1892 v Ireland	2–0
	2 Apr 1892 v Scotland	4–1
	1 Apr 1893 v Scotland	5–2
	1 Mar 1894 v Ireland	2–2
	7 Apr 1894 v Scotland	2–2
	6 Apr 1895 v Scotland	3–0
	17 Mar 1900 v Ireland	2–0

168. Edmund Samuel Currey
Inside forward
Born   Lewes, 28 June 1868
Died   4 March 1920
Clubs   Oxford University; Old Carthusians; Corinthians

Caps	2	Result	Goals
	15 Mar 1890 v Wales	3–1	2
	5 Apr 1890 v Scotland	1–1	

169. Harry Wood
Inside forward
Born   Walsall, 26 June 1868
Died   5 July 1951
Clubs   Walsall Town Swifts; Wolverhampton Wanderers;
        Southampton; Portsmouth

Caps	3	Result	Goals
	15 Mar 1890 v Wales	3–1	
	5 Apr 1890 v Scotland	1–1	1
	4 Apr 1896 v Scotland	1–2	

170. John Barton
Right half
Born   Blackburn, 5 October 1866
Died   22 April 1910
Clubs   Witton FC; Blackburn West End; Blackburn Rovers

Caps	1	Result	Goals
	15 Mar 1890 v Ireland	9–1	1

171. Charles Perry
Centre half
Born   West Bromwich, 16 January 1866
Died   2 July 1927
Clubs   West Bromwich Strollers; West Bromwich Albion

Caps	3	Result
	15 Mar 1890 v Ireland	9–1
	7 Mar 1891 v Ireland	6–1
	13 Mar 1893 v Wales	6–0

172. Fred Geary
Centre forward
Born Hyson Green, 23 January 1868
Died 8 January 1955
Clubs Balmoral FC; Notts Rangers; Grimsby Town; Notts County; Everton; Liverpool

Caps 2	Result	Goals
15 Mar 1890 v Ireland	9–1	3
6 Apr 1891 v Scotland	2–1	

173. Nathaniel Walton
Inside forward
Born Preston, 30 November 1867
Died 3 March 1930
Clubs Witton FC; Blackburn Rovers; Nelson

Caps 1	Result
15 Mar 1890 v Ireland	9–1

174. Leonard Rodwell Wilkinson
Goalkeeper
Born Highgate, London, 15 October 1868
Died 9 February 1913
Clubs Oxford University; Old Carthusians; Corinthians

Caps 1	Result
7 Mar 1891 v Wales	4–1

175. Thomas Stoddard Porteous
Right back
Born Newcastle-upon-Tyne, 1 May 1865
Died 23 February 1919
Clubs Heart of Midlothian; Kilmarnock; Sunderland; Rotherham Town; Manchester City

Caps 1	Result
7 Mar 1891 v Wales	4–1

176. Elphinstone Jackson
Fullback
Born Calcutta, India, 9 October 1868
Died 20 December 1945
Clubs Oxford University; Corinthians

Caps 1	Result
7 Mar 1891 v Wales	4–1

177. Albert Smith
Right half
Born Nottingham, 23 July 1869
Died 18 April 1921
Clubs Notts Rangers; Long Eaton Rangers; Derby County; Nottingham Forest; Notts County; Blackburn Rovers

Caps 3	Result
7 Mar 1891 v Wales	4–1
6 Apr 1891 v Scotland	2–1
25 Feb 1893 v Ireland	6–1

178. Alfred Weatherell Milward
Outside left
Born Great Marlow, 12 September 1870
Died 10 November 1934
Clubs Old Borlasians; Marlow; Everton; New Brighton Tower; Southampton; New Brompton

Caps 4	Result	Goals
7 Mar 1891 v Wales	4–1	1
6 Apr 1891 v Scotland	2–1	
29 Mar 1897 v Wales	4–0	2
3 Apr 1897 v Scotland	1–2	

179. Edgar Wallace Chadwick
Inside left
Born Blackburn, 14 June 1869
Died 14 February 1942
Clubs Little Dots FC; Blackburn Olympic; Blackburn Rovers; Everton; Burnley; Southampton; Liverpool; Blackpool; Glossop; Darwen

Caps 7	Result	Goals
7 Mar 1891 v Wales	4–1	1

	Result	Goals
6 Apr 1891 v Scotland	2–1	1
2 Apr 1892 v Scotland	4–1	1
1 Apr 1893 v Scotland	5–2	
7 Apr 1894 v Scotland	2–2	
7 Mar 1896 v Ireland	2–0	
3 Apr 1897 v Scotland	1–2	

180. Joseph Thomas Marsden
Right back
Born Darwen, 24 July 1868
Died 18 January 1897
Clubs Darwen; Everton

Caps 1	Result
7 Mar 1891 v Ireland	6–1

181. Alfred Underwood
Left back
Born Newcastle-under-Lyme, 2 August 1868
Died 8 October 1928
Clubs Hanley Tabernacle; Etruria FC; Stoke

Caps 2	Result
7 Mar 1891 v Ireland	6–1
5 Mar 1892 v Ireland	2–0

182. Albert Edward James Matthias 'Jem' Bayliss
Inside right/Centre forward
Born Tipton, 30 August 1863
Died 19 August 1933
Clubs Great Bridge Unity; Tipton Providence; Wednesbury Old Athletic; West Bromwich Albion

Caps 1	Result
7 Mar 1891 v Ireland	6–1

183. George Huth Cotterill
Centre forward
Born Brighton, 4 April 1868
Died 1 October 1950
Clubs Cambridge University; Corinthians; Old Brightonians; Weybridge; Burgess Hill; Surrey; Sussex

Caps 4	Result	Goals
7 Mar 1891 v Ireland	6–1	1
5 Mar 1892 v Wales	2–0	
25 Feb 1893 v Ireland	6–1	
1 Apr 1893 v Scotland	5–2	1

184. Arthur George Henfrey
Halfback/Forward
Born Wellingborough, 22 November 1868
Died 17 October 1929
Clubs Cambridge University; Finedon FC; Corinthians; Northamptonshire

Caps 5	Result	Goals
7 Mar 1891 v Ireland	6–1	1
5 Mar 1892 v Wales	2–0	1
18 Mar 1895 v Wales	1–1	
16 Mar 1896 v Wales	9–1	
4 Apr 1896 v Scotland	1–2	

185. George Toone
Goalkeeper
Born Nottingham, 10 June 1868
Died 1 September 1943
Clubs Notts Rangers; Notts County; Bedminster; Bristol City

Caps 2	Result
5 Mar 1892 v Wales	2–0
2 Apr 1892 v Scotland	4–1

🌐 DID YOU KNOW...?

At Blackburn on 6 April 1891, thousands of spectators stayed away from the England v Scotland match as there was no Blackburn Rovers player in the side. England won 2–1 and the second goal was scored by Everton's Edgar Chadwick, a native of Blackburn.

186. Henry Lilley
Left back
Born Staveley, 20 October 1873
Clubs Staveley FC; Sheffield Utd; Gainsborough Trinity

Caps	1	*Result*
	5 Mar 1892 v Wales	2–0

187. Anthony Henry Hossack
Right half
Born Walsall, 2 May 1867
Died 24 January 1926
Clubs Cambridge University; Corinthians

Caps	2	*Result*
	5 Mar 1892 v Wales	2–0
	12 Mar 1894 v Wales	5–1

188. William Norman Winckworth
Right half
Born London, 9 February 1870
Died 9 November 1941
Clubs Old Westminsters; Corinthians

Caps	2	*Result*	*Goals*
	5 Mar 1892 v Wales	2–0	
	25 Feb 1893 v Ireland	6–1	1

189. George Kinsey
Left half
Born Burton-on-Trent, 20 June 1866
Died 16 January 1911
Clubs Burton Crusaders; Burton Swifts; Mitchell St George's; Wolverhampton Wanderers; Aston Villa; Derby County; Notts County; Bristol Eastville Rovers

Caps	4	*Result*
	5 Mar 1892 v Wales	2–0
	1 Apr 1893 v Scotland	5–2
	7 Mar 1894 v Ireland	2–0
	16 Mar 1896 v Wales	9–1

190. Robert Cunliffe Gosling
Inside forward
Born Farnham, 15 June 1868
Died 18 April 1922
Clubs Cambridge University; Old Etonians; Corinthians

Caps	5	*Result*	*Goals*
	5 Mar 1892 v Wales	2–0	
	1 Apr 1893 v Scotland	5–2	1
	12 Mar 1894 v Wales	5–1	1
	18 Mar 1895 v Wales	1–1	
	6 Apr 1895 v Scotland	3–0	

191. Joseph Alfred Schofield
Outside left
Born Hanley, 1 January 1871
Died 29 September 1929
Clubs Stoke

Caps	3	*Result*	*Goals*
	5 Mar 1892 v Wales	2–0	
	13 Mar 1893 v Wales	6–0	1
	9 Mar 1895 v Ireland	9–0	

192. Rupert Renorden Sandilands
Outside left
Born Thrapston, 7 August 1868
Died 20 April 1946
Clubs Old Westminsters; Casuals; Corinthians; London; Kent

Caps	5	*Result*	*Goals*
	5 Mar 1892 v Wales	2–0	1
	25 Feb 1893 v Ireland	6–1	1
	12 Mar 1894 v Wales	5–1	
	18 Mar 1895 v Wales	1–1	
	16 Mar 1896 v Wales	9–1	

193. John Davies Cox
Right half
Born Spondon, 13 November 1870
Died 20 June 1957

Clubs Spondon FC; Long Eaton Rangers; Derby County

Caps	1	*Result*
	5 Mar 1892 v Ireland	2–0

194. Michael Whitham
Right back
Born Ecclesfield, 6 November 1867
Died 6 May 1924
Clubs Ecclesfield FC; Rotherham Swifts; Sheffield Utd

Caps	1	*Result*
	5 Mar 1892 v Ireland	2–0

195. William Charles Athersmith
Outside right
Born Bloxwich, 10 May 1872
Died 18 September 1910
Clubs Unity Gas Depot; Aston Villa; Small Heath; Grimsby Town

Caps	12	*Result*	*Goals*
	5 Mar 1892 v Ireland	2–0	
	20 Feb 1897 v Ireland	6–0	1
	29 Mar 1897 v Wales	4–0	
	3 Apr 1897 v Scotland	1–2	
	5 Mar 1898 v Ireland	3–2	1
	28 Mar 1898 v Wales	3–0	
	2 Apr 1898 v Scotland	3–1	
	18 Feb 1899 v Ireland	13–2	1
	20 Mar 1899 v Wales	4–0	
	8 Apr 1899 v Scotland	2–1	
	26 Mar 1900 v Wales	1–1	
	7 Apr 1900 v Scotland	1–4	

196. John Hargreaves Pearson
Inside right
Born Crewe, 25 January 1868
Died 22 June 1931
Clubs Crewe Alexandra

Caps	1	*Result*
	5 Mar 1892 v Ireland	2–0

197. John Henry George Devey
Inside right/Centre forward
Born Birmingham, 26 December 1866
Died 11 October 1940
Clubs Excelsior FC; Aston Unity; Mitchell St George's; Aston Villa

Caps	2	*Result*	*Goals*
	5 Mar 1892 v Ireland	2–0	
	1 Mar 1894 v Ireland	2–2	1

198. John Reynolds
Right half
Born Blackburn, 21 February 1869
Died 12 March 1917
Clubs Park Road; Witton FC; Blackburn Rovers; Belfast Distillery; Ulster; West Bromwich Albion; Droitwich FC; Aston Villa; Celtic; Southampton; Bristol St George's; Stockport County; Willesden Town FC

Caps	8	*Result*	*Goals*
	2 Apr 1892 v Scotland	4–1	
	13 Mar 1893 v Wales	6–0	1
	1 Apr 1893 v Scotland	5–2	1
	1 Mar 1894 v Ireland	2–2	
	7 Apr 1894 v Scotland	2–2	1
	6 Apr 1895 v Scotland	3–0	
	29 Mar 1897 v Wales	4–0	
	3 Apr 1897 v Scotland	1–2	

199. Charles Christopher Charsley
Goalkeeper
Born Leicester, 7 November 1864
Died 10 January 1945
Clubs Stafford Rangers; Small Heath; West Bromwich Albion

Caps	1	*Result*
	25 Feb 1893 v Ireland	6–1

DID YOU KNOW...?

Excluding own goals, Jack Reynolds remains the only player to have scored for and against England, as he also played several games for Ireland in the late nineteenth century.

200. Alban Hugh Harrison
Right back
Born   Bredhurst, 30 November 1869
Died   15 August 1943
Clubs   Cambridge University; Old Westminsters; Corinthians

Caps	2	Result
	25 Feb 1893 v Ireland	6–1
	1 Apr 1893 v Scotland	5–2

201. Frederick Raymond Pelly
Left back
Born   Upminster, 11 August 1868
Died   16 October 1940
Clubs   Old Foresters; Corinthians; Casuals; Essex; London

Caps	3	Result
	25 Feb 1893 v Ireland	6–1
	12 Mar 1894 v Wales	5–1
	7 Apr 1894 v Scotland	2–2

202. Norman Charles Cooper
Wing half
Born   Long Ditton, 12 July 1870
Died   30 July 1920
Clubs   Cambridge University; Old Brightonians; Corinthians

Caps	1	Result
	25 Feb 1893 v Ireland	6–1

203. Robert Topham
Outside right
Born   Ellesmere, 3 November 1867
Died   31 August 1931
Clubs   Oxford University; Oswestry FC; Wolverhampton Wanderers; Casuals; Chiswick Park; Corinthians

Caps	2	Result
	25 Feb 1893 v Ireland	6–1
	12 Mar 1894 v Wales	5–1

204. Gilbert Oswald Smith
Centre forward
Born   Croydon, 25 November 1872
Died   6 December 1943
Clubs   Oxford University; Old Carthusians; Corinthians

Caps	20	Result	Goals
	25 Feb 1893 v Ireland	6–1	1
	12 Mar 1894 v Wales	5–1	
	7 Apr 1894 v Scotland	2–2	
	18 Mar 1895 v Wales	1–1	1
	7 Mar 1896 v Ireland	2–0	1
	16 Mar 1896 v Wales	9–1	2
	4 Apr 1896 v Scotland	1–2	
	20 Feb 1897 v Ireland	6–0	
	29 Mar 1897 v Wales	4–0	
	3 Apr 1897 v Scotland	1–2	
	5 Mar 1898 v Ireland	3–2	1
	28 Mar 1898 v Wales	3–0	1
	2 Apr 1898 v Scotland	3–1	
	18 Feb 1899 v Ireland	13–2	4
	20 Mar 1899 v Wales	4–0	
	8 Apr 1899 v Scotland	2–1	1
	17 Mar 1900 v Ireland	2–0	
	26 Mar 1900 v Wales	1–1	
	7 Apr 1900 v Scotland	1–4	
	30 Mar 1901 v Scotland	2–2	

205. Walter Evelyn Gilliat
Inside forward
Born   Stoke Poges, 22 July 1869
Died   2 January 1963
Clubs   Oxford University; Old Carthusians; Woking

Caps	1	Result	Goals
	25 Feb 1893 v Ireland	6–1	3

206. John William Sutcliffe
Goalkeeper
Born   Shibden, 14 April 1898
Died   7 July 1947
Clubs   Bolton Wanderers; Millwall Athletic; Manchester Utd; Plymouth Argyle; Southend Utd

Caps	5	Result
	13 Mar 1893 v Wales	6–0
	9 Mar 1895 v Ireland	9–0
	6 Apr 1895 v Scotland	3–0
	30 Mar 1901 v Scotland	2–2
	2 Mar 1903 v Wales	2–1

207. James Albert Turner
Left half
Born   Blackbull, 11 June 1866
Died   9 April 1904
Clubs   Black Lane Rovers; Bolton Wanderers; Stoke; Derby County

Caps	3	Result
	13 Mar 1893 v Wales	6–0
	9 Mar 1895 v Ireland	9–0
	5 Mar 1898 v Ireland	3–2

208. James Whitehead
Inside right
Born   Church, 14 May 1870
Died   22 August 1929
Clubs   Peel Bank; Accrington; Blackburn Rovers; Manchester City

Caps	2	Result
	13 Mar 1893 v Wales	6–0
	1 Mar 1894 v Ireland	2–2

209. Frederick Spiksley
Outside left
Born   Gainsborough, 25 January 1870
Died   28 July 1948
Clubs   Jubilee Swifts; Gainsborough Trinity; Sheffield Wednesday; Glossop; Leeds City; Southend Utd; Watford

Caps	7	Result	Goals
	13 Mar 1893 v Wales	6–0	2
	1 Apr 1893 v Scotland	5–2	2
	1 Mar 1894 v Ireland	2–2	1
	7 Apr 1894 v Scotland	2–2	
	7 Mar 1896 v Ireland	2–0	
	28 Mar 1898 v Wales	3–0	
	2 Apr 1898 v Scotland	3–1	

210. Leslie Hewitt Gay
Goalkeeper
Born   Brighton, 24 March 1871
Died   1 November 1949
Clubs   Cambridge University; Old Brightonians; Corinthians

Caps	3	Result
	1 Apr 1893 v Scotland	5–2
	12 Mar 1894 v Wales	5–1
	7 Apr 1894 v Scotland	2–2

211. Joseph Reader
Goalkeeper
Born   West Bromwich, 27 February 1866
Died   8 March 1954
Clubs   Carters Green FC; West Bromwich Albion

Caps	1	Result
	1 Mar 1894 v Ireland	2–2

212. James William Crabtree
Fullback/Halfback

Born   Burnley, 23 December 1871
Died   18 June 1908
Clubs   Burnley Royal Swifts; Rossendale; Heywood
        Central; Burnley; Aston Villa; Plymouth Argyle

Caps	14	Result	
	1 Mar 1894 v Ireland	2–2	
	9 Mar 1895 v Ireland	9–0	
	6 Apr 1895 v Scotland	3–0	
	7 Mar 1896 v Ireland	2–0	
	16 Mar 1896 v Wales	9–1	
	4 Apr 1896 v Scotland	1–2	
	18 Feb 1899 v Ireland	13–2	
	20 Mar 1899 v Wales	4–0	
	8 Apr 1899 v Scotland	2–1	
	17 Mar 1900 v Ireland	2–0	
	26 Mar 1900 v Wales	1–1	
	7 Apr 1900 v Scotland	1–4	
	18 Mar 1901 v Wales	6–0	
	3 Mar 1902 v Wales	0–0	

213. Harry Chippendale
Outside right

Born   Blackburn, 2 October 1870
Died   29 September 1952
Clubs   Nelson; Blackburn Rovers

Caps	1	Result
	1 Mar 1894 v Ireland	2–2

214. Lewis Vaughan Lodge
Fullback

Born   Aycliffe, 21 December 1872
Died   21 October 1916
Clubs   Cambridge University; Corinthians; Casuals

Caps	5	Result
	12 Mar 1894 v Wales	5–1
	18 Mar 1895 v Wales	1–1
	6 Apr 1895 v Scotland	3–0
	7 Mar 1896 v Ireland	2–0
	4 Apr 1896 v Scotland	1–2

215. Arthur George Topham
Halfback

Born   Ellesmere, 19 February 1869
Died   18 May 1931
Clubs   Oxford University; Casuals; Eastbourne; Chiswick
        Park; Corinthians

Caps	1	Result
	12 Mar 1894 v Wales	5–1

216. John Gould Veitch
Inside left/Outside left

Born   Kingston Hill, 19 July 1869
Died   3 October 1914
Clubs   Cambridge University; Old Westminsters;
        Corinthians

Caps	1	Result	Goals
	12 Mar 1894 v Wales	5–1	3

217. Ernest 'Nudger' Needham
Left half

Born   Newbold Moor, 21 January 1873
Died   8 March 1936
Clubs   Waverley FC; Staveley Wanderers; Staveley Town;
        Sheffield Utd

Caps	16	Result	Goals
	7 Apr 1894 v Scotland	2–2	
	6 Apr 1895 v Scotland	3–0	
	20 Feb 1897 v Ireland	6–0	
	29 Mar 1897 v Wales	4–0	1
	3 Apr 1897 v Scotland	1–2	
	28 Mar 1898 v Wales	3–0	
	2 Apr 1898 v Scotland	3–1	
	18 Feb 1899 v Ireland	13–2	
	20 Mar 1899 v Wales	4–0	1

	8 Apr 1899 v Scotland	2–1	
	17 Mar 1900 v Ireland	2–0	
	7 Apr 1900 v Scotland	1–4	
	9 Mar 1901 v Ireland	3–0	
	18 Mar 1901 v Wales	6–0	1
	30 Mar 1901 v Scotland	2–2	
	3 Mar 1902 v Wales	0–0	

218. Raby Howell
Right half

Born   Wincobank, 12 October 1869
Died   20 June 1937
Clubs   Ecclesfield; Rotherham Swifts; Sheffield Utd;
        Liverpool; Preston North End

Caps	2	Result	Goals
	9 Mar 1895 v Ireland	9–0	1
	8 Apr 1899 v Scotland	2–1	

219. Thomas Henry Crawshaw
Centre half

Born   Sheffield, 27 December 1872
Died   25 November 1960
Clubs   Park Grange; Attercliffe; Heywood Central; Sheffield
        Wednesday; Chesterfield Town

Caps	10	Result	Goals
	9 Mar 1895 v Ireland	9–0	
	7 Mar 1896 v Ireland	2–0	
	16 Mar 1896 v Wales	9–1	
	4 Apr 1896 v Scotland	1–2	
	20 Feb 1897 v Ireland	6–0	
	29 Mar 1897 v Wales	4–0	
	3 Apr 1897 v Scotland	1–2	
	9 Mar 1901 v Ireland	3–0	1
	29 Feb 1904 v Wales	2–2	
	12 Mar 1904 v Ireland	3–1	

220. Stephen Bloomer
Inside right

Born   Cradley Heath, 20 January 1874
Died   16 April 1938
Clubs   Derby Swifts; Derby County; Middlesbrough

Caps	23	Result	Goals
	9 Mar 1895 v Ireland	9–0	2
	6 Apr 1895 v Scotland	3–0	1
	7 Mar 1896 v Ireland	2–0	1
	16 Mar 1896 v Wales	9–1	5
	20 Feb 1897 v Ireland	6–0	2
	29 Mar 1897 v Wales	4–0	1
	3 Apr 1897 v Scotland	1–2	1
	2 Apr 1898 v Scotland	3–1	2
	18 Feb 1899 v Ireland	13–2	2
	20 Mar 1899 v Wales	4–0	2
	8 Apr 1899 v Scotland	2–1	
	7 Apr 1900 v Scotland	1–4	1
	18 Mar 1901 v Wales	6–0	4
	30 Mar 1901 v Scotland	2–2	1
	3 Mar 1902 v Wales	0–0	
	22 Mar 1902 v Ireland	1–0	
	3 May 1902 v Scotland	2–2	
	9 Apr 1904 v Scotland	1–0	1
	25 Feb 1905 v Ireland	1–1	1
	27 Mar 1905 v Wales	3–1	
	1 Apr 1905 v Scotland	1–0	
	18 Mar 1907 v Wales	1–1	
	6 Apr 1907 v Scotland	1–1	1

221. Francis Becton
Inside forward

Born   Preston, 15 November 1873
Died   6 November 1909
Clubs   Fishwick Ramblers; Preston North End; Liverpool;
        Sheffield Utd; Bedminster; Swindon Town; Ashton
        Town; New Brighton Tower

Caps	2	Result	Goals
	9 Mar 1895 v Ireland	9–0	2
	29 Mar 1897 v Wales	4–0	

222. George Berkeley Raikes
Goalkeeper

Born	Carleton-Forehoe, 14 March 1873
Died	18 December 1966
Clubs	Oxford University; Corinthians; Wymondham FC; Norfolk

Caps	4	Result
	18 Mar 1895 v Wales	1–1
	7 Mar 1896 v Ireland	2–0
	16 Mar 1896 v Wales	9–1
	4 Apr 1896 v Scotland	1–2

223. William John Oakley
Fullback

Born	Shrewsbury, 27 April 1873
Died	20 September 1934
Clubs	Oxford University; Corinthians; Casuals

Caps	16	Result
	18 Mar 1895 v Wales	1–1
	7 Mar 1896 v Ireland	2–0
	16 Mar 1896 v Wales	9–1
	4 Apr 1896 v Scotland	1–2
	20 Feb 1897 v Ireland	6–0
	29 Mar 1897 v Wales	4–0
	3 Apr 1897 v Scotland	1–2
	5 Mar 1898 v Ireland	3–2
	28 Mar 1898 v Wales	3–0
	2 Apr 1898 v Scotland	3–1
	17 Mar 1900 v Ireland	2–0
	26 Mar 1900 v Wales	1–1
	7 Apr 1900 v Scotland	1–4
	9 Mar 1901 v Ireland	3–0
	18 Mar 1901 v Wales	6–0
	30 Mar 1901 v Scotland	2–2

224. Richard Raine Barker
Wing half

Born	Kensington, 29 May 1869
Died	1 October 1940
Clubs	Casuals; Corinthians

Caps	1	Result
	18 Mar 1895 v Wales	1–1

225. Maurice Hugh Stanbrough
Outside left

Born	Cleobury, 2 September 1870
Died	15 December 1904
Clubs	Cambridge University; Old Carthusians; Corinthians; Eastbourne

Caps	1	Result
	18 Mar 1895 v Wales	1–1

226. Gerald Powys Dewhurst
Inside forward

Born	London, 14 February 1872
Died	29 March 1956
Clubs	Cambridge University; Liverpool Ramblers; Corinthians

Caps	1	Result
	18 Mar 1895 v Wales	1–1

227. Stephen Smith
Outside left

Born	Abbots Bromley, 14 January 1874
Died	19 May 1935
Clubs	Cannock Town; Rugeley; Ceal FC; Aston Villa; Portsmouth; New Brompton

Caps	1	Result	Goals
	6 Apr 1895 v Scotland	3–0	1

228. Cuthbert James Burnup
Outside left

Born	Blackheath, 21 November 1875
Died	5 April 1960
Clubs	Cambridge University; Old Malvernians; Corinthians

Caps	1	Result
	4 Apr 1896 v Scotland	1–2

229. John William Robinson
Goalkeeper

Born	Derby, 22 April 1870
Died	28 October 1931
Clubs	Derby Midland; Lincoln City; Derby County; New Brighton Tower; Southampton; Plymouth Argyle; Exeter City; Millwall Athletic; Green Waves FC; Stoke

Caps	11	Result
	20 Feb 1897 v Ireland	6–0
	3 Apr 1897 v Scotland	1–2
	5 Mar 1898 v Ireland	3–2
	28 Mar 1898 v Wales	3–0
	2 Apr 1898 v Scotland	3–1
	20 Mar 1899 v Wales	4–0
	8 Apr 1899 v Scotland	2–1
	17 Mar 1900 v Ireland	2–0
	26 Mar 1900 v Wales	1–1
	7 Apr 1900 v Scotland	1–4
	9 Mar 1901 v Ireland	3–0

230. William Williams
Fullback

Born	West Smethwick, 20 January 1876
Died	22 January 1929
Clubs	Hawthorn Villa; West Smethwick; Old Hill Wanderers; West Bromwich Albion

Caps	6	Result
	20 Feb 1897 v Ireland	6–0
	5 Mar 1898 v Ireland	3–2
	28 Mar 1898 v Wales	3–0
	2 Apr 1898 v Scotland	3–1
	18 Feb 1899 v Ireland	13–2
	20 Mar 1899 v Wales	4–0

231. Bernard Middleditch
Right half

Born	Highgate, 22 February 1871
Died	3 October 1949
Clubs	Cambridge University; Corinthians

Caps	1	Result
	20 Feb 1897 v Ireland	6–0

232. George Frederick Wheldon
Inside left

Born	Langley Green, 1 November 1869
Died	13 January 1924
Clubs	Langley Green Victoria; Small Heath; Aston Villa; West Bromwich Albion; Queen's Park Rangers; Portsmouth; Worcester City; Coventry City

Caps	4	Result	Goals
	20 Feb 1897 v Ireland	6–0	3
	5 Mar 1898 v Ireland	3–2	
	28 Mar 1898 v Wales	3–0	2
	2 Apr 1898 v Scotland	3–1	1

233. Thomas Henry Bradshaw
Outside left

Born	Liverpool, 24 August 1873
Died	25 December 1899
Clubs	Northwich Victoria; Liverpool; Tottenham Hotspur; Thames Ironworks

Caps	1	Result
	20 Feb 1897 v Ireland	6–0

234. William Henry Foulke
Goalkeeper

Born	Dawley, 12 April 1874
Died	1 May 1916
Clubs	Alfreton FC; Blackwell Colliery; Sheffield Utd; Chelsea; Bradford City

Caps	1	Result
	29 Mar 1897 v Wales	4–0

235. Howard Spencer
Right back
Born   Birmingham, 23 August 1875
Died   14 January 1940
Clubs   Stamford FC; Birchfield Trinity; Aston Villa
Caps   6

	Result
29 Mar 1897 v Wales	4–0
3 Apr 1897 v Scotland	1–2
26 Mar 1900 v Wales	1–1
14 Feb 1903 v Ireland	4–0
27 Mar 1905 v Wales	3–1
1 Apr 1905 v Scotland	1–0

236. Frank Forman
Right half/Centre half
Born   Aston-on-Trent, 23 May 1875
Died   4 December 1961
Clubs   Aston-on-Trent FC; Beeston Town; Derby County; Nottingham Forest
Caps   9

	Result	Goals
5 Mar 1898 v Ireland	3–2	
2 Apr 1898 v Scotland	3–1	
18 Feb 1899 v Ireland	13–2	1
20 Mar 1899 v Wales	4–0	
8 Apr 1899 v Scotland	2–1	
30 Mar 1901 v Scotland	2–2	
22 Mar 1902 v Ireland	1–0	
3 May 1902 v Scotland	2–2	
2 Mar 1903 v Wales	2–1	

237. Thomas Morren
Centre half
Born   Sunderland, 11 May 1871
Died   31 January 1929
Clubs   Middlesbrough Victoria; Middlesbrough Ironopolis; Middlesbrough FC; Barnsley St Peters; Sheffield Utd
Caps   1

	Result	Goals
5 Mar 1898 v Ireland	3–2	1

238. Charles Henry Richards
Inside right
Born   Burton-on-Trent, 9 August 1875
Clubs   Gresley Rovers; Notts County; Nottingham Forest; Grimsby Town; Leicester Fosse; Newton Heath
Caps   1

	Result
5 Mar 1898 v Ireland	3–2

239. Ben Walter Garfield
Outside left
Born   Burton-on-Trent, 4 April 1872
Died   23 February 1942
Clubs   Kettering Burton Wanderers; West Bromwich Albion; Brighton & Hove Albion
Caps   1

	Result
5 Mar 1898 v Ireland	3–2

240. Thomas Perry
Right half
Born   West Bromwich, 3 November 1871
Died   18 July 1927
Clubs   Christ Church FC; Stourbridge; West Bromwich Albion; Aston Villa
Caps   1

	Result
28 Mar 1898 v Wales	3–0

241. Thomas Edward Booth
Centre half
Born   Ardwick, 25 April 1874
Died   7 September 1939
Clubs   Hooley Hill; Ashton North End; Blackburn Rovers; Everton; Preston North End; Carlisle Utd
Caps   2

	Result
28 Mar 1898 v Wales	3–0
14 Apr 1903 v Scotland	1–2

242. John Hillman
Goalkeeper
Born   Tavistock, 15 November 1871
Died   1 August 1955
Clubs   Burnley; Everton; Dundee; Manchester City; Millwall Athletic
Caps   1

	Result
18 Feb 1899 v Ireland	13–2

243. Philip Bach
Fullback
Born   Ludlow, 20 June 1872
Died   30 December 1937
Clubs   Middlesbrough; Reading; Sunderland; Bristol City
Caps   1

	Result
18 Feb 1899 v Ireland	13–2

244. James Settle
Inside left/Outside left
Born   Millom, 5 March 1875
Clubs   Bolton Wanderers; Halliwell Rovers; Bury; Everton; Stockport County
Caps   6

	Result	Goals
18 Feb 1899 v Ireland	13–2	3
20 Mar 1899 v Wales	4–0	
8 Apr 1899 v Scotland	2–1	1
22 Mar 1902 v Ireland	1–0	1
3 Mar 1902 v Scotland	2–2	1
14 Feb 1903 v Ireland	4–0	

245. Frederick Ralph Forman
Outside right
Born   Aston-on-Trent, 8 November 1873
Died   14 June 1910
Clubs   Aston-on-Trent; Beeston Town; Derby County; Nottingham Forest
Caps   3

	Result	Goals
18 Feb 1899 v Ireland	13–2	2
20 Mar 1899 v Wales	4–0	1
8 Apr 1899 v Scotland	2–1	

246. Henry Thickett
Right back
Born   Hexthorpe, 14 May 1873
Died   15 November 1920
Clubs   Hexthorpe FC; Sheffield Utd; Rotherham Town; Bristol City
Caps   2

	Result
20 Mar 1899 v Wales	4–0
8 Apr 1899 v Scotland	2–1

247. William Harrison Johnson
Wing half
Born   Ecclesfield, 4 January 1876
Died   17 July 1940
Clubs   Atlas and Norfolk Works; Ecclesfield Church; Sheffield Utd
Caps   6

	Result	Goals
17 Mar 1900 v Ireland	2–0	1
26 Mar 1900 v Wales	1–1	
7 Apr 1900 v Scotland	1–4	
14 Feb 1903 v Ireland	4–0	
2 Mar 1903 v Wales	2–1	
14 Apr 1903 v Scotland	1–2	

248. Arthur Turner
Outside right
Born   Farnborough, 20 June 1877
Died   4 April 1925
Clubs   Aldershot North End; South Farnborough; Camberley St Michael's; Southampton; Derby County; Newcastle Utd; Tottenham Hotspur
Caps   2

	Result
17 Mar 1900 v Ireland	2–0
9 Mar 1901 v Ireland	3–0

249. Daniel Cunliffe
Inside right
Born   Bolton, 11 November 1875
Died   28 December 1937
Clubs Little Lever; Middleton Borough; Oldham County;
       Liverpool; New Brighton Tower; Portsmouth; New
       Brompton; Millwall Athletic; Heywood; Rochdale

Caps	1	Result
	17 Mar 1900 v Ireland	2–0

250. Charles Sagar
Centre forward/Inside forward
Born   Edgworth, 28 March 1878
Died   4 December 1919
Clubs Edgworth Rovers; Turton FC; Bury; Manchester Utd;
       Haslingden FC

Caps	2	Result	Goals
	17 Mar 1900 v Ireland	2–0	1
	3 Mar 1902 v Wales	0–0	

251. Alfred Ernest 'Fred' Priest
Inside left/Outside left
Born   Guisborough, 8 August 1875
Died   5 May 1922
Clubs Darlington; South Bank; Sheffield Utd;
       Middlesbrough; Hartlepool Utd

Caps	1	Result
	17 Mar 1900 v Ireland	2–0

252. Arthur Chadwick
Centre half
Born   Church, 12 September 1875
Died   21 March 1936
Clubs Church FC; Accrington; Burton Swifts;
       Southampton; Portsmouth; Northampton Town;
       Exeter City

Caps	2	Result
	26 Mar 1900 v Wales	1–1
	7 Apr 1900 v Scotland	1–4

253. Reginald Erskine 'Tip' Foster
Inside forward
Born   Malvern, 16 April 1878
Died   13 May 1914
Clubs Oxford University; Old Malvernians; Corinthians

Caps	5	Result	Goals
	26 Mar 1900 v Wales	1–1	
	9 Mar 1901 v Ireland	3–0	2
	18 Mar 1901 v Wales	6–0	1
	30 Mar 1901 v Scotland	2–2	
	3 Mar 1902 v Wales	0–0	

254. George Plumpton Wilson
Inside left
Born   Bourne, 21 February 1878
Died   30 July 1934
Clubs Corinthians; Southampton; Casuals; London Hospital

Caps	2	Result	Goals
	26 Mar 1900 v Wales	1–1	1
	7 Apr 1900 v Scotland	1–4	

255. William Alfred Spouncer
Outside left
Born   Gainsborough, 1 July 1877
Died   31 August 1962
Clubs Gainsborough Trinity; Sheffield Utd; Nottingham
       Forest

Caps	1	Result
	26 Mar 1900 v Wales	1–1

256. John Plant
Outside left
Born   Bollington, 3 September 1871
Clubs Denton FC; Bollington FC; Bury; Reading

Caps	1	Result
	7 Apr 1900 v Scotland	1–4

257. Charles Burgess Fry
Right back
Born   Croydon, 25 April 1872
Died   7 September 1956
Clubs West Kent FC; Casuals; Oxford University; Old
       Reptonians; Corinthians; Southampton; Portsmouth

Caps	1	Result
	9 Mar 1901 v Ireland	3–0

258. William Jones
Right half
Born   Brighton, 6 March 1876
Died   3 September 1908
Clubs Heaton Rovers; Willington Athletic; Loughborough
       Town; Bristol City; Tottenham Hotspur; Swindon Town

Caps	1	Result
	9 Mar 1901 v Ireland	3–0

259. George Albert Hedley
Centre forward
Born   South Bank, 20 July 1876
Died   16 August 1942
Clubs South Bank FC; Sheffield Utd; Southampton;
       Wolverhampton Wanderers

Caps	1	Result
	9 Mar 1901 v Ireland	3–0

260. Herbert Ernest Banks
Inside left
Born   Coventry, 22 February 1874
Died   14 November 1947
Clubs Everton; Third Lanark; Millwall Athletic; Aston Villa;
       Bristol City; Watford

Caps	1	Result
	9 Mar 1901 v Ireland	3–0

261. John Cox
Outside left
Born   Blackpool, 21 November 1876
Clubs South Shore FC; Blackpool; Liverpool

Caps	3	Result
	9 Mar 1901 v Ireland	3–0
	3 May 1902 v Scotland	2–2
	14 Apr 1903 v Scotland	1–2

262. Matthew Kingsley
Goalkeeper
Born   Turton, 15 November 1875
Died   27 March 1960
Clubs Edgworth; Turton FC; Darwen; Newcastle Utd; West
       Ham Utd; Queen's Park Rangers; Rochdale; Barrow

Caps	1	Result
	18 Mar 1901 v Wales	6–0

263. Albert Wilkes
Wing half
Born   Birmingham, 11 May 1874
Died   9 December 1936
Clubs Oldbury Town; Walsall; Aston Villa; Fulham

Caps	5	Result	Goals
	18 Mar 1901 v Wales	6–0	
	30 Mar 1901 v Scotland	2–2	
	3 Mar 1902 v Wales	0–0	
	22 Mar 1902 v Ireland	1–0	
	3 May 1902 v Scotland	2–2	1

264. William Bannister
Centre half
Born   Burnley, 14 April 1879
Died   26 March 1942
Clubs Earley FC; Burnley; Bolton Wanderers; Woolwich
       Arsenal; Leicester Fosse

Caps	2	Result
	18 Mar 1901 v Wales	6–0
	22 Mar 1902 v Ireland	1–0

265. Walter 'Cocky' Bennett
Outside right

Born	Mexborough, 7 March 1874	
Died	6 April 1908	
Clubs	Mexborough FC; Sheffield Utd; Bristol City; Denaby Utd	
Caps	2	*Result*
	18 Mar 1901 v Wales	6–0
	30 Mar 1901 v Scotland	2–2

266. William Edwin Beats
Centre forward

Born	Wolstanton, 13 November 1871	
Died	13 April 1939	
Clubs	Port Hill; Port Vale Rovers; Burslem Port Vale; Wolverhampton Wanderers; Bristol Rovers; Reading	
Caps	2	*Result*
	18 Mar 1901 v Wales	6–0
	3 May 1902 v Scotland	2–2

267. Bertram Oswald Corbett
Outside left

Born	Thame, 15 May 1875	
Died	30 November 1967	
Clubs	Oxford University; Corinthians; Reading; Slough	
Caps	1	*Result*
	18 Mar 1901 v Wales	6–0

268. James Iremonger
Fullback

Born	Norton, 5 March 1876	
Died	25 March 1956	
Clubs	Wilford FC; Jardine's FC; Nottingham Forest	
Caps	2	*Result*
	30 Mar 1901 v Scotland	2–2
	22 Mar 1902 v Ireland	1–0

269. Frederick Blackburn
Outside left

Born	Mellor, 23 September 1879	
Clubs	Blackburn Rovers; West Ham Utd	
Caps	3	*Result* Goals
	30 Mar 1901 v Scotland	2–2 1
	22 Mar 1902 v Ireland	1–0
	9 Apr 1904 v Scotland	1–0

270. William George
Goalkeeper

Born	Shrewsbury, 29 June 1874	
Died	4 December 1933	
Clubs	Woolwich Ramblers; Trowbridge Town; Aston Villa	
Caps	3	*Result*
	3 Mar 1902 v Wales	0–0
	22 Mar 1902 v Ireland	1–0
	3 May 1902 v Scotland	2–2

271. Robert Crompton
Right back

Born	Blackburn, 26 September 1879	
Died	15 March 1941	
Clubs	Blackburn Rovers	
Caps	41	*Result*
	3 Mar 1902 v Wales	0–0
	22 Mar 1902 v Ireland	1–0
	3 May 1902 v Scotland	2–2
	2 Mar 1903 v Wales	2–1
	14 Apr 1903 v Scotland	1–2
	29 Feb 1904 v Wales	2–2
	12 Mar 1904 v Ireland	3–1
	9 Apr 1904 v Scotland	1–0
	17 Feb 1906 v Ireland	5–0
	19 Mar 1906 v Wales	1–0
	7 Apr 1906 v Scotland	1–2
	16 Feb 1907 v Ireland	1–0
	18 Mar 1907 v Wales	1–1
	6 Apr 1907 v Scotland	1–1
	15 Feb 1908 v Ireland	3–1
	16 Mar 1908 v Wales	7–1
	4 Apr 1908 v Scotland	1–1
	6 Jun 1908 v Austria	6–1
	8 Jun 1908 v Austria	11–1
	10 Jun 1908 v Hungary	7–0
	13 Jun 1908 v Bohemia	4–0
	13 Feb 1909 v Ireland	4–0
	15 Mar 1909 v Wales	2–0
	3 Apr 1909 v Scotland	2–0
	29 May 1909 v Hungary	4–2
	31 May 1909 v Hungary	8–2
	1 Jun 1909 v Austria	8–1
	14 Mar 1910 v Wales	1–0
	2 Apr 1910 v Scotland	0–2
	11 Feb 1911 v Ireland	2–1
	13 Mar 1911 v Wales	3–0
	1 Apr 1911 v Scotland	1–1
	10 Feb 1912 v Ireland	6–1
	11 Mar 1912 v Wales	2–0
	23 Mar 1912 v Scotland	1–1
	15 Feb 1913 v Ireland	1–2
	17 Mar 1913 v Wales	4–3
	5 Apr 1913 v Scotland	1–0
	14 Feb 1914 v Ireland	0–3
	16 Mar 1914 v Wales	2–0
	4 Apr 1914 v Scotland	1–3

272. Walter Abbott
Left half/Inside left

Born	Birmingham, 7 December 1877	
Died	1 February 1941	
Clubs	Rosewood Victoria; Small Heath; Everton; Burnley	
Caps	1	*Result*
	3 Mar 1902 v Wales	0–0

273. William Hogg
Outside right

Born	Newcastle-upon-Tyne, 29 May 1879	
Died	30 January 1937	
Clubs	Willington Athletic; Sunderland; Rangers; Dundee; Raith Rovers; Montrose	
Caps	3	*Result*
	3 Mar 1902 v Wales	0–0
	22 Mar 1902 v Ireland	1–0
	3 May 1902 v Scotland	2–2

274. Herbert Broughall Lipsham
Outside left

Born	Chester, 29 April 1878	
Died	16 June 1932	
Clubs	Chester; Crewe Alexandra; Sheffield Utd; Fulham; Millwall Athletic	
Caps	1	*Result*
	3 Mar 1902 v Wales	0–0

275. John Calvey
Centre forward

Born	South Bank, 23 June 1875	
Died	11 January 1937	
Clubs	Millwall Athletic; Nottingham Forest	
Caps	1	*Result*
	22 Mar 1902 v Ireland	1–0

276. George Molyneux
Left back

Born	Liverpool, 21 March 1875	
Died	14 April 1942	
Clubs	Third Grenadiers; South Shore; Wigan County; Stoke; Everton; Southampton; Portsmouth; Southend Utd; Colchester Utd	
Caps	4	*Result*
	3 May 1902 v Scotland	2–2
	14 Feb 1903 v Ireland	4–0
	2 Mar 1903 v Wales	2–1
	14 Apr 1903 v Scotland	1–2

277. Albert Edward 'Kelly' Houlker
Left half
Born   Blackburn, 27 April 1872
Died   27 May 1962
Clubs   Blackburn Rovers; Portsmouth; Southampton; Colne FC

Caps	5	Result
	3 May 1902 v Scotland	2–2
	2 Mar 1903 v Wales	2–1
	14 Apr 1903 v Scotland	1–2
	17 Feb 1906 v Ireland	5–0
	19 Mar 1906 v Wales	1–0

278. Thomas Baddeley
Goalkeeper
Born   Burslem, 2 November 1874
Died   24 September 1946
Clubs   Burslem Swifts; Burslem Port Vale; Wolverhampton
        Wanderers; Bradford Park Avenue; Stoke

Caps	5	Result
	14 Feb 1903 v Ireland	4–0
	14 Apr 1903 v Scotland	1–2
	29 Feb 1904 v Wales	2–2
	12 Mar 1904 v Ireland	3–1
	9 Apr 1904 v Scotland	1–0

279. Thomas Holford
Centre half/Left half
Born   Hanley, 28 January 1878
Died   6 April 1964
Clubs   Stoke; Manchester City; Port Vale

Caps	1	Result
	14 Feb 1903 v Ireland	4–0

280. Harry Hadley
Left half
Born   Barrow-in-Furness, 2 April 1877
Died   September 1942
Clubs   Colley Gate Utd; Halesowen; West Bromwich
        Albion; Aston Villa; Nottingham Forest;
        Southampton; Croydon Common

Caps	1	Result
	14 Feb 1903 v Ireland	4–0

281. Harry Davis
Outside right
Born   Wombwell, 23 March 1880
Clubs   Barnsley; Sheffield Wednesday

Caps	3	Result	Goals
	14 Feb 1903 v Ireland	4–0	1
	2 Mar 1903 v Wales	2–1	
	14 Apr 1903 v Scotland	1–2	

282. John Sharp
Outside right
Born   Hereford, 15 February 1878
Died   28 January 1938
Clubs   Hereford Thistle; Aston Villa; Everton

Caps	2	Result	Goals
	14 Feb 1903 v Ireland	4–0	1
	1 Apr 1905 v Scotland	1–0	

283. Vivian John Woodward
Centre forward/Inside forward
Born   Kennington, 3 June 1879
Died   31 January 1954
Clubs   Clacton FC; Harwich & Parkeston; Chelmsford;
        Tottenham Hotspur; Chelsea

Caps	23	Result	Goals
	14 Feb 1903 v Ireland	4–0	2
	2 Mar 1903 v Wales	2–1	1
	14 Apr 1903 v Scotland	1–2	1
	12 Mar 1904 v Ireland	3–1	
	9 Apr 1904 v Scotland	1–0	
	25 Feb 1905 v Ireland	1–1	
	27 Mar 1905 v Wales	3–1	2
	1 Apr 1905 v Scotland	1–0	
	6 Apr 1907 v Scotland	1–1	

	15 Feb 1908 v Ireland	3–1	1
	16 Mar 1908 v Wales	7–1	3
	4 Apr 1908 v Scotland	1–1	
	6 Jun 1908 v Austria	6–1	1
	8 Jun 1908 v Austria	11–1	4
	10 Jun 1908 v Hungary	7–0	1
	13 Jun 1908 v Bohemia	4–0	
	13 Feb 1909 v Ireland	4–0	2
	15 Mar 1909 v Wales	2–0	
	29 May 1909 v Hungary	4–2	2
	31 May 1909 v Hungary	8–2	4
	1 Jun 1909 v Austria	8–1	3
	12 Feb 1910 v Ireland	1–1	
	13 Mar 1911 v Wales	3–0	2

284. Arthur Lockett
Outside left
Born   Alsagers Bank, 3 October 1875
Died   1957
Clubs   Alsagers Bank FC; Crewe Alexandra; Stoke; Aston
        Villa; Preston North End; Watford

Caps	1	Result
	14 Feb 1903 v Ireland	4–0

285. William Garratty
Inside right/Centre forward
Born   Saltley, 6 October 1878
Died   6 May 1931
Clubs   Highfield Villa; Aston Shakespeare; Aston Villa;
        Leicester Fosse; West Bromwich Albion; Lincoln City

Caps	1	Result
	2 Mar 1903 v Wales	2–1

286. Joseph William Bache
Inside left
Born   Stourbridge, 8 February 1880
Died   10 November 1960
Clubs   Stourbridge FC; Aston Villa; Mid-Rhondda; Grimsby
        Town

Caps	7	Result	Goals
	2 Mar 1903 v Wales	2–1	1
	29 Feb 1904 v Wales	2–2	1
	12 Mar 1904 v Ireland	3–1	1
	1 Apr 1905 v Scotland	1–0	1
	16 Feb 1907 v Ireland	1–0	
	12 Feb 1910 v Ireland	1–1	
	1 Apr 1911 v Scotland	1–1	

> ⚽ **DID YOU KNOW...?**
>
> During the 1960s, England's most famous mascot was
> actually a man – Ken Baily – who used to dress up in
> a top hat, Union Jack waistcoat and red hunting
> jacket and parade around the ground before games.

287. Reginald 'Rex' Corbett
Inside left/Outside left
Born   Thame, 31 August 1879
Died   2 September 1967
Clubs   Old Malvernians; Corinthians

Caps	1	Result
	2 Mar 1903 v Wales	2–1

288. Percy Humphreys
Inside right
Born   Cambridge, 3 December 1880
Died   13 April 1959
Clubs   Queen's Park Rangers; Notts County; Leicester
        Fosse; Chelsea; Tottenham Hotspur; Hartlepool Utd

Caps	1	Result
	14 Apr 1903 v Scotland	1–2

289. Arthur John Capes
Inside left
Born Burton-on-Trent, 23 February 1875
Died 26 February 1945
Clubs Burton Wanderers; Nottingham Forest; Stoke; Bristol City; Swindon Town

Caps	1	Result	
	14 Apr 1903 v Scotland	1–2	

290. Herbert Burgess
Left back
Born Manchester, 2 July 1883
Died 1954
Clubs Glossop; Manchester City; Manchester Utd

Caps	4	Result	
	29 Feb 1904 v Wales	2–2	
	12 Mar 1904 v Ireland	3–1	
	9 Apr 1904 v Scotland	1–0	
	7 Apr 1906 v Scotland	1–2	

291. Ernest Albert Lee
Right half
Born Bridport, 20 June 1879
Died 14 January 1958
Clubs Poole FC; Southampton; Dundee

Caps	1	Result	
	9 Feb 1904 v Wales	2–2	

292. Herod Ruddlesdin
Wing half
Born Birdwell, 10 January 1876
Died 26 March 1910
Clubs Birdwell FC; Sheffield Wednesday

Caps	3	Result	
	29 Feb 1904 v Wales	2–2	
	12 Mar 1904 v Ireland	3–1	
	1 Apr 1905 v Scotland	1–0	

293. William Frederick Brawn
Outside right
Born Wellingborough, 1 August 1878
Died 18 August 1932
Clubs Wellingborough FC; Northampton Town; Sheffield Utd; Aston Villa; Middlesbrough; Chelsea; Brentford

Caps	2	Result	
	29 Feb 1904 v Wales	2–2	
	12 Mar 1904 v Ireland	3–1	

294. Alfred Common
Inside right
Born Sunderland, 25 May 1880
Died 3 April 1946
Clubs Jarrow; Sunderland; Sheffield Utd; Middlesbrough; Woolwich Arsenal; Preston North End

Caps	3	Result	Goals
	29 Feb 1904 v Wales	2–2	1
	12 Mar 1904 v Ireland	3–1	1
	19 Mar 1906 v Wales	1–0	

295. Arthur Samuel Brown
Centre forward
Born Gainsborough, 6 April 1885
Died 27 June 1944
Clubs Gainsborough Trinity; Sheffield Utd; Sunderland; Fulham; Middlesbrough

Caps	2	Result	Goals
	29 Feb 1904 v Wales	2–2	
	17 Feb 1906 v Ireland	5–0	1

296. George Henry Davis
Outside left
Born Alfreton, 5 June 1881
Died 28 April 1969
Clubs Alfreton Town; Derby County; Calgary Hillhurst (Canada)

Caps	2	Result	Goals
	29 Feb 1904 v Wales	2–2	
	12 Mar 1904 v Ireland	3–1	1

297. Alexander Leake
Centre half/Left half
Born Birmingham, 11 July 1871
Died 29 March 1938
Clubs Old Hill Wanderers; Small Heath; Aston Villa; Burnley; Wednesbury Old Athletic

Caps	5	Result	
	12 Mar 1904 v Ireland	3–1	
	9 Apr 1904 v Scotland	1–0	
	25 Feb 1905 v Ireland	1–1	
	27 Mar 1905 v Wales	3–1	
	1 Apr 1905 v Scotland	1–0	

298. Samuel Wolstenholme
Right half
Born Little Lever, 25 November 1876
Clubs Darley Vale; Farnworth FC; Farnworth Alliance; Horwich; Everton; Blackburn Rovers; Croydon Common; Norwich City

Caps	3	Result	
	9 Apr 1904 v Scotland	1–0	
	25 Feb 1905 v Ireland	1–1	
	27 Mar 1905 v Wales	3–1	

299. Bernard Wilkinson
Centre half
Born Thorpe Hesley, 12 September 1879
Died 28 May 1949
Clubs Shiregreen; Sheffield Utd; Rotherham Town

Caps	1	Result	
	9 Apr 1904 v Scotland	1–0	

300. John 'Jock' Rutherford
Outside right
Born Percy Main, 12 October 1884
Died 21 April 1963
Clubs Willington Athletic; Newcastle Utd; Woolwich Arsenal

Caps	11	Result	Goals
	9 Apr 1904 v Scotland	1–0	
	16 Feb 1907 v Ireland	1–0	
	18 Mar 1907 v Wales	1–1	
	6 Apr 1907 v Scotland	1–1	
	15 Feb 1908 v Ireland	3–1	
	16 Mar 1908 v Wales	7–1	
	4 Apr 1908 v Scotland	1–1	
	6 Jun 1908 v Austria	6–1	
	8 Jun 1908 v Austria	11–1	1
	10 Jun 1908 v Hungary	7–0	1
	13 Jun 1908 v Bohemia	4–0	1

301. Stanley Shute Harris
Inside left
Born Bristol, 19 July 1881
Died 4 May 1926
Clubs Cambridge University; Old Westminsters; Casuals; Worthing; Corinthians; Portsmouth

Caps	6	Result	Goals
	9 Apr 1904 v Scotland	1–0	
	25 Feb 1905 v Ireland	1–1	
	27 Mar 1905 v Wales	3–1	1
	17 Feb 1906 v Ireland	5–0	1
	19 Mar 1906 v Wales	1–0	
	7 Apr 1906 v Scotland	1–2	

302. Reginald Garnet 'Tim' Williamson
Goalkeeper
Born North Ormesby, 6 June 1884
Died 1 August 1943
Clubs Redcar Crusaders; Middlesbrough

Caps	7	Result	
	25 Feb 1905 v Ireland	1–1	

11 Feb 1911 v Ireland	2–1	
13 Mar 1911 v Wales	3–0	
1 Apr 1911 v Scotland	1–1	
11 Mar 1912 v Wales	2–0	
23 Mar 1912 v Scotland	1–1	
15 Feb 1913 v Ireland	1–2	

303. William Balmer
Right back
Born Liverpool, 24 June 1877
Died 1937
Clubs South Shore; Everton; Croydon Common

Caps	1	Result
	25 Feb 1905 v Ireland	1–1

304. John Carr
Left back
Born Seaton Burn, 1 October 1876
Died 17 March 1948
Clubs Seaton Burn FC; Newcastle Utd

Caps	2	Result
	25 Feb 1905 v Ireland	1–1
	16 Feb 1907 v Ireland	1–0

305. Charles Roberts
Centre half
Born Darlington, 6 April 1883
Died 7 August 1939
Clubs Darlington St Augustine's; Bishop Auckland; Grimsby Town; Manchester Utd; Oldham Athletic

Caps	3	Result
	25 Feb 1905 v Ireland	1–1
	27 Mar 1905 v Wales	3–1
	1 Apr 1905 v Scotland	1–0

306. Richard Bond
Outside right
Born Garstang, 14 December 1883
Died 25 April 1955
Clubs Preston North End; Bradford City; Blackburn Rovers; Lancaster Town; Garstang FC

Caps	8	Result	Goals
	25 Feb 1905 v Ireland	1–1	
	27 Mar 1905 v Wales	3–1	
	17 Feb 1906 v Ireland	5–0	2
	19 Mar 1906 v Wales	1–0	
	7 Apr 1906 v Scotland	1–2	
	12 Feb 1910 v Ireland	1–1	
	14 Mar 1910 v Wales	1–0	
	2 Apr 1910 v Scotland	0–2	

307. Frank Booth
Outside left
Born Hyde, 30 September 1882
Died 22 June 1919
Clubs Hyde FC; Glossop; Stockport County; Manchester City; Bury; Clyde

Caps	1	Result
	25 Feb 1905 v Ireland	1–1

308. James Henry Linacre
Goalkeeper
Born Aston-on-Trent, 26 March 1881
Died 11 May 1957
Clubs Aston-on-Trent FC; Draycott Mills; Derby County; Nottingham Forest

Caps	2	Result
	27 Mar 1905 v Wales	3–1
	1 Apr 1905 v Scotland	1–0

309. Herbert Smith
Left back
Born Witney, 22 November 1879
Died 6 January 1951
Clubs Witney FC; Reading; Oxford City; Derby County; Stoke; Richmond; Oxfordshire

Caps	4	Result
	27 Mar 1905 v Wales	3–1
	1 Apr 1905 v Scotland	1–0
	17 Feb 1906 v Ireland	5–0
	19 Mar 1906 v Wales	1–0

310. Harold Payne Hardman
Outside left
Born Manchester, 4 April 1882
Died 9 June 1965
Clubs Northern Nomads; Blackpool; Everton; Manchester Utd; Bradford City; Stoke

Caps	4	Result	Goals
	27 Mar 1905 v Wales	3–1	
	16 Feb 1907 v Ireland	1–0	1
	6 Apr 1907 v Scotland	1–1	
	16 Mar 1908 v Wales	7–1	

311. Arthur Bridgett
Outside left
Born Forsbrook, 22 October 1882
Died 1954
Clubs Burslem Park; Trentham; Stoke; Sunderland; South Shields; Port Vale

Caps	11	Result	Goals
	1 Apr 1905 v Scotland	1–0	
	4 Apr 1908 v Scotland	1–1	
	6 Jun 1908 v Austria	6–1	1
	8 Jun 1908 v Austria	11–1	1
	10 Jun 1908 v Hungary	7–0	
	13 Jun 1908 v Bohemia	4–0	
	13 Feb 1909 v Ireland	4–0	
	15 Mar 1909 v Wales	2–0	
	29 May 1909 v Hungary	4–2	1
	31 May 1908 v Hungary	8–2	
	1 Jun 1909 v Austria	8–1	

312. James Ashcroft
Goalkeeper
Born Liverpool, 12 September 1878
Died 9 April 1943
Clubs Garston Copper Works; Gravesend Utd; Woolwich Arsenal; Blackburn Rovers; Tranmere Rovers

Caps	3	Result
	17 Feb 1906 v Ireland	5–0
	19 Mar 1906 v Wales	1–0
	7 Apr 1906 v Scotland	1–2

313. Benjamin Warren
Right half
Born Newhall, 14 July 1879
Died 15 January 1917
Clubs Newhall Town; Newhall Swifts; Derby County; Chelsea

Caps	22	Result	Goals
	17 Feb 1906 v Ireland	5–0	
	19 Mar 1906 v Wales	1–0	
	7 Apr 1906 v Scotland	1–2	
	16 Feb 1907 v Ireland	1–0	
	18 Mar 1907 v Wales	1–1	
	6 Apr 1907 v Scotland	1–1	
	15 Feb 1908 v Ireland	3–1	
	16 Mar 1908 v Wales	7–1	
	4 Apr 1908 v Scotland	1–1	
	6 Jun 1908 v Austria	6–1	
	8 Jun 1908 v Austria	11–1	1
	10 Jun 1908 v Hungary	7–0	
	13 Jun 1908 v Bohemia	4–0	
	13 Feb 1909 v Ireland	4–0	
	15 Mar 1909 v Wales	2–0	
	3 Apr 1909 v Scotland	2–0	
	29 May 1909 v Hungary	4–2	
	31 May 1909 v Hungary	8–2	
	1 Jun 1909 v Austria	8–1	1
	11 Feb 1911 v Ireland	2–1	
	13 Mar 1911 v Wales	3–0	
	1 Apr 1911 v Scotland	1–1	

314. Colin Campbell Veitch
Halfback

Born　Newcastle-upon-Tyne, 22 May 1881
Died　26 August 1938
Clubs　Newcastle Utd
Caps　6

	Result
17 Feb 1906 v Ireland	5–0
19 Mar 1906 v Wales	1–0
7 Apr 1906 v Scotland	1–2
18 Mar 1907 v Wales	1–1
6 Apr 1907 v Scotland	1–1
15 Mar 1909 v Wales	2–0

315. Samuel Hulme Day
Inside forward

Born　Peckham Rye, 29 December 1878
Died　21 February 1950
Clubs　Cambridge University; Corinthians; Old Malvernians
Caps　3

	Result	Goals
17 Feb 1906 v Ireland	5–0	1
19 Mar 1906 v Wales	1–0	1
7 Apr 1906 v Scotland	1–2	

316. Albert Arthur Gosnell
Outside left

Born　Colchester, 10 February 1880
Died　6 January 1972
Clubs　Colchester Town; New Brompton; Chatham; Newcastle Utd; Tottenham Hotspur; Darlington; Burslem Port Vale
Caps　1

	Result
17 Feb 1906 v Ireland	5–0

317. Edward Gordon Dundas Wright
Outside left

Born　Earlsfield Green, 3 October 1884
Died　5 June 1947
Clubs　Cambridge University; Corinthians; Portsmouth; Hull City; Leyton; Worthing; Reigate Priory
Caps　1

	Result
19 Mar 1906 v Wales	1–0

318. Harry Makepeace
Wing half

Born　Middlesbrough, 22 August 1881
Died　19 December 1952
Clubs　Bootle Amateurs; Everton
Caps　4

	Result
7 Apr 1908 v Scotland	1–2
2 Apr 1910 v Scotland	0–2
11 Mar 1912 v Wales	2–0
23 Mar 1912 v Scotland	1–1

319. Albert Shepherd
Centre forward

Born　Bolton, 10 September 1885
Died　8 November 1929
Clubs　Bolton St Luke's; Bolton Wanderers; Newcastle Utd; Bradford City
Caps　2

	Result	Goals
7 Apr 1906 v Scotland	1–2	1
11 Feb 1911 v Ireland	2–1	1

320. James Conlin
Outside left

Born　Consett, 6 July 1881
Died　23 June 1917
Clubs　Cambuslang; Hibernian; Falkirk; Albion Rovers; Bradford City; Manchester City; Birmingham; Airdrieonians
Caps　1

	Result
7 Apr 1906 v Scotland	1–2

321. Samuel Hardy
Goalkeeper

Born　Newbold, 26 August 1883
Died　24 October 1966
Clubs　Newbold White Star; Chesterfield Town; Liverpool; Aston Villa; Nottingham Forest
Caps　21

	Result
16 Feb 1907 v Ireland	1–0
18 Mar 1907 v Wales	1–1
6 Apr 1907 v Scotland	1–1
4 Apr 1908 v Scotland	1–1
13 Feb 1909 v Ireland	4–0
15 Mar 1909 v Wales	2–0
3 Apr 1909 v Scotland	2–0
29 May 1909 v Hungary	4–2
31 May 1909 v Hungary	8–2
1 Jun 1909 v Austria	8–1
12 Feb 1910 v Ireland	1–1
14 Mar 1910 v Wales	1–0
2 Apr 1910 v Scotland	0–2
10 Feb 1912 v Ireland	6–1
5 Apr 1913 v Scotland	1–0
14 Feb 1914 v Ireland	0–3
16 Mar 1914 v Wales	2–0
4 Apr 1914 v Scotland	1–3
25 Oct 1919 v Ireland	1–1
15 Mar 1920 v Wales	1–2
10 Apr 1920 v Scotland	5–4

322. William John Wedlock
Centre half

Born　Bedminster, 28 October 1880
Died　24 January 1965
Clubs　Bristol Melrose; Arlington Rovers; Bristol City; Aberdare
Caps　26

	Result	Goals
16 Feb 1907 v Ireland	1–0	
18 Mar 1907 v Wales	1–1	
6 Apr 1907 v Scotland	1–1	
15 Feb 1908 v Ireland	3–1	
16 Mar 1908 v Wales	7–1	1
4 Apr 1908 v Scotland	1–1	
6 Jun 1908 v Austria	6–1	
8 Jun 1908 v Austria	11–1	
10 Jun 1908 v Hungary	7–0	
13 Jun 1908 v Bohemia	4–0	
13 Feb 1909 v Ireland	4–0	
15 Mar 1909 v Wales	2–0	
3 Apr 1909 v Scotland	2–0	
29 May 1909 v Hungary	4–2	
31 May 1909 v Hungary	8–2	
1 Jun 1909 v Austria	8–1	
12 Feb 1910 v Ireland	1–1	
14 Mar 1910 v Wales	1–0	
2 Apr 1910 v Scotland	0–2	
11 Feb 1911 v Ireland	2–1	
13 Mar 1911 v Wales	3–0	
1 Apr 1911 v Scotland	1–1	
10 Feb 1912 v Ireland	6–1	
11 Mar 1912 v Wales	2–0	
23 Mar 1912 v Scotland	1–1	
16 Mar 1914 v Wales	2–0	1

323. Robert Murray Hawkes
Left half

Born　Breachwood Green, 18 October 1880
Died　12 September 1945
Clubs　Luton Town; Bedford Town; Hertfordshire
Caps　5

	Result
16 Feb 1907 v Ireland	1–0
6 Jun 1908 v Austria	6–1
8 Jun 1908 v Austria	11–1
10 Jun 1908 v Hungary	7–0
13 Jun 1908 v Bohemia	4–0

324. John George 'Tim' Coleman
Inside forward

Born　Kettering, 26 October 1881
Died　20 November 1940
Clubs　Kettering FC; Northampton Town; Woolwich Arsenal; Everton; Sunderland; Fulham; Nottingham Forest

Caps	1	Result
	16 Feb 1907 v Ireland	1–0

325. George Richard Hilsdon
Centre forward

Born Bow, 10 August 1885
Died 10 September 1941
Clubs South-West Ham FC; Clapton Orient; Luton Town; West Ham Utd; Chelsea; Chatham

Caps	8	Result	Goals
	16 Feb 1907 v Ireland	1–0	
	15 Feb 1908 v Ireland	3–1	2
	16 Mar 1908 v Wales	7–1	2
	4 Apr 1908 v Scotland	1–1	
	6 Jun 1908 v Austria	6–1	2
	10 Jun 1908 v Hungary	7–0	4
	13 Jun 1908 v Bohemia	4–0	2
	13 Feb 1909 v Ireland	4–0	2

326. Jesse Pennington
Left back

Born West Bromwich, 23 August 1883
Died 5 September 1970
Clubs Smethwick Centaur; Langley Villa; Langley St Michael's; Dudley Town; West Bromwich Albion

Caps	25	Result
	18 Mar 1907 v Wales	1–1
	6 Apr 1907 v Scotland	1–1
	15 Feb 1908 v Ireland	3–1
	16 Mar 1908 v Wales	7–1
	4 Apr 1908 v Scotland	1–1
	8 Jun 1908 v Austria	11–1
	15 Mar 1909 v Wales	2–0
	3 Apr 1908 v Scotland	2–0
	29 May 1909 v Hungary	4–2
	31 May 1909 v Hungary	8–2
	1 Jun 1909 v Austria	8–1
	14 Mar 1910 v Wales	1–0
	2 Apr 1910 v Scotland	0–2
	11 Feb 1911 v Ireland	2–1
	13 Mar 1911 v Wales	3–0
	1 Apr 1911 v Scotland	1–1
	10 Feb 1912 v Ireland	6–1
	11 Mar 1912 v Wales	2–0
	23 Mar 1912 v Scotland	1–1
	17 Mar 1913 v Wales	4–3
	5 Apr 1913 v Scotland	1–0
	14 Feb 1914 v Ireland	0–3
	4 Apr 1914 v Scotland	1–3
	15 Mar 1920 v Wales	1–2
	10 Apr 1920 v Scotland	5–4

327. Irvine Thornley
Centre forward

Born Hayfield, 30 November 1883
Died 24 April 1955
Clubs Glossop Villa; Glossop St James; Glossop North End; Manchester City; South Shields; Hamilton Academicals

Caps	1	Result
	18 Mar 1907 v Wales	1–1

328. James Stewart
Inside forward

Born Newcastle-upon-Tyne, 4 May 1883
Died 23 May 1957
Clubs Gateshead NER; Sheffield Wednesday; Newcastle Utd; Rangers; North Shields Athletic

Caps	3	Result	Goals
	18 Mar 1907 v Wales	1–1	1
	6 Apr 1907 v Scotland	1–1	
	1 Apr 1911 v Scotland	1–1	1

329. George Wall
Outside left

Born Bolden Colliery, 20 February 1885
Died 1962

Clubs Whitburn; Jarrow; Barnsley; Manchester Utd; Oldham Athletic; Hamilton Academicals; Rochdale; Ashton National

Caps	7	Result	Goals
	18 Mar 1907 v Wales	1–1	
	15 Feb 1908 v Ireland	3–1	
	3 Apr 1909 v Scotland	2–0	2
	14 Mar 1910 v Wales	1–0	
	2 Apr 1910 v Scotland	0–2	
	23 Mar 1912 v Scotland	1–1	
	15 Feb 1913 v Ireland	1–2	

330. Harry Mart Maskrey
Goalkeeper

Born Unstone, 8 October 1880
Died 21 April 1927
Clubs Ripley Athletic; Derby County; Bradford City; Ripley Town; Burton All Saints

Caps	1	Result
	15 Feb 1908 v Ireland	3–1

331. Evelyn Henry Lintott
Left half

Born Godalming, 2 November 1883
Died 1 July 1916
Clubs Plymouth Argyle; Queen's Park Rangers; Bradford City; Leeds City

Caps	7	Result
	15 Feb 1908 v Ireland	3–1
	16 Mar 1908 v Wales	7–1
	4 Apr 1908 v Scotland	1–1
	13 Feb 1909 v Ireland	4–0
	3 Apr 1909 v Scotland	2–0
	29 May 1909 v Hungary	4–2
	31 May 1909 v Hungary	8–2

332. James Edward Windridge
Inside left

Born Birmingham, 21 October 1882
Died 23 September 1939
Clubs Small Heath; Chelsea; Middlesbrough

Caps	8	Result	Goals
	15 Feb 1908 v Ireland	3–1	
	16 Mar 1908 v Wales	7–1	1
	4 Apr 1908 v Scotland	1–1	1
	6 Jun 1908 v Austria	6–1	2
	8 Jun 1908 v Austria	11–1	1
	10 Jun 1908 v Hungary	7–0	1
	13 Jun 1908 v Bohemia	4–0	1
	13 Feb 1909 v Ireland	4–0	

333. Horace Peter Bailey
Goalkeeper

Born Derby, 3 July 1881
Died 1 August 1960
Clubs Ripley Athletic; Leicester Imperial; Leicester Fosse; Derby County; Birmingham

Caps	5	Result
	16 Mar 1908 v Wales	7–1
	6 Jun 1908 v Austria	6–1
	8 Jun 1908 v Austria	11–1
	10 Jun 1908 v Hungary	7–0
	13 Jun 1908 v Bohemia	4–0

334. Walter Samuel Corbett
Fullback

Born Wellington, 26 November 1880
Died 1955
Clubs Astbury Richmond; Bournbrook; Aston Villa; Birmingham; Queen's Park Rangers; Wellington Town

Caps	3	Result
	6 Jun 1908 v Austria	6–1
	10 Jun 1908 v Hungary	7–0
	13 Jun 1908 v Bohemia	4–0

335. Frank Bradshaw
Inside left
Born   Sheffield, 31 May 1885
Clubs Sheffield Wednesday; Northampton Town; Everton;
         Arsenal

Caps	1	*Result*	*Goals*
	8 Jun 1908 v Austria	11–1	3

336. Joseph Richard Cottle
Left back
Born   Bedminster, 4 March 1886
Died   3 February 1958
Clubs Eclipse FC; Dolphin FC; Bristol City

Caps	1	*Result*
	13 Feb 1909 v Ireland	4–0

337. Arthur Berry
Winger
Born   Liverpool, 3 January 1888
Died   15 March 1953
Clubs Oxford University; Fulham; Everton; Oxford City;
         Liverpool; Wrexham; Northern Nomads

Caps	1	*Result*
	13 Feb 1909 v Ireland	4–0

338. Frederick Beaconsfield Pentland
Outside right
Born   Wolverhampton, 8 August 1883
Died   16 March 1962
Clubs Small Heath; Blackpool; Blackburn Rovers; Brentford;
         Queen's Park Rangers; Halifax Town; Stoke

Caps	5	*Result*
	15 Mar 1909 v Wales	2–0
	3 Apr 1909 v Scotland	2–0
	29 May 1909 v Hungary	4–2
	31 May 1909 v Hungary	8–2
	1 Jun 1909 v Austria	8–1

339. Bertram Clewley Freeman
Centre forward
Born   Handsworth, 2 October 1885
Died   11 August 1955
Clubs Aston Manor; Aston Villa; Woolwich Arsenal;
         Everton; Burnley; Wigan Borough; Kettering Town

Caps	5	*Result*	*Goals*
	15 Mar 1909 v Wales	2–0	1
	3 Apr 1909 v Scotland	2–0	
	10 Feb 1912 v Ireland	6–1	1
	11 Mar 1912 v Wales	2–0	1
	23 Mar 1912 v Scotland	1–1	

340. George Holley
Inside forward
Born   Seaham Harbour, 20 November 1885
Died   27 August 1942
Clubs Seaham Athletic; Seaham Villa; Seaham White Star;
         Sunderland; Brighton & Hove Albion

Caps	10	*Result*	*Goals*
	15 Mar 1909 v Wales	2–0	1
	3 Apr 1909 v Scotland	2–0	
	29 May 1909 v Hungary	4–2	
	31 May 1909 v Hungary	8–2	1
	1 Jun 1909 v Austria	8–1	2
	14 Mar 1910 v Wales	1–0	
	10 Feb 1912 v Ireland	6–1	1
	11 Mar 1912 v Wales	2–0	1
	23 Mar 1912 v Scotland	1–1	1
	5 Apr 1913 v Scotland	1–0	

341. Harold John Fleming
Inside right
Born   Downton, 30 April 1887
Died   23 August 1955
Clubs Swindon Town

Caps	11	*Result*	*Goals*
	3 Apr 1909 v Scotland	2–0	
	29 May 1909 v Hungary	4–2	1

	31 May 1909 v Hungary	8–2	2
	12 Feb 1910 v Ireland	1–1	1
	14 Mar 1910 v Wales	1–0	
	11 Feb 1911 v Ireland	2–1	
	13 Mar 1911 v Wales	3–0	
	10 Feb 1912 v Ireland	6–1	3
	17 Mar 1913 v Wales	4–3	1
	5 Apr 1913 v Scotland	1–0	
	4 Apr 1914 v Scotland	1–3	1

342. George Henry Richards
Left half/Inside left
Born   Castle Donington, 10 May 1880
Died   1 November 1959
Clubs Whitwick White Star; Derby County

Caps	1	*Result*
	1 Jun 1909 v Austria	8–1

343. Harold James Halse
Inside right/Centre forward
Born   Leytonstone, 16 January 1886
Died   25 April 1951
Clubs Newportians FC; Wanstead FC; Barking Town;
         Clapton Orient; Southend Utd; Manchester Utd;
         Aston Villa; Chelsea; Charlton Athletic

Caps	1	*Result*	*Goals*
	1 Jun 1909 v Austria	8–1	2

344. Herbert Morley
Right back
Born   Kiveton Park, 2 October 1882
Died   15 July 1957
Clubs Kiveton Park FC; Grimsby Town; Notts County

Caps	1	*Result*
	12 Feb 1910 v Ireland	1–1

345. Arthur Cowell
Left back
Born   Blackburn, 20 May 1886
Died   12 February 1959
Clubs Nelson; Blackburn Rovers

Caps	1	*Result*
	12 Feb 1910 v Ireland	1–1

346. Andrew Ducat
Right half
Born   Brixton, 16 February 1886
Died   23 July 1942
Clubs Southend Athletic; Woolwich Arsenal; Aston Villa;
         Fulham

Caps	6	*Result*	*Goals*
	12 Feb 1910 v Ireland	1–1	
	14 Mar 1910 v Wales	1–0	1
	2 Apr 1910 v Scotland	0–2	
	15 Mar 1920 v Wales	1–2	
	10 Apr 1920 v Scotland	5–4	
	23 Oct 1920 v Ireland	2–0	

347. William Bradshaw
Left half
Born   Padiham, 22 October 1884
Clubs Padiham FC; Accrington Stanley; Blackburn Rovers;
         Rochdale

Caps	4	*Result*
	12 Feb 1910 v Ireland	1–1
	14 Mar 1910 v Wales	1–0
	10 Feb 1912 v Ireland	6–1
	17 Mar 1913 v Wales	4–3

348. Albert Edward Hall
Outside left
Born   Wordsley, 5 March 1882
Died   17 October 1957
Clubs Stourbridge; Aston Villa; Millwall Athletic

Caps	1	*Result*
	12 Feb 1910 v Ireland	1–1

349. John Parkinson
Centre forward
Born Bootle, 23 September 1883
Died 13 September 1942
Clubs Liverpool; Bury

Caps	2	Result
	14 Mar 1910 v Wales	1–0
	2 Apr 1910 v Scotland	0–2

350. William Hibbert
Inside right
Born Golborne, 21 September 1884
Died 16 March 1949
Clubs Newton-le-Willows; Bryn Central; Bury; Newcastle Utd; Bradford City; Oldham Athletic

Caps	1	Result
	2 Apr 1910 v Scotland	0–2

351. Harold Thomas Walter Hardinge
Inside left
Born Greenwich, 25 February 1886
Died 8 May 1965
Clubs Maidstone; Newcastle Utd; Sheffield Utd; Arsenal

Caps	1	Result
	2 Apr 1910 v Scotland	0–2

352. Albert Sturgess
Wing half
Born Stoke-on-Trent, 21 October 1882
Died 16 July 1957
Clubs Tunstall Cresswells; Stoke; Sheffield Utd; Norwich City

Caps	2	Result
	11 Feb 1911 v Ireland	2–1
	4 Apr 1914 v Scotland	1–3

353. John 'Jock' Simpson
Outside right
Born Pendleton, 25 December 1885
Died 4 January 1959
Clubs Falkirk; Blackburn Rovers

Caps	8	Result	Goals
	11 Feb 1911 v Ireland	2–1	
	13 Mar 1911 v Wales	3–0	
	1 Apr 1911 v Scotland	1–1	
	10 Feb 1912 v Ireland	6–1	1
	11 Mar 1912 v Wales	2–0	
	23 Mar 1912 v Scotland	1–1	
	5 Apr 1913 v Scotland	1–0	
	16 Mar 1914 v Wales	2–0	

354. George Woodger
Inside left/Outside left
Born Croydon, 3 September 1883
Died 1961
Clubs Thornton Heath Wednesday; Croydon Glenrose; Croydon Wanderers; Crystal Palace; Oldham Athletic; Tottenham Hotspur

Caps	1	Result
	11 Feb 1911 v Ireland	2–1

355. Robert Ernest Evans
Outside left
Born Chester, 21 November 1885
Died 28 November 1965
Clubs Saltney Ferry; Wrexham; Aston Villa; Sheffield Utd

Caps	4	Result	Goals
	11 Feb 1911 v Ireland	2–1	1
	13 Mar 1911 v Wales	3–0	
	1 Apr 1911 v Scotland	1–1	
	11 Mar 1912 v Wales	2–0	

356. Kenneth Reginald Hunt
Wing half/Centre half
Born Oxford, 24 February 1884
Died 28 April 1949
Clubs Oxford University; Corinthians; Wolverhampton Wanderers; Leyton; Crystal Palace; Oxford City

Caps	2	Result
	13 Mar 1911 v Wales	3–0
	1 Apr 1911 v Scotland	1–1

357. George William Webb
Centre forward
Born London, 3 November 1888
Died 28 March 1915
Clubs Ilford Alliance; Ilford FC; Wanstead; West Ham Utd; Manchester City

Caps	2	Result	Goals
	13 Mar 1911 v Wales	3–0	1
	1 Apr 1911 v Scotland	1–1	

358. John Thomas Brittleton
Right half
Born Winsford, 23 April 1882
Died 22 February 1955
Clubs Winsford Celtic; Winsford Utd; Stockport County; Sheffield Wednesday; Stoke

Caps	5	Result
	10 Feb 1912 v Ireland	6–1
	11 Mar 1912 v Wales	2–0
	23 Mar 1912 v Scotland	1–1
	5 Apr 1913 v Scotland	1–0
	16 Mar 1914 v Wales	2–0

359. John Mordue
Winger
Born Edmondsley, 4 August 1887
Died 14 December 1957
Clubs Sacriston FC; Spennymoor Utd; Barnsley; Woolwich Arsenal; Sunderland; Middlesbrough; Durham City

Caps	2	Result
	10 Feb 1912 v Ireland	6–1
	15 Feb 1913 v Ireland	1–2

360. Frank Jefferis
Inside right
Born Fordingbridge, 3 July 1884
Died 21 May 1938
Clubs Fordingbridge Turks; Southampton; Everton; Preston North End; Southport

Caps	2	Result
	11 Mar 1912 v Wales	2–0
	23 Mar 1912 v Scotland	1–1

361. Robert William Benson
Fullback
Born Whitehaven, 9 February 1883
Died 19 February 1916
Clubs Swalwell FC; Newcastle Utd; Southampton; Sheffield Utd; Woolwich Arsenal

Caps	1	Result
	15 Feb 1913 v Ireland	1–2

362. Francis Cuggy
Right half
Born Walker, 16 June 1889
Died 27 March 1965
Clubs Willingham Athletic; Sunderland; Wallsend

Caps	2	Result
	15 Feb 1913 v Ireland	1–2
	14 Feb 1914 v Ireland	0–3

363. Thomas Wilkinson Boyle
Centre half
Born Barnsley, 29 January 1888
Died 5 January 1940
Clubs Hoyland Star; Elsecar FC; Barnsley; Burnley; Wrexham

Caps	1	Result
	15 Feb 1913 v Ireland	1–2

364. George Utley
Left half
Born   Barnsley, 4 March 1887
Died   8 January 1966
Clubs Elsecar FC; Wentworth FC; Sheffield Wednesday;
         Barnsley; Sheffield Utd; Manchester City

Caps	1	Result
	15 Feb 1913 v Ireland	1–2

365. Charles Murray Buchan
Inside right
Born   Plumstead, 22 September 1891
Died   25 June 1960
Clubs Northfleet; Leyton; Sunderland; Arsenal

Caps	6	Result	Goals
	15 Feb 1913 v Ireland	1–2	1
	15 Mar 1920 v Wales	1–2	1
	14 Mar 1921 v Wales	0–0	
	21 May 1921 v Belgium	2–0	1
	10 May 1923 v France	4–1	1
	12 Apr 1924 v Scotland	1–1	

366. George Washington Elliott
Centre forward
Born   Sunderland, 7 March 1889
Died   27 November 1948
Clubs Redcar Crusaders; South Bank; Middlesbrough

Caps	3	Result
	15 Feb 1913 v Ireland	1–2
	14 Feb 1914 v Ireland	0–3
	15 Mar 1920 v Wales	1–2

367. Joseph Smith
Inside left
Born   Dudley Port, 25 June 1889
Died   11 August 1971
Clubs Bolton Wanderers; Stockport County; Darwen;
         Manchester Central; Hyde Utd

Caps	5	Result	Goals
	15 Feb 1913 v Ireland	1–2	
	16 Mar 1914 v Wales	2–0	1
	4 Apr 1914 v Scotland	1–3	
	25 Oct 1919 v Ireland	1–1	
	15 Mar 1920 v Wales	1–2	

368. Joseph McCall
Centre half
Born   Kirkham, 6 July 1886
Died   3 February 1965
Clubs Kirkham FC; Preston North End

Caps	5	Result	Goals
	17 Mar 1913 v Wales	4–3	1
	5 Apr 1913 v Scotland	1–0	
	4 Apr 1914 v Scotland	1–3	
	10 Apr 1920 v Scotland	5–4	
	23 Oct 1920 v Ireland	2–0	

369. Ernald Oak Scattergood
Goalkeeper
Born   Riddings, 29 May 1887
Died   2 July 1932
Clubs Ripley Athletic; Derby County; Bradford Park Avenue

Caps	1	Result
	17 Mar 1913 v Wales	4–3

370. Hugh Moffat
Wing half
Born   Congleton, 20 January 1885
Died   14 November 1952
Clubs Burnley; Oldham Athletic

Caps	1	Result
	17 Mar 1913 v Wales	4–3

371. Charles William Wallace
Outside right
Born   Sunderland, 20 January 1885
Died   7 January 1970

Clubs Southwick FC; Crystal Palace; Aston Villa; Oldham
         Athletic

Caps	3	Result
	17 Mar 1913 v Wales	4–3
	14 Feb 1914 v Ireland	0–3
	10 Apr 1920 v Scotland	5–4

372. Harry Hampton
Centre forward
Born   Wellington 21 April 1885
Died   15 March 1963
Clubs Wellington Town; Aston Villa; Birmingham;
         Newport County

Caps	4	Result	Goals
	17 Mar 1913 v Wales	4–3	1
	5 Apr 1913 v Scotland	1–0	1
	16 Mar 1914 v Wales	2–0	
	4 Apr 1914 v Scotland	1–3	

373. Edwin Gladstone 'Pinky' Latheron
Inside forward
Born   Grangetown, 6 September 1887
Died   14 October 1917
Clubs Grangetown FC; Blackburn Rovers

Caps	2	Result	Goals
	17 Mar 1913 v Wales	4–3	1
	14 Feb 1914 v Ireland	0–3	

374. Joseph Hodkinson
Outside left
Born   Lancaster, 1 April 1889
Died   18 June 1954
Clubs Lancaster Town; Glossop; Blackburn Rovers

Caps	3	Result
	17 Mar 1913 v Wales	4–3
	5 Apr 1913 v Scotland	1–0
	25 Oct 1919 v Ireland	1–1

375. William Watson
Left half
Born   Southport, 11 September 1890
Died   1 September 1955
Clubs Southport Central; Burnley; Blackburn Rovers

Caps	3	Result
	5 Apr 1913 v Scotland	1–0
	14 Feb 1914 v Ireland	0–3
	25 Oct 1919 v Ireland	1–1

376. Franklin Charles Buckley
Centre half
Born   Urmston, 9 November 1882
Died   22 December 1964
Clubs Aston Villa; Brighton & Hove Albion; Manchester
         Utd; Manchester City; Birmingham; Derby County;
         Bradford City

Caps	1	Result
	14 Feb 1914 v Ireland	0–3

377. Daniel Shea
Inside right
Born   Wapping, 6 November 1887
Died   25 December 1960
Clubs Pearl Utd; Manor Park Albion; West Ham Utd;
         Blackburn Rovers; Fulham; Coventry City; Clapton
         Orient; Sheppey Utd

Caps	2	Result
	14 Feb 1914 v Ireland	0–3
	16 Mar 1914 v Wales	2–0

378. Henry Martin
Outside left
Born   Selston, 5 December 1891
Died   1974
Clubs Sutton Junction; Sunderland; Nottingham Forest;
         Rochdale

Caps	1	Result
	14 Feb 1914 v Ireland	0–3

379. Henry Colclough
Left back
Born   Longton, 4 October 1891
Died   1941
Clubs Crewe Alexandra; Crystal Palace
Caps   1   Result
       16 Mar 1914 v Wales   2–0

380. Robert McNeal
Left half
Born   Stanley, 15 January 1891
Died   15 May 1956
Clubs Hobson Wanderers; West Bromwich Albion
Caps   2   Result
       16 Mar 1914 v Wales   2–0
       4 Apr 1914 v Scotland   1–3

381. Edwin Mosscrop
Outside left
Born   Southport, 16 June 1892
Died   14 March 1980
Clubs Blowick FC; Shepherd's Bush; Southport YMCA;
       Southport Central; Burnley
Caps   2   Result
       16 Mar 1914 v Wales   2–0
       4 Apr 1914 v Scotland   1–3

382. Frederick Ingram 'Fanny' Walden
Outside right
Born   Wellingborough, 1 March 1888
Died   3 May 1949
Clubs Northampton Town; Tottenham Hotspur
Caps   2   Result
       4 Apr 1914 v Scotland   1–3
       13 Mar 1922 v Wales   1–0

383. Joseph Smith
Right back
Born   Dudley, 10 April 1890
Died   9 June 1956
Clubs Darby End Victoria; Cradley Heath St Luke's; West
       Bromwich Albion; Birmingham; Worcester
Caps   2   Result
       25 Oct 1919 v Ireland   1–1
       21 Oct 1922 v Ireland   2–0

384. Arthur Egerton Knight
Left back
Born   Godalming, 7 September 1887
Died   10 March 1956
Clubs Portsmouth; Corinthians
Caps   1   Result
       25 Oct 1919 v Ireland   1–1

385. John James Bagshaw
Right half
Born   Derby, 25 December 1885
Died   25 August 1966
Clubs Fletcher's Athletic; Graham Street Primitives; Derby
       County; Notts County; Watford; Grantham; Ilkeston
       Utd
Caps   1   Result
       25 Oct 1919 v Ireland   1–1

386. Sidney Bowser
Inside forward/Centre half
Born   Handsworth, 6 April 1891
Died   25 February 1961
Clubs Astbury Richmond; Willenhall; West Bromwich
       Albion; Belfast Distillery; Walsall
Caps   1   Result
       25 Oct 1919 v Ireland   1–1

387. Robert Joseph Turnbull
Outside right
Born   Middlesbrough, 17 December 1885
Died   18 March 1952
Clubs South Bank East End; Bradford Park Avenue; Leeds
       Utd; Rhyl Athletic
Caps   1   Result
       25 Oct 1919 v Ireland   1–1

388. Jack Carr
Outside right/Inside forward
Born   Middlesbrough, 26 November 1892
Died   10 May 1942
Clubs South Bank FC; Middlesbrough; Blackpool;
       Hartlepool Utd
Caps   2   Result
       25 Oct 1919 v Ireland   1–1
       5 Mar 1923 v Wales   2–2

389. John Gilbert Cock
Centre forward
Born   Hayle, 14 November 1893
Died   19 April 1966
Clubs West Kensington Utd; Forest Gate; Old
       Kingstonians; Huddersfield Town; Chelsea; Everton;
       Plymouth Argyle; Millwall, Folkestone; Walton
Caps   2   Result Goals
       25 Oct 1919 v Ireland   1–1   1
       10 Apr 1920 v Scotland   5–4   1

390. Thomas Clay
Right back
Born   Leicester, 19 November 1892
Died   21 February 1949
Clubs Leicester Fosse; Tottenham Hotspur
Caps   4   Result
       15 Mar 1920 v Wales   1–2
       22 Oct 1921 v Ireland   1–1
       13 Mar 1922 v Wales   1–0
       8 Apr 1922 v Scotland   0–1

391. Frank Barson
Centre half
Born   Sheffield, 10 April 1891
Died   13 September 1968
Clubs Albion FC; Cammell Laird's FC; Barnsley; Aston
       Villa; Manchester Utd; Watford; Hartlepool Utd;
       Wigan Borough; Rhyl Athletic
Caps   1   Result
       15 Mar 1920 v Wales   1–2

392. Arthur Grimsdell
Left half
Born   Watford, 23 March 1894
Died   12 March 1963
Clubs Watford St Stephens; Watford; Tottenham Hotspur;
       Clapton Orient
Caps   6   Result
       15 Mar 1920 v Wales   1–2
       10 Apr 1920 v Scotland   5–4
       23 Oct 1920 v Ireland   2–0
       19 Apr 1921 v Scotland   0–3
       21 Oct 1922 v Ireland   2–0
       5 Mar 1923 v Wales   2–2

 DID YOU KNOW...?

Standing at only 5 feet 2 inches, Spurs' Fanny
Walden, who played two games for England, was
the smallest player ever to represent his country.
Walden also played more than 250 games for
Northamptonshire County Cricket Club, and went on
to become a first-class cricket umpire.

393. Samuel Chedgzoy
Outside right

Born Ellesmere Port, 27 January 1889
Died 15 January 1967
Clubs Birnell's Ironworks; Everton; New Bedford (USA);
Carsteel FC (Canada)

Caps	8	Result
	15 Mar 1920 v Wales	1–2
	23 Oct 1920 v Ireland	2–0
	14 Mar 1921 v Wales	0–0
	19 Apr 1921 v Scotland	0–3
	22 Oct 1921 v Ireland	1–1
	14 Apr 1923 v Scotland	2–2
	3 Mar 1924 v Wales	1–2
	22 Oct 1924 v N. Ireland	3–1

394. Alfred Edward Quantrill
Outside left

Born Punjab, India, 22 January 1897
Died 19 April 1968
Clubs Boston Swifts; Derby County; Preston North End;
Chorley; Bradford Park Avenue; Nottingham
Forest

Caps	4	Result	Goals
	15 Mar 1920 v Wales	1–2	
	10 Apr 1920 v Scotland	5–4	1
	23 Oct 1920 v Ireland	2–0	
	14 Mar 1921 v Wales	0–0	

395. Ephraim Longworth
Right back

Born Bolton, 2 October 1887
Died 7 January 1968
Clubs Bolton St Luke's; Hyde St George's; Bolton
Wanderers; Leyton; Liverpool

Caps	5	Result
	10 Apr 1920 v Scotland	5–4
	21 May 1921 v Belgium	2–0
	5 Mar 1923 v Wales	2–2
	19 Mar 1923 v Belgium	6–1
	14 Apr 1923 v Scotland	2–2

396. Robert Kelly
Outside right/Inside right

Born Ashton-in-Makerfield, 16 November 1893
Died 22 September 1969
Clubs Ashton White Star; Ashton Central; Earlstown; St
Helens Town; Burnley; Sunderland; Huddersfield
Town; Preston North End; Carlisle Utd

Caps	14	Result	Goals
	10 Apr 1920 v Scotland	5–4	2
	23 Oct 1920 v Ireland	2–0	
	14 Mar 1921 v Wales	0–0	
	19 Apr 1921 v Scotland	0–3	
	13 Mar 1922 v Wales	1–0	1
	8 Apr 1922 v Scotland	0–1	
	14 Apr 1923 v Scotland	2–2	1
	20 Oct 1923 v N. Ireland	1–2	
	22 Oct 1924 v N. Ireland	3–1	1
	28 Feb 1925 v Wales	2–1	
	4 Apr 1925 v Scotland	0–2	
	1 Mar 1926 v Wales	1–3	
	21 May 1927 v Luxembourg	5–2	1
	31 Mar 1928 v Scotland	1–5	1

397. Frederick Morris
Inside left

Born Tipton, 27 August 1893
Died 4 July 1962
Clubs Tipton Victoria; Redditch; West Bromwich Albion;
Coventry City; Oakengates Town

Caps	2	Result	Goals
	10 Apr 1920 v Scotland	5–4	1
	23 Oct 1920 v Ireland	2–0	

⚽ **DID YOU KNOW...?**

On 10 April 1920, England debutants Bob Kelly and
Fred Morris scored three goals in seven minutes as
England came back from 4–2 behind to beat
Scotland 5–4 at Hillsborough.

398. John William Mew
Goalkeeper

Born Sunderland, 30 March 1889
Died 1963
Clubs Blaydon Utd; Marley Hill Colliery; Manchester Utd;
Barrow

Caps	1	Result
	23 Oct 1920 v Ireland	2–0

399. John Thomas 'Dicky' Downs
Right back

Born Middridge, 13 August 1886
Died 24 March 1949
Clubs Crook; Shildon Athletic; Barnsley; Everton; Brighton
& Hove Albion

Caps	1	Result
	23 Oct 1920 v Ireland	2–0

400. Frederick Edwin Bullock
Left back

Born Hounslow, 5 May 1886
Died 15 November 1922
Clubs Hounslow Town; Ilford; Huddersfield Town

Caps	1	Result
	23 Oct 1920 v Ireland	2–0

401. William Henry Walker
Inside left

Born Wednesbury, 29 October 1897
Died 28 November 1964
Clubs Hednesford Town; Darlaston; Wednesbury Old Park;
Aston Villa

Caps	18	Result	Goals
	23 Oct 1920 v Ireland	2–0	1
	22 Oct 1921 v Ireland	1–1	
	13 Mar 1922 v Wales	1–0	
	8 Apr 1922 v Scotland	0–1	
	21 May 1923 v Sweden	4–2	2
	24 May 1923 v Sweden	3–1	
	12 Apr 1924 v Scotland	1–1	1
	22 Oct 1924 v N. Ireland	3–1	1
	8 Dec 1924 v Belgium	4–0	2
	28 Feb 1925 v Wales	2–1	
	4 Apr 1925 v Scotland	0–2	
	21 May 1925 v France	3–2	
	24 Oct 1925 v N. Ireland	0–0	
	1 Mar 1926 v Wales	1–3	1
	17 Apr 1926 v Scotland	0–1	
	20 Oct 1926 v N. Ireland	3–3	
	12 Feb 1927 v Wales	3–3	1
	7 Dec 1932 v Austria	4–3	

402. Ernest Herbert Coleman
Goalkeeper

Born Steyning, 19 October 1889
Died 15 June 1958
Clubs Dulwich Hamlet; Surrey; London

Caps	1	Result
	14 Mar 1921 v Wales	0–0

403. Warneford Cresswell
Fullback

Born South Shields, 5 November 1897
Died 20 October 1973

Clubs	South Shields; Sunderland; Everton	
Caps	7	Result
	14 Mar 1921 v Wales	0–0
	10 May 1923 v France	4–1
	1 Nov 1923 v Belgium	2–2
	22 Oct 1924 v N. Ireland	3–1
	1 Mar 1926 v Wales	1–3
	20 Oct 1926 v N. Ireland	3–3
	19 Oct 1929 v N. Ireland	3–0

404. John Silcock
Left back

Born	Wigan 15 January 1898	
Died	28 June 1966	
Clubs	Manchester Utd; Oldham Athletic; Droylsden Utd	
Caps	3	Result
	14 Mar 1921 v Wales	0–0
	19 Apr 1921 v Scotland	0–3
	24 May 1923 v Sweden	3–1

405. John Bamber
Half back

Born	Peasley Cross, 11 April 1895	
Died	28 July 1971	
Clubs	St Helens Recreation; Heywood; Liverpool; Leicester City; Tranmere Rovers; Prescot Cables	
Caps	1	Result
	14 Mar 1921 v Wales	0–0

406. George Wilson
Centre half

Born	Blackpool, 14 January 1892	
Died	25 November 1961	
Clubs	Fleetwood; Morecambe; Blackpool; Sheffield Wednesday; Nelson	
Caps	12	Result
	14 Mar 1921 v Wales	0–0
	19 Apr 1921 v Scotland	0–3
	21 May 1921 v Belgium	2–0
	22 Oct 1921 v Ireland	1–1
	8 Apr 1922 v Scotland	0–1
	21 Oct 1922 v Ireland	2–0
	5 Mar 1923 v Wales	2–2
	19 Mar 1923 v Belgium	6–1
	14 Apr 1923 v Scotland	2–2
	20 Oct 1923 v N. Ireland	1–2
	3 Mar 1924 v Wales	1–2
	17 May 1924 v France	3–1

407. Thomas George Bromilow
Left half

Born	Liverpool, 7 October 1894	
Died	4 March 1959	
Clubs	United West Dingle Presbyterian Club; Liverpool	
Caps	5	Result
	14 Mar 1921 v Wales	0–0
	13 Mar 1922 v Wales	1–0
	8 Apr 1922 v Scotland	0–1
	19 Mar 1923 v Belgium	6–1
	24 Oct 1925 v N. Ireland	0–0

408. Henry Chambers
Centre forward

Born	Willington Quay, 17 November 1896		
Died	29 June 1949		
Clubs	North Shields Athletic; Liverpool; West Bromwich Albion; Oakengates Town		
Caps	8	Result	Goals
	14 Mar 1921 v Wales	0–0	
	19 Apr 1921 v Scotland	0–3	
	21 May 1921 v Belgium	2–0	1
	21 Oct 1922 v Ireland	2–0	2
	5 Mar 1923 v Wales	2–2	1
	19 Mar 1923 v Belgium	6–1	1

	14 Apr 1923 v Scotland	2–2
	20 Oct 1923 v N. Ireland	1–2

409. Harold Gough
Goalkeeper

Born	Chesterfield, 31 December 1890	
Died	16 June 1970	
Clubs	Spital Olympic; Castleford Town; Bradford Park Avenue; Sheffield Utd; Harrogate; Oldham Athletic; Bolton Wanderers; Torquay Utd	
Caps	1	Result
	19 Apr 1921 v Scotland	0–3

410. Thomas Smart
Right back

Born	Blackheath, 20 September 1896	
Died	16 June 1968	
Clubs	Blackheath Town; Halesowen; Aston Villa; Brierley Hill Alliance	
Caps	5	Result
	19 Apr 1921 v Scotland	0–3
	3 Mar 1924 v Wales	1–2
	12 Apr 1924 v Scotland	1–1
	24 Oct 1925 v N. Ireland	0–0
	20 Nov 1929 v Wales	6–0

411. Bertram Smith
Right half

Born	Higham, 7 March 1892	
Died	23 September 1969	
Clubs	Vanbrugh Park; Crawford Utd; Metrogas FC; Huddersfield Town; Tottenham Hotspur	
Caps	2	Result
	19 Apr 1921 v Scotland	0–3
	13 Mar 1922 v Wales	1–0

412. Herbert Bliss
Inside left

Born	Willenhall, 29 March 1890	
Died	14 June 1968	
Clubs	Willenhall Swifts; Tottenham Hotspur; Clapton Orient; Bournemouth	
Caps	1	Result
	19 Apr 1921 v Scotland	0–3

413. James Henry Dimmock
Outside left

Born	Edmonton, 5 December 1900	
Died	23 December 1972	
Clubs	Park Avenue FC; Gothic Works; Tottenham Hotspur; Thames; Clapton Orient; Ashford	
Caps	3	Result
	19 Apr 1921 v Scotland	0–3
	1 Mar 1926 v Wales	1–3
	24 May 1926 v Belgium	5–3

414. Benjamin Howard Baker
Goalkeeper

Born	Aigburth, 13 February 1892	
Died	10 September 1987	
Clubs	Northern Nomads; Blackburn Rovers; Preston North End; Corinthians; Liverpool; Everton; Chelsea; Oldham Athletic	
Caps	2	Result
	21 May 1921 v Belgium	2–0
	24 Oct 1925 v N. Ireland	0–0

415. John Fort
Right back

Born	Leigh, 15 April 1888	
Died	23 November 1965	
Clubs	Atherton; Exeter City; Millwall Athletic	
Caps	1	Result
	21 May 1921 v Belgium	2–0

416. Albert Read
Right half/Centre half
Born Ealing, 22 November 1899
Clubs Tufnell Park; Queen's Park Rangers; Reading

Caps	1	*Result*
	21 May 1921 v Belgium	2–0

417. Percival Henry Barton
Left half
Born Edmonton, 19 August 1895
Died 12 October 1961
Clubs Tottenham Thursday; Sultan FC; Birmingham; Stourbridge

Caps	7	*Result*
	21 May 1921 v Belgium	2–0
	22 Oct 1921 v Ireland	1–1
	10 May 1923 v France	4–1
	1 Nov 1923 v Belgium	2–2
	3 Mar 1924 v Wales	1–2
	12 Apr 1924 v Scotland	1–1
	22 Oct 1924 v N. Ireland	3–1

418. Archibald Rawlings
Outside right
Born Leicester, 2 October 1891
Died 11 June 1952
Clubs Wombwell; Shirebrook; Northampton Town; Barnsley; Rochdale; Dundee; Preston North End; Liverpool; Walsall; Bradford Park Avenue; Southport; Dick Kerr's FC; Burton Tower

Caps	1	*Result*
	21 May 1921 v Belgium	2–0

419. James Marshall Seed
Inside right
Born Blackhill, 25 March 1895
Died 16 July 1966
Clubs Whitburn; Sunderland; Mid-Rhondda; Tottenham Hotspur; Sheffield Wednesday

Caps	5	*Result*	*Goals*
	21 May 1921 v Belgium	2–0	
	21 Oct 1922 v Ireland	2–0	
	5 Mar 1923 v Wales	2–2	
	19 Mar 1923 v Belgium	6–1	1
	4 Apr 1925 v Scotland	0–2	

420. George 'Jud' Harrison
Outside left
Born Church Gresley, 18 July 1892
Died 12 March 1939
Clubs Gresley Rovers; Leicester Fosse; Everton; Preston North End; Blackpool

Caps	2	*Result*
	21 May 1921 v Belgium	2–0
	22 Oct 1921 v Ireland	1–1

421. Jeremiah Dawson
Goalkeeper
Born Holme, 18 March 1888
Died 8 August 1970
Clubs Holme FC; Cliviger FC; Burnley

Caps	2	*Result*
	22 Oct 1921 v Ireland	1–1
	8 Apr 1922 v Scotland	0–1

422. Thomas Lucas
Full back
Born St Helens, 20 September 1895
Died 11 December 1953
Clubs Sherdley Villa; Sutton Commercial; Heywood Utd; Peasley Cross; Eccles Borough; Liverpool; Clapton Orient

Caps	3	*Result*
	22 Oct 1921 v Ireland	1–1
	17 May 1924 v France	3–1
	24 May 1926 v Belgium	5–3

423. Frank Moss
Wing half
Born Aston, 17 April 1895
Died 15 September 1965
Clubs Walsall; Aston Villa; Cardiff City; Bromsgrove Rovers; Worcester City

Caps	5	*Result*
	22 Oct 1921 v Ireland	1–1
	8 Apr 1922 v Scotland	0–1
	21 Oct 1922 v Ireland	2–0
	1 Nov 1923 v Belgium	2–2
	12 Apr 1924 v Scotland	1–1

424. William John Kirton
Inside right
Born Newcastle-upon-Tyne, 2 December 1896
Died 27 September 1970
Clubs North Shields; Pandon Temperance; Leeds City; Aston Villa; Coventry City; Kidderminster Harriers; Leamington Town

Caps	1	*Result*	*Goals*
	22 Oct 1921 v Ireland	1–1	1

425. Ernest Simms
Centre forward
Born South Shields, 23 July 1891
Died 1971
Clubs South Shields Adelaide; Murton Colliery; Barnsley; Luton Town; Stockport County; Scunthorpe Utd; York City; Vauxhall Motors

Caps	1	*Result*
	22 Oct 1921 v Ireland	1–1

426. John Edward Davison
Goalkeeper
Born Gateshead, 2 September 1887
Died 1971
Clubs Gateshead St Chad's; Sheffield Wednesday; Mansfield Town

Caps	1	*Result*
	13 Mar 1922 v Wales	1–0

427. Frederick Titmuss
Left back
Born Pirton, 15 February 1898
Died 2 October 1966
Clubs Pirton Utd; Hitchen Town; Southampton; Plymouth Argyle; St Austell FC

Caps	2	*Result*
	13 Mar 1922 v Wales	1–0
	5 Mar 1923 v Wales	2–2

428. Maxwell Woosnam
Centre half
Born Liverpool, 6 September 1892
Died 14 July 1965
Clubs Cambridge University; Corinthians Chelsea; Manchester City; Northwich Victoria

Caps	1	*Result*
	13 Mar 1922 v Wales	1–0

429. William Ernest Rawlings
Centre forward
Born Andover, 3 January 1896
Died 25 September 1972
Clubs Andover FC; Southampton; Manchester Utd; Port Vale

Caps	2	*Result*
	13 Mar 1922 v Wales	1–0
	8 Apr 1922 v Scotland	0–1

430. William Henry Smith
Outside left
Born Tantobie, 23 May 1895
Died 13 April 1951

Clubs Hobson Wanderers; Huddersfield Town; Rochdale

Caps	3	Result
	13 Mar 1922 v Wales	1–0
	8 Apr 1922 v Scotland	0–1
	31 Mar 1928 v Scotland	1–5

431. Samuel John Wadsworth
Left back
Born   Darwen, 13 September 1896
Died   1 September 1961
Clubs   Darwen; Blackburn Rovers; Nelson; Huddersfield Town; Burnley; Lytham

Caps	9	Result
	6 Apr 1922 v Scotland	0–1
	19 Mar 1923 v Belgium	6–1
	14 Apr 1923 v Scotland	2–2
	20 Oct 1923 v N. Ireland	1–2
	12 Apr 1924 v Scotland	1–1
	22 Oct 1924 v N. Ireland	3–1
	4 Apr 1925 v Scotland	0–2
	1 Mar 1926 v Wales	1–3
	20 Oct 1926 v N. Ireland	3–3

432. Richard Ernest York
Outside right
Born   Birmingham, 25 April 1899
Died   9 December 1969
Clubs   Aston Villa; Port Vale; Brierley Hill Alliance

Caps	2	Result
	8 Apr 1922 v Scotland	0–1
	17 Apr 1926 v Scotland	0–1

433. Edward Hallows Taylor
Goalkeeper
Born   Liverpool, 7 March 1887
Died   5 July 1956
Clubs   Liverpool Balmoral; Oldham Athletic; Huddersfield Town; Everton; Ashton National; Wrexham

Caps	8	Result
	21 Oct 1922 v Ireland	2–0
	5 Mar 1923 v Wales	2–2
	19 Mar 1923 v Belgium	6–1
	14 Apr 1923 v Scotland	2–2
	20 Oct 1923 v N. Ireland	1–2
	12 Apr 1924 v Scotland	1–1
	17 May 1924 v France	3–1
	17 Apr 1926 v Scotland	0–1

434. Jack Harry Harrow
Left back
Born   Beddington, 8 October 1888
Died   19 July 1958
Clubs   Mill Green Rovers; Croydon Common; Chelsea

Caps	2	Result
	21 Oct 1922 v Ireland	2–0
	21 May 1923 v Sweden	4–2

435. David William Mercer
Outside right
Born   St Helens, 20 March 1893
Died   4 June 1950
Clubs   Prescot Athletic; Skelmersdale; Hull City; Sheffield Utd; Shirebrook; Torquay Utd

Caps	2	Result	Goals
	21 Oct 1922 v Ireland	2–0	
	19 Mar 1923 v Belgium	6–1	1

436. Frank Raymond Osborne
Outside right/Centre forward
Born   South Africa, 14 October 1896
Died   8 March 1988
Clubs   Bromley; Fulham; Tottenham Hotspur; Southampton

Caps	4	Result	Goals
	21 Oct 1922 v Ireland	2–0	
	10 May 1923 v France	4–1	

	8 Dec 1924 v Belgium	4–0	
	24 May 1926 v Belgium	5–3	3

437. Owen Williams
Outside left
Born   Ryhope, 23 September 1896
Died   9 December 1960
Clubs   Ryhope Colliery; Easington Colliery; Clapton Orient; Middlesbrough; Southend Utd; Shildon

Caps	2	Result
	21 Oct 1922 v Ireland	2–0
	5 Mar 1923 v Wales	2–2

438. Thomas Patrick Magee
Right half
Born   Widnes, 6 May 1898
Died   4 May 1974
Clubs   West Bromwich Albion; Crystal Palace

Caps	5	Result
	5 Mar 1923 v Wales	2–2
	24 May 1923 v Sweden	3–1
	8 Dec 1924 v Belgium	4–0
	4 Apr 1925 v Scotland	0–2
	21 May 1925 v France	3–2

439. Victor Martin Watson
Centre forward
Born   Chesterton, 10 November 1897
Died   3 August 1988
Clubs   Girton FC; Cambridge Town; Peterborough and Fletton Utd; Brotherhood Engineering Works; Wellingborough Town; West Ham Utd; Southampton

Caps	5	Result	Goals
	5 Mar 1923 v Wales	2–2	1
	14 Apr 1923 v Scotland	2–2	1
	5 Apr 1930 v Scotland	5–2	2
	10 May 1930 v Germany	3–3	
	14 May 1930 v Austria	0–0	

440. Frederick William Kean
Right half/Centre half
Born   Sheffield, 10 December 1898
Died   28 October 1973
Clubs   Sheffield Hallam; Portsmouth; Sheffield Wednesday; Bolton Wanderers; Luton Town; Sutton Town

Caps	9	Result
	19 Mar 1923 v Belgium	6–1
	14 Apr 1923 v Scotland	2–2
	3 Mar 1924 v Wales	1–2
	22 Oct 1924 v N. Ireland	3–1
	24 Oct 1925 v N. Ireland	0–0
	24 May 1926 v Belgium	5–3
	21 May 1927 v Luxembourg	5–2
	9 May 1929 v France	4–1
	15 May 1929 v Spain	3–4

441. Norman Bullock
Centre forward
Born   Monkton, 8 September 1900
Died   27 October 1970
Clubs   Sedgley Park; Bury

Caps	3	Result	Goals
	19 Mar 1923 v Belgium	6–1	1
	1 Mar 1926 v Wales	1–3	
	20 Oct 1926 v N. Ireland	3–3	1

442. Kenneth Edward Hegan
Winger
Born   Coventry, 24 January 1901
Clubs   Corinthians

Caps	4	Result	Goals
	19 Mar 1923 v Belgium	6–1	2
	10 May 1923 v France	4–1	2
	20 Oct 1923 v N. Ireland	1–2	
	1 Nov 1923 v Belgium	2–2	

443. John Tresadern
Left half
Born   Leytonstone, 26 September 1890
Died   26 September 1959
Clubs   Barking Town; West Ham Utd; Burnley;
        Northampton Town

Caps	2	Result
	14 Apr 1923 v Scotland	2–2
	21 May 1923 v Sweden	4–2

444. Frederick Edward Tunstall
Outside left
Born   Gravesend, 29 March 1900
Died   18 November 1965
Clubs   Darfield St George's; Scunthorpe Utd; Sheffield Utd;
        Halifax Town; Boston Utd

Caps	7	Result
	14 Apr 1923 v Scotland	2–2
	20 Oct 1923 v Ireland	1–2
	3 Mar 1924 v Wales	1–2
	12 Apr 1924 v Scotland	1–1
	17 May 1924 v France	3–1
	22 Oct 1924 v N. Ireland	3–1
	4 Apr 1925 v Scotland	0–2

445. John Thomas Alderson
Goalkeeper
Born   Crook, 28 November 1891
Died   17 February 1972
Clubs   Crook Town; Shildon Athletic; Newcastle Utd;
        Crystal Palace; Pontypridd; Sheffield Utd; Exeter
        City; Torquay Utd

Caps	1	Result
	10 May 1923 v France	4–1

446. Harry Jones
Left back
Born   Blackwell, 24 May 1891
Clubs   Blackwell Colliery; Nottingham Forest;
        Sutton Town

Caps	1	Result
	10 May 1923 v France	4–1

447. Seth Lewis Plum
Wing half
Born   Edmonton, 15 July 1899
Died   29 November 1969
Clubs   Mildway Athletic; Tottenham Park Avondale;
        Barnet; Charlton Athletic; Chelsea; Southend Utd

Caps	1	Result
	10 May 1923 v France	4–1

448. James Seddon
Centre half
Born   Bolton, 20 May 1895
Died   21 October 1971
Clubs   Hamilton Central Chorley; Bolton Wanderers;
        Dordrecht FC (Holland)

Caps	6	Result
	10 May 1923 v France	4–1
	21 May 1923 v Sweden	4–2
	24 May 1923 v Sweden	3–1
	1 Nov 1923 v Belgium	2–2
	12 Feb 1927 v Wales	3–3
	13 Apr 1929 v Scotland	0–1

449. Frederick Norman Smith Creek
Inside right/Centre forward
Born   Darlington, 12 January 1898
Died   26 July 1980
Clubs   Cambridge University; Corinthians; Darlington

Caps	1	Result	Goals
	10 May 1923 v France	4–1	1

450. Frank Hartley
Inside forward
Born   Shipton-under-Wychwood, 20 July 1896

Died   20 October 1965
Clubs   Oxford City; Tottenham Hotspur; Corinthians

Caps	1	Result
	10 May 1923 v France	4–1

451. Ernest Clarke 'Tim' Williamson
Goalkeeper
Born   Murton Colliery, 24 May 1890
Died   30 April 1964
Clubs   Murton Red Star; Wingate Albion; Croydon
        Common; Arsenal; Norwich City

Caps	2	Result
	21 May 1923 v Sweden	4–2
	24 May 1923 v Sweden	3–1

452. William Ashurst
Right back
Born   Willington, 4 May 1894
Died   26 January 1947
Clubs   Durham City; Leeds City; Lincoln City; Notts
        County; West Bromwich Albion; Newark Town

Caps	5	Result
	21 May 1923 v Sweden	4–2
	24 May 1923 v Sweden	3–1
	8 Dec 1924 v Belgium	4–0
	28 Feb 1925 v Wales	2–1
	4 Apr 1925 v Scotland	0–2

453. Basil Clement Patchitt
Fullback/Halfback
Born   London, 12 August 1900
Clubs   Cambridge University; Corinthians; Castleford Town

Caps	2	Result
	21 May 1923 v Sweden	4–2
	24 May 1923 v Sweden	3–1

454. George Thornewell
Outside right
Born   Romiley, 8 July 1898
Died   6 March 1986
Clubs   Rolls-Royce; Derby County; Blackburn Rovers;
        Chesterfield; Newark Town

Caps	4	Result	Goals
	21 May 1923 v Sweden	4–2	1
	24 May 1923 v Sweden	3–1	
	17 May 1924 v France	3–1	
	21 May 1924 v France	3–2	

455. James Moore
Inside forward
Born   Birmingham, 11 May 1889
Died   1972
Clubs   Glossop; Derby County; Chesterfield; Mansfield
        Town; Worcester City

Caps	1	Result	Goals
	21 May 1923 v Sweden	4–2	1

456. Harry Bedford
Inside right/Centre forward
Born   Calow, 15 October 1899
Died   24 June 1976
Clubs   Grassmoor Ivanhoe; Nottingham Forest; Blackpool;
        Derby County; Newcastle Utd; Sunderland;
        Bradford Park Avenue; Chesterfield; Heanor Town

Caps	2	Result	Goals
	21 May 1923 v Sweden	4–2	
	22 Oct 1924 v N. Ireland	3–1	1

457. Thomas Urwin
Winger
Born   Haswell, 5 February 1896
Died   7 May 1968
Clubs   Fulwell FC; Lambton Star; Shildon; Middlesbrough;
        Newcastle Utd

Caps	4	Result
	21 May 1923 v Sweden	4–2
	24 May 1923 v Sweden	3–1

1 Nov 1923 v Belgium	2–2	
1 Mar 1926 v Wales	1–3	

458. William Gray Bruce Moore
Inside left
Born Newcastle-upon-Tyne, 6 October 1894
Died 26 September 1968
Clubs Seaton Delaval; Sunderland; West Ham Utd

Caps 1	*Result*	*Goals*
24 May 1923 v Sweden	3–1	2

459. Harold Sidney Miller
Inside left
Born Watford, 20 May 1902
Died 24 October 1988
Clubs St Albans City; Charlton Athletic; Chelsea; Northampton Town

Caps 1	*Result*	*Goals*
24 May 1923 v Sweden	3–1	1

460. Alfred George Bower
Fullback
Born Bromley, 10 November 1895
Died 30 June 1970
Clubs Old Carthusians; Corinthians; Chelsea; Casuals

Caps 5	*Result*
20 Oct 1923 v N. Ireland	1–2
1 Nov 1923 v Belgium	2–2
8 Dec 1924 v Belgium	4–0
28 Feb 1925 v Wales	2–1
12 Feb 1927 v Wales	3–3

461. Harry Harold Pantling
Right half
Born Leighton Buzzard, 2 May 1891
Died 21 December 1952
Clubs Watford; Sheffield Utd; Rotherham Utd; Heanor Town

Caps 1	*Result*
20 Oct 1923 v N. Ireland	1–2

462. Thomas Meehan
Left half
Born Harpurhey, 4 February 1896
Died 18 August 1924
Clubs Newtown; Walkden Central; Rochdale; Manchester Utd; Chelsea

Caps 1	*Result*
20 Oct 1923 v N. Ireland	1–2

463. Joseph Bradford
Centre forward
Born Pegg's Green, 22 January 1901
Died 6 September 1980
Clubs Pegg's Green Victoria; Birmingham; Bristol City

Caps 12	*Result*	*Goals*
20 Oct 1923 v N. Ireland	1–2	1
8 Dec 1924 v Belgium	4–0	2
31 Mar 1928 v Scotland	1–5	
22 Oct 1928 v N. Ireland	2–1	
17 Nov 1928 v Wales	3–2	
9 May 1929 v France	4–1	
15 May 1929 v Spain	3–4	1
19 Oct 1929 v N. Ireland	3–0	
5 Apr 1930 v Scotland	5–2	
10 May 1930 v Germany	3–3	2
14 May 1930 v Austria	0–0	
22 Nov 1930 v Wales	4–0	1

464. Arthur Edward Hufton
Goalkeeper
Born Southwell, 25 November 1892
Died 2 February 1967
Clubs Atlas & Norfolk Works; Sheffield Utd; West Ham Utd; Watford

Caps 6	*Result*
1 Nov 1923 v Belgium	2–2
22 Oct 1927 v N. Ireland	0–2

31 Mar 1928 v Scotland	1–5	
9 May 1929 v France	4–1	
11 May 1929 v Belgium	5–1	
15 May 1929 v Spain	3–4	

465. William Brown
Inside right
Born Fence Houses, 22 August 1899
Died 17 January 1985
Clubs Hetton FC; West Ham Utd; Chelsea; Fulham; Stockport County; Hartlepool Utd

Caps 1	*Result*	*Goals*
1 Nov 1923 v Belgium	2–2	1

466. William Thomas Roberts
Centre forward
Born Handsworth, 29 November 1898
Died 13 October 1965
Clubs Soho Villa; Leicester Fosse; Preston North End; Burnley; Tottenham Hotspur; Dick Kerr's FC; Chorley

Caps 2	*Result*	*Goals*
1 Nov 1923 v Belgium	2–2	1
3 Mar 1924 v Wales	1–2	1

467. Alexander Graham Doggart
Inside left
Born Bishop Auckland, 2 June 1897
Died 7 June 1963
Clubs Cambridge University; Corinthians: Darlington; Bishop Auckland

Caps 1	*Result*
1 Nov 1923 v Belgium	2–2

468. William Ronald Sewell
Goalkeeper
Born Middlesbrough, 19 July 1890
Died 4 February 1945
Clubs Wingate Albion; Gainsborough Trinity; Burnley; Blackburn Rovers

Caps 1	*Result*
3 Mar 1924 v Wales	1–2

469. Thomas Mort
Left back
Born Kearsley, 1 December 1897
Died 6 June 1967
Clubs Altrincham; Rochdale; Aston Villa

Caps 3	*Result*
3 Mar 1924 v Wales	1–2
17 May 1924 v France	3–1
17 Apr 1926 v Scotland	0–1

470. David Bone Nightingale Jack
Inside right
Born Bolton, 3 April 1899
Died 10 September 1958
Clubs Bolton Wanderers; Arsenal

Caps 9	*Result*	*Goals*
3 Mar 1924 v Wales	1–2	
12 Apr 1924 v Scotland	1–1	
17 May 1928 v France	5–1	1
19 May 1928 v Belgium	3–1	
5 Apr 1930 v Scotland	5–2	1
10 May 1930 v Germany	3–3	1
14 May 1930 v Austria	0–0	
16 Nov 1932 v Wales	0–0	
7 Dec 1932 v Austria	4–3	

471. Clement Stephenson
Inside left
Born New Delaval, 6 February 1890
Died 24 October 1961
Clubs New Delaval Villa; West Stanley; Blyth Spartans; Aston Villa; Huddersfield Town

Caps 1	*Result*
3 Mar 1924 v Wales	1–2

472. Charles William Spencer
Centre half
Born   Washington, 4 December 1899
Died   9 February 1953
Clubs Glebe Rovers; Washington Chemical Works;
       Newcastle Utd; Tunbridge Wells Rangers; Wigan
       Athletic

Caps	2	Result
	12 Apr 1924 v Scotland	1–1
	28 Feb 1925 v Wales	2–1

473. William Butler
Outside right
Born   Atherton, 27 March 1900
Died   11 July 1966
Clubs Howe Bridge FC; Atherton Collieries; Bolton
       Wanderers; Reading

Caps	1	Result
	12 Apr 1924 v Scotland	1–1

474. Frederick Harold Ewer
Wing half
Born   West Ham, 30 September 1898
Died   29 January 1971
Clubs Casuals; Corinthians

Caps	2	Result
	17 Mar 1924 v France	3–1
	8 Dec 1924 v Belgium	4–0

475. George Frederick Blackburn
Left half
Born   Willesden Green, 8 March 1899
Died   3 July 1957
Clubs Hampstead Town; Aston Villa; Cardiff City;
       Mansfield Town; Cheltenham Town

Caps	1	Result
	17 May 1924 v France	3–1

476. Stanley George James Earle
Inside right
Born   Stratford, 6 September 1897
Died   26 September 1971
Clubs Clapton Orient; West Ham Utd; Clapton Orient

Caps	2	Result
	17 May 1924 v France	3–1
	22 Oct 1927 v N. Ireland	0–2

477. Vivian Talbot Gibbins
Centre forward/Inside forward
Born   Forest Gate, 10 August 1901
Died   21 November 1979
Clubs Clapton Orient; West Ham Utd; Brentford; Bristol
       Rovers; Southampton; Leyton Orient; Catford
       Wanderers

Caps	2	Result	Goals
	17 May 1924 v France	3–1	2
	21 May 1925 v France	3–2	1

478. Harry Storer
Left half/Inside left
Born   West Derby, 2 February 1898
Died   1 September 1967
Clubs Ripley Town; Eastwood FC; Grimsby Town; Derby
       County; Burnley

Caps	2	Result	Goals
	17 May 1924 v France	3–1	1
	22 Oct 1927 v N. Ireland	0–2	

479. James Frederick Mitchell
Goalkeeper
Born   Manchester, 18 November 1897
Died   30 May 1975
Clubs Blackpool; Northern Nomads; Manchester University;
       Preston North End; Manchester City; Leicester City

Caps	1	Result
	22 Oct 1924 v N. Ireland	3–1

480. Harry Healless
Centre half/Wing half
Born   Blackburn, 10 February 1893
Died   11 January 1972
Clubs Blackburn Athletic; Victoria Cross; Blackburn Trinity;
       Blackburn Rovers

Caps	2	Result
	22 Oct 1924 v N. Ireland	3–1
	31 Mar 1928 v Scotland	1–5

481. Henry Hardy
Goalkeeper
Born   Stockport, 14 January 1895
Died   17 February 1969
Clubs Alderley Edge FC; Stockport County; Everton; Bury

Caps	1	Result
	8 Dec 1924 v Belgium	4–0

482. John Dennis Butler
Centre half
Born   Colombo, Sri Lanka, 14 August 1894
Died   5 January 1961
Clubs Fulham; Dartford; Arsenal; Torquay Utd

Caps	1	Result
	8 Dec 1924 v Belgium	4–0

483. Frank Roberts
Inside right/Centre forward
Born   Sandbach, 3 April 1893
Died   23 May 1961
Clubs Sandbach Villa; Sandbach Ramblers; Crewe
       Alexandra; Bolton Wanderers; Manchester City;
       Manchester Central; Horwich RMI

Caps	4	Result	Goals
	8 Dec 1924 v Belgium	4–0	
	28 Feb 1925 v Wales	2–1	2
	4 Apr 1925 v Scotland	0–2	
	21 May 1925 v France	3–2	

484. Arthur Reginald Dorrell
Outside left
Born   Small Heath, 30 March 1896
Died   13 September 1942
Clubs Aston Villa; Port Vale

Caps	4	Result	Goals
	8 Dec 1924 v Belgium	4–0	
	28 Feb 1925 v Wales	2–1	
	21 May 1925 v France	3–2	1
	24 Oct 1925 v N. Ireland	0–0	

485. Richard Henry 'Pincher' Pym
Goalkeeper
Born   Topsham, 2 February 1893
Died   23 September 1988
Clubs Exeter City; Bolton Wanderers

Caps	3	Result
	28 Feb 1925 v Wales	2–1
	4 Apr 1925 v Scotland	0–2
	1 Mar 1926 v Wales	1–3

486. John Henry Hill
Centre half
Born   Hetton-le-Hole, 2 March 1897
Died   25 April 1972
Clubs Durham City; Plymouth Argyle; Burnley; Newcastle
       Utd; Bradford City; Hull City

Caps	11	Result
	28 Feb 1925 v Wales	2–1
	17 Apr 1926 v Scotland	0–1
	20 Oct 1926 v N. Ireland	3–3
	2 Apr 1927 v Scotland	2–1
	11 May 1927 v Belgium	9–1
	26 May 1927 v France	6–0
	22 Oct 1927 v N. Ireland	0–2
	28 Nov 1927 v Wales	1–2
	9 May 1929 v France	4–1

11 May 1929 v Belgium	5–1	
15 May 1929 v Spain	3–4	

487. Leonard Graham
Left half
Born   Leyton, 20 August 1901
Died   21 December 1962
Clubs   Capworth Utd; Leytonstone; Millwall Athletic
Caps   2   *Result*
        28 Feb 1925 v Wales   2–1
        4 Apr 1925 v Scotland   0–2

488. Thomas Edwin Reed Cook
Centre forward
Born   Cuckfield, 5 February 1901
Died   15 January 1950
Clubs   Cuckfield FC; Brighton & Hove Albion; Northfleet;
        Bristol Rovers
Caps   1   *Result*
        28 Feb 1925 v Wales   2–1

489. John Edward Townrow
Centre half
Born   West Ham, 28 March 1901
Died   11 April 1969
Clubs   Clapton Orient; Chelsea; Bristol Rovers
Caps   2   *Result*
        4 Apr 1925 v Scotland   0–2
        1 Mar 1926 v Wales   1–3

490. Frederick Samuel Fox
Goalkeeper
Born   Highworth, 22 November 1898
Died   15 May 1968
Clubs   Swindon Town; Abertillery; Preston North End;
        Gillingham; Millwall; Halifax Town; Brentford
Caps   1   *Result*
        21 May 1925 v France   3–2

491. Thomas Robert Parker
Right back
Born   Southampton, 19 November 1897
Died   1 November 1987
Clubs   Sholing Rangers; Sholing Athletic; Southampton;
        Arsenal
Caps   1   *Result*
        21 May 1925 v France   3–2

492. William Felton
Right back
Born   Heworth, 1 August 1900
Died   22 April 1977
Cubs   Pelaw Albion; Pandon Temperance; Wardley
        Colliery; Jarrow; Grimsby Town; Sheffield
        Wednesday; Manchester City; Tottenham Hotspur;
        Altrincham
Caps   1   *Result*
        21 May 1925 v France   3–2

493. William Ingram Bryant
Centre half
Born   Ghent, Belgium, 1 March 1899
Died   21 January 1986
Clubs   Chelmsford, Clapton Orient; Millwall
Caps   1   *Result*
        21 May 1925 v France   3–2

494. George Henry Green
Left half
Born   Leamington, 2 May 1901
Died   16 June 1980
Clubs   Nuneaton; Sheffield Utd; Leamington Town
Caps   8   *Result*
        21 May 1925 v France   3–2
        1 Mar 1926 v Wales   1–3
        17 Apr 1926 v Scotland   0–1

24 May 1926 v Belgium	5–3	
20 Oct 1926 v N. Ireland	3–3	
12 Feb 1927 v Wales	3–3	
17 May 1928 v France	5–1	
19 May 1928 v Belgium	3–1	

495. Francis Carr Hudspeth
Left back
Born   Percy Main, 20 April 1890
Died   8 February 1963
Clubs   Scotswood; Newburn; Clare Vale; North Shields
        Athletic; Newcastle Utd; Stockport County; Crook
        Town
Caps   1   *Result*
        24 Oct 1925 v N. Ireland   0–0

496. George Henry Armitage
Centre half
Born   Stoke Newington, 17 January 1898
Died   28 August 1936
Clubs   St Saviour's FC; Wimbledon; Charlton Athletic;
        Leyton
Caps   1   *Result*
        24 Oct 1925 v N. Ireland   0–0

497. Samuel William Austin
Outside right
Born   Arnold, 29 April 1900
Died   2 April 1979
Clubs   Arnold Utd; Arnold St Mary's; Norwich City;
        Manchester City; Chesterfield; Kidderminster
        Harriers
Caps   1   *Result*
        24 Oct 1925 v N. Ireland   0–0

498. Sydney Charles Puddefoot
Inside right/Centre forward
Born   Limehouse, 17 October 1894
Died   2 October 1972
Clubs   Conder Athletic; Limehouse Town; West Ham Utd;
        Falkirk; Blackburn Rovers
Caps   2   *Result*
        24 Oct 1925 v N. Ireland   0–0
        17 Apr 1926 v Scotland   0–1

499. Claude Thesiger Ashton
Centre forward
Born   Calcutta, India, 19 February 1901
Died   31 October 1942
Clubs   Cambridge University; Corinthians; Old
        Wykehamists
Caps   1   *Result*
        24 Oct 1925 v N. Ireland   0–0

500. Willis Edwards
Right half
Born   Newton, 28 April 1903
Died   27 September 1988
Clubs   Newton Rangers; Chesterfield; Leeds Utd
Caps   16   *Result*
        1 Mar 1926 v Wales   1–3
        17 Apr 1926 v Scotland   0–1
        20 Oct 1926 v N. Ireland   3–3
        12 Feb 1927 v Wales   3–3
        2 Apr 1927 v Scotland   2–1
        1 May 1927 v Belgium   9–1
        21 May 1927 v Luxembourg   5–2
        26 May 1927 v France   6–0
        31 Mar 1928 v Scotland   1–5
        17 May 1928 v France   5–1
        19 May 1928 v Belgium   3–1
        22 Oct 1928 v Wales   2–1
        17 Nov 1928 v Wales   3–2
        13 Apr 1929 v Scotland   0–1
        19 Oct 1929 v N. Ireland   3–0
        20 Nov 1929 v Wales   6–0

501. Frederick Roy Goodall
Right back
Born   Dronfield, 31 December 1902
Died   19 January 1982
Clubs   Dronfield Woodhouse FC; Huddersfield Town

Caps	25	Result
	17 Apr 1926 v Scotland	0–1
	2 Apr 1927 v Scotland	2–1
	11 May 1927 v Belgium	9–1
	21 May 1927 v Luxembourg	5–2
	26 May 1927 v France	6–0
	28 Nov 1927 v Wales	1–2
	31 Mar 1928 v Scotland	1–5
	17 May 1928 v France	5–1
	19 May 1928 v Belgium	3–1
	5 Apr 1930 v Scotland	5–2
	10 May 1930 v Germany	3–3
	14 May 1930 v Austria	0–0
	20 Oct 1930 v N. Ireland	5–1
	22 Nov 1930 v Wales	4–0
	28 Mar 1931 v Scotland	0–2
	16 May 1931 v Belgium	4–1
	17 Oct 1931 v N. Ireland	6–2
	17 Oct 1932 v N. Ireland	1–0
	16 Nov 1932 v Wales	0–0
	7 Dec 1932 v Austria	4–3
	13 May 1933 v Italy	1–1
	20 May 1933 v Switzerland	4–0
	14 Oct 1933 v N. Ireland	3–0
	15 Nov 1933 v Wales	1–2
	6 Dec 1933 v France	4–1

502. Edward Cashfield Harper
Centre forward
Born   Sheerness, 22 August 1901
Died   22 July 1959
Clubs   Sheppey Utd; Blackburn Rovers; Sheffield
        Wednesday; Tottenham Hotspur; Preston North End

Caps	1	Result
	17 Apr 1926 v Scotland	0–1

503. James William Ruffell
Outside left
Born   Barnsley, 8 August 1900
Died   5 September 1989
Clubs   Fuller's FC; Chadwell Heath; Manor Park Albion;
        Wall End Utd; West Ham Utd; Aldershot

Caps	6	Result
	17 Apr 1926 v Scotland	0–1
	20 Oct 1926 v N. Ireland	3–3
	22 Oct 1928 v N. Ireland	2–1
	17 Nov 1928 v Wales	3–2
	13 Apr 1929 v Scotland	0–1
	20 Nov 1929 v Wales	6–0

504. George Samuel Ashmore
Goalkeeper
Born   Plymouth, 5 May 1898
Died   19 May 1973
Clubs   Nineveh Wesley; West Bromwich Albion;
        Chesterfield

Caps	1	Result
	24 May 1926 v Belgium	5–3

505. Richard Henry Hill
Left back
Born   Mapperley, 26 November 1893
Died   25 April 1971
Clubs   Millwall Athletic; Torquay Utd; Newark Town

Caps	1	Result
	24 May 1926 v Belgium	5–3

506. Samuel Cowan
Centre half
Born   Chesterfield, 10 May 1901
Died   4 October 1964

Clubs   Bulcroft Colliery; Denaby Utd; Doncaster Rovers;
        Manchester City; Bradford City; Mossley

Caps	3	Result
	24 May 1926 v Belgium	5–3
	14 May 1930 v Austria	0–0
	16 May 1931 v Belgium	4–1

507. Joseph Walter Spence
Outside right/Centre forward
Born   Throckley, 15 December 1898
Died   31 December 1966
Clubs   Throckley Celtic; Scotswood; Manchester Utd;
        Bradford City; Chesterfield

Caps	2	Result	Goals
	24 May 1926 v Belgium	5–3	
	20 Oct 1926 v N. Ireland	3–3	1

508. Joseph Henry Carter
Inside right
Born   Aston, 22 April 1901
Died   21 January 1977
Clubs   Westbourne Celtic; West Bromwich Albion;
        Tranmere Rovers; Walsall; Vono Sports

Caps	3	Result	Goals
	24 May 1926 v Belgium	5–3	1
	11 May 1929 v Belgium	5–1	1
	15 May 1929 v Spain	3–4	2

509. Thomas Clark Fisher Johnson
Inside left
Born   Dalton-in-Furness, 19 August 1900
Died   28 January 1973
Clubs   Dalton Athletic; Dalton Casuals; Manchester City;
        Everton; Liverpool; Darwen

Caps	5	Result	Goals
	24 May 1926 v Belgium	5–3	1
	20 Nov 1929 v Wales	6–0	2
	9 Dec 1931 v Spain	7–1	2
	9 Apr 1932 v Scotland	3–0	
	17 Oct 1932 v N. Ireland	1–0	

510. Albert McInroy
Goalkeeper
Born   Walton-le-Dale, 23 April 1901
Died   7 January 1985
Clubs   Coppell Central; Preston North End; Great
        Harwood; Leyland Motors; Sunderland; Newcastle
        Utd; Leeds Utd; Gateshead

Caps	1	Result
	20 Oct 1926 v N. Ireland	3–3

511. George Brown
Inside right/Centre forward
Born   Mickley, 22 June 1903
Died   10 June 1948
Clubs   Mickley Colliery; Huddersfield Town; Aston Villa;
        Burnley; Leeds Utd; Darlington

Caps	9	Result	Goals
	20 Oct 1926 v N. Ireland	3–3	
	12 Feb 1927 v Wales	3–3	
	2 Apr 1927 v Scotland	2–1	
	11 May 1927 v Belgium	9–1	2
	21 May 1927 v Luxembourg	5–2	
	26 May 1927 v France	6–0	2
	28 Nov 1927 v Wales	1–2	
	13 Apr 1929 v Scotland	0–1	
	16 Nov 1932 v Wales	0–0	

512. John Henry Brown
Goalkeeper
Born   Hodthorpe, 19 March 1899
Died   10 April 1962
Clubs   Manton Colliery; Worksop Town; Sheffield
        Wednesday; Hartlepool Utd

Caps	6	Result
	12 Feb 1927 v Wales	3–3

2 Apr 1927 v Scotland	2–1
11 May 1927 v Belgium	9–1
21 May 1927 v Luxembourg	5–2
26 May 1927 v France	6–0
19 Oct 1929 v N. Ireland	3–0

513. George Smith Waterfield
Left back
Born   Swinton, near Rotherham, 2 June 1901
Died   1988
Clubs   Swinton FC; Mexborough; Burnley; Crystal Palace

Caps 1	*Result*
12 Feb 1927 v Wales	3–3

514. William Harold Pease
Outside right
Born   Leeds, 30 September 1899
Died   2 October 1955
Clubs   Leeds City; Northampton Town; Middlesbrough; Luton Town

Caps 1	*Result*
12 Feb 1927 v Wales	3–3

515. William Ralph 'Dixie' Dean
Centre forward
Born   Birkenhead, 22 January 1907
Died   1 March 1980
Clubs   Heswall; Pensby Utd; Tranmere Rovers; Everton; Notts County; Sligo Rovers; Hurst

Caps 16	*Result*	*Goals*
12 Feb 1927 v Wales	3–3	2
2 Apr 1927 v Scotland	2–1	2
11 May 1927 v Belgium	9–1	3
21 May 1927 v Luxembourg	5–2	3
26 May 1927 v France	6–0	2
22 Oct 1927 v N. Ireland	0–2	
28 Nov 1927 v Wales	1–2	
31 Mar 1928 v Scotland	1–5	
17 May 1928 v France	5–1	2
19 May 1928 v Belgium	3–1	2
22 Oct 1928 v N. Ireland	2–1	1
17 Nov 1928 v Wales	3–2	
13 Apr 1929 v Scotland	0–1	
28 Mar 1931 v Scotland	0–2	
9 Dec 1931 v Spain	7–1	1
17 Oct 1932 v N. Ireland	1–0	

516. Louis Antonio Page
Outside left
Born   Kirkdale, 27 March 1899
Died   12 October 1959
Clubs   South Liverpool; Stoke; Northampton Town; Burnley; Manchester Utd; Port Vale; Yeovil & Petters

Caps 7	*Result*	*Goals*
12 Feb 1927 v Wales	3–3	
2 Apr 1927 v Scotland	2–1	
11 May 1927 v Belgium	9–1	1
21 May 1927 v Luxembourg	5–2	
26 May 1927 v France	6–0	
22 Oct 1927 v Ireland	0–2	
28 Nov 1927 v Wales	1–2	

517. Herbert Jones
Left back
Born   Blackpool, 3 September 1896
Died   11 September 1973
Clubs   South Shore Strollers; Fleetwood; Blackpool; Blackburn Rovers; Brighton & Hove Albion

Caps 6	*Result*
2 Apr 1927 v Scotland	2–1
11 May 1927 v Belgium	9–1
21 May 1927 v Luxembourg	5–2
26 May 1927 v France	6–0
22 Oct 1927 v Ireland	0–2
31 Mar 1928 v Scotland	1–5

> ⚽ **DID YOU KNOW...?**
>
> The last player to score a hat-trick in consecutive England matches was Dixie Dean in May 1927. The feat was achieved during a summer tour of northern Europe against Belgium (9–1) and Luxembourg (5–2).

518. Sidney Macdonald Bishop
Wing half
Born   Stepney, 10 February 1900
Died   4 May 1949
Clubs   Ilford; Crystal Palace; West Ham Utd; Leicester City; Chelsea

Caps 4	*Result*	*Goals*
2 Apr 1927 v Scotland	2–1	
11 May 1927 v Belgium	9–1	
21 May 1917 v Luxembourg	5–2	1
26 May 1927 v France	6–0	

519. Joseph Harold Anthony Hulme
Outside right
Born   Stafford, 26 August 1904
Died   26 September 1991
Clubs   York City; Blackburn Rovers; Arsenal; Huddersfield Town

Caps 9	*Result*	*Goals*
2 Apr 1927 v Scotland	2–1	
11 May 1927 v Belgium	9–1	1
26 May 1927 v France	6–0	
22 Oct 1927 v N. Ireland	0–2	
28 Nov 1927 v Wales	1–2	
31 Mar 1928 v Scotland	1–5	
22 Oct 1928 v N. Ireland	2–1	1
17 Nov 1928 v Wales	3–2	2
1 Apr 1933 v Scotland	1–2	

520. Arthur Rigby
Inside left/Outside left
Born   Chorlton, 7 June 1900
Died   25 March 1960
Clubs   Stockport County; Crewe Alexandra; Bradford City; Blackburn Rovers; Everton; Middlesbrough; Clapton Orient

Caps 5	*Result*	*Goals*
2 Apr 1927 v Scotland	2–1	
11 May 1927 v Belgium	9–1	2
21 May 1927 v Luxembourg	5–2	
26 May 1927 v France	6–0	1
28 Nov 1927 v Wales	1–2	

521. Thomas Cooper
Right back
Born   Fenton, 9 April 1904
Died   25 June 1940
Clubs   Trentham FC; Port Vale; Derby County; Liverpool

Caps 15	*Result*
22 Oct 1927 v N. Ireland	0–2
22 Oct 1928 v N. Ireland	2–1
17 Nov 1928 v Wales	3–2
13 Apr 1929 v Scotland	0–1
9 May 1929 v France	4–1
11 May 1929 v Belgium	5–1
15 May 1929 v Spain	3–4
14 May 1931 v France	2–5
18 Nov 1931 v Wales	3–1
9 Dec 1931 v Spain	7–1
1 Apr 1933 v Scotland	1–2
14 Apr 1934 v Scotland	3–0
10 May 1934 v Hungary	1–2
16 May 1934 v Czechoslovakia	1–2
29 Sep 1934 v Wales	4–0

522. Henry Nuttall
Wing half

Born Bolton, 9 November 1897
Died 25 April 1969
Clubs Fleetwood; Bolton Wanderers; Rochdale; Nelson

Caps	3	Result
	22 Oct 1927 v N. Ireland	0–2
	28 Nov 1927 v Wales	1–2
	13 Apr 1929 v Scotland	0–1

523. John Ball
Inside left

Born Hazel Grove, 29 September 1900
Died 1989
Clubs Silverwood Colliery; Sheffield Utd; Bristol Rovers; Wath Athletic; Bury; West Ham Utd; Coventry City; Stourbridge

Caps	1	Result
	22 Oct 1927 v N. Ireland	0–2

524. Daniel Richard Tremelling
Goalkeeper

Born Burton-on-Trent, 12 November 1897
Died 15 August 1970
Clubs Langwith Colliery; Shirebrook; Lincoln City; Birmingham; Bury

Caps	1	Result
	28 Nov 1927 v Wales	1–2

525. Reginald Osborne
Left back

Born Wynberg, South Africa, 23 July 1898
Died 18 April 1977
Clubs Leicester City; Folkestone

Caps	1	Result
	28 Nov 1927 v Wales	1–2

526. Alfred Baker
Right back/Right half

Born Ilkeston, 27 April 1898
Died 1 April 1955
Clubs Cossall St Catherine's; Long Eaton; Eastwood Rangers; Arsenal

Caps	1	Result
	28 Nov 1927 v Wales	1–2

527. Thomas Wilson
Centre half

Born Seaham, 16 April 1896
Died 2 February 1948
Clubs Seaham Colliery; Sunderland; Huddersfield Town; Blackpool

Caps	1	Result
	31 Mar 1928 v Scotland	1–5

528. Benjamin Albert Olney
Goalkeeper

Born Holborn, 30 March 1899
Died 23 September 1943
Clubs Fairley's Athletic; Aston Park Rangers; Brierley Hill Alliance; Stourbridge; Derby County; Aston Villa; Bilston Utd; Walsall; Shrewsbury Town; Moor Green

Caps	2	Result
	17 May 1928 v France	5–1
	19 May 1928 v Belgium	3–1

529. Ernest Blenkinsop
Left back

Born Cudworth, 20 April 1902
Died 24 April 1969
Clubs Cudworth United Methodists; Hull City; Sheffield Wednesday; Liverpool; Cardiff City; Buxton

Caps	26	Result
	17 May 1928 v France	5–1
	19 May 1928 v Belgium	3–1

	22 Oct 1928 v N. Ireland	2–1
	17 Nov 1928 v Wales	3–2
	13 Apr 1929 v Scotland	0–1
	9 May 1929 v France	4–1
	11 May 1929 v Belgium	5–1
	15 May 1929 v Spain	3–4
	19 Oct 1929 v N. Ireland	3–0
	20 Nov 1929 v Wales	6–0
	5 Apr 1930 v Scotland	5–2
	10 May 1930 v Germany	3–3
	14 May 1930 v Austria	0–0
	20 Oct 1930 v N. Ireland	5–1
	22 Nov 1930 v Wales	4–0
	28 Mar 1931 v Scotland	0–2
	14 May 1931 v France	2–5
	16 May 1931 v Belgium	4–1
	17 Oct 1931 v N. Ireland	6–2
	18 Nov 1931 v Wales	3–1
	9 Dec 1931 v Spain	7–1
	9 Apr 1932 v Scotland	3–0
	17 Oct 1932 v N. Ireland	1–0
	16 Nov 1932 v Wales	0–0
	7 Dec 1932 v Austria	4–3
	1 Apr 1933 v Scotland	1–2

530. Vincent Matthews
Centre half

Born Oxford, 15 January 1896
Died 15 November 1950
Clubs St Frideville FC; Oxford City; Bournemouth; Bolton Wanderers; Tranmere Rovers; Sheffield Utd; Shamrock Rovers; Oswestry Town; Shrewsbury Town

Caps	2	Result	Goals
	17 May 1928 v France	5–1	
	19 May 1928 v Belgium	3–1	1

531. John Bruton
Outside right

Born Westhoughton, 21 November 1903
Died 13 March 1896
Clubs Hindley Green; Wigan Borough; Horwich RMI; Burnley; Blackburn Rovers

Caps	3	Result
	17 May 1928 v France	5–1
	19 May 1928 v Belgium	3–1
	13 Apr 1929 v Scotland	0–1

532. George Ternent Stephenson
Inside forward

Born New Delaval, 3 September 1900
Died 18 August 1971
Clubs New Delaval Villa; Leeds City; Aston Villa; Derby County; Sheffield Wednesday; Preston North End; Charlton Athletic

Caps	3	Result	Goals
	17 May 1928 v France	5–1	2
	19 May 1928 v Belgium	3–1	
	14 May 1931 v France	2–5	

533. Leonard James Barry
Outside left

Born Sneiton, Nottingham, 27 October 1901
Died 17 April 1970
Clubs Notts County; Leicester City; Nottingham Forest

Caps	5	Result
	17 May 1928 v France	5–1
	19 May 1928 v Belgium	3–1
	9 May 1929 v France	4–1
	11 May 1929 v Belgium	5–1
	15 May 1929 v Spain	3–4

534. John Hacking
Goalkeeper

Born Blackburn, 22 December 1897
Died 31 May 1955

Clubs Blackburn Co-op; Blackpool; Fleetwood; Oldham
Athletic; Manchester Utd; Accrington Stanley

Caps	3	*Result*
	22 Oct 1928 v N. Ireland	2–1
	17 Nov 1928 v Wales	3–2
	13 Apr 1929 v Scotland	0–1

535. James William 'Tiny' Barrett
Centre half
Born Stratford, 19 January 1907
Died 25 November 1970
Clubs West Ham Utd

Caps	1	*Result*
	22 Oct 1928 v N. Ireland	2–1

 DID YOU KNOW...?

Jimmy Barrett of West Ham United has the
shortest England career. He was carried off after
eight minutes of the game against Northern
Ireland on 22 October 1928 and never played for
England again.

536. Austen Fenwick Campbell
Left half
Born Hamsterley, 5 May 1901
Died 8 September 1981
Clubs Spen Black & White; Leadgate Park; Coventry City;
Blackburn Rovers; Huddersfield Town; Hull City

Caps	8	*Result*
	22 Oct 1928 v N. Ireland	2–1
	17 Nov 1928 v Wales	3–2
	20 Oct 1930 v N. Ireland	5–1
	22 Nov 1930 v Wales	4–0
	28 Mar 1931 v Scotland	0–2
	17 Oct 1931 v N. Ireland	6–2
	18 Nov 1931 v Wales	3–1
	9 Dec 1931 v Spain	7–1

537. Ernest William Hine
Inside forward
Born Smithy Cross, 9 April 1901
Died 25 April 1974
Clubs Staincross Station; Barnsley; Leicester City;
Huddersfield Town; Manchester Utd

Caps	6	*Result*	*Goals*
	22 Oct 1928 v N. Ireland	2–1	
	17 Nov 1928 v Wales	3–2	1
	19 Oct 1929 v N. Ireland	3–0	1
	20 Nov 1929 v Wales	6–0	
	17 Oct 1931 v N. Ireland	6–2	1
	18 Nov 1931 v Wales	3–1	1

538. Ernest Arthur Hart
Centre half
Born Overseal, 3 January 1902
Died 21 July 1954
Clubs Woodlands Wesleyans; Leeds Utd; Mansfield
Town

Caps	8	*Result*
	17 Nov 1928 v Wales	3–2
	19 Oct 1929 v N. Ireland	3–0
	20 Nov 1929 v Wales	6–0
	7 Dec 1932 v Austria	4–3
	1 Apr 1933 v Scotland	1–2
	14 Apr 1934 v Scotland	3–0
	10 May 1934 v Hungary	1–2
	16 May 1934 v Czechoslovakia	1–2

539. William Russell Wainscoat
Inside left
Born East Retford, 28 July 1898
Died 4 July 1967
Clubs Maltby Main Colliery; Barnsley; Middlesbrough;
Leeds Utd; Hull City

Caps	1	*Result*
	13 Apr 1929 v Scotland	0–1

540. John 'Joe' Peacock
Wing half
Born Wigan, 15 March 1897
Died 4 March 1979
Clubs Wigan Recreation; Atherton; Everton;
Middlesbrough; Sheffield Wednesday; Clapton Orient

Caps	3	*Result*
	9 May 1929 v France	4–1
	11 May 1929 v Belgium	5–1
	15 May 1929 v Spain	3–4

541. Hugh Adcock
Outside right
Born Coalville, 10 April 1903
Died 16 October 1975
Clubs Coalville Town; Loughborough Corinthians;
Leicester City; Bristol Rovers; Folkestone

Caps	5	*Result*	*Goals*
	9 May 1929 v France	4–1	
	11 May 1929 v Belgium	5–1	
	15 May 1929 v Spain	3–4	
	19 Oct 1929 v N. Ireland	3–0	
	20 Nov 1929 v Wales	6–0	1

542. Edgar Isaac Lewis Kail
Inside right
Born Camberwell, 26 November 1900
Died 16 January 1976
Clubs Dulwich Hamlet; Chelsea

Caps	3	*Result*	*Goals*
	9 May 1929 v France	4–1	2
	11 May 1929 v Belgium	5–1	
	15 May 1929 v Spain	3–4	

543. George Henry Camsell
Centre forward
Born Framwellgate Moor, 27 November 1902
Died 7 March 1966
Clubs Esh Winning; Tow Law Town; Durham City;
Middlesbrough

Caps	9	*Result*	*Goals*
	9 May 1929 v France	4–1	2
	11 May 1929 v Belgium	5–1	4
	19 Oct 1929 v N. Ireland	3–0	2
	20 Nov 1929 v Wales	6–0	3
	6 Dec 1933 v France	4–1	2
	4 Dec 1935 v Germany	3–0	2
	4 Apr 1936 v Scotland	1–1	1
	6 May 1936 v Austria	1–2	1
	9 May 1936 v Belgium	2–3	1

544. Leonard Frederick Oliver
Right half
Born Fulham, 1 August 1905
Died 22 August 1967
Clubs Alma Athletic; Tufnell Park; Fulham

Caps	1	*Result*
	11 May 1929 v Belgium	5–1

545. Albert Frank Barrett
Left half
Born West Ham, 11 November 1903
Died 1989
Clubs West Ham Utd; Southampton; Fulham

Caps	1	*Result*
	19 Oct 1929 v N. Ireland	3–0

546. Eric Fred Brook
Outside left

Born	Mexborough, 27 November 1907		
Died	29 March 1965		
Clubs	Mexborough FC; Dearne Valley Old Boys; Wath Athletic; Barnsley; Manchester City		

Caps	18	Result	Goals
	19 Oct 1929 v N. Ireland	3–0	
	20 May 1933 v Switzerland	4–0	
	14 Oct 1933 v N. Ireland	3–0	1
	15 Nov 1933 v Wales	1–2	1
	6 Dec 1933 v France	4–1	1
	14 Apr 1934 v Scotland	3–0	1
	10 May 1934 v Hungary	1–2	
	16 May 1934 v Czechoslovakia	1–2	
	29 Sep 1934 v Wales	4–0	1
	14 Nov 1934 v Italy	3–2	2
	6 Feb 1935 v N. Ireland	2–1	
	6 Apr 1935 v Scotland	0–2	
	19 Oct 1935 v N. Ireland	3–1	1
	5 Feb 1936 v Wales	1–2	
	4 Apr 1936 v Scotland	1–1	
	2 Dec 1936 v Hungary	6–2	1
	23 Oct 1937 v N. Ireland	5–1	1
	17 Nov 1937 v Wales	2–1	

547. Henry Edward Hibbs
Goalkeeper

Born	Wilnecote, 27 May 1906	
Died	23 April 1984	
Clubs	Tamworth Castle; Birmingham	

Caps	25	Result
	20 Nov 1929 v Wales	6–0
	5 Apr 1930 v Scotland	5–2
	10 May 1930 v Germany	3–3
	14 May 1930 v Austria	0–0
	20 Oct 1930 v N. Ireland	5–1
	22 Nov 1930 v Wales	4–0
	28 Mar 1931 v Scotland	0–2
	17 Oct 1931 v N. Ireland	6–2
	18 Nov 1931 v Wales	3–1
	9 Dec 1931 v Spain	7–1
	17 Oct 1932 v N. Ireland	1–0
	16 Nov 1932 v Wales	0–0
	7 Dec 1932 v Austria	4–3
	1 Apr 1933 v Scotland	1–2
	13 May 1933 v Italy	1–1
	20 May 1933 v Switzerland	4–0
	14 Oct 1933 v N. Ireland	3–0
	15 Nov 1933 v Wales	1–2
	6 Dec 1933 v France	4–1
	29 Sep 1934 v Wales	4–0
	6 Feb 1935 v N. Ireland	2–1
	6 Apr 1935 v Scotland	0–2
	18 May 1935 v Holland	1–0
	4 Dec 1935 v Germany	3–0
	5 Feb 1936 v Wales	1–2

548. William Marsden
Left half

Born	Silksworth, 10 November 1901	
Died	20 June 1983	
Clubs	Silksworth Colliery; Sunderland; Sheffield Wednesday	

Caps	3	Result
	20 Nov 1929 v Wales	6–0
	5 Apr 1930 v Scotland	5–2
	10 May 1930 v Germany	3–3

549. Alfred Henry Strange
Right half

Born	Marehey, 2 April 1900	
Died	3 October 1978	
Clubs	Marehey Colliery; Portsmouth; Port Vale; Sheffield Wednesday; Bradford Park Avenue	

Caps	20	Result
	5 Apr 1930 v Scotland	5–2
	10 May 1930 v Germany	3–3
	14 May 1930 v Austria	0–0
	20 Oct 1930 v N. Ireland	5–1
	22 Nov 1930 v Wales	4–0
	28 Mar 1931 v Scotland	0–2
	14 May 1931 v France	2–5
	16 May 1931 v Belgium	4–1
	17 Oct 1931 v N. Ireland	6–2
	18 Nov 1931 v Wales	3–1
	9 Dec 1931 v Spain	7–1
	9 Apr 1932 v Scotland	3–0
	17 Oct 1932 v N. Ireland	1–0
	7 Dec 1932 v Austria	4–3
	1 Apr 1933 v Scotland	1–2
	13 May 1933 v Italy	1–1
	20 May 1933 v Switzerland	4–0
	14 Oct 1933 v N. Ireland	3–0
	15 Nov 1933 v Wales	1–2
	6 Dec 1933 v France	4–1

> ⚽ **DID YOU KNOW...?**
>
> In May 1936, England's George Camsell ended his international career with the best average goal-scoring figures ever attained by a British international. He played for England nine times between 1929 and 1936, and scored a total of eighteen goals.

550. Maurice Webster
Centre half

Born	Blackpool, 13 November 1899	
Died	14 February 1978	
Clubs	Bloomfield Villa; South Shore Wednesday; Fleetwood; Lytham; Stalybridge Celtic; Middlesbrough; Carlisle Utd	

Caps	3	Result
	5 Apr 1930 v Scotland	5–2
	10 May 1930 v Germany	3–3
	14 May 1930 v Austria	0–0

551. Samuel Dickinson Crooks
Outside right

Born	Bearpark, 16 January 1908	
Died	5 February 1981	
Clubs	Bearpark Colliery; Brandon Juniors; Tow Law Town; Durham City; Derby County	

Caps	26	Result	Goals
	5 Apr 1930 v Scotland	5–2	
	10 May 1930 v Germany	3–3	
	14 May 1930 v Austria	0–0	
	20 Oct 1930 v N. Ireland	5–1	1
	22 Nov 1930 v Wales	4–0	
	28 Mar 1931 v Scotland	0–2	
	14 May 1931 v France	2–5	1
	16 May 1931 v Belgium	4–1	
	17 Oct 1931 v N. Ireland	6–2	
	18 Nov 1931 v Wales	3–1	1
	9 Dec 1931 v Spain	7–1	2
	9 Apr 1932 v Scotland	3–0	1
	17 Oct 1932 v N. Ireland	1–0	
	16 Nov 1932 v Wales	0–0	
	7 Dec 1932 v Austria	4–3	1
	14 Oct 1933 v N. Ireland	3–0	
	15 Nov 1933 v Wales	1–2	
	6 Dec 1933 v France	4–1	
	14 Apr 1934 v Scotland	3–0	
	10 May 1934 v Hungary	1–2	

16 May 1934 v Czechoslovakia	1–2	
6 Feb 1935 v N. Ireland	2–1	
5 Feb 1936 v Wales	1–2	
4 Apr 1936 v Scotland	1–1	
17 Oct 1936 v Wales	1–2	
2 Dec 1936 v Hungary	6–2	

552. Ellis James Rimmer
Outside left
Born Birkenhead, 2 January 1907
Died 16 March 1965
Clubs Parkside FC; Northern Nomads; Whitchurch; Tranmere Rovers; Sheffield Wednesday; Ipswich Town

Caps	4	Result	Goals
	5 Apr 1930 v Scotland	5–2	2
	10 May 1930 v Germany	3–3	
	14 May 1930 v Austria	0–0	
	9 Dec 1931 v Spain	7–1	

553. Thomas 'Tony' Leach
Centre half
Born Wincobank, 23 September 1903
Died 2 February 1970
Clubs Wath Athletic; Sheffield Wednesday; Newcastle Utd; Stockport County: Carlisle Utd; Lincoln City

Caps	2	Result
	20 Oct 1930 v N. Ireland	5–1
	22 Nov 1930 v Wales	4–0

554. Gordon Hodgson
Inside right
Born Johannesburg, South Africa, 16 April 1904
Died 14 June 1951
Clubs Transvaal FC (South Africa); Liverpool; Aston Villa; Leeds Utd

Caps	3	Result	Goals
	20 Oct 1930 v N. Ireland	5–1	
	22 Nov 1930 v Wales	4–0	1
	28 Mar 1931 v Scotland	0–2	

555. James Hampson
Centre forward
Born Little Hulton, 23 March 1906
Died 10 January 1938
Clubs Walkden Park; Little Hulton St Johns; Nelson; Blackpool

Caps	3	Result	Goals
	20 Oct 1930 v N. Ireland	5–1	1
	22 Nov 1930 v Wales	4–0	2
	7 Dec 1932 v Austria	4–3	2

556. Harry Burgess
Inside forward
Born Alderley Edge, 20 August 1904
Died 1968
Clubs Alderley Edge FC; Stockport County; Sandbach Ramblers; Sheffield Wednesday; Chelsea

Caps	4	Result	Goals
	20 Oct 1930 v N. Ireland	5–1	2
	28 Mar 1931 v Scotland	0–2	
	14 May 1931 v France	2–5	
	16 May 1931 v Belgium	4–1	2

557. William Eric 'Coog' Houghton
Outside left
Born Billingborough, 29 June 1910
Died 1 May 1996
Clubs Billingborough FC; Boston Town; Aston Villa; Notts County

Caps	7	Result	Goals
	20 Oct 1930 v N. Ireland	5–1	1
	22 Nov 1930 v Wales	4–0	
	14 May 1931 v France	2–5	
	16 May 1931 v Belgium	4–1	1

17 Oct 1931 v N. Ireland	6–2	2
9 Apr 1932 v Scotland	3–0	
7 Dec 1932 v Austria	4–3	1

558. Herbert Roberts
Centre half
Born Oswestry, 19 February 1905
Died 19 June 1944
Clubs Oswestry Town; Arsenal

Caps	1	Result
	28 Mar 1931 v Scotland	0–2

559. John Forsyth Crawford
Winger
Born Jarrow, 26 September 1896
Died 27 September 1975
Clubs Palmer's Works FC; Jarrow Town; Hull City; Chelsea; Queen's Park Rangers

Caps	1	Result
	28 Mar 1931 v Scotland	0–2

560. Hugh Turner
Goalkeeper
Born Wigan, 6 August 1904
Died 1997
Clubs Felling Colliery; Darlington; High Fell FC; Huddersfield Town; Fulham

Caps	2	Result
	14 May 1931 v France	2–5
	16 May 1931 v Belgium	4–1

561. Joseph Thomas Tate
Left half
Born Old Hill, 4 August 1904
Died 18 May 1973
Clubs Round Oak; Cradley Heath; Aston Villa; Brierley Hill Alliance

Caps	3	Result
	14 May 1931 v France	2–5
	16 May 1931 v Belgium	4–1
	16 Nov 1932 v Wales	0–0

562. Thomas Graham
Centre half
Born Hamsterley, 12 March 1905
Died 29 March 1983
Clubs Hamsterley Swifts; Consett Celtic; Nottingham Forest

Caps	2	Result
	14 May 1931 v France	2–5
	17 Oct 1931 v N. Ireland	6–2

563. Thomas 'Pongo' Waring
Centre forward
Born High Tranmere, 12 October 1906
Died 20 December 1980
Clubs Tranmere Celtic; Tranmere Rovers; Aston Villa; Barnsley; Wolverhampton Wanderers; Accrington Stanley; Bath City

Caps	5	Result	Goals
	14 May 1931 v France	2–5	1
	16 May 1931 v Belgium	4–1	
	17 Oct 1931 v N. Ireland	6–2	2
	18 Nov 1931 v Wales	3–1	
	9 Apr 1932 v Scotland	3–0	1

564. Henry Roberts
Inside right
Born Barrow-in-Furness, 1 September 1907
Died 2 October 1984
Clubs Barrow Wireworks; Barrow FC; Chesterfield; Lincoln City; Port Vale; Millwall; Sheffield Wednesday

Caps	1	Result	Goals
	16 May 1931 v Belgium	4–1	1

565. John William Smith
Inside right
Born   Whitburn, 28 October 1898
Died   19 January 1977
Clubs Whitburn FC; North Shields Athletic; Portsmouth;
         Bournemouth; Clapton Orient

Caps	3	Result	Goals
	17 Oct 1931 v N. Ireland	6–2	1
	18 Nov 1931 v Wales	3–1	1
	9 Dec 1931 v Spain	7–1	2

566. Charles William Gee
Centre half
Born   Stockport, 6 April 1909
Died   20 June 1981
Clubs Stockport County; Everton

Caps	3	Result
	18 Nov 1931 v Wales	3–1
	9 Dec 1931 v Spain	7–1
	18 Nov 1936 v N. Ireland	3–1

567. Clifford Sydney Bastin
Outside left
Born   Exeter, 14 March 1912
Died   4 December 1991
Clubs Exeter City; Arsenal

Caps	21	Result	Goals
	18 Nov 1931 v Wales	3–1	
	13 May 1933 v Italy	1–1	1
	20 May 1933 v Switzerland	4–0	2
	14 Oct 1933 v N. Ireland	3–0	
	15 Nov 1933 v Wales	1–2	
	14 Apr 1934 v Scotland	3–0	1
	10 May 1934 v Hungary	1–2	
	16 May 1934 v Czechoslovakia	1–2	
	14 Nov 1934 v Italy	3–2	
	6 Feb 1935 v N. Ireland	2–1	2
	6 Apr 1935 v Scotland	0–2	
	4 Dec 1935 v Germany	3–0	1
	5 Feb 1936 v Wales	1–2	
	4 Apr 1936 v Scotland	1–1	
	6 May 1936 v Austria	1–2	
	17 Oct 1936 v Wales	1–2	1
	18 Nov 1936 v N. Ireland	3–1	1
	9 Apr 1938 v Scotland	0–1	
	14 May 1938 v Germany	6–3	1
	21 May 1938 v Switzerland	1–2	1
	26 May 1938 v France	4–2	1

568. Harold Frederick Pearson
Goalkeeper
Born   Tamworth, 7 May 1908
Died   2 November 1994
Clubs Tamworth Castle; Bromsgrove Rovers; West
         Bromwich Albion; Millwall

Caps	1	Result
	9 Apr 1932 v Scotland	3–0

569. George Edward Shaw
Right back
Born   Swinton 13 October 1899
Died   4 March 1973
Clubs Gillingham; Rossington Main Colliery; Doncaster
         Rovers; Huddersfield Town; West Bromwich Albion;
         Stalybridge; Celtic; Worcester City

Caps	1	Result
	9 Apr 1932 v Scotland	3–0

570. James Peter O'Dowd
Centre half
Born   Halifax, 26 February 1908
Died   8 May 1964
Clubs Apperley Bridge; Selby Town; Bradford Park
         Avenue; Blackburn Rovers; Burnley; Chelsea;
         Valenciennes FC (France); Torquay Utd

Caps	3	Result
	9 Apr 1932 v Scotland	3–0
	17 Oct 1932 v N. Ireland	1–0
	20 May 1933 v Switzerland	4–0

571. Samuel Weaver
Left half
Born   Pilsley, 8 February 1909
Died   15 April 1985
Clubs Pilsley Red Rose; Sutton Town; Hull City; Newcastle
         Utd; Chelsea; Stockport County

Caps	3	Result
	9 Apr 1932 v Scotland	3–0
	17 Oct 1932 v N. Ireland	1–0
	1 Apr 1933 v Scotland	1–2

572. Robert Barclay
Inside forward
Born   Scotswood, 27 October 1906
Died   13 July 1969
Clubs Allendale; Scotswood FC; Derby County; Sheffield
         Utd; Huddersfield Town

Caps	3	Result	Goals
	9 Apr 1932 v Scotland	3–0	1
	17 Oct 1932 v N. Ireland	1–0	1
	4 Apr 1936 v Scotland	1–1	

573. Arthur Cunliffe
Outside left
Born   Blackrod, 5 February 1909
Died   28 August 1986
Clubs Adlington; Chorley; Blackburn Rovers; Aston Villa;
         Middlesbrough; Burnley; Hull City; Rochdale

Caps	2	Result
	17 Oct 1932 v N. Ireland	1–0
	16 Nov 1932 v Wales	0–0

574. Lewis Stoker
Right half
Born   Wheatley Hill, 31 March 1910
Died   15 May 1979
Clubs Bearpark; West Stanley; Birmingham; Nottingham
         Forest

Caps	3	Result
	16 Nov 1932 v Wales	0–0
	14 Apr 1934 v Scotland	3–0
	10 May 1934 v Hungary	1–2

575. Alfred Young
Centre half
Born   Sunderland, 4 November 1905
Died   30 August 1977
Clubs Durham City; Huddersfield Town; York City

Caps	9	Result
	16 Nov 1932 v Wales	0–0
	2 Dec 1936 v Hungary	6–2
	17 Apr 1937 v Scotland	1–3
	14 May 1937 v Norway	6–0
	17 May 1937 v Sweden	4–0
	14 May 1938 v Germany	6–3
	21 May 1938 v Switzerland	1–2
	26 May 1938 v France	4–2
	22 Oct 1938 v Wales	2–4

576. Edward Sandford
Inside left
Born   Handsworth, 22 October 1910
Died   1995
Clubs Tantany Athletic; Overend Wesley; Birmingham
         Carriage Works; Smethwick Highfield; West
         Bromwich Albion; Sheffield Utd

Caps	1	Result
	16 Nov 1932 v Wales	0–0

577. Errington Ridley Liddell Keen
Left half
Born   Walker, 4 September 1910
Died   28 July 1984
Clubs   Newcastle Utd; Derby County; Chelmsford City;
          Hereford Utd; Leeds Utd; Bacup Borough

Caps 4	*Result*
7 Dec 1932 v Austria	4–3
17 Oct 1936 v Wales	1–2
18 Nov 1936 v N. Ireland	3–1
2 Dec 1936 v Hungary	6–2

578. Ronald William Starling
Inside forward
Born   Pelaw, 11 October 1909
Died   17 December 1991
Clubs   Washington Colliery; Hull City; Newcastle Utd;
          Sheffield Wednesday; Aston Villa

Caps 2	*Result*
1 Apr 1933 v Scotland	1–2
17 Apr 1937 v Scotland	1–3

579. George Samuel Hunt
Inside right/Centre forward
Born   Mexborough, 22 February 1910
Died   19 September 1996
Clubs   Chesterfield; Tottenham Hotspur; Arsenal; Bolton
          Wanderers; Sheffield Wednesday

Caps 3	*Result*	*Goals*
1 Apr 1933 v Scotland	1–2	1
13 May 1933 v Italy	1–1	
20 May 1933 v Switzerland	4–0	

580. John Pickering
Inside left
Born   Mortomley, 18 December 1908
Died   10 May 1977
Clubs   Mortemley St Saviour's FC; Sheffield Utd

Caps 1	*Result*
1 Apr 1933 v Scotland	1–2

581. John Arnold
Outside left
Born   Cowley, 30 November 1907
Died   3 April 1984
Clubs   Oxford City; Southampton; Fulham

Caps 1	*Result*
1 Apr 1933 v Scotland	1–2

582. Edris Albert Hapgood
Left back
Born   Bristol, 24 September 1908
Died   20 April 1973
Clubs   Bristol Rovers; Kettering Town; Arsenal; Blackburn
          Rovers

Caps 30	*Result*
13 May 1933 v Italy	1–1
20 May 1933 v Switzerland	4–0
14 Oct 1933 v N. Ireland	3–0
15 Nov 1933 v Wales	1–2
14 Apr 1934 v Scotland	3–0
10 May 1934 v Hungary	1–2
16 May 1934 v Czechoslovakia	1–2
29 Sep 1934 v Wales	4–0
14 Nov 1934 v Italy	3–2
6 Feb 1935 v N. Ireland	2–1
6 Apr 1935 v Scotland	0–2
18 May 1935 v Holland	1–0
19 Oct 1935 v N. Ireland	3–1
4 Dec 1935 v Germany	3–0
5 Feb 1936 v Wales	1–2
4 Apr 1936 v Scotland	1–1
6 May 1936 v Austria	1–2
9 May 1936 v Belgium	2–3
20 May 1937 v Finland	8–0
9 Apr 1938 v Scotland	0–1
14 May 1938 v Germany	6–3
21 May 1938 v Switzerland	1–2
26 May 1938 v France	4–2
22 Oct 1938 v Wales	2–4
26 Oct 1938 v FIFA	3–0
9 Nov 1938 v Norway	4–0
16 Nov 1938 v N. Ireland	7–0
15 Apr 1939 v Scotland	2–1
13 May 1939 v Italy	2–2
18 May 1939 v Yugoslavia	1–2

583. Thomas Angus White
Centre half
Born   Manchester, 29 July 1908
Died   13 August 1967
Clubs   Southport; Everton; Northampton Town; New Brighton

Caps 1	*Result*
13 May 1933 v Italy	1–1

584. Wilfred Copping
Left half
Born   Barnsley, 17 August 1907
Died   20 June 1980
Clubs   Dearne Valley Old Boys; Middlecliffe Rovers; Leeds
          Utd; Arsenal

Caps 20	*Result*
13 May 1933 v Italy	1–1
20 May 1933 v Switzerland	4–0
14 Oct 1933 v N. Ireland	3–0
15 Nov 1933 v Wales	1–2
6 Dec 1933 v France	4–1
14 Apr 1934 v Scotland	3–0
14 Nov 1934 v Italy	3–2
6 Feb 1935 v N. Ireland	2–1
6 May 1936 v Austria	1–2
9 May 1936 v Belgium	2–3
14 May 1937 v Norway	6–0
17 May 1937 v Sweden	4–0
20 May 1937 v Finland	8–0
23 Oct 1937 v N. Ireland	5–1
17 Nov 1937 v Wales	2–1
1 Dec 1937 v Czechoslovakia	5–4
9 Apr 1938 v Scotland	0–1
22 Oct 1938 v Wales	2–4
26 Oct 1938 v FIFA	3–0
24 May 1939 v Romania	2–0

585. Albert Geldard
Outside right
Born   Bradford, 11 April 1914
Died   19 October 1989
Clubs   Manningham Mills; Bradford Park Avenue; Everton;
          Bolton Wanderers; Darwen

Caps 4	*Result*
13 May 1933 v Italy	1–1
20 May 1933 v Switzerland	4–0
6 Apr 1935 v Scotland	0–2
23 Oct 1937 v N. Ireland	5–1

586. James Robert Richardson
Inside forward
Born   Ashington, 8 February 1911
Died   28 August 1964
Clubs   Blyth Spartans; Newcastle Utd; Huddersfield Town;
          Millwall; Leyton Orient

Caps 2	*Result*
13 May 1933 v Italy	1–1
20 May 1933 v Switzerland	4–0

587. William Isaac Furness
Inside forward
Born   New Washington, 8 June 1909
Died   29 August 1980
Clubs   Usworth Colliery; Leeds Utd; Norwich City

Caps 1	*Result*
13 May 1933 v Italy	1–1

588. James Phillips Allen
Centre half

Born	Poole, 16 October 1909	
Died	February 1995	
Clubs	Poole Central; Poole Town; Portsmouth; Aston Villa	
Caps	2	Result
	14 Oct 1933 v N. Ireland	3–0
	15 Nov 1933 v Wales	1–2

589. Arthur Thomas Grosvenor
Inside right

Born	Netherton, 22 November 1908		
Died	31 October 1972		
Clubs	Tippity Green Vics; Vono Works; Stourbridge; Birmingham; Sheffield Wednesday; Bolton Wanderers		
Caps	3	Result	Goals
	14 Oct 1933 v N. Ireland	3–0	1
	15 Nov 1933 v Wales	1–2	
	6 Dec 1933 v France	4–1	1

590. John William Bowers
Centre forward

Born	Low Santon, 22 February 1908		
Died	4 July 1970		
Clubs	Appleby Works; Scunthorpe Utd; Derby County; Leicester City		
Caps	3	Result	Goals
	14 Oct 1933 v N. Ireland	3–0	1
	15 Nov 1933 v Wales	1–2	
	14 Apr 1934 v Scotland	3–0	1

591. David Liddle Fairhurst
Left back

Born	Blyth, 20 July 1906	
Died	26 October 1972	
Clubs	New Delaval Villa; Blyth Spartans; Newcastle Utd	
Caps	1	Result
	6 Dec 1933 v France	4–1

592. Arthur Sydney Rowe
Centre half

Born	Tottenham, 1 September 1906	
Died	8 November 1993	
Clubs	Northfleet; Tottenham Hotspur	
Caps	1	Result
	6 Dec 1933 v France	4–1

593. George William Hall
Inside forward

Born	Newark, 12 March 1912		
Died	22 May 1967		
Clubs	Ransome & Marles FC; Notts County; Tottenham Hotspur		
Caps	10	Result	Goals
	6 Dec 1933 v France	4–1	
	23 Oct 1937 v N. Ireland	5–1	
	17 Nov 1937 v Wales	2–1	1
	1 Dec 1937 v Czechoslovakia	5–4	
	9 Apr 1938 v Scotland	0–1	
	26 Oct 1938 v FIFA	3–0	1
	16 Nov 1938 v N. Ireland	7–0	5
	15 Apr 1939 v Scotland	2–1	
	13 May 1939 v Italy	2–2	1
	18 May 1939 v Yugoslavia	1–2	

594. Frank Moss
Goalkeeper

Born	Leyland, 5 November 1909	
Died	7 February 1970	
Clubs	Lostock Hall; Leyland Motors; Preston North End; Oldham Athletic; Arsenal	
Caps	4	Result
	14 Apr 1934 v Scotland	3–0
	10 May 1934 v Hungary	1–2
	16 May 1934 v Czechoslovakia	1–2
	14 Nov 1934 v Italy	3–2

595. Horatio Stratton 'Raich' Carter
Inside forward

Born	Hendon, 21 December 1913		
Died	9 October 1994		
Clubs	Sunderland Forge; Sunderland; Derby County; Hull City		
Caps	13	Result	Goals
	14 Apr 1934 v Scotland	3–0	
	10 May 1934 v Hungary	1–2	
	4 Dec 1935 v Germany	3–0	
	18 Nov 1936 v N. Ireland	3–1	1
	2 Dec 1936 v Hungary	6–2	1
	17 Apr 1937 v Scotland	1–3	
	28 Sep 1946 v N. Ireland	7–2	1
	30 Sep 1946 v Eire	1–0	
	19 Oct 1946 v Wales	3–0	
	27 Nov 1946 v Holland	8–2	2
	12 Apr 1947 v Scotland	1–1	1
	3 May 1947 v France	3–0	1
	18 May 1947 v Switzerland	0–1	

596. Horace Burrows
Left half

Born	Sutton-in-Ashfield, 1 March 1910	
Died	22 March 1969	
Clubs	Sutton Junction; Coventry City; Mansfield Town; Sheffield Wednesday	
Caps	3	Result
	10 May 1934 v Hungary	1–2
	16 May 1934 v Czechoslovakia	1–2
	18 May 1934 v Holland	1–0

597. Samuel Frederick Tilson
Centre forward/Inside left

Born	Barnsley, 19 April 1904		
Died	21 November 1972		
Clubs	Barnsley; Manchester City; Northampton Town; York City		
Caps	4	Result	Goals
	10 May 1934 v Hungary	1–2	1
	16 May 1934 v Czechoslovakia	1–2	1
	29 Sep 1934 v Wales	4–0	2
	19 Oct 1935 v N. Ireland	3–1	2

598. Thomas Gardner
Right half

Born	Huyton, 28 May 1910	
Died	22 May 1970	
Clubs	Orrell FC; Liverpool; Grimsby Town; Hull City; Aston Villa; Burnley; Wrexham; Wellington Town; Oswestry Town	
Caps	2	Result
	16 May 1934 v Czechoslovakia	1–2
	18 May 1935 v Holland	1–0

599. Joseph Beresford
Inside forward

Born	Chesterfield, 26 February 1906	
Died	11 June 1978	
Clubs	Mexborough Athletic; Mansfield Town; Aston Villa; Preston North End; Swansea Town	
Caps	1	Result
	16 May 1934 v Czechoslovakia	1–2

600. Clifford Samuel Britton
Right half

Born	Hanham, 29 August 1909		
Died	1 December 1975		
Clubs	Hanham Athletic; Hanham Utd; Methodists; Bristol St George's FC; Bristol Rovers; Everton		
Caps	9	Result	Goals
	29 Sep 1934 v Wales	4–0	
	14 Nov 1934 v Italy	3–2	
	6 Feb 1935 v N. Ireland	2–1	
	6 Apr 1935 v Scotland	0–2	
	18 Nov 1936 v N. Ireland	3–1	
	2 Dec 1936 v Hungary	6–2	1
	17 Apr 1937 v Scotland	1–3	
	14 May 1937 v Norway	6–0	
	17 May 1937 v Sweden	4–0	

DID YOU KNOW...?

Willie Hall scored a hat-trick in just three and a half minutes against Northern Ireland at Old Trafford on 16 November 1938. Hall went on to net five times in England's 7–0 win.

601. John William Barker
Centre half
Born   Denaby, 27 February 1907
Died   20 January 1982
Clubs   Denaby Utd; Derby County

Caps 11	Result
29 Sep 1934 v Wales	4–0
14 Nov 1934 v Italy	3–2
6 Feb 1935 v N. Ireland	2–1
6 Apr 1935 v Scotland	0–2
18 May 1935 v Holland	1–0
19 Oct 1935 v N. Ireland	3–1
4 Dec 1935 v Germany	3–0
5 Feb 1936 v Wales	1–2
4 Apr 1936 v Scotland	1–1
6 May 1936 v Austria	1–2
17 Oct 1936 v Wales	1–2

602. John Bray
Left half
Born   Oswaldtwistle, 22 April 1909
Died   20 November 1982
Clubs   Manchester Central; Manchester City

Caps 6	Result
29 Sep 1934 v Wales	4–0
19 Oct 1935 v N. Ireland	3–1
4 Dec 1935 v Germany	3–0
5 Feb 1936 v Wales	1–2
4 Apr 1936 v Scotland	1–1
17 Apr 1937 v Scotland	1–3

603. Stanley Matthews
Outside right
Born   Hanley, 1 February 1915
Died   5 May 1999
Clubs   Stoke St Peters; Stoke City; Blackpool

Caps 54	Result	Goals
29 Sep 1934 v Wales	4–0	1
14 Nov 1934 v Italy	3–2	
4 Dec 1935 v Germany	3–0	
17 Apr 1937 v Scotland	1–3	
17 Nov 1937 v Wales	2–1	1
1 Dec 1937 v Czechoslovakia	5–4	3
9 Apr 1938 v Scotland	0–1	
14 May 1938 v Germany	6–3	1
21 May 1938 v Switzerland	1–2	
26 May 1938 v France	4–2	
22 Oct 1938 v Wales	2–4	1
26 Oct 1938 v FIFA	3–0	
9 Nov 1938 v Norway	4–0	
16 Nov 1938 v N. Ireland	7–0	1
15 Apr 1939 v Scotland	2–1	
13 May 1939 v Italy	2–2	
18 May 1939 v Yugoslavia	1–2	
12 Apr 1947 v Scotland	1–1	
18 May 1947 v Switzerland	0–1	
27 May 1947 v Portugal	10–0	1
21 Sep 1947 v Belgium	5–2	
18 Oct 1947 v Wales	3–0	
5 Nov 1947 v N. Ireland	2–2	
10 Apr 1948 v Scotland	2–0	
16 May 1948 v Italy	4–0	
26 Sep 1948 v Denmark	0–0	
9 Oct 1948 v N. Ireland	6–2	1
10 Nov 1948 v Wales	1–0	
1 Dec 1948 v Switzerland	6–0	
9 Apr 1949 v Scotland	1–3	

	Result	
2 Jul 1950 v Spain	0–1	
7 Oct 1950 v N. Ireland	4–1	
14 Apr 1951 v Scotland	2–3	
21 Oct 1953 v Rest of Europe	4–4	
11 Nov 1953 v N. Ireland	3–1	
25 Nov 1953 v Hungary	3–6	
17 Jun 1954 v Belgium	4–4	
26 Jun 1954 v Uruguay	2–4	
2 Oct 1954 v N. Ireland	2–0	
10 Nov 1954 v Wales	3–2	
1 Dec 1954 v W. Germany	3–1	
2 Apr 1955 v Scotland	7–2	
11 May 1955 v France	0–1	
18 May 1955 v Spain	1–1	
22 May 1955 v Portugal	1–3	
22 Oct 1955 v Wales	1–2	
9 May 1956 v Brazil	4–2	
6 Oct 1956 v N. Ireland	1–1	1
14 Nov 1956 v Wales	3–1	
28 Nov 1956 v Yugoslavia	3–0	
5 Dec 1956 v Denmark	5–2	
6 Apr 1957 v Scotland	2–1	
8 May 1957 v Eire	5–1	
15 May 1957 v Denmark	4–1	

604. Edwin Raymond Bowden
Inside right/Centre forward
Born   Looe, 13 September 1909
Died   23 September 1998
Clubs   Looe FC; Plymouth Argyle; Arsenal; Newcastle Utd

Caps 6	Result	Goals
29 Sep 1934 v Wales	4–0	
14 Nov 1934 v Italy	3–2	
19 Oct 1935 v N. Ireland	3–1	
5 Feb 1936 v Wales	1–2	1
6 May 1936 v Austria	1–2	
2 Dec 1936 v Hungary	6–2	

605. Raymond William Westwood
Inside left/Outside left
Born   Brierley Hill, 14 April 1912
Died   16 January 1982
Clubs   Stourbridge; Brierley Hill Alliance; Bolton Wanderers; Chester; Darwen

Caps 6	Result
29 Sep 1934 v Wales	4–0
6 Apr 1935 v Scotland	0–2
18 May 1935 v Holland	1–0
19 Oct 1935 v N. Ireland	3–1
4 Dec 1935 v Germany	3–0
17 Oct 1936 v Wales	1–2

606. George Charles Male
Right back
Born   West Ham, 8 May 1910
Died   19 February 1998
Clubs   Clapton Orient; Arsenal

Caps 19	Result
14 Nov 1934 v Italy	3–2
6 Feb 1935 v N. Ireland	2–1
6 Apr 1935 v Scotland	0–2
18 May 1935 v Holland	1–0
19 Oct 1935 v N. Ireland	3–1
4 Dec 1935 v Germany	3–0
5 Feb 1936 v Wales	1–2
4 Apr 1936 v Scotland	1–1
6 May 1936 v Austria	1–2
9 May 1936 v Belgium	2–3
18 Nov 1936 v N. Ireland	3–1
2 Dec 1936 v Hungary	6–2
17 Apr 1937 v Scotland	1–3
14 May 1937 v Norway	6–0
17 May 1937 v Sweden	4–0
20 May 1937 v Finland	8–0
13 May 1939 v Italy	2–2
18 May 1939 v Yugoslavia	1–2
24 May 1939 v Romania	2–0

607. Edward Joseph Drake
Centre forward

Born Southampton, 16 August 1912
Died 31 May 1995
Clubs Winchester City; Southampton; Arsenal

Caps	5	Result	Goals
	14 Nov 1934 v Italy	3–2	1
	6 Feb 1935 v N. Ireland	2–1	
	5 Feb 1936 v Wales	1–2	
	2 Dec 1936 v Hungary	6–2	3
	26 May 1938 v France	4–2	2

608. John Gilbert Bestall
Inside forward

Born Beighton, near Sheffield, 24 June 1900
Died 1 April 1985
Clubs Beighton Miners' Welfare; Rotherham Utd; Grimsby Town

Caps	1	Result
	6 Feb 1935 v N. Ireland	2–1

609. Walter John Alsford
Left half

Born Edmonton, 6 November 1911
Died 3 June 1968
Clubs Cheshunt; Northfleet; Tottenham Hotspur; Nottingham Forest

Caps	1	Result
	6 Apr 1935 v Scotland	0–2

610. Robert Gurney
Centre forward

Born Silksworth, 13 October 1907
Clubs Seaham Harbour; Bishop Auckland; Sunderland

Caps	1	Result
	6 Apr 1935 v Scotland	0–2

611. Frederick Worrall
Outside right

Born Warrington, 8 September 1910
Died 13 April 1979
Clubs Witton Albion; Nantwich; Oldham Athletic; Portsmouth; Crewe Alexandra

Caps	2	Result	Goals
	18 May 1935 v Holland	1–0	1
	18 Nov 1936 v N. Ireland	3–1	1

612. George Richard Eastham
Inside forward

Born Blackpool, 13 September 1913
Died 20 January 2000
Clubs South Shore Wednesday; Bolton Wanderers; Brentford; Blackpool; Swansea Town; Rochdale; Lincoln City; Hyde Utd; Ards

Caps	1	Result
	18 May 1935 v Holland	1–0

613. William Richardson
Centre forward

Born Framwellgate Moor, 29 May 1909
Died 29 March 1959
Clubs Horden Wednesday; Bus Co FC; Hartlepool Utd; West Bromwich Albion; Shrewsbury Town

Caps	1	Result
	18 May 1935 v Holland	1–0

614. Walter Edward Boyes
Outside left

Born Sheffield, 5 January 1913
Died 16 September 1960
Clubs Woodhouse Mills Utd; West Bromwich Albion; Everton; Notts County; Scunthorpe Utd; Retford Town

Caps	3	Result
	18 May 1935 v Holland	1–0

	22 Oct 1938 v Wales	2–4
	26 Oct 1938 v FIFA	3–0

615. Edward Sagar
Goalkeeper

Born Moorends, Doncaster, 7 February 1910
Died 16 October 1986
Clubs Thorne Colliery; Everton

Caps	4	Result
	19 Oct 1935 v N. Ireland	3–1
	4 Apr 1936 v Scotland	1–1
	6 May 1936 v Austria	1–2
	9 May 1936 v Belgium	2–3

616. Septimus Charles Smith
Right half

Born Whitburn, 15 March 1912
Clubs Whitburn FC; Leicester City

Caps	1	Result
	19 Oct 1935 v N. Ireland	3–1

617. Ralph James Evans Birkett
Outside right

Born Newton Abbot, 9 January 1913
Died 8 July 2002
Clubs Dartmouth Utd; Torquay Utd; Arsenal; Middlesbrough; Newcastle Utd

Caps	1	Result
	19 Oct 1935 v N. Ireland	3–1

618. William John Crayston
Right half

Born Grange-over-Sands, 9 October 1910
Died 26 December 1992
Clubs Ulverston; Barrow; Bradford Park Avenue; Arsenal; North End; Barnsley

Caps	8	Result	Goals
	4 Dec 1935 v Germany	3–0	
	5 Feb 1936 v Wales	1–2	
	4 Apr 1936 v Scotland	1–1	
	6 May 1936 v Austria	1–2	
	9 May 1936 v Belgium	2–3	
	23 Oct 1937 v N. Ireland	5–1	
	17 Nov 1937 v Wales	2–1	
	1 Dec 1937 v Czechoslovakia	5–4	1

619. Richard Spence
Outside right

Born Platt's Common, 18 July 1908
Died 4 March 1983
Clubs Thorpe Colliery; Platt's Common WMC; Barnsley; Chelsea

Caps	2	Result
	6 May 1936 v Austria	1–2
	9 May 1936 v Belgium	2–3

620. Harold Henry Hobbis
Outside left

Born Dartford, 9 March 1913
Died 30 June 1991
Clubs Bromley; Charlton Athletic; Tonbridge

Caps	2	Result	Goals
	6 May 1936 v Austria	1–2	
	9 May 1936 v Belgium	2–3	1

 DID YOU KNOW...?

Aged 42 years and 103 days, Stanley Matthews became England's oldest international when he played his last game against Denmark in May 1957. With a career lasting 22 years and 228 days, he has also played for England for the longest period of time.

621. Bernard Joy
Centre half
Born Fulham, 29 October 1911
Died 18 July 1984
Clubs Casuals; Southend Utd; Fulham; Corinthians; Arsenal

Caps	1	*Result*
	9 May 1936 v Belgium	2–3

622. Samuel Barkas
Left back
Born Wardley Colliery, 29 December 1909
Died 8 December 1989
Clubs Bradford City; Manchester City

Caps	5	*Result*
	9 May 1936 v Belgium	2–3
	23 Oct 1937 v N. Ireland	5–1
	17 Nov 1937 v Wales	2–1
	1 Dec 1937 v Czechoslovakia	5–4
	17 Apr 1937 v Scotland	1–3

623. George Henry Holdcroft
Goalkeeper
Born Burslem, 23 January 1909
Died 17 April 1983
Clubs Biddulph FC; Norton Druids; Whitfield Colliery; Port Vale; Darlington; Everton; Preston North End; Barnsley

Caps	2	*Result*
	17 Oct 1936 v Wales	1–2
	18 Nov 1936 v N. Ireland	3–1

624. James Nathaniel Cunliffe
Inside right
Born Blackrod, 5 July 1912
Died 21 November 1986
Clubs Haslingden; Adlington; Everton; Rochdale

Caps	1	*Result*
	9 May 1936 v Belgium	2–3

625. Bert Sproston
Right back
Born Elworth, near Sandbach, 22 June 1915
Died 27 January 2000
Clubs Sandbach Ramblers; Leeds Utd; Tottenham Hotspur; Manchester City

Caps	11	*Result*
	17 Oct 1936 v Wales	1–2
	23 Oct 1937 v N. Ireland	5–1
	17 Nov 1937 v Wales	2–1
	1 Dec 1937 v Czechoslovakia	5–4
	9 Apr 1938 v Scotland	0–1
	14 May 1938 v Germany	6–3
	21 May 1938 v Switzerland	1–2
	26 May 1938 v France	4–2
	22 Oct 1938 v France	4–2
	26 Oct 1938 v FIFA	3–0
	9 Nov 1938 v Norway	4–0

626. Arthur Edward Catlin
Left back
Born South Bank, 11 January 1910
Died 5 July 1990
Clubs South Bank FC; Sheffield Wednesday

Caps	5	*Result*
	17 Oct 1936 v Wales	1–2
	18 Nov 1936 v N. Ireland	3–1
	2 Dec 1936 v Hungary	6–2
	14 May 1937 v Norway	6–0
	17 May 1937 v Sweden	4–0

627. Tom Smalley
Wing half
Born Hemsworth, 13 January 1912
Died 1 April 1984

Clubs South Kirkby Colliery; Wolverhampton Wanderers; Norwich City; Northampton Town

Caps	1	*Result*
	17 Oct 1936 v Wales	1–2

628. William Reed Scott
Inside forward
Born Willington Quay, 6 December 1907
Died 18 October 1969
Clubs Howden Bridge British Legion; Middlesbrough; Brentford; Aldershot; Dover

Caps	1	*Result*
	17 Oct 1936 v Wales	1–2

629. Frederick Charles Steele
Centre forward
Born Hanley, 6 May 1916
Died 23 April 1976
Clubs Downing's Tileries; Stoke City; Mansfield Town; Port Vale

Caps	6	*Result*	*Goals*
	17 Oct 1936 v Wales	1–2	
	18 Nov 1936 v N. Ireland	3–1	
	17 Apr 1937 v Scotland	1–3	1
	14 May 1937 v Norway	6–0	2
	17 May 1937 v Sweden	4–0	3
	20 May 1937 v Finland	8–0	2

630. Joseph Alfred Johnson
Outside left
Born Grimsby, 4 April 1911
Died 8 August 1983
Clubs Scunthorpe Utd; Bristol City; Stoke City; West Bromwich Albion; Northwich Victoria; Hereford Utd

Caps	5	*Result*	*Goals*
	18 Nov 1936 v N. Ireland	3–1	
	17 Apr 1937 v Scotland	1–3	
	14 May 1937 v Norway	6–0	
	17 May 1937 v Sweden	4–0	1
	20 May 1937 v Finland	8–0	1

631. George Jacob Tweedy
Goalkeeper
Born Willington, 8 January 1913
Died 23 April 1987
Clubs Willington Town; Grimsby Town

Caps	1	*Result*
	2 Dec 1936 v Hungary	6–2

632. Victor Robert Woodley
Goalkeeper
Born Slough, 26 February 1910
Died 23 October 1978
Clubs Windsor & Eton; Chelsea; Bath City; Derby County

Caps	19	*Result*
	17 Apr 1937 v Scotland	1–3
	14 Mar 1937 v Norway	6–0
	17 May 1937 v Sweden	4–0
	20 May 1937 v Finland	8–0
	23 Oct 1937 v N. Ireland	5–1
	17 Nov 1937 v Wales	2–1
	1 Dec 1937 v Czechoslovakia	5–4
	9 Apr 1938 v Scotland	0–1
	14 May 1938 v Germany	6–3
	21 May 1938 v Switzerland	1–2
	26 May 1938 v France	4–2
	22 Oct 1938 v Wales	2–4
	26 Oct 1938 v FIFA	3–0
	9 Nov 1938 v Norway	4–0
	16 Nov 1938 v N. Ireland	7–0
	15 Apr 1939 v Scotland	2–1
	13 May 1939 v Italy	2–2
	18 May 1939 v Yugoslavia	1–2
	24 May 1939 v Romania	2–0

DID YOU KNOW...?

The last amateur to win a full international cap for England was Bernard Joy, who appeared in the 3–2 defeat by Belgium in Brussels on 9 May 1936.

633. Alfred John Kirchen
Outside right
Born	Shouldham, 26 April 1913		
Died	18 August 1999		
Clubs	Shouldham FC; Norwich City; Arsenal		
Caps	3	Result	Goals
	14 May 1937 v Norway	6–0	1
	17 May 1937 v Sweden	4–0	
	20 May 1937 v Finland	8–0	1

634. Thomas Galley
Right half/Inside forward
Born	Hednesford, 4 August 1915		
Died	2000		
Clubs	Cannock Town; Notts County; Wolverhampton Wanderers; Grimsby Town; Kidderminster Harriers; Clacton Town		
Caps	2	Result	Goals
	14 May 1937 v Norway	6–0	1
	17 May 1937 v Sweden	4–0	

635. Leonard Arthur Goulden
Inside left
Born	Hackney, 16 July 1912		
Died	14 February 1995		
Clubs	Chelmsford; Leyton; West Ham Utd; Chelsea		
Caps	14	Result	Goals
	14 May 1937 v Norway	6–0	1
	17 May 1937 v Sweden	4–0	
	23 Oct 1937 v N. Ireland	5–1	
	17 Nov 1937 v Wales	2–1	
	1 Dec 1937 v Czechoslovakia	5–4	
	14 May 1938 v Germany	6–3	1
	21 May 1938 v Switzerland	1–2	
	26 May 1938 v France	4–2	
	22 Oct 1938 v Wales	2–4	
	26 Oct 1938 v FIFA	3–0	1
	15 Apr 1939 v Scotland	2–1	
	13 May 1939 v Italy	2–2	
	18 May 1939 v Yugoslavia	1–2	
	24 May 1939 v Romania	2–0	1

636. Charles Kenneth Willingham
Right half
Born	Sheffield, 1 December 1912		
Died	6 May 1975		
Clubs	Ecclesfield; Worksop Town; Huddersfield Town; Sunderland; Leeds Utd		
Caps	12	Result	Goals
	20 May 1937 v Finland	8–0	1
	9 Apr 1938 v Scotland	0–1	
	14 May 1938 v Germany	6–3	
	21 May 1938 v Switzerland	1–2	
	26 May 1938 v France	4–2	
	22 Oct 1938 v Wales	2–4	
	26 Oct 1938 v FIFA	3–0	
	9 Nov 1938 v Norway	4–0	
	16 Nov 1938 v N. Ireland	7–0	
	15 Apr 1939 v Scotland	2–1	
	13 May 1929 v Italy	2–2	
	18 May 1939 v Yugoslavia	1–2	

637. Harry Betmead
Centre half
Born	Grimsby, 11 April 1912		
Died	26 August 1984		
Clubs	Hay Cross FC; Grimsby Town		
Caps	1	Result	
	20 May 1937 v Finland	8–0	

638. John 'Jackie' Robinson
Inside right
Born	Shiremoor, 10 August 1917		
Died	22 October 1979		
Clubs	Sheffield Wednesday; Sunderland; Lincoln City		
Caps	4	Result	Goals
	20 May 1937 v Finland	8–0	1
	14 May 1938 v Germany	6–3	2
	21 May 1938 v Switzerland	1–2	
	22 Oct 1938 v Wales	2–4	

639. Joseph Payne
Centre forward
Born	Chesterfield, 17 January 1914		
Died	22 April 1975		
Clubs	Bolsover Colliery; Biggleswade Town; Luton Town; Chelsea; West Ham Utd; Millwall; Worcester City		
Caps	1	Result	Goals
	20 May 1937 v Finland	8–0	2

640. Stanley Cullis
Centre half
Born	Ellesmere Port, 25 October 1916	
Died	27 February 2001	
Clubs	Ellesmere Port Wednesday; Wolverhampton Wanderers	
Caps	12	Result
	23 Oct 1937 v N. Ireland	5–1
	17 Nov 1937 v Wales	2–1
	1 Dec 1937 v Czechoslovakia	5–4
	9 Apr 1938 v Scotland	0–1
	26 May 1938 v France	4–2
	26 Oct 1938 v FIFA	3–0
	9 Nov 1938 v Norway	4–0
	16 Nov 1938 v N. Ireland	7–0
	15 Apr 1939 v Scotland	2–1
	13 May 1939 v Italy	2–2
	18 May 1939 v Yugoslavia	1–2
	24 May 1939 v Romania	2–0

641. George Robert Mills
Inside right/Centre forward
Born	Deptford, 29 December 1908		
Died	15 July 1970		
Clubs	Emerald Athletic; Bromley; Chelsea		
Caps	3	Result	Goals
	23 Oct 1937 v N. Ireland	5–1	3
	17 Nov 1937 v Wales	2–1	
	1 Dec 1937 v Czechoslovakia	5–4	

642. John Morton
Winger
Born	Sheffield, 26 February 1914		
Died	8 March 1986		
Clubs	Woodhouse Alliance FC; Gainsborough Trinity; West Ham Utd		
Caps	1	Result	Goals
	1 Dec 1937 v Czechoslovakia	5–4	1

643. Michael Fenton
Centre forward
Born	Stockton-on-Tees, 30 October 1913	
Died	5 February 2003	
Clubs	South Bank East End; Middlesbrough	
Caps	1	Result
	9 Apr 1938 v Scotland	0–1

644. Joseph Eric Stephenson
Inside left
Born	Bexleyheath, 23 September 1914	
Died	8 September 1944	
Clubs	Harrogate; Leeds Utd	
Caps	2	Result
	9 Apr 1938 v Scotland	0–1
	16 Nov 1938 v N. Ireland	7–0

645. Donald Welsh
Left half/Inside left
Born	Manchester, 25 February 1911
Died	2 February 1990
Clubs	Torquay Utd; Charlton Athletic

Caps	3	Result	Goals
	14 May 1938 v Germany	6–3	
	21 May 1938 v Switzerland	1–2	
	24 May 1939 v Romania	2–0	1

646. Frank Henry Broome
Winger/Centre forward
Born Berkhamsted, 11 June 1915
Died 23 September 1994
Clubs Boxmoor Utd; Berkhamsted Town; Aston Villa; Derby County; Notts County; Brentford; Crewe Alexandra; Shelbourne

Caps	7	Result	Goals
	14 May 1938 v Germany	6–3	1
	21 May 1938 v Switzerland	1–2	
	26 May 1938 v France	4–2	1
	9 Nov 1938 v Norway	4–0	
	13 May 1939 v Italy	2–2	
	18 May 1939 v Yugoslavia	1–2	1
	24 May 1929 v Romania	2–0	

647. Thomas Lawton
Centre forward
Born Bolton, 6 October 1919
Died 6 November 1996
Clubs Hayes Athletic; Rossendale Utd; Burnley; Everton; Chelsea; Notts County; Brentford; Arsenal; Kettering Town

Caps	23	Result	Goals
	22 Oct 1938 v Wales	2–4	1
	26 Oct 1938 v FIFA	3–0	1
	9 Nov 1938 v Norway	4–0	1
	16 Nov 1938 v N. Ireland	7–0	1
	15 Apr 1939 v Scotland	2–1	1
	13 May 1939 v Italy	2–2	1
	18 May 1939 v Yugoslavia	1–2	
	24 May 1939 v Romania	2–0	
	28 Sep 1946 v N. Ireland	7–2	1
	30 Sep 1946 v Eire	1–0	
	19 Oct 1946 v Wales	3–0	1
	27 Nov 1946 v Holland	8–2	4
	12 Apr 1947 v Scotland	1–1	
	3 May 1947 v France	3–0	
	18 May 1947 v Switzerland	0–1	
	27 May 1947 v Portugal	10–0	4
	21 Sep 1947 v Belgium	5–2	2
	18 Oct 1947 v Wales	3–0	1
	5 Nov 1947 v N. Ireland	2–2	1
	19 Nov 1947 v Sweden	4–2	1
	10 Apr 1948 v Scotland	2–0	
	16 May 1948 v Italy	4–0	1
	26 Sep 1948 v Denmark	0–0	

648. John Douglas Wright
Wing half
Born Southend-on-Sea, 29 April 1917
Died 28 December 1992
Clubs Southend Utd; Newcastle Utd; Lincoln City; Blyth Spartans

Caps	1	Result
	9 Nov 1938 v Norway	4–0

649. Ronald William Dix
Inside forward
Born Bristol, 5 September 1912
Died 2 April 1998
Clubs Bristol Rovers; Blackburn Rovers; Aston Villa; Derby County; Tottenham Hotspur; Reading

⚽ **DID YOU KNOW...?**

The fastest ever England goal was scored by Tommy Lawton. He scored the first of his four goals after just seventeen seconds in a 10–0 win against Portugal in May 1947.

Caps	1	Result	Goals
	9 Nov 1938 v Norway	4–0	1

650. James Reginald Smith
Outside left
Born Battersea, 20 January 1912
Clubs Hitchin Town; Millwall; Dundee; Corby Town

Caps	2	Result	Goals
	9 Nov 1938 v Norway	4–0	2
	16 Nov 1938 v N. Ireland	7–0	

651. William Walker Morris
Right back
Born Handsworth, 26 March 1913
Died 4 October 1995
Clubs Halesowen Town; Wolverhampton Wanderers

Caps	3	Result
	16 Nov 1938 v N. Ireland	7–0
	15 Apr 1939 v Scotland	2–1
	24 May 1939 v Romania	2–0

652. Joseph Mercer
Wing half
Born Ellesmere Port, 9 August 1914
Died 9 August 1990
Clubs Elton Green FC; Shell-Mex FC; Ellesmere Port Town; Runcorn; Everton; Arsenal

Caps	5	Result
	16 Nov 1938 v N. Ireland	7–0
	15 Apr 1939 v Scotland	2–1
	13 May 1939 v Italy	2–2
	18 May 1939 v Yugoslavia	1–2
	24 May 1939 v Romania	2–0

653. Albert 'Pat' Beasley
Winger
Born Stourbridge, 16 July 1913
Died 27 February 1986
Clubs Stourbridge FC; Arsenal; Huddersfield Town; Fulham; Bristol City

Caps	1	Result	Goals
	15 Apr 1939 v Scotland	2–1	1

654. Leslie George Smith
Outside left
Born Ealing, 13 March 1918
Died 24 May 1995
Clubs Petersham; Wimbledon; Hayes; Brentford; Aston Villa; Kidderminster Harriers

Caps	1	Result
	24 May 1939 v Romania	2–0

655. Frank Victor Swift
Goalkeeper
Born Blackpool, 24 December 1913
Died 6 February 1958
Clubs Blackpool Gasworks; Fleetwood; Manchester City

Caps	19	Result
	28 Sep 1946 v N. Ireland	7–2
	30 Sep 1946 v Eire	1–0
	19 Oct 1946 v Wales	3–0
	27 Nov 1946 v Holland	8–2
	12 Apr 1947 v Scotland	1–1
	3 May 1947 v France	3–0
	18 May 1947 v Switzerland	0–1
	27 May 1947 v Portugal	10–0
	21 Sep 1947 v Belgium	5–2
	18 Oct 1947 v Wales	3–0
	5 Nov 1947 v N. Ireland	2–2
	19 Nov 1947 v Sweden	4–2
	10 Apr 1948 v Scotland	2–0
	16 May 1948 v Italy	4–0
	26 Sep 1948 v Denmark	0–0
	9 Oct 1948 v N. Ireland	6–2
	10 Nov 1948 v Wales	1–0
	9 Apr 1949 v Scotland	1–3
	18 May 1949 v Norway	4–1

656. Lawrence Scott
Right back

Born	Sheffield, 23 April 1917	
Died	28 July 1999	
Clubs	Bradford City; Arsenal; Crystal Palace	
Caps	17	Result
	28 Sep 1946 v N. Ireland	7–2
	30 Sep 1946 v Eire	1–0
	19 Oct 1946 v Wales	3–0
	27 Nov 1946 v Holland	8–2
	12 Apr 1947 v Scotland	1–1
	3 May 1947 v France	3–0
	18 May 1947 v Switzerland	0–1
	27 May 1947 v Portugal	10–0
	21 Sep 1947 v Belgium	5–2
	18 Oct 1947 v Wales	3–0
	5 Nov 1947 v N. Ireland	2–2
	19 Nov 1947 v Sweden	4–2
	10 Apr 1948 v Scotland	2–0
	16 May 1948 v Italy	4–0
	26 Sep 1948 v Denmark	0–0
	9 Oct 1948 v N. Ireland	6–2
	10 Nov 1948 v Wales	1–0

657. George Francis Hardwick
Left back

Born	Saltburn, 2 February 1920	
Died	19 April 2003	
Clubs	South Bank East End; Middlesbrough; Oldham Athletic	
Caps	13	Result
	28 Sep 1946 v N. Ireland	7–2
	30 Sep 1946 v Eire	1–0
	19 Oct 1946 v Wales	3–0
	27 Nov 1946 v Holland	8–2
	12 Apr 1947 v Scotland	1–1
	3 May 1947 v France	3–0
	18 May 1947 v Switzerland	0–1
	27 May 1947 v Portugal	10–0
	21 Sep 1947 v Belgium	5–2
	18 Oct 1947 v Wales	3–0
	5 Nov 1947 v N. Ireland	2–2
	19 Nov 1947 v Sweden	4–2
	10 Apr 1948 v Scotland	2–0

658. William Ambrose Wright
Left half/Centre half

Born	Ironbridge, 6 February 1924		
Died	3 September 1994		
Clubs	Wolverhampton Wanderers		
Caps	105	Result	Goals
	28 Sep 1946 v N. Ireland	7–2	
	30 Sep 1946 v Eire	1–0	
	19 Oct 1946 v Wales	3–0	
	27 Nov 1946 v Holland	8–2	
	12 Apr 1947 v Scotland	1–1	
	3 May 1947 v France	3–0	
	18 May 1947 v Switzerland	0–1	
	27 May 1947 v Portugal	10–0	
	21 Sep 1947 v Belgium	5–2	
	18 Oct 1947 v Wales	3–0	
	5 Nov 1947 v N. Ireland	2–2	
	19 Nov 1947 v Sweden	4–2	
	10 Apr 1948 v Scotland	2–0	
	16 May 1948 v Italy	4–0	
	26 Sep 1948 v Denmark	0–0	
	9 Oct 1948 v N. Ireland	6–2	
	10 Nov 1948 v Wales	1–0	
	1 Dec 1948 v Switzerland	6–0	
	9 Apr 1949 v Scotland	1–3	
	13 May 1949 v Sweden	1–3	
	18 May 1949 v Norway	4–1	
	22 May 1949 v France	3–1	1
	21 Sep 1949 v Eire	0–2	
	15 Oct 1949 v Wales	4–1	

16 Nov 1949 v N. Ireland	9–2	
30 Nov 1949 v Italy	2–0	1
15 Apr 1950 v Scotland	1–0	
14 May 1950 v Portugal	5–3	
18 May 1950 v Belgium	4–1	
25 Jun 1950 v Chile	2–0	
29 Jun 1950 v USA	0–1	
2 Jul 1950 v Spain	0–1	
7 Oct 1950 v N. Ireland	4–1	1
14 Apr 1951 v Scotland	2–3	
9 May 1951 v Argentina	2–1	
3 Oct 1951 v France	2–2	
20 Oct 1951 v Wales	1–1	
14 Nov 1951 v N. Ireland	2–0	
28 Nov 1951 v Austria	2–2	
5 Apr 1952 v Scotland	2–1	
18 May 1952 v Italy	1–1	
25 May 1952 v Austria	3–2	
28 May 1952 v Switzerland	3–0	
4 Oct 1952 v N. Ireland	2–2	
12 Nov 1952 v Wales	5–2	
26 Nov 1952 v Belgium	5–0	
18 Apr 1953 v Scotland	2–2	
17 May 1953 v Argentina	0–0	
24 May 1953 v Chile	2–1	
31 May 1953 v Uruguay	1–2	
8 Jun 1953 v USA	6–3	
10 Oct 1953 v Wales	4–1	
21 Oct 1953 v Rest of Europe	4–4	
11 Nov 1953 v N. Ireland	3–1	
25 Nov 1953 v Hungary	3–6	
3 Apr 1954 v Scotland	4–2	
16 May 1954 v Yugoslavia	0–1	
23 May 1954 v Hungary	1–7	
17 Jun 1954 v Belgium	4–4	
20 Jun 1954 v Switzerland	2–0	
26 Jun 1954 v Uruguay	2–4	
2 Oct 1954 v N. Ireland	2–0	
10 Nov 1954 v Wales	3–2	
1 Dec 1954 v W. Germany	3–1	
2 Apr 1955 v Scotland	7–2	
11 May 1955 v France	0–1	
18 May 1955 v Spain	1–1	
22 May 1955 v Portugal	1–3	
2 Oct 1955 v Denmark	5–1	
22 Oct 1955 v Wales	1–2	
2 Nov 1955 v N. Ireland	3–0	
30 Nov 1955 v Spain	4–1	
14 Apr 1956 v Scotland	1–1	
9 May 1956 v Brazil	4–2	
16 May 1956 v Sweden	0–0	
20 May 1956 v Finland	5–1	
26 May 1956 v W. Germany	3–1	
6 Oct 1956 v N. Ireland	1–1	
14 Nov 1956 v Wales	3–1	
28 Nov 1956 v Yugoslavia	3–0	
5 Dec 1956 v Denmark	5–2	
6 Apr 1957 v Scotland	2–1	
8 May 1957 v Eire	5–1	
15 May 1957 v Denmark	4–1	
19 May 1957 v Eire	1–1	
19 Oct 1957 v Wales	4–0	
6 Nov 1957 v N. Ireland	2–3	
27 Nov 1957 v France	4–0	
19 Apr 1958 v Scotland	4–0	
7 May 1958 v Portugal	2–1	
11 May 1958 v Yugoslavia	0–5	
18 May 1958 v Soviet Union	1–1	
8 Jun 1958 v Soviet Union	2–2	
11 Jun 1958 v Brazil	0–0	
15 Jun 1958 v Austria	2–2	
17 Jun 1958 v Soviet Union	0–1	
4 Oct 1958 v N. Ireland	3–3	
22 Oct 1958 v Soviet Union	5–0	
26 Nov 1958 v Wales	2–2	

11 Apr 1959 v Scotland	1–0	
6 May 1959 v Italy	2–2	
13 May 1959 v Brazil	0–2	
17 May 1959 v Peru	1–4	
24 May 1959 v Mexico	1–2	
28 May 1959 v USA	8–1	

659. Cornelius 'Neil' Franklin
Centre half

Born	Stoke-on-Trent, 24 January 1922
Died	17 February 1996
Clubs	Stoke City; Sante Fe (Colombia) Hull City; Crewe Alexandra; Stockport County; Wellington Town; Sankeys FC
Caps	27

	Result
28 Sep 1946 v N. Ireland	7–2
30 Sep 1946 v Eire	1–0
19 Oct 1946 v Wales	3–0
27 Nov 1946 v Holland	8–2
12 Apr 1947 v Scotland	1–1
3 May 1947 v France	3–0
18 May 1947 v Switzerland	0–1
27 May 1947 v Portugal	10–0
21 Sep 1947 v Belgium	5–2
18 Oct 1947 v Wales	3–0
5 Nov 1947 v N. Ireland	2–2
19 Nov 1947 v Sweden	4–2
10 Apr 1948 v Scotland	2–0
16 May 1948 v Italy	4–0
26 Sep 1948 v Denmark	0–0
9 Oct 1948 v N. Ireland	6–2
10 Nov 1948 v Wales	1–0
1 Dec 1948 v Switzerland	6–0
9 Apr 1949 v Scotland	1–3
13 May 1949 v Sweden	1–3
18 May 1949 v Norway	4–1
22 May 1949 v France	3–1
21 Sep 1949 v Eire	0–2
15 Oct 1949 v Wales	4–1
16 Nov 1949 v N. Ireland	9–2
30 Nov 1949 v Italy	2–0
15 Apr 1950 v Scotland	1–0

660. Henry Cockburn
Wing half

Born	Ashton-under-Lyne, 14 September 1923
Died	2 February 2004
Clubs	Goslings FC; Manchester Utd; Bury; Peterborough Utd; Corby Town; Sankey's FC
Caps	13

	Result
28 Sep 1946 v N. Ireland	7–2
30 Sep 1946 v Eire	1–0
19 Oct 1946 v Wales	3–0
10 Apr 1948 v Scotland	2–0
16 May 1948 v Italy	4–0
26 Sep 1948 v Denmark	0–0
9 Oct 1948 v N. Ireland	6–2
1 Dec 1948 v Switzerland	6–0
9 Apr 1949 v Scotland	1–3
13 May 1949 v Sweden	1–3
9 May 1951 v Argentina	2–1
19 May 1951 v Portugal	5–2
3 Oct 1951 v France	2–2

661. Thomas Finney
Outside right

Born	Preston, 5 April 1922
Clubs	Preston North End
Caps	76

	Result	Goals
28 Sep 1946 v N. Ireland	7–2	1
30 Sep 1946 v Eire	1–0	1
19 Oct 1946 v Wales	3–0	
27 Nov 1946 v Holland	8–2	1
3 May 1947 v France	3–0	1
27 May 1947 v Portugal	10–0	1

21 Sep 1947 v Belgium	5–2	2
18 Oct 1947 v Wales	3–0	1
5 Nov 1947 v N. Ireland	2–2	
19 Nov 1947 v Sweden	4–2	
10 Apr 1948 v Scotland	2–0	1
16 May 1948 v Italy	4–0	2
9 Oct 1948 v N. Ireland	6–2	
10 Nov 1948 v Wales	1–0	1
9 Apr 1949 v Scotland	1–3	
13 May 1949 v Sweden	1–3	1
18 May 1949 v Norway	4–1	1
22 May 1949 v France	3–1	
21 Sep 1949 v Eire	0–2	
15 Oct 1949 v Wales	4–1	
16 Nov 1949 v N. Ireland	9–2	
30 Nov 1949 v Italy	2–0	
15 Apr 1950 v Scotland	1–0	
14 May 1950 v Portugal	5–3	4
18 May 1950 v Belgium	4–1	
25 Jun 1950 v Chile	2–0	
29 Jun 1950 v USA	0–1	
2 Jul 1950 v Spain	0–1	
15 Nov 1950 v Wales	4–2	
14 Apr 1951 v Scotland	2–3	1
9 May 1951 v Argentina	2–1	
19 May 1951 v Portugal	5–2	1
3 Oct 1951 v France	2–2	
20 Oct 1951 v Wales	1–1	
14 Nov 1951 v N. Ireland	2–0	
5 Apr 1952 v Scotland	2–1	
18 May 1952 v Italy	1–1	
25 May 1952 v Austria	3–2	
28 May 1952 v Switzerland	3–0	
4 Oct 1952 v N. Ireland	2–2	
12 Nov 1952 v Wales	5–2	1
26 Nov 1952 v Belgium	5–0	
18 Apr 1953 v Scotland	2–2	
17 May 1953 v Argentina	0–0	
24 May 1953 v Chile	2–1	
31 May 1953 v Uruguay	1–2	
8 Jun 1953 v USA	6–3	2
10 Oct 1953 v Wales	4–1	
3 Apr 1954 v Scotland	4–2	
16 May 1954 v Yugoslavia	0–1	
23 May 1954 v Hungary	1–7	
17 Jun 1954 v Belgium	4–4	
20 Jun 1954 v Switzerland	2–0	
26 Jun 1954 v Uruguay	2–4	1
1 Dec 1954 v W. Germany	3–1	
2 Oct 1955 v Denmark	5–1	
22 Oct 1955 v Wales	1–2	
2 Nov 195 v N. Ireland	3–0	1
30 Nov 1955 v Spain	4–1	1
14 Apr 1956 v Scotland	1–1	
14 Nov 1956 v Wales	3–1	1
28 Nov 1956 v Yugoslavia	3–0	
5 Dec 1956 v Denmark	5–2	
6 Apr 1957 v Scotland	2–1	
8 May 1957 v Eire	5–1	
15 May 1957 v Denmark	4–1	
19 May 1957 v Eire	1–1	
19 Oct 1957 v Wales	4–0	1
27 Nov 1957 v France	4–0	
19 Apr 1958 v Scotland	4–0	
7 May 1958 v Portugal	2–1	
11 May 1958 v Yugoslavia	0–5	
18 May 1958 v Soviet Union	1–1	
8 Jun 1958 v Soviet Union	2–2	1
4 Oct 1958 v N. Ireland	3–3	1
22 Oct 1958 v Soviet Union	5–0	

662. Wilfred Mannion
Inside forward

Born Middlesbrough, 16 May 1918
Died 14 April 2000
Clubs South Bank St Peters; Middlesbrough; Hull City; Poole Town; Cambridge Utd; King's Lynn; Haverhill Rovers; Earlstown

Caps	26	Result	Goals
	28 Sep 1946 v N. Ireland	7–2	3
	30 Sep 1946 v Eire	1–0	
	19 Oct 1946 v Wales	3–0	2
	27 Nov 1946 v Holland	8–2	1
	12 Apr 1947 v Scotland	1–1	
	3 May 1947 v France	3–0	1
	18 May 1947 v Switzerland	0–1	
	27 May 1947 v Portugal	10–0	
	21 Sep 1947 v Belgium	5–2	
	18 Oct 1947 v Wales	3–0	
	5 Nov 1947 v N. Ireland	2–2	1
	19 Nov 1947 v Sweden	4–2	
	16 May 1948 v Italy	4–0	
	18 May 1949 v Norway	4–1	
	22 May 1949 v France	3–1	
	21 Sep 1949 v Eire	0–2	
	15 Apr 1950 v Scotland	1–0	
	14 May 1950 v Portugal	5–3	
	18 May 1950 v Belgium	4–1	1
	25 Jun 1950 v Chile	2–0	1
	29 Jun 1950 v USA	0–1	
	7 Oct 1950 v N. Ireland	4–1	
	15 Nov 1950 v Wales	4–2	1
	22 Nov 1950 v Yugoslavia	2–2	
	14 Apr 1951 v Scotland	2–3	
	3 Oct 1951 v France	2–2	

663. Robert Langton
Outside left

Born Burscough, 8 September 1918
Died 15 November 1996
Clubs Burscough Victoria; Blackburn Rovers; Preston North End; Bolton Wanderers; Ards; Wisbech Town; Kidderminster Harriers

Caps	11	Result	Goals
	28 Sep 1946 v N. Ireland	7–2	1
	30 Sep 1946 v Eire	1–0	
	19 Oct 1946 v Wales	3–0	
	27 Nov 1946 v Holland	8–2	
	3 May 1947 v France	3–0	
	18 May 1947 v Switzerland	0–1	
	19 Nov 1947 v Sweden	4–2	
	26 Sep 1948 v Denmark	0–0	
	13 May 1949 v Sweden	1–3	
	15 Apr 1950 v Scotland	1–0	
	7 Oct 1950 v N. Ireland	4–1	

664. Harry Johnston
Centre half/Wing half

Born Droylsden, 26 September 1919
Died 12 October 1973
Clubs Droylsden Athletic; Blackpool

Caps	10	Result
	27 Nov 1946 v Holland	8–2
	12 Apr 1947 v Scotland	1–1
	14 Apr 1951 v Scotland	2–3
	17 May 1953 v Argentina	0–0
	24 May 1953 v Chile	2–1
	31 May 1953 v Uruguay	1–2
	8 Jun 1953 v USA	6–3
	10 Oct 1953 v Wales	4–1
	11 Nov 1953 v N. Ireland	3–1
	25 Nov 1953 v Hungary	3–6

665. James Mullen
Outside left

Born Newcastle-upon-Tyne, 6 January 1923
Died 2 October 1987
Clubs Wolverhampton Wanderers

Caps	12	Result	Goals
	12 Apr 1947 v Scotland	1–1	
	18 May 1949 v Norway	4–1	1
	22 May 1949 v France	3–1	
	18 May 1950 v Belgium	4–1	1
	25 Jun 1950 v Chile	2–0	
	29 Jun 1950 v USA	0–1	
	10 Oct 1953 v Wales	4–1	
	21 Oct 1953 v Rest of Europe	4–4	2
	11 Nov 1953 v N. Ireland	3–1	
	3 Apr 1954 v Scotland	4–2	1
	16 May 1954 v Yugoslavia	0–1	
	20 Jun 1954 v Switzerland	2–0	1

666. Edmund Lowe
Left half

Born Halesowen, 11 July 1925
Clubs Finchley; Aston Villa; Fulham; Notts County

Caps	3	Result
	3 May 1947 v France	3–0
	18 May 1947 v Switzerland	0–1
	27 May 1947 v Portugal	10–0

667. Stanley Harding Mortensen
Centre forward/Inside forward

Born South Shields, 26 May 1921
Died 22 May 1991
Clubs South Shields; Blackpool; Hull City; Southport; Bath City; Lancaster City

Caps	25	Result	Goals
	27 May 1947 v Portugal	10–0	4
	21 Sep 1947 v Belgium	5–2	1
	18 Oct 1947 v Wales	3–0	1
	5 Nov 1947 v N. Ireland	2–2	
	19 Nov 1947 v Sweden	4–2	3
	10 Apr 1948 v Scotland	2–0	1
	16 May 1948 v Italy	4–0	1
	9 Oct 1948 v N. Ireland	5–2	3
	10 Nov 1948 v Wales	1–0	
	9 Apr 1949 v Scotland	1–3	
	13 May 1949 v Sweden	1–3	
	18 May 1949 v Norway	4–1	
	15 Oct 1949 v Wales	4–1	1
	16 Nov 1949 v N. Ireland	9–2	2
	30 Nov 1949 v Italy	2–0	
	15 Apr 1950 v Scotland	1–0	
	14 May 1950 v Portugal	5–3	1
	18 May 1950 v Belgium	4–1	1
	25 Jun 1950 v Chile	2–0	1
	29 Jun 1950 v USA	0–1	
	2 Jul 1950 v Spain	0–1	
	14 Apr 1951 v Scotland	2–3	
	9 May 1951 v Argentina	2–1	1
	21 Oct 1953 v Rest of Europe	4–4	1
	25 Nov 1953 v Hungary	3–6	1

⚽ **DID YOU KNOW...?**

Stan Mortensen made his international debut for Wales against his own country, England, at Wembley in an unofficial wartime match on 25 September 1943. He was England's reserve, but when Wales lost injured Ivor Powell it was agreed that Mortensen would take his place.

668. Timothy Victor Ward
Wing half

Born Cheltenham, 17 September 1917
Died 28 January 1993
Clubs Cheltenham Town; Derby County; Barnsley

Caps	2	Result

21 Sep 1947 v Belgium	5–2
10 Nov 1948 v Wales	1–0

669. Philip Henry Taylor
Right half
Born   Bristol, 18 September 1917
Clubs   Bristol Rovers; Liverpool

Caps	3	Result
18 Oct 1947 v Wales		3–0
5 Nov 1947 v N. Ireland		2–2
19 Nov 1947 v Sweden		4–2

670. Stanley Pearson
Inside forward
Born   Salford, 15 January 1919
Died   20 February 1997
Clubs   Manchester Utd; Bury; Chester

Caps	8	Result	Goals
10 Apr 1948 v Scotland		2–0	
9 Oct 1948 v N. Ireland		6–2	1
9 Apr 1949 v Scotland		1–3	
16 Nov 1949 v N. Ireland		9–2	2
30 Nov 1949 v Italy		2–0	
19 May 1951 v Portugal		5–2	
5 Apr 1952 v Scotland		2–1	2
18 May 1952 v Italy		1–1	

671. John Robert Howe
Fullback
Born   West Hartlepool, 7 October 1915
Died   5 April 1987
Clubs   Hartlepool Utd; Derby County; Huddersfield Town;
        King's Lynn; Long Sutton; Wisbech Town

Caps	3	Result
16 May 1948 v Italy		4–0
9 Oct 1948 v N. Ireland		6–2
9 Apr 1949 v Scotland		1–3

672. John Aston
Left back
Born   Manchester, 3 September 1921
Died   31 July 2003
Clubs   Clayton Methodists; Manchester Utd

Caps	17	Result
26 Sep 1948 v Denmark		0–0
10 Nov 1948 v Wales		1–0
1 Dec 1948 v Switzerland		6–0
9 Apr 1949 v Scotland		1–3
13 May 1949 v Sweden		1–3
18 May 1949 v Norway		4–1
22 May 1949 v France		3–1
21 Sep 1949 v Eire		0–2
15 Oct 1949 v Wales		4–1
16 Nov 1949 v N. Ireland		9–2
30 Nov 1949 v Italy		2–0
15 Apr 1950 v Scotland		1–0
14 May 1950 v Portugal		5–3
18 May 1950 v Belgium		4–1
25 Jun 1950 v Chile		2–0
29 Jun 1950 v USA		0–1
7 Oct 1950 v N. Ireland		4–1

673. James Hagan
Inside forward
Born   Washington, 21 January 1918
Died   27 February 1998
Clubs   Liverpool; Derby County; Sheffield Utd

Caps	1	Result
26 Sep 1948 v Denmark		0–0

674. Leonard Francis Shackleton
Inside forward
Born   Bradford, 3 May 1922
Died   28 November 2000
Clubs   Kippax Utd; Arsenal; Bradford Park Avenue;
        Newcastle Utd; Sunderland

Caps	5	Result	Goals

26 Sep 1948 v Denmark	0–0
10 Nov 1948 v Wales	1–0
15 Oct 1949 v Wales	4–1
10 Nov 1954 v Wales	3–2
1 Dec 1954 v W. Germany	3–1 1

675. John Edward Thompson Milburn
Outside right/Centre forward
Born   Ashington, 1 May 1924
Died   8 October 1988
Clubs   Ashington; Newcastle Utd; Linfield; Yiewsley

Caps	13	Result	Goals
9 Oct 1948 v N. Ireland		6–2	1
10 Nov 1948 v Wales		1–0	
1 Dec 1948 v Switzerland		6–0	1
9 Apr 1949 v Scotland		1–3	1
15 Oct 1949 v Wales		4–1	3
14 May 1950 v Portugal		5–3	
18 May 1950 v Belgium		4–1	
2 Jul 1950 v Spain		0–1	
15 Nov 1950 v Wales		4–2	1
9 May 1951 v Argentina		2–1	1
19 May 1951 v Portugal		5–2	2
3 Oct 1951 v France		2–2	
2 Oct 1955 v Denmark		5–1	

676. Edwin George Ditchburn
Goalkeeper
Born   Gillingham, 24 October 1921
Died   26 December 2005
Clubs   Northfleet Paper Mills; Tottenham Hotspur;
        Romford; Brentwood

Caps	6	Result
1 Dec 1948 v Switzerland		6–0
13 May 1949 v Sweden		1–3
8 Jun 1953 v USA		6–3
14 Nov 1956 v Wales		3–1
28 Nov 1956 v Yugoslavia		3–0
5 Dec 1956 v Denmark		5–2

677. Alfred Ernest Ramsey
Right back
Born   Dagenham, 22 January 1920
Died   28 April 1999
Clubs   Southampton; Tottenham Hotspur

Caps	32	Result	Goals
1 Dec 1948 v Switzerland		6–0	
30 Nov 1949 v Italy		2–0	
15 Apr 1950 v Scotland		1–0	
14 May 1950 v Portugal		5–3	
18 May 1950 v Belgium		4–1	
25 Jun 1950 v Chile		2–0	
29 Jun 1950 v USA		0–1	
2 Jul 1950 v Spain		0–1	
7 Oct 1950 v N. Ireland		4–1	
15 Nov 1950 v Wales		4–2	
22 Nov 1950 v Yugoslavia		2–2	
14 Apr 1951 v Scotland		2–3	
9 May 1951 v Argentina		2–1	
19 May 1951 v Portugal		5–2	
3 Oct 1951 v France		2–2	
20 Oct 1951 v Wales		1–1	
14 Nov 1951 v N. Ireland		2–0	
28 Nov 1951 v Austria		2–2	1
5 Apr 1952 v Scotland		2–1	
18 May 1952 v Italy		1–1	
25 May 1952 v Austria		3–2	
28 May 1952 v Switzerland		3–0	
4 Oct 1952 v N. Ireland		2–2	
12 Nov 1952 v Wales		5–2	
26 Nov 1952 v Belgium		5–0	
18 Apr 1953 v Scotland		2–2	
17 May 1953 v Argentina		0–0	
24 May 1953 v Chile		2–1	
31 May 1953 v Uruguay		1–2	
8 Jun 1953 v USA		6–3	
21 Oct 1953 v Rest of Europe		4–4	1
25 Nov 1953 v Hungary		3–6	1

678. John Frederick Rowley
Forward
Born   Wolverhampton, 7 October 1920
Died   28 June 1998
Clubs   Wolverhampton Wanderers; Cradley Heath;
        Bournemouth; Manchester Utd; Plymouth Argyle

Caps	6	Result	Goals
	1 Dec 1948 v Switzerland	6–0	1
	13 May 1949 v Sweden	1–3	
	18 May 1949 v Norway	4–1	
	22 May 1949 v France	3–1	
	16 Nov 1949 v N. Ireland	9–2	4
	30 Nov 1949 v Italy	2–0	1

679. John Haines
Inside forward
Born   Wickhamford, 24 April 1920
Died   19 March 1987
Clubs   Evesham Town; Cheltenham Town; Liverpool;
        Swansea Town; Leicester City; West Bromwich
        Albion; Bradford Park Avenue; Rochdale; Chester;
        Wellington Town; Kidderminster Harriers

Caps	1	Result	Goals
	1 Dec 1948 v Switzerland	6–0	2

680. John Hancocks
Outside right
Born   Oakengates, 30 April 1919
Died   14 February 1994
Clubs   Oakengates Town; Walsall; Wolverhampton
        Wanderers; Wellington Town; Cambridge Utd;
        Oswestry; Sankey's FC

Caps	3	Result	Goals
	1 Dec 1948 v Switzerland	6–0	2
	15 Oct 1949 v Wales	4–1	
	22 Nov 1950 v Yugoslavia	2–2	

681. Edmund Shimwell
Right back
Born   Wirksworth, 27 February 1920
Died   2 October 1988
Clubs   Wirksworth FC; Sheffield Utd; Blackpool; Oldham
        Athletic; Burton Albion

Caps	1	Result
	13 May 1949 v Sweden	1–3

682. Roy Thomas Frank Bentley
Centre forward
Born   Bristol, 17 May 1924
Clubs   Bristol Rovers; Bristol City; Newcastle Utd; Chelsea;
        Fulham; Queen's Park Rangers

Caps	12	Result	Goals
	13 May 1949 v Sweden	1–3	
	15 Apr 1950 v Scotland	1–0	1
	14 May 1950 v Portugal	5–3	
	18 May 1950 v Belgium	4–1	1
	25 Jun 1950 v Chile	2–0	
	29 Jun 1950 v USA	0–1	
	12 Nov 1952 v Wales	5–2	1
	26 Nov 1952 v Belgium	5–0	
	10 Nov 1954 v Wales	3–2	3
	1 Dec 1954 v W. Germany	3–1	1
	18 May 1955 v Spain	1–1	1
	22 May 1955 v Portugal	1–3	1

DID YOU KNOW...?

In May 1950, during England's 4–1 victory against
Belgium in Brussels, Jimmy Mullen became the
national team's first ever substitute, when he replaced
Jackie Milburn. He also became the first sub to score,
when he found the net shortly after the interval.

683. William Ellerington
Right back
Born   Southampton, 30 June 1923
Clubs   Southampton

Caps	2	Result
	18 May 1949 v Norway	4–1
	22 May 1949 v France	3–1

684. James William Dickinson
Left half
Born   Alton, 24 April 1925
Died   9 November 1982
Clubs   Portsmouth

Caps	48	Result
	18 May 1949 v Norway	4–1
	22 May 1949 v France	3–1
	21 Sep 1949 v Eire	0–2
	15 Oct 1949 v Wales	4–1
	15 Apr 1950 v Scotland	1–0
	14 May 1950 v Portugal	5–3
	18 May 1950 v Belgium	4–1
	25 Jun 1950 v Chile	2–0
	29 Jun 1950 v USA	0–1
	2 Jul 1950 v Spain	0–1
	7 Oct 1950 v N. Ireland	4–1
	15 Nov 1950 v Wales	4–2
	22 Nov 1950 v Yugoslavia	2–2
	20 Oct 1951 v Wales	1–1
	14 Nov 1951 v N. Ireland	2–0
	28 Nov 1951 v Austria	2–2
	5 Apr 1952 v Scotland	2–1
	18 May 1952 v Italy	1–1
	25 May 1952 v Austria	3–2
	28 May 1952 v Switzerland	3–0
	4 Oct 1952 v N. Ireland	2–2
	12 Nov 1952 v Wales	5–2
	26 Nov 1952 v Belgium	5–0
	18 Apr 1953 v Scotland	2–2
	17 May 1953 v Argentina	0–0
	24 May 1953 v Chile	2–1
	31 May 1953 v Uruguay	1–2
	8 Jun 1953 v USA	6–3
	10 Oct 1953 v Wales	4–1
	21 Oct 1953 v Rest of Europe	4–4
	1 Nov 1953 v N. Ireland	3–1
	25 Nov 1953 v Hungary	3–6
	3 Apr 1954 v Scotland	4–2
	16 May 1954 v Yugoslavia	0–1
	23 May 1954 v Hungary	1–7
	17 Jun 1954 v Belgium	4–4
	20 Jun 1954 v Switzerland	2–0
	26 Jun 1954 v Uruguay	2–4
	18 May 1955 v Spain	1–1
	22 May 1955 v Portugal	1–3
	2 Oct 1955 v Denmark	5–1
	22 Oct 1955 v Wales	1–2
	2 Nov 1955 v N. Ireland	3–0
	30 Nov 1955 v Spain	4–1
	14 Apr 1956 v Scotland	1–1
	14 Nov 1956 v Wales	3–1
	28 Nov 1956 v Yugoslavia	3–0
	5 Dec 1956 v Denmark	5–2

685. John Morris
Inside right/Right half
Born   Radcliffe, 27 September 1923
Clubs   Manchester Utd; Derby County; Leicester City;
        Corby Town; Kettering Town

Caps	3	Result	Goals
	18 May 1949 v Norway	4–1	1
	22 May 1949 v France	3–1	2
	21 Sep 1949 v Eire	0–2	

686. Bert Frederick Williams
Goalkeeper
Born   Bilston, 31 January 1920
Clubs   Thompson's FC; Walsall; Wolverhampton Wanderers

Caps	24	Result
	22 May 1949 v France	3–1
	21 Sep 1949 v Eire	0–2
	15 Oct 1949 v Wales	4–1
	30 Nov 1949 v Italy	2–0
	15 Apr 1950 v Scotland	1–0
	14 May 1950 v Portugal	5–3
	18 May 1950 v Belgium	4–1
	25 Jun 1950 v Chile	2–0
	29 Jun 1950 v USA	0–1
	2 Jul 1950 v Spain	0–1
	7 Oct 1950 v N. Ireland	4–1
	15 Nov 1950 v Wales	4–2
	22 Nov 1950 v Yugoslavia	2–2
	14 Apr 1951 v Scotland	2–3
	9 May 1951 v Argentina	2–1
	19 May 1951 v Portugal	5–2
	3 Oct 1951 v France	2–2
	20 Oct 1951 v Wales	1–1
	1 Dec 1954 v W. Germany	3–1
	2 Apr 1955 v Scotland	7–2
	15 May 1955 v France	0–1
	18 May 1955 v Spain	1–1
	22 May 1955 v Portugal	1–3
	22 Oct 1955 v Wales	1–2

687. Bertram Mozley
Right back
Born Derby, 21 September 1923
Clubs Shelton Utd; Derby County

Caps	3	Result
	21 Sep 1949 v Eire	0–2
	15 Oct 1949 v Wales	4–1
	16 Nov 1949 v N. Ireland	9–2

688. Peter Philip Harris
Outside right
Born Southsea, 19 December 1925
Died 17 December 2002
Clubs Gosport Borough; Portsmouth

Caps	2	Result
	21 Sep 1949 v Eire	0–2
	23 May 1954 v Hungary	1–7

689. Jesse Pye
Centre forward/Inside forward
Born Rotherham, 22 December 1918
Died 20 February 1984
Clubs Treeton FC; Sheffield Utd; Notts County;
Wolverhampton Wanderers; Luton Town; Derby
County; Wisbech Town

Caps	1	Result
	21 Sep 1949 v Eire	0–2

690. Bernard Streten
Goalkeeper
Born Gillingham, 14 January 1921
Died 6 May 1994
Clubs Notts County; Shrewsbury Town; Luton Town;
King's Lynn; Wisbech Town; Cambridge City; North
Walsham FC

Caps	1	Result
	16 Nov 1949 v N. Ireland	9–2

691. William Watson
Right half
Born Bolton-on-Dearne, 7 March 1920
Died 24 April 2004
Clubs Huddersfield Town; Sunderland; Halifax Town

Caps	4	Result
	16 Nov 1949 v N. Ireland	9–2
	30 Nov 1949 v Italy	2–0
	15 Nov 1950 v Wales	4–2
	22 Nov 1950 v Yugoslavia	2–2

692. Jack Froggatt
Centre half/Outside left
Born Sheffield, 17 November 1922
Died 26 December 2003
Clubs Portsmouth; Leicester City; Kettering Town

Caps	13	Result	Goals
	16 Nov 1949 v N. Ireland	9–2	1
	30 Nov 1949 v Italy	2–0	
	14 Apr 1951 v Scotland	2–3	
	28 Nov 1951 v Austria	2–2	
	5 Apr 1952 v Scotland	2–1	
	18 May 1952 v Italy	1–1	
	25 May 1952 v Austria	3–2	
	28 May 1952 v Switzerland	3–0	
	4 Oct 1952 v N. Ireland	2–2	
	12 Nov 1952 v Wales	5–2	1
	26 Nov 1952 v Belgium	5–0	
	18 Apr 1953 v Scotland	2–2	
	8 Jun 1953 v USA	6–3	

693. William Jones
Centre half
Born Whaley Bridge, 13 May 1921
Clubs Hayfield St Matthew's; Liverpool; Ellesmere Port Town

Caps	2	Result
	14 May 1950 v Portugal	5–3
	18 May 1950 v Belgium	4–1

694. Lawrence Hughes
Centre half
Born Waterloo, 2 March 1924
Clubs Tranmere Rovers; Liverpool

Caps	3	Result
	25 Jun 1950 v Chile	2–0
	29 Jun 1950 v USA	0–1
	2 Jul 1950 v Spain	0–1

695. William Eckersley
Left back
Born Southport, 16 July 1925
Died 25 October 1982
Clubs High Park FC; Blackburn Rovers

Caps	17	Result
	2 Jul 1950 v Spain	0–1
	22 Nov 1950 v Yugoslavia	2–2
	14 Apr 1951 v Scotland	2–3
	9 May 1951 v Argentina	2–1
	19 May 1951 v Portugal	5–2
	28 Nov 1951 v Austria	2–2
	25 May 1952 v Austria	3–2
	28 May 1952 v Switzerland	3–0
	4 Oct 1952 v N. Ireland	2–2
	17 May 1953 v Argentina	0–0
	24 May 1953 v Chile	2–1
	31 May 1953 v Uruguay	1–2
	8 Jun 1953 v USA	6–3
	10 Oct 1953 v Wales	4–1
	21 Oct 1953 v Rest of Europe	4–4
	11 Nov 1953 v N. Ireland	3–1
	25 Nov 1953 v Hungary	3–6

696. Edward Francis Baily
Inside left
Born London, 6 August 1925
Clubs Finchley; Tottenham Hotspur; Port Vale; Nottingham
Forest; Leyton Orient

Caps	9	Result	Goals
	2 Jul 1950 v Spain	0–1	
	7 Oct 1950 v N. Ireland	4–1	2
	15 Nov 1950 v Wales	4–2	2
	22 Nov 1950 v Yugoslavia	2–2	
	20 Oct 1951 v Wales	1–1	1
	28 Nov 1951 v Austria	2–2	
	25 May 1952 v Austria	3–2	
	28 May 1952 v Switzerland	3–0	
	4 Oct 1952 v N. Ireland	2–2	

DID YOU KNOW...?

Billy Wright became the first England player to register 100 appearances for his country in April 1959. At Wembley Stadium, the assembled crowd waiting to watch the match against Scotland gave him a standing ovation.

697. Allenby Chilton
Centre half
Born South Hylton, 16 September 1918
Died 16 June 1996
Clubs Seaham Colliery; Manchester Utd; Grimsby Town

Caps	2	Result
	7 Oct 1950 v N. Ireland	4–1
	3 Oct 1951 v France	2–2

698. Jack Lee
Inside right/Centre forward
Born Sileby, 4 November 1920
Died 15 January 1995
Clubs Quorn Methodists; Leicester City; Derby County; Coventry City

Caps	1	Result	Goals
	7 Oct 1950 v N. Ireland	4–1	1

699. Lionel Smith
Left back
Born Mexborough, 23 August 1920
Died 15 November 1980
Clubs Arsenal; Watford; Gravesend

Caps	6	Result
	15 Nov 1950 v Wales	4–2
	20 Oct 1951 v Wales	1–1
	14 Nov 1951 v N. Ireland	2–0
	12 Nov 1952 v Wales	5–2
	26 Nov 1952 v Belgium	5–0
	18 Apr 1953 v Scotland	2–2

700. Leslie Harry Compton
Centre half
Born Woodford, 12 September 1912
Died 27 December 1984
Clubs Hampstead Town; Arsenal

Caps	2	Result
	15 Nov 1950 v Wales	4–2
	22 Nov 1950 v Yugoslavia	2–2

701. Leslie Dennis Medley
Outside left
Born Lower Edmonton, 3 September 1920
Clubs Tottenham Hotspur; Toronto Greenbacks (Canada); Ulster Utd (Canada)

Caps	6	Result	Goals
	15 Nov 1950 v Wales	4–2	
	22 Nov 1950 v Yugoslavia	2–2	
	3 Oct 1951 v France	2–2	1
	20 Oct 1951 v Wales	1–1	
	14 Nov 1951 v N. Ireland	2–0	
	28 Nov 1951 v Austria	2–2	

702. Nathaniel Lofthouse
Centre forward
Born Bolton, 27 August 1925
Clubs Bolton Wanderers

Caps	33	Result	Goals
	22 Nov 1950 v Yugoslavia	2–2	2
	20 Oct 1951 v Wales	1–1	
	14 Nov 1951 v N. Ireland	2–0	2
	28 Nov 1951 v Austria	2–2	1
	5 Apr 1952 v Scotland	2–1	
	18 May 1952 v Italy	1–1	
	25 May 1952 v Austria	3–2	2
	28 May 1952 v Switzerland	3–0	2
	4 Oct 1952 v N. Ireland	2–2	1
	12 Nov 1952 v Wales	5–2	2
	26 Nov 1952 v Belgium	5–0	2
	18 Apr 1953 v Scotland	2–2	
	17 May 1953 v Argentina	0–0	
	24 May 1953 v Chile	2–1	1
	31 May 1953 v Uruguay	1–2	
	8 Jun 1953 v USA	6–3	2
	10 Oct 1953 v Wales	4–1	2
	21 Oct 1953 v Rest of Europe	4–4	
	11 Nov 1953 v N. Ireland	3–1	1
	17 Jun 1954 v Belgium	4–4	2
	26 Jun 1954 v Uruguay	2–4	1
	2 Oct 1954 v N. Ireland	2–0	
	2 Apr 1955 v Scotland	7–2	2
	15 May 1955 v France	0–1	
	18 May 1955 v Spain	1–1	
	22 May 1955 v Portugal	1–3	
	2 Oct 1955 v Denmark	5–1	2
	22 Oct 1955 v Wales	1–2	
	30 Nov 1955 v Spain	4–1	
	14 Apr 1956 v Scotland	1–1	
	20 May 1956 v Finland	5–1	2
	22 Oct 1958 v Soviet Union	5–0	1
	26 Nov 1958 v Wales	2–2	

703. Harold William Hassall
Inside left
Born Tyldesley, 4 March 1929
Clubs Astley & Tyldesley Collieries; Huddersfield Town; Bolton Wanderers

Caps	5	Result	Goals
	14 Apr 1951 v Scotland	2–3	1
	9 May 1951 v Argentina	2–1	
	19 May 1951 v Portugal	5–2	1
	3 Oct 1951 v France	2–2	
	11 Nov 1953 v N. Ireland	3–1	2

704. James Guy Taylor
Centre half
Born Hillingdon, 5 November 1917
Died 6 March 2001
Clubs Hillingdon Town; Fulham; Queen's Park Rangers; Tunbridge Wells Rangers

Caps	2	Result
	9 May 1951 v Argentina	2–1
	19 May 1951 v Portugal	5–2

705. Victor Metcalfe
Outside left
Born Barrow-in-Furness, 3 February 1922
Died 6 April 2003
Clubs Ravensthorpe Albion; Huddersfield Town; Hull City

Caps	2	Result
	9 May 1951 v Argentina	2–1
	19 May 1951 v Portugal	5–2

 DID YOU KNOW...?

England's oldest 'new' cap was won by Arsenal's Leslie Compton, who, at the age of thirty-eight years and two months, made his international debut in England's 4–2 win over Wales at Roker Park on 15 November 1950.

706. William Edward Nicholson
Right half
Born Scarborough, 26 January 1919
Died 23 October 2004
Clubs Tottenham Hotspur; Northfleet

Caps	1	Result	Goals
	19 May 1951 v Portugal	5–2	1

707. Arthur Willis
Fullback
Born   Denaby, 2 February 1920
Died   7 November 1987
Clubs   Finchley; Tottenham Hotspur; Swansea Town;
        Haverfordwest FC

Caps	1	Result
	3 Oct 1951 v France	2–2

708. Malcolm Williamson Barrass
Centre half
Born   Blackpool, 13 December 1924
Clubs   Ford Motors; Bolton Wanderers; Sheffield Utd;
        Wigan Athletic; Nuneaton Borough; Pwllheli

Caps	3	Result
	20 Oct 1951 v Wales	1–1
	14 Nov 1951 v N. Ireland	2–0
	18 Apr 1953 v Scotland	2–2

709. Thomas Thompson
Inside right
Born   Fence Houses, 10 November 1928
Clubs   Newcastle Utd; Aston Villa; Preston North End;
        Stoke City; Barrow

Caps	2	Result
	20 Oct 1951 v Wales	1–1
	6 Apr 1957 v Scotland	2–1

710. Gilbert Harold Merrick
Goalkeeper
Born   Birmingham, 26 January 1922
Clubs   Solihull Town; Birmingham City

Caps	23	Result
	14 Nov 1951 v N. Ireland	2–0
	28 Nov 1951 v Austria	2–2
	5 Apr 1952 v Scotland	2–1
	18 May 1952 v Italy	1–1
	25 May 1952 v Austria	3–2
	28 May 1952 v Switzerland	3–0
	4 Oct 1952 v N. Ireland	2–2
	12 Nov 1952 v Wales	5–2
	26 Nov 1952 v Belgium	5–0
	18 Apr 1953 v Scotland	2–2
	17 May 1953 v Argentina	0–0
	24 May 1953 v Chile	2–1
	31 May 1953 v Uruguay	1–2
	10 Oct 1953 v Wales	4–1
	21 Oct 1953 v Rest of Europe	4–4
	11 Nov 1953 v N. Ireland	3–1
	25 Nov 1953 v Hungary	3–6
	3 Apr 1954 v Scotland	4–2
	16 May 1954 v Yugoslavia	0–1
	23 May 1954 v Hungary	1–7
	17 Jun 1954 v Belgium	4–4
	20 Jun 1954 v Switzerland	2–0
	26 Jun 1954 v Uruguay	2–4

711. John Sewell
Inside forward
Born   Whitehaven, 24 January 1927
Clubs   Whitehaven Town; Notts County; Sheffield
        Wednesday; Aston Villa; Hull City; Lusaka City
        (Zambia)

Caps	6	Result	Goals
	14 Nov 1951 v N. Ireland	2–0	
	25 May 1952 v Austria	3–2	1
	28 May 1952 v Switzerland	3–0	1
	4 Oct 1952 v N. Ireland	2–2	
	25 Nov 1953 v Hungary	3–6	1
	23 May 1954 v Hungary	1–7	

712. Leonard Phillips
Inside left
Born   Hackney, 11 September 1922
Clubs   Portsmouth; Poole Town; Chelmsford City; Bath City

Caps	3	Result
	14 Nov 1951 v N. Ireland	2–0

	10 Nov 1954 v Wales	3–2
	1 Dec 1954 v W. Germany	3–1

713. Clement Arthur Milton
Outside right
Born   Bedminster, 10 March 1928
Clubs   Arsenal; Bristol City

Caps	1	Result
	28 Nov 1951 v Austria	2–2

> ⚽ **DID YOU KNOW…?**
>
> Arthur Milton, who played football for Arsenal and cricket for Gloucestershire, was the last player to win a cap in both sports for England. He earned his football cap in a 1951 match against Austria.

714. Ivan Arthur 'Ivor' Broadis
Inside forward
Born   Isle of Dogs, 18 December 1922
Clubs   Finchley; Northfleet; Carlisle Utd; Sunderland;
        Manchester City; Newcastle Utd; Queen of the
        South

Caps	14	Result	Goals
	28 Nov 1951 v Austria	2–2	
	5 Apr 1952 v Scotland	2–1	
	18 May 1952 v Italy	1–1	1
	18 Apr 1953 v Scotland	2–2	2
	17 May 1953 v Argentina	0–0	
	24 May 1953 v Chile	2–1	
	31 May 1953 v Uruguay	1–2	
	8 Jun 1953 v USA	6–3	1
	3 Apr 1954 v Scotland	4–2	1
	16 May 1954 v Yugoslavia	0–1	
	23 May 1954 v Hungary	1–7	1
	17 Jun 1954 v Belgium	4–4	2
	20 Jun 1954 v Switzerland	2–0	
	26 Jun 1954 v Uruguay	2–4	

715. Thomas Garrett
Fullback
Born   Sunderland, 28 February 1927
Clubs   Horden Colliery; Blackpool; Millwall; Fleetwood

Caps	3	Result
	5 Apr 1952 v Scotland	2–1
	18 May 1952 v Italy	1–1
	10 Oct 1953 v Wales	4–1

716. William Henry Elliott
Outside left
Born   Bradford, 20 March 1925
Clubs   Bradford Park Avenue; Burnley; Sunderland;
        Wisbech Town

Caps	5	Result	Goals
	18 May 1952 v Italy	1–1	
	25 May 1952 v Austria	3–2	
	4 Oct 1952 v N. Ireland	2–2	1
	12 Nov 1952 v Wales	5–2	
	26 Nov 1952 v Belgium	5–0	2

717. Ronald Allen
Centre forward
Born   Fenton, 15 January 1929
Died   9 June 2001
Clubs   Port Vale; West Bromwich Albion; Crystal Palace

Caps	5	Result	Goals
	28 Sep 1952 v Switzerland	3–0	
	3 Apr 1954 v Scotland	4–2	1
	16 May 1954 v Yugoslavia	0–1	
	10 Nov 1954 v Wales	3–2	
	1 Dec 1954 v W. Germany	3–1	1

718. Redfern Froggatt
Inside forward
Born Sheffield, 23 August 1924
Died 26 December 2003
Clubs Sheffield Wednesday; Stalybridge Celtic
Caps 4

		Result	Goals
12 Nov 1952 v Wales		5–2	
26 Nov 1952 v Belgium		5–0	1
18 Apr 1953 v Scotland		2–2	
8 Jun 1953 v USA		6–3	1

⚽ **DID YOU KNOW...?**

Billy Wright never refused to sign autographs. The Wolves player was ambidextrous and often signed two books at a time.

719. Thomas Taylor
Centre forward
Born Barnsley, 29 January 1932
Died 6 February 1958
Clubs Smithies Utd; Barnsley; Manchester Utd
Caps 19

	Result	Goals
17 May 1953 v Argentina	0–0	
24 May 1953 v Chile	2–1	1
31 May 1953 v Uruguay	1–2	1
17 Jun 1954 v Belgium	4–4	
20 Jun 1954 v Switzerland	2–0	
14 Apr 1956 v Scotland	1–1	
9 May 1956 v Brazil	4–2	2
16 May 1956 v Sweden	0–0	
20 May 1956 v Finland	5–1	
26 May 1956 v W. Germany	3–1	
6 Oct 1956 v N. Ireland	1–1	
28 Nov 1956 v Yugoslavia	3–0	2
5 Dec 1956 v Denmark	5–2	3
8 May 1957 v Eire	5–1	3
15 May 1957 v Denmark	4–1	2
19 May 1957 v Eire	1–1	
19 Oct 1957 v Wales	4–0	
6 Nov 1957 v N. Ireland	2–3	
27 Nov 1957 v France	4–0	2

720. John Berry
Outside right
Born Aldershot, 1 June 1926
Died 15 September 1994
Clubs Birmingham City; Manchester Utd
Caps 4

	Result
17 May 1953 v Argentina	0–0
24 May 1953 v Chile	2–1
31 May 1953 v Uruguay	1–2
16 May 1956 v Sweden	0–0

721. Albert Quixall
Inside forward
Born Sheffield, 9 August 1933
Clubs Sheffield Wednesday; Manchester Utd; Oldham Athletic; Stockport County; Altrincham
Caps 5

	Result
10 Oct 1953 v Wales	4–1
21 Oct 1953 v Rest of Europe	4–4
11 Nov 1953 v N. Ireland	3–1
18 May 1955 v Spain	1–1
22 May 1955 v Portugal	1–3

722. Dennis Wilshaw
Centre forward/Inside forward
Born Stoke-on-Trent, 11 March 1926
Died 10 May 2004
Clubs Wolverhampton Wanderers; Walsall; Stoke City

Caps 12	Result	Goals
10 Oct 1953 v Wales	4–1	2
20 Jun 1954 v Switzerland	2–0	1
26 Jun 1954 v Uruguay	2–4	
2 Apr 1955 v Scotland	7–2	4
15 May 1955 v France	0–1	
18 May 1955 v Spain	1–1	
22 May 1955 v Portugal	1–3	
22 Oct 1955 v Wales	1–2	
2 Nov 195 v N. Ireland	3–0	2
20 May 1956 v Finland	5–1	1
26 May 1956 v W. Germany	3–1	
6 Oct 1956 v N. Ireland	1–1	

723. Derek Gilbert Ufton
Centre half/Left half
Born Crayford, 31 May 1928
Clubs Borough Utd; Dulwich Hamlet; Cardiff City; Bexleyheath & Welling; Charlton Athletic
Caps 1

	Result
21 Oct 1953 v Rest of Europe	4–4

724. Stanley Rickaby
Right back
Born Stockton-on-Tees, 12 March 1924
Clubs South Bank; West Bromwich Albion; Poole Town; Weymouth; Newton Abbot Spurs
Caps 1

	Result
11 Nov 1953 v N. Ireland	3–1

725. Ernest Taylor
Inside right
Born Sunderland, 2 September 1925
Died 9 April 1985
Clubs Newcastle Utd; Blackpool; Manchester Utd; Sunderland; Altrincham; Derry City
Caps 1

	Result
25 Nov 1953 v Hungary	3–6

726. George Robb
Outside left
Born Finsbury Park, 1 June 1926
Clubs Finchley; Tottenham Hotspur
Caps 1

	Result
25 Nov 1953 v Hungary	3–6

727. Ronald Staniforth
Right back
Born Newton Heath, 13 April 1924
Died 1988
Clubs Newton Albion; Stockport County; Huddersfield Town; Sheffield Wednesday; Barrow
Caps 8

	Result
3 Apr 1954 v Scotland	4–2
16 May 1954 v Yugoslavia	0–1
23 May 1954 v Hungary	1–7
17 Jun 1954 v Belgium	4–4
20 Jun 1954 v Switzerland	2–0
26 Jun 1954 v Uruguay	2–4
10 Nov 1954 v Wales	3–2
1 Dec 1954 v W. Germany	3–1

728. Roger William Byrne
Left back
Born Manchester, 8 February 1929
Died 6 February 1958
Clubs Manchester Utd
Caps 33

	Result
3 Apr 1954 v Scotland	4–2
16 May 1954 v Yugoslavia	0–1
23 May 1954 v Hungary	1–7
17 Jun 1954 v Belgium	4–4
20 Jun 1954 v Switzerland	2–0
26 Jun 1954 v Uruguay	2–4
2 Oct 1954 v N. Ireland	2–0
10 Nov 1954 v Wales	3–2

1 Dec 1954 v W. Germany	3–1
2 Apr 1955 v Scotland	7–2
15 May 1955 v France	0–1
18 May 1955 v Spain	1–1
22 May 1955 v Portugal	1–3
2 Oct 1955 v Denmark	5–1
22 Oct 1955 v Wales	1–2
2 Nov 1955 v N. Ireland	3–0
30 Nov 1955 v Spain	4–1
14 Apr 1956 v Scotland	1–1
9 May 1956 v Brazil	4–2
16 May 1956 v Sweden	0–0
20 May 1956 v Finland	5–1
26 May 1956 v W. Germany	3–1
6 Oct 1956 v N. Ireland	1–1
14 Nov 1956 v Wales	3–1
28 Nov 1956 v Yugoslavia	3–0
5 Dec 1956 v Denmark	5–2
6 Apr 1957 v Scotland	2–1
8 May 1957 v Eire	5–1
15 May 1957 v Denmark	4–1
19 May 1957 v Eire	1–1
19 Oct 1957 v Wales	4–0
6 Nov 1957 v N. Ireland	2–3
27 Nov 1957 v France	4–0

729. Henry Alfred Clarke
Centre half

Born Woodford Green, 23 February 1923
Died 16 April 2000
Clubs Lovell's Athletic; Tottenham Hotspur; Llanelli

Caps 1	*Result*
3 Apr 1954 v Scotland	4–2

730. John Nicholls
Inside forward

Born Wolverhampton, 3 April 1931
Died 1 April 1995
Clubs Heath Town Wesley; Heath Town Utd; Wolverhampton Wanderers; West Bromwich Albion; Cardiff City; Exeter City; Worcester City; Wellington Town; Oswestry Town; Sankey's FC

Caps 2	*Result*	*Goals*
3 Apr 1954 v Scotland	4–2	1
16 May 1954 v Yugoslavia	0–1	

731. Sidney William Owen
Centre half

Born Birmingham, 29 September 1922
Died 16 January 1999
Clubs Birmingham City; Luton Town

Caps 3	*Result*
16 May 1954 v Yugoslavia	0–1
23 May 1954 v Hungary	1–7
17 Jun 1954 v Belgium	4–4

732. Bedford Jezzard
Centre forward/Inside left

Born Clerkenwell, 19 October 1927
Died 21 May 2005
Clubs Fulham

Caps 2	*Result*
23 May 1954 v Hungary	1–7
2 Nov 1955 v N. Ireland	3–0

733. William Harry McGarry
Right half

Born Stoke-on-Trent, 10 June 1927
Died 15 March 2005
Clubs Port Vale; Huddersfield Town; Bournemouth

Caps 4	*Result*
20 Jun 1954 v Switzerland	2–0
26 Jun 1954 v Uruguay	2–4
2 Oct 1955 v Denmark	5–1
22 Oct 1955 v Wales	1–2

734. Raymond Wood
Goalkeeper

Born Hebburn, 11 June 1931
Died 7 July 2002
Clubs Newcastle Utd; Darlington; Manchester Utd; Huddersfield Town; Bradford City; Barnsley

Caps 3	*Result*
2 Oct 1954 v N. Ireland	2–0
10 Nov 1954 v Wales	3–2
20 May 1956 v Finland	5–1

735. William Anthony Foulkes
Right back/Centre half

Born St Helens, 5 January 1932
Clubs Manchester Utd

Caps 1	*Result*
2 Oct 1954 v N. Ireland	2–0

736. John Wheeler
Right half

Born Crosby, 26 July 1928
Clubs Carlton FC; Tranmere Rovers; Bolton Wanderers; Liverpool; New Brighton

Caps 1	*Result*
2 Oct 1954 v N. Ireland	2–0

737. Raymond John Barlow
Left half

Born Swindon, 17 August 1926
Clubs Garland's FC; West Bromwich Albion; Birmingham City; Stourbridge

Caps 1	*Result*
2 Oct 1954 v N. Ireland	2–0

738. Donald George Revie
Wing half/Inside forward

Born Middlesbrough, 10 July 1927
Died 26 May 1989
Clubs Middlesbrough Swifts; Leicester City; Hull City; Manchester City; Sunderland; Leeds Utd

Caps 6	*Result*	*Goals*
2 Oct 1954 v N. Ireland	2–0	1
2 Apr 1955 v Scotland	7–2	1
15 May 1955 v France	0–1	
2 Oct 1955 v Denmark	5–1	2
22 Oct 1955 v Wales	1–2	
6 Oct 1956 v N. Ireland	1–1	

🌐 DID YOU KNOW...?

In October 1953, Alf Ramsey scored a last-minute penalty to spare England's blushes as they came back from 3–1 down to salvage a 4–4 draw with the Rest of Europe as part of the FA's anniversary celebrations at Wembley.

739. John Norman Haynes
Inside forward

Born Kentish Town, 17 October 1934
Clubs Feltham Utd; Wimbledon; Woodford Town; Fulham; Durban City (South Africa)

Caps 56	*Result*	*Goals*
2 Oct 1954 v N. Ireland	2–0	1
2 Nov 1955 v N. Ireland	3–0	
30 Nov 1955 v Spain	4–1	
14 Apr 1956 v Scotland	1–1	1
9 May 1956 v Brazil	4–2	
16 May 1956 v Sweden	0–0	
20 May 1956 v Finland	5–1	1
26 May 1956 v W. Germany	3–1	1

14 Nov 1956 v Wales	3–1	1
28 Nov 1956 v Yugoslavia	3–0	
8 May 1957 v Eire	5–1	
15 May 1957 v Denmark	4–1	1
19 May 1957 v Eire	1–1	
19 Oct 1957 v Wales	4–0	2
6 Nov 1957 v N. Ireland	2–3	
27 Nov 1957 v France	4–0	
19 Apr 1958 v Scotland	4–0	
7 May 1958 v Portugal	2–1	
11 May 1958 v Yugoslavia	0–5	
18 May 1958 v Soviet Union	1–1	
8 Jun 1958 v Soviet Union	2–2	
11 Jun 1958 v Brazil	0–0	
15 Jun 1958 v Austria	2–2	1
17 Jun 1958 v Soviet Union	0–1	
4 Oct 1958 v N. Ireland	3–3	
22 Oct 1958 v Soviet Union	5–0	3
11 Apr 1959 v Scotland	1–0	
6 May 1959 v Italy	2–2	
13 May 1959 v Brazil	0–2	
17 May 1959 v Peru	1–4	
24 May 1959 v Mexico	1–2	
28 May 1959 v USA	8–1	1
18 Nov 1959 v N. Ireland	2–1	
11 May 1960 v Yugoslavia	3–3	1
15 May 1960 v Spain	0–3	
22 May 1960 v Hungary	0–2	
8 Oct 1960 v N. Ireland	5–2	
19 Oct 1960 v Luxembourg	9–0	1
26 Oct 1960 v Spain	4–2	
23 Nov 1960 v Wales	5–1	1
15 Apr 1961 v Scotland	9–3	2
10 May 1961 v Mexico	8–0	
21 May 1961 v Portugal	1–1	
24 May 1961 v Italy	3–2	
27 May 1961 v Austria	1–3	
14 Oct 1961 v Wales	1–1	
25 Oct 1961 v Portugal	2–0	
22 Nov 1961 v N. Ireland	1–1	
4 Apr 1962 v Austria	3–1	
14 Apr 1962 v Scotland	0–2	
9 May 1962 v Switzerland	3–1	
20 May 1962 v Peru	4–0	
31 May 1962 v Hungary	1–2	
2 Jun 1962 v Argentina	3–1	
7 Jun 1962 v Bulgaria	0–0	
10 Jun 1962 v Brazil	1–3	

740. Brian Pilkington
Outside left
Born Leyland, 12 February 1933
Clubs Leyland Motors; Burnley; Bolton Wanderers; Bury; Barrow; Chorley

Caps 1	*Result*
2 Oct 1954 v N. Ireland	2–0

741. William John Slater
Halfback/Inside left
Born Clitheroe, 29 April 1927
Clubs Blackpool; Brentford; Wolverhampton Wanderers; Northern Nomads

Caps 12	*Result*
10 Nov 1954 v Wales	3–2
1 Dec 1954 v W. Germany	3–1
19 Apr 1958 v Scotland	4–0
7 May 1958 v Portugal	2–1
11 May 1958 v Yugoslavia	0–5
18 May 1958 v Soviet Union	1–1
8 Jun 1958 v Soviet Union	2–2
11 Jun 1958 v Brazil	0–0
15 Jun 1958 v Austria	2–2
17 Jun 1958 v Soviet Union	0–1
22 Oct 1958 v Soviet Union	5–0
18 Apr 1960 v Scotland	1–1

742. Frank Blunstone
Outside left
Born Crewe, 17 October 1934
Clubs Crewe Alexandra; Chelsea

Caps 5	*Result*
10 Nov 1954 v Wales	3–2
2 Apr 1955 v Scotland	7–2
15 May 1955 v France	0–1
22 May 1955 v Portugal	1–3
26 Nov 1956 v Yugoslavia	3–0

743. James Meadows
Right back
Born Bolton, 21 July 1931
Died 16 January 1994
Clubs Manchester City

Caps 1	*Result*
2 Apr 1955 v Scotland	7–2

744. Kenneth Armstrong
Right half
Born Bradford, 3 June 1924
Died 13 June 1984
Clubs Bradford Rovers; Chelsea; Eastern Union (New Zealand); GisBorne City (New Zealand); North Shore Utd (New Zealand)

Caps 1	*Result*
2 Apr 1955 v Scotland	7–2

745. Duncan Edwards
Left half
Born Dudley, 1 October 1936
Died 21 February 1958
Clubs Manchester Utd

Caps 18	*Result*	*Goals*
2 Apr 195 v Scotland	7–2	
15 May 1955 v France	0–1	
18 May 1955 v Spain	1–1	
22 May 1955 v Portugal	1–3	
14 Apr 1956 v Scotland	1–1	
9 May 1956 v Brazil	4–2	
16 May 1956 v Sweden	0–0	
20 May 1956 v Finland	5–1	
26 May 1956 v W. Germany	3–1	1
6 Oct 1956 v N. Ireland	1–1	
5 Dec 1956 v Denmark	5–2	2
6 Apr 1957 v Scotland	2–1	1
8 May 1957 v Eire	5–1	
15 May 1957 v Denmark	4–1	
19 May 1957 v Eire	1–1	
19 Oct 1957 v Wales	4–0	
6 Nov 1957 v N. Ireland	2–3	1
27 Nov 1957 v France	4–0	

746. Richard Peter Sillett
Right back
Born Southampton, 1 February 1933
Died 14 March 1998
Clubs Land FC; Southampton; Chelsea; Guildford City; Ashford Town

Caps 3	*Result*
15 May 1955 v France	0–1
18 May 1955 v Spain	1–1
22 May 1955 v Portugal	1–3

747. Ronald Flowers
Left half
Born Edlington, 28 July 1934
Clubs Doncaster Rovers; Wath Wanderers; Wolverhampton Wanderers; Northampton Town; Telford Utd

Caps 49	*Result*	*Goals*
15 May 1955 v France	0–1	
26 Nov 1958 v Wales	2–2	
11 Apr 1959 v Scotland	1–0	
6 May 1959 v Italy	2–2	

13 May 1959 v Brazil	0–2	
17 May 1959 v Peru	1–4	
24 May 1959 v Mexico	1–2	
28 May 1959 v USA	8–1	2
17 Oct 1959 v Wales	1–1	
28 Oct 1959 v Sweden	2–3	
18 Nov 1959 v N. Ireland	2–1	
19 Apr 1960 v Scotland	1–1	
11 May 1960 v Yugoslavia	3–3	
15 May 1960 v Spain	0–3	
22 May 1960 v Hungary	0–2	
8 Oct 1960 v N. Ireland	5–2	
19 Oct 1960 v Luxembourg	9–0	
26 Oct 1960 v Spain	4–2	
23 Nov 1960 v Wales	5–1	
15 Apr 1961 v Scotland	9–3	
10 May 1961 v Mexico	8–0	1
21 May 1961 v Portugal	1–1	1
24 May 1961 v Italy	3–2	
27 May 1961 v Austria	1–3	
28 Sep 1961 v Luxembourg	4–1	
14 Oct 1961 v Wales	1–1	
25 Oct 1961 v Portugal	2–0	
22 Nov 1961 v N. Ireland	1–1	
4 Apr 1962 v Austria	3–1	1
14 Apr 1962 v Scotland	0–2	
9 May 1962 v Switzerland	3–1	1
20 May 1962 v Peru	4–0	1
31 May 1962 v Hungary	1–2	1
2 Jun 1962 v Argentina	3–1	1
7 Jun 1962 v Bulgaria	0–0	
10 Jun 1962 v Brazil	1–3	
3 Oct 1962 v France	1–1	1
20 Oct 1962 v N. Ireland	3–1	
21 Nov 1962 v Wales	4–0	
27 Feb 1963 v France	2–5	
6 Apr 1963 v Scotland	1–2	
5 Jun 1963 v Switzerland	8–1	
24 May 1964 v Eire	3–1	
27 May 1964 v USA	10–0	
4 Jun 1964 v Portugal	1–1	
18 Nov 1964 v Wales	2–1	
9 Dec 1964 v Holland	1–1	
12 May 1965 v W. Germany	1–0	
29 Jun 1966 v Norway	6–1	

748. Ronald Leslie Baynham

Goalkeeper

Born   Birmingham, 10 June 1929
Clubs Erdington Rovers; Bromford Amateurs; Worcester
       City; Luton Town

Caps	3	Result
	2 Oct 1955 v Denmark	5–1
	2 Nov 1955 v N. Ireland	3–0
	30 Nov 1955 v Spain	4–1

749. Jeffrey James Hall

Right back

Born   Scunthorpe, 7 September 1929
Died   4 April 1959
Clubs Wilsden; Bank Top; Birmingham City

Caps	17	Result
	2 Oct 1955 v Denmark	5–1
	22 Oct 1955 v Wales	1–2
	2 Nov 1955 v N. Ireland	3–0
	30 Nov 1955 v Spain	4–1
	14 Apr 1956 v Scotland	1–1
	9 May 1956 v Brazil	4–2
	16 May 1956 v Sweden	0–0
	20 May 1956 v Finland	5–1
	26 May 1956 v W. Germany	3–1
	6 Oct 1956 v N. Ireland	1–1
	14 Nov 1956 v Wales	3–1
	28 Nov 1956 v Yugoslavia	3–0
	5 Dec 1956 v Denmark	5–2
	6 Apr 1957 v Scotland	2–1

8 May 1957 v Eire	5–1	
15 May 1957 v Denmark	4–1	
19 May 1957 v Eire	1–1	

750. Geoffrey Reginald Bradford

Centre forward/Inside forward

Born   Frenchay, 18 July 1927
Died   31 December 1994
Clubs Soundwell FC; Bristol Rovers

Caps	1	Result	Goals
	2 Oct 1955 v Denmark	5–1	1

751. Ronald Clayton

Right half

Born   Preston, 5 August 1934
Clubs Blackburn Rovers; Morecambe; Great Harwood

Caps	35	Result
	2 Nov 1955 v N. Ireland	3–0
	30 Nov 1955 v Spain	4–1
	9 May 1956 v Brazil	4–2
	16 May 1956 v Sweden	0–0
	20 May 1956 v Finland	5–1
	26 May 1956 v W. Germany	3–1
	6 Oct 1956 v N. Ireland	1–1
	14 Nov 1956 v Wales	3–1
	28 Nov 1956 v Yugoslavia	3–0
	5 Dec 1956 v Denmark	5–2
	6 Apr 1957 v Scotland	2–1
	8 May 1957 v Eire	5–1
	15 May 1957 v Denmark	4–1
	19 May 1957 v Eire	1–1
	19 Oct 1957 v Wales	4–0
	6 Nov 1957 v N. Ireland	2–3
	27 Nov 1957 v France	4–0
	19 Apr 1958 v Scotland	4–0
	7 May 1958 v Portugal	2–1
	11 May 1958 v Yugoslavia	0–5
	17 Jun 1958 v Soviet Union	0–1
	4 Oct 1958 v N. Ireland	3–3
	22 Oct 1958 v Soviet Union	5–0
	26 Nov 1958 v Wales	2–2
	11 Apr 1959 v Scotland	1–0
	6 May 1959 v Italy	2–2
	13 May 1959 v Brazil	0–2
	17 May 1959 v Peru	1–4
	24 May 1959 v Mexico	1–2
	28 May 1959 v USA	8–1
	17 Oct 1959 v Wales	1–1
	28 Oct 1959 v Sweden	2–3
	18 Nov 1959 v N. Ireland	2–1
	19 Apr 1960 v Scotland	1–1
	11 May 1960 v Yugoslavia	3–3

752. William Perry

Outside left

Born   Johannesburg, 10 September 1930
Clubs Johannesburg Rangers; Blackpool; Southport;
       Hereford Utd; South Coast Utd (Australia);
       Holyhead Town

Caps	3	Result	Goals
	2 Nov 1955 v N. Ireland	3–0	
	30 Nov 1955 v Spain	4–1	2
	14 Apr 1956 v Scotland	1–1	

753. Peter John Walter Atyeo

Inside right/Centre forward

Born   Westbury, 7 February 1932
Died   16 June 1993
Clubs Westbury Utd; Portsmouth; Bristol City

Caps	6	Result	Goals
	30 Nov 1955 v Spain	4–1	1
	9 May 1956 v Brazil	4–2	
	16 May 1956 v Sweden	0–0	
	8 May 1957 v Eire	5–1	2
	15 May 1957 v Denmark	4–1	1
	19 May 1957 v Eire	1–1	1

754. Reginald Matthews
Goalkeeper

Born Coventry, 20 December 1932
Died 7 October 2002
Clubs Coventry City; Chelsea; Derby County; Rugby Town

Caps	5	Result
	14 Apr 1956 v Scotland	1–1
	9 May 1956 v Brazil	4–2
	16 May 1956 v Sweden	0–0
	26 May 1956 v W. Germany	3–1
	6 Oct 1956 v N. Ireland	1–1

755. Colin Grainger
Outside left

Born Havercroft, 10 June 1933
Clubs South Elmsall; Wrexham; Sheffield Utd; Sunderland; Leeds Utd; Port Vale; Doncaster Rovers; Macclesfield

Caps	7	Result	Goals
	9 May 1956 v Brazil	4–2	2
	16 May 1956 v Sweden	0–0	
	20 May 1956 v Finland	5–1	
	26 May 1956 v W. Germany	3–1	1
	6 Oct 1956 v N. Ireland	1–1	
	14 Nov 1956 v Wales	3–1	
	6 Apr 1957 v Scotland	2–1	

⚽ **DID YOU KNOW...?**

Colin Grainger scored twice on his England debut in the first England–Brazil match at Wembley on 9 May 1956. England won 4–2 and two penalties that were missed that night might have made it 6–2.

756. Gordon Astall
Outside right

Born Horwich, 22 September 1927
Clubs Plymouth Argyle; Birmingham City; Torquay Utd

Caps	2	Result	Goals
	20 May 1956 v Finland	5–1	1
	26 May 1956 v W. Germany	3–1	1

757. John Brooks
Inside forward

Born Reading, 23 December 1931
Clubs Reading; Tottenham Hotspur; Chelsea; Brentford; Crystal Palace; Stevenage Town; Knebworth FC

Caps	3	Result	Goals
	14 Nov 1956 v Wales	3–1	1
	28 Nov 1956 v Yugoslavia	3–0	1
	5 Dec 1956 v Denmark	5–2	

758. Alan Hodgkinson
Goalkeeper

Born Rotherham, 16 August 1936
Clubs Worksop Town; Sheffield Utd

Caps	5	Result
	6 Apr 1957 v Scotland	2–1
	8 May 1957 v Eire	5–1
	15 May 1957 v Denmark	4–1
	19 May 1957 v Eire	1–1
	23 Nov 1960 v Wales	5–1

759. Derek Tennyson Kevan
Centre forward/Inside forward

Born Ripon, 6 March 1935
Clubs Bradford Park Avenue; West Bromwich Albion; Chelsea; Manchester City; Crystal Palace; Peterborough Utd; Luton Town; Stockport County; Macclesfield Town; Boston Utd; Stourbridge; Ancell's FC

Caps	14	Result	Goals
	6 Apr 1957 v Scotland	2–1	1
	19 Oct 1957 v Wales	4–0	
	6 Nov 1957 v N. Ireland	2–3	
	19 Apr 1958 v Scotland	4–0	2
	7 May 1958 v Portugal	2–1	
	1 May 1958 v Yugoslavia	0–5	
	18 May 1958 v Soviet Union	1–1	1
	8 Jun 1958 v Soviet Union	2–2	1
	11 Jun 1958 v Brazil	0–0	
	15 Jun 1958 v Austria	2–2	1
	17 Jun 1958 v Soviet Union	0–1	
	24 May 1959 v Mexico	1–2	1
	28 May 1959 v USA	8–1	1
	10 May 1961 v Mexico	8–0	

760. David Pegg
Outside left

Born Doncaster, 20 September 1935
Died 6 February 1958
Clubs Manchester Utd

Caps	1	Result
	19 May 1957 v Eire	1–1

761. Edward Hopkinson
Goalkeeper

Born Wheatley Hill, 19 October 1935
Died 25 April 2004
Clubs Oldham Athletic; Bolton Wanderers

Caps	14	Result
	19 Oct 1957 v Wales	4–0
	6 Nov 1957 v N. Ireland	2–3
	27 Nov 1957 v France	4–0
	19 Apr 1958 v Scotland	4–0
	7 May 1958 v Portugal	2–1
	11 May 1958 v Yugoslavia	0–5
	11 Apr 1959 v Scotland	1–0
	6 May 1959 v Italy	2–2
	13 May 1959 v Brazil	0–2
	17 May 1959 v Peru	1–4
	24 May 1959 v Mexico	1–2
	28 May 1959 v USA	8–1
	17 Oct 1959 v Wales	1–1
	28 Oct 1959 v Sweden	2–3

762. Donald Howe
Right back

Born Wolverhampton, 12 October 1935
Clubs West Bromwich Albion; Arsenal

Caps	23	Result
	19 Oct 1957 v Wales	4–0
	6 Nov 1957 v N. Ireland	2–3
	27 Nov 1957 v France	4–0
	19 Apr 1958 v Scotland	4–0
	7 May 1958 v Portugal	2–1
	11 May 1958 v Yugoslavia	0–5
	18 May 1958 v Soviet Union	1–1
	8 Jun 1958 v Soviet Union	2–2
	11 Jun 1958 v Brazil	0–0
	15 Jun 1958 v Austria	2–2
	17 Jun 1958 v Soviet Union	0–1
	4 Oct 1958 v N. Ireland	3–3
	22 Oct 1958 v Soviet Union	5–0
	26 Nov 1958 v Wales	2–2
	11 Apr 1959 v Scotland	1–0
	6 May 1959 v Italy	2–2
	13 May 1959 v Brazil	0–2
	17 May 1959 v Peru	1–4
	24 May 1959 v Mexico	1–2
	28 May 1959 v USA	8–1
	17 Oct 1959 v Wales	1–1
	28 Oct 1959 v Sweden	2–3
	18 Nov 1959 v N. Ireland	2–1

763. Bryan Douglas
Outside right/Inside forward

Born   Blackburn, 27 May 1934
Clubs   Blackburn Rovers; Great Harwood
Caps   36

	Result	Goals
19 Oct 1957 v Wales	4–0	
6 Nov 1957 v N. Ireland	2–3	
27 Nov 1957 v France	4–0	
19 Apr 1958 v Scotland	4–0	1
7 May 1958 v Portugal	2–1	
11 May 1958 v Yugoslavia	0–5	
18 May 1958 v Soviet Union	1–1	
8 Jun 1958 v Soviet Union	2–2	
11 Jun 1958 v Brazil	0–0	
15 Jun 1958 v Austria	2–2	
22 Oct 1958 v Soviet Union	5–0	
11 Apr 1959 v Scotland	1–0	
11 May 1960 v Yugoslavia	3–3	1
22 May 1960 v Hungary	0–2	
8 Oct 1960 v N. Ireland	5–2	1
19 Oct 1960 v Luxembourg	9–0	
26 Oct 1960 v Spain	4–2	1
23 Nov 1960 v Wales	5–1	
15 Apr 1961 v Scotland	9–3	1
10 May 1961 v Mexico	8–0	2
21 May 1961 v Portugal	1–1	
24 May 1961 v Italy	3–2	
27 May 1961 v Austria	1–3	
28 Sep 1961 v Luxembourg	4–1	
14 Oct 1961 v Wales	1–1	1
25 Oct 1961 v Portugal	2–0	
22 Nov 1961 v N. Ireland	1–1	
14 Apr 1962 v Scotland	0–2	
20 May 1962 v Peru	4–0	
31 May 1962 v Hungary	1–2	
2 Jun 1962 v Argentina	3–1	
7 Jun 1962 v Bulgaria	0–0	
10 Jun 1962 v Brazil	1–3	
6 Apr 1963 v Scotland	1–2	1
8 May 1963 v Brazil	1–1	1
5 Jun 1963 v Switzerland	8–1	1

764. Alan A'Court
Outside left

Born   Rainhill, 30 September 1934
Clubs   Prescot Celtic; Prescot Cables; Liverpool; Tranmere
Rovers; Norwich City
Caps   5

	Result	Goals
6 Nov 1957 v N. Ireland	2–3	1
11 Jun 1958 v Brazil	0–0	
15 Jun 1958 v Austria	2–2	
17 Jun 1958 v Soviet Union	0–1	
26 Nov 1958 v Wales	2–2	

765. Robert William Robson
Right half

Born   Langley Park, 18 February 1933
Clubs   Fulham; West Bromwich Albion; Vancouver Royals
(Canada)
Caps   20

	Result	Goals
27 Nov 1957 v France	4–0	2
18 May 1958 v Soviet Union	1–1	
8 Jun 1958 v Soviet Union	2–2	
11 Jun 1958 v Brazil	0–0	
15 Jun 1958 v Austria	2–2	
15 May 1960 v Spain	0–3	
22 May 1960 v Hungary	0–2	
8 Oct 1960 v N. Ireland	5–2	
19 Oct 1960 v Luxembourg	9–0	
26 Oct 1960 v Spain	4–2	
23 Nov 1960 v Wales	5–1	
15 Apr 1961 v Scotland	9–3	1
10 May 1961 v Mexico	8–1	1
21 May 1961 v Portugal	1–1	
24 May 1961 v Italy	3–2	

28 Sep 1961 v Luxembourg	4–1	
14 Oct 1961 v Wales	1–1	
25 Oct 1961 v Portugal	2–0	
22 Nov 1961 v N. Ireland	1–1	
9 May 1962 v Switzerland	3–1	

766. Ernest James Langley
Left back

Born   Kilburn, 7 February 1929
Clubs   Yiewsley; Hounslow Town; Uxbridge; Hayes;
Ruislip; Guildford City; Leeds Utd; Brighton & Hove
Albion; Fulham; Queen's Park Rangers; Hillingdon
Borough
Caps   3

	Result
19 Apr 1958 v Scotland	4–0
7 May 1958 v Portugal	2–1
11 May 1958 v Yugoslavia	0–5

767. Robert Charlton
Inside forward/Outside left

Born   Ashington, 11 October 1937
Clubs   Manchester Utd; Preston North End
Caps   106

	Result	Goals
19 Apr 1958 v Scotland	4–0	1
7 May 1958 v Portugal	2–1	2
11 May 1958 v Yugoslavia	0–5	
4 Oct 1958 v N. Ireland	3–3	2
22 Oct 1958 v Soviet Union	5–0	1
26 Nov 1958 v Wales	2–2	
11 Apr 1959 v Scotland	1–0	1
6 May 1959 v Italy	2–2	1
13 May 1959 v Brazil	0–2	
17 May 1959 v Peru	1–4	
24 May 1959 v Mexico	1–2	
28 May 1959 v USA	8–1	3
17 Oct 1959 v Wales	1–1	
28 Oct 1959 v Sweden	2–3	1
19 Apr 1960 v Scotland	1–1	1
11 May 1960 v Yugoslavia	3–3	
15 May 1960 v Spain	0–3	
22 May 1960 v Hungary	0–2	
8 Oct 1960 v N. Ireland	5–2	1
19 Oct 1960 v Luxembourg	9–0	3
26 Oct 1960 v Spain	4–2	
23 Nov 1960 v Wales	5–1	1
15 Apr 1961 v Scotland	9–3	
10 May 1961 v Mexico	8–0	3
21 May 1961 v Portugal	1–1	
24 May 1961 v Italy	3–2	
27 May 1961 v Austria	1–3	
28 Sep 1961 v Luxembourg	4–1	2
14 Oct 1961 v Wales	1–1	
25 Oct 1961 v Portugal	2–0	
22 Nov 1961 v N. Ireland	1–1	1
4 Apr 1962 v Austria	3–1	
14 Apr 1962 v Scotland	0–2	
9 May 1962 v Switzerland	3–1	
20 May 1962 v Peru	4–0	
31 May 1962 v Hungary	1–2	
2 Jun 1962 v Argentina	3–1	1
7 Jun 1962 v Bulgaria	0–0	
10 Jun 1962 v Brazil	1–3	
27 Feb 1963 v France	2–5	
6 Apr 1963 v Scotland	1–2	
8 May 1963 v Brazil	1–1	
20 May 1963 v Czechoslovakia	4–2	1
2 Jun 1963 v E. Germany	2–1	1
5 Jun 1963 v Switzerland	8–1	3
12 Oct 1963 v Wales	4–0	1
23 Oct 1963 v Rest of World	2–1	
20 Nov 1963 v N. Ireland	8–3	
11 Apr 1964 v Scotland	0–1	
6 May 1964 v Uruguay	2–1	
17 May 1964 v Portugal	4–3	1
24 May 1964 v Eire	3–1	

27 May 1964 v USA	10–0	1
30 May 1964 v Brazil	1–5	
6 Jun 1964 v Argentina	0–1	
3 Oct 1964 v N. Ireland	4–3	
9 Dec 1964 v Holland	1–1	
10 Apr 1965 v Scotland	2–2	1
2 Oct 1965 v Wales	0–0	
20 Oct 1965 v Austria	2–3	1
10 Nov 1965 v N. Ireland	2–1	
8 Dec 1965 v Spain	2–0	
23 Feb 1966 v W. Germany	1–0	
2 Apr 1966 v Scotland	4–3	1
4 May 1966 v Yugoslavia	2–0	1
26 Jun 1966 v Finland	3–0	
29 Jun 1966 v Norway	6–1	
5 Jul 1966 v Poland	1–0	
11 Jul 1966 v Uruguay	0–0	
16 Jul 1966 v Mexico	2–0	1
20 Jul 1966 v France	2–0	
23 Jul 1966 v Argentina	1–0	
26 Jul 1966 v Portugal	2–1	2
30 Jul 1966 v W. Germany	4–2	
22 Oct 1966 v N. Ireland	2–0	
2 Nov 1966 v Czechoslovakia	0–0	
16 Nov 1966 v Wales	5–1	1
15 Apr 1967 v Scotland	2–3	
21 Oct 1967 v Wales	3–0	1
22 Nov 1967 v N. Ireland	2–0	1
6 Dec 1967 v Soviet Union	2–2	
24 Feb 1968 v Scotland	1–1	
3 Apr 1968 v Spain	1–0	1
8 May 1968 v Spain	2–1	
22 May 1968 v Sweden	3–1	1
5 Jun 1968 v Yugoslavia	0–1	
8 Jun 1968 v Soviet Union	2–0	1
6 Nov 1968 v Romania	0–0	
11 Dec 1968 v Bulgaria	1–1	
15 Jan 1969 v Romania	1–1	
3 May 1969 v N. Ireland	3–1	
7 May 1969 v Wales	2–1	1
10 May 1969 v Scotland	4–1	
1 Jun 1969 v Mexico	0–0	
12 Jun 1969 v Brazil	1–2	
5 Nov 1969 v Holland	1–0	
10 Dec 1969 v Portugal	1–0	
14 Jan 1970 v Holland	0–0	
18 Apr 1970 v Wales	1–1	
21 Apr 1970 v N. Ireland	3–1	1
20 May 1970 v Colombia	4–0	1
24 May 1970 v Ecuador	2–0	
2 Jun 1970 v Romania	1–0	
7 Jun 1970 v Brazil	0–1	
11 Jun 1970 v Czechoslovakia	1–0	
14 Jun 1970 v W. Germany	2–3	

⚽ **DID YOU KNOW...?**

When Bobby Charlton scored a cracking goal in England's World Cup 1966 semi-final defeat of Portugal, several Portuguese players shook his hand to congratulate him on the strike.

768. Colin Agnew McDonald
Goalkeeper
Born Summerseat, 15 October 1930
Clubs Burnley; Headington Utd

Caps	8	Result
	18 May 1958 v Soviet Union	1–1
	8 Jun 1958 v Soviet Union	2–2

11 Jun 1958 v Brazil	0–0	
15 Jun 1958 v Austria	2–2	
17 Jun 1958 v Soviet Union	0–1	
4 Oct 1958 v N. Ireland	3–3	
22 Oct 1958 v Soviet Union	5–0	
26 Nov 1958 v Wales	2–2	

769. Thomas Banks
Left back
Born Farnworth, 10 November 1929
Clubs Prestwich's XI; Bolton Wanderers; Bangor City

Caps	6	Result
	18 May 1958 v Soviet Union	1–1
	8 Jun 1958 v Soviet Union	2–2
	11 Jun 1958 v Brazil	0–0
	15 Jun 1958 v Austria	2–2
	17 Jun 1958 v Soviet Union	0–1
	4 Oct 1958 v N. Ireland	3–3

770. Edwin Clamp
Wing half
Born Coalville, 14 September 1934
Died 11 December 1995
Clubs Wolverhampton Wanderers; Arsenal; Stoke City; Peterborough Utd; Worcester City; Lower Gornal FC

Caps	4	Result
	18 May 1958 v Soviet Union	1–1
	8 Jun 1958 v Soviet Union	2–2
	11 Jun 1958 v Brazil	0–0
	15 Jun 1958 v Austria	2–2

771. Peter Brabrook
Outside right
Born Greenwich, 8 November 1937
Clubs Chelsea; West Ham Utd; Orient; Romford

Caps	3	Result
	17 Jun 1958 v Soviet Union	0–1
	4 Oct 1958 v N. Ireland	3–3
	15 May 1960 v Spain	0–3

772. Peter Frank Broadbent
Inside forward
Born Elvington, 15 May 1933
Clubs Dover; Brentford; Wolverhampton Wanderers; Shrewsbury Town; Aston Villa; Stockport County; Bromsgrove Rovers

Caps	7	Result	Goals
	17 Jun 1958 v Soviet Union	0–1	
	4 Oct 1958 v N. Ireland	3–3	
	26 Nov 1958 v Wales	2–2	2
	11 Apr 1959 v Scotland	1–0	
	6 May 1959 v Italy	2–2	
	13 May 1959 v Brazil	0–2	
	19 Apr 1960 v Scotland	1–1	

773. Wilfred McGuinness
Left half
Born Manchester, 25 October 1937
Clubs Manchester Utd

Caps	2	Result
	4 Oct 1958 v N. Ireland	3–3
	24 May 1959 v Mexico	1–2

774. Graham Shaw
Left back
Born Sheffield, 9 July 1934
Clubs Oaks Fold; Sheffield Utd; Doncaster Rovers; Scarborough

Caps	5	Result
	22 Oct 1958 v Soviet Union	5–0
	26 Nov 1958 v Wales	2–2
	11 Apr 1959 v Scotland	1–0
	6 May 1959 v Italy	2–2
	21 Nov 1962 v Wales	4–0

DID YOU KNOW...?

On the occasion of his 100th international appearance at Wembley on 21 April 1970, Bobby Charlton captained England and scored a goal in the 3–1 victory over Northern Ireland.

775. Daniel Robert Clapton
Outside right
Born Aldgate, 22 July 1934
Died 20 June 1986
Clubs Leytonstone; Arsenal; Luton Town; Corinthians FC Sydney (Australia)

Caps	1	Result
	26 Nov 1958 v Wales	2–2

776. Albert Douglas Holden
Winger
Born Manchester, 28 September 1930
Clubs Bolton Wanderers; Preston North End; Hakoah (Australia)

Caps	5	Result
	11 Apr 1959 v Scotland	1–0
	6 May 1959 v Italy	2–2
	13 May 1959 v Brazil	0–2
	17 May 1959 v Peru	1–4
	24 May 1959 v Mexico	1–2

777. James Christopher Armfield
Right back
Born Denton, 21 September 1935
Clubs Blackpool

Caps	43	Result
	13 May 1950 v Brazil	0–2
	17 May 1959 v Peru	1–4
	24 May 1959 v Mexico	1–2
	28 May 1959 v USA	8–1
	19 Apr 1960 v Scotland	1–1
	11 May 1960 v Yugoslavia	3–3
	15 May 1960 v Spain	0–3
	22 May 1960 v Hungary	0–2
	8 Oct 1960 v N. Ireland	5–2
	19 Oct 1960 v Luxembourg	9–0
	26 Oct 1960 v Spain	4–2
	23 Nov 1960 v Wales	5–1
	15 Apr 1961 v Scotland	9–3
	10 May 1961 v Mexico	8–0
	21 May 1961 v Portugal	1–1
	24 May 1961 v Italy	3–2
	27 May 1961 v Austria	1–3
	28 Sep 1961 v Luxembourg	4–1
	14 Oct 1961 v Wales	1–1
	25 Oct 1961 v Portugal	2–0
	22 Nov 1961 v N. Ireland	1–1
	4 Apr 1962 v Austria	3–1
	14 Apr 1962 v Scotland	0–2
	9 May 1962 v Switzerland	3–1
	20 May 1962 v Peru	4–0
	31 May 1962 v Hungary	1–2
	2 Jun 1962 v Argentina	3–1
	7 Jun 1962 v Bulgaria	0–0
	10 Jun 1962 v Brazil	1–3
	3 Oct 1962 v France	1–1
	20 Oct 1962 v N. Ireland	3–1
	21 Nov 1962 v Wales	4–0
	27 Feb 1963 v France	2–5
	6 Apr 1963 v Scotland	1–2
	8 May 1963 v Brazil	1–1
	2 Jun 1963 v E. Germany	2–1
	5 Jun 1963 v Switzerland	8–1
	12 Oct 1963 v Wales	4–0
	23 Oct 1963 v Rest of World	2–1
	20 Nov 1963 v N. Ireland	8–3

11 Apr 1964 v Scotland	0–1	
4 May 1966 v Yugoslavia	2–0	
26 Jun 1966 v Finland	3–0	

778. Norman Victor Deeley
Winger
Born Wednesbury, 30 November 1933
Clubs Wolverhampton Wanderers; Leyton Orient; Worcester City; Bromsgrove Rovers; Darlaston

Caps	2	Result
	13 May 1959 v Brazil	0–2
	17 May 1959 v Peru	1–4

779. James Peter Greaves
Inside forward
Born Poplar, 20 February 1940
Clubs Chelsea; AC Milan; Tottenham Hotspur; West Ham Utd; Chelmsford City; Barnet

Caps	57	Result	Goals
	17 May 1959 v Peru	1–4	1
	24 May 1959 v Mexico	1–2	
	28 May 1959 v USA	8–1	
	17 Oct 1959 v Wales	1–1	1
	28 Oct 1959 v Sweden	2–3	
	11 May 1960 v Yugoslavia	3–3	1
	15 May 1960 v Spain	0–3	
	8 Oct 1960 v N. Ireland	5–2	2
	19 Oct 1960 v Luxembourg	9–0	3
	26 Oct 1960 v Spain	4–2	1
	23 Nov 1960 v Wales	5–1	2
	15 Apr 1961 v Scotland	9–3	3
	21 May 1961 v Portugal	1–1	
	24 May 1961 v Italy	3–2	1
	27 May 1961 v Austria	1–3	1
	14 Apr 1962 v Scotland	0–2	
	9 May 1962 v Switzerland	3–1	
	20 May 1962 v Peru	4–0	3
	31 May 1962 v Hungary	1–2	
	2 Jun 1962 v Argentina	3–1	1
	7 Jun 1962 v Bulgaria	0–0	
	10 Jun 1962 v Brazil	1–3	
	3 Oct 1962 v France	1–1	
	20 Oct 1962 v N. Ireland	3–1	1
	21 Nov 1962 v Wales	4–0	1
	27 Feb 1963 v France	2–5	
	6 Apr 1963 v Scotland	1–2	
	8 May 1963 v Brazil	1–1	
	20 May 1963 v Czechoslovakia	4–2	2
	5 Jun 1963 v Switzerland	8–1	
	12 Oct 1963 v Wales	4–0	1
	23 Oct 1963 v Rest of World	2–1	1
	20 Nov 1963 v N. Ireland	8–3	4
	6 May 1964 v Uruguay	2–1	
	17 May 1964 v Portugal	4–3	
	24 May 1964 v Eire	3–1	1
	30 May 1964 v Brazil	1–5	1
	4 Jun 1964 v Portugal	1–1	
	6 Jun 1964 v Argentina	0–1	
	3 Oct 1964 v N. Ireland	4–3	3
	21 Oct 1964 v Belgium	2–2	
	9 Dec 1964 v Holland	1–1	1
	10 Apr 1965 v Scotland	2–2	1
	5 May 1965 v Hungary	1–0	1
	9 May 1965 v Yugoslavia	1–1	
	2 Oct 1965 v Wales	0–0	
	20 Oct 1965 v Austria	2–3	
	4 May 1966 v Yugoslavia	2–0	1
	29 Jun 1966 v Norway	6–1	4
	3 Jul 1966 v Denmark	2–0	
	5 Jul 1966 v Poland	1–0	
	11 Jul 1966 v Uruguay	0–0	
	16 Jul 1966 v Mexico	2–0	
	20 Jul 1966 v France	2–0	
	15 Apr 1967 v Scotland	2–3	
	24 May 1967 v Spain	2–0	1
	27 May 1967 v Austria	1–0	

780. Warren Bradley
Outside right

Born Hyde, 20 June 1933
Clubs Durham City; Bolton Wanderers; Bishop Auckland; Manchester Utd; Bury; Northwich Victoria; Macclesfield; Bangor City

Caps	3	Result	Goals
	6 May 1959 v Italy	2–2	1
	24 May 1959 v Mexico	1–2	
	28 May 1959 v USA	8–1	1

781. Anthony Allen
Left back

Born Stoke-on-Trent, 27 November 1939
Clubs Stoke City; Bury; Hellenic FC (South Africa); Stafford Rangers

Caps	3	Result
	17 Oct 1959 v Wales	1–1
	28 Oct 1959 v Sweden	2–3
	18 Nov 1959 v N. Ireland	2–1

782. Trevor Smith
Centre half

Born Quarry Bank, 13 April 1936
Died 9 August 2003
Clubs Birmingham City; Walsall

Caps	2	Result
	17 Oct 1959 v Wales	1–1
	28 Oct 1959 v Sweden	2–3

783. John Michael Connelly
Winger

Born St Helens, 18 July 1938
Clubs St Helens Town; Burnley; Manchester Utd; Blackburn Rovers; Bury

Caps	20	Result	Goals
	17 Oct 1959 v Wales	1–1	
	28 Oct 1959 v Sweden	2–3	1
	18 Nov 1959 v N. Ireland	2–1	
	19 Apr 1960 v Scotland	1–1	
	14 Oct 1961 v Wales	1–1	
	25 Oct 1961 v Portugal	2–0	1
	4 Apr 1962 v Austria	3–1	
	9 May 1962 v Switzerland	3–1	1
	21 Nov 1962 v Wales	4–0	1
	27 Feb 1963 v France	2–5	
	5 May 1965 v Hungary	1–0	
	9 May 1965 v Yugoslavia	1–1	
	16 May 1965 v Sweden	2–1	1
	2 Oct 1965 v Wales	0–0	
	20 Oct 1965 v Austria	2–3	1
	10 Nov 1965 v N. Ireland	2–1	
	2 Apr 1966 v Scotland	4–3	
	29 Jun 1966 v Norway	6–1	1
	3 Jul 1966 v Denmark	2–0	
	11 Jul 1966 v Uruguay	0–0	

784. Brian Howard Clough
Centre forward

Born Middlesbrough, 21 March 1935
Died 20 September 2004
Clubs Great Broughton; Middlesbrough; Sunderland

Caps	2	Result
	17 Oct 1959 v Wales	1–1
	28 Oct 1959 v Sweden	2–3

785. Edwin Holliday
Outside left

Born Leeds 7 June 1939
Clubs Middlesbrough; Sheffield Wednesday; Hereford Utd; Workington; Peterborough Utd

Caps	3	Result
	17 Oct 1959 v Wales	1–1
	28 Oct 1959 v Sweden	2–3
	18 Nov 1959 v N. Ireland	2–1

786. Ronald Springett
Goalkeeper

Born Fulham, 22 July 1935
Clubs Victoria Utd; Queen's Park Rangers; Sheffield Wednesday; Ashford Town

Caps	33	Result
	18 Nov 1959 v N. Ireland	2–1
	19 Apr 1960 v Scotland	1–1
	11 May 1960 v Yugoslavia	3–3
	15 May 1960 v Spain	0–3
	22 May 1960 v Hungary	0–2
	8 Oct 1960 v N. Ireland	5–2
	19 Oct 1960 v Luxembourg	9–0
	26 Oct 1960 v Spain	4–2
	15 Apr 1961 v Scotland	9–3
	10 May 1961 v Mexico	8–0
	21 May 1961 v Portugal	1–1
	24 May 1961 v Italy	3–2
	27 May 1961 v Austria	1–3
	28 Sep 1961 v Luxembourg	4–1
	14 Oct 1961 v Wales	1–1
	25 Oct 1961 v Portugal	2–0
	22 Nov 1961 v N. Ireland	1–1
	4 Apr 1962 v Austria	3–1
	14 Apr 1962 v Scotland	0–2
	9 May 1962 v Switzerland	3–1
	20 May 1962 v Peru	4–0
	31 May 1962 v Hungary	1–2
	2 Jun 1962 v Argentina	3–1
	7 Jun 1962 v Bulgaria	0–0
	10 Jun 1962 v Brazil	1–3
	3 Oct 1962 v France	1–1
	20 Oct 1962 v N. Ireland	3–1
	21 Nov 1962 v Wales	4–0
	27 Feb 1963 v France	2–5
	5 Jun 1963 v Switzerland	8–1
	2 Oct 1965 v Wales	0–0
	20 Oct 1965 v Austria	2–3
	29 Jun 1966 v Norway	6–1

787. Kenneth Brown
Centre half

Born Forest Gate, 16 February 1934
Clubs Neville Utd; West Ham Utd; Torquay Utd; Hereford Utd

Caps	1	Result
	18 Nov 1959 v N. Ireland	2–1

788. Joseph Henry Baker
Centre forward

Born Liverpool 17 July 1940
Died 6 October 2003
Clubs Edinburgh Thistle; Coltness Utd; Armadale Thistle; Hibernian; AC Torino (Italy); Arsenal; Nottingham Forest; Sunderland; Raith Rovers

Caps	8	Result	Goals
	18 Nov 1959 v N. Ireland	2–1	1
	19 Apr 1960 v Scotland	1–1	
	11 May 1960 v Yugoslavia	3–3	
	15 May 1960 v Spain	0–3	
	22 May 1960 v Hungary	0–2	
	10 Nov 1965 v N. Ireland	2–1	1
	8 Dec 1965 v Spain	2–0	1
	5 Jan 1966 v Poland	1–1	

⚽ **DID YOU KNOW...?**

Joe Baker of Hibernian became the first player of a Scottish club to represent England. He scored on his debut, on 18 November 1959, when England beat Northern Ireland 2–1.

789. Raymond Alan Parry

Inside left/Outside left

Born Derby, 19 January 1936
Died 23 May 2003
Clubs Bolton Wanderers; Blackpool; Bury

Caps	2	Result	Goals
	18 Nov 1959 v N. Ireland	2–1	1
	19 Apr 1960 v Scotland	1–1	

790. Ramon Wilson

Left back

Born Shirebrook, 17 December 1934
Clubs Huddersfield Town; Everton; Oldham Athletic; Bradford City

Caps	63	Result
	19 Apr 1960 v Scotland	1–1
	11 May 1960 v Yugoslavia	3–3
	15 May 1960 v Spain	0–3
	22 May 1960 v Hungary	0–2
	14 Oct 1961 v Wales	1–1
	25 Oct 1961 v Portugal	2–0
	22 Nov 1961 v N. Ireland	1–1
	4 Apr 1962 v Austria	3–1
	14 Apr 1962 v Scotland	0–2
	9 May 1962 v Switzerland	3–1
	20 May 1962 v Peru	4–0
	31 May 1962 v Hungary	1–2
	2 Jun 1962 v Argentina	3–1
	7 Jun 1962 v Bulgaria	0–0
	10 Jun 1962 v Brazil	1–3
	3 Oct 1962 v France	1–1
	20 Oct 1962 v N. Ireland	3–1
	8 May 1963 v Brazil	1–1
	20 May 1963 v Czechoslovakia	4–2
	2 Jun 1963 v E. Germany	2–1
	5 Jun 1963 v Switzerland	8–1
	12 Oct 1963 v Wales	4–0
	23 Oct 1963 v Rest of World	2–1
	11 Apr 1964 v Scotland	0–1
	6 May 1964 v Uruguay	2–1
	17 May 1964 v Portugal	4–3
	24 May 1964 v Eire	3–1
	30 May 1964 v Brazil	1–5
	4 Jun 1964 v Portugal	1–1
	6 Jun 1964 v Argentina	0–1
	10 Apr 1965 v Scotland	2–2
	5 May 1965 v Hungary	1–0
	9 May 1965 v Yugoslavia	1–1
	12 May 1965 v W. Germany	1–0
	16 May 1965 v Sweden	2–1
	2 Oct 1965 v Wales	0–0
	20 Oct 1965 v Austria	2–3
	10 Nov 1965 v N. Ireland	2–1
	8 Dec 1965 v Spain	2–0
	5 Jan 1966 v Poland	1–1
	23 Feb 1966 v W. Germany	1–0
	4 May 1966 v Yugoslavia	2–0
	26 Jun 1966 v Finland	3–0
	3 Jul 1966 v Denmark	2–0
	5 Jul 1966 v Poland	1–0
	11 Jul 1966 v Uruguay	0–0
	16 Jul 1966 v Mexico	2–0
	20 Jul 1966 v France	2–0
	23 Jul 1966 v Argentina	1–0
	26 Jul 1966 v Portugal	2–1
	30 Jul 1966 v W. Germany	4–2
	22 Oct 1966 v N. Ireland	2–0
	2 Nov 1966 v Czechoslovakia	0–0
	16 Nov 1966 v Wales	5–1
	15 Apr 1967 v Scotland	2–3
	27 May 1967 v Austria	1–0
	22 Nov 1967 v N. Ireland	2–0
	6 Dec 1967 v Soviet Union	2–2
	24 Feb 1968 v Scotland	1–1
	3 Apr 1968 v Spain	1–0
	8 May 1968 v Spain	2–1
	5 Jun 1968 v Yugoslavia	0–1
	8 Jun 1968 v Soviet Union	2–0

791. Peter Swan

Centre half

Born South Elmsall, 8 October 1936
Clubs Sheffield Wednesday; Bury; Matlock Town

Caps	19	Result
	11 May 1960 v Yugoslavia	3–3
	15 May 1960 v Spain	0–3
	22 May 1960 v Hungary	0–2
	8 Oct 1960 v N. Ireland	5–2
	19 Oct 1960 v Luxembourg	9–0
	26 Oct 1960 v Spain	4–2
	23 Nov 1960 v Wales	5–1
	15 Apr 1961 v Scotland	9–3
	10 May 1961 v Mexico	8–0
	21 May 1961 v Portugal	1–1
	24 May 1961 v Italy	3–2
	27 May 1961 v Austria	1–3
	28 Sep 1961 v Luxembourg	4–1
	14 Oct 1961 v Wales	1–1
	25 Oct 1961 v Portugal	2–0
	22 Nov 1961 v N. Ireland	1–1
	4 Apr 1962 v Austria	3–1
	14 Apr 1962 v Austria	0–2
	9 May 1962 v Switzerland	3–1

792. Dennis Sydney Viollet

Centre forward/Inside forward

Born Manchester, 20 September 1933
Died 6 March 1999
Clubs Manchester Utd; Stoke City; Baltimore Bays (USA); Witton Albion; Linfield

Caps	2	Result	Goals
	22 May 1960 v Hungary	0–2	
	28 Sep 1961 v Luxembourg	4–1	1

793. Michael McNeil

Left back

Born Middlesbrough, 7 February 1940
Clubs Cargo Fleet FC; Middlesbrough; Ipswich Town; Cambridge City

Caps	9	Result
	8 Oct 1960 v N. Ireland	5–2
	19 Oct 1960 v Luxembourg	9–0
	26 Oct 1960 v Spain	4–2
	23 Nov 1960 v Wales	5–1
	15 Apr 1961 v Scotland	9–3
	10 May 1961 v Mexico	8–0
	21 May 1961 v Portugal	1–1
	24 May 1961 v Italy	3–2
	28 Sep 1961 v Luxembourg	4–1

794. Robert Alfred Smith

Centre forward

Born Lingdale, 22 February 1933
Clubs Redcar Utd; Tudor Rose; Chelsea; Tottenham Hotspur; Brighton & Hove Albion; Hastings Utd; Banbury Utd

Caps	15	Result	Goals
	8 Oct 1960 v N. Ireland	5–2	1
	19 Oct 1960 v Luxembourg	9–0	2
	26 Oct 1960 v Spain	4–2	2
	23 Nov 1960 v Wales	5–1	1
	15 Apr 1961 v Scotland	9–3	2
	21 May 1961 v Portugal	1–1	
	14 Apr 1962 v Scotland	0–2	
	27 Feb 1963 v France	2–5	1
	6 Apr 1963 v Scotland	1–2	
	8 May 1963 v Brazil	1–2	
	20 May 1963 v Czechoslovakia	4–2	1
	2 Jun 1963 v E. Germany	2–1	
	12 Oct 1963 v Wales	4–0	2
	23 Oct 1963 v Rest of World	2–1	
	20 Nov 1963 v N. Ireland	8–3	1

795. Gerald Archibald Hitchens
Centre forward

Born	Rawnsley, 8 October 1934	
Died	13 April 1983	
Clubs	Highley Miners Welfare; Kidderminster Harriers; Cardiff City; Aston Villa; Inter Milan (Italy); Torino (Italy); Atalanta (Italy); Cagliari (Italy); Worcester City; Merthyr Tydfil	

Caps	7	Result	Goals
	10 May 1961 v Mexico	8–0	1
	24 May 1961 v Italy	3–2	2
	27 May 1961 v Austria	1–3	
	9 May 1962 v Switzerland	3–1	1
	20 May 1962 v Peru	4–0	
	31 May 1962 v Hungary	1–2	
	10 Jun 1962 v Brazil	1–3	1

796. John Angus
Right back

Born	Amble, 2 September 1938	
Clubs	Burnley	

Caps	1	Result
	27 May 1961 v Austria	1–3

797. Brian George Miller
Left half

Born	Hapton, 19 January 1937	
Clubs	Burnley	

Caps	1	Result
	27 May 1961 v Austria	1–3

798. John Fantham
Inside forward

Born	Sheffield, 6 February 1939	
Clubs	Sheffield Wednesday; Rotherham Utd; Macclesfield	

Caps	1	Result
	28 Sep 1961 v Luxembourg	4–1

799. Raymond Pointer
Centre forward

Born	Cramlington, 10 October 1936	
Clubs	Burnley; Bury; Coventry City; Portsmouth	

Caps	3	Result	Goals
	28 Sep 1961 v Luxembourg	4–1	1
	14 Oct 1961 v Wales	1–1	
	25 Oct 1961 v Portugal	2–0	1

800. John Joseph Byrne
Inside right/Centre forward

Born	West Horsley, 13 May 1939	
Died	27 October 1999	
Clubs	Epsom Town; Guildford City; Crystal Palace; West Ham Utd; Fulham; Durban City (South Africa)	

Caps	11	Result	Goals
	22 Nov 1961 v N. Ireland	1–1	
	5 Jun 1963 v Switzerland	8–1	2
	11 Apr 1964 v Scotland	0–1	
	6 May 1964 v Uruguay	2–1	1
	17 May 1964 v Portugal	4–3	2
	24 May 1964 v Eire	3–1	1
	30 May 1964 v Brazil	1–5	
	4 Jun 1964 v Portugal	1–1	
	6 Jun 1964 v Argentina	0–1	
	18 Nov 1964 v Wales	2–1	
	10 Apr 1965 v Scotland	2–2	

801. Raymond Crawford
Centre forward

Born	Portsmouth, 13 July 1936	
Clubs	Portsmouth; Ipswich Town; Wolverhampton Wanderers; West Bromwich Albion; Charlton Athletic; Kettering Town; Colchester Utd; Durban City (South Africa)	

Caps	2	Result	Goals
	22 Nov 1961 v N. Ireland	1–1	
	4 Apr 1962 v Austria	3–1	1

802. Stanley Anderson
Right half

Born	Horden, 27 February 1933	
Clubs	Horden Colliery Welfare; Sunderland; Newcastle Utd; Middlesbrough	

Caps	2	Result
	4 Apr 1962 v Austria	3–1
	14 Apr 1962 v Scotland	0–2

803. Roger Hunt
Inside forward

Born	Golborne, 20 July 1938	
Clubs	Stockton Heath; Liverpool; Bolton Wanderers	

Caps	34	Result	Goals
	4 Apr 1962 v Austria	3–1	1
	2 Jun 1963 v E. Germany	2–1	1
	11 Apr 1964 v Scotland	0–1	
	27 May 1964 v USA	10–0	4
	4 Jun 1964 v Portugal	1–1	1
	18 Nov 1964 v Wales	2–1	
	8 Dec 1965 v Spain	2–0	1
	5 Jan 1966 v Poland	1–1	
	23 Feb 1966 v W. Germany	1–0	
	2 Apr 1966 v Scotland	4–3	2
	26 Jun 1966 v Finland	3–0	1
	29 Jun 1966 v Norway	6–1	
	5 Jul 1966 v Poland	1–0	1
	11 Jul 1966 v Uruguay	0–0	
	16 Jul 1966 v Mexico	2–0	1
	20 Jul 1966 v France	2–0	2
	23 Jul 1966 v Argentina	1–0	
	26 Jul 1966 v Portugal	2–1	
	30 Jul 1966 v W. Germany	4–2	
	22 Oct 1966 v N. Ireland	2–0	1
	2 Nov 1966 v Czechoslovakia	0–0	
	16 Nov 1966 v Wales	5–1	
	24 May 1967 v Spain	2–0	1
	27 May 1967 v Austria	1–0	
	21 Oct 1967 v Wales	3–0	
	22 Nov 1967 v N. Ireland	2–0	
	6 Dec 1967 v Soviet Union	2–2	
	3 Apr 1968 v Spain	1–0	
	8 May 1968 v Spain	2–1	
	22 May 1968 v Sweden	3–1	1
	5 Jun 1968 v Yugoslavia	0–1	
	8 Jun 1968 v Soviet Union	2–0	
	6 Nov 1968 v Romania	0–0	
	15 Jan 1969 v Romania	1–1	

⚽ **DID YOU KNOW...?**

Billy Wright and Bobby Moore each captained England a record ninety times. Wright was skipper from 9 October 1948 until 28 May 1959, while Moore's tenure started on 20 May 1963 against Czechoslovakia and ended on 14 November 1973 at Wembley, when he played his last international against Italy.

804. Robert Frederick Moore
Left half

Born	Barking, 12 April 1941	
Died	24 February 1993	
Clubs	West Ham Utd; Fulham; Herning FC (Denmark)	

Caps	108	Result	Goals
	20 May 1962 v Peru	4–0	
	31 May 1962 v Hungary	1–2	
	2 Jun 1962 v Argentina	3–1	
	7 Jun 1962 v Bulgaria	0–0	
	10 Jun 1962 v Brazil	1–3	

3 Oct 1962 v France	1–1	
20 Oct 1962 v N. Ireland	3–1	
21 Nov 1962 v Wales	4–0	
27 Feb 1963 v France	2–5	
6 Apr 1963 v Scotland	1–2	
8 May 1963 v Brazil	1–1	
20 May 1963 v Czechoslovakia	4–2	
2 Jun 1963 v E. Germany	2–1	
5 Jun 1963 v Switzerland	8–1	
12 Oct 1963 v Wales	4–0	
23 Oct 1963 v Rest of World	2–1	
20 Nov 1963 v N. Ireland	8–3	
11 Apr 1964 v Scotland	0–1	
6 May 1964 v Uruguay	2–1	
17 May 1964 v Portugal	4–3	
24 May 1964 v Eire	3–1	
30 May 1964 v Brazil	1–5	
4 Jun 1964 v Portugal	1–1	
6 Jun 1964 v Argentina	0–1	
3 Oct 1964 v N. Ireland	4–3	
21 Oct 1964 v Belgium	2–2	
10 Apr 1965 v Scotland	2–2	
5 May 1965 v Hungary	1–0	
9 May 1965 v Yugoslavia	1–1	
12 May 1965 v W. Germany	1–0	
16 May 1965 v Sweden	2–1	
2 Oct 1965 v Wales	0–0	
20 Oct 1965 v Austria	2–3	
10 Nov 1965 v N. Ireland	2–1	
8 Dec 1965 v Spain	2–0	
5 Jan 1966 v Poland	1–1	1
23 Feb 1966 v W. Germany	1–0	
2 Apr 1966 v Scotland	4–3	
29 Jun 1966 v Norway	6–1	1
3 Jul 1966 v Denmark	2–0	
5 Jul 1966 v Poland	1–0	
11 Jul 1966 v Uruguay	0–0	
16 Jul 1966 v Mexico	2–0	
20 Jul 1966 v France	2–0	
23 Jul 1966 v Argentina	1–0	
26 Jul 1966 v Portugal	2–1	
30 Jul 1966 v W. Germany	4–2	
22 Oct 1966 v N. Ireland	2–0	
2 Nov 1966 v Czechoslovakia	0–0	
16 Nov 1966 v Wales	5–1	
15 Apr 1967 v Scotland	2–3	
24 May 1967 v Spain	2–0	
27 May 1967 v Austria	1–0	
21 Oct 1967 v Wales	3–0	
22 Nov 1967 v N. Ireland	2–0	
6 Dec 1967 v Soviet Union	2–2	
24 Feb 1968 v Scotland	1–1	
3 Apr 1968 v Spain	1–0	
8 May 1968 v Spain	2–1	
22 May 1968 v Sweden	3–1	
1 Jun 1968 v W. Germany	0–1	
5 Jun 1968 v Yugoslavia	0–1	
8 Jun 1968 v Soviet Union	2–0	
6 Nov 1968 v Romania	0–0	
11 Dec 1968 v Bulgaria	1–1	
12 Mar 1969 v France	5–0	
3 May 1969 v N. Ireland	3–1	
7 May 1969 v Wales	2–1	
10 May 1969 v Scotland	4–1	
1 Jun 1969 v Mexico	0–0	
8 Jun 1969 v Uruguay	2–1	
12 Jun 1969 v Brazil	1–2	
5 Nov 1969 v Holland	1–0	
10 Dec 1969 v Portugal	1–0	
25 Feb 1970 v Belgium	3–1	
18 Apr 1970 v Wales	1–1	
21 Apr 1970 v N. Ireland	3–1	
25 Apr 1970 v Scotland	0–0	
20 May 1970 v Colombia	4–0	
24 May 1970 v Ecuador	2–0	

2 Jun 1970 v Romania	1–0
7 Jun 1970 v Brazil	0–1
11 Jun 1970 v Czechoslovakia	1–0
14 Jun 1970 v W. Germany	2–3
25 Nov 1970 v E. Germany	3–1
21 Apr 1971 v Greece	3–0
12 May 1971 v Malta	5–0
15 May 1971 v N. Ireland	1–0
22 May 1971 v Scotland	3–1
13 Oct 1971 v Switzerland	3–2
10 Nov 1971 v Switzerland	1–1
1 Dec 1971 v Greece	2–0
29 Apr 1972 v W. Germany	1–3
13 May 1972 v W. Germany	0–0
20 May 1972 v Wales	3–0
27 May 1972 v Scotland	1–0
11 Oct 1972 v Yugoslavia	1–1
15 Nov 1972 v Wales	1–0
24 Jan 1973 v Wales	1–1
14 Feb 1973 v Scotland	5–0
12 May 1973 v N. Ireland	2–1
15 May 1973 v Wales	3–0
19 May 1973 v Scotland	1–0
27 May 1973 v Czechoslovakia	1–1
6 Jun 1973 v Poland	0–2
10 Jun 1973 v Soviet Union	2–1
14 Jun 1973 v Italy	0–2
14 Nov 1973 v Italy	0–1

 DID YOU KNOW...?

In February 1973, Bobby Moore celebrated his 100th international appearance by leading England to a 5–0 victory over Scotland at Hampden Park. The game, part of the Scottish FA's centenary celebrations, was England's biggest victory north of the border since 1888.

805. Maurice Norman
Centre half

Born Mulbarton, 8 May 1934
Clubs Mulbarton FC; Wymondham Minors; Norwich City; Tottenham Hotspur

Caps 23	*Result*
20 May 1962 v Peru	4–0
31 May 1962 v Hungary	1–2
2 Jun 1962 v Argentina	3–1
7 Jun 1962 v Bulgaria	0–0
10 Jun 1962 v Brazil	1–3
3 Oct 1962 v France	1–1
6 Apr 1963 v Scotland	1–2
8 May 1963 v Brazil	1–1
20 May 1963 v Czechoslovakia	4–2
2 Jun 1963 v E. Germany	2–1
12 Oct 1963 v Wales	4–0
23 Oct 1963 v Rest of World	2–1
20 Nov 1963 v N. Ireland	8–3
11 Apr 1964 v Scotland	0–1
6 May 1964 v Uruguay	2–1
17 May 1964 v Portugal	4–3
27 May 1964 v USA	10–0
30 May 1964 v Brazil	1–5
4 Jun 1964 v Portugal	1–1
6 Jun 1964 v Argentina	0–1
3 Oct 1964 v N. Ireland	4–3
21 Oct 1964 v Belgium	2–2
9 Dec 1964 v Holland	1–1

806. Alan Peacock
Centre forward
Born Middlesbrough, 29 October 1937
Clubs Middlesbrough; Leeds Utd; Plymouth Argyle

Caps	6	Result	Goals
	2 Jun 1962 v Argentina	3–1	
	7 Jun 1962 v Bulgaria	0–0	
	20 Oct 1962 v N. Ireland	3–1	
	21 Nov 1962 v Wales	4–0	2
	2 Oct 1965 v Wales	0–0	
	10 Nov 1965 v N. Ireland	2–1	1

807. Michael Stephen Hellawell
Outside right
Born Keighley, 30 June 1938
Clubs Salts FC; Huddersfield Town; Queen's Park Rangers; Birmingham City; Sunderland; Peterborough Utd; Bromsgrove Rovers

Caps	2	Result
	3 Oct 1962 v France	1–1
	20 Oct 1962 v N. Ireland	3–1

808. Christopher Crowe
Outside right/Inside forward
Born Newcastle-upon-Tyne, 1 June 1939
Died 20 June 2003
Clubs Leeds Utd; Blackburn Rovers; Wolverhampton Wanderers; Nottingham Forest; Bristol City; Auburn FC (Australia); Walsall

Caps	1	Result
	3 Oct 1962 v France	1–1

809. Raymond Ogden Charnley
Centre forward
Born Lancaster, 29 May 1935
Clubs Bolton-le-Sands FC; Morecambe; Blackpool; Preston North End; Wrexham; Bradford City

Caps	1	Result
	3 Oct 1962 v France	1–1

810. Alan Thomas Hinton
Outside left
Born Wednesbury, 6 October 1942
Clubs Wolverhampton Wanderers; Nottingham Forest; Derby County

Caps	3	Result	Goals
	3 Oct 1962 v France	1–1	
	21 Oct 1964 v Belgium	2–2	1
	18 Nov 1964 v Wales	2–1	

811. Brian Leslie Labone
Centre half
Born Liverpool, 23 January 1940
Clubs Everton

Caps	26	Result
	20 Oct 1962 v N. Ireland	3–1
	21 Nov 1962 v Wales	4–0
	27 Feb 1963 v France	2–5
	24 May 1967 v Spain	2–0
	27 May 1967 v Austria	1–0
	24 Feb 1968 v Scotland	1–1
	8 May 1968 v Spain	2–1
	22 May 1968 v Sweden	3–1
	1 Jun 1968 v W. Germany	0–1
	5 Jun 1968 vYugoslavia	0–1
	8 Jun 1968 v Soviet Union	2–0
	6 Nov 1968 v Romania	0–0
	11 Dec 1968 v Bulgaria	1–1
	3 May 1969 v N. Ireland	3–1
	10 May 1969 v Scotland	4–1
	1 Jun 1969 v Mexico	0–0
	8 Jun 1969 v Uruguay	2–1
	12 Jun 1969 v Brazil	1–2
	25 Feb 1970 v Belgium	3–1
	18 Apr 1970 v Wales	1–1
	25 Apr 1970 v Scotland	0–0
	20 May 1970 v Colombia	4–0
	24 May 1970 v Ecuador	2–0
	2 Jun 1970 v Romania	1–0
	7 Jun 1970 v Brazil	0–1
	14 Jun 1970 v W. Germany	2–3

812. Frederick Hill
Inside forward
Born Sheffield, 17 January 1940
Clubs Bolton Wanderers; Halifax Town; Manchester City; Peterborough Utd; Droylsden

Caps	2	Result
	20 Oct 1962 v N. Ireland	3–1
	21 Nov 1962 v Wales	4–0

813. Michael O'Grady
Outside left
Born Leeds, 11 October 1942
Clubs Huddersfield Town; Leeds Utd; Wolverhampton Wanderers; Birmingham City; Rotherham Utd

Caps	2	Result	Goals
	20 Oct 1962 v N. Ireland	3–1	2
	12 Mar 1969 v France	5–0	1

814. Robert Victor Tambling
Forward
Born Storrington, 18 September 1941
Clubs Chelsea; Crystal Palace; Cork Celtic; Waterford; Shamrock Rovers

Caps	3	Result	Goals
	21 Nov 1962 v Wales	4–0	
	27 Feb 1963 v France	2–5	1
	4 May 1966 v Yugoslavia	2–0	

815. Ronald Patrick Henry
Left back
Born Shoreditch, 17 August 1934
Clubs Harpenden Town; Redbourne FC; Tottenham Hotspur

Caps	1	Result
	27 Feb 1963 v France	2–5

⚽ **DID YOU KNOW...?**

Gordon Banks kept a record seven consecutive clean sheets for England in 1966. Only Eusebio's late penalty in the semi-final of the 1966 World Cup stopped him from making it eight.

---

816. Gordon Banks
Goalkeeper
Born Sheffield, 30 December 1937
Clubs Millspout Steel Works; Chesterfield; Leicester City; Stoke City

Caps	73	Result
	6 Apr 1963 v Scotland	1–2
	8 May 1963 v Brazil	1–1
	20 May 1963 v Czechoslovakia	4–2
	2 Jun 1963 v E. Germany	2–1
	12 Oct 1963 v Wales	4–0
	23 Oct 1963 v Rest of World	2–1
	20 Nov 1963 v N. Ireland	8–3
	11 Apr 1964 v Scotland	0–1
	6 May 1964 v Uruguay	2–1
	17 May 1964 v Portugal	4–3
	27 May 1964 v USA	10–0
	4 Jun 1964 v Portugal	1–1
	6 Jun 1964 v Argentina	0–1
	3 Oct 1964 v N. Ireland	4–3

10 Apr 1965 v Scotland	2–2
5 May 1965 v Hungary	1–0
9 May 1965 v Yugoslavia	1–1
12 May 1965 v W. Germany	1–0
16 May 1965 v Sweden	2–1
10 Nov 1965 v N. Ireland	2–1
8 Dec 1965 v Spain	2–0
5 Jan 1966 v Poland	1–1
23 Feb 1966 v W. Germany	1–0
2 Apr 1966 v Scotland	4–3
4 May 1966 v Yugoslavia	2–0
26 Jun 1966 v Finland	3–0
5 Jul 1966 v Poland	1–0
11 Jul 1966 v Uruguay	0–0
16 Jul 1966 v Mexico	2–0
20 Jul 1966 v France	2–0
23 Jul 1966 v Argentina	1–0
26 Jul 1966 v Portugal	2–1
30 Jul 1966 v W. Germany	4–2
22 Oct 1966 v N. Ireland	2–0
2 Nov 1966 v Czechoslovakia	0–0
16 Nov 1966 v Wales	5–1
15 Apr 1967 v Scotland	2–3
21 Oct 1967 v Wales	3–0
22 Nov 1967 v N. Ireland	2–0
5 Dec 1967 v Soviet Union	2–2
24 Feb 1968 v Scotland	1–1
3 Apr 1968 v Spain	1–0
1 Jun 1968 v W. Germany	0–1
5 Jun 1968 v Yugoslavia	0–1
8 Jun 1968 v Soviet Union	2–0
6 Nov 1968 v Romania	0–0
15 Jan 1969 v Romania	1–1
12 Mar 1969 v France	5–0
3 May 1969 v N. Ireland	3–1
10 May 1969 v Scotland	4–1
8 Jun 1969 v Uruguay	2–1
12 Jun 1969 v Brazil	1–2
14 Jan 1970 v Holland	0–0
25 Feb 1970 v Belgium	3–1
18 Apr 1970 v Wales	1–1
21 Apr 1970 v N. Ireland	3–1
25 Apr 1970 v Scotland	0–0
20 May 1970 v Colombia	4–0
24 May 1970 v Ecuador	2–0
2 Jun 1970 v Romania	1–0
7 Jun 1970 v Brazil	0–1
11 Jun 1970 v Czechoslovakia	1–0
3 Feb 1971 v Malta	1–0
21 Apr 1971 v Greece	3–0
12 May 1971 v Malta	5–0
15 May 1971 v N. Ireland	1–0
22 May 1971 v Scotland	3–1
13 Oct 1971 v Switzerland	3–2
1 Dec 1971 v Greece	2–0
29 Apr 1972 v W. Germany	1–3
13 May 1972 v W. Germany	0–0
20 May 1972 v Wales	3–0
27 May 1972 v Scotland	1–0

817. Gerald Byrne
Fullback

Born Liverpool, 29 August 1938
Clubs Liverpool

Caps	2	Result
	6 Apr 1963 v Scotland	1–2
	29 Jun 1966 v Norway	6–1

818. James Melia
Inside left

Born Liverpool, 1 November 1937
Clubs Liverpool; Wolverhampton Wanderers;
Southampton; Aldershot; Crewe Alexandra

Caps	2	Result	Goals
	6 Apr 1963 v Scotland	1–2	
	5 Jun 1963 v Switzerland	8–1	1

DID YOU KNOW...?

The greatest ever save must surely be the one made by Gordon Banks in the 1970 World Cup match against Brazil. How he managed to get across his goal and turn Pele's downward header round the post is still something of a mystery.

819. Gordon Milne
Right half

Born Preston, 29 March 1937
Clubs Morecambe; Preston North End; Liverpool;
Blackpool; Wigan Athletic

Caps	14	Result
	8 May 1963 v Brazil	1–1
	20 May 1963 v Czechoslovakia	4–2
	2 Jun 1963 v E. Germany	2–1
	12 Oct 1963 v Wales	4–0
	23 Oct 1963 v Rest of World	2–1
	20 Nov 1963 v N. Ireland	8–3
	11 Apr 1964 v Scotland	0–1
	6 May 1964 v Uruguay	2–1
	17 May 1964 v Portugal	4–3
	24 May 1964 v Eire	3–1
	30 May 1964 v Brazil	1–5
	6 Jun 1964 v Argentina	0–1
	3 Oct 1964 v N. Ireland	4–3
	21 Oct 1964 v Belgium	2–2

820. George Edward Eastham
Inside right

Born Blackpool, 23 September 1936
Clubs Ards; Newcastle Utd; Arsenal; Stoke City; Hellenic
FC (South Africa)

Caps	19	Result	Goals
	8 May 1963 v Brazil	1–1	
	20 May 1963 v Czechoslovakia	4–2	
	2 Jun 1963 v E. Germany	2–1	
	12 Oct 1963 v Wales	4–0	
	23 Oct 1963 v Rest of World	2–1	
	20 Nov 1963 v N. Ireland	8–3	
	11 Apr 1964 v Scotland	0–1	
	6 May 1964 v Uruguay	2–1	
	17 May 1964 v Portugal	4–3	
	24 May 1964 v Eire	3–1	1
	27 May 1964 v USA	10–0	
	30 May 1964 v Brazil	1–5	
	6 Jun 1964 v Argentina	0–1	
	5 May 1965 v Hungary	1–0	
	12 May 1965 v W. Germany	1–0	
	16 May 1965 v Sweden	2–1	
	8 Dec 1965 v Spain	2–0	
	5 Jan 1966 v Poland	1–1	
	3 July 1966 v Denmark	2–0	1

821. Kenneth John Shellito
Right back

Born East Ham, 18 April 1940
Clubs Chelsea

Caps	1	Result
	20 May 1963 v Czechoslovakia	4–2

DID YOU KNOW...?

Alan Mullery had to miss England's 1964 tour of Brazil because he managed to rick his back while cleaning his teeth.

822. Terence Lionel Paine
Outside right
Born Winchester, 23 March 1939
Clubs Winchester Corinthians; Winchester City; Southampton; Hereford Utd

Caps	19	Result	Goals
	20 May 1963 v Czechoslovakia	4–2	
	2 Jun 1963 v E. Germany	2–1	
	12 Oct 1963 v Wales	4–0	
	23 Oct 1963 v Rest of World	2–1	1
	20 Nov 1963 v N. Ireland	8–3	3
	11 Apr 1964 v Scotland	0–1	
	6 May 1964 v Uruguay	2–1	
	27 May 1964 v USA	10–0	2
	4 Jun 1964 v Portugal	1–1	
	3 Oct 1964 v N. Ireland	4–3	
	5 May 1965 v Hungary	1–0	
	9 May 1965 v Yugoslavia	1–1	
	12 May 1965 v W. Germany	1–0	1
	16 May 1965 v Sweden	2–1	
	2 Oct 1965 v Wales	0–0	
	20 Oct 1965 v Austria	2–3	
	4 May 1966 v Yugoslavia	2–0	
	29 Jun 1966 v Norway	6–1	
	16 Jul 1966 v Mexico	2–0	

823. Anthony Herbert Kay
Left half
Born Attercliffe, 13 May 1937
Clubs Sheffield Wednesday; Everton

Caps	1	Result	Goals
	5 Jun 1963 v Switzerland	8–1	1

824. Robert Anthony Thomson
Left back
Born Smethwick, 5 December 1943
Clubs Wolverhampton Wanderers; Birmingham City; Walsall; Luton Town

Caps	8	Result
	20 Nov 1963 v N. Ireland	8–3
	27 May 1964 v USA	10–0
	4 Jun 1964 v Portugal	1–1
	6 Jun 1964 v Argentina	0–1
	3 Oct 1964 v N. Ireland	4–3
	21 Oct 1964 v Belgium	2–2
	18 Nov 1964 v Wales	2–1
	9 Dec 1964 v Holland	1–1

825. George Reginald Cohen
Right back
Born Kensington, 22 October 1939
Clubs Fulham

Caps	37	Result
	6 May 1964 v Uruguay	2–1
	17 May 1964 v Portugal	4–3
	24 May 1964 v Eire	3–1
	27 May 1964 v USA	10–0
	30 May 1964 v Brazil	1–5
	3 Oct 1964 v N. Ireland	4–3
	21 Oct 1964 v Belgium	2–2
	18 Nov 1964 v Wales	2–1
	9 Dec 1964 v Holland	1–1
	10 Apr 1965 v Scotland	2–2
	5 May 1965 v Hungary	1–0
	9 May 1965 v Yugoslavia	1–1
	12 May 1965 v W. Germany	1–0
	16 May 1965 v Sweden	2–1
	2 Oct 1965 v Wales	0–0
	20 Oct 1965 v Austria	2–3
	10 Nov 1965 v N. Ireland	2–1
	8 Dec 1965 v Spain	2–0
	5 Jan 1966 v Poland	1–1
	23 Feb 1966 v W. Germany	1–0
	2 Apr 1966 v Scotland	4–3
	29 Jun 1966 v Norway	6–1

	3 Jul 1966 v Denmark	2–0
	5 Jul 1966 v Poland	1–0
	11 Jul 1966 v Uruguay	0–0
	16 Jul 1966 v Mexico	2–0
	20 Jul 1966 v France	2–0
	23 Jul 1966 v Argentina	1–0
	26 Jul 1966 v Portugal	2–1
	30 Jul 1966 v W. Germany	4–2
	22 Oct 1966 v N. Ireland	2–0
	2 Nov 1966 v Czechoslovakia	0–0
	16 Nov 1966 v Wales	5–1
	15 Apr 1967 v Scotland	2–3
	24 May 1967 v Spain	2–0
	21 Oct 1967 v Wales	3–0
	22 Nov 1967 v N. Ireland	2–0

826. Peter Thompson
Outside left
Born Carlisle, 27 November 1942
Clubs Preston North End; Liverpool; Bolton Wanderers

Caps	16	Result
	17 May 1964 v Portugal	4–3
	24 May 1964 v Eire	3–1
	27 May 1964 v USA	10–0
	30 May 1964 v Brazil	1–5
	4 Jun 1964 v Portugal	1–1
	6 Jun 1964 v Argentina	0–1
	3 Oct 1964 v N. Ireland	4–3
	21 Oct 1964 v Belgium	2–2
	18 Nov 1964 v Wales	2–1
	9 Dec 1964 v Holland	1–1
	10 Apr 1965 v Scotland	2–2
	10 Nov 1965 v N. Ireland	2–1
	22 Nov 1967 v N. Ireland	2–0
	1 Jun 1968 v W. Germany	0–1
	5 Jun 1969 v Holland	1–0
	25 Apr 1970 v Scotland	0–0

827. Anthony Keith Waiters
Goalkeeper
Born Southport, 1 February 1937
Clubs Bishop Auckland; Macclesfield; Blackpool; Burnley

Caps	5	Result
	24 May 1964 v Eire	3–1
	30 May 1964 v Brazil	1–5
	21 Oct 1964 v Belgium	2–2
	18 Nov 1964 v Wales	2–1
	9 Dec 1964 v Holland	1–1

828. Michael Alfred Bailey
Right half
Born Wisbech, 27 February 1942
Clubs Charlton Athletic; Wolverhampton Wanderers; Minnesota Kicks (USA); Hereford Utd

Caps	2	Result
	27 May 1964 v USA	10–0
	18 Nov 1965 v Wales	2–1

829. Frederick Pickering
Centre forward
Born Blackburn, 19 January 1941
Clubs Blackburn Rovers; Everton; Birmingham City; Blackpool; Brighton & Hove Albion

Caps	3	Result	Goals
	27 May 1964 v USA	10–0	3
	3 Oct 1964 v N. Ireland	4–3	1
	21 Oct 1964 v Belgium	2–2	

830. Terence Frederick Venables
Right half/Inside left
Born Bethnal Green, 6 January 1943
Clubs Chelsea; Tottenham Hotspur; Queen's Park Rangers; Crystal Palace

Caps	2	Result
	21 Oct 1964 v Belgium	2–2
	9 Dec 1964 v Holland	1–1

831. Gerald Morton Young
Left half
Born South Shields, 1 October 1936
Clubs Hawthorn Leslie FC; Sheffield Wednesday

Caps	1	Result
	18 Nov 1964 v Wales	2–1

832. Frank Wignall
Centre forward/Inside forward
Born Blackrod, 21 August 1939
Clubs Blackrod FC; Horwich RMI; Everton; Nottingham
Forest; Wolverhampton Wanderers; Derby County;
Mansfield Town; King's Lynn; Burton Albion

Caps	2	Result	Goals
	18 Nov 1964 v Wales	2–1	2
	9 Dec 1964 v Holland	1–1	

833. Alan Patrick Mullery
Right half
Born Notting Hill, 23 November 1941
Clubs Fulham; Tottenham Hotspur

Caps	35	Result	Goals
	9 Dec 1964 v Holland	1–1	
	24 May 1967 v Spain	2–0	
	27 May 1967 v Austria	1–0	
	21 Oct 1967 v Wales	3–0	
	22 Nov 1967 v N. Ireland	2–0	
	6 Dec 1967 v Soviet Union	2–2	
	24 Feb 1968 v Scotland	1–1	
	3 Apr 1968 v Spain	1–0	
	8 May 1968 v Spain	2–1	
	22 May 1968 v Sweden	3–1	
	6 Jun 1968 v Yugoslavia	0–1	
	6 Nov 1968 v Romania	0–0	
	11 Dec 1968 v Bulgaria	1–1	
	12 Mar 1969 v France	5–0	
	3 May 1969 v N. Ireland	3–1	
	10 May 1969 v Scotland	4–1	
	1 Jun 1969 v Mexico	0–0	
	8 Jun 1969 v Uruguay	2–1	
	12 Jun 1969 v Brazil	1–2	
	5 Nov 1969 v Holland	1–0	
	10 Dec 1969 v Portugal	1–0	
	14 Jan 1970 v Holland	0–0	
	18 Apr 1970 v Wales	1–1	
	21 Apr 1970 v N. Ireland	3–1	
	25 Apr 1970 v Scotland	0–0	
	20 May 1970 v Colombia	4–0	
	24 May 1970 v Ecuador	2–0	
	2 Jun 1970 v Romania	1–0	
	7 Jun 1970 v Brazil	0–1	
	11 Jun 1970 v Czechoslovakia	1–0	
	14 Jun 1970 v W. Germany	2–3	1
	25 Nov 1970 v E. Germany	3–1	
	3 Feb 1971 v Malta	1–0	
	21 Apr 1971 v Greece	3–0	
	13 Oct 1971 v Switzerland	3–2	

⚽ **DID YOU KNOW...?**

In June 1968, Alan Mullery gained the unwanted
distinction of becoming the first England player to
be sent off in a full international, when he was
dismissed during a European Nations Cup match
against Yugoslavia in Italy.

834. Norbert Peter 'Nobby' Stiles
Wing half
Born Manchester, 18 May 1942
Clubs Manchester Utd; Middlesbrough; Preston North End

Caps	28	Result	Goals
	10 Apr 1965 v Scotland	2–2	
	5 May 1965 v Hungary	1–0	
	9 May 1965 v Yugoslavia	1–1	
	16 May 1965 v Sweden	2–1	
	2 Oct 1965 v Wales	0–0	
	20 Oct 1965 v Austria	2–3	
	10 Nov 1965 v N. Ireland	2–1	
	8 Dec 1965 v Spain	2–0	
	5 Jan 1966 v Poland	1–1	
	23 Feb 1966 v W. Germany	1–0	1
	2 Apr 1966 v Scotland	4–3	
	29 Jun 1966 v Norway	6–1	
	3 Jul 1966 v Denmark	2–0	
	5 Jul 1966 v Poland	1–0	
	11 Jul 1966 v Uruguay	0–0	
	16 Jul 1966 v Mexico	2–0	
	20 Jul 1966 v France	2–0	
	23 Jul 1966 v Argentina	1–0	
	26 Jul 1966 v Portugal	2–1	
	30 Jul 1966 v W. Germany	4–2	
	22 Oct 1966 v N. Ireland	2–0	
	2 Nov 1966 v Czechoslovakia	0–0	
	16 Nov 1966 v Wales	5–1	
	15 Apr 1967 v Scotland	2–3	
	8 Jun 1967 v Soviet Union	2–0	
	15 Jan 1969 v Romania	1–1	
	21 Apr 1970 v N. Ireland	3–1	
	25 Apr 1970 v Scotland	0–0	

835. Jack Charlton
Centre half
Born Ashington, 8 May 1935
Clubs Ashington YMCA; Ashington Welfare; Leeds Utd

Caps	35	Result	Goals
	10 Apr 1965 v Scotland	2–2	
	5 May 1965 v Hungary	1–0	
	9 May 1965 v Yugoslavia	1–1	
	12 May 1965 v W. Germany	1–0	
	16 May 1965 v Sweden	2–1	
	2 Oct 1965 v Wales	0–0	
	20 Oct 1965 v Austria	2–3	
	10 Nov 1965 v N. Ireland	2–1	
	8 Dec 1965 v Spain	2–0	
	5 Jan 1966 v Poland	1–1	
	23 Feb 1966 v W. Germany	1–0	
	2 Apr 1966 v Scotland	4–3	
	4 May 1966 v Yugoslavia	2–0	
	26 Jun 1966 v Finland	3–0	1
	3 Jul 1966 v Denmark	2–0	1
	5 Jul 1966 v Poland	1–0	
	11 Jul 1966 v Uruguay	0–0	
	16 Jul 1966 v Mexico	2–0	
	20 Jul 1966 v France	2–0	
	23 Jul 1966 v Argentina	1–0	
	26 Jul 1966 v Portugal	2–1	
	30 Jul 1966 v W. Germany	4–2	
	22 Oct 1966 v N. Ireland	2–0	
	2 Nov 1966 v Czechoslovakia	0–0	
	16 Nov 1966 v Wales	5–1	1
	15 Apr 1967 v Scotland	2–3	1
	21 Oct 1967 v Wales	3–0	
	3 Apr 1968 v Spain	1–0	
	15 Jan 1969 v Romania	1–1	1
	12 Mar 1969 v France	5–0	
	7 May 1969 v Wales	2–1	
	5 Nov 1969 v Holland	1–0	
	10 Dec 1969 v Portugal	1–0	1
	14 Jan 1970 v Holland	0–0	
	1 Jun 1970 v Czechoslovakia	1–0	

836. Barry John Bridges
Outside right/Centre forward

Born Horsford, 29 April 1941
Clubs Chelsea; Birmingham City; Queen's Park Rangers;
        Millwall; Brighton & Hove Albion; Highland Park
        (South Africa); St Patrick's Athletic

Caps	4	Result	Goals
	10 Apr 1965 v Scotland	2–2	
	5 May 1965 v Hungary	1–0	
	9 May 1965 v Yugoslavia	1–1	1
	20 Oct 1965 v Austria	2–3	

837. Alan James Ball
Inside forward

Born Farnworth, 12 May 1945
Clubs Bolton Wanderers; Blackpool; Everton; Arsenal;
        Southampton; Vancouver Whitecaps (Canada);
        Bristol Rovers

Caps	72	Result	Goals
	9 May 1965 v Yugoslavia	1–1	
	12 May 1965 v W. Germany	1–0	
	16 May 1965 v Sweden	2–1	1
	8 Dec 1965 v Spain	2–0	
	5 Jan 1966 v Poland	1–1	
	23 Feb 1966 v W. Germany	1–0	
	2 Apr 1966 v Scotland	4–3	
	26 Jun 1966 v Finland	3–0	
	3 Jul 1966 v Denmark	2–0	
	5 Jul 1966 v Poland	1–0	
	11 Jul 1966 v Uruguay	0–0	
	23 Jul 1966 v Argentina	1–0	
	26 Jul 1966 v Portugal	2–1	
	30 Jul 1966 v W. Germany	4–2	
	22 Oct 1966 v N. Ireland	2–0	
	2 Nov 1966 v Czechoslovakia	0–0	
	16 Nov 1966 v Wales	5–1	
	15 Apr 1967 v Scotland	2–3	
	24 May 1967 v Spain	2–0	
	27 May 1967 v Austria	1–0	1
	21 Oct 1967 v Wales	3–0	1
	6 Dec 1967 v Soviet Union	2–2	1
	24 Feb 1968 v Scotland	1–1	
	3 Apr 1968 v Spain	1–0	
	8 May 1968 v Spain	2–1	
	1 Jun 1968 v W. Germany	0–1	
	5 Jun 1968 v Yugoslavia	0–1	
	6 Nov 1968 v Romania	0–0	
	15 Jan 1969 v Romania	1–1	
	3 May 1969 v N. Ireland	3–1	
	7 May 1969 v Wales	2–1	
	10 May 1969 v Scotland	4–1	
	1 Jun 1969 v Mexico	0–0	
	8 Jun 1969 v Uruguay	2–1	
	12 Jun 1969 v Brazil	1–2	
	10 Dec 1969 v Portugal	1–0	
	25 Feb 1970 v Belgium	3–1	2
	18 Apr 1970 v Wales	1–1	
	25 Apr 1970 v Scotland	0–0	
	20 May 1970 v Colombia	4–0	1
	24 May 1970 v Ecuador	2–0	
	2 Jun 1970 v Romania	1–0	
	7 Jun 1970 v Brazil	0–1	
	11 Jun 1970 v Czechoslovakia	1–0	
	14 Jun 1970 v W. Germany	2–3	
	25 Nov 1970 v E. Germany	3–1	
	3 Feb 1971 v Malta	1–0	
	21 Apr 1971 v Greece	3–0	
	12 May 1971 v Malta	5–0	
	15 May 1971 v N. Ireland	1–0	
	22 May 1971 v Scotland	3–1	
	10 Nov 1971 v Switzerland	1–1	
	1 Dec 1971 v Greece	2–0	
	29 Apr 1972 v W. Germany	1–3	
	13 May 1972 v W. Germany	0–0	
	27 May 1972 v Scotland	1–0	1
	11 Oct 1972 v Yugoslavia	1–1	

15 Nov 1972 v Wales	1–0	
24 Jan 1973 v Wales	1–1	
14 Feb 1973 v Scotland	5–0	
12 May 1973 v N. Ireland	2–1	
15 May 1973 v Wales	3–0	
19 May 1973 v Scotland	1–0	
27 May 1973 v Czechoslovakia	1–1	
6 Jun 1973 v Poland	0–2	
3 Apr 1974 v Portugal	0–0	
12 Mar 1975 v W. Germany	2–0	
16 Apr 1975 v Cyprus	5–0	
1 May 1975 v Cyprus	1–0	
17 May 1975 v N. Ireland	0–0	
21 May 1975 v Wales	2–2	
24 May 1975 v Scotland	5–1	

838. Michael David Jones
Centre forward

Born Worksop, 24 April 1945
Clubs Dinnington Miners Welfare; Sheffield Utd;
        Leeds Utd

Caps	3	Result
	12 May 1965 v W. Germany	1–0
	16 May 1965 v Sweden	2–1
	14 Jan 1970 v Holland	0–0

839. Derek William Temple
Outside left

Born Liverpool, 13 November 1938
Clubs Everton; Preston North End; Wigan Athletic

Caps	1	Result
	12 May 1965 v W. Germany	1–0

⚽ **DID YOU KNOW...?**

The first player to win an England cap as a substitute was Norman Hunter when he came on against Spain in Madrid on 8 December 1965.

840. Norman Hunter
Left half

Born Eighton Banks, 29 October 1943
Clubs Leeds Utd; Bristol City; Barnsley

Caps	28	Result	Goals
	8 Dec 1965 v Spain	2–0	
	23 Feb 1966 v W. Germany	1–0	
	4 May 1966 v Yugoslavia	2–0	
	26 Jun 1966 v Finland	3–0	
	27 May 1967 v Austria	1–0	
	8 May 1968 v Spain	2–1	1
	22 May 1968 v Sweden	3–1	
	1 Jun 1968 v W. Germany	0–1	
	5 Jun 1968 v Yugoslavia	0–1	
	8 Jun 1968 v Soviet Union	2–0	
	15 Jan 1969 v Romania	1–1	
	7 May 1969 v Wales	2–1	
	14 Jan 1970 v Holland	0–0	
	14 Jun 1970 v W. Germany	2–3	
	3 Feb 1971 v Malta	1–0	
	29 Apr 1972 v W. Germany	1–3	
	13 May 1972 v W. Germany	0–0	
	20 May 1972 v Wales	3–0	
	23 May 1972 v N. Ireland	0–1	
	27 May 1972 v Scotland	1–0	
	15 Nov 1972 v Wales	1–0	
	24 Jan 1973 v Wales	1–1	1
	10 Jun 1973 v Soviet Union	2–1	
	26 Sep 1973 v Austria	7–0	
	17 Oct 1973 v Poland	1–1	
	15 May 1974 v N. Ireland	1–0	

18 May 1974 v Scotland	0–2
30 Oct 1974 v Czechoslovakia	3–0

841. Gordon Harris
Outside left
Born   Worksop, 2 June 1940
Clubs Firbeck Colliery; Burnley; Sunderland; South
Shields

Caps	1	Result
	5 Jan 1966 v Poland	1–1

842. Keith Robert Newton
Fullback
Born   Manchester, 23 June 1941
Died   16 June 1998
Clubs Blackburn Rovers; Everton; Burnley

Caps	27	Result
	23 Feb 1966 v W. Germany	1–0
	2 Apr 1966 v Scotland	4–3
	24 May 1967 v Spain	2–0
	21 Oct 1967 v Wales	3–0
	24 Feb 1968 v Scotland	1–1
	8 May 1968 v Spain	2–1
	22 May 1968 v Sweden	3–1
	1 Jun 1968 v W. Germany	0–1
	5 Jun 1968 v Yugoslavia	0–1
	6 Nov 1968 v Romania	0–0
	11 Dec 1968 v Bulgaria	1–1
	12 Mar 1969 v France	5–0
	3 May 1969 v N. Ireland	3–1
	7 May 1969 v Wales	2–1
	10 May 1969 v Scotland	4–1
	1 Jun 1969 v Mexico	0–0
	8 Jun 1969 v Uruguay	2–1
	12 Jun 1969 v Brazil	1–2
	14 Jan 1970 v Holland	0–0
	25 Feb 1970 v Belgium	3–1
	21 Apr 1970 v N. Ireland	3–1
	25 Apr 1970 v Scotland	0–0
	20 May 1970 v Colombia	4–0
	24 May 1970 v Ecuador	2–0
	2 Jun 1970 v Romania	1–0
	11 Jun 1970 v Czechoslovakia	1–0
	14 Jun 1970 v W. Germany	2–3

843. Geoffrey Charles Hurst
Centre forward/Inside left
Born   Ashton-under-Lyne, 8 December 1941
Clubs West Ham Utd; Stoke City; West Bromwich Albion;
Cork Celtic; Telford Utd

Caps	49	Result	Goals
	23 Feb 1966 v W. Germany	1–0	
	2 Apr 1966 v Scotland	4–3	1
	4 May 1966 v Yugoslavia	2–0	
	26 Jun 1966 v Finland	3–0	
	3 Jul 1966 v Denmark	2–0	
	23 Jul 1966 v Argentina	1–0	1
	26 Jul 1966 v Portugal	2–1	
	30 Jul 1966 v W. Germany	4–2	3
	22 Oct 1966 v N. Ireland	2–0	
	2 Nov 1966 v Czechoslovakia	0–0	
	16 Nov 1966 v Wales	5–1	2
	15 Apr 1967 v Scotland	2–3	1
	24 May 1967 v Spain	2–0	
	27 May 1967 v Austria	1–0	
	21 Oct 1967 v Wales	3–0	
	22 Nov 1967 v N. Ireland	2–0	1
	6 Dec 1967 v Soviet Union	2–2	
	24 Feb 1968 v Scotland	1–1	
	22 May 1968 v Sweden	3–1	
	1 Jun 1968 v W. Germany	0–1	
	8 Jun 1968 v Soviet Union	2–0	1
	6 Nov 1968 v Romania	0–0	
	11 Dec 1968 v Bulgaria	1–1	1
	15 Jan 1969 v Romania	1–1	
	12 Mar 1969 v France	5–0	3

3 May 1969 v N. Ireland	3–1	1	
10 May 1969 v Scotland	4–1	2	
1 Jun 1969 v Mexico	0–0		
8 Jun 1969 v Uruguay	2–1	1	
12 Jun 1969 v Brazil	1–2		
5 Nov 1969 v Holland	1–0		
14 Jan 1970 v Holland	0–0		
25 Feb 1970 v Belgium	3–1	1	
18 Apr 1970 v Wales	1–1		
21 Apr 1970 v N. Ireland	3–1	1	
25 Apr 1970 v Scotland	0–0		
20 May 1970 v Colombia	4–0		
24 May 1970 v Ecuador	2–0		
2 Jun 1970 v Romania	1–0	1	
7 Jun 1970 v Brazil	0–1		
14 Jun 1970 v W. Germany	2–3		
25 Nov 1970 v E. Germany	3–1		
21 Apr 1971 v Greece	3–0	1	
19 May 1971 v Wales	0–0		
22 May 1971 v Scotland	3–1		
13 Oct 1971 v Switzerland	3–2	1	
10 Nov 1971 v Switzerland	1–1		
1 Dec 1971 v Greece	2–0	1	
29 Apr 1972 v W. Germany	1–3		

⚽ **DID YOU KNOW...?**

Geoff Hurst's three goals at Wembley in July 1966 were the first hat-trick ever scored in a World Cup Final and remain so to this day, four decades later.

844. Martin Stanford Peters
Midfielder
Born   Plaistow, 8 November 1943
Clubs West Ham Utd; Tottenham Hotspur; Norwich City;
Sheffield Utd

Caps	67	Result	Goals
	4 May 1966 v Yugoslavia	2–0	
	26 Jun 1966 v Finland	3–0	1
	5 Jul 1966 v Poland	1–0	
	16 Jul 1966 v Mexico	2–0	
	20 Jul 1966 v France	2–0	
	23 Jul 1966 v Argentina	1–0	
	26 Jul 1966 v Portugal	2–1	
	30 Jul 1966 v W. Germany	4–2	1
	22 Oct 1966 v N. Ireland	2–0	1
	2 Nov 1966 v Czechoslovakia	0–0	
	16 Nov 1966 v Wales	5–1	
	15 Apr 1967 v Scotland	2–3	
	21 Oct 1967 v Wales	3–0	1
	22 Nov 1967 v N. Ireland	2–0	
	6 Dec 1967 v Soviet Union	2–2	1
	24 Feb 1968 v Scotland	1–1	
	3 Apr 1968 v Spain	1–0	
	8 May 1968 v Spain	2–1	1
	22 May 1968 v Sweden	3–1	1
	5 Jun 1968 v Yugoslavia	0–1	
	8 Jun 1968 v Soviet Union	2–0	
	6 Nov 1968 v Romania	0–0	
	11 Dec 1968 v Bulgaria	1–1	
	12 Mar 1969 v France	5–0	
	3 May 1969 v N. Ireland	3–1	1
	10 May 1969 v Scotland	4–1	2
	1 Jun 1969 v Mexico	0–0	
	8 Jun 1969 v Uruguay	2–1	
	12 Jun 1969 v Brazil	1–2	
	5 Nov 1969 v Holland	1–0	
	10 Dec 1969 v Portugal	1–0	
	14 Jan 1970 v Holland	0–0	

25 Feb 1970 v Belgium	3–1	
18 Apr 1970 v Wales	1–1	
21 Apr 1970 v N. Ireland	3–1	1
25 Apr 1970 v Scotland	0–0	
20 May 1970 v Colombia	4–0	2
24 May 1970 v Ecuador	2–0	
2 Jun 1970 v Romania	1–0	
7 Jun 1970 v Brazil	0–1	
1 Jun 1970 v Czechoslovakia	1–0	
14 Jun 1970 v W. Germany	2–3	1
25 Nov 1970 v E. Germany	3–1	1
3 Feb 1971 v Malta	1–0	1
21 Apr 1971 v Greece	3–0	
12 May 1971 v Malta	5–0	
15 May 1971 v N. Ireland	1–0	
19 May 1971 v Wales	0–0	
22 May 1971 v Scotland	3–1	1
13 Oct 1971 v Switzerland	3–2	
1 Dec 1971 v Greece	2–0	
29 Apr 1972 v W. Germany	1–3	
13 May 1972 v W. Germany	0–0	
23 May 1972 v N. Ireland	0–1	
14 Feb 1973 v Scotland	5–0	
12 May 1973 v N. Ireland	2–1	
15 May 1973 v Wales	3–0	1
19 May 1973 v Scotland	1–0	1
27 May 1973 v Czechoslovakia	1–1	
6 Jun 1973 v Poland	0–2	
10 Jun 1973 v Soviet Union	2–1	
14 Jun 1973 v Italy	0–2	
26 Sep 1973 v Austria	7–0	
17 Oct 1973 v Poland	1–1	
14 Nov 1973 v Italy	0–1	
3 Apr 1974 v Portugal	0–0	
18 May 1974 v Scotland	0–2	

845. Ian Robert Callaghan
Outside right/Midfielder

Born Liverpool, 10 April 1942
Clubs Liverpool; Swansea City; Cork Utd; Soudifjord (Norway); Crewe Alexandra

Caps 4	Result
26 Jun 1966 v Finland	3–0
20 Jul 1966 v France	2–0
7 Sep 1977 v Switzerland	0–0
12 Oct 1977 v Luxembourg	2–0

846. Peter Philip Bonetti
Goalkeeper

Born Putney, 27 September 1941
Clubs Chelsea; Dundee Utd

Caps 7	Result
3 Jul 1966 v Denmark	2–0
24 May 1967 v Spain	2–0
27 May 1967 v Austria	1–0
8 May 1968 v Spain	2–1
5 Nov 1969 v Holland	1–0
10 Dec 1969 v Portugal	1–0
14 Jun 1970 v W. Germany	2–3

847. John William Hollins
Right half/Midfielder

Born Guildford, 16 July 1946
Clubs Chelsea; Queen's Park Rangers; Arsenal

Caps 1	Result
24 May 1967 v Spain	2–0

848. David Sadler
Centre half

Born Yalding, 5 February 1946
Clubs Maidstone Utd; Manchester Utd; Preston North End

Caps 4	Result
22 Nov 1967 v N. Ireland	2–0
6 Dec 1967 v Soviet Union	2–2

24 May 1970 v Ecuador	2–0
25 Nov 1970 v E. Germany	3–1

849. Cyril Barry Knowles
Fullback

Born Fitzwilliam, 13 July 1944
Died 31 August 1991
Clubs Hemsworth FC; Monkton Colliery; Middlesbrough; Tottenham Hotspur

Caps 4	Result
6 Dec 1967 v Soviet Union	2–2
3 Apr 1968 v Spain	1–0
22 May 1968 v Sweden	3–1
1 Jun 1968 v W. Germany	0–1

850. Michael George Summerbee
Outside right/Centre forward

Born Preston, 15 December 1942
Clubs Swindon Town; Manchester City; Burnley; Blackpool; Stockport County; Mossley

Caps 8	Result	Goals
24 Feb 1968 v Scotland	2–2	
3 Apr 1968 v Spain	1–0	
1 Jun 1968 v W. Germany	0–1	
10 Nov 1971 v Switzerland	1–1	1
13 May 1972 v W. Germany	0–0	
20 May 1972 v Wales	3–0	
23 May 1972 v N. Ireland	0–1	
10 Jun 1973 v Soviet Union	2–1	

851. Alex Cyril Stepney
Goalkeeper

Born Mitcham, 18 September 1944
Clubs Tooting & Mitcham; Millwall; Chelsea; Manchester Utd; Dallas Tornado (USA); Altrincham

Caps 1	Result
22 May 1968 v Sweden	3–1

852. Colin Bell
Midfielder

Born Hesleden, 26 February 1946
Clubs Horden Colliery; Bury; Manchester City

Caps 48	Result	Goals
22 May 1968 v Sweden	3–1	
1 Jun 1968 v W. Germany	0–1	
11 Dec 1968 v Bulgaria	1–1	
12 Mar 1969 v France	5–0	
7 May 1969 v Wales	2–1	
8 Jun 1969 v Uruguay	2–1	
12 Jun 1969 v Brazil	1–2	1
5 Nov 1969 v Holland	1–0	1
10 Dec 1969 v Portugal	1–0	
14 Jan 1970 v Holland	0–0	
21 Apr 1970 v N. Ireland	3–1	
7 Jun 1970 v Brazil	0–1	
11 Jun 1970 v Czechoslovakia	1–0	
14 Jun 1970 v W. Germany	2–3	
1 Dec 1971 v Greece	2–0	
29 Apr 1972 v W. Germany	1–3	
13 May 1972 v W. Germany	0–0	
20 May 1972 v Wales	3–0	1
23 May 1972 v N. Ireland	0–1	
27 May 1972 v Scotland	1–0	
11 Oct 1972 v Yugoslavia	1–1	
15 Nov 1972 v Wales	1–0	1
24 Jan 1973 v Wales	1–1	
14 Feb 1973 v Scotland	5–0	
12 May 1973 v N. Ireland	2–1	
15 May 1973 v Wales	3–0	
19 May 1973 v Scotland	1–0	
27 May 1973 v Czechoslovakia	1–1	
6 Jun 1973 v Poland	0–2	
26 Sep 1973 v Austria	7–0	1
17 Oct 1973 v Poland	1–1	
14 Nov 1973 v Italy	0–1	

11 May 1974 v Wales	2–0
15 May 1974 v N. Ireland	1–0
18 May 1974 v Scotland	0–2
22 May 1974 v Argentina	2–2
29 May 1974 v E. Germany	1–1
1 Jun 1974 v Bulgaria	1–0
5 Jun 1974 v Yugoslavia	2–2
30 Oct 1974 v Czechoslovakia	3–0	2
20 Nov 1974 v Portugal	0–0
12 Mar 1975 v W. Germany	2–0	1
16 Apr 1975 v Cyprus	5–0
11 May 1975 v Cyprus	1–0
17 May 1975 v N. Ireland	0–0
24 May 1975 v Scotland	5–1	1
3 Sep 1975 v Switzerland	2–1
30 Oct 1975 v Czechoslovakia	1–2

853. Thomas James Wright
Right back
Born Liverpool, 21 October 1944
Clubs Everton

Caps 11	Result
8 Jun 1968 v Soviet Union	2–0
6 Nov 1968 v Romania	0–0
15 Jan 1969 v Romania	1–1
1 Jun 1969 v Mexico	0–0
8 Jun 1969 v Uruguay	2–1
12 Jun 1969 v Brazil	1–2
5 Nov 1969 v Holland	1–0
18 Apr 1970 v Wales	1–1
2 Jun 1970 v Romania	1–0
7 Jun 1970 v Brazil	0–1
25 Feb 1970 v Belgium	3–1

854. Robert McNab
Left back
Born Huddersfield, 20 July 1943
Clubs Huddersfield Town; Arsenal; Wolverhampton Wanderers; Barnet

Caps 4	Result
6 Nov 1968 v Romania	0–0
11 Dec 1968 v Bulgaria	1–1
15 Jan 1969 v Romania	1–1
3 May 1969 v N. Ireland	3–1

855. Gordon West
Goalkeeper
Born Barnsley, 24 April 1943
Clubs Blackpool; Everton; Tranmere Rovers

Caps 3	Result
11 Dec 1968 v Bulgaria	1–1
7 May 1969 v Wales	2–1
1 Jun 1969 v Mexico	0–0

856. Paul Reaney
Right back
Born Fulham, 22 October 1944
Clubs Leeds Utd; Bradford City; Newcastle UB (Australia)

Caps 3	Result
11 Dec 1968 v Bulgaria	1–1
10 Dec 1969 v Portugal	1–0
3 Feb 1971 v Malta	1–0

857. John Radford
Centre forward
Born Hemsworth, 22 February 1947
Clubs Arsenal; West Ham Utd; Blackburn Rovers; Bishop's Stortford

Caps 2	Result
15 Jan 1969 v Romania	1–1
13 Oct 1971 v Switzerland	3–2

858. Terence Cooper
Left back
Born Castleford, 12 July 1944
Clubs Ferrybridge Amateurs; Leeds Utd; Middlesbrough; Bristol City; Bristol Rovers

Caps 20	Result
12 Mar 1969 v France	5–0
7 May 1969 v Wales	2–1
10 May 1969 v Scotland	4–1
1 Jun 1969 v Mexico	0–0
14 Jan 1970 v Holland	0–0
25 Feb 1970 v Belgium	3–1
20 May 1970 v Colombia	4–0
24 May 1970 v Ecuador	2–0
2 Jun 1970 v Romania	1–0
7 Jun 1970 v Brazil	0–1
11 Jun 1970 v Czechoslovakia	1–0
14 Jun 1970 v W. Germany	2–3
25 Nov 1970 v E. Germany	3–1
12 May 1971 v Malta	5–0
15 May 1971 v N. Ireland	1–0
19 May 1971 v Wales	0–0
22 May 1971 v Scotland	3–1
13 Oct 1971 v Switzerland	3–2
10 Nov 1971 v Switzerland	1–1
20 Nov 1974 v Portugal	0–0

859. Francis Henry Lee
Outside right/Centre forward
Born Westhoughton, 29 April 1944
Clubs Bolton Wanderers; Manchester City; Derby County

Caps 27	Result	Goals
11 Dec 1968 v Bulgaria	1–1	
12 Mar 1969 v France	5–0	1
3 May 1969 v N. Ireland	3–1	1
7 May 1969 v Wales	2–1	1
10 May 1969 v Scotland	4–1	
1 Jun 1969 v Mexico	0–0	
8 Jun 1969 v Uruguay	2–1	1
5 Nov 1969 v Holland	1–0	
10 Dec 1969 v Portugal	1–0	
14 Jan 1970 v Holland	0–0	
25 Feb 1970 v Belgium	3–1	
18 Apr 1970 v Wales	1–1	1
20 May 1970 v Colombia	4–0	
24 May 1970 v Ecuador	2–0	1
2 Jun 1970 v Romania	1–0	
7 Jun 1970 v Brazil	0–1	
14 Jun 1970 v W. Germany	2–3	
25 Nov 1970 v E. Germany	3–1	1
21 Apr 1971 v Greece	3–0	1
12 May 1971 v Malta	5–0	1
15 May 1971 v N. Ireland	1–0	
19 May 1971 v Wales	0–0	
22 May 1971 v Scotland	3–1	
13 Oct 1971 v Switzerland	3–2	
10 Nov 1971 v Switzerland	1–1	
1 Dec 1971 v Greece	2–0	
29 Apr 1972 v W. Germany	1–3	1

860. Jeffrey Astle
Centre forward
Born Eastwood, 13 May 1942
Died 19 January 2002
Clubs Notts County; West Bromwich Albion; Dunstable Town; Weymouth; Atherstone Town; Hillingdon Borough

Caps 5	Result
7 May 1969 v Wales	2–1
10 Dec 1969 v Portugal	1–0
25 Apr 1970 v Scotland	0–0
7 Jun 1970 v Brazil	0–1
11 Jun 1970 v Czechoslovakia	1–0

861. Emlyn Walter Hughes
Left back/Midfielder

Born	Barrow-in-Furness, 28 August 1947
Died	9 November 2004
Clubs	Roose FC; Blackpool; Liverpool; Wolverhampton Wanderers; Rotherham Utd; Hull City; Mansfield Town; Swansea City

Caps 62	Result	Goals
5 Nov 1969 v Holland	1–0	
10 Dec 1969 v Portugal	1–0	
25 Feb 1970 v Belgium	3–1	
18 Apr 1970 v Wales	1–1	
21 Apr 1970 v N. Ireland	3–1	
25 Apr 1970 v Scotland	0–0	
25 Nov 1970 v E. Germany	3–1	
3 Feb 1971 v Malta	1–0	
21 Apr 1971 v Greece	3–0	
12 May 1971 v Malta	5–0	
19 May 1971 v Wales	0–0	
10 Nov 1971 v Switzerland	1–1	
1 Dec 1971 v Greece	2–0	
29 Apr 1972 v W. Germany	1–3	
13 May 1972 v W. Germany	0–0	
20 May 1972 v Wales	3–0	1
23 May 1972 v N. Ireland	0–1	
27 May 1972 v Scotland	1–0	
15 Nov 1972 v Wales	1–0	
24 Jan 1973 v Wales	1–1	
14 Feb 1973 v Scotland	5–0	
15 May 1973 v Wales	3–0	
19 May 1973 v Scotland	1–0	
6 Jun 1973 v Poland	0–2	
10 Jun 1973 v Soviet Union	2–1	
14 Jun 1973 v Italy	0–2	
26 Sep 1973 v Austria	7–0	
17 Oct 1973 v Poland	1–1	
14 Nov 1973 v Italy	0–1	
11 May 1974 v Wales	2–0	
15 May 1974 v N. Ireland	1–0	
18 May 1974 v Scotland	0–2	
22 May 1974 v Argentina	2–2	
29 May 1974 v E. Germany	1–1	
1 Jun 1974 v Bulgaria	1–0	
5 Jun 1974 v Yugoslavia	2–2	
30 Oct 1974 v Czechoslovakia	3–0	
20 Nov 1974 v Portugal	0–0	
11 May 1975 v Cyprus	1–0	
17 May 1975 v N. Ireland	0–0	
17 Nov 1976 v Italy	0–2	
30 Mar 1977 v Luxembourg	5–0	
31 May 1977 v Wales	0–1	
4 Jun 1977 v Scotland	1–2	
8 Jun 197 v Brazil	0–0	
12 Jun 1977 v Argentina	1–1	
15 Jun 1977 v Uruguay	0–0	
7 Sep 1977 v Switzerland	0–0	
12 Oct 1977 v Luxembourg	2–0	
16 Nov 1977 v Italy	2–0	
22 Feb 1978 v W. Germany	1–2	
16 May 1978 v N. Ireland	1–0	
20 May 1978 v Scotland	1–0	
24 May 1978 v Hungary	4–1	
20 Sep 1978 v Denmark	4–3	
25 Oct 1978 v Eire	1–1	
7 Feb 1979 v N. Ireland	4–0	
23 May 1979 v Wales	0–0	
10 Jun 1979 v Sweden	0–0	
26 Mar 1980 v Spain	2–0	
20 May 1980 v N. Ireland	1–1	
24 May 1980 v Scotland	2–0	

862. Ian Storey-Moore
Outside left

Born	Ipswich, 17 January 1945
Clubs	Nottingham Forest; Manchester Utd; Burton Albion

Caps 1	Result
14 Jan 1970 v Holland	0–0

863. Peter Leslie Osgood
Centre forward

Born	Windsor, 20 February 1947
Clubs	Windsor Corinthians; Chelsea; Southampton; Norwich City; Philadelphia Fury (USA)

Caps 4	Result
25 Feb 1970 v Belgium	3–1
2 Jun 1970 v Romania	1–0
11 Jun 1970 v Czechoslovakia	1–0
14 Nov 1973 v Italy	0–1

864. Ralph Coates
Midfielder

Born	Hetton-le-Hole, 26 April 1946
Clubs	Burnley; Tottenham Hotspur; Orient

Caps 4	Result
21 Apr 1970 v N. Ireland	3–1
21 Apr 1971 v Greece	3–0
12 May 1971 v Malta	5–0
19 May 1971 v Wales	0–0

865. Brian Kidd
Forward

Born	Manchester, 29 May 1949
Clubs	Manchester Utd; Arsenal; Manchester City; Everton; Bolton Wanderers; Lauderdale Strikers (USA); Atlanta Chiefs (USA)

Caps 2	Result	Goals
21 Apr 1970 v N. Ireland	3–1	
24 May 1970 v Ecuador	2–0	1

⚽ **DID YOU KNOW...?**

When Allan Clarke made his debut for England in a full international match against Czechoslovakia in a World Cup game in June 1970, he scored the only goal of the match from a penalty. The day in question also happened to be his wife's birthday, his wedding anniversary and the anniversary of his transfer from Fulham to Leicester City.

866. Allan John Clarke
Forward

Born	Willenhall, 31 July 1946
Clubs	Walsall; Fulham; Leicester City; Leeds Utd; Barnsley

Caps 19	Result	Goals
11 Jun 1970 v Czechoslovakia	1–0	1
25 Nov 1970 v E. Germany	3–1	1
12 May 1971 v Malta	5–0	1
15 May 1971 v N. Ireland	1–0	1
19 May 1971 v Wales	0–0	
22 May 1971 v Scotland	3–1	
14 Feb 1973 v Scotland	5–0	2
15 May 1973 v Wales	3–0	
19 May 1973 v Scotland	1–0	
27 May 1973 v Czechoslovakia	1–1	1
6 Jun 1973 v Poland	0–2	
10 Jun 1973 v Soviet Union	2–1	
14 Jun 1973 v Italy	0–2	
26 Sep 1973 v Austria	7–0	2
17 Oct 1973 v Poland	1–1	1
14 Nov 1973 v Italy	0–1	
20 Nov 1974 v Portugal	0–0	
30 Oct 1975 v Czechoslovakia	1–2	
19 Nov 1975 v Portugal	1–1	

867. Peter Leslie Shilton

Goalkeeper

Born Leicester, 18 September 1949
Clubs Leicester City; Stoke City; Nottingham Forest;
Southampton; Derby County; Plymouth Argyle;
Wimbledon; Bolton Wanderers; Coventry City;
West Ham Utd; Leyton Orient
Caps 125

Date	Result
25 Nov 1970 v E. Germany	3–1
19 May 1971 v Wales	0–0
10 Nov 1971 v Switzerland	1–1
23 May 1972 v N. Ireland	0–1
11 Oct 1972 v Yugoslavia	1–1
14 Feb 1973 v Scotland	5–0
12 May 1973 v N. Ireland	2–1
15 May 1973 v Wales	3–0
19 May 1973 v Scotland	1–0
23 May 1973 v Czechoslovakia	1–1
6 Jun 1973 v Poland	0–2
10 Jun 1973 v Soviet Union	2–1
14 Jun 1973 v Italy	0–2
26 Sep 1973 v Austria	7–0
17 Oct 1973 v Poland	1–1
14 Nov 1973 v Italy	0–1
11 May 1974 v Wales	2–0
15 May 1974 v N. Ireland	1–0
18 May 1974 v Scotland	0–2
22 May 1974 v Argentina	2–2
16 Apr 1975 v Cyprus	5–0
28 May 1977 v N. Ireland	2–1
31 May 1977 v Wales	0–1
13 May 1978 v Wales	3–1
24 May 1978 v Hungary	4–1
29 Nov 1978 v Czechoslovakia	1–0
10 Jun 1979 v Sweden	0–0
13 Jun 1979 v Austria	3–4
17 Oct 1979 v N. Ireland	5–1
26 Mar 1980 v Spain	2–0
15 Jun 1980 v Italy	0–1
10 Sep 1980 v Norway	4–0
19 Nov 1980 v Switzerland	2–1
29 Apr 1981 v Romania	0–0
18 Nov 1981 v Hungary	1–0
25 May 1982 v Holland	2–0
29 May 1982 v Scotland	1–0
16 Jun 1982 v France	3–1
20 Jun 1982 v Czechoslovakia	2–0
25 Jun 1982 v Kuwait	1–0
29 Jun 1982 v W. Germany	0–0
5 Jul 1982 v Spain	0–0
22 Sep 1982 v Denmark	2–2
13 Oct 1982 v W. Germany	1–2
17 Nov 1982 v Greece	3–0
23 Feb 1983 v Wales	2–1
30 Mar 1983 v Greece	0–0
27 Apr 1983 v Hungary	2–0
28 May 1983 v N. Ireland	0–0
1 Jun 1983 v Scotland	2–0
12 Jun 1983 v Australia	0–0
15 Jun 1983 v Australia	1–0
19 Jun 1983 v Australia	1–1
21 Sep 1983 v Denmark	0–1
12 Oct 1983 v Hungary	3–0
29 Feb 1984 v France	0–2
4 Apr 1984 v N. Ireland	1–0
2 May 1984 v Wales	0–1
26 May 1984 v Scotland	1–1
2 Jun 1984 v Soviet Union	0–2
10 Jun 1984 v Brazil	2–0
13 Jun 1984 v Uruguay	0–2
17 Jun 1984 v Chile	0–0
12 Sep 1984 v E. Germany	1–0
17 Oct 1984 v Finland	5–0
14 Nov 1984 v Turkey	8–0
27 Feb 1985 v N. Ireland	1–0
1 May 1985 v Romania	0–0
22 May 1985 v Finland	1–1
25 May 1985 v Scotland	0–1
6 Jun 1985 v Italy	1–2
12 Jun 1985 v W. Germany	3–0
11 Sep 1985 v Romania	1–1
16 Oct 1985 v Turkey	5–0
13 Nov 1985 v N. Ireland	0–0
29 Jan 1986 v Egypt	4–0
26 Feb 1986 v Israel	2–1
26 Mar 1986 v Soviet Union	0–1
23 Apr 1986 v Scotland	2–1
17 May 1986 v Mexico	3–0
24 May 1986 v Canada	1–0
3 Jun 1986 v Portugal	0–1
6 Jun 1986 v Morocco	0–0
11 Jun 1986 v Poland	3–0
18 Jun 1986 v Paraguay	3–0
22 Jun 1986 v Argentina	1–2
10 Sep 1986 v Sweden	0–1
15 Oct 1986 v N. Ireland	3–0
18 Feb 1987 v Spain	4–2
1 Apr 1987 v N. Ireland	2–0
19 May 1987 v Brazil	1–1
9 Sep 1987 v W. Germany	1–3
14 Oct 1987 v Turkey	8–0
11 Nov 1987 v Yugoslavia	4–1
23 Mar 1988 v Holland	2–2
21 May 1988 v Scotland	1–0
24 May 1988 v Colombia	1–1
28 May 1988 v Switzerland	1–0
12 Jun 1988 v Eire	0–1
15 Jun 1988 v Holland	1–3
14 Sep 1988 v Denmark	1–0
19 Oct 1988 v Sweden	0–0
8 Feb 1989 v Greece	2–1
8 Mar 1989 v Albania	2–0
26 Apr 1989 v Albania	5–0
23 May 1989 v Chile	2–0
27 May 1989 v Scotland	2–0
3 Jun 1989 v Poland	3–0
7 Jun 1989 v Denmark	1–1
6 Sep 1989 v Sweden	0–0
11 Oct 1989 v Poland	0–0
15 Nov 1989 v Italy	0–0
13 Dec 1989 v Yugoslavia	2–1
28 Mar 1990 v Brazil	1–0
25 Apr 1990 v Czechoslovakia	4–2
15 May 1990 v Denmark	1–0
22 May 1990 v Uruguay	1–2
2 Jun 1990 v Tunisia	1–1
11 Jun 1990 v Eire	1–1
16 Jun 1990 v Holland	0–0
21 Jun 1990 v Egypt	1–0
26 Jun 1990 v Belgium	1–0
1 Jul 1990 v Cameroon	3–2
4 Jul 1990 v W. Germany	1–1
7 Jul 1990 v Italy	1–2

 DID YOU KNOW...?

Legendary goalkeeper Peter Shilton still holds the record number of international caps for an England player. He appeared no fewer than 125 times between 1971 and 1990, despite the fact that his rival Ray Clemence also played for England a total of 61 times in that period.

868. Roy Leslie McFarland
Centre half
Born   Liverpool, 5 April 1948
Clubs   Tranmere Rovers; Derby County; Bradford City
Caps   28   Result
        3 Feb 1971 v Malta   1–0
        21 Apr 1971 v Greece   3–0
        12 May 1971 v Malta   5–0
        15 May 1971 v N. Ireland   1–0
        22 May 1971 v Scotland   3–1
        13 Oct 1971 v Switzerland   3–2
        1 Dec 1971 v Greece   2–0
        13 May 1972 v W. Germany   0–0
        20 May 1972 v Wales   3–0
        27 May 1972 v Scotland   1–0
        15 Nov 1972 v Wales   1–0
        24 Jan 1973 v Wales   1–1
        12 May 1973 v N. Ireland   2–1
        15 May 1973 v Wales   3–0
        19 May 1973 v Scotland   1–0
        27 May 1973 v Czechoslovakia   1–1
        6 Jun 1973 v Poland   0–2
        10 Jun 1973 v Soviet Union   2–1
        14 Jun 1973 v Italy   0–2
        26 Sep 1973 v Austria   7–0
        17 Oct 1973 v Poland   1–1
        14 Nov 1973 v Italy   0–1
        11 May 1974 v Wales   2–0
        15 May 1974 v N. Ireland   1–0
        30 Oct 1975 v Czechoslovakia   1–2
        15 May 1976 v Scotland   1–2
        8 Sep 1976 v Eire   1–1
        17 Nov 1976 v Italy   0–2

869. Martin Harcourt Chivers
Centre forward
Born   Southampton, 27 April 1945
Clubs   Southampton; Tottenham Hotspur; Servette
        (Switzerland); Norwich City; Brighton & Hove
        Albion; Dorchester Town; Barnet
Caps   24   Result Goals
        3 Feb 1971 v Malta   1–0
        21 Apr 1971 v Greece   3–0   1
        12 May 1971 v Malta   5–0   2
        15 May 1971 v N. Ireland   1–0
        22 May 1971 v Scotland   3–1   2
        13 Oct 1971 v Switzerland   3–2   1
        10 Nov 1971 v Switzerland   1–1
        1 Dec 1971 v Greece   2–0   1
        29 Apr 1972 v W. Germany   1–3
        13 May 1972 v W. Germany   0–0
        23 May 1972 v N. Ireland   0–1
        27 May 1972 v Scotland   1–0
        15 Nov 1972 v Wales   1–0
        24 Jan 1973 v Wales   1–1
        14 Feb 1973 v Scotland   5–0   1
        12 May 1973 v N. Ireland   2–1   2
        15 May 1973 v Wales   3–0   1
        19 May 1973 v Scotland   1–0
        27 May 1973 v Czechoslovakia 1–1
        6 Jun 1973 v Poland   0–2
        10 Jun 1973 v Soviet Union 2–1   1
        14 Jun 1973 v Italy   0–2
        26 Sep 1973 v Austria   7–0   1
        17 Oct 1973 v Poland   1–1

870. Joseph Royle
Centre forward
Born   Liverpool, 8 April 1949
Clubs   Everton; Manchester City; Bristol City; Norwich City
Caps   6   Result Goals
        3 Feb 1971 v Malta   1–0
        11 Oct 1972 v Yugoslavia   1–1   1
        11 May 1976 v N. Ireland   4–0
        28 May 1976 v Italy   3–2

        13 Oct 1976 v Finland   2–1   1
        30 Mar 1977 v Luxembourg   5–0

871. James Colin Harvey
Midfielder
Born   Liverpool, 16 November 1944
Clubs   Everton; Sheffield Wednesday
Caps   1   Result
        3 Feb 1971 v Malta   1–0

872. Peter Edwin Storey
Right back/Midfielder
Born   Farnham, 7 September 1945
Clubs   Arsenal; Fulham
Caps   19   Result
        21 Apr 1971 v Greece   3–0
        15 May 1971 v N. Ireland   1–0
        22 May 1971 v Scotland   3–1
        10 Nov 1971 v Switzerland   1–1
        13 May 1972 v W. Germany   0–0
        20 May 1972 v Wales   3–0
        23 May 1972 v N. Ireland   0–1
        27 May 1972 v Scotland   1–0
        1 Oct 1972 v Yugoslavia   1–1
        15 Nov 1972 v Wales   1–0
        24 Jan 1973 v Wales   1–1
        14 Feb 1973 v Scotland   5–0
        12 May 1973 v N. Ireland   2–1
        15 May 1973 v Wales   3–0
        19 May 1973 v Scotland   1–0
        27 May 1973 v Czechoslovakia   1–1
        6 Jun 1973 v Poland   0–2
        10 Jun 1973 v Soviet Union   2–1
        14 Jun 1973 v Italy   0–2

873. Christopher Lawler
Right back
Born   Liverpool, 20 October 1943
Clubs   Liverpool; Portsmouth; Stockport County; Bangor
        City
Caps   4   Result Goals
        12 May 1971 v Malta   5–0   1
        19 May 1971 v Wales   0–0
        22 May 1971 v Scotland   3–1
        13 Oct 1971 v Switzerland   3–2

874. Paul Edward Madeley
Defender
Born   Beeston, 20 September 1944
Clubs   Farsley Celtic; Leeds Utd
Caps   24   Result
        15 May 1971 v N. Ireland   1–0
        13 Oct 1971 v Switzerland   3–2
        10 Nov 1971 v Switzerland   1–1
        1 Dec 1971 v Greece   2–0
        29 Apr 1972 v W. Germany   1–3
        13 May 1972 v W. Germany   0–0
        20 May 1972 v Wales   3–0
        27 May 1972 v Scotland   5–0
        14 Feb 1973 v Scotland   5–0
        27 May 1973 v Czechoslovakia   1–1
        6 Jun 1973 v Poland   0–2
        10 Jun 1973 v Soviet Union   2–1
        14 Jun 1973 v Italy   0–2
        26 Sep 1973 v Austria   7–0
        17 Oct 1973 v Poland   1–1
        14 Nov 1973 v Italy   0–2
        30 Oct 1974 v Czechoslovakia   3–0
        20 Nov 1974 v Portugal   0–0
        16 Apr 1975 v Cyprus   5–0
        30 Oct 1975 v Czechoslovakia   1–2
        19 Nov 1975 v Portugal   1–1
        13 Jun 1976 v Finland   4–1
        8 Sep 1976 v Eire   1–1
        9 Feb 1977 v Holland   0–2

875. Thomas Smith

Defender

Born Liverpool, 5 April 1945
Clubs Liverpool; Swansea City

Caps	1	*Result*
	19 May 1971 v Wales	0–0

876. Laurence Valentine Lloyd

Centre half

Born Bristol, 6 October 1948
Clubs Bristol Rovers; Liverpool; Coventry City; Nottingham Forest; Wigan Athletic

Caps	4	*Result*
	19 May 1971 v Wales	0–0
	10 Nov 1971 v Switzerland	1–1
	23 May 1971 v N. Ireland	0–1
	17 May 1980 v Wales	1–4

877. Anthony Brown

Forward

Born Oldham, 3 October 1945
Clubs West Bromwich Albion; Torquay Utd; Stafford Rangers

Caps	1	*Result*
	19 May 1971 v Wales	0–0

878. Rodney Marsh

Inside forward

Born Hatfield, 11 October 1944
Clubs West Ham Utd; Fulham; Queen's Park Rangers; Manchester City; Tampa Bay Rowdies (USA)

Caps	9	*Result*	*Goals*
	10 Nov 1971 v Switzerland	1–1	
	29 Apr 1972 v W. Germany	1–3	
	13 May 1972 v W. Germany	0–0	
	20 May 1972 v Wales	3–0	1
	23 May 1972 v N. Ireland	0–1	
	27 May 1972 v Scotland	1–0	
	11 Oct 1972 v Yugoslavia	1–1	
	15 Nov 1972 v Wales	1–0	
	24 Jan 1973 v Wales	1–1	

879. Malcolm Macdonald

Centre forward

Born Fulham, 7 January 1950
Clubs Tonbridge; Fulham; Luton Town; Newcastle Utd; Arsenal

Caps	14	*Result*	*Goals*
	20 May 1972 v Wales	3–0	
	23 May 1972 v N. Ireland	0–1	
	27 May 1972 v Scotland	1–0	
	10 Jun 1973 v Soviet Union	2–1	
	3 Apr 1974 v Portugal	0–0	
	18 May 1974 v Scotland	0–2	
	5 Jun 1974 v Yugoslavia	2–2	
	12 Mar 1975 v W. Germany	2–0	1
	16 Apr 1975 v Cyprus	5–0	5
	11 May 1975 v Cyprus	1–0	
	17 May 1975 v N. Ireland	0–0	
	3 Sep 1975 v Switzerland	2–1	
	30 Oct 1975 v Czechoslovakia	1–2	
	19 Nov 1975 v Portugal	1–1	

880. Colin Todd

Defender

Born Chester-le-Street, 12 December 1948
Clubs Sunderland; Derby County; Everton; Birmingham City; Nottingham Forest; Oxford Utd; Vancouver Whitecaps (Canada); Luton Town

Caps	27	*Result*
	23 May 1972 v N. Ireland	0–1
	3 Apr 1974 v Portugal	0–0
	11 May 1974 v Wales	2–0
	15 May 1974 v N. Ireland	1–0
	18 May 1974 v Scotland	0–2

	22 May 1974 v Argentina	2–2
	29 May 1974 v E. Germany	1–1
	1 Jun 1974 v Bulgaria	1–0
	5 Jun 1974 v Yugoslavia	2–2
	20 Nov 1974 v Portugal	0–0
	12 Mar 1975 v W. Germany	2–0
	16 Apr 1975 v Cyprus	5–0
	11 May 1975 v Cyprus	1–0
	17 May 1975 v N. Ireland	0–0
	21 May 1975 v Wales	2–2
	24 May 1975 v Scotland	5–1
	3 Sep 1975 v Switzerland	2–1
	30 Oct 1975 v Czechoslovakia	1–2
	19 Nov 1975 v Portugal	1–1
	11 May 1976 v N. Ireland	4–0
	15 May 1976 v Scotland	1–2
	23 May 1976 v Brazil	0–1
	13 Jun 1976 v Finland	4–1
	8 Sep 1976 v Eire	1–1
	13 Oct 1976 v Finland	2–1
	9 Feb 1977 v Holland	0–2
	28 May 1977 v N. Ireland	2–1

881. Anthony William Currie

Midfielder

Born Edgware, 1 January 1950
Clubs Watford; Sheffield Utd; Leeds Utd; Queen's Park Rangers; Chesham Utd; Torquay Utd; Hendon; Goole Town

Caps	17	*Result*	*Goals*
	23 May 1972 v N. Ireland	0–1	
	10 Jun 1973 v Soviet Union	2–1	
	14 Jun 1973 v Italy	0–2	
	26 Sep 1973 v Austria	7–0	1
	17 Oct 1973 v Poland	1–1	
	14 Nov 1973 v Italy	0–1	
	3 Sep 1975 v Switzerland	2–1	
	19 Apr 1978 v Brazil	1–1	
	13 May 1978 v Wales	3–1	1
	16 May 1978 v N. Ireland	1–0	
	20 May 1978 v Scotland	1–0	
	24 May 1978 v Hungary	4–1	1
	29 Nov 1978 v Czechoslovakia	1–0	
	7 Feb 1979 v N. Ireland	4–0	
	19 May 1979 v N. Ireland	2–0	
	23 May 1979 v Wales	0–0	
	10 Jun 1979 v Sweden	0–0	

882. Michael Denis Mills

Fullback

Born Godalming, 4 January 1949
Clubs Portsmouth; Ipswich Town; Southampton; Stoke City

Caps	42	*Result*
	11 Oct 1972 v Yugoslavia	1–1
	24 Mar 1976 v Wales	2–1
	8 May 1976 v Wales	1–0
	11 May 1976 v N. Ireland	4–0
	15 May 1976 v Scotland	1–2
	23 May 1976 v Brazil	0–1
	28 May 1976 v Italy	3–2
	13 Jun 1976 v Finland	4–1
	13 Oct 1976 v Finland	2–1
	17 Nov 1976 v Italy	0–2
	28 May 1977 v N. Ireland	2–1
	31 May 1977 v Wales	0–1
	4 Jun 1977 v Scotland	1–2
	23 Feb 1978 v W. Germany	1–2
	19 Apr 1978 v Brazil	1–1
	13 May 1978 v Wales	3–1
	16 May 1978 v N. Ireland	1–0
	20 May 1978 v Scotland	1–0
	24 May 1978 v Hungary	4–1
	20 Sep 1978 v Denmark	4–3
	25 Oct 1978 v Eire	1–1
	7 Feb 1979 v N. Ireland	4–0

19 May 1979 v N. Ireland	2–0
26 May 1979 v Scotland	3–1
6 Jun 1979 v Bulgaria	3–0
13 Jun 1979 v Austria	3–4
9 Sep 1979 v Denmark	1–0
17 Oct 1979 v N. Ireland	5–1
26 Mar 1980 v Spain	2–0
18 Jun 1980 v Spain	2–1
19 Nov 1980 v Switzerland	2–1
30 May 1981 v Switzerland	1–2
6 Jun 1981 v Hungary	3–1
9 Sep 1981 v Norway	1–2
18 Nov 1981 v Hungary	1–0
29 May 1982 v Scotland	1–0
3 Jun 1982 v Finland	4–1
16 Jun 1982 v France	3–1
20 Jun 1982 v Czechoslovakia	2–0
25 Jun 1982 v Kuwait	1–0
29 Jun 1982 v W. Germany	0–0
5 Jul 1982 v Spain	0–0

883. Frank Richard Lampard Snr
Left back
Born West Ham, 20 September 1948
Clubs West Ham Utd; Southend Utd

Caps	2	Result
11 Oct 1972 v Yugoslavia		1–1
31 May 1980 v Australia		2–1

884. Jeffrey Paul Blockley
Centre half
Born Leicester, 12 September 1949
Clubs Midland Athletic; Coventry City; Arsenal; Leicester City; Derby County; Notts County

Caps	1	Result
11 Oct 1972 v Yugoslavia		1–1

885. Michael Roger Channon
Forward
Born Orcheston, 28 November 1948
Clubs Southampton; Manchester City; Caroline Hills FC (Hong Kong); Newcastle Utd; Bristol Rovers; Norwich City; Portsmouth

Caps	46	Result	Goals
11 Oct 1972 v Yugoslavia		1–1	
14 Feb 1973 v Scotland		5–0	1
12 May 1973 v N. Ireland		2–1	
15 May 1973 v Wales		3–0	1
19 May 1973 v Scotland		1–0	
27 May 1973 v Czechoslovakia		1–1	
10 Jun 1973 v Soviet Union		2–1	
14 Jun 1973 v Italy		0–2	
26 Sep 1973 v Austria		7–0	2
17 Oct 1973 v Poland		1–1	
14 Nov 1973 v Italy		0–1	
3 Apr 1974 v Portugal		0–0	
11 May 1974 v Wales		2–0	
15 May 1974 v N. Ireland		1–0	
18 May 1974 v Scotland		0–2	
22 May 1974 v Argentina		2–2	1
29 May 1974 v E. Germany		1–1	1
1 Jun 1974 v Bulgaria		1–0	
5 Jun 1974 v Yugoslavia		2–2	1
30 Oct 1974 v Czechoslovakia		3–0	1
20 Nov 1974 v Portugal		0–0	
12 Mar 1975 v W. Germany		2–0	
16 Apr 1975 v Cyprus		5–0	
11 May 1975 v Cyprus		1–0	
17 May 1975 v N. Ireland		0–0	
21 May 1975 v Wales		2–2	
24 May 1975 v Scotland		5–1	
3 Sep 1975 v Switzerland		2–1	1
30 Oct 1975 v Czechoslovakia		1–2	1
19 Nov 1975 v Portugal		1–1	1
24 Mar 1976 v Wales		2–1	

11 May 1976 v N. Ireland	4–0	2
15 May 1976 v Scotland	1–2	1
23 May 1976 v Brazil	0–1	
28 May 1976 v Italy	3–2	2
13 Jun 1976 v Finland	4–1	1
13 Oct 1976 v Finland	2–1	
17 Nov 1976 v Italy	0–2	
30 Mar 1977 v Luxembourg	5–0	2
28 May 1977 v N. Ireland	2–1	1
31 May 1977 v Wales	0–1	
4 Jun 1977 v Scotland	1–2	1
8 Jun 1977 v Brazil	0–0	
12 Jun 1977 v Argentina	1–1	
15 Jun 1977 v Uruguay	0–0	
7 Sep 1977 v Switzerland	0–0	

886. Raymond Clemence
Goalkeeper
Born Skegness, 5 August 1948
Clubs Notts County; Scunthorpe Utd; Liverpool; Tottenham Hotspur

Caps	61	Result
15 Nov 1972 v Wales		1–0
24 Jan 1973 v Wales		1–1
29 May 1974 v E. Germany		1–1
1 Jun 1974 v Bulgaria		1–0
5 Jun 1974 v Yugoslavia		2–2
30 Oct 1974 v Czechoslovakia		3–0
20 Nov 1974 v Portugal		0–0
12 Mar 1975 v W. Germany		2–0
11 May 1975 v Cyprus		1–0
17 May 1975 v N. Ireland		0–0
21 May 1975 v Wales		2–2
24 May 1975 v Scotland		5–1
3 Sep 1975 v Switzerland		2–1
30 Oct 1975 v Czechoslovakia		1–2
19 Nov 1975 v Portugal		1–1
24 Mar 1976 v Wales		2–1
8 May 1976 v Wales		1–0
11 May 1976 v N. Ireland		4–0
15 May 1976 v Scotland		1–2
23 May 1976 v Brazil		0–1
13 Jun 1976 v Finland		4–1
8 Sep 1976 v Eire		1–1
13 Oct 1976 v Finland		2–1
17 Nov 1976 v Italy		0–2
9 Feb 1977 v Holland		0–2
30 Mar 1977 v Luxembourg		5–0
4 Jun 1977 v Scotland		1–2
8 Jun 1977 v Brazil		0–0
12 Jun 1977 v Argentina		1–1
15 Jun 1977 v Uruguay		0–0
7 Sep 1977 v Switzerland		0–0
12 Oct 1977 v Luxembourg		2–0
16 Nov 1977 v Italy		2–0
22 Feb 1978 v W. Germany		1–2
16 May 1978 v N. Ireland		1–0
20 May 1978 v Scotland		1–0
20 Sep 1978 v Denmark		4–3
25 Oct 1978 v Eire		1–1
7 Feb 1979 v N. Ireland		4–0
19 May 1979 v N. Ireland		2–0
26 May 1979 v Scotland		3–1
6 Jun 1979 v Bulgaria		3–0
13 Jun 1979 v Austria		3–4
9 Sep 1979 v Denmark		1–0
22 Nov 1979 v Bulgaria		2–0
6 Feb 1980 v Eire		2–0
13 May 1980 v Argentina		3–1
17 May 1980 v Wales		1–4
24 May 1980 v Scotland		2–0
12 Jun 1980 v Belgium		1–1
18 Jun 1980 v Spain		2–1
15 Oct 1980 v Romania		1–2
25 Mar 1981 v Spain		1–2

12 May 1981 v Brazil	0–1
30 May 1981 v Switzerland	1–2
6 Jun 1981 v Hungary	3–1
9 Sep 1981 v Norway	1–2
23 Feb 1982 v N. Ireland	4–0
3 Jun 1982 v Finland	4–1
15 Dec 1982 v Luxembourg	9–0
16 Nov 1983 v Luxembourg	4–0

887. Joseph Kevin Keegan
Forward/Midfielder
Born   Armthorpe, 14 February 1951
Clubs   Scunthorpe Utd; Liverpool; SV Hamburg (Germany);
        Southampton; Newcastle Utd

Caps	63	Result	Goals
	15 Nov 1972 v Wales	1–0	
	24 Jan 1973 v Wales	1–1	
	11 May 1974 v Wales	2–0	1
	15 May 1974 v N. Ireland	1–0	
	22 May 1974 v Argentina	2–2	
	29 May 1974 v E. Germany	1–1	
	1 Jun 1974 v Bulgaria	1–0	
	5 Jun 1974 v Yugoslavia	2–2	1
	30 Oct 1974 v Czechoslovakia	3–0	
	12 Mar 1975 v W. Germany	2–0	
	16 Apr 1975 v Cyprus	5–0	
	11 May 1975 v Cyprus	1–0	1
	17 May 1975 v N. Ireland	0–0	
	24 May 1975 v Scotland	5–1	
	3 Sep 1975 v Switzerland	2–1	1
	30 Oct 1975 v Czechoslovakia	1–2	
	19 Nov 1975 v Portugal	1–1	
	24 Mar 1976 v Wales	2–1	
	8 May 1976 v Wales	1–0	
	11 May 1976 v N. Ireland	4–0	
	15 May 1976 v Scotland	1–2	
	23 May 1976 v Brazil	0–1	
	13 Jun 1976 v Finland	4–1	2
	8 Sep 1976 v Eire	1–1	
	13 Oct 1976 v Finland	2–1	
	17 Nov 1976 v Italy	0–2	
	9 Feb 1977 v Holland	0–2	
	30 Mar 1977 v Luxembourg	5–0	1
	31 May 1977 v Wales	0–1	
	8 Jun 1977 v Brazil	0–0	
	12 Jun 1977 v Argentina	1–1	
	15 Jun 1977 v Uruguay	0–0	
	7 Sep 1977 v Switzerland	0–0	
	16 Nov 1977 v Italy	2–0	1
	22 Feb 1978 v W. Germany	1–2	
	19 Apr 1978 v Brazil	1–1	1
	24 May 1978 v Hungary	4–1	
	20 Sep 1978 v Denmark	4–3	2
	25 Oct 1978 v Eire	1–1	
	29 Nov 1978 v Czechoslovakia	1–0	
	7 Feb 1979 v N. Ireland	4–0	1
	23 May 1979 v Wales	0–0	
	26 May 1979 v Scotland	3–1	1
	6 Jun 1979 v Bulgaria	3–0	1
	10 Jun 1979 v Sweden	0–0	
	13 Jun 1979 v Austria	3–4	1
	9 Sep 1979 v Denmark	1–0	1
	17 Oct 1979 v N. Ireland	5–1	
	6 Feb 1980 v Eire	2–0	2
	26 Mar 1980 v Spain	2–0	
	13 May 1980 v Argentina	3–1	1
	12 Jun 1980 v Belgium	1–1	
	15 Jun 1980 v Italy	0–1	
	18 Jun 1980 v Spain	2–1	
	25 Mar 1981 v Spain	1–2	
	30 May 1981 v Switzerland	1–2	
	6 Jun 1981 v Hungary	3–1	1
	9 Sep 1981 v Norway	1–2	
	18 Nov 1981 v Hungary	1–0	
	23 Feb 1982 v N. Ireland	4–0	1

29 May 1982 v Scotland	1–0
3 Jun 1982 v Finland	4–1
5 Jul 1982 v Spain	0–0

888. David Nish
Fullback
Born   Burton-on-Trent, 26 September 1947
Clubs   Measham Imperial; Leicester City; Derby County;
        Tulsa Roughnecks (USA); Seattle Sounders (USA);
        Shepshed Charterhouse

Caps	5	Result
	12 May 1973 v N. Ireland	2–1
	3 Apr 1974 v Portugal	0–0
	11 May 1974 v Wales	2–0
	15 May 1974 v N. Ireland	1–0
	18 May 1974 v Scotland	0–2

889. John Peter Richards
Centre forward
Born   Warrington, 9 November 1950
Clubs   Wolverhampton Wanderers; Derby County;
        Maritimo (Portugal)

Caps	1	Result
	12 May 1973 v N. Ireland	2–1

890. Kevin Hector
Inside left
Born   Leeds, 2 November 1944
Clubs   Bradford Park Avenue; Derby County; Vancouver
        Whitecaps (Canada); Boston Utd; Burton Albion;
        Shepshed Charterhouse; Belper Town

Caps	2	Result
	17 Oct 1973 v Poland	1–1
	14 Nov 1973 v Italy	0–1

891. Philip Parkes
Goalkeeper
Born   Sedgeley, 8 August 1950
Clubs   Walsall; Brierley Hill Alliance; Queen's Park
        Rangers; West Ham Utd; Ipswich Town

Caps	1	Result
	3 Apr 1974 v Portugal	0–0

892. Michael Pejic
Left back
Born   Chesterton, 25 January 1950
Clubs   Stoke City; Everton; Aston Villa

Caps	4	Result
	3 Apr 1974 v Portugal	0–0
	1 May 1974 v Wales	2–0
	15 May 1974 v N. Ireland	1–0
	18 May 1974 v Scotland	0–2

893. Martin Dobson
Midfielder
Born   Blackburn, 14 February 1948
Clubs   Bolton Wanderers; Burnley; Everton; Bury

Caps	5	Result
	3 Apr 1974 v Portugal	0–0
	29 May 1974 v E. Germany	1–1
	1 Jun 1974 v Bulgaria	1–0
	5 Jun 1974 v Yugoslavia	2–2
	30 Oct 1974 v Czechoslovakia	3–0

894. David Vernon Watson
Centre half
Born   Stapleford, 5 October 1946
Clubs   Notts County; Rotherham Utd; Sunderland;
        Manchester City; Werder Bremen (Germany);
        Southampton; Stoke City; Vancouver Whitecaps
        (Canada); Fort Lauderdale (USA); Kettering Town

Caps	65	Result	Goals
	3 Apr 1974 v Portugal	0–0	
	18 May 1974 v Scotland	0–2	
	22 May 1974 v Argentina	2–2	

29 May 1974 v E. Germany	1–1
1 Jun 1974 v Bulgaria	1–0
5 Jun 1974 v Yugoslavia	2–2
30 Oct 1974 v Czechoslovakia	3–0
20 Nov 1974 v Portugal	0–0
12 Mar 1975 v W. Germany	2–0
16 Apr 1975 v Cyprus	5–0
11 May 1975 v Cyprus	1–0
17 May 1975 v N. Ireland	0–0
21 May 1975 v Wales	2–2
24 May 1975 v Scotland	5–1
3 Sep 1975 v Switzerland	2–1
30 Oct 1975 v Czechoslovakia	1–2
19 Nov 1975 v Portugal	1–1
9 Feb 1977 v Holland	0–2
30 Mar 1977 v Luxembourg	5–0
28 May 1977 v N. Ireland	2–1
31 May 1977 v Wales	0–1
4 Jun 1977 v Scotland	1–2
8 Jun 1977 v Brazil	0–0
12 Jun 1977 v Argentina	1–1
15 Jun 1977 v Uruguay	0–0
7 Sep 1977 v Switzerland	0–0
12 Oct 1977 v Luxembourg	2–0
16 Nov 1977 v Italy	2–0
22 Feb 1978 v W. Germany	1–2
19 Apr 1978 v Brazil	1–1
13 May 1978 v Wales	3–1
16 May 1978 v N. Ireland	1–0
20 May 1978 v Scotland	1–0
24 May 1978 v Hungary	4–1
20 Sep 1978 v Denmark	4–3
25 Oct 1978 v Eire	1–1
29 Nov 1978 v Czechoslovakia	1–0

7 Feb 1979 v N. Ireland	4–0	1
19 May 1979 v N. Ireland	2–0	1
23 May 1979 v Wales	0–0	
26 May 1979 v Scotland	3–1	
6 Jun 1979 v Bulgaria	3–0	1
10 Jun 1979 v Sweden	0–0	
13 Jun 1979 v Austria	3–4	
9 Sep 1979 v Denmark	1–0	
17 Oct 1979 v N. Ireland	5–1	
22 Nov 1979 v Bulgaria	2–0	1
6 Feb 1980 v Eire	2–0	
26 Mar 1980 v Spain	2–0	
13 May 1980 v Argentina	3–1	
20 May 1980 v N. Ireland	1–1	
24 May 1980 v Scotland	2–0	
12 Jun 1980 v Belgium	1–1	
15 Jun 1980 v Italy	0–1	
18 Jun 1980 v Spain	2–1	
10 Sep 1980 v Norway	4–0	
15 Oct 1980 v Romania	1–2	
19 Nov 1980 v Switzerland	2–1	
29 Apr 1981 v Romania	0–0	
20 May 1981 v Wales	0–0	
23 May 1981 v Scotland	0–1	
30 May 1981 v Switzerland	1–2	
6 Jun 1981 v Hungary	3–1	
23 Feb 1982 v N. Ireland	4–0	
2 Jun 1982 v Iceland	1–1	

895. Stanley Bowles
Forward/Midfielder
Born Moston, 24 December 1948
Clubs Manchester City; Crewe Alexandra; Carlisle Utd; Queen's Park Rangers; Nottingham Forest; Orient; Brentford

Caps	5	*Result*	*Goals*
3 Apr 1974 v Portugal		0–0	
11 May 1974 v Wales		2–0	1
15 May 1974 v N. Ireland		1–0	
17 Nov 1976 v Italy		0–2	
9 Feb 1977 v Holland		0–2	

896. Trevor David Brooking
Midfielder
Born Barking, 2 October 1948
Clubs West Ham Utd

Caps	47	*Result*	*Goals*
3 Apr 1974 v Portugal		0–0	
22 May 1974 v Argentina		2–2	
29 May 1974 v E. Germany		1–1	
1 Jun 1974 v Bulgaria		1–0	
5 Jun 1974 v Yugoslavia		3–0	
30 Oct 1974 v Czechoslovakia		3–0	
20 Nov 1974 v Portugal		0–0	
19 Nov 1975 v Portugal		1–1	
24 Mar 1976 v Wales		2–1	
23 May 1976 v Brazil		0–1	
28 May 1976 v Italy		3–2	
13 Jun 1976 v Finland		4–1	
8 Sep 1976 v Eire		1–1	
13 Oct 1976 v Finland		2–1	
17 Nov 1976 v Italy		0–2	
9 Feb 1977 v Holland		0–2	
28 May 1977 v N. Ireland		2–1	
31 May 1977 v Wales		0–1	
16 Nov 1977 v Italy		2–0	1
22 Feb 1978 v W. Germany		1–2	
13 May 1978 v Wales		3–1	
20 May 1978 v Scotland		1–0	
24 May 1978 v Hungary		4–1	
20 Sep 1978 v Denmark		4–3	
25 Oct 1978 v Eire		1–1	
7 Feb 1979 v N. Ireland		4–0	
23 May 1979 v Wales		0–0	
26 May 1979 v Scotland		3–1	
6 Jun 1979 v Bulgaria		3–0	
10 Jun 1979 v Sweden		0–0	
13 Jun 1979 v Austria		3–4	
9 Sep 1979 v Denmark		1–0	
17 Oct 1979 v N. Ireland		5–1	
13 May 1980 v Argentina		3–1	
17 May 1980 v Wales		1–4	
20 May 1980 v N. Ireland		1–1	
24 May 1980 v Scotland		2–0	1
12 Jun 1980 v Belgium		1–1	
18 Jun 1980 v Spain		2–1	1
19 Nov 1980 v Switzerland		2–1	
25 Mar 1981 v Spain		1–2	
29 Apr 1981 v Romania		0–0	
6 Jun 1981 v Hungary		3–1	2
18 Sep 1981 v Hungary		1–0	
29 May 1982 v Scotland		1–0	
3 Jun 1982 v Finland		4–1	
5 Jul 1982 v Spain		0–0	

897. Keith Weller
Forward
Born Islington, 11 June 1946
Died 12 November 2004
Clubs Tottenham Hotspur; Millwall; Chelsea; Leicester City; New England Teamen (USA)

Caps	4	*Result*	*Goals*
1 May 1974 v Wales		2–0	
15 May 1974 v N. Ireland		1–0	1
18 May 1974 v Scotland		0–2	
22 May 1974 v Argentina		2–2	

898. Frank Stuart Worthington
Forward
Born Halifax, 23 November 1948
Clubs Huddersfield Town; Leicester City; Bolton Wanderers; Birmingham City; Tampa Bay Rowdies (USA); Leeds Utd; Sunderland; Southampton; Brighton & Hove Albion; Tranmere Rovers; Preston North End; Stalybridge Celtic; Chorley

Caps	8	*Result*	*Goals*
15 May 1974 v N. Ireland		1–0	

18 May 1974 v Scotland	0–2	
22 May 1974 v Argentina	2–2	1
29 May 1974 v E. Germany	1–1	
1 Jun 1974 v Bulgaria	1–0	1
5 Jun 1974 v Yugoslavia	2–2	
30 Oct 1974 v Czechoslovakia	3–0	
20 Nov 1974 v Portugal	0–0	

899. Alec Lindsay
Left back
Born Bury, 27 February 1948
Clubs Bury; Liverpool; Stoke City; Oakland (USA); Newton FC

Caps	4	Result
	22 May 1974 v Argentina	2–2
	29 May 1974 v E. Germany	1–1
	1 Jun 1974 v Bulgaria	1–0
	5 Jun 1974 v Yugoslavia	2–2

900. Gerald Charles James Francis
Midfielder
Born Hammersmith, 6 December 1951
Clubs Queen's Park Rangers; Crystal Palace; Coventry City; Exeter City; Cardiff City; Swansea City; Portsmouth; Wimbledon; Bristol Rovers

Caps	12	Result	Goals
	30 Oct 1974 v Czechoslovakia	3–0	
	20 Nov 1974 v Portugal	0–0	
	21 May 1975 v Wales	2–2	
	24 May 1975 v Scotland	5–1	2
	3 Sep 1975 v Switzerland	2–1	
	30 Oct 1975 v Czechoslovakia	1–2	
	19 Nov 1975 v Portugal	1–1	
	8 May 1976 v Wales	1–0	
	11 May 1976 v N. Ireland	4–0	1
	15 May 1976 v Scotland	1–2	
	23 May 1976 v Brazil	0–1	
	13 Jun 1976 v Finland	4–1	

901. David Thomas
Winger
Born Kirkby-in-Ashfield, 5 October 1950
Clubs Burnley; Queen's Park Rangers; Everton; Wolverhampton Wanderers; Middlesbrough; Portsmouth

Caps	8	Result
	30 Oct 1974 v Czechoslovakia	3–0
	20 Nov 1974 v Portugal	0–0
	16 Apr 1975 v Cyprus	5–0
	11 May 1975 v Cyprus	1–0
	21 May 1975 v Wales	2–2
	24 May 1975 v Scotland	5–1
	30 Oct 1975 v Czechoslovakia	1–2
	19 Nov 1975 v Portugal	1–1

902. Stephen Whitworth
Right back
Born Coalville, 20 March 1952
Clubs Leicester City; Sunderland; Bolton Wanderers; Mansfield Town

Caps	7	Result
	12 Mar 1975 v W. Germany	2–0
	11 May 1975 v Cyprus	1–0
	17 May 1975 v N. Ireland	0–0
	21 May 1975 v Wales	2–2
	24 May 1975 v Scotland	5–1
	3 Sep 1975 v Switzerland	2–1
	19 Nov 1975 v Portugal	1–1

903. Ian Terry Gillard
Left back
Born Hammersmith, 9 October 1950
Clubs Queen's Park Rangers; Aldershot

Caps	3	Result
	12 Mar 1975 v W. Germany	2–0

21 May 1975 v Wales	2–2	
30 Oct 1975 v Czechoslovakia	1–2	

904. Alan Anthony Hudson
Midfielder
Born Chelsea, 21 June 1951
Clubs Chelsea; Stoke City; Arsenal; Seattle Sounders (USA)

Caps	2	Result
	12 Mar 1975 v W. Germany	2–0
	16 Apr 1975 v Cyprus	5–0

905. Thomas Kevin Beattie
Left half/Left back
Born Carlisle, 18 December 1953
Clubs Ipswich Town; Colchester Utd; Middlesbrough

Caps	9	Result	Goals
	16 Apr 1975 v Cyprus	5–0	
	11 May 1975 v Cyprus	1–0	
	24 May 1975 v Scotland	5–1	1
	3 Sep 1975 v Switzerland	2–1	
	19 Nov 1975 v Portugal	1–1	
	13 Oct 1976 v Finland	2–1	
	17 Nov 1976 v Italy	0–2	
	9 Feb 1977 v Holland	0–2	
	12 Oct 1977 v Luxembourg	2–0	

906. Dennis Tueart
Forward
Born Newcastle, 27 November 1949
Clubs Sunderland; Manchester City; New York Cosmos (USA); Stoke City; Burnley

Caps	6	Result	Goals
	11 May 1975 v Cyprus	1–0	
	17 May 1975 v N. Ireland	0–0	
	13 Oct 1976 v Finland	2–1	1
	28 May 1977 v N. Ireland	2–1	1
	31 May 1977 v Wales	0–1	
	4 Jun 1977 v Scotland	1–2	

907. Colin Viljoen
Midfielder
Born Johannesburg, 20 June 1948
Clubs Southern Transvaal (South Africa); Ipswich Town; Manchester City; Chelsea

Caps	2	Result
	17 May 1975 v N. Ireland	0–0
	21 May 1975 v Wales	2–2

908. David Edward Johnson
Centre forward
Born Liverpool, 23 October 1951
Clubs Everton; Ipswich Town; Liverpool; Barnsley; Manchester City; Tulsa Roughnecks (USA); Preston North End

Caps	8	Result	Goals
	24 May 1975 v Scotland	5–1	1
	3 Sep 1975 v Switzerland	2–1	
	24 Mar 1976 v Wales	2–1	2
	6 Feb 1980 v Eire	2–0	
	13 May 1980 v Argentina	3–1	2
	20 May 1980 v N. Ireland	1–1	1
	24 May 1980 v Scotland	2–0	
	12 Jun 1980 v Belgium	1–1	

909. Brian Little
Forward
Born Peterlee, 25 November 1953
Clubs Aston Villa

Caps	1	Result
	21 May 1975 v Wales	2–2

910. Trevor Cherry
Fullback/Midfielder
Born Huddersfield, 23 February 1948
Clubs Huddersfield Town; Leeds Utd; Bradford City

Caps	27	Result
	24 Mar 1976 v Wales	2–1
	15 May 1976 v Scotland	1–2
	23 May 1976 v Brazil	0–1
	13 Jun 1976 v Finland	4–1
	8 Sep 1976 v Eire	1–1
	17 Nov 1976 v Italy	0–2
	30 Mar 1977 v Luxembourg	5–0
	28 May 1977 v N. Ireland	2–1
	4 Jun 1977 v Scotland	1–2
	8 Jun 1977 v Brazil	0–0
	12 Jun 1977 v Argentina	1–1
	15 Jun 1977 v Uruguay	0–0
	7 Sep 1977 v Switzerland	0–0
	12 Oct 1977 v Luxembourg	2–0
	16 Nov 1977 v Italy	2–0
	19 Apr 1978 v Brazil	1–1
	13 May 1978 v Wales	3–1
	29 Nov 1978 v Czechoslovakia	1–0
	23 May 1979 v Wales	0–0
	10 Jun 1979 v Sweden	0–0
	6 Feb 1980 v Eire	2–0
	13 May 1980 v Argentina	3–1
	17 May 1980 v Wales	1–4
	20 May 1980 v N. Ireland	1–1
	24 May 1980 v Scotland	2–0
	31 May 1980 v Australia	2–1
	18 Jun 1980 v Spain	2–1

911. Philip George Neal
Right back
Born Irchester, 20 February 1951
Clubs Irchester FC; Northampton Town; Liverpool; Bolton Wanderers

Caps	50	Result	Goals
	24 Mar 1976 v Wales	2–1	
	28 May 1976 v Italy	3–2	
	31 May 1977 v Wales	0–1	
	4 Jun 1977 v Scotland	1–2	
	8 Jun 1977 v Brazil	0–0	
	12 Jun 1977 v Argentina	1–1	
	15 Jun 1977 v Uruguay	0–0	
	7 Sep 1977 v Switzerland	0–0	
	16 Nov 1977 v Italy	2–0	
	22 Feb 1978 v W. Germany	1–2	
	16 May 1978 v N. Ireland	1–0	1
	20 May 1978 v Scotland	1–0	
	24 May 1978 v Hungary	4–1	1
	20 Sep 1978 v Denmark	4–3	1
	25 Oct 1978 v Eire	1–1	
	7 Feb 1979 v N. Ireland	4–0	
	19 May 1979 v N. Ireland	2–0	
	26 May 1979 v Scotland	3–1	
	6 Jun 1979 v Bulgaria	3–0	
	13 Jun 1979 v Austria	3–4	
	9 Sep 1979 v Denmark	1–0	
	17 Oct 1979 v N. Ireland	5–1	
	26 Mar 1980 v Spain	2–0	
	13 May 1980 v Argentina	3–1	
	17 May 1980 v Wales	1–4	
	12 Jun 1980 v Belgium	1–1	
	15 Jun 1980 v Italy	0–1	
	15 Oct 1980 v Romania	1–2	
	19 Nov 1980 v Switzerland	2–1	
	25 Mar 1981 v Spain	1–2	
	12 May 1981 v Brazil	0–1	
	6 Jun 1981 v Hungary	3–1	
	9 Sep 1981 v Norway	1–2	
	18 Nov 1981 v Hungary	1–0	
	27 Apr 1982 v Wales	1–0	
	25 May 1982 v Holland	2–0	
	2 Jun 1982 v Iceland	1–1	
	16 Jun 1982 v France	3–1	
	25 Jun 1982 v Kuwait	1–0	
	22 Sep 1982 v Denmark	2–2	

	17 Nov 1982 v Greece	3–0
	15 Dec 1982 v Luxembourg	9–0
	23 Feb 1983 v Wales	2–1
	30 Mar 1983 v Greece	0–0
	27 Apr 1983 v Hungary	2–0
	28 May 1983 v N. Ireland	0–0
	1 Jun 1983 v Scotland	2–0
	15 Jun 1983 v Australia	1–0
	19 Jun 1983 v Australia	1–1
	21 Sep 1983 v Denmark	0–1

912. Philip Bernard Thompson
Central defender
Born Liverpool, 21 January 1954
Clubs Liverpool; Sheffield Utd

Caps	42	Result	Goals
	24 Mar 1976 v Wales	2–1	
	8 May 1976 v Wales	1–0	
	11 May 1976 v N. Ireland	4–0	
	15 May 1976 v Scotland	1–2	
	23 May 1976 v Brazil	0–1	
	28 May 1976 v Italy	3–2	1
	13 Jun 1976 v Finland	4–1	
	13 Oct 1976 v Finland	2–1	
	25 Oct 1978 v Eire	1–1	
	29 Nov 1978 v Czechoslovakia	1–0	
	19 May 1979 v N. Ireland	2–0	
	26 May 1979 v Scotland	3–1	
	6 Jun 1979 v Bulgaria	3–0	
	10 Jun 1979 v Sweden	0–0	
	13 Jun 1979 v Austria	3–4	
	9 Sep 1979 v Denmark	1–0	
	17 Oct 1979 v N. Ireland	5–1	
	22 Nov 1979 v Bulgaria	2–0	
	6 Feb 1980 v Eire	2–0	
	26 Mar 1980 v Spain	2–0	
	13 May 1980 v Argentina	3–1	
	17 May 1980 v Wales	1–4	
	24 May 1980 v Scotland	2–0	
	12 Jun 1980 v Belgium	1–1	
	15 Jun 1980 v Italy	0–1	
	18 Jun 1980 v Spain	2–1	
	10 Sep 1980 v Norway	4–0	
	15 Oct 1980 v Romania	1–2	
	6 Jun 1981 v Hungary	3–1	
	9 Sep 1981 v Norway	1–2	
	18 Nov 1981 v Hungary	1–0	
	27 Apr 1982 v Wales	1–0	
	25 May 1982 v Holland	2–0	
	29 May 1982 v Scotland	1–0	
	3 Jun 1982 v Finland	4–1	
	16 Jun 1982 v France	3–1	
	20 Jun 1982 v Czechoslovakia	2–0	
	25 Jun 1982 v Kuwait	1–0	
	29 Jun 1982 v W. Germany	0–0	
	5 Jul 1982 v Spain	0–0	
	13 Oct 1982 v W. Germany	1–2	
	17 Nov 1982 v Greece	3–0	

913. Michael Doyle
Right half
Born Manchester, 25 November 1946
Clubs Manchester City; Stoke City; Bolton Wanderers; Rochdale

Caps	5	Result
	24 Mar 1976 v Wales	2–1
	15 May 1976 v Scotland	1–2
	23 May 1976 v Brazil	0–1
	28 May 1976 v Italy	3–2
	9 Feb 1977 v Holland	0–2

914. Philip John Boyer
Forward
Born Nottingham, 25 January 1949
Clubs Derby County; York City; Bournemouth; Norwich

City; Southampton; Manchester City; Bulova FC (Hong Kong); Grantham; Stamford; Shepshed Charterhouse

Caps	1	Result
	24 Mar 1976 v Wales	2–1

915. Raymond Kennedy
Inside forward
Born Seaton Delaval, 28 July 1951
Clubs Arsenal; Liverpool; Swansea City; Hartlepool Utd

Caps	17	Result	Goals
	24 Mar 1976 v Wales	2–1	1
	8 May 1976 v Wales	1–0	
	11 May 1976 v N. Ireland	4–0	
	15 May 1976 v Scotland	1–2	
	30 Mar 1977 v Luxembourg	5–0	1
	31 May 1977 v Wales	0–1	
	4 Jun 1977 v Scotland	1–2	
	8 Jun 1977 v Brazil	0–0	
	12 Jun 1977 v Argentina	1–1	
	7 Sep 1977 v Switzerland	0–0	
	12 Oct 1977 v Luxembourg	2–0	1
	22 Nov 1979 v Bulgaria	2–0	
	26 Mar 1980 v Spain	2–0	
	13 May 1980 v Argentina	3–1	
	17 May 1980 v Wales	1–4	
	12 Jun 1980 v Belgium	1–1	
	15 Jun 1980 v Italy	0–1	

916. David Thomas Clement
Right back
Born Battersea, 2 February 1948
Died 31 March 1982
Clubs Queen's Park Rangers; Bolton Wanderers; Fulham; Wimbledon

Caps	5	Result
	24 Mar 1976 v Wales	2–1
	8 May 1976 v Wales	1–0
	28 May 1976 v Italy	3–2
	17 Nov 1976 v Italy	0–2
	9 Feb 1977 v Holland	0–2

917. Peter John Taylor
Winger
Born Southend-on-Sea, 3 January 1953
Clubs Canvey Island FC; Southend Utd; Crystal Palace; Tottenham Hotspur; Orient; Oldham Athletic (on loan); Maidstone Utd; Exeter City

Caps	4	Result	Goals
	24 Mar 1976 v Wales	2–1	1
	8 May 1976 v Wales	1–0	1
	11 May 1976 v N. Ireland	4–0	
	15 May 1976 v Scotland	1–2	

918. Mark Anthony Towers
Midfielder
Born Manchester, 13 April 1952
Clubs Manchester City; Sunderland; Birmingham City; Montreal Manic (Canada)

Caps	3	Result
	8 May 1976 v Wales	1–0
	11 May 1976 v N. Ireland	4–0
	28 May 1976 v Italy	3–2

919. Brian Greenhoff
Central defender
Born Barnsley, 28 April 1953
Clubs Manchester Utd; Leeds Utd; Rochdale

Caps	18	Result
	8 May 1976 v Wales	1–0
	11 May 1976 v N. Ireland	4–0
	8 Sep 1976 v Eire	1–1
	13 Oct 1976 v Finland	2–1
	17 Nov 1976 v Italy	0–2
	9 Feb 1977 v Holland	0–2

	28 May 1977 v N. Ireland	2–1
	31 May 1977 v Wales	0–1
	4 Jun 1977 v Scotland	1–2
	8 Jun 1977 v Brazil	0–0
	12 Jun 197 v Argentina	1–1
	15 Jun 1977 v Uruguay	0–0
	19 Apr 1978 v Brazil	1–1
	13 May 1978 v Wales	3–1
	16 May 1978 v N. Ireland	1–0
	20 May 1978 v Scotland	1–0
	24 May 1978 v Hungary	4–1
	31 May 1980 v Australia	2–1

920. James Stuart Pearson
Centre forward
Born Hull, 21 June 1949
Clubs Hull City; Manchester Utd; West Ham Utd

Caps	15	Result	Goals
	8 May 1976 v Wales	1–0	
	11 May 1976 v N. Ireland	4–0	1
	15 May 1976 v Scotland	1–2	
	23 May 1976 v Brazil	0–1	
	13 Jun 1976 v Finland	4–1	1
	8 Sep 1976 v Eire	1–1	1
	9 Feb 1977 v Holland	0–2	
	31 May 1977 v Wales	0–1	
	4 Jun 1977 v Scotland	1–2	
	8 Jun 1977 v Brazil	0–0	
	12 Jun 1977 v Argentina	1–1	1
	15 Jun 1977 v Uruguay	0–0	
	16 Nov 1977 v Italy	2–0	
	22 Feb 1978 v W. Germany	1–2	1
	16 May 1978 v N. Ireland	1–0	

921. John James Rimmer
Goalkeeper
Born Southport, 10 February 1948
Clubs Manchester Utd; Swansea City; Arsenal; Aston Villa; Luton Town

Caps	1	Result
	28 May 1976 v Italy	3–2

922. Raymond Colin Wilkins
Midfielder
Born Hillingdon, 14 September 1956
Clubs Chelsea; Manchester Utd; AC Milan (Italy) Saint-Germain (France); Glasgow Rangers; Queen's Park Rangers; Crystal Palace; Wycombe Wanderers; Hibernian; Millwall; Leyton Orient

Caps	84	Result	Goals
	28 May 1976 v Italy	3–2	
	8 Sep 1976 v Eire	1–1	
	13 Oct 1976 v Finland	2–1	
	28 May 1977 v N. Ireland	2–1	
	8 Jun 1977 v Brazil	0–0	
	12 Jun 1977 v Argentina	1–1	
	15 Jun 1977 v Uruguay	0–0	
	7 Sep 1977 v Switzerland	0–0	
	12 Oct 1977 v Luxembourg	2–0	
	16 Nov 1977 v Italy	2–0	
	22 Feb 1978 v W. Germany	1–2	
	13 May 1978 v Wales	3–1	
	16 May 1978 v N. Ireland	1–0	
	20 May 1978 v Scotland	1–0	
	24 May 1978 v Hungary	4–1	
	20 Sep 1978 v Denmark	4–3	
	25 Oct 1978 v Eire	1–1	
	29 Nov 1978 v Czechoslovakia	1–0	
	19 May 1979 v N. Ireland	2–0	
	23 May 1979 v Wales	0–0	
	26 May 1979 v Scotland	3–1	
	6 Jun 1979 v Bulgaria	3–0	
	10 Jun 1979 v Sweden	0–0	
	13 Jun 1979 v Austria	3–4	1
	9 Sep 1979 v Denmark	1–0	

17 Oct 1979 v N. Ireland	5–1	
22 Nov 1979 v Bulgaria	2–0	
26 Mar 1980 v Spain	2–0	
13 May 1980 v Argentina	3–1	
17 May 1980 v Wales	1–4	
20 May 1980 v N. Ireland	1–1	
24 May 1980 v Scotland	2–0	
12 Jun 1980 v Belgium	1–1	1
15 Jun 1980 v Italy	0–1	
18 Jun 1980 v Spain	2–1	
25 Mar 1981 v Spain	1–2	
29 Apr 1981 v Romania	0–0	
12 May 1981 v Brazil	0–1	
20 May 1981 v Wales	0–0	
23 May 1981 v Scotland	0–1	
30 May 1981 v Switzerland	1–2	
6 Jun 1981 v Hungary	3–1	
23 Feb 1982 v N. Ireland	4–0	1
27 Apr 1982 v Wales	1–0	
25 May 1982 v Holland	2–0	
29 May 1982 v Scotland	2–0	
3 Jun 1982 v Finland	4–1	
16 Jun 1982 v France	3–1	
20 Jun 1982 v Czechoslovakia	2–0	
25 Jun 1982 v Kuwait	1–0	
29 Jun 1982 v W. Germany	0–0	
5 Jul 1982 v Spain	0–0	
22 Sep 1982 v Denmark	2–2	
13 Oct 1982 v W. Germany	1–2	
21 Sep 1983 v Denmark	0–1	
4 Apr 1984 v N. Ireland	1–0	
2 May 1984 v Wales	0–1	
26 May 1984 v Scotland	1–1	
2 Jun 1984 v Soviet Union	0–2	
10 Jun 1984 v Brazil	2–0	
13 Jun 1984 v Uruguay	0–2	
17 Jun 1984 v Chile	0–0	
12 Sep 1984 v E. Germany	1–0	
17 Oct 1984 v Finland	5–0	
14 Nov 1984 v Turkey	8–0	
27 Feb 1985 v N. Ireland	1–0	
26 Mar 1985 v Eire	2–1	
1 May 1985 v Romania	0–0	
22 May 1985 v Finland	1–1	
25 May 1985 v Scotland	0–1	
6 Jun 1985 v Italy	1–2	
9 Jun 1985 v Mexico	0–1	
16 Oct 1985 v Turkey	5–0	
13 Nov 1985 v N. Ireland	0–0	
29 Jan 1986 v Egypt	4–0	
26 Feb 1986 v Israel	2–1	
26 Mar 1986 v Soviet Union	1–0	
23 Apr 1986 v Scotland	2–1	
17 May 1986 v Mexico	3–0	
24 May 1986 v Canada	1–0	
3 Jun 1986 v Portugal	0–1	
6 Jun 1986 v Morocco	0–0	
10 Sep 1986 v Sweden	0–1	
12 Nov 1986 v Yugoslavia	2–0	

923. Gordon Alec Hill
Outside left
Born Sunbury-on-Thames, 1 April 1954
Clubs Staines Town; Southall; Millwall; Manchester Utd;
Derby County; Queen's Park Rangers; Montreal
Manic (Canada); Chicago Sting (USA); Stafford
Rangers; Northwich Victoria

Caps	6	Result
28 May 1976 v Italy		3–2
8 Sep 1976 v Eire		1–1
13 Oct 1976 v Finland		2–1
30 Mar 1977 v Luxembourg		5–0
7 Sep 1977 v Switzerland		0–0
12 Oct 1977 v Luxembourg		2–0

924. Joseph Thomas Corrigan
Goalkeeper
Born Manchester, 18 November 1948
Clubs Sale FC; Manchester City; Seattle Sounders (USA);
Brighton & Hove Albion; Norwich City; Stoke City

Caps	9	Result
28 May 1976 v Italy		3–2
19 Apr 1978 v Brazil		1–1
23 May 1979 v Wales		0–0
20 May 1980 v N. Ireland		1–1
31 May 1980 v Australia		2–1
20 May 1981 v Wales		0–0
23 May 1981 v Scotland		0–1
27 Apr 1982 v Wales		1–0
2 Jun 1982 v Iceland		1–1

925. Charles Frederick George
Forward
Born Islington, 10 October 1950
Clubs Arsenal; Derby County; Southampton; Nottingham
Forest; Bulova FC (Hong Kong); Bournemouth

Caps	1	Result
8 Sept 1976 v Eire		1–1

926. Trevor John Francis
Forward
Born Plymouth, 19 April 1954
Clubs Birmingham City; Nottingham Forest; Manchester
City; Sampdoria (Italy); Atalanta (Italy); Glasgow
Rangers; Queen's Park Rangers

Caps	52	Result	Goals
9 Feb 1977 v Holland		0–2	
30 Mar 1977 v Luxembourg		5–0	1
4 Jun 1977 v Scotland		1–2	
8 Jun 1977 v Brazil		0–0	
7 Sep 1977 v Switzerland		0–0	
12 Oct 1977 v Luxembourg		2–0	
16 Nov 1977 v Italy		2–0	
22 Feb 1978 v W. Germany		1–2	
19 Apr 1978 v Brazil		1–1	
13 May 1978 v Wales		3–1	
20 May 1978 v Scotland		1–0	
24 May 1978 v Hungary		4–1	1
6 Jun 1979 v Bulgaria		3–0	
10 Jun 1979 v Sweden		0–0	
13 Jun 1979 v Austria		3–4	
17 Oct 1979 v N. Ireland		5–1	2
22 Nov 1979 v Bulgaria		2–0	
26 Mar 1980 v Spain		1–2	1
25 Mar 1981 v Spain		2–1	
29 Apr 1981 v Romania		0–0	
29 May 1981 v Scotland		0–1	
30 May 1981 v Switzerland		1–2	
9 Sep 1981 v Norway		1–2	
23 Feb 1982 v N. Ireland		4–0	
27 Apr 1982 v Wales		1–0	1
29 May 1982 v Scotland		1–0	
3 Jun 1982 v Finland		4–1	
16 Jun 1982 v France		3–1	
20 Jun 1982 v Czechoslovakia		2–0	1
25 Jun 1982 v Kuwait		1–0	1
29 Jun 1982 v W. Germany		0–0	
5 Jul 1982 v Spain		0–0	
22 Sep 1982 v Denmark		2–2	2
30 Mar 1983 v Greece		0–0	
27 Apr 1983 v Hungary		2–0	1
28 May 1983 v N. Ireland		0–0	
1 Jun 1983 v Scotland		2–0	
12 Jun 1983 v Australia		0–0	
15 Jun 1983 v Australia		1–0	
19 Jun 1983 v Australia		1–1	1
21 Sep 1983 v Denmark		0–1	
4 Apr 1984 v N. Ireland		1–0	
2 Jun 1984 v Soviet Union		0–2	
12 Sep 1984 v E. Germany		1–0	
14 Nov 1984 v Turkey		8–0	

27 Feb 1985 v N. Ireland	1–0	
1 May 1985 v Romania	0–0	
22 May 1985 v Finland	1–1	
25 May 1985 v Scotland	0–1	
6 Jun 1985 v Italy	1–2	
9 Jun 1985 v Mexico	0–1	
23 Apr 1986 v Scotland	2–1	

927. John Gidman
Right back
Born   Liverpool, 10 January 1954
Clubs   Liverpool; Aston Villa; Everton; Manchester Utd;
        Manchester City; Stoke City

Caps	1	Result	
	30 Mar 1977 v Luxembourg	5–0	

928. Paul Mariner
Centre forward
Born   Bolton, 22 May 1953
Clubs   Chorley; Plymouth Argyle; Ipswich Town; Arsenal;
        Portsmouth; Colchester Utd

Caps	35	Result	Goals
	30 Mar 1977 v Luxembourg	5–0	
	28 May 1977 v N. Ireland	2–1	
	12 Oct 1977 v Luxembourg	2–0	1
	13 May 1978 v Wales	3–1	
	20 May 1978 v Scotland	1–0	
	17 May 1980 v Wales	1–4	1
	20 May 1980 v N. Ireland	1–1	
	24 May 1980 v Scotland	2–0	
	31 May 1980 v Australia	2–1	1
	15 Jun 1980 v Italy	0–1	
	18 May 1980 v Spain	2–1	
	10 Sep 1980 v Norway	4–0	1
	19 Nov 1980 v Switzerland	2–1	1
	25 Mar 1981 v Spain	1–2	
	30 May 1981 v Switzerland	1–2	
	6 Jun 1981 v Hungary	3–1	
	9 Sep 1981 v Norway	1–2	
	18 Nov 1981 v Hungary	1–0	1
	25 May 1982 v Holland	2–0	1
	29 May 1982 v Scotland	1–0	1
	3 Jun 1982 v Finland	4–1	2
	16 Jun 1982 v France	3–1	1
	20 Jun 1982 v Czechoslovakia	2–0	
	25 Jun 1982 v Kuwait	1–0	
	29 Jun 1982 v W. Germany	0–0	
	5 Jul 1982 v Spain	0–0	
	22 Sep 1982 v Denmark	2–2	
	13 Oct 1982 v W. Germany	1–2	
	17 Nov 1982 v Greece	3–0	
	23 Feb 1983 v Wales	2–1	
	21 Sep 1983 v Denmark	0–1	
	12 Oct 1983 v Hungary	3–0	1
	16 Nov 1983 v Luxembourg	4–0	1
	12 Nov 1984 v E. Germany	1–0	
	1 May 1985 v Romania	0–0	

929. Brian Ernest Talbot
Midfielder
Born   Ipswich, 21 July 1953
Clubs   Ipswich Town; Arsenal; Watford; Stoke City; West
        Bromwich Albion

Caps	6	Result
	28 May 1977 v N. Ireland	2–1
	4 Jun 1977 v Scotland	1–2
	8 Jun 1977 v Brazil	0–0
	12 Jun 1977 v Argentina	1–1
	15 Jun 1977 v Uruguay	0–0
	31 May 1980 v Australia	2–1

930. Terence McDermott
Midfielder
Born   Kirkby, 8 December 1951
Clubs   Bury; Newcastle Utd; Liverpool

Caps	25	Result	Goals
	7 Sep 1977 v Switzerland	0–0	

12 Oct 1977 v Luxembourg	2–0	
19 May 1979 v N. Ireland	2–0	
23 May 1979 v Wales	0–0	
10 Jun 1979 v Sweden	0–0	
9 Sep 1979 v Denmark	1–0	
17 Oct 1979 v N. Ireland	5–1	
6 Feb 1980 v Eire	2–0	
20 May 1980 v N. Ireland	1–1	
24 May 1980 v Scotland	2–0	
12 Jun 1980 v Belgium	1–1	
18 Jun 1980 v Spain	2–1	
10 Sep 1980 v Norway	4–0	2
15 Oct 1980 v Romania	1–2	
19 Nov 1980 v Switzerland	2–1	
29 Apr 1981 v Romania	0–0	
12 May 1981 v Brazil	0–1	
30 May 1981 v Switzerland	1–2	1
6 Jun 1981 v Hungary	3–1	
9 Sep 1981 v Norway	1–2	
18 Nov 1981 v Hungary	1–0	
27 Apr 1982 v Wales	1–0	
25 May 1982 v Holland	2–0	
29 May 1982 v Scotland	1–0	
2 Jun 1982 v Iceland	1–1	

931. Trevor John Whymark
Forward
Born   Burston, 4 May 1950
Clubs   Diss Town; Ipswich Town; Vancouver Whitecaps
        (Canada); Sparta Rotterdam (Holland); Derby
        County; Grimsby Town; Southend Utd;
        Peterborough Utd; Colchester Utd

Caps	1	Result
	12 Oct 1977 v Luxembourg	2–0

932. Stephen James Coppell
Midfielder/Forward
Born   Liverpool, 9 July 1955
Clubs   Tranmere Rovers; Manchester Utd

Caps	42	Result	Goals
	16 Nov 1977 v Italy	2–0	
	22 Feb 1978 v W. Germany	1–2	
	19 Apr 1978 v Brazil	1–1	
	13 May 1978 v Wales	3–1	
	16 May 1978 v N. Ireland	1–0	
	20 May 1978 v Scotland	1–0	1
	24 May 1978 v Hungary	4–1	
	20 Sep 1978 v Denmark	4–3	
	25 Oct 1978 v Eire	1–1	
	29 Nov 1978 v Czechoslovakia	1–0	1
	7 Feb 1979 v N. Ireland	4–0	
	19 May 1979 v N. Ireland	4–0	
	23 May 1979 v Wales	0–0	
	26 May 1979 v Scotland	3–1	1
	6 Jun 1979 v Bulgaria	3–0	
	13 Jun 1979 v Austria	3–4	1
	9 Sep 1979 v Denmark	1–0	
	17 Oct 1979 v N. Ireland	5–1	
	6 Feb 1980 v Eire	2–0	
	26 Mar 1980 v Spain	2–0	
	13 May 1980 v Argentina	3–1	
	17 May 1980 v Wales	1–4	
	24 May 1980 v Scotland	2–0	1
	12 Jun 1980 v Belgium	1–1	
	15 Jun 1980 v Italy	0–1	
	15 Oct 1980 v Romania	1–2	
	19 Nov 1980 v Switzerland	2–1	
	29 Apr 1981 v Romania	0–0	
	12 May 1981 v Brazil	0–1	
	20 May 1981 v Wales	0–0	
	23 May 1981 v Scotland	0–1	
	30 May 1981 v Switzerland	1–2	
	6 Jun 1981 v Hungary	3–1	
	18 Nov 1981 v Hungary	1–0	
	29 May 1982 v Scotland	1–0	
	3 Jun 1982 v Finland	4–1	

16 Jun 1982 v France	3–1	
20 Jun 1982 v Czechoslovakia	2–0	
25 Jun 1982 v Kuwait	1–0	
29 Jun 1982 v W. Germany	0–0	
30 Mar 1983 v Greece	0–0	
15 Dec 1983 v Luxembourg	9–0	1

933. Robert Dennis Latchford
Centre forward
Born Birmingham, 18 January 1951
Clubs Birmingham City; Everton; Swansea City; NAC Breda (Holland); Coventry City; Lincoln City; Newport County; Merthyr Tydfil

Caps 12	*Result*	*Goals*
16 Nov 1977 v Italy	2–0	
19 Apr 1978 v Brazil	1–1	
13 May 1978 v Wales	3–1	1
20 Sep 1978 v Denmark	4–3	1
25 Oct 1978 v Eire	1–1	1
29 Nov 1978 v Czechoslovakia	1–0	
7 Feb 1979 v N. Ireland	4–0	2
19 May 1979 v N. Ireland	2–0	
23 May 1970 v Wales	0–0	
26 May 1979 v Scotland	3–1	
6 Jun 1979 v Bulgaria	3–0	
13 Jun 1979 v Austria	3–4	

934. Peter Simon Barnes
Winger
Born Manchester, 10 June 1957
Clubs Manchester City; West Bromwich Albion; Leeds Utd; Real Betis (Spain); Coventry City; Manchester Utd; Bolton Wanderers (on loan); Port Vale (on loan); Wimbledon; Hull City; Sunderland; Stockport County

Caps 22	*Result*	*Goals*
16 Nov 1977 v Italy	2–0	
22 Feb 1978 v W. Germany	1–2	
19 Apr 1978 v Brazil	1–1	
13 May 1978 v Wales	3–1	1
20 May 1978 v Scotland	1–0	
24 May 1978 v Hungary	4–1	
20 Sep 1978 v Denmark	4–3	
25 Oct 1978 v Eire	1–1	
29 Nov 1978 v Czechoslovakia	1–0	
7 Feb 1979 v N. Ireland	4–0	
19 Mar 1979 v N. Ireland	2–0	
26 May 1979 v Scotland	3–1	1
6 Jun 1979 v Bulgaria	3–0	1
13 Jun 1979 v Austria	3–4	
9 Sep 1979 v Denmark	1–0	
17 May 1980 v Wales	1–4	
25 Mar 1981 v Spain	1–2	
12 May 1981 v Brazil	0–1	
20 May 1981 v Wales	0–0	
30 May 1981 v Switzerland	1–2	
9 Sep 1981 v Norway	1–2	
25 May 1982 v Holland	2–0	

935. Anthony Stewart Woodcock
Forward
Born Nottingham, 6 December 1955
Clubs Nottingham Forest; Lincoln City; Doncaster Rovers; FC Cologne (Germany); Arsenal

Caps 42	*Result*	*Goals*
16 May 1978 v N. Ireland	1–0	
25 Oct 1978 v Eire	1–1	
29 Nov 1978 v Czechoslovakia	1–0	
6 Jun 1979 v Bulgaria	3–0	
10 Jun 1979 v Sweden	0–0	
17 Oct 1979 v N. Ireland	5–1	2
22 Nov 1979 v Bulgaria	2–0	
6 Feb 1980 v Eire	2–0	
26 Mar 1980 v Spain	2–0	1
13 May 1980 v Argentina	3–1	

12 Jun 1980 v Belgium	1–1	
15 Jun 1980 v Italy	0–1	
18 Jun 1980 v Spain	2–1	1
10 Sep 1980 v Norway	4–0	1
15 Oct 1980 v Romania	1–2	1
19 Nov 1980 v Switzerland	2–1	
29 Apr 1981 v Romania	0–0	
20 May 1981 v Wales	0–0	
23 May 1981 v Scotland	0–1	
23 Feb 1982 v N. Ireland	4–0	
25 May 1982 v Holland	2–0	1
3 Jun 1982 v Finland	4–1	
29 Jun 1982 v W. Germany	0–0	
5 Jul 1982 v Spain	0–0	
13 Oct 1982 v W. Germany	1–2	1
17 Nov 1982 v Greece	3–0	2
15 Dec 1982 v Luxembourg	9–0	1
30 Mar 1983 v Greece	0–0	
16 Nov 1983 v Luxembourg	4–0	
29 Feb 1984 v France	0–2	
4 Apr 1984 v N. Ireland	1–0	1
2 May 1984 v Wales	0–1	
26 May 1984 v Scotland	1–1	1
10 Jun 1984 v Brazil	2–0	
13 Jun 1984 v Uruguay	0–2	
12 Sep 1984 v E. Germany	1–0	
17 Oct 1984 v Finland	5–0	1
14 Nov 1984 v Turkey	8–0	2
27 Feb 1985 v N. Ireland	1–0	
11 Sep 1985 v Romania	1–1	
16 Oct 1985 v Turkey	5–0	
26 Feb 1986 v Israel	2–1	

⚽ **DID YOU KNOW...?**

Viv Anderson of Nottingham Forest became the first black player to wear an England shirt when he made his debut against Czechoslovakia in November 1978.

936. Vivian Alexander Anderson
Right back
Born Nottingham, 29 August 1956
Clubs Nottingham Forest; Arsenal; Manchester Utd; Sheffield Wednesday; Barnsley; Middlesbrough

Caps 30	*Result*	*Goals*
29 Nov 1978 v Czechoslovakia	1–0	
10 Jun 1979 v Sweden	0–0	
22 Nov 1979 v Bulgaria	2–0	
18 Jun 1980 v Spain	2–1	
10 Sep 1980 v Norway	4–0	
29 Apr 1981 v Romania	0–0	
20 May 1981 v Wales	0–0	
23 May 1981 v Scotland	0–1	
23 Feb 1982 v N. Ireland	4–0	
2 Jun 1982 v Iceland	1–1	
4 Apr 1984 v N. Ireland	1–0	
14 Nov 1984 v Turkey	8–0	1
27 Feb 1985 v N. Ireland	1–0	
26 Mar 1985 v Eire	2–1	
1 May 1985 v Romania	0–0	
22 May 1985 v Finland	1–1	
25 May 1985 v Scotland	0–1	
9 Jun 1985 v Mexico	0–1	
16 Jun 1985 v USA	5–0	
26 Mar 1986 v Soviet Union	1–0	
17 May 1986 v Mexico	3–0	
10 Sep 1986 v Sweden	0–1	

17 May 1986 v Mexico	3–0
10 Sep 1986 v Sweden	0–1
15 Oct 1986 v N. Ireland	3–0
12 Nov 1986 v Yugoslavia	2–0	1
18 Feb 1987 v Spain	4–2
1 Apr 1987 v N. Ireland	2–0
29 Apr 1987 v Turkey	0–0
9 Sep 1987 v W. Germany	1–3
27 Apr 1988 v Hungary	0–0
24 May 1988 v Colombia	1–1

937. Kenneth Graham Sansom
Left back
Born   Camberwell, 26 September 1958
Clubs   Crystal Palace; Arsenal; Newcastle Utd; Queen's Park
Rangers; Coventry City; Everton; Brentford; Watford

Caps 86	Result	Goals
23 May 1979 v Wales	0–0	
22 Nov 1979 v Bulgaria	2–0	
6 Feb 1980 v Eire	2–0	
13 May 1980 v Argentina	3–1	
17 May 1980 v Wales	1–4	
20 May 1980 v N. Ireland	1–1	
24 May 1980 v Scotland	2–0	
12 Jun 1980 v Belgium	1–1	
15 Jun 1980 v Italy	0–1	
10 Sep 1980 v Norway	4–0	
15 Oct 1980 v Romania	1–2	
19 Nov 1980 v Switzerland	2–1	
25 Mar 1981 v Spain	1–2	
29 Apr 1981 v Romania	0–0	
12 May 1981 v Brazil	0–1	
20 May 1981 v Wales	0–0	
23 May 1981 v Scotland	0–1	
30 May 1981 v Switzerland	1–2	
23 Feb 1982 v N. Ireland	4–0	
27 Apr 1982 v Wales	1–0	
25 May 1982 v Holland	2–0	
29 May 1982 v Scotland	1–0	
3 Jun 1982 v Finland	4–1	
16 Jun 1982 v France	3–1	
20 Jun 1982 v Czechoslovakia	2–0	
29 Jun 1982 v W. Germany	0–0	
5 Jul 1982 v Spain	0–0	
22 Sep 1982 v Denmark	2–2	
13 Oct 1982 v W. Germany	1–2	
17 Nov 1982 v Greece	3–0	
15 Dec 1982 v Luxembourg	9–0	
30 Mar 1983 v Greece	0–0	
27 Apr 1983 v Hungary	2–0	
28 May 1983 v N. Ireland	0–0	
1 Jun 1983 v Scotland	2–0	
21 Sep 1983 v Denmark	0–1	
12 Oct 1983 v Hungary	3–0	
16 Nov 1983 v Luxembourg	4–0	
29 Feb 1984 v France	0–2	
26 May 1984 v Scotland	1–1	
2 Jun 1984 v Soviet Union	0–2	
10 Jun 1984 v Brazil	2–0	
13 Jun 1984 v Uruguay	0–2	
17 Jun 1984 v Chile	0–0	
12 Sep 1984 v E. Germany	1–0	
17 Oct 1984 v Finland	5–0	1
14 Nov 1984 v Turkey	8–0	
27 Feb 1985 v N. Ireland	1–0	
26 Mar 1985 v Eire	2–1	
1 May 1985 v Romania	0–0	
22 May 1985 v Finland	1–1	
25 May 1985 v Scotland	0–1	
6 Jun 1985 v Italy	1–2	
9 Jun 1985 v Mexico	0–1	
12 Jun 1985 v W. Germany	3–0	
16 Jun 1985 v USA	5–0	
11 Sep 1985 v Romania	1–1	
16 Oct 1985 v Turkey	5–0	

13 Nov 1985 v N. Ireland	0–0
29 Jan 1986 v Egypt	4–0
26 Feb 1986 v Israel	2–1
26 Mar 1986 v Soviet Union	1–0
23 Apr 1986 v Scotland	2–1
17 May 1986 v Mexico	3–0
24 May 1986 v Canada	1–0
3 Jun 1986 v Portugal	0–1
6 Jun 1986 v Morocco	0–0
11 Jun 1986 v Poland	3–0
18 Jun 1986 v Paraguay	3–0
22 Jun 1986 v Argentina	1–2
10 Sep 1986 v Sweden	0–1
15 Oct 1986 v N. Ireland	3–0
12 Nov 1986 v Yugoslavia	2–0
18 Feb 1987 v Spain	4–2
1 Apr 1987 v N. Ireland	2–0
29 Apr 1987 v Turkey	0–0
9 Sep 1987 v W. Germany	1–3
14 Oct 1987 v Turkey	8–0
11 Nov 1987 v Yugoslavia	4–1
23 Mar 1988 v Holland	2–2
21 May 1988 v Scotland	1–0
24 May 1988 v Colombia	1–1
28 May 1988 v Switzerland	1–0
12 Jun 1988 v Eire	0–1
15 Jun 1988 v Holland	1–3
18 Jun 1988 v Soviet Union	1–3

938. Lawrence Paul Cunningham
Forward
Born   London, 8 March 1956
Died   15 July 1989
Clubs   West Bromwich Albion; Real Madrid (Spain);
Manchester Utd; Olympique Marseilles (France);
Leicester City; Sporting Gijon (Spain); Charleroi
(Belgium); Wimbledon

Caps 6	Result
23 May 1979 v Wales	0–0
10 Jun 1979 v Sweden	0–0
13 Jun 1979 v Austria	3–4
6 Feb 1980 v Eire	2–0
26 Mar 1980 v Spain	2–0
15 Oct 1980 v Romania	1–2

939. Kevin Philip Reeves
Forward
Born   Burley, 20 October 1957
Clubs   Bournemouth; Norwich City; Manchester City;
Burnley

Caps 2	Result
22 Nov 1979 v Bulgaria	2–0
20 May 1980 v N. Ireland	1–1

940. Glenn Hoddle
Midfielder
Born   Hayes, 27 October 1957
Clubs   Tottenham Hotspur; Monaco (France); Swindon
Town; Chelsea

Caps 53	Result	Goals
22 Nov 1979 v Bulgaria	2–0	1
17 May 1980 v Wales	1–4	
31 May 1980 v Australia	2–1	1
18 Jun 1980 v Spain	2–1	
25 Mar 1981 v Spain	1–2	1
20 May 1981 v Wales	0–0	
23 May 1981 v Scotland	0–1	
9 Sep 1981 v Norway	1–2	
23 Feb 1981 v N. Ireland	4–0	1
27 Apr 1982 v Wales	1–0	
2 Jun 1982 v Iceland	1–1	
20 Jun 1982 v Czechoslovakia	2–0	
25 Jun 1982 v Kuwait	1–0	
15 Dec 1982 v Luxembourg	9–0	1
28 May 1982 v N. Ireland	0–0	

Date	Opponent	Result	Goals
1 Jun 1983	v Scotland	2–0	
12 Oct 1983	v Hungary	3–0	1
16 Nov 1983	v Luxembourg	4–0	
29 Feb 1984	v France	0–2	
26 Mar 1985	v Eire	2–1	
25 May 1985	v Scotland	0–1	
6 Jun 1985	v Italy	1–2	
9 Jun 1985	v Mexico	0–1	
12 Jun 1985	v W. Germany	3–0	
16 Jun 1985	v USA	5–0	
11 Sep 1985	v Romania	1–1	1
13 Oct 1985	v N. Ireland	0–0	
16 Oct 1985	v Turkey	5–0	
26 Feb 1986	v Israel	2–1	
26 Mar 1986	v Soviet Union	1–0	
23 Apr 1986	v Scotland	2–1	1
17 May 1986	v Mexico	3–0	
24 May 1986	v Canada	1–0	
3 Jun 1986	v Portugal	0–1	
6 Jun 1986	v Morocco	0–0	
11 Jun 1986	v Poland	3–0	
18 Jun 1986	v Paraguay	3–0	
22 Jun 1986	v Argentina	1–2	
10 Sep 1986	v Sweden	0–1	
15 Oct 1986	v N. Ireland	3–0	
12 Nov 1986	v Yugoslavia	2–0	
18 Feb 1987	v Spain	4–2	
29 Apr 1987	v Turkey	0–0	
23 May 1987	v Scotland	0–0	
9 Sep 1987	v W. Germany	1–3	
14 Oct 1987	v Turkey	8–0	
11 Nov 1987	v Yugoslavia	4–1	
23 Mar 1988	v Holland	2–2	
27 Apr 1988	v Hungary	0–0	
24 May 1988	v Colombia	1–1	
12 Jun 1988	v Eire	0–1	
15 Jun 1988	v Holland	1–3	
18 Jun 1988	v Soviet Union	1–3	

 DID YOU KNOW...?

When England beat Turkey 8–0 in Istanbul on 14 November 1984 in a World Cup qualifying match, it was the side's biggest away victory since 1960. Bryan Robson scored a hat-trick, the first England captain to achieve the feat since 1909.

941. Bryan Robson
Midfielder

Born   Chester-le-Street, 11 January 1957
Clubs   West Bromwich Albion; Manchester Utd; Middlesbrough

Caps	90	Result	Goals
6 Feb 1980	v Eire	2–0	
31 May 1980	v Australia	2–1	
10 Sep 1980	v Norway	4–0	
15 Oct 1980	v Romania	1–2	
19 Nov 1980	v Switzerland	2–1	
25 Mar 1981	v Spain	1–2	
29 Apr 1981	v Romania	0–0	
12 May 1981	v Brazil	0–1	
20 May 1981	v Wales	0–0	
23 May 1981	v Scotland	0–1	
30 May 1981	v Switzerland	1–2	
6 Jun 1981	v Hungary	3–1	
9 Sep 1981	v Norway	1–2	1
18 Nov 1981	v Hungary	1–0	
23 Feb 1982	v N. Ireland	4–0	1
27 Apr 1982	v Wales	1–0	
25 May 1982	v Holland	2–0	
29 May 1982	v Scotland	1–0	
3 Jun 1982	v Finland	4–1	2
16 Jun 1982	v France	3–1	2
20 Jun 1982	v Czechoslovakia	2–0	
29 Jun 1982	v W. Germany	0–0	
5 Jul 1982	v Spain	0–0	
22 Sep 1982	v Denmark	2–2	
17 Nov 1982	v Greece	3–0	
15 Dec 1982	v Luxembourg	9–0	
1 Jun 1983	v Scotland	1–0	1
12 Oct 1983	v Hungary	3–0	
16 Nov 1983	v Luxembourg	4–0	2
29 Feb 1984	v France	0–2	
4 Apr 1984	v N. Ireland	1–0	
26 May 1984	v Scotland	1–1	
2 Jun 1984	v Soviet Union	0–2	
10 Jun 1984	v Brazil	2–0	
13 Jun 1984	v Uruguay	0–2	
17 Jun 1984	v Chile	0–0	
12 Sep 1984	v E. Germany	1–0	1
17 Oct 1984	v Finland	5–0	1
14 Nov 1984	v Turkey	8–0	3
26 Mar 1985	v Eire	2–1	
1 May 1985	v Romania	0–0	
22 May 1985	v Finland	1–1	
25 May 1985	v Scotland	0–1	
6 Jun 1985	v Italy	1–2	
9 Jun 1985	v Mexico	0–1	
12 Jun 1985	v W. Germany	3–0	1
16 Jun 1985	v USA	5–0	
11 Sep 1985	v Romania	1–1	
16 Oct 1985	v Turkey	5–0	1
26 Feb 1986	v Israel	2–1	2
17 May 1986	v Mexico	3–0	
3 Jun 1986	v Portugal	0–1	
6 Jun 1986	v Morocco	0–0	
15 Oct 1986	v N. Ireland	3–0	
18 Feb 1987	v Spain	4–2	
1 Apr 1987	v N. Ireland	2–0	1
29 Apr 1987	v Turkey	0–0	
19 May 1987	v Brazil	1–1	
23 May 1987	v Scotland	0–0	
14 Oct 1987	v Turkey	8–0	1
11 Nov 1987	v Yugoslavia	4–1	1
23 Mar 1988	v Holland	2–2	
27 Apr 1988	v Hungary	0–0	
21 May 1988	v Scotland	1–0	
24 May 1988	v Colombia	1–1	
28 May 1988	v Switzerland	1–0	
12 Jun 1988	v Eire	0–1	
15 Jun 1988	v Holland	1–3	1
18 Jun 1988	v Soviet Union	1–3	
14 Sep 1988	v Denmark	1–0	
19 Oct 1988	v Sweden	0–0	
16 Nov 1988	v Saudi Arabia	1–1	
8 Feb 1989	v Greece	2–1	1
8 Mar 1989	v Albania	2–0	1
26 Apr 1989	v Albania	5–0	
23 May 1989	v Chile	0–0	
27 May 1989	v Scotland	2–0	
3 Jun 1989	v Poland	3–0	
7 Jun 1989	v Denmark	1–1	
11 Oct 1989	v Poland	0–0	
15 Nov 1989	v Italy	0–0	
13 Dec 1989	v Yugoslavia	2–1	2
25 Apr 1990	v Czechoslovakia	4–2	
22 May 1990	v Uruguay	1–2	
2 Jun 1990	v Tunisia	1–1	
11 Jun 1990	v Eire	1–1	
16 Jun 1990	v Holland	0–0	
6 Feb 1991	v Cameroon	2–0	
27 Mar 1991	v Eire	1–1	
16 Oct 1991	v Turkey	1–0	

DID YOU KNOW...?

On 16 June 1982, the fastest England World Cup goal was scored by Bryan Robson, after just twenty-seven seconds in a group match against France in Bilbao.

942. Garry Birtles
Forward
Born   Nottingham, 27 July 1956
Clubs   Long Eaton Utd; Nottingham Forest; Manchester Utd; Notts County; Grimsby Town

Caps	3	Result
	13 May 1980 v Argentina	3–1
	15 Jun 1980 v Italy	0–1
	15 Oct 1980 v Romania	1–2

943. Alan Ernest Devonshire
Midfielder
Born   Park Royal, London, 13 April 1956
Clubs   West Ham Utd; Watford

Caps	8	Result
	20 May 1980 v N. Ireland	1–1
	31 May 1980 v Australia	2–1
	25 May 1982 v Holland	2–0
	2 Jun 1982 v Iceland	1–1
	31 Oct 1982 v W. Germany	1–2
	23 Feb 1983 v Wales	2–1
	30 Mar 1983 v Greece	0–0
	16 Nov 1983 v Luxembourg	4–0

944. Russell Charles Osman
Central defender
Born   Repton, 14 February 1959
Clubs   Ipswich Town; Leicester City; Southampton; Bristol City; Brighton & Hove Albion; Cardiff City

Caps	11	Result
	31 May 1980 v Australia	2–1
	25 Mar 1981 v Spain	1–2
	29 Apr 1981 v Romania	0–0
	30 May 1981 v Switzerland	1–2
	9 Sep 1981 v Norway	1–2
	2 Jun 1982 v Iceland	1–1
	22 Sep 1982 v Denmark	2–2
	12 Jun 1983 v Australia	0–0
	15 Jun 1983 v Australia	1–0
	19 Jun 1983 v Australia	1–1
	21 Sep 1983 v Denmark	0–1

945. Terence Ian Butcher
Central defender
Born   Singapore, 28 December 1958
Clubs   Ipswich Town; Glasgow Rangers; Coventry City; Sunderland

Caps	77	Result	Goals
	31 May 1980 v Australia	2–1	
	25 Mar 1981 v Spain	1–2	
	27 Apr 1982 v Wales	1–0	
	29 May 1982 v Scotland	1–0	
	16 Jun 1982 v France	3–1	
	20 Jun 1982 v Czechoslovakia	2–0	
	29 Jun 1982 v W. Germany	0–0	
	5 Jul 1982 v Spain	0–0	
	22 Sep 1982 v Denmark	2–2	
	13 Oct 1982 v W. Germany	1–2	
	15 Dec 1982 v Luxembourg	9–0	
	23 Feb 1983 v Wales	2–1	1
	30 Mar 1983 v Greece	0–0	
	27 Apr 1983 v Hungary	2–0	
	28 May 1983 v N. Ireland	0–0	
	1 Jun 1983 v Scotland	2–0	
	12 Jun 1983 v Australia	0–0	
	15 Jun 1983 v Australia	1–0	
	19 Jun 1983 v Australia	1–1	
	21 Sep 1983 v Denmark	0–1	
	17 Oct 1984 v Finland	5–0	
	16 Nov 1984 v Luxembourg	4–0	1
	29 Feb 1984 v France	0–2	
	4 Apr 1984 v N. Ireland	1–0	
	12 Sep 1984 v E. Germany	1–0	
	12 Oct 1984 v Finland	5–0	
	14 Nov 1984 v Turkey	8–0	
	27 Feb 1985 v N. Ireland	1–0	
	26 Mar 1985 v Eire	2–1	
	1 May 1985 v Romania	0–0	
	22 May 1985 v Finland	1–1	
	25 May 1985 v Scotland	0–1	
	6 Jun 1985 v Italy	1–2	
	12 Jun 1985 v W. Germany	3–0	
	16 Jun 1985 v USA	5–0	
	26 Feb 1986 v Israel	2–1	
	26 Mar 1986 v Soviet Union	1–0	
	23 Apr 1986 v Scotland	2–1	1
	17 May 1986 v Mexico	3–0	
	24 May 1986 v Canada	1–0	
	3 Jun 1986 v Portugal	0–1	
	6 Jun 1986 v Morocco	0–0	
	11 Jun 1986 v Poland	3–0	
	18 Jun 1986 v Paraguay	3–0	
	22 Jun 1986 v Argentina	1–2	
	10 Sep 1986 v Sweden	0–1	
	15 Oct 1986 v N. Ireland	3–0	
	12 Nov 1986 v Yugoslavia	2–0	
	18 Feb 1987 v Spain	4–2	
	1 Apr 1987 v N. Ireland	2–0	
	19 May 1987 v Brazil	1–1	
	23 May 1987 v Scotland	0–0	
	14 Oct 1987 v Turkey	8–0	
	11 Nov 1987 v Yugoslavia	4–1	
	14 Sep 1988 v Denmark	1–0	
	19 Oct 1988 v Sweden	0–0	
	8 Feb 1989 v Greece	2–1	
	8 Mar 1989 v Albania	2–0	
	26 Apr 1989 v Albania	5–0	
	23 May 1989 v Chile	0–0	
	27 May 1989 v Scotland	2–0	
	3 June 1989 v Poland	3–0	
	7 June 1989 v Denmark	1–1	
	6 Sep 1989 v Sweden	0–0	
	11 Oct 1989 v Poland	0–0	
	15 Nov 1989 v Italy	0–0	
	13 Dec 1989 v Yugoslavia	2–1	
	28 Mar 1990 v Brazil	1–0	
	25 Apr 1990 v Czechoslovakia	4–2	
	15 May 1990 v Denmark	1–0	
	22 May 1990 v Uruguay	1–2	
	2 Jun 1990 v Tunisia	1–1	
	11 Jun 1990 v Eire	1–1	
	16 Jun 1990 v Holland	0–0	
	26 Jun 1990 v Belgium	1–0	
	1 Jul 1990 v Cameroon	3–2	
	4 Jul 1990 v W. Germany	1–1	

946. Alan Sunderland
Forward
Born   Mexborough, 1 July 1953
Clubs   Wolverhampton Wanderers; Arsenal; Ipswich Town

Caps	1	Result
	31 May 1980 v Australia	2–1

947. David Armstrong
Midfielder
Born   Durham, 26 December 1954
Clubs   Middlesbrough; Southampton; Bournemouth

Caps	3	Result
	31 May 1980 v Australia	2–1
	13 Oct 1982 v W. Germany	1–2
	2 May 1984 v Wales	0–1

948. Peter David Ward
Forward
Born Derby, 27 July 1955
Clubs Burton Albion; Brighton & Hove Albion;
Nottingham Forest

Caps	1	Result
	31 May 1980 v Australia	2–1

949. Eric Lazenby Gates
Forward
Born Ferryhill, 28 June 195
Clubs Ipswich Town; Sunderland; Carlisle Utd

Caps	2	Result
	10 Sep 1980 v Norway	4–0
	15 Oct 1980 v Romania	1–2

950. Graham Rix
Midfielder
Born Doncaster, 23 October 1957
Clubs Arsenal; Brentford; Caen (France); Le Havre
(France); Dundee; Chelsea

Caps	17	Result
	10 Sep 1980 v Norway	4–0
	15 Oct 1980 v Romania	1–2
	19 Nov 1980 v Switzerland	2–1
	12 May 1981 v Brazil	0–1
	20 May 1981 v Wales	0–0
	23 May 1981 v Scotland	0–1
	25 May 1982 v Holland	2–0
	3 Jun 1982 v Finland	4–1
	16 Jun 1982 v France	3–1
	20 Jun 1982 v Czechoslovakia	2–0
	25 Jun 1982 v Kuwait	1–0
	29 Jun 1982 v W. Germany	0–0
	5 Jul 1982 v Spain	0–0
	22 Sep 1982 v Denmark	2–2
	13 Oct 1982 v W. Germany	1–2
	30 Mar 1983 v Greece	0–0
	4 Apr 1984 v N. Ireland	1–0

951. Alvin Edward Martin
Central defender
Born Bootle, 29 July 1958
Clubs West Ham Utd; Leyton Orient

Caps	17	Result
	12 May 1981 v Brazil	0–1
	23 May 1981 v Scotland	0–1
	18 Nov 1981 v Hungary	1–0
	17 Nov 1982 v Greece	3–0
	3 Jun 1982 v Finland	4–1
	15 Dec 1982 v Luxembourg	9–0
	23 Feb 1983 v Wales	2–1
	30 Mar 1983 v Greece	0–0
	27 Apr 1983 v Hungary	2–0
	12 Oct 1983 v Hungary	3–0
	16 Nov 1983 v Luxembourg	4–0
	2 May 1984 v Wales	0–1
	27 Feb 1985 v N. Ireland	1–0
	26 Feb 1986 v Israel	2–1
	24 May 1986 v Canada	1–0
	18 Jun 1986 v Paraguay	3–0
	10 Sep 1986 v Sweden	0–1

952. Peter Withe
Centre forward
Born Liverpool, 30 August 1951
Clubs Southport; Barrow; Wolverhampton Wanderers;
Birmingham City; Nottingham Forest; Newcastle
Utd; Aston Villa; Sheffield Utd; Huddersfield Town

Caps	11	Result	Goals
	12 May 1981 v Brazil	0–1	
	20 May 1981 v Wales	0–0	
	23 May 1981 v Scotland	0–1	
	9 Sep 1981 v Norway	1–2	
	27 Apr 1982 v Wales	1–0	
	2 Jun 1982 v Iceland	1–1	

	27 Apr 1983 v Hungary	2–0	1
	28 May 1983 v N. Ireland	0–0	
	1 Jun 1983 v Scotland	2–0	
	12 Oct 1983 v Hungary	3–0	
	14 Nov 1984 v Turkey	8–0	

953. Anthony William Morley
Forward
Born Ormskirk, 26 August 1954
Clubs Preston North End; Burnley; Aston Villa; West
Bromwich Albion; Birmingham City (on loan); Den
Haag (Holland)

Caps	6	Result
	18 Nov 1981 v Hungary	1–0
	23 Feb 1982 v N. Ireland	4–0
	27 Apr 1982 v Wales	1–0
	2 Jun 1982 v Iceland	1–1
	22 Sep 1982 v Denmark	2–2
	17 Nov 1982 v Greece	3–0

954. Stephen Brian Foster
Central defender
Born Portsmouth, 24 September 1957
Clubs Portsmouth; Brighton & Hove Albion; Aston Villa;
Luton Town; Oxford Utd

Caps	3	Result
	23 Feb 1982 v N. Ireland	4–0
	25 May 1982 v Holland	2–0
	25 Jun 1982 v Kuwait	1–0

955. Cyrille Regis
Forward
Born French Guyana, 9 February1958
Clubs West Bromwich Albion; Coventry City; Aston Villa;
Wolverhampton Wanderers; Wycombe Wanderers;
Chester City

Caps	5	Result
	23 Feb 1982 v N. Ireland	4–0
	27 Apr 1982 v Wales	1–0
	2 Jun 1982 v Iceland	1–1
	13 Oct 1982 v W. Germany	1–2
	14 Oct 1987 v Turkey	8–0

956. Stephen John Perryman
Midfielder/Defender
Born Ealing, 21 December 1951
Clubs Tottenham Hotspur; Oxford Utd; Brentford

Caps	1	Result
	2 Jun 1982 v Iceland	1–1

957. Paul Goddard
Forward
Born Harlington, 12 October 1959
Clubs Queen's Park Rangers; West Ham Utd; Newcastle
Utd; Derby County; Millwall; Ipswich Town

Caps	1	Result	Goals
	2 Jun 1982 v Iceland	1–1	1

958. Ricky Anthony Hill
Midfielder
Born London, 5 March 1959
Clubs Luton Town; Le Havre (France); Leicester City

Caps	3	Result
	22 Sep 1982 v Denmark	2–2
	13 Oct 1982 v W. Germany	1–2
	29 Jan 1986 v Egypt	4–0

⚽ DID YOU KNOW...?

Paul Goddard is the only England goalscorer with an
international career of less than 90 minutes. He scored
after coming on as a 40th-minute substitute against
Iceland in June 1982 and was never picked again.

959. Luther Loide Blissett
Forward
Born Jamaica, 1 February 1958
Clubs Watford; AC Milan (Italy); Bournemouth; West Bromwich Albion; Bury; Mansfield Town

Caps 14	Result	Goals
13 Oct 1982 v W. Germany	1–2	
15 Dec 1982 v Luxembourg	9–0	3
23 Feb 1983 v Wales	2–1	
30 Mar 1983 v Greece	0–0	
27 Apr 1983 v Hungary	2–0	
28 May 1983 v N. Ireland	0–0	
1 Jun 1983 v Scotland	2–0	
12 Jun 1983 v Australia	0–0	
19 Jun 1983 v Australia	1–1	
21 Sep 1983 v Denmark	0–1	
12 Oct 1983 v Hungary	3–0	
2 May 1984 v Wales	0–1	
26 May 1984 v Scotland	1–1	
2 Jun 1984 v Soviet Union	0–2	

960. Samuel Lee
Midfielder
Born Liverpool, 7 February 1959
Clubs Liverpool; Queen's Park Rangers; Osasuna (Spain); Southampton; Bolton Wanderers

Caps 14	Result	Goals
17 Nov 1982 v Greece	3–0	1
15 Dec 1982 v Luxembourg	9–0	
23 Feb 1983 v Wales	2–1	
30 Mar 1983 v Greece	0–0	
27 Apr 1983 v Hungary	2–0	
1 Jun 1983 v Scotland	2–0	
19 Jun 1983 v Australia	1–1	
21 Sep 1983 v Denmark	0–1	
12 Oct 1983 v Hungary	3–0	1
16 Nov 1983 v Luxembourg	4–0	
29 Feb 1984 v France	0–2	
4 Apr 1984 v N. Ireland	1–0	
2 May 1984 v Wales	0–1	
17 Jun 1984 v Chile	0–0	

961. Gary Vincent Mabbutt
Central defender
Born Bristol, 23 August 1961
Clubs Bristol Rovers; Tottenham Hotspur

Caps 16	Result	Goals
13 Oct 1982 v W. Germany	1–2	
17 Nov 1982 v Greece	3–0	
15 Dec 1982 v Luxembourg	9–0	
23 Feb 1983 v Wales	2–1	
30 Mar 1983 v Greece	0–0	
27 Apr 1983 v Hungary	2–0	
28 May 1983 v N. Ireland	0–0	
1 Jun 1983 v Scotland	2–0	
12 Oct 1983 v Hungary	3–0	
12 Nov 1986 v Yugoslavia	2–0	1
1 Apr 1987 v N. Ireland	2–0	
29 Apr 1987 v Turkey	0–0	
9 Sep 1987 v W. Germany	1–3	
16 October 1991 v Turkey	1–0	
13 November 1991 v Poland	1–1	
25 March 1992 v Czechoslovakia	2–2	

962. Mark Valentine Chamberlain
Winger
Born Stoke-on-Trent, 19 November 1961
Clubs Port Vale; Stoke City; Sheffield Wednesday; Portsmouth; Brighton & Hove Albion; Exeter City

Caps 8	Result	Goals
15 Dec 1982 v Luxembourg	9–0	1
21 Sep 1983 v Denmark	0–1	
26 May 1984 v Scotland	1–1	
2 Jun 1984 v Soviet Union	0–2	
10 Jun 1984 v Brazil	2–0	
13 Jun 1984 v Uruguay	0–2	

17 Jun 1984 v Chile	0–0	
17 Oct 1984 v Finland	5–0	

963. Derek James Statham
Left back
Born Wolverhampton, 24 March 1959
Clubs West Bromwich Albion; Southampton; Stoke City; Walsall

Caps 3	Result
23 Feb 1983 v Wales	2–1
12 Jun 1983 v Australia	0–0
15 Jun 1983 v Australia	1–0

964. Gordon Sidney Cowans
Midfielder
Born Durham, 27 October 1958
Clubs Aston Villa; Bari (Italy); Blackburn Rovers; Derby County; Wolverhampton Wanderers; Sheffield Utd; Bradford City; Stockport County; Burnley

Caps 10	Result	Goals
23 Feb 1983 v Wales	2–1	
28 May 1983 v N. Ireland	0–0	
1 Jun 1983 v Scotland	2–0	1
12 Jun 1983 v Australia	0–0	
15 Jun 1983 v Australia	1–0	
19 Jun 1983 v Australia	1–1	
27 Apr 1983 v Hungary	2–0	
29 Jan 1986 v Egypt	4–0	1
26 Mar 1986 v Soviet Union	1–0	
14 Nov 1990 v Eire	1–1	

965. Graham Paul Roberts
Central defender
Born Southampton, 3 July 1959
Clubs Portsmouth; Tottenham Hotspur; Glasgow Rangers; Chelsea; West Bromwich Albion

Caps 6	Result
28 May 1983 v N. Ireland	0–0
1 Jun 1983 v Scotland	2–0
29 Feb 1984 v France	0–2
4 Apr 1984 v N. Ireland	1–0
26 May 1984 v Scotland	1–1
2 Jun 1984 v Soviet Union	0–2

966. John Charles Bryan Barnes
Forward
Born Jamaica, 7 November 1963
Clubs Watford; Liverpool; Newcastle Utd; Charlton Athletic

Caps 79	Result	Goals
28 May 1983 v N. Ireland	0–0	
12 Jun 1983 v Australia	0–0	
15 Jun 1983 v Australia	1–0	
19 Jun 1983 v Australia	1–1	
21 Sep 1983 v Denmark	0–1	
16 Nov 1983 v Luxembourg	4–0	
29 Feb 1984 v France	0–2	
26 May 1984 v Scotland	1–1	
2 Jun 1984 v Soviet Union	0–2	
10 Jun 1984 v Brazil	2–0	1
13 Jun 1984 v Uruguay	0–2	
17 Jun 1984 v Chile	0–0	
12 Sep 1984 v E. Germany	1–0	
17 Oct 1984 v Finland	5–0	
14 Nov 1984 v Turkey	8–0	2
27 Feb 1984 v N. Ireland	1–0	
1 May 1985 v Romania	0–0	
22 May 1985 v Finland	1–1	
25 May 1985 v Scotland	0–1	
6 Jun 1985 v Italy	1–2	
9 Jun 1985 v Mexico	0–1	
12 Jun 1985 v W. Germany	3–0	
16 Jun 1985 v USA	5–0	
11 Sep 1985 v Romania	1–1	
26 Feb 1986 v Israel	2–1	
17 May 1986 v Mexico	3–0	
24 May 1986 v Canada	1–0	

22 Jun 1986 v Argentina	1–2	
10 Sep 1986 v Sweden	0–1	
29 Apr 1987 v Turkey	0–0	
19 May 1987 v Brazil	1–1	
9 Sep 1987 v W. Germany	1–3	
14 Oct 1987 v Turkey	8–0	2
11 Nov 1987 v Yugoslavia	4–1	1
17 Feb 1988 v Israel	0–0	
23 Mar 1988 v Holland	2–2	
21 May 1988 v Scotland	1–0	
24 May 1988 v Colombia	1–1	
28 May 1988 v Switzerland	1–0	
12 Jun 1988 v Eire	0–1	
15 Jun 1988 v Holland	1–3	
18 Jun 1988 v Soviet Union	1–3	
19 Oct 1988 v Sweden	0–0	
8 Feb 1989 v Greece	2–1	1
8 Mar 1989 v Albania	2–0	1
3 Jun 1989 v Poland	3–0	1
7 Jun 1989 v Denmark	1–1	
6 Sep 1989 v Sweden	0–0	
15 Nov 1989 v Italy	0–0	
28 Mar 1990 v Brazil	1–0	
15 May 1990 v Denmark	1–0	
22 May 1990 v Uruguay	1–2	1
2 Jun 1990 v Tunisia	1–1	
11 Jun 1990 v Eire	1–1	
16 Jun 1990 v Holland	0–0	
21 Jun 1990 v Egypt	1–0	
26 Jun 1990 v Belgium	1–0	
1 Jul 1990 v Cameroon	3–2	
12 Sep 1990 v Hungary	1–0	
17 Oct 1990 v Poland	2–0	
6 Feb 1991 v Cameroon	2–0	
27 Mar 1991 v Eire	1–1	
1 May 1991 v Turkey	1–0	
21 May 1991 v Soviet Union	3–1	
25 May 1991 v Argentina	2–2	
25 Mar 1992 v Czechoslovakia	2–2	
3 Jun 1992 v Finland	2–1	
17 Feb 1993 v San Marino	6–0	
31 Mar 1993 v Turkey	2–0	
28 Apr 1993 v Holland	2–2	1
29 May 1993 v Poland	1–1	
9 Jun 1993 v USA	0–2	
19 Jun 1993 v Germany	1–2	
7 Sep 1994 v USA	2–0	
12 Oct 1994 v Romania	1–1	
16 Nov 1994 v Nigeria	1–0	
29 Mar 1995 v Uruguay	0–0	
8 Jun 1995 v Sweden	3–3	
6 Sep 1995 v Colombia	0–0	

⚽ DID YOU KNOW...?

In June 1984, John Barnes became the scorer of one of England's greatest ever goals. Aged just twenty, he ran at and single-handedly beat the entire Brazilian defence in Rio's Maracanã Stadium, and coolly slotted the ball past the keeper.

967. Daniel Joseph Thomas
Fullback
Born Worksop, 12 November 1961
Clubs Coventry City; Tottenham Hotspur

Caps 2	*Result*
12 Jun 1983 v Australia	0–0
19 Jun 1983 v Australia	1–1

968. Steven Charles Williams
Midfielder
Born London, 12 July 1958

Clubs Southampton; Arsenal; Luton Town; Exeter City

Caps 6	*Result*
12 Jun 1983 v Australia	0–0
15 Jun 1983 v Australia	1–0
29 Feb 1984 v France	0–2
12 Sep 1984 v E. Germany	1–0
17 Oct 1984 v Finland	5–0
14 Nov 1984 v Turkey	8–0

969. Mark Francis Barham
Midfielder/Winger
Born Folkestone, 12 July 1962
Clubs Norwich City; Huddersfield Town; Middlesbrough; West Bromwich Albion; Brighton & Hove Albion; Shrewsbury Town

Caps 2	*Result*
12 Jun 1983 v Australia	0–0
15 Jun 1983 v Australia	1–0

970. John Charles Gregory
Midfielder
Born Scunthorpe, 11 May 1954
Clubs Northampton Town; Aston Villa; Brighton & Hove Albion; Queen's Park Rangers; Derby County; Portsmouth; Plymouth Argyle; Bolton Wanderers

Caps 6	*Result*
12 Jun 1983 v Australia	0–0
15 Jun 1983 v Australia	1–0
19 Jun 1983 v Australia	1–1
21 Sep 1983 v Denmark	0–1
12 Oct 1983 v Hungary	3–0
2 May 1984 v Wales	0–1

971. Paul Anthony Walsh
Forward
Born Plumstead, 1 October 1962
Clubs Charlton Athletic; Luton Town; Liverpool; Tottenham Hotspur; Queen's Park Rangers (on loan); Portsmouth; Manchester City

Caps 5	*Result*	*Goals*
12 Jun 1983 v Australia	0–0	
15 Jun 1983 v Australia	1–0	1
19 Jun 1983 v Australia	1–1	
29 Feb 1984 v France	0–2	
2 May 1984 v Wales	0–1	

972. Nicholas Pickering
Midfielder
Born Newcastle-upon-Tyne, 4 August 1963
Clubs Sunderland; Coventry City; Derby County; Darlington; Burnley

Caps 1	*Result*
19 Jun 1983 v Australia	1–1

973. Nigel Philip Spink
Goalkeeper
Born Chelmsford, 8 August 1958
Clubs Chelmsford City; Aston Villa; West Bromwich Albion; Millwall

Caps 1	*Result*
19 Jun 1983 v Australia	1–1

974. Michael Duxbury
Defender
Born Blackburn, 1 September 1959
Clubs Manchester Utd; Blackburn Rovers; Bradford City

Caps 10	*Result*
16 Nov 1983 v Luxembourg	4–0
29 Feb 1984 v France	0–2
2 May 1984 v Wales	0–1
26 May 1984 v Scotland	1–1
2 Jun 1984 v Soviet Union	0–2
10 Jun 1984 v Brazil	2–0
13 Jun 1984 v Uruguay	0–2
17 Jun 1984 v Chile	0–0
12 Sep 1984 v E. Germany	1–0
17 Oct 1984 v Finland	5–0

975. Brian Stein
Forward

Born   Cape Town, 19 October 1957
Clubs   Edgware Town; Luton Town; Annecy (France); Barnet

Caps	1	Result
	29 Feb 1984 v France	0–2

976. Alan Philip Kennedy
Left back

Born   Sunderland, 31 August 1954
Clubs   Newcastle Utd; Liverpool; Sunderland; Hartlepool Utd; Beerschot (Belgium); Wigan Athletic; Wrexham

Caps	2	Result
	4 Apr 1984 v N. Ireland	1–0
	2 May 1984 v Wales	0–1

977. Mark Wright
Central defender

Born   Dorchester, 1 August 1963
Clubs   Oxford Utd; Southampton; Derby County; Liverpool

Caps	45	Result	Goals
	2 May 1984 v Wales	0–1	
	12 Sep 1984 v E. Germany	1–0	
	14 Oct 1984 v Turkey	8–0	
	17 Oct 1984 v Finland	5–0	
	26 Mar 1985 v Eire	2–1	
	1 May 1985 v Romania	0–0	
	6 Jun 1985 v Italy	1–2	
	12 Jun 1985 v W. Germany	3–0	
	11 Sep 1985 v Romania	1–1	
	16 Oct 1985 v Turkey	5–0	
	13 Nov 1985 v N. Ireland	0–0	
	29 Jan 1986 v Egypt	4–0	
	26 Mar 1986 v Soviet Union	1–0	
	12 Nov 1986 v Yugoslavia	2–0	
	1 Apr 1986 v N. Ireland	2–0	
	23 May 1986 v Scotland	0–0	
	17 Feb 1988 v Israel	0–0	
	23 Mar 1988 v Holland	2–2	
	24 May 1988 v Colombia	1–1	
	28 May 1988 v Switzerland	1–0	
	12 Jun 1988 v Eire	0–1	
	15 Jun 1988 v Holland	1–3	
	25 Apr 1990 v Czechoslovakia	4–2	
	2 Jun 1990 v Tunisia	1–1	
	16 Jun 1990 v Holland	0–0	
	21 Jun 1990 v Egypt	1–0	1
	26 Jun 1990 v Belgium	1–0	
	1 Jul 1990 v Cameroon	3–2	
	4 Jul 1990 v W. Germany	1–1	
	7 Jul 1990 v Italy	1–2	
	12 Sep 1990 v Hungary	1–0	
	17 Oct 1990 v Poland	2–0	
	14 Nov 1990 v Eire	1–1	
	6 Feb 1991 v Cameroon	2–0	
	27 Mar 1991 v Eire	1–1	
	21 May 1991 v Soviet Union	3–1	
	25 May 1991 v Argentina	2–2	
	1 Jun 1991 v Australia	1–0	
	8 Jun 1991 v New Zealand	2–0	
	12 Jun 1991 v Malaysia	4–2	
	19 Feb 1992 v France	2–0	
	3 Jun 1992 v Finland	2–1	
	9 Sep 1992 v Spain	0–1	
	24 Apr 1996 v Croatia	0–0	
	18 May 1996 v Hungary	3–0	

978. Terence William Fenwick
Defender

Born   Durham, 17 November 1959
Clubs   Crystal Palace; Queen's Park Rangers; Tottenham Hotspur; Leicester City (on loan); Swindon Town

Caps	20	Result
	2 May 1984 v Wales	0–1
	26 May 1984 v Scotland	1–1
	2 Jun 1984 v Soviet Union	0–2
	10 Jun 1984 v Brazil	2–0
	13 Jun 1984 v Uruguay	0–2
	17 Jun 1984 v Chile	0–0
	22 May 1985 v Finland	1–1
	25 May 1985 v Scotland	0–1
	9 Jun 1985 v Mexico	0–1
	16 Jun 1985 v USA	5–0
	11 Sep 1985 v Romania	1–1
	16 Oct 1985 v Turkey	5–0
	13 Nov 1985 v N. Ireland	0–0
	29 Jan 1986 v Egypt	4–0
	17 May 1986 v Mexico	3–0
	3 Jun 1986 v Portugal	0–1
	6 Jun 1986 v Morocco	0–0
	11 Jun 1986 v Portugal	3–0
	22 Jun 1986 v Argentina	1–2
	17 Feb 1988 v Israel	0–0

979. Gary Winston Lineker
Forward

Born   Leicester, 30 November 1960
Clubs   Leicester City; Everton; Barcelona (Spain); Tottenham Hotspur; Grampus Eight (Japan)

Caps	80	Result	Goals
	26 May 1984 v Scotland	1–1	
	26 Mar 1985 v Eire	2–1	1
	1 May 1985 v Romania	0–0	
	25 May 1985 v Scotland	0–1	
	6 Jun 1985 v Italy	1–2	
	12 Jun 1985 v W. Germany	3–0	
	16 Jun 1985 v USA	5–0	2
	11 Sep 1985 v Romania	1–1	
	16 Oct 1985 v Turkey	5–0	3
	13 Nov 1985 v N. Ireland	0–0	
	29 Jan 1986 v Egypt	4–0	
	26 Mar 1986 v Soviet Union	1–0	
	24 May 1986 v Canada	1–0	
	3 Jun 1986 v Portugal	0–1	
	6 Jun 1986 v Morocco	0–0	
	11 Jun 1986 v Poland	3–0	3
	18 Jun 1986 v Paraguay	3–0	2
	22 Jun 1986 v Argentina	1–2	1
	15 Oct 1986 v N. Ireland	3–0	2
	12 Nov 1986 v Yugoslavia	2–0	
	18 Feb 1987 v Spain	4–2	4
	1 Apr 1987 v N. Ireland	2–0	
	29 Apr 1987 v Turkey	0–0	
	19 May 1987 v Brazil	1–1	1
	9 Sep 1987 v W. Germany	1–3	1
	14 Oct 1987 v Turkey	8–0	3
	11 Nov 1987 v Yugoslavia	4–1	
	23 Mar 1988 v Holland	2–2	1
	27 Apr 1988 v Hungary	0–0	
	21 May 1988 v Scotland	1–0	
	24 May 1988 v Colombia	1–1	1
	28 May 1988 v Switzerland	1–0	1
	12 Jun 1988 v Eire	0–1	
	15 Jun 1988 v Holland	1–3	
	18 Jun 1988 v Soviet Union	1–3	
	19 Oct 1988 v Sweden	0–0	
	16 Nov 1988 v Saudi Arabia	1–1	
	8 Feb 1989 v Greece	2–1	
	8 Mar 1989 v Albania	2–0	
	26 Apr 1989 v Albania	5–0	1
	3 Jun 1989 v Poland	3–0	1
	7 Jun 1989 v Denmark	1–1	1
	6 Sep 1989 v Sweden	0–0	
	1 Oct 1989 v Poland	0–0	
	15 Nov 1989 v Italy	0–0	
	13 Dec 1989 v Yugoslavia	2–1	
	28 Mar 1990 v Brazil	1–0	1
	25 Apr 1990 v Czechoslovakia	4–2	
	15 May 1990 v Denmark	1–0	1
	22 May 1990 v Uruguay	1–2	
	2 Jun 1990 v Tunisia	1–1	

11 Jun 1990 v Eire	1–1	1
16 Jun 1990 v Holland	0–0	
21 Jun 1990 v Egypt	1–0	
26 Jun 1990 v Belgium	1–0	
1 Jul 1990 v Cameroon	3–2	2
4 Jul 1990 v W. Germany	1–1	1
7 Jul 1990 v Italy	1–2	
12 Sep 1990 v Hungary	1–0	1
17 Oct 1990 v Poland	2–1	1
14 Nov 1990 v Eire	1–1	
6 Feb 1991 v Cameroon	2–0	2
27 Mar 1991 v Eire	1–1	
1 May 1991 v Turkey	1–0	
25 May 1991 v Argentina	2–2	1
1 Jun 1991 v Australia	1–0	
3 Jun 1991 v New Zealand	1–0	1
12 Jun 1991 v Malaysia	4–2	4
11 Sep 1991 v Germany	0–1	
16 Oct 1991 v Turkey	1–0	
13 Nov 1991 v Poland	1–1	1
19 Feb 1992 v France	2–0	1
25 Mar 1992 v Czechoslovakia	2–2	
29 Apr 1992 v CIS	2–2	1
12 May 1992 v Hungary	1–0	
17 May 1992 v Brazil	1–1	
3 Jun 1992 v Finland	2–1	
11 Jun 1992 v Denmark	0–0	
14 Jun 1992 v France	0–0	
17 Jun 1992 v Sweden	1–2	

980. Stephen Kenneth Hunt
Midfielder
Born Witton, 4 August 1956
Clubs Aston Villa; New York Cosmos (USA); Coventry City; West Bromwich Albion

Caps 2	Result
26 May 1984 v Scotland	1–1
2 Jun 1984 v Soviet Union	0–2

981. Mark Wayne Hateley
Centre forward
Born Liverpool, 7 November 1961
Clubs Coventry City; Portsmouth; AC Milan (Italy); Monaco (France); Glasgow Rangers; Queen's Park Rangers; Leeds Utd; Hull City

Caps 32	Result	Goals
2 Jun 1984 v Soviet Union	0–2	
10 Jun 1984 v Brazil	2–0	1
13 Jun 1984 v Uruguay	0–2	
17 Jun 1984 v Chile	0–0	
12 Sep 1984 v E. Germany	1–0	
17 Oct 1984 v Finland	5–0	2
27 Feb 1985 v N. Ireland	1–0	1
26 Mar 1985 v Eire	2–1	
22 May 1985 v Finland	1–1	1
25 May 1985 v Scotland	0–1	
6 Jun 1985 v Italy	1–2	1
9 Jun 1985 v Mexico	0–1	
11 Sep 1985 v Romania	1–1	
16 Oct 1985 v Turkey	5–0	
29 Jan 1986 v Egypt	4–0	
23 Apr 1986 v Scotland	2–1	
17 May 1986 v Mexico	3–0	2
24 May 1986 v Canada	1–0	1
3 Jun 1986 v Portugal	0–1	
6 Jun 1986 v Morocco	0–0	
18 Jun 1986 v Paraguay	3–0	
29 Apr 1987 v Turkey	0–0	
19 May 1987 v Brazil	1–1	
23 May 1987 v Scotland	0–0	
9 Sep 1987 v W. Germany	1–3	
23 Mar 1988 v Holland	2–2	
27 Apr 1988 v Hungary	0–0	
24 May 1988 v Colombia	1–1	
12 Jun 1988 v Eire	0–1	
15 Jun 1988 v Holland	1–3	

18 Jun 1988 v Soviet Union	1–3	
25 Mar 1992 v Czechoslovakia	2–2	

982. David Watson
Central defender
Born Liverpool, 20 November 1960
Clubs Liverpool; Norwich City; Everton

Caps 12	Result
10 Jun 1984 v Brazil	2–0
13 Jun 1984 v Uruguay	0–2
17 Jun 1984 v Chile	0–0
9 Jun 1985 v Mexico	0–1
16 Jun 1985 v USA	5–0
23 Apr 1986 v Scotland	2–1
15 Oct 1986 v N. Ireland	3–0
17 Feb 1988 v Israel	0–0
23 Mar 1988 v Holland	2–2
21 May 1988 v Scotland	1–0
28 May 1988 v Switzerland	1–0
18 Jun 1988 v Soviet Union	1–3

983. Clive Darren Allen
Forward
Born London, 20 May 1961
Clubs Queen's Park Rangers; Arsenal; Crystal Palace; Tottenham Hotspur; Bordeaux (France); Manchester City; Chelsea; West Ham Utd; Millwall; Carlisle Utd

Caps 5	Result
10 Jun 1984 v Brazil	2–0
13 Jun 1984 v Uruguay	0–2
17 Jun 1984 v Chile	0–0
29 Apr 1987 v Turkey	0–0
17 Feb 1988 v Israel	0–0

984. Gary Andrew Stevens
Defender/Midfielder
Born Hillingdon, 30 March 1962
Clubs Brighton & Hove Albion; Tottenham Hotspur; Portsmouth

Caps 7	Result
17 Oct 1984 v Finland	5–0
14 Nov 1984 v Turkey	8–0
27 Feb 1985 v N. Ireland	1–0
23 Apr 1988 v Scotland	2–0
17 May 1986 v Mexico	3–0
6 Jun 1986 v Morocco	0–0
18 Jun 1986 v Paraguay	3–0

985. Trevor McGregor Steven
Midfielder
Born Berwick, 21 September 1963
Clubs Burnley; Everton; Glasgow Rangers; Olympique Marseilles (France)

Caps 36	Result	Goals
27 Feb 1985 v N. Ireland	1–0	
26 Mar 1985 v Eire	2–1	1
1 May 1985 v Romania	0–0	
22 May 1985 v Finland	1–1	
6 Jun 1985 v Italy	1–2	
16 Jun 1985 v USA	5–0	1
16 Oct 1985 v Turkey	5–0	
29 Jan 1986 v Egypt	4–0	1
26 Mar 1986 v Soviet Union	1–0	
17 May 1986 v Mexico	3–0	
11 Jun 1986 v Poland	3–0	
18 Jun 1986 v Paraguay	3–0	
22 Jun 1986 v Argentina	1–2	
10 Sep 1986 v Sweden	0–0	
12 Nov 1986 v Yugoslavia	2–0	
18 Feb 1987 v Spain	4–2	
14 Oct 1987 v Turkey	8–0	
17 Feb 1988 v Yugoslavia	4–1	
23 Mar 1988 v Holland	2–2	
27 Apr 1988 v Hungary	0–0	
21 May 1988 v Scotland	1–0	
28 May 1988 v Switzerland	1–0	
15 Jun 1988 v Holland	1–3	

18 Jun 1988 v Soviet Union	1–3
27 May 1989 v Scotland	2–0
25 Apr 1990 v Czechoslovakia	4–2
1 Jul 1990 v Cameroon	3–2
4 Jul 1990 v W. Germany	1–1
7 Jul 1990 v Italy	1–2
6 Feb 1991 v Cameroon	2–0
11 Sep 1991 v Germany	0–1
29 Apr 1992 v CIS	2–2 1
17 May 1992 v Brazil	1–1
3 Jun 1992 v Finland	2–1
11 Jun 1992 v Denmark	0–0
14 Jun 1992 v France	0–0

986. Gary Richard Bailey
Goalkeeper
Born Ipswich, 9 August 1958
Clubs Witts University (South Africa); Manchester Utd
Caps 2   *Result*

26 Mar 1985 v Eire	2–1
9 Jun 1985 v Mexico	0–1

987. Christopher Roland Waddle
Winger
Born Hepworth, 14 December 1960
Clubs Tow Law Town; Newcastle Utd; Tottenham Hotspur;
Marseille (France); Sheffield Wednesday; Falkirk;
Bradford City; Sunderland; Burnley
Caps 62   *Result* *Goals*

26 Mar 1985 v Eire	2–1	
1 May 1985 v Romania	0–0	
22 May 1985 v Finland	1–1	
25 May 1985 v Scotland	0–1	
6 Jun 1985 v Italy	1–2	
9 Jun 1985 v Mexico	0–1	
12 Jun 1985 v W. Germany	3–0	
16 Jun 1985 v USA	5–0	
11 Sep 1985 v Romania	1–1	
16 Oct 1985 v Turkey	5–0	1
13 Nov 1985 v N. Ireland	0–0	
26 Feb 1986 v Israel	2–1	
26 Mar 1986 v Soviet Union	1–0	1
23 Apr 1986 v Scotland	2–1	
17 May 1986 v Mexico	3–0	
24 May 1986 v Canada	1–0	
3 Jun 1986 v Portugal	0–1	
6 Jun 1986 v Morocco	0–0	
11 Jun 1986 v Poland	3–0	
22 Jun 1986 v Argentina	1–2	
10 Sep 1986 v Sweden	0–0	
15 Oct 1986 v N. Ireland	3–0	1
12 Nov 1986 v Yugoslavia	2–0	
18 Feb 1987 v Spain	4–2	
1 Apr 1987 v N. Ireland	2–0	1
29 Apr 1987 v Turkey	0–0	
19 May 1987 v Brazil	1–1	
23 May 1987 v Scotland	0–0	
9 Sep 1987 v W. Germany	1–3	
17 Feb 1988 v Israel	0–0	
27 Apr 1988 v Hungary	0–0	
21 May 1988 v Scotland	1–0	
24 May 1988 v Colombia	1–1	
28 May 1988 v Switzerland	1–0	
12 Jun 1988 v Eire	0–1	
15 Jun 1988 v Holland	1–3	
19 Oct 1988 v Sweden	0–0	
16 Nov 1988 v Saudi Arabia	1–1	
8 Mar 1989 v Albania	2–0	
26 Apr 1989 v Albania	5–0	1
23 May 1989 v Chile	0–0	
27 May 1989 v Scotland	2–0	1
3 Jun 1989 v Poland	3–0	
7 Jun 1989 v Denmark	1–1	
6 Sep 1989 v Sweden	0–0	
11 Oct 1989 v Poland	0–0	
15 Nov 1989 v Italy	0–0	

13 Dec 1989 v Yugoslavia	2–1
28 Mar 1990 v Brazil	1–0
15 May 1990 v Denmark	1–0
22 May 1990 v Uruguay	1–2
2 Jun 1990 v Tunisia	1–1
11 Jun 1990 v Eire	1–1
16 Jun 1990 v Holland	0–0
21 Jun 1990 v Egypt	1–0
26 Jun 1990 v Belgium	1–0
1 Jul 1990 v Cameroon	3–2
4 Jul 1990 v W. Germany	1–1
7 Jul 1990 v Italy	1–2
12 Sep 1990 v Hungary	1–0
17 Oct 1990 v Poland	2–0
16 Oct 1991 v Turkey	1–0

988. Peter Davenport
Forward
Born Birkenhead, 24 March 1961
Clubs Everton; Cammell Laird; Nottingham Forest;
Manchester Utd; Middlesbrough; Sunderland;
St Johnstone; Stockport County; Macclesfield
Caps 1   *Result*

26 Mar 1985 v Eire	2–1

989. Michael Gary Stevens
Right back
Born Barrow, 27 March 1963
Clubs Everton; Glasgow Rangers; Tranmere Rovers
Caps 46   *Result*

6 Jun 1985 v Italy	1–2
12 Jun 1985 v W. Germany	3–0
11 Sep 1985 v Romania	1–1
16 Oct 1985 v Turkey	5–0
13 Nov 1985 v N. Ireland	0–0
29 Jan 1986 v Egypt	4–0
26 Feb 1986 v Israel	2–1
23 Apr 1986 v Scotland	2–1
24 May 1986 v Canada	1–0
3 Jun 1986 v Portugal	0–1
6 Jun 1986 v Morocco	0–0
11 Jun 1986 v Poland	3–0
18 Jun 1986 v Paraguay	3–0
22 Jun 1986 v Argentina	1–2
19 May 1987 v Brazil	1–1
23 May 1987 v Scotland	0–0
14 Oct 1987 v Turkey	8–0
11 Nov 1987 v Yugoslavia	4–1
17 Feb 1988 v Israel	0–0
23 Mar 1988 v Holland	2–2
27 Apr 1988 v Hungary	0–0
21 May 1988 v Scotland	1–0
28 May 1988 v Switzerland	1–0
12 Jun 1988 v Eire	0–1
15 Jun 1988 v Holland	1–3
18 Jun 1988 v Soviet Union	1–3
14 Sep 1988 v Denmark	1–0
19 Oct 1988 v Sweden	0–0
8 Feb 1989 v Greece	2–1
8 Mar 1989 v Albania	2–0
26 Apr 1989 v Albania	5–0
27 May 1989 v Scotland	2–0
3 Jun 1989 v Poland	3–0
6 Sep 1989 v Sweden	0–0
11 Oct 1989 v Poland	0–0
15 Nov 1989 v Italy	0–0
28 Mar 1990 v Brazil	1–0
15 May 1990 v Denmark	1–0
2 Jun 1990 v Tunisia	1–1
11 Jun 1990 v Eire	1–1
7 Jul 1990 v Italy	1–2
21 May 1991 v Soviet Union	3–1
29 Apr 1992 v CIS	2–2
12 May 1992 v Hungary	1–0
17 May 1992 v Brazil	1–1
3 June 1992 v Finland	2–1

990. Peter Reid
Midfielder
Born   Huyton, 20 June 1956
Clubs   Bolton Wanderers; Everton; Queen's Park Rangers;
        Manchester City; Southampton; Notts County; Bury

Caps	13	Result
	9 Jun 1985 v Mexico	0–1
	12 Jun 1985 v W. Germany	3–0
	16 Jun 1985 v USA	5–0
	11 Sep 1985 v Romania	1–1
	23 Apr 1986 v Scotland	2–1
	24 May 1986 v Canada	1–0
	11 Jun 1986 v Poland	3–0
	18 Jun 1986 v Paraguay	3–0
	22 Jun 1986 v Argentina	1–2
	19 May 1987 v Brazil	1–1
	9 Sep 1987 v W. Germany	1–3
	11 Nov 1987 v Yugoslavia	4–1
	28 May 1988 v Switzerland	1–0

991. Kerry Michael Dixon
Forward
Born   Luton, 24 July 1961
Clubs   Tottenham Hotspur; Dunstable; Reading; Chelsea;
        Southampton; Luton Town; Millwall; Watford;
        Doncaster Rovers

Caps	8	Result	Goals
	9 Jun 1985 v Mexico	0–1	
	12 Jun 1985 v W. Germany	3–0	2
	16 Jun 1985 v USA	5–0	2
	13 Nov 1985 v N. Ireland	0–0	
	26 Feb 1986 v Israel	2–1	
	17 May 1986 v Mexico	3–0	
	11 Jun 1986 v Poland	3–0	
	10 Sep 1986 v Sweden	0–1	

992. Paul William Bracewell
Midfielder
Born   Stoke-on-Trent, 19 July 1962
Clubs   Stoke City; Sunderland; Everton; Newcastle Utd;
        Fulham

Caps	3	Result
	12 Jun 1985 v W. Germany	3–0
	16 Jun 1985 v USA	5–0
	13 Nov 1985 v N. Ireland	0–0

993. Christopher Charles Eric Woods
Goalkeeper
Born   Boston, 14 November 1959
Clubs   Nottingham Forest; Queen's Park Rangers; Norwich
        City; Glasgow Rangers; Sheffield Wednesday;
        Reading; Southampton; Sunderland; Burnley

Caps	43	Result
	16 Jun 1985 v USA	5–0
	29 Jan 1986 v Egypt	4–0
	26 Feb 1986 v Israel	2–1
	24 May 1986 v Canada	1–0
	12 Nov 1986 v Yugoslavia	2–0
	18 Feb 1987 v Spain	4–2
	1 Apr 1987 v N. Ireland	2–0
	29 Apr 1987 v Turkey	0–0
	23 May 1987 v Scotland	0–0
	17 Feb 1988 v Israel	0–0
	27 Apr 1988 v Hungary	0–0
	28 May 1988 v Switzerland	1–0
	18 Jun 1988 v Soviet Union	1–3
	14 Sep 1988 v Denmark	1–0
	28 Mar 1990 v Brazil	1–0
	15 May 1990 v Denmark	1–0
	12 Sep 1990 v Hungary	1–0
	17 Oct 1990 v Poland	2–0
	14 Nov 1990 v Eire	1–1
	21 May 1991 v Soviet Union	3–1
	1 Jun 1991 v Australia	1–0
	3 Jun 1991 v New Zealand	1–0

	8 Jun 1991 v New Zealand	2–0
	12 Jun 1991 v Malaysia	4–2
	11 Sep 1991 v Germany	0–1
	16 Oct 1991 v Turkey	1–0
	13 Nov 1991 v Poland	1–1
	19 Feb 1992 v France	2–0
	29 Apr 1992 v CIS	2–2
	17 May 1992 v Brazil	1–1
	3 Jun 1992 v Finland	2–1
	11 Jun 1992 v Denmark	0–0
	14 Jun 1992 v France	0–0
	17 Jun 1992 v Sweden	1–2
	9 Sep 1992 v Spain	0–1
	14 Oct 1992 v Norway	1–1
	18 Nov 1992 v Turkey	4–0
	17 Feb 1993 v San Marino	6–0
	31 Mar 1993 v Turkey	2–0
	28 Apr 1993 v Holland	2–2
	29 May 1993 v Poland	1–1
	2 Jun 1993 v Norway	0–2
	9 Jun 1993 v USA	0–2

994. David Lloyd 'Danny' Wallace
Forward
Born   Greenwich, 21 January 1964
Clubs   Southampton; Manchester Utd; Millwall;
        Birmingham City; Wycombe Wanderers

Caps	1	Result	Goals
	29 Jan 1986 v Egypt	4–0	1

995. Peter Andrew Beardsley
Forward
Born   Newcastle-upon-Tyne, 18 January 1961
Clubs   Carlisle Utd; Vancouver Whitecaps (Canada);
        Manchester Utd; Newcastle Utd; Liverpool; Everton;
        Bolton Wanderers; Manchester City (on loan);
        Fulham (on loan); Hartlepool Utd

Caps	59	Result	Goals
	29 Jan 1986 v Egypt	4–0	
	26 Feb 1986 v Israel	2–1	
	26 Mar 1986 v Soviet Union	1–0	
	17 May 1986 v Mexico	3–0	1
	24 May 1986 v Canada	1–0	
	3 Jun 1986 v Portugal	0–1	
	11 Jun 1986 v Poland	3–0	
	18 Jun 1986 v Paraguay	3–0	1
	22 Jun 1986 v Argentina	1–2	
	15 Oct 1986 v N. Ireland	3–0	
	12 Nov 1986 v Yugoslavia	2–0	
	18 Feb 1987 v Spain	4–2	
	1 Apr 1987 v N. Ireland	2–0	
	19 May 1987 v Brazil	1–1	
	23 May 1987 v Scotland	0–0	
	9 Sep 1987 v W. Germany	1–3	
	14 Oct 1987 v Turkey	8–0	1
	11 Nov 1987 v Yugoslavia	4–1	1
	17 Feb 1988 v Israel	0–0	
	23 Mar 1988 v Holland	2–2	
	27 Apr 1988 v Hungary	0–0	
	21 May 1988 v Scotland	1–0	1
	24 May 1988 v Colombia	1–1	
	28 May 1988 v Switzerland	1–0	
	12 Jun 1988 v Eire	0–1	
	15 Jun 1988 v Holland	1–3	
	14 Sep 1988 v Denmark	1–0	
	19 Oct 1988 v Sweden	0–0	
	16 Nov 1988 v Saudi Arabia	1–1	
	8 Feb 1989 v Greece	2–1	
	8 Mar 1989 v Albania	2–0	
	26 Apr 1989 v Albania	5–0	2
	3 Jun 1989 v Poland	3–0	
	7 Jun 1989 v Denmark	1–1	
	6 Sep 1989 v Sweden	0–0	
	11 Oct 1989 v Poland	0–0	
	15 Nov 1989 v Italy	0–0	

28 Mar 1990 v Brazil	1–0
22 May 1990 v Uruguay	1–2
2 Jun 1990 v Tunisia	1–1
11 Jun 1990 v Eire	1–1
21 Jun 1990 v Egypt	1–0
1 Jul 1990 v Cameroon	3–2
4 Jul 1990 v W. Germany	1–1
7 Jul 1990 v Italy	1–2
17 Oct 1990 v Poland	2–0 1
14 Nov 1990 v Eire	1–1
27 Mar 1991 v Eire	1–1
21 May 1991 v Soviet Union	3–1
9 Mar 1994 v Denmark	1–0
17 May 1994 v Greece	5–0 1
22 May 1994 v Norway	0–0
16 Nov 1994 v Nigeria	1–0
15 Feb 1995 v Eire	0–1
29 Mar 1995 v Uruguay	0–0
3 Jun 1995 v Japan	2–1
8 Jun 1995 v Sweden	3–3
12 Dec 1995 v Portugal	1–1
23 May 1996 v China	3–0

996. Stephen Brian Hodge
Midfielder

Born   Nottingham, 25 October 1962
Clubs   Nottingham Forest; Aston Villa; Tottenham Hotspur; Leeds Utd; Derby County (on loan); Queen's Park Rangers; Watford; Leyton Orient

Caps 24	*Result*
26 Mar 1986 v Soviet Union	1–0
23 Apr 1986 v Scotland	2–1
24 May 1986 v Canada	1–0
3 Jun 1986 v Portugal	0–1
6 Jun 1986 v Morocco	0–0
11 Jun 1986 v Poland	3–0
18 Jun 1986 v Paraguay	3–0
22 Jun 1986 v Argentina	1–2
10 Sep 1986 v Sweden	0–1
15 Oct 1986 v N. Ireland	3–0
12 Nov 1986 v Yugoslavia	2–0
18 Feb 1987 v Spain	4–2
1 Apr 1987 v N. Ireland	2–0
29 Apr 1987 v Turkey	0–0
23 May 1987 v Scotland	0–0
14 Sep 1988 v Denmark	1–0
15 Nov 1989 v Italy	0–0
13 Dec 1989 v Yugoslavia	2–1
25 Apr 1990 v Czechoslovakia	4–2
15 May 1990 v Denmark	1–0
22 May 1990 v Uruguay	1–2
2 Jun 1990 v Tunisia	1–1
6 Feb 1991 v Cameroon	2–0
1 May 1991 v Turkey	1–0

997. Anthony Richard Cottee
Forward

Born   West Ham, 11 July 1965
Clubs   West Ham Utd; Everton; Leicester City; Birmingham City; Barnet; Millwall

Caps 7	*Result*
10 Sep 1986 v Sweden	0–1
15 Oct 1986 v N. Ireland	3–0
27 Apr 1988 v Hungary	0–0
14 Sep 1988 v Denmark	1–0
19 Oct 1988 v Sweden	0–0
23 May 1989 v Chile	0–0
27 May 1989 v Scotland	2–0

998. Tony Alexander Adams
Central defender

Born   Romford, 10 October 1966
Clubs   Arsenal

Caps 66	*Result*	*Goals*
18 Feb 1987 v Spain	4–2	

29 Apr 1987 v Turkey	0–0	
19 May 1987 v Brazil	1–1	
9 Sep 1987 v W. Germany	1–3	
14 Oct 1987 v Turkey	8–0	
11 Nov 1987 v Yugoslavia	4–1	1
23 Mar 1988 v Holland	1–1	1
27 Apr 1988 v Hungary	0–0	
21 May 1988 v Scotland	1–0	
24 May 1988 v Colombia	1–1	
28 May 1988 v Switzerland	1–0	
12 Jun 1988 v Eire	0–1	
15 Jun 1988 v Holland	1–3	
18 Jun 1988 v Soviet Union	1–3	1
14 Sep 1988 v Denmark	1–0	
19 Oct 1988 v Sweden	0–0	
16 Nov 1988 v Saudi Arabia	1–1	1
14 Nov 1990 v Eire	1–1	
27 Mar 1991 v Eire	1–1	
14 Oct 1992 v Norway	1–1	
18 Nov 1992 v Turkey	4–0	
17 Feb 1993 v San Marino	6–0	
31 Mar 1993 v Turkey	2–0	
28 Apr 1993 v Holland	2–2	
29 May 1993 v Poland	1–1	
2 Jun 1993 v Norway	0–2	
8 Sep 1993 v Poland	3–0	
13 Oct 1993 v Holland	0–2	
9 Mar 1994 v Denmark	1–0	
17 May 1994 v Greece	5–0	
22 May 1994 v Norway	0–0	
7 Sep 1994 v USA	2–0	
12 Oct 1994 v Romania	1–1	
15 Feb 1995 v Eire	0–1	
29 Mar 1995 v Uruguay	0–0	
6 Sep 1995 v Colombia	0–0	
11 Oct 1995 v Norway	0–0	
15 Nov 1995 v Switzerland	3–1	
12 Dec 1995 v Portugal	1–1	
23 May 1996 v China	3–0	
8 Jun 1996 v Switzerland	1–1	
15 Jun 1996 v Scotland	2–0	
18 Jun 1996 v Holland	4–1	
22 Jun 1996 v Spain	0–0	
26 Jun 1996 v Germany	1–1	
9 Nov 1996 v Georgia	2–0	
30 Apr 1997 v Georgia	2–0	
11 Oct 1997 v Italy	0–0	
11 Feb 1998 v Chile	0–2	
22 Apr 1998 v Portugal	3–0	
23 May 1998 v Saudi Arabia	0–0	
15 Jun 1998 v Tunisia	2–0	
22 Jun 1998 v Romania	1–2	
26 Jun 1998 v Colombia	2–0	
30 Jun 1998 v Argentina	2–2	
10 Feb 1999 v France	0–2	
5 Jun 1999 v Sweden	0–0	
4 Sep 1999 v Luxembourg	6–0	
8 Sep 1999 v Poland	0–0	
10 Oct 1999 v Belgium	2–1	
13 Nov 1999 v Scotland	2–0	
17 Nov 1999 v Scotland	0–1	
31 May 2000 v Ukraine	2–0	1
12 Jun 2000 v Portugal	2–3	
2 Sep 2000 v France	1–1	
7 Oct 2000 v Germany	0–1	

999. Stuart Pearce
Left back

Born   Hammersmith, 24 April 1962
Clubs   Coventry City; Nottingham Forest; Newcastle Utd; West Ham Utd; Manchester City

Caps 78	*Result*	*Goals*
19 May 1987 v Brazil	1–1	
23 May 1987 v Scotland	0–0	
9 Sep 1987 v W. Germany	1–3	

17 Feb 1988 v Israel	0–0	
27 Apr 1988 v Hungary	0–0	
14 Sep 1988 v Denmark	1–0	
19 Oct 1988 v Sweden	0–0	
16 Nov 1988 v Saudi Arabia	1–1	
8 Feb 1989 v Greece	2–1	
8 Mar 1989 v Albania	2–0	
26 Apr 1989 v Albania	5–0	
23 May 1989 v Chile	0–0	
27 May 1989 v Scotland	2–0	
3 Jun 1989 v Poland	3–0	
7 Jun 1989 v Denmark	1–1	
6 Sep 1989 v Sweden	0–0	
11 Oct 1989 v Poland	0–0	
15 Nov 1989 v Italy	0–0	
13 Dec 1989 v Yugoslavia	2–1	
28 Mar 1990 v Brazil	1–0	
25 Apr 1990 v Czechoslovakia	4–2	1
15 May 1990 v Denmark	1–0	
22 May 1990 v Uruguay	1–2	
2 Jun 1990 v Tunisia	1–1	
11 Jun 1990 v Eire	1–1	
16 Jun 1990 v Holland	0–0	
21 Jun 1990 v Egypt	1–0	
26 Jun 1990 v Belgium	1–0	
1 Jul 1990 v Cameroon	3–2	
4 Jul 1990 v W. Germany	1–1	
12 Sep 1990 v Hungary	1–0	
17 Oct 1990 v Poland	2–0	
14 Nov 1990 v Eire	1–1	
6 Feb 1991 v Cameroon	2–0	
27 Mar 1991 v Eire	1–1	
1 May 1991 v Turkey	1–0	
25 May 1991 v Argentina	2–2	
1 Jun 1991 v Australia	1–0	
3 Jun 1991 v New Zealand	1–0	
8 Jun 1991 v New Zealand	2–0	1
12 Jun 1991 v Malaysia	4–2	
16 Oct 1991 v Turkey	1–0	
13 Nov 1991 v Poland	1–1	
19 Feb 1992 v France	2–0	
25 Mar 1992 v Czechoslovakia	2–2	
17 May 1992 v Brazil	1–1	
3 Jun 1992 v Finland	2–1	
11 Jun 1992 v Denmark	0–0	
14 Jun 1992 v France	0–0	
17 Jun 1992 v Sweden	1–2	
9 Sep 1992 v Spain	0–1	
14 Oct 1992 v Norway	1–1	
18 Nov 1992 v Turkey	4–0	1
8 Sep 1993 v Poland	3–0	1
17 Nov 1993 v San Marino	7–1	
17 May 1994 v Greece	5–0	
12 Oct 1994 v Romania	1–1	
3 Jun 1995 v Japan	2–1	
11 Jun 1995 v Brazil	1–3	
11 Oct 1995 v Norway	0–0	
15 Nov 1995 v Switzerland	3–1	1
12 Dec 1995 v Portugal	1–1	
27 Mar 1996 v Bulgaria	1–0	
24 Apr 1996 v Croatia	0–0	
18 May 1996 v Hungary	3–0	
8 Jun 1996 v Switzerland	1–1	
15 Jun 1996 v Scotland	2–0	
18 Jun 1996 v Holland	4–1	
22 Jun 1996 v Spain	0–0	
26 Jun 1996 v Germany	1–1	
1 Sep 1996 v Moldova	3–0	
9 Oct 1996 v Poland	2–1	
12 Feb 1997 v Italy	0–1	
29 Mar 1997 v Mexico	2–0	
24 May 1997 v South Africa	2–1	
4 Jun 1997 v Italy	2–0	
4 Sep 1999 v Luxembourg	6–0	
8 Sep 1999 v Poland	0–0	

1000. Neil John Webb

Midfielder

Born Reading, 30 July 1963
Clubs Reading; Portsmouth; Nottingham Forest; Manchester Utd; Swindon Town; Grimsby Town; Aldershot

Caps 26	*Result*	*Goals*
9 Sep 1987 v W. Germany	1–3	
14 Oct 1987 v Turkey	8–0	1
11 Nov 1987 v Yugoslavia	4–1	
17 Feb 1988 v Israel	0–0	
23 Mar 1988 v Holland	2–2	
21 May 1988 v Scotland	1–0	
28 May 1988 v Switzerland	1–0	
12 Jun 1988 v Eire	0–1	
18 Jun 1988 v Soviet Union	1–3	
14 Sep 1988 v Denmark	1–0	1
19 Oct 1988 v Sweden	0–0	
8 Feb 1989 v Greece	2–1	
8 Mar 1989 v Albania	2–0	
26 Apr 1989 v Albania	5–0	
23 May 1989 v Chile	0–0	
27 May 1989 v Scotland	2–0	
3 Jun 1989 v Poland	3–0	1
7 Jun 1989 v Denmark	1–1	
6 Sep 1989 v Sweden	0–0	
15 Nov 1989 v Italy	0–0	
19 Feb 1992 v France	2–0	
12 May 1992 v Hungary	1–0	1
17 May 1992 v Brazil	1–1	
3 Jun 1992 v Finland	2–1	
11 Jun 1992 v Denmark	0–0	
17 Jun 1992 v Sweden	1–2	

⚽ DID YOU KNOW...?

Nottingham Forest's Neil Webb became the 1,000th player to be used in an England international when he won his first cap as a substitute for Glenn Hoddle during the 3–1 defeat away to West Germany in September 1987.

1001. Michael Gordon Harford

Forward

Born Sunderland, 12 February 1959
Clubs Lincoln City; Newcastle Utd; Bristol City; Birmingham City; Luton Town; Derby County; Chelsea; Sunderland; Coventry City; Wimbledon

Caps 2	*Result*
17 Feb 1988 v Israel	0–0
14 Sep 1988 v Denmark	1–0

1002. Stephen McMahon

Midfielder

Born Liverpool, 20 August 1961
Clubs Everton; Aston Villa; Liverpool; Manchester City; Swindon Town

Caps 17	*Result*
17 Feb 1988 v Israel	0–0
27 Apr 1988 v Hungary	0–0
24 May 1988 v Colombia	1–1
18 Jun 1988 v Soviet Union	1–3
7 Jun 1989 v Denmark	1–1
6 Sep 1989 v Sweden	0–0
11 Oct 1989 v Poland	0–0
15 Nov 1989 v Italy	0–0
13 Dec 1989 v Yugoslavia	2–1
28 Mar 1990 v Brazil	1–0
25 Apr 1990 v Czechoslovakia	4–2
15 May 1990 v Denmark	1–0

11 Jun 1990 v Eire	1–1
21 Jun 1990 v Egypt	1–0
26 Jun 1990 v Belgium	1–0
7 Jul 1990 v Italy	1–2
14 Nov 1990 v Eire	1–1

1003. Gary Andrew Pallister
Central defender
Born Ramsgate, 30 June 1965
Clubs Middlesbrough; Darlington; Manchester Utd

Caps	22	Result
	27 Apr 1988 v Hungary	0–0
	16 Nov 1988 v Saudi Arabia	1–1
	6 Feb 1991 v Cameroon	2–0
	1 May 1991 v Turkey	1–0
	11 Sep 1991 v Germany	0–1
	2 Jun 1993 v Norway	0–2
	9 Jun 1993 v USA	0–2
	13 Jun 1993 v Brazil	1–1
	19 Jun 1993 v Germany	1–2
	8 Sep 1993 v Poland	3–0
	13 Oct 1993 v Holland	0–2
	17 Nov 1993 v San Marino	7–1
	9 Mar 1994 v Denmark	1–0
	7 Sep 1994 v USA	2–0
	12 Oct 1994 v Romania	1–1
	15 Feb 1995 v Eire	0–1
	29 Mar 1995 v Uruguay	0–0
	8 Jun 1995 v Sweden	3–3
	11 Oct 1995 v Norway	0–0
	15 Nov 1995 v Switzerland	3–1
	1 Sep 1996 v Moldova	3–0
	9 Oct 1996 v Poland	2–1

1004. Paul John Gascoigne
Midfielder
Born Gateshead, 27 May 1967
Clubs Newcastle Utd; Tottenham Hotspur; Lazio (Italy); Glasgow Rangers; Middlesbrough; Everton; Burnley; Boston Utd

Caps	57	Result	Goals
	14 Sep 1988 v Denmark	1–0	
	16 Nov 1988 v Saudi Arabia	1–1	
	26 Apr 1989 v Albania	5–0	1
	23 May 1989 v Chile	0–0	
	27 May 1989 v Scotland	2–0	
	6 Sep 1989 v Sweden	0–0	
	28 Mar 1990 v Brazil	1–0	
	25 Apr 1990 v Czechoslovakia	4–2	1
	15 May 1990 v Denmark	1–0	
	22 May 1990 v Uruguay	1–2	
	2 Jun 1990 v Tunisia	1–1	
	11 Jun 1990 v Eire	1–1	
	16 Jun 1990 v Holland	0–0	
	21 Jun 1990 v Egypt	1–0	
	26 Jun 1990 v Belgium	1–0	
	1 Jul 1990 v Cameroon	3–2	
	4 Jul 1990 v W. Germany	1–1	
	12 Sep 1990 v Hungary	1–0	
	17 Oct 1990 v Poland	2–0	
	6 Feb 1991 v Cameroon	2–0	
	14 Oct 1992 v Norway	1–1	
	18 Nov 1992 v Turkey	4–0	2
	17 Feb 1993 v San Marino	6–0	
	31 Mar 1993 v Turkey	2–0	1
	28 Apr 1993 v Holland	2–2	
	29 May 1993 v Poland	1–1	
	2 Jun 1993 v Norway	0–2	
	8 Sep 1993 v Poland	3–0	1
	9 Mar 1994 v Denmark	1–0	
	3 Jun 1995 v Japan	2–1	
	8 Jun 1995 v Sweden	3–3	
	11 Jun 1995 v Brazil	1–3	
	6 Sep 1995 v Colombia	0–0	
	15 Nov 1995 v Switzerland	3–1	
	12 Dec 1995 v Portugal	1–1	
	27 Mar 1996 v Bulgaria	1–0	
	24 Apr 1996 v Croatia	0–0	
	23 May 1996 v China	3–0	1
	8 Jun 1996 v Switzerland	1–1	
	15 Jun 1996 v Scotland	2–0	1
	18 Jun 1996 v Holland	4–1	
	22 Jun 1996 v Spain	0–0	
	26 Jun 1996 v Germany	1–1	
	1 Sep 1996 v Moldova	3–0	1
	9 Oct 1996 v Poland	2–1	
	9 Nov 1996 v Georgia	2–0	
	24 May 1997 v South Africa	2–1	
	31 May 1997 v Poland	2–0	
	4 Jun 1997 v Italy	2–0	
	7 Jun 1997 v France	1–0	
	10 Jun 1997 v Brazil	0–1	
	10 Sep 1997 v Moldova	4–0	1
	11 Oct 1997 v Italy	0–0	
	15 Nov 1997 v Cameroon	2–0	
	23 May 1998 v Saudi Arabia	0–0	
	27 May 1998 v Morocco	1–0	
	29 May 1998 v Belgium	0–0	

1005. David Carlyle Rocastle
Midfielder
Born Lewisham, 2 May 1967
Died 31 March 2001
Clubs Arsenal; Leeds Utd; Manchester City; Chelsea; Norwich City (on loan); Hull City (on loan)

Caps	14	Result
	14 Sep 1988 v Denmark	1–0
	16 Nov 1988 v Saudi Arabia	1–1
	8 Feb 1989 v Greece	2–1
	8 Mar 1989 v Albania	2–0
	26 Apr 1989 v Albania	5–0
	3 Jun 1989 v Poland	3–0
	7 Jun 1989 v Denmark	1–1
	6 Sep 1989 v Sweden	0–0
	11 Oct 1989 v Poland	0–0
	13 Dec 1989 v Yugoslavia	2–1
	15 May 1990 v Denmark	1–0
	13 Nov 1991 v Poland	1–1
	25 Mar 1992 v Czechoslovakia	2–2
	17 May 1992 v Brazil	1–1

1006. Desmond Sinclair Walker
Central defender
Born Hackney, 26 November 1965
Clubs Nottingham Forest; Sampdoria (Italy); Sheffield Wednesday

Caps	59	Result
	14 Sep 1988 v Denmark	1–0
	19 Oct 1988 v Sweden	0–0
	8 Feb 1989 v Greece	2–1
	8 Mar 1989 v Albania	2–0
	26 Apr 1989 v Albania	5–0
	23 May 1989 v Chile	0–0
	27 May 1989 v Scotland	2–0
	3 Jun 1989 v Poland	3–0
	7 Jun 1989 v Denmark	1–1
	6 Sep 1989 v Sweden	0–0
	11 Oct 1989 v Poland	0–0
	15 Nov 1989 v Italy	0–0
	13 Dec 1989 v Yugoslavia	2–1
	28 Mar 1990 v Brazil	1–0
	25 Apr 1990 v Czechoslovakia	4–2
	15 May 1990 v Denmark	1–0
	22 May 1990 v Uruguay	1–2
	2 Jun 1990 v Tunisia	1–1
	11 Jun 1990 v Eire	1–1
	16 Jun 1990 v Holland	0–0
	21 Jun 1990 v Egypt	1–0
	26 Jun 1990 v Belgium	1–0
	1 Jul 1990 v Cameroon	3–2

4 Jul 1990 v W. Germany	1–1
7 Jul 1990 v Italy	1–2
12 Sep 1990 v Hungary	1–0
17 Oct 1990 v Poland	2–0
14 Nov 1990 v Eire	1–1
6 Feb 1991 v Cameroon	2–0
27 Mar 1991 v Eire	1–1
1 May 1991 v Turkey	1–0
25 May 1991 v Argentina	2–2
1 Jun 1991 v Australia	1–0
3 Jun 1991 v New Zealand	1–0
8 Jun 1991 v New Zealand	2–0
12 Jun 1991 v Malaysia	4–2
16 Oct 1991 v Turkey	1–0
13 Nov 1991 v Poland	1–1
19 Feb 1992 v France	2–0
25 Mar 1992 v Czechoslovakia	2–2
29 Apr 1992 v CIS	2–2
12 May 1992 v Hungary	1–0
17 May 1992 v Brazil	1–1
3 Jun 1992 v Finland	2–1
11 Jun 1992 v Denmark	0–0
14 Jun 1992 v France	0–0
17 Jun 1992 v Sweden	1–2
9 Sep 1992 v Spain	0–1
14 Oct 1992 v Norway	1–1
18 Nov 1992 v Turkey	4–0
17 Feb 1993 v San Marino	6–0
31 Mar 1993 v Turkey	2–0
28 Apr 1993 v Holland	2–2
29 May 1993 v Poland	1–1
2 Jun 1993 v Norway	0–2
9 Jun 1993 v USA	0–2
13 Jun 1993 v Brazil	1–1
19 Jun 1993 v Germany	1–2
17 Nov 1993 v San Marino	7–1

1007. David Andrew Seaman
Goalkeeper

Born Rotherham, 19 September 1963
Clubs Leeds Utd; Peterborough Utd; Birmingham City; Queen's Park Rangers; Arsenal; Manchester City

Caps	75	*Result*
	16 Nov 1988 v Saudi Arabia	1–1
	7 Jun 1989 v Denmark	1–1
	25 Apr 1990 v Czechoslovakia	4–2
	6 Feb 1991 v Cameroon	2–0
	27 Mar 1991 v Eire	1–1
	1 May 1991 v Turkey	1–0
	25 May 1991 v Argentina	2–2
	25 Mar 1992 v Czechoslovakia	2–2
	12 May 1992 v Hungary	1–0
	8 Sep 1993 v Poland	3–0
	13 Oct 1993 v Holland	0–2
	17 Nov 1993 v San Marino	7–1
	9 Mar 1994 v Denmark	1–0
	22 May 1994 v Norway	0–0
	7 Sep 1994 v USA	2–0
	12 Oct 1994 v Romania	1–1
	15 Feb 1995 v Eire	0–1
	6 Sep 1995 v Colombia	0–0
	11 Oct 1995 v Norway	0–0
	15 Nov 1995 v Switzerland	3–1
	12 Dec 1995 v Portugal	1–1
	27 Mar 1995 v Bulgaria	1–0
	24 Apr 1996 v Croatia	0–0
	18 May 1996 v Hungary	3–0
	8 Jun 1996 v Switzerland	1–1
	15 Jun 1996 v Scotland	2–0
	18 Jun 1996 v Holland	4–1
	22 Jun 1996 v Spain	0–0
	26 Jun 1996 v Germany	1–1
	1 Sep 1996 v Moldova	3–0
	9 Oct 1996 v Poland	2–1
	9 Nov 1996 v Georgia	2–0
	30 Apr 1997 v Georgia	2–0

31 May 1997 v Poland	2–0
7 Jun 1997 v France	1–0
10 Jun 1997 v Brazil	0–1
10 Sep 1997 v Moldova	4–0
11 Oct 1997 v Italy	0–0
22 Apr 1998 v Portugal	3–0
23 May 1998 v Saudi Arabia	0–0
15 Jun 1998 v Tunisia	2–0
22 Jun 1998 v Romania	1–2
26 Jun 1998 v Colombia	2–0
30 Jun 1998 v Argentina	2–2
5 Sep 1998 v Sweden	1–2
10 Oct 1998 v Bulgaria	0–0
14 Oct 1998 v Luxembourg	3–0
10 Feb 1999 v France	0–2
27 Mar 1999 v Poland	3–1
28 Apr 1999 v Hungary	1–1
5 Jun 1999 v Sweden	0–0
9 Jun 1999 v Bulgaria	1–1
10 Oct 1999 v Belgium	2–1
13 Nov 1999 v Scotland	2–0
17 Nov 1999 v Scotland	0–1
23 Feb 2000 v Argentina	0–0
27 May 2000 v Brazil	1–1
12 Jun 2000 v Portugal	2–3
17 Jun 2000 v Germany	1–0
2 Sep 2000 v France	1–1
7 Oct 2000 v Germany	0–1
11 Oct 2000 v Finland	0–0
24 Mar 2001 v Finland	2–1
28 Mar 2001 v Albania	3–1
6 Jun 2001 v Greece	2–0
1 Sep 2001 v Germany	5–1
5 Sep 2001 v Albania	2–0
17 Apr 2002 v Paraguay	4–0
2 Jun 2002 v Sweden	1–1
7 Jun 2002 v Argentina	1–0
12 Jun 2002 v Nigeria	0–0
15 Jun 2002 v Denmark	3–0
21 Jun 2002 v Brazil	1–2
12 Oct 2002 v Slovakia	2–1
16 Oct 2002 v Macedonia	2–2

1008. Melvyn Sterland
Right back

Born Sheffield, 1 October 1961
Clubs Sheffield Wednesday; Glasgow Rangers; Leeds Utd

Caps	1	*Result*
	16 Nov 1988 v Saudi Arabia	1–1

1009. Michael Lauriston Thomas
Midfielder

Born Lambeth, 24 August 1967
Clubs Arsenal; Portsmouth; Liverpool; Benfica (Portugal); Middlesbrough; Wimbledon

Caps	2	*Result*
	16 Nov 1988 v Saudi Arabia	1–1
	13 Dec 1989 v Yugoslavia	2–1

1010. Alan Martin Smith
Forward

Born Bromsgrove, 21 November 1962
Clubs Alvechurch; Leicester City; Arsenal

Caps	13	*Result*	*Goals*
	16 Nov 1988 v Saudi Arabia	1–1	
	8 Feb 1989 v Greece	2–1	
	8 Mar 1989 v Albania	2–0	
	3 Jun 1989 v Poland	3–0	
	1 May 1991 v Turkey	1–0	
	21 May 1991 v Soviet Union	3–1	1
	25 May 1991 v Argentina	2–2	
	11 Sep 1991 v Germany	0–1	
	16 Oct 1991 v Turkey	1–0	1
	13 Nov 1991 v Poland	1–1	
	12 May 1992 v Hungary	1–0	

11 Jun 1992 v Denmark	0–0
17 Jun 1992 v Sweden	1–2

1011. Brian Marwood
Winger
Born   Seaham, 5 February 1960
Clubs   Hull City; Sheffield Wednesday; Arsenal; Sheffield
        Utd; Middlesbrough; Swindon Town; Barnet

Caps	1	Result
	16 Nov 1988 v Saudi Arabia	1–1

1012. Paul Andrew Parker
Defender
Born   West Ham, 4 April 1964
Clubs   Fulham; Queen's Park Rangers; Manchester Utd;
        Derby County; Sheffield Utd

Caps	19	Result
	26 Apr 1989 v Albania	5–0
	23 May 1989 v Chile	0–0
	7 Jun 1989 v Denmark	1–1
	13 Dec 1989 v Yugoslavia	2–1
	22 May 1990 v Uruguay	1–2
	16 Jun 1990 v Holland	0–0
	21 Jun 1990 v Egypt	1–0
	26 Jun 1990 v Belgium	1–0
	1 Jul 1990 v Cameroon	3–2
	4 Jul 1990 v W. Germany	1–1
	7 Jul 1990 v Italy	1–2
	12 Sep 1990 v Hungary	1–0
	17 Oct 1990 v Poland	2–0
	21 May 1991 v Soviet Union	3–1
	1 Jun 1991 v Australia	1–0
	3 Jun 1991 v New Zealand	1–0
	11 Sep 1991 v Germany	0–1
	13 Oct 1993 v Holland	0–2
	9 Mar 1994 v Denmark	1–0

1013. Nigel Howard Clough
Forward
Born   Sunderland, 19 March 1966
Clubs   Nottingham Forest; Liverpool; Manchester City;
        Sheffield Wednesday (on loan)

Caps	14	Result
	23 May 1989 v Chile	0–0
	25 May 1991 v Argentina	2–2
	1 Jun 1991 v Australia	1–0
	12 Jun 1991 v Malaysia	4–2
	19 Feb 1992 v France	2–0
	25 Mar 1992 v Czechoslovakia	2–2
	29 Apr 1992 v CIS	2–2
	9 Sep 1992 v Spain	0–1
	31 Mar 1993 v Turkey	2–0
	29 May 1993 v Poland	1–1
	2 Jun 1993 v Norway	0–2
	9 Jun 1993 v USA	0–2
	13 Jun 1993 v Brazil	1–1
	19 Jun 1993 v Germany	1–2

1014. John Fashanu
Forward
Born   Kensington, 18 September 1962
Clubs   Norwich City; Crystal Palace (on loan); Lincoln City;
        Millwall; Wimbledon; Aston Villa

Caps	2	Result
	23 May 1989 v Chile	0–0
	27 May 1989 v Scotland	2–0

1015. Stephen George Bull
Forward
Born   Tipton, 28 March 1965
Clubs   West Bromwich Albion; Wolverhampton Wanderers

Caps	13	Result	Goals
	27 May 1989 v Scotland	2–0	1
	7 Jun 1989 v Denmark	1–1	
	13 Dec 1989 v Yugoslavia	2–1	
	25 Apr 1990 v Czechoslovakia	4–2	2
	15 May 1990 v Denmark	1–0	

22 May 1990 v Uruguay	1–2	
2 Jun 1990 v Tunisia	1–1	1
11 Jun 1990 v Eire	1–1	
16 Jun 1990 v Holland	0–0	
21 Jun 1990 v Egypt	1–0	
26 Jun 1990 v Belgium	1–0	
12 Sep 1990 v Hungary	1–0	
17 Oct 1990 v Poland	2–0	

1016. David John Beasant
Goalkeeper
Born   Wimbledon, 20 March 1959
Clubs   Wimbledon; Newcastle Utd; Chelsea; Grimsby Town
        (on loan); Wolverhampton Wanderers (on loan);
        Southampton; Nottingham Forest; Portsmouth;
        Wigan Athletic; Brighton & Hove Albion

Caps	2	Result
	15 Nov 1989 v Italy	0–0
	13 Dec 1989 v Yugoslavia	2–1

1017. Michael Christopher Phelan
Midfielder
Born   Nelson, 24 September 1962
Clubs   Burnley; Norwich City; Manchester Utd; West
        Bromwich Albion

Caps	1	Result
	15 Nov 1989 v Italy	0–0

1018. David Andrew Platt
Midfielder/Forward
Born   Oldham, 10 June 1966
Clubs   Manchester Utd; Crewe Alexandra; Aston Villa; Bari
        (Italy); Sampdoria (Italy); Arsenal

Caps	62	Result	Goals
	15 Nov 1989 v Italy	0–0	
	13 Dec 1989 v Yugoslavia	2–1	
	28 Mar 1990 v Brazil	1–0	
	15 May 1990 v Denmark	1–0	
	2 Jun 1990 v Tunisia	1–1	
	16 Jun 1990 v Holland	0–0	
	21 Jun 1990 v Egypt	1–0	
	26 Jun 1990 v Belgium	1–0	1
	1 Jul 1990 v Cameroon	3–2	1
	4 Jul 1990 v W. Germany	1–1	
	7 Jul 1990 v Italy	1–2	1
	12 Sep 1990 v Hungary	1–0	
	17 Oct 1990 v Poland	2–0	
	14 Nov 1990 v Eire	1–1	1
	27 Mar 1991 v Eire	1–1	
	1 May 1991 v Turkey	1–0	
	21 May 1991 v Soviet Union	3–1	2
	25 May 1991 v Argentina	2–2	1
	1 Jun 1991 v Australia	1–0	
	3 Jun 1991 v New Zealand	1–0	
	8 Jun 1991 v New Zealand	2–0	
	12 Jun 1991 v Malaysia	4–2	
	11 Sep 1991 v Germany	0–1	
	16 Oct 1991 v Turkey	1–0	
	13 Nov 1991 v Poland	1–1	
	25 Mar 1992 v Czechoslovakia	2–2	
	29 Apr 1992 v CIS	2–2	
	17 May 1992 v Brazil	1–1	1
	3 Jun 1992 v Finland	2–1	2
	11 Jun 1992 v Denmark	0–0	
	14 Jun 1992 v France	0–0	
	17 Jun 1992 v Sweden	1–2	1
	9 Sep 1992 v Spain	0–1	
	14 Oct 1992 v Norway	1–1	1
	18 Nov 1992 v Turkey	4–0	
	17 Feb 1993 v San Marino	6–0	4
	31 Mar 1993 v Turkey	2–0	1
	28 Apr 1993 v Holland	2–2	1
	29 May 1993 v Poland	1–1	
	2 Jun 1993 v Norway	0–2	
	13 Jun 1993 v Brazil	1–1	1
	19 Jun 1993 v Germany	1–2	1

8 Sep 1993 v Poland	3–0	
13 Oct 1993 v Holland	0–2	
17 Nov 1993 v San Marino	7–1	
9 Mar 1994 v Denmark	1–0	1
17 May 1994 v Greece	5–0	2
22 May 1994 v Norway	0–0	
7 Sep 1994 v USA	2–0	
16 Nov 1994 v Nigeria	1–0	1
15 Feb 1995 v Eire	0–1	
29 Mar 1995 v Uruguay	0–0	
3 Jun 1995 v Japan	2–1	1
8 Jun 1995 v Sweden	3–3	1
11 Jun 1995 v Brazil	1–3	
27 Mar 1996 v Bulgaria	1–0	
24 Apr 1996 v Croatia	0–0	
18 May 1996 v Hungary	3–0	1
8 Jun 1996 v Switzerland	1–1	
18 Jun 1996 v Holland	4–1	
22 Jun 1996 v Spain	0–0	
26 Jun 1996 v Germany	1–1	

1019. Nigel Winterburn
Left back
Born Nuneaton, 11 December 1963
Clubs Birmingham City; Wimbledon; Arsenal; West Ham Utd

Caps 2	*Result*
15 Nov 1989 v Italy	0–0
19 Jun 1993 v Germany	1–2

1020. Anthony Robert Dorigo
Left back
Born Melbourne, Australia, 31 December 1965
Clubs Aston Villa; Chelsea; Leeds Utd

Caps 15	*Result*
13 Dec 1989 v Yugoslavia	2–1
25 Apr 1990 v Czechoslovakia	4–2
15 May 1990 v Denmark	1–0
7 Jul 1990 v Italy	1–2
12 Sep 1990 v Hungary	1–0
21 May 1991 v Soviet Union	3–1
11 Sep 1991 v Germany	0–1
25 Mar 1992 v Czechoslovakia	2–2
12 May 1992 v Hungary	1–0
17 May 1992 v Brazil	1–1
17 Feb 1993 v San Marino	6–0
29 May 1993 v Poland	1–1
9 Jun 1993 v USA	0–2
13 Jun 1993 v Brazil	1–1
13 Oct 1993 v Holland	0–2

1021. Lee Michael Dixon
Right back
Born Manchester, 17 March 1964
Clubs Burnley; Chester City; Bury; Stoke City; Arsenal

Caps 22	*Result*	*Goals*
25 Apr 1990 v Czechoslovakia	4–2	
12 Sep 1990 v Hungary	1–0	
17 Oct 1990 v Poland	2–0	
14 Nov 1990 v Eire	1–1	
6 Feb 1991 v Cameroon	2–0	
27 Mar 1991 v Eire	1–1	1
1 May 1991 v Turkey	1–0	
25 May 1991 v Argentina	2–2	
11 Sep 1991 v Germany	0–1	
16 Oct 1991 v Turkey	1–0	
13 Nov 1991 v Poland	1–1	
25 Mar 1992 v Czechoslovakia	2–2	
9 Sep 1992 v Spain	0–1	
14 Oct 1992 v Norway	1–1	
18 Nov 1992 v Turkey	4–0	
17 Feb 1993 v San Marino	6–0	
31 Mar 1993 v Turkey	2–0	
28 Apr 1993 v Holland	2–2	
2 Jun 1993 v Norway	0–2	

9 Jun 1993 v USA	0–2
17 Nov 1993 v San Marino	7–1
10 Feb 1999 v France	0–2

1022. Ian Edward Wright
Forward
Born Woolwich, 3 November 1963
Clubs Crystal Palace, Arsenal, West Ham Utd, Nottingham Forest (on loan), Glasgow Celtic, Burnley

Caps 33	*Result*	*Goals*
6 Feb 1991 v Cameroon	2–0	
27 Mar 1991 v Eire	1–1	
21 May 1991 v Soviet Union	3–1	
8 Jun 1991 v New Zealand	2–0	
12 May 1992 v Hungary	1–0	
14 Oct 1992 v Norway	1–1	
18 Nov 1992 v Turkey	4–0	
31 Mar 1993 v Turkey	2–0	
29 May 1993 v Poland	1–1	1
2 Jun 1993 v Norway	0–2	
9 Jun 1993 v USA	0–2	
13 Jun 1993 v Brazil	1–1	
19 Jun 1993 v Germany	1–2	
8 Sep 1993 v Poland	3–0	
13 Oct 1993 v Holland	0–2	
17 Nov 1993 v San Marino	7–1	4
17 May 1994 v Greece	5–0	
22 May 1994 v Norway	0–0	
7 Sep 1994 v USA	2–0	
12 Oct 1994 v Romania	1–1	
9 Nov 1996 v Georgia	2–0	
12 Feb 1997 v Italy	0–1	
29 Mar 1997 v Mexico	2–0	
24 May 1997 v South Africa	2–1	1
4 Jun 1997 v Italy	2–0	1
7 Jun 1997 v France	1–0	
10 Jun 1997 v Brazil	0–1	
10 Sep 1997 v Moldova	4–0	2
11 Oct 1997 v Italy	0–0	
23 May 1998 v Saudia Arabia	0–0	
27 May 1998 v Morocco	1–0	
14 Oct 1998 v Luxembourg	3–0	
18 Nov 1998 v Czech Republic	2–0	

1023. Lee Stuart Sharpe
Left winger
Born Halesowen, 27 May 1971
Clubs Torquay Utd; Manchester Utd; Leeds Utd; Bradford City; Portsmouth; Exeter City

Caps 8	*Result*
27 Mar 1991 v Eire	1–1
31 Mar 1993 v Turkey	2–0
2 Jun 1993 v Norway	0–2
9 Jun 1993 v USA	0–2
13 Jun 1993 v Brazil	1–1
19 Jun 1993 v Germany	1–2
8 Sep 1993 v Poland	3–0
13 Oct 1993 v Holland	0–2

1024. Geoffrey Robert Thomas
Midfielder
Born Manchester, 5 August 1964
Clubs Rochdale; Crewe Alexandra; Crystal Palace; Wolverhampton Wanderers; Nottingham Forest; Barnsley; Notts County

Caps 9	*Result*
1 May 1991 v Turkey	1–0
21 May 1991 v Soviet Union	3–1
25 May 1991 v Argentina	2–2
1 Jun 1991 v Australia	1–0
3 Jun 1991 v New Zealand	1–0
8 Jun 1991 v New Zealand	2–0
12 Jun 1991 v Malaysia	4–2
13 Nov 1991 v Poland	1–1
19 Feb 1992 v France	2–0

1025. Dennis Frank Wise
Midfielder

Born   Kensington, 15 December 1966
Clubs Wimbledon; Chelsea; Leicester City; Millwall

Caps	21	Result	Goals
	1 May 1991 v Turkey	1–0	1
	21 May 1991 v Soviet Union	3–1	
	1 Jun 1991 v Australia	1–0	
	3 Jun 1991 v New Zealand	1–0	
	8 Jun 1991 v New Zealand	2–0	
	22 May 1994 v Norway	0–0	
	12 Oct 1994 v Romania	1–1	
	16 Nov 1994 v Nigeria	1–0	
	6 Sep 1995 v Colombia	0–0	
	11 Oct 1995 v Norway	0–0	
	12 Dec 1995 v Portugal	1–1	
	18 May 1996 v Hungary	3–0	
	10 Oct 1999 v Belgium	2–1	
	23 Feb 2000 v Argentina	0–0	
	27 May 2000 v Brazil	1–1	
	3 Jun 2000 v Malta	2–1	
	12 Jun 2000 v Portugal	2–3	
	17 Jun 2000 v Germany	1–0	
	20 Jun 2000 v Romania	2–3	
	2 Sep 2000 v France	1–1	
	11 Oct 2000 v Finland	0–0	

1026. David Batty
Midfielder

Born   Leeds, 2 December 1968
Clubs Leeds Utd; Blackburn Rovers; Newcastle Utd

Caps	42	Result
	21 May 1991 v Soviet Union	3–1
	25 May 1991 v Argentina	2–2
	1 Jun 1991 v Australia	1–0
	3 Jun 1991 v New Zealand	1–0
	12 Jun 1991 v Malaysia	4–2
	11 Sep 1991 v Germany	0–1
	16 Oct 1991 v Turkey	1–0
	12 May 1992 v Hungary	1–0
	14 Jun 1992 v France	0–0
	17 Jun 1992 v Sweden	1–2
	14 Oct 1992 v Norway	1–1
	17 Feb 1993 v San Marino	6–0
	9 Jun 1993 v USA	0–2
	13 Jun 1993 v Brazil	1–1
	9 Mar 1994 v Denmark	1–0
	3 Jun 1995 v Japan	2–1
	11 Jun 1995 v Brazil	1–3
	1 Sep 1996 v Moldova	3–0
	9 Nov 1996 v Georgia	2–0
	12 Feb 1997 v Italy	0–1
	29 Mar 1997 v Mexico	3–0
	30 Apr 1997 v Georgia	2–0
	24 May 1997 v South Africa	2–1
	31 May 1997 v Poland	2–0
	7 Jun 1997 v France	1–0
	10 Sep 1997 v Moldova	4–0
	11 Oct 1997 v Italy	0–0
	11 Feb 1998 v Chile	0–2
	25 Mar 1998 v Switzerland	1–1
	22 Apr 1998 v Portugal	3–0
	23 May 1998 v Saudi Arabia	0–0
	15 Jun 1998 v Tunisia	2–0
	22 Jun 1998 v Romania	1–2
	26 Jun 1996 v Colombia	2–0
	30 Jun 1998 v Argentina	2–2
	10 Oct 1998 v Bulgaria	0–0
	14 Oct 1998 v Luxembourg	3–0
	28 Apr 1999 v Hungary	1–1
	5 Jun 1999 v Sweden	0–0
	9 Jun 1999 v Bulgaria	1–1
	4 Sep 1999 v Luxembourg	6–0
	8 Sep 1999 v Poland	0–0

1027. David Eric Hirst
Forward

Born   Cudworth, 7 December 1967
Clubs Barnsley; Sheffield Wednesday; Southampton

Caps	3	Result	Goals
	1 Jun 1991 v Australia	1–0	
	8 Jun 1991 v New Zealand	2–0	1
	19 Feb 1992 v France	2–0	

1028. John Akin Salako
Left winger

Born   Nigeria, 11 February 1969
Clubs Crystal Palace; Swansea City (on loan); Coventry
       City; Bolton Wanderers; Fulham; Charlton Athletic;
       Reading; Brentford

Caps	5	Result
	1 Jun 1991 v Australia	1–0
	3 Jun 1991 v New Zealand	1–0
	8 Jun 1991 v New Zealand	2–0
	12 Jun 1991 v Malaysia	4–2
	11 Sep 1991 v Germany	0–1

1029. Mark Everton Walters
Left winger

Born   Birmingham, 2 June 1964
Clubs Aston Villa; Glasgow Rangers; Liverpool; Stoke City
       (on loan); Wolverhampton Wanderers (on loan);
       Southampton; Swindon Town

Caps	1	Result
	3 Jun 1991 v New Zealand	1-0

1030. Gary Andrew Charles
Fullback

Born   Newham, 13 April 1970
Clubs Nottingham Forest; Leicester City; Derby County;
       Aston Villa; Benfica (Portugal)

Caps	2	Result
	8 Jun 1991 v New Zealand	2–0
	12 Jun 1991 v Malaysia	4–2

1031. Earl Delisser Barrett
Defender

Born   Rochdale, 28 April 1967
Clubs Manchester City; Chester City (on loan); Oldham
       Athletic; Aston Villa; Everton; Sheffield Utd (on
       loan); Sheffield Wednesday

Caps	3	Result
	3 Jun 1991 v New Zealand	1–0
	13 Jun 1993 v Brazil	1–1
	19 Jun 1993 v Germany	1–2

1032. Brian Christopher Deane
Forward

Born   Leeds, 7 February 1968
Clubs Doncaster Rovers; Sheffield Utd; Leeds Utd; Benfica
       (Portugal); Middlesbrough; Leicester City; West
       Ham Utd; Sunderland

Caps	3	Result
	3 Jun 1991 v New Zealand	1–0
	8 Jun 1991 v New Zealand	2–0
	9 Sep 1992 v Spain	0–1

1033. Paul Charles Merson
Forward

Born   Harlsden, 20 March 1968
Clubs Arsenal; Brentford (on loan); Middlesbrough; Aston
       Villa; Portsmouth; Walsall

Caps	21	Result	Goals
	11 Sep 1991 v Germany	0–1	
	25 Mar 1992 v Czechoslovakia	2–2	1
	12 May 1992 v Hungary	1–0	
	17 May 1992 v Brazil	1–1	
	3 Jun 1992 v Finland	2–1	
	11 Jun 1992 v Denmark	0–0	
	17 Jun 1992 v Sweden	1–2	

9 Sep 1992 v Spain	0–1	
14 Oct 1992 v Norway	1–1	
28 Apr 1993 v Holland	2–2	
13 Jun 1993 v Brazil	1–1	
19 Jun 1993 v Germany	1–2	
13 Oct 1993 v Holland	0–2	
17 May 1994 v Greece	5–0	
12 Feb 1997 v Italy	0–1	
25 Mar 1998 v Switzerland	1–1	1
22 Apr 1998 v Portugal	3–0	
29 May 1998 v Belgium	0–0	
30 Jun 1998 v Argentina	2–2	
5 Sep 1998 v Sweden	1–2	
18 Nov 1998 v Czech Republic	2–0	1

1034. Paul Andrew Stewart
Forward
Born   Manchester, 7 October 1964
Clubs Blackpool; Manchester City; Tottenham Hotspur;
Liverpool; Crystal Palace (on loan); Wolverhampton
Wanderers (on loan); Burnley (on loan); Sunderland
(on loan); Stoke City; Workington

Caps	3	Result
11 Sep 1991 v Germany	0–1	
25 Mar 1992 v Czechoslovakia	2–2	
29 Apr 1992 v CIS	2–2	

1035. Anthony Mark Daley
Winger
Born   Birmingham, 18 October 1967
Clubs Aston Villa; Wolverhampton Wanderers; Watford;
Walsall

Caps	7	Result
13 Nov 1991 v Poland	1–1	
29 Apr 1992 v CIS	2–2	
12 May 1992 v Hungary	1–0	
17 May 1992 v Brazil	1–1	
3 Jun 1992 v Finland	2–1	
11 Jun 1992 v Denmark	0–0	
17 Jun 1992 v Sweden	1–2	

1036. Andrew Arthur Gray
Midfielder
Born   Lambeth, 22 February 1964
Clubs Crystal Palace; Aston Villa; Queen's Park Rangers;
Tottenham Hotspur; Marbella (Spain); Swindon
Town (on loan); Falkirk; Bury; Millwall

Caps	1	Result
13 Nov 1991 v Poland	1–1	

1037. Andrew Sinton
Left winger
Born   Cramlington, 19 March 1966
Clubs Cambridge Utd; Brentford; Queen's Park Rangers;
Sheffield Wednesday; Tottenham Hotspur;
Wolverhampton Wanderers; Burton Albion

Caps	12	Result
13 Nov 1991 v Poland	1–1	
29 Apr 1992 v CIS	2–2	
12 May 1992 v Hungary	1–0	
17 May 1992 v Brazil	1–1	
14 Jun 1992 v France	0–0	
17 Jun 1992 v Sweden	1–2	
9 Sep 1992 v Spain	0–1	
31 Mar 1993 v Turkey	2–0	
13 Jun 1993 v Brazil	1–1	
19 Jun 1993 v Germany	1–2	
13 Oct 1993 v Holland	0–2	
17 Nov 1993 v San Marino	7–1	

1038. Robert Marc Jones
Right back
Born   Wrexham, 5 November 1971
Clubs Crewe Alexandra; Liverpool

Caps	8	Result
19 Feb 1992 v France	2–0	
8 Sep 1993 v Poland	3–0	
17 May 1994 v Greece	5–0	
22 May 1994 v Norway	0–0	
7 Sep 1994 v USA	2–0	
12 Oct 1994 v Romania	1–1	
16 Nov 1994 v Nigeria	1–0	
29 Mar 1995 v Uruguay	0–0	

1039. Martin Raymond Keown
Central defender
Born   Oxford, 24 July 1966
Clubs Arsenal; Brighton & Hove Albion (on loan); Aston
Villa; Everton; Leicester City; Reading

Caps	43	Result	Goals
19 Feb 1992 v France	2–0	
25 Mar 1992 v Czechoslovakia	2–2	1
29 Apr 1992 v CIS	2–2	
12 May 1992 v Hungary	1–0	
17 May 1992 v Brazil	1–1	
3 Jun 1992 v Finland	2–1	
11 Jun 1992 v Denmark	0–0	
14 Jun 1992 v France	0–0	
17 Jun 1992 v Sweden	1–2	
28 Apr 1993 v Holland	2–2	
19 Jun 1993 v Germany	1–2	
29 Mar 1997 v Mexico	2–0	
24 May 1997 v South Africa	2–1	
4 Jun 1997 v Italy	2–0	
10 Jun 1997 v Brazil	0–1	
25 Mar 1998 v Switzerland	1–1	
27 May 1998 v Morocco	1–0	
29 May 1998 v Belgium	0–0	
18 Nov 1998 v Czech Republic	2–0	
10 Feb 1999 v France	0–2	
27 Mar 1999 v Poland	3–1	
28 Apr 1999 v Hungary	1–1	
5 Jun 1999 v Sweden	0–0	
4 Sep 1999 v Luxembourg	6–0	
8 Sep 1999 v Poland	0–0	
10 Oct 1999 v Belgium	2–1	
17 Nov 1999 v Scotland	0–1	
23 Feb 2000 v Argentina	0–0	
27 May 2000 v Brazil	1–1	
3 Jun 2000 v Malta	2–1	1
12 Jun 2000 v Portugal	2–3	
17 Jun 2000 v Germany	1–0	
20 Jun 2000 v Romania	2–3	
2 Sep 2000 v France	1–1	
7 Oct 2000 v Germany	0–1	
11 Oct 2000 v Finland	0–0	
25 May 2001 v Mexico	4–0	
6 Jun 2001 v Greece	2–0	
15 Aug 2001 v Holland	0–2	
6 Oct 2001 v Greece	2–2	
17 Apr 2002 v Paraguay	4–0	
21 May 2002 v South Korea	1–1	
26 May 2002 v Cameroon	2–2	

1040. Alan Shearer
Forward
Born   Newcastle, 13 August 1970
Clubs Southampton; Blackburn Rovers; Newcastle Utd

Caps	63	Result	Goals
19 Feb 1992 v France	2–0	1
29 Apr 1992 v CIS	2–2	
14 Jun 1992 v France	0–0	
9 Sep 1992 v Spain	0–1	
14 Oct 1992 v Norway	1–1	
18 Nov 1992 v Turkey	4–0	1
13 Oct 1993 v Holland	0–2	
9 Mar 1994 v Denmark	1–0	
17 May 1994 v Greece	5–0	1

Dixie Dean (*left*), Everton's legendary forward, scored 18 goals in 16 appearances for England between 1927 and 1932.

Right: Stanley Matthews became England's oldest international when he took to the field against Denmark in May 1957 aged 42 years and 103 days.

Centre forward Tommy Lawton (*above left*) scored 22 goals in 23 appearances for his country during the 1930s and 1940s.

Left: Tom Finney, the Preston plumber, played in three World Cups (1950, 1954 and 1958), and scored 30 goals in 76 appearances for England.

Willie Hall (*above*) found the back of the net five times during England's 7–1 defeat of Northern Ireland in 1938.

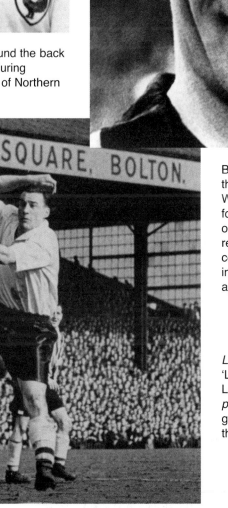

Billy Wright (*above*), the Wolverhampton Wanderers star, played for England on 105 occasions and set a record of 70 consecutive international appearances.

Left: Known as the 'Lion of Vienna', Nat Lofthouse (*centre of picture*) scored 30 goals in 33 games for the national side.

At Berlin's Olympic Stadium on 14 May 1938, England beat Germany 6–3 before a 115,000 strong crowd. When the British anthem was played before the game, the England players gave a Nazi salute as a sign of respect towards their hosts.

The Battle of Highbury: On 14 November 1934, at Arsenal's Highbury Stadium, England recorded a 3–2 win over Italy to maintain their unbeaten home record.

On 25 November 1953, fans witnessed a heavy defeat for England at Wembley, when the national side lost 6–3 to Hungary. Stan Mortensen (*above left*) looks on as Hungarian goalkeeper Gyula Grosics retains possession.

In the presence of Queen Elizabeth II, England were victorious over Scotland in April 1961, during a 9–3 rout at Wembley. Captain Johnny Haynes is pictured holding the trophy, held aloft by teammates Peter Swan (*left*) and Jimmy Armfield (*middle*), with Mike McNeil (*right*) by his side.

On 23 July 1966, England faced Argentina in the World Cup quarter-final. During the ill-tempered encounter, in which Antonio Rattin (*third from right*) was sent off, England scored a single goal to record a 1−0 victory.

Spurs legend Jimmy Greaves (*right*) sustained a nasty injury in the final group match against France, which resulted in his last ever World Cup appearance. Three games later, after earning his 57th cap, he retired from international football.

Twenty-four-year-old Geoff Hurst (*below*) marked the start of his 1966 World Cup campaign with a goal against Argentina. Two games later, the West Ham player would score a hat-trick in the final.

Members of England's World Cup-winning side: brothers Jack and Bobby Charlton (*above*), Nobby Stiles (*below left*) and Martin Peters (*below right*).

On 30 July 1966, England were crowned World Cup winners after beating West Germany 4–2 in an unforgettable final. Jubilant captain Bobby Moore is held aloft by teammates Geoff Hurst (*left*) and Ray Wilson (*right*).

The England team pose with the Jules Rimet Cup. *Back row, from left to right:* trainer Harold Shepherdson, Nobby Stiles, Roger Hunt, Gordon Banks, Jack Charlton, George Cohen, Ray Wilson, and manager Alf Ramsey. *Front row, from left to right:* Martin Peters, Geoff Hurst, Bobby Moore, Alan Ball and Bobby Charlton.

22 May 1994 v Norway	0–0	
7 Sep 1994 v USA	2–0	2
12 Oct 1994 v Romania	1–1	
16 Nov 1994 v Nigeria	1–0	
15 Feb 1995 v Eire	0–1	
3 Jun 1995 v Japan	2–1	
8 Jun 1995 v Sweden	3–3	
11 Jun 1995 v Brazil	1–3	
6 Sep 1995 v Colombia	0–0	
11 Oct 1995 v Norway	0–0	
15 Nov 1995 v Switzerland	3–1	
12 Dec 1995 v Portugal	1–1	
18 May 1996 v Hungary	3–0	
23 May 1996 v China	3–0	
8 Jun 1996 v Switzerland	1–1	1
15 Jun 1996 v Scotland	2–0	1
18 Jun 1996 v Holland	4–1	2
22 Jun 1996 v Spain	0–0	
26 Jun 1996 v Germany	1–1	1
1 Sep 1996 v Moldova	3–0	1
9 Oct 1996 v Poland	2–1	2
12 Feb 1997 v Italy	0–1	
30 Apr 1997 v Georgia	2–0	1
31 May 1997 v Poland	2–0	1
7 Jun 1997 v France	1–0	1
10 Jun 1997 v Brazil	0–1	
11 Feb 1998 v Chile	0–2	
25 Mar 1998 v Switzerland	1–1	
22 Apr 1998 v Portugal	3–0	2
23 May 1998 v Saudi Arabia	0–0	
15 Jun 1998 v Tunisia	2–0	1
22 Jun 1998 v Romania	1–2	
26 Jun 1998 v Colombia	2–0	
30 Jun 1998 v Argentina	2–2	1
5 Sep 1998 v Sweden	1–2	1
10 Oct 1998 v Bulgaria	0–0	
14 Oct 1998 v Luxembourg	3–0	1
10 Feb 1999 v France	0–2	
27 Mar 1999 v Poland	3–1	
28 Apr 1999 v Hungary	1–1	1
5 Jun 1999 v Sweden	0–0	
9 Jun 1999 v Bulgaria	1–1	1
4 Sep 1999 v Luxembourg	6–0	3
8 Sep 1999 v Poland	0–0	
10 Oct 1999 v Belgium	2–1	1
13 Nov 1999 v Scotland	2–0	
17 Nov 1999 v Scotland	0–1	
23 Feb 2000 v Argentina	0–0	
27 May 2000 v Brazil	1–1	
31 May 2000 v Ukraine	2–0	
3 Jun 2000 v Malta	2–1	
12 Jun 2000 v Portugal	2–3	
17 Jun 2000 v Germany	1–0	1
20 Jun 2000 v Romania	2–3	1

1041. Keith Curle
Central defender
Born Bristol, 14 November 1963
Clubs Bristol Rovers; Torquay Utd; Bristol City; Reading; Wimbledon; Manchester City; Wolverhampton Wanderers; Sheffield Utd; Barnsley; Mansfield Town

Caps	3	*Result*
	29 Apr 1992 v CIS	2–2
	12 May 1992 v Hungary	1–0
	11 Jun 1992 v Denmark	0–0

1042. Nigel Anthony Martyn
Goalkeeper
Born St Austell, 11 August 1966
Clubs Bristol Rovers; Crystal Palace; Leeds Utd; Everton

Caps	23	*Result*
	29 Apr 1992 v CIS	2–2
	12 May 1992 v Hungary	1–0
	19 Jun 1993 v Germany	1–2

24 May 1997 v South Africa	2–1	
15 Nov 1997 v Cameroon	2–0	
11 Feb 1998 v Chile	0–2	
29 May 1998 v Belgium	0–0	
18 Nov 1998 v Czech Republic	2–0	
10 Feb 1999 v France	0–2	
4 Sep 1999 v Luxembourg	6–0	
8 Sep 1999 v Poland	0–0	
10 Oct 1999 v Belgium	2–1	
31 May 2000 v Ukraine	2–0	
20 Jun 2000 v Romania	2–3	
28 Feb 2001 v Spain	3–0	
25 May 2001 v Mexico	4–0	
15 Aug 2001 v Holland	0–2	
6 Oct 2001 v Greece	2–2	
10 Nov 2001 v Sweden	1–1	
13 Feb 2002 v Holland	1–1	
27 Mar 2002 v Italy	1–2	
21 May 2002 v South Korea	1–1	
26 May 2002 v Cameroon	2–2	

1043. Carlton Lloyd Palmer
Defender/Midfielder
Born Rowley Regis, 5 December 1965
Clubs West Bromwich Albion; Sheffield Wednesday; Leeds Utd; Southampton; Nottingham Forest; Coventry City; Watford; Stockport County

Caps	18	*Result*	*Goals*
	29 Apr 1992 v CIS	2–2	
	12 May 1992 v Hungary	1–0	
	17 May 1992 v Brazil	1–1	
	3 Jun 1992 v Finland	2–1	
	11 Jun 1992 v Denmark	0–0	
	14 Jun 1992 v France	0–0	
	17 Jun 1992 v Sweden	1–2	
	9 Sep 1992 v Spain	0–1	
	14 Oct 1992 v Norway	1–1	
	18 Nov 1992 v Turkey	4–0	
	17 Feb 1993 v San Marino	6–0	1
	31 Mar 1993 v Turkey	2–0	
	28 Apr 1993 v Holland	2–2	
	29 May 1993 v Poland	1–1	
	2 Jun 1993 v Norway	0–2	
	9 Jun 1992 v USA	0–2	
	13 Jun 1993 v Brazil	1–1	
	13 Oct 1993 v Holland	0–2	

1044. Timothy David Flowers
Goalkeeper
Born Kenilworth, 3 February 1967
Clubs Wolverhampton Wanderers; Southampton; Swindon Town (on loan); Blackburn Rovers; Leicester City; Stockport County; Coventry City

Caps	11	*Result*
	13 Jun 1993 v Brazil	1–1
	17 May 1994 v Greece	5–0
	16 Nov 1994 v Nigeria	1–0
	29 Mar 1995 v Uruguay	0–0
	3 Jun 1995 v Japan	2–1
	8 Jun 1995 v Sweden	3–3
	11 Jun 1995 v Brazil	1–3
	23 May 1996 v China	3–0
	12 Feb 1997 v Italy	0–1
	25 Mar 1998 v Switzerland	1–1
	27 May 1998 v Morocco	1–0

1045. David John Bardsley
Right back
Born Manchester, 11 September 1964
Clubs Blackpool; Watford; Oxford Utd; Queen's Park Rangers

Caps	2	*Result*
	9 Sep 1992 v Spain	0–1
	29 May 1993 v Poland	1–1

1046. Paul Emerson Carlyle Ince
Midfielder
Born Ilford, 21 October 1967
Clubs West Ham Utd; Manchester Utd; Inter Milan (Italy); Liverpool; Middlesbrough; Wolverhampton Wanderers

Caps	53	Result	Goals
	9 Sep 1992 v Spain	0–1	
	14 Oct 1992 v Norway	1–1	
	18 Nov 1992 v Turkey	4–0	
	31 Mar 1993 v Turkey	2–0	
	28 Apr 1993 v Holland	2–2	
	29 May 1993 v Poland	1–1	
	9 Jun 1993 v USA	0–2	
	13 Jun 1993 v Brazil	1–1	
	19 Jun 1993 v Germany	1–2	
	8 Sep 1993 v Poland	3–0	
	13 Oct 1993 v Holland	0–2	
	17 Nov 1993 v San Marino	7–1	2
	9 Mar 1994 v Denmark	1–0	
	22 May 1994 v Norway	0–0	
	12 Oct 1994 v Romania	1–1	
	15 Feb 1995 v Eire	0–1	
	27 Mar 1996 v Bulgaria	1–0	
	24 Apr 1996 v Croatia	0–0	
	18 May 1996 v Hungary	3–0	
	8 Jun 1996 v Switzerland	1–1	
	15 Jun 1996 v Scotland	2–0	
	18 Jun 1996 v Holland	4–1	
	26 Jun 1996 v Germany	1–1	
	1 Sep 1996 v Moldova	3–0	
	9 Oct 1996 v Poland	2–1	
	9 Nov 1996 v Georgia	2–0	
	12 Feb 1997 v Italy	0–1	
	29 Mar 1997 v Mexico	2–0	
	30 Apr 1997 v Georgia	2–0	
	31 May 1997 v Poland	2–0	
	4 Jun 1997 v Italy	2–0	
	7 Jun 1997 v France	1–0	
	10 Jun 1997 v Brazil	0–1	
	11 Oct 1997 v Italy	0–0	
	15 Nov 1997 v Cameroon	2–0	
	11 Feb 1998 v Chile	0–2	
	25 Mar 1998 v Switzerland	1–1	
	22 Apr 1998 v Portugal	3–0	
	27 May 1998 v Morocco	1–0	
	15 Jun 1998 v Tunisia	2–0	
	22 Jun 1998 v Romania	1–2	
	26 Jun 1998 v Colombia	2–0	
	30 Jun 1998 v Argentina	2–2	
	5 Sep 1998 v Sweden	1–2	
	10 Feb 1999 v France	0–2	
	10 Oct 1999 v Belgium	2–1	
	13 Nov 1999 v Scotland	2–0	
	17 Nov 1999 v Scotland	0–1	
	27 May 2000 v Brazil	1–1	
	3 Jun 2000 v Malta	2–1	
	12 Jun 2000 v Portugal	2–3	
	17 Jun 2000 v Germany	1–0	
	20 Jun 2000 v Romania	2–3	

1047. David White
Winger/Forward
Born Manchester, 30 October 1967
Clubs Manchester City; Leeds Utd; Sheffield Utd

Caps	1	Result
	9 Sep 1992 v Spain	0–1

1048. Leslie Ferdinand
Forward
Born Acton, 8 December 1966
Clubs Queen's Park Rangers; Brentford (on loan); Besiktas (Turkey); Newcastle Utd; Tottenham Hotspur; West Ham Utd; Leicester City; Bolton Wanderers; Reading

Caps	17	Result	Goals
	17 Feb 1993 v San Marino	6–0	1

	28 Apr 1993 v Holland	2–2	
	2 Jun 1993 v Norway	0–2	
	9 Jun 1993 v USA	0–2	
	8 Sep 1993 v Poland	3–0	1
	17 Nov 1993 v San Marino	7–1	1
	7 Sep 1994 v USA	2–0	
	12 Dec 1995 v Portugal	1–1	
	27 Mar 1996 v Bulgaria	1–0	1
	18 May 1996 v Hungary	3–0	
	9 Oct 1996 v Poland	2–1	
	9 Nov 1996 v Georgia	2–0	1
	4 Jun 1997 v Italy	2–0	
	10 Sep 1997 v Moldova	4–0	
	23 May 1998 v Saudi Arabia	0–0	
	27 May 1998 v Morocco	1–0	
	29 May 1998 v Belgium	0–0	

1049. Edward Paul Sheringham
Forward
Born Highams Park, 2 April 1966
Clubs Millwall; Aldershot (on loan); Nottingham Forest; Tottenham Hotspur; Manchester Utd; Portsmouth; West Ham Utd

Caps	51	Result	Goals
	29 May 1993 v Poland	1–1	
	2 Jun 1993 v Norway	0–2	
	7 Sep 1994 v USA	2–0	
	12 Oct 1994 v Romania	1–1	
	16 Nov 1994 v Nigeria	1–0	
	29 Mar 1995 v Uruguay	0–0	
	3 Jun 1995 v Japan	2–1	
	8 Jun 1995 v Sweden	3–3	1
	11 Jun 1995 v Brazil	1–3	
	6 Sep 1995 v Colombia	0–0	
	11 Oct 1995 v Norway	0–0	
	15 Nov 1995 v Switzerland	3–1	1
	27 Mar 1996 v Bulgaria	1–0	
	24 Apr 1996 v Croatia	0–0	
	18 May 1996 v Hungary	3–0	
	8 Jun 1996 v Switzerland	1–1	
	15 Jun 1996 v Scotland	2–0	
	18 Jun 1996 v Holland	4–1	2
	22 Jun 1996 v Spain	0–0	
	26 Jun 1996 v Germany	1–1	
	9 Nov 1996 v Georgia	2–0	1
	29 Mar 1997 v Mexico	2–0	1
	30 Apr 1997 v Georgia	2–0	1
	24 May 1997 v South Africa	2–1	
	31 May 1997 v Poland	2–0	1
	4 Jun 1997 v Italy	2–0	
	7 Jun 1997 v France	1–0	
	10 Jun 1997 v Brazil	0–1	
	11 Oct 1997 v Italy	0–0	
	11 Feb 1998 v Chile	0–2	
	25 Mar 1998 v Switzerland	1–1	
	22 Apr 1998 v Portugal	3–0	1
	23 May 1998 v Saudi Arabia	0–0	
	15 Jun 1998 v Tunisia	2–0	
	22 Jun 1998 v Romania	1–2	
	5 Sep 1998 v Sweden	1–2	
	10 Oct 1998 v Bulgaria	0–0	
	9 Jun 1999 v Bulgaria	1–1	
	24 Mar 2001 v Finland	2–1	
	28 Mar 2001 v Albania	3–1	
	25 May 2001 v Mexico	4–0	1
	6 Oct 2001 v Greece	2–2	1
	10 Nov 2001 v Sweden	1–1	
	27 May 2002 v Italy	1–2	
	17 Apr 2002 v Paraguay	4–0	
	21 May 2002 v South Korea	1–1	
	26 May 2002 v Cameroon	2–2	
	7 Jun 2002 v Argentina	1–0	
	12 Jun 2002 v Nigeria	0–0	
	15 Jun 2002 v Denmark	3–0	
	21 Jun 2002 v Brazil	1–2	

1050. Stuart Edward Ripley
Winger
Born Middlesbrough, 20 November 1967
Clubs Middlesbrough; Bolton Wanderers (on loan); Blackburn Rovers; Southampton; Barnsley; Sheffield Wednesday

Caps	2	*Result*
	17 Nov 1993 v San Marino	7–1
	10 Sep 1997 v Moldova	4–0

1051. Darren Robert Anderton
Winger
Born Southampton, 3 March 1972
Clubs Portsmouth; Tottenham Hotspur; Birmingham City

Caps	30	*Result*	*Goals*
	9 Mar 1994 v Denmark	1–0	
	17 May 1994 v Greece	5–0	1
	22 May 1994 v Norway	0–0	
	7 Sep 1994 v USA	2–0	
	15 Feb 1995 v Eire	0–1	
	29 Mar 1995 v Uruguay	0–0	
	3 Jun 1995 v Japan	2–1	1
	8 Jun 1995 v Sweden	3–3	1
	11 Jun 1995 v Brazil	1–3	
	18 May 1996 v Hungary	3–0	2
	23 May 1996 v China	3–0	
	8 Jun 1996 v Switzerland	1–1	
	15 Jun 1996 v Scotland	2–0	
	18 Jun 1996 v Holland	4–1	
	22 Jun 1996 v Spain	0–0	
	26 Jun 1996 v Germany	1–1	
	23 May 1998 v Saudi Arabia	0–0	
	27 May 1998 v Morocco	1–0	
	15 Jun 1998 v Tunisia	2–0	
	22 Jun 1998 v Romania	1–2	
	26 Jun 1998 v Colombia	2–0	1
	30 Jun 1998 v Argentina	2–2	
	5 Sep 1998 v Sweden	1–2	
	10 Oct 1998 v Bulgaria	0–0	
	14 Oct 1998 v Luxembourg	3–0	
	18 Nov 1998 v Czech Republic	2–0	1
	10 Feb 1999 v France	0–2	
	2 Sep 2000 v France	1–1	
	15 Nov 2000 v Italy	0–1	
	10 Nov 2001 v Sweden	1–1	

1052. Graham Pierre Le Saux
Left back
Born Jersey, 17 October 1968
Clubs Chelsea; Blackburn Rovers; Southampton

Caps	36	*Result*	*Goals*
	9 Mar 1994 v Denmark	1–0	
	17 May 1994 v Greece	5–0	
	22 May 1994 v Norway	0–0	
	7 Sep 1994 v USA	2–0	
	12 Oct 1994 v Romania	1–1	
	16 Nov 1994 v Nigeria	1–0	
	15 Feb 1995 v Eire	0–1	
	29 Mar 1995 v Uruguay	0–0	
	8 Jun 1995 v Sweden	3–3	
	11 Jun 1995 v Brazil	1–3	1
	6 Sep 1995 v Colombia	0–0	
	12 Dec 1995 v Portugal	1–1	
	12 Feb 1997 v Italy	0–1	
	29 Mar 1997 v Mexico	2–0	
	30 Apr 1997 v Georgia	2–0	
	24 May 1997 v South Africa	2–1	
	31 May 1997 v Poland	2–0	
	4 Jun 1997 v Italy	2–0	
	7 Jun 1997 v France	1–0	
	10 Jun 1997 v Brazil	0–1	
	11 Oct 1997 v Italy	0–0	
	11 Feb 1998 v Chile	0–2	
	22 Apr 1998 v Portugal	3–0	
	27 May 1998 v Morocco	1–0	
	29 May 1998 v Belgium	0–0	
	15 Jun 1998 v Tunisia	2–0	
	22 Jun 1998 v Romania	1–2	
	26 Jun 1998 v Colombia	2–0	
	30 Jun 1998 v Argentina	2–2	
	5 Sep 1998 v Sweden	1–2	
	10 Oct 1998 v Bulgaria	0–0	
	18 Nov 1998 v Czech Republic	2–0	
	10 Feb 1999 v France	0–2	
	27 Mar 1999 v Poland	3–1	
	5 Jun 1999 v Sweden	0–0	
	7 Oct 2000 v Germany	0–1	

1053. Matthew Paul Le Tissier
Forward
Born St Peter Port, 14 October 1968
Clubs Southampton

Caps	8	*Result*
	9 Mar 1994 v Denmark	1–0
	17 May 1994 v Greece	5–0
	22 May 1994 v Norway	0–0
	12 Oct 1994 v Romania	1–1
	16 Nov 1994 v Nigeria	1–0
	15 Feb 1995 v Eire	0–1
	1 Sep 1996 v Moldova	3–0
	12 Feb 1997 v Italy	0–1

1054. Stephen Andrew Bould
Central defender
Born Stoke-on-Trent, 16 November 1962
Clubs Stoke City; Torquay Utd; Arsenal; Sunderland

Caps	2	*Result*
	17 May 1994 v Greece	5–0
	22 May 1994 v Norway	0–0

1055. Kevin Richardson
Midfielder
Born Newcastle, 4 December 1962
Clubs Everton; Watford; Arsenal; Real Sociedad (Spain); Aston Villa; Coventry City; Southampton; Barnsley; Blackpool

Caps	1	*Result*
	17 May 1994 v Greece	5–0

1056. Barry Venison
Right back
Born Consett, 16 August 1964
Clubs Sunderland; Liverpool; Newcastle Utd; Galatasaray (Turkey); Southampton

Caps	2	*Result*
	7 Sep 1994 v USA	2–0
	29 Mar 1994 v Uruguay	0–0

1057. Robert Martin Lee
Midfielder
Born West Ham, 1 February 1966
Clubs Charlton Athletic; Newcastle Utd; Derby County; West Ham Utd; Oldham Athletic; Wycombe Wanderers

Caps	21	*Result*	*Goals*
	12 Oct 1994 v Romania	1–1	1
	16 Nov 1994 v Nigeria	1–0	
	6 Sep 1995 v Colombia	0–0	
	11 Oct 1995 v Norway	0–0	
	15 Nov 1995 v Switzerland	3–1	
	27 Mar 1996 v Bulgaria	1–0	
	18 May 1996 v Hungary	3–0	
	29 Mar 1997 v Mexico	2–0	
	30 Apr 1997 v Georgia	2–0	
	24 May 1997 v South Africa	2–1	1
	31 May 1997 v Poland	2–0	
	7 Jun 1997 v France	1–0	
	10 Jun 1997 v Brazil	0–1	
	15 Nov 1997 v Cameroon	2–0	
	11 Feb 1998 v Chile	0–2	
	25 Mar 1998 v Switzerland	1–1	
	29 May 1998 v Belgium	0–0	

26 Jun 1998 v Colombia	2–0	
5 Sep 1998 v Sweden	0–0	
9 Jun 1999 v Bulgaria	1–1	
4 Sep 1999 v Luxembourg	6–0	

1058. Stephen Norman Howey
Central defender
Born   Sunderland, 26 October 1971
Clubs   Newcastle Utd; Manchester City; Leicester City; Bolton Wanderers; New England Revolution (USA); Hartlepool Utd

Caps 4	*Result*
16 Nov 1994 v Nigeria	1–0
6 Sep 1995 v Colombia	0–0
12 Dec 1995 v Portugal	1–1
27 Mar 1996 v Bulgaria	1–1

1059. Neil Ruddock
Central defender
Born   Wandsworth, 9 May 1968
Clubs   Millwall; Tottenham Hotspur; Southampton; Liverpool; Queen's Park Rangers (on loan); West Ham Utd; Crystal Palace; Swindon Town

Caps 1	*Result*
16 Nov 1994 v Nigeria	1–0

1060. Steven McManaman
Forward
Born   Bootle, 11 February 1972
Clubs   Liverpool; Real Madrid (Spain); Manchester City

Caps 37	*Result*	*Goals*
16 Nov 1994 v Nigeria	1–0	
29 Mar 1994 v Uruguay	0–0	
3 Jun 1995 v Japan	2–1	
6 Sep 1995 v Colombia	0–0	
11 Oct 1995 v Norway	0–0	
15 Nov 1995 v Switzerland	3–1	
12 Dec 1995 v Portugal	1–1	
27 Mar 1996 v Bulgaria	1–0	
24 Apr 1996 v Croatia	0–0	
23 May 1996 v China	3–0	
8 Jun 1996 v Switzerland	1–1	
15 Jun 1996 v Scotland	2–0	
18 Jun 1996 v Holland	4–1	
22 Jun 1996 v Spain	0–0	
26 Jun 1996 v Germany	1–1	
9 Oct 1996 v Poland	2–1	
12 Feb 1997 v Italy	0–1	
29 Mar 1997 v Mexico	2–0	
15 Nov 1997 v Cameroon	2–0	
25 Mar 1998 v Switzerland	1–1	
27 May 1998 v Morocco	1–0	
26 Jun 1998 v Colombia	2–0	
27 Mar 1999 v Poland	3–1	
28 Apr 1999 v Hungary	1–1	
4 Sep 1999 v Luxembourg	6–0	2
8 Sep 1999 v Poland	0–0	
31 May 2000 v Ukraine	2–0	
3 Jun 2000 v Malta	2–1	
12 Jun 2000 v Portugal	2–3	1
2 Sep 2000 v France	1–1	
11 Oct 2000 v Finland	0–0	
24 Mar 2001 v Finland	2–1	
28 Mar 2001 v Albania	3–1	
6 Jun 2001 v Greece	2–0	
1 Sep 2001 v Germany	5–1	
5 Sep 2001 v Albania	2–0	
6 Oct 2001 v Greece	2–2	

1061. Warren Dean Barton
Right back
Born   Stoke Newington, 19 March 1969
Clubs   Leytonstone and Ilford; Maidstone Utd; Wimbledon; Newcastle Utd; Derby County; Dagenham and Redbridge

Caps 3	*Result*
15 Feb 1995 v Eire	0–1
8 Jun 1995 v Sweden	3–3
11 Jun 1995 v Brazil	1–3

1062. Nicholas Jonathan Barmby
Midfielder
Born   Hull, 11 February 1974
Clubs   Tottenham Hotspur; Middlesbrough; Everton; Liverpool; Leeds Utd; Nottingham Forest; Hull City

Caps 23	*Result*	*Goals*
29 Mar 1995 v Uruguay	0–0	
8 Jun 1995 v Sweden	3–3	
6 Sep 1995 v Colombia	0–0	
11 Oct 1995 v Norway	0–0	
12 Dec 1995 v Portugal	1–1	
23 May 1996 v China	3–0	2
8 Jun 1996 v Switzerland	1–1	
18 Jun 1996 v Holland	4–1	
22 Jun 1996 v Spain	0–0	
1 Sep 1996 v Moldova	3–0	1
27 May 2000 v Brazil	1–1	
31 May 2000 v Ukraine	2–0	
3 Jun 2000 v Malta	2–1	
17 Jun 2000 v Germany	1–0	
20 Jun 2000 v Romania	2–3	
2 Sep 2000 v France	1–1	
7 Oct 2000 v Germany	0–1	
15 Nov 2000 v Italy	0–1	
28 Feb 2001 v Spain	3–0	1
15 Aug 2001 v Holland	0–2	
1 Sep 2001 v Germany	5–1	
5 Sep 2001 v Albania	2–0	
6 Oct 2001 v Greece	2–2	

1063. Andrew Alexander Cole
Forward
Born   Nottingham, 15 October 1971
Clubs   Arsenal; Fulham (on loan); Bristol City; Newcastle Utd; Manchester Utd; Blackburn Rovers; Manchester City

Caps 15	*Result*	*Goals*
29 Mar 1995 v Uruguay	0–0	
12 Feb 1997 v Italy	0–1	
10 Feb 1999 v France	0–2	
27 Mar 1999 v Poland	3–1	
5 Jun 1999 v Sweden	0–0	
13 Nov 1999 v Scotland	2–0	
23 Feb 2000 v Argentina	0–0	
2 Sep 2000 v France	1–1	
7 Oct 2000 v Germany	0–1	
11 Oct 2000 v Finland	0–0	
28 Feb 2001 v Spain	3–0	
24 Mar 2001 v Finland	2–1	
28 Mar 2001 v Albania	3–1	1
15 Aug 2001 v Holland	0–2	
6 Oct 2001 v Greece	2–2	

1064. Stanley Victor Collymore
Forward
Born   Cannock, 22 January 1971
Clubs   Wolverhampton Wanderers; Crystal Palace; Southend Utd; Nottingham Forest; Liverpool; Aston Villa; Fulham; Leicester City; Bradford City; Real Oviedo (Spain)

Caps 3	*Result*
3 Jun 1995 v Japan	2–1
11 Jun 1995 v Brazil	1–3
10 Sep 1997 v Moldova	4–0

1065. Gary Alexander Neville
Right back
Born   Bury, 18 February 1975
Clubs   Manchester Utd

Caps 77	*Result*
3 Jun 1995 v Japan	2–1

11 Jun 1995 v Brazil	1–3
6 Sep 1995 v Colombia	0–0
11 Oct 1995 v Norway	0–0
15 Nov 1995 v Switzerland	3–1
12 Dec 1995 v Portugal	1–1
27 Mar 1996 v Bulgaria	1–0
24 Apr 1996 v Croatia	0–0
18 May 1996 v Hungary	3–0
23 May 1996 v China	3–0
8 Jun 1996 v Switzerland	1–1
15 Jun 1996 v Scotland	2–0
18 Jun 1996 v Holland	4–1
22 Jun 1996 v Spain	0–0
1 Sep 1996 v Moldova	3–0
9 Oct 1996 v Poland	2–1
12 Feb 1997 v Italy	0–1
30 Apr 1997 v Georgia	2–0
31 May 1997 v Poland	2–0
4 Jun 1997 v Italy	2–0
7 Jun 1997 v France	1–0
10 Jun 1997 v Brazil	0–1
10 Sep 1997 v Moldova	4–0
11 Feb 1998 v Chile	0–2
22 Apr 1998 v Portugal	3–0
23 May 1998 v Saudi Arabia	0–0
29 May 1998 v Belgium	0–0
22 Jun 1998 v Romania	1–2
26 Jun 1998 v Colombia	2–0
30 Jun 1998 v Argentina	2–2
10 Oct 1998 v Bulgaria	0–0
27 Mar 1999 v Poland	2–1
4 Sep 1999 v Luxembourg	6–0
8 Sep 1999 v Poland	0–0
27 May 2000 v Brazil	1–1
3 Jun 2000 v Malta	2–1
12 Jun 2000 v Portugal	2–3
17 Jun 2000 v Germany	1–0
20 Jun 2000 v Romania	2–3
7 Oct 2000 v Germany	0–1
15 Nov 2000 v Italy	0–1
28 Feb 2001 v Spain	3–0
24 Mar 2001 v Finland	2–1
28 Mar 2001 v Albania	3–1
15 Aug 2001 v Holland	0–2
1 Sep 2001 v Germany	5–1
5 Sep 2001 v Albania	2–0
6 Oct 2001 v Greece	2–2
10 Nov 2001 v Sweden	1–1
13 Feb 2002 v Holland	1–1
27 Mar 2002 v Italy	1–2
17 Apr 2002 v Paraguay	4–0
12 Oct 2002 v Slovakia	2–1
16 Oct 2002 v Macedonia	2–2
12 Feb 2003 v Australia	1–3
29 Mar 2003 v Liechtenstein	2–0
2 Apr 2003 v Turkey	2–0
6 Sep 2003 v Macedonia	2–1
10 Sep 2003 v Liechtenstein	2–0
11 Oct 2003 v Turkey	0–0
16 Nov 2003 v Denmark	2–3
1 Jun 2004 v Japan	1–1
5 Jun 2004 v Iceland	6–1
13 Jun 2004 v France	1–2
17 Jun 2004 v Switzerland	3–0
20 Jun 2004 v Croatia	4–2
24 Jun 2004 v Portugal	2–2
18 Aug 2004 v Ukraine	3–0
4 Sep 2004 v Austria	2–2
8 Sep 2004 v Poland	2–1
9 Oct 2004 v Wales	2–0
13 Oct 2004 v Azerbaijan	1–0
17 Nov 2004 v Spain	0–1
9 Feb 2005 v Holland	0–0
26 March 2005 v N. Ireland	4–0
30 Mar 2005 v Azerbaijan	2–0
17 Aug 2005 v Denmark	1–4

 DID YOU KNOW...?

When Phil Neville lined up alongside brother Gary for the match against China on 23 May 1996, the pair became the first siblings to represent England since Bobby and Jack Charlton at the 1970 World Cup Finals in Mexico.

1066. John Robert Scales
Defender
Born Harrogate, 4 July 1966
Clubs Leeds Utd; Bristol Rovers; Wimbledon; Liverpool; Tottenham Hotspur; Ipswich Town

Caps 3	*Result*
3 Jun 1995 v Japan	2–1
8 Jun 1995 v Sweden	3–3
11 Jun 1995 v Brazil	1–3

1067. David Gerald Unsworth
Defender
Born Chorley, 16 October 1973
Clubs Everton; West Ham Utd; Aston Villa; Portsmouth; Ipswich Town (on loan)

Caps 1	*Result*
3 Jun 1995 v Japan	2–1

1068. Colin Terence Cooper
Defender
Born Sedgefield, 28 February 1967
Clubs Middlesbrough; Millwall; Nottingham Forest; Sunderland

Caps 2	*Result*
8 Jun 1995 v Sweden	3–3
11 Jun 1995 v Brazil	1–3

1069. Jamie Frank Redknapp
Midfielder
Born Barton-on-Sea, 25 June 1973
Clubs Bournemouth; Liverpool; Tottenham Hotspur; Southampton

Caps 17	*Result*	*Goals*
8 Sep 1995 v Colombia	0–0	
11 Oct 1995 v Norway	0–0	
15 Nov 1995 v Switzerland	3–1	
23 May 1996 v China	3–0	
15 Jun 1996 v Scotland	2–0	
29 Mar 1997 v Mexico	2–0	
30 Apr 1997 v Georgia	2–0	
24 May 1997 v South Africa	2–1	
5 Sep 1998 v Sweden	1–2	
10 Oct 1998 v Bulgaria	0–0	
10 Feb 1999 v France	0–2	
27 Mar 1999 v Poland	3–1	
28 Apr 1999 v Hungary	1–1	
9 Jun 1999 v Bulgaria	1–1	
10 Oct 1999 v Belgium	2–1	1
13 Nov 1999 v Scotland	2–0	
17 Nov 1999 v Scotland	0–1	

1070. Steven Brian Stone
Winger
Born Gateshead, 20 August 1971
Clubs Nottingham Forest; Aston Villa; Portsmouth

Caps 9	*Result*	*Goals*
11 Oct 1995 v Norway	0–0	
15 Nov 1995 v Switzerland	3–1	1
12 Dec 1995 v Portugal	1–1	1
27 Mar 1996 v Bulgaria	1–0	
24 Apr 1996 v Croatia	0–0	
23 May 1996 v China	3–0	
8 Jun 1996 v Switzerland	1–1	
15 Jun 1996 v Scotland	2–0	
22 Jun 1996 v Spain	0–0	

1071. Gareth Southgate
Defender
Born Watford, 3 September 1970
Clubs Crystal Palace; Aston Villa; Middlesbrough
Caps 57   *Result* *Goals*

12 Dec 1995 v Portugal	1–1	
27 Mar 1996 v Bulgaria	1–0	
18 May 1996 v Hungary	3–0	
23 May 1996 v China	3–0	
8 Jun 1996 v Switzerland	1–1	
15 Jun 1996 v Scotland	2–0	
18 Jun 1996 v Holland	4–1	
22 Jun 1996 v Spain	0–0	
26 Jun 1996 v Germany	1–1	
1 Sep 1996 v Moldova	3–0	
9 Oct 1996 v Poland	2–1	
9 Nov 1996 v Georgia	2–0	
29 Mar 1997 v Mexico	2–0	
30 Apr 1997 v Georgia	2–0	
24 May 1997 v South Africa	2–1	
31 May 1997 v Poland	2–0	
4 Jun 1997 v Italy	2–0	
7 Jun 1997 v France	1–0	
10 Jun 1997 v Brazil	0–1	
10 Sep 1997 v Moldova	4–0	
1 Oct 1997 v Italy	0–0	
15 Nov 1997 v Cameroon	2–0	
25 Mar 1998 v Switzerland	1–1	
23 May 1998 v Saudi Arabia	0–0	
27 May 1998 v Morocco	1–0	
15 Jun 1998 v Tunisia	2–0	
30 Jun 1998 v Argentina	2–2	
5 Sep 1998 v Sweden	1–2	
10 Oct 1998 v Bulgaria	0–0	
14 Oct 1998 v Luxembourg	3–0	1
9 Jun 1999 v Bulgaria	1–1	
10 Oct 1999 v Belgium	2–1	
13 Nov 1999 v Scotland	2–0	
23 Feb 2000 v Argentina	0–0	
31 May 2000 v Ukraine	2–0	
3 Jun 2000 v Malta	2–1	
20 Jun 2000 v Romania	2–3	
2 Sep 2000 v France	1–1	
7 Oct 2000 v Germany	0–1	
11 Oct 2000 v Finland	0–0	
15 Nov 2000 v Italy	0–1	
25 May 2001 v Mexico	4–0	
15 Aug 2001 v Holland	0–2	
10 Nov 2001 v Sweden	1–1	
13 Feb 2002 v Holland	1–1	
27 Mar 2002 v Italy	1–2	
17 Apr 2002 v Paraguay	4–0	
21 May 2002 v South Korea	1–1	
26 May 2002 v Cameroon	2–2	
7 Sep 2002 v Portugal	1–1	
12 Oct 2002 v Slovakia	2–1	
29 Mar 2003 v Liechtenstein	2–0	
22 May 2003 v South Africa	2–1	1
3 Jun 2003 v Serbia	2–1	
11 Jun 2003 v Slovakia	2–1	
18 Feb 2004 v Portugal	1–1	
31 Mar 2004 v Sweden	0–1	

1072. Robert Bernard Fowler
Forward
Born Liverpool, 9 April 1975
Clubs Liverpool, Leeds Utd; Manchester City
Caps 26   *Result* *Goals*

27 Mar 1996 v Bulgaria	1–0	
24 Apr 1996 v Croatia	0–0	
23 May 1996 v China	3–0	
18 Jun 1996 v Holland	4–1	
22 Jun 1996 v Spain	0–0	
29 Mar 1997 v Mexico	2–0	1
15 Nov 1997 v Cameroon	2–0	1
18 Nov 1998 v Czech Republic	2–0	

9 Jun 1999 v Bulgaria	1–1	
4 Sep 1999 v Luxembourg	6–0	
8 Sep 1999 v Poland	0–0	
27 May 2000 v Brazil	1–1	
31 May 2000 v Ukraine	2–0	1
3 Jun 2000 v Malta	2–1	
15 Nov 2000 v Italy	0–1	
24 Mar 2001 v Finland	2–1	
25 May 2001 v Mexico	4–0	1
6 Jun 2001 v Greece	2–0	
15 Aug 2001 v Holland	0–2	
5 Sep 2001 v Albania	2–0	1
6 Oct 2001 v Greece	2–2	
10 Nov 2001 v Sweden	1–1	
27 Mar 2002 v Italy	1–2	1
17 Apr 2002 v Paraguay	4–0	
26 May 2002 v Cameroon	2–2	1
15 Jun 2002 v Denmark	3–0	

1073. Philip John Neville
Defender/Midfielder
Born Bury, 21 January 1977
Clubs Manchester Utd; Everton
Caps 52   *Result*

23 May 1996 v China	3–0
24 May 1997 v South Africa	2–1
31 May 1997 v Poland	2–0
4 Jun 1997 v Italy	2–0
7 Jun 1997 v France	1–0
10 Jun 1997 v Brazil	0–1
10 Sep 1997 v Moldova	4–0
15 Nov 1997 v Cameroon	2–0
11 Feb 1998 v Chile	0–2
22 Apr 1998 v Portugal	3–0
23 May 1998 v Saudi Arabia	0–0
29 May 1998 v Belgium	0–0
14 Oct 1998 v Luxembourg	3–0
27 Mar 1999 v Poland	3–1
28 Apr 1999 v Hungary	1–1
5 Jun 1999 v Sweden	0–0
9 Jun 1999 v Bulgaria	1–1
4 Sep 1999 v Luxembourg	6–0
8 Sep 1999 v Poland	0–0
10 Oct 1999 v Belgium	2–1
13 Nov 1999 v Scotland	2–0
17 Nov 1999 v Scotland	0–1
23 Feb 2000 v Argentina	0–0
27 May 2000 v Brazil	1–1
31 May 2000 v Ukraine	2–0
3 Jun 2000 v Malta	2–1
12 Jun 2000 v Portugal	2–3
17 Jun 2000 v Germany	1–0
29 Jun 2000 v Romania	2–3
11 Oct 2000 v Finland	0–0
28 Feb 2001 v Spain	3–0
25 May 2001 v Mexico	4–0
6 Jun 2001 v Greece	2–0
10 Nov 2001 v Sweden	1–1
13 Feb 2002 v Holland	1–1
27 Mar 2002 v Italy	1–2
17 Apr 2002 v Paraguay	4–0
22 May 2003 v South Africa	2–1
3 Jun 2003 v Serbia	2–1
11 Jun 2002 v Slovakia	2–1
20 Aug 2003 v Croatia	3–1
6 Sep 2003 v Macedonia	2–1
10 Sep 2003 v Liechtenstein	2–0
16 Nov 2003 v Denmark	2–3
18 Feb 2004 v Portugal	1–1
31 Mar 2004 v Sweden	0–1
1 Jun 2004 v Japan	1–1
5 Jun 2004 v Iceland	6–1
20 Jun 2004 v Croatia	4–2
24 Jun 2004 v Portugal	2–2
28 May 2005 v USA	2–1
31 May 2005 v Colombia	3–2

1074. Ugochuku Ehiogu
Defender
Born Hackney, 3 November 1972
Clubs West Bromwich Albion; Aston Villa; Middlesbrough

Caps 4	Result	Goals
23 May 1996 v China	3–0	
28 Feb 2001 v Spain	3–0	1
13 Feb 2002 v Holland	1–1	
27 Mar 2002 v Italy	1–2	

1075. Sulzeer 'Sol' Jeremiah Campbell
Central defender
Born Newham, 16 September 1974
Clubs Tottenham Hotspur; Arsenal

Caps 66	Result	Goals
18 May 1996 v Hungary	3–0	
15 Jun 1996 v Scotland	2–0	
9 Nov 1996 v Georgia	2–0	
12 Feb 1997 v Italy	0–1	
30 Apr 1997 v Georgia	2–0	
24 May 1997 v South Africa	2–1	
31 May 1997 v Poland	2–0	
7 Jun 1997 v France	1–0	
10 Jun 1997 v Brazil	0–1	
10 Sep 1997 v Moldova	4–0	
11 Oct 1997 v Italy	0–0	
15 Nov 1997 v Cameroon	2–0	
11 Feb 1998 v Chile	0–2	
22 Apr 1998 v Portugal	3–0	
27 May 1998 v Morocco	1–0	
29 May 1998 v Belgium	0–0	
15 Jun 1998 v Tunisia	2–0	
22 Jun 1998 v Romania	1–2	
26 Jun 1998 v Colombia	2–0	
30 Jun 1998 v Argentina	2–2	
5 Sep 1998 v Sweden	1–2	
10 Oct 1998 v Bulgaria	0–0	
14 Oct 1998 v Luxembourg	3–0	
18 Nov 1998 v Czech Republic	2–0	
27 Mar 1999 v Poland	3–1	
5 Jun 1999 v Sweden	0–0	
9 Jun 1999 v Bulgaria	1–1	
13 Nov 1999 v Scotland	2–0	
17 Nov 1999 v Scotland	0–1	
23 Feb 2000 v Argentina	0–0	
27 May 2000 v Brazil	1–1	
31 May 2000 v Ukraine	2–0	
3 Jun 2000 v Malta	2–1	
12 Jun 2000 v Portugal	2–3	
17 Jun 2000 v Germany	1–0	
20 Jun 2000 v Romania	2–3	
2 Sep 2000 v France	1–1	
28 Feb 2001 v Spain	3–0	
24 Mar 2001 v Finland	2–1	
28 Mar 2001 v Albania	3–1	
1 Sep 2001 v Germany	5–1	
5 Sep 2001 v Albania	2–0	
13 Feb 2002 v Holland	1–1	
27 Mar 2002 v Italy	1–2	
21 May 2002 v South Korea	1–1	
26 May 2002 v Cameroon	2–2	
2 Jun 2002 v Sweden	1–1	1
7 Jun 2002 v Argentina	1–0	
12 Jun 2002 v Nigeria	0–0	
15 Jun 2002 v Denmark	3–0	
21 Jun 2002 v Brazil	1–2	
16 Oct 2002 v Macedonia	2–2	
12 Feb 2003 v Australia	1–3	
2 Apr 2003 v Turkey	2–0	
6 Sep 2003 v Macedonia	2–1	
11 Oct 2003 v Turkey	0–0	
1 Jun 2004 v Japan	1–1	
5 Jun 2004 v Iceland	6–1	
13 Jun 2004 v France	1–2	
17 Jun 2004 v Switzerland	3–0	
20 Jun 2004 v Croatia	4–2	
24 Jun 2004 v Portugal	2–2	
9 Oct 2004 v Wales	2–0	
13 Oct 2004 v Azerbaijan	1–0	
28 May 2005 v USA	2–1	
8 Oct 2005 v Austria	1–0	

1076. Ian Michael Walker
Goalkeeper
Born Watford, 31 October 1971
Clubs Tottenham Hotspur; Oxford Utd (on loan); Leicester City; Bolton Wanderers

Caps 3	Result
18 May 1996 v Hungary	3–0
23 May 1996 v China	3–0
12 Feb 1997 v Italy	0–1

1077. Jason Malcolm Wilcox
Winger
Born Farnworth, 15 July 1971
Clubs Blackburn Rovers; Leeds Utd; Leicester City

Caps 3	Result
18 May 1996 v Hungary	3–0
10 Feb 1999 v France	0–2
23 Feb 2000 v Argentina	0–0

1078. David Robert Joseph Beckham
Midfielder
Born Leytonstone, 2 May 1975
Clubs Manchester Utd; Preston North End (on loan); Real Madrid

Caps 86	Result	Goals
1 Sep 1996 v Moldova	3–0	
9 Oct 1996 v Poland	2–1	
9 Nov 1996 v Georgia	2–0	
12 Feb 1997 v Italy	0–1	
30 Apr 1997 v Georgia	2–0	
24 May 1997 v South Africa	2–1	
31 May 1997 v Poland	2–0	
4 Jun 1997 v Italy	2–0	
7 Jun 1997 v France	1–0	
10 Sep 1997 v Moldova	4–0	
11 Oct 1997 v Italy	0–0	
15 Nov 1997 v Cameroon	2–0	
22 Apr 1998 v Portugal	3–0	
23 May 1998 v Saudi Arabia	0–0	
29 May 1998 v Belgium	0–0	
22 Jun 1998 v Romania	1–2	
26 Jun 1998 v Colombia	2–0	1
30 Jun 1998 v Argentina	2–2	
14 Oct 1998 v Luxembourg	3–0	
18 Nov 1998 v Czech Republic	2–0	
10 Feb 1999 v France	0–2	
27 Mar 1999 v Poland	3–1	
5 Jun 1999 v Sweden	0–0	
4 Sep 1999 v Luxembourg	6–0	
8 Sep 1999 v Poland	0–0	
13 Nov 1999 v Scotland	2–0	
17 Nov 1999 v Scotland	0–1	
23 Feb 2000 v Argentina	0–0	
27 May 2000 v Brazil	1–1	
31 May 2000 v Ukraine	2–0	
3 Jun 2000 v Malta	2–1	
12 Jun 2000 v Portugal	2–3	
17 Jun 2000 v Germany	1–0	
20 Jun 2000 v Romania	2–3	
2 Sep 2000 v France	1–1	
7 Oct 2000 v Germany	0–1	
15 Nov 2000 v Italy	0–1	
28 Feb 2001 v Spain	3–0	
24 Mar 2001 v Finland	2–1	1
28 Mar 2001 v Albania	3–1	
25 May 2001 v Mexico	4–0	1
6 Jun 2001 v Greece	3–0	1
15 Aug 2001 v Holland	0–2	
1 Sep 2001 v Germany	5–1	
5 Sep 2001 v Albania	2–0	
6 Oct 2001 v Greece	2–2	1

10 Nov 2001 v Sweden	1–1	1
13 Feb 2002 v Holland	1–1	
27 Mar 2002 v Italy	1–2	
2 Jun 2002 v Sweden	1–1	
7 Jun 2002 v Argentina	1–0	1
12 Jun 2002 v Nigeria	0–0	
15 Jun 2002 v Denmark	3–0	
21 Jun 2002 v Brazil	1–2	
12 Oct 2002 v Slovakia	2–1	1
16 Oct 2002 v Macedonia	2–2	1
12 Feb 2003 v Australia	1–3	
29 Mar 2003 v Liechtenstein	2–0	1
2 Apr 2003 v Turkey	2–0	1
22 May 2003 v South Africa	2–1	
20 Aug 2003 v Croatia	3–1	1
6 Sep 2003 v Macedonia	2–1	1
10 Sep 2003 v Liechtenstein	2–0	
11 Oct 2003 v Turkey	0–0	
16 Nov 2003 v Denmark	2–3	
18 Feb 2004 v Portugal	1–1	
1 Jun 2004 v Japan	1–1	
5 Jun 2004 v Iceland	6–1	
13 Jun 2004 v France	1–2	
17 Jun 2004v Switzerland	3–0	
21 Jun 2004 v Croatia	4–2	
24 Jun 2004 v Portugal	2–2	
18 Aug 2004 v Ukraine	3–0	1
4 Sep 2004 v Austria	2–2	
8 Sep 2004 v Poland	2–1	
9 Oct 2004 v Wales	2–0	1
17 Nov 2004 v Spain	0–1	
9 Feb 2005 v Holland	0–0	
26 Mar 2005 v N. Ireland	4–0	
30 Mar 2005 v Azerbaijan	2–0	1
31 May 2005 v Colombia	3–2	
17 Aug 2005 v Denmark	1–4	
3 Sep 2005 v Wales	1–0	
7 Sep 2005 v N. Ireland	0–1	
8 Oct 2005 v Austria	1–0	
12 Nov 2005 v Argentina	3–2	

1079. Andrew George Hinchcliffe
Left back
Born   Manchester, 5 February 1969
Clubs   Manchester City; Everton; Sheffield Wednesday

Caps 7	Result
1 Sep 1996 v Moldova	3–0
9 Oct 1996 v Poland	2–1
9 Nov 1996 v Georgia	2–0
15 Nov 1997 v Cameroon	2–0
25 Mar 1998 v Switzerland	1–1
23 May 1997 v Saudi Arabia	0–0
9 Jun 1999 v Bulgaria	1–1

1080. David Benjamin James
Goalkeeper
Born   Welwyn Garden City, 1 August 1970
Clubs   Watford; Liverpool; Aston Villa; West Ham Utd;
        Manchester City

Caps 33	Result
1 Sep 1996 v Moldova	3–0
15 Nov 2000 v Italy	0–1
28 Feb 2001 v Spain	3–0
25 May 2001 v Mexico	4–0
15 Aug 2001 v Holland	0–2
13 Feb 2002 v Holland	1–1
27 Mar 2002 v Italy	1–2
21 May 2002 v South Korea	1–1
26 May 2002 v Cameroon	2–2
7 Sep 2002 v Portugal	1–1
12 Feb 2003 v Australia	1–3
29 Mar 2003 v Liechtenstein	2–0
2 Apr 2003 v Turkey	2–0
22 May 2003 v South Africa	2–1
3 Jun 2003 v Serbia	2–1
11 Jun 2003 v Slovakia	2–1

20 Aug 2003 v Croatia	3–1
6 Sep 2003 v Macedonia	2–1
10 Sep 2003 v Liechtenstein	2–0
11 Oct 2003 v Turkey	0–0
16 Nov 2003 v Denmark	2–3
18 Feb 2004 v Portugal	1–1
21 Mar 2004 v Sweden	0–1
1 Jun 2004 v Japan	1–1
13 Jun 2004 v France	1–2
17 Jun 2004 v Switzerland	3–0
21 Jun 2004 v Croatia	4–2
24 Jun 2004 v Portugal	2–2
18 Aug 2004 v Ukraine	3–0
4 Sep 2004 v Austria	2–2
28 May 2005 v USA	2–1
31 May 2005 v Colombia	3–2
17 Aug 2005 v Denmark	1–4

1081. Nicholas Butt
Midfielder
Born   Manchester, 21 January 1975
Clubs   Manchester Utd; Newcastle Utd; Birmingham City

Caps 39	Result
29 Mar 1997 v Mexico	2–0
24 May 1997 v South Africa	2–1
10 Sep 1997 v Moldova	4–0
11 Oct 1997 v Italy	0–0
11 Feb 1998 v Chile	0–2
29 May 1998 v Belgium	0–0
18 Nov 1998 v Czech Republic	2–0
28 Apr 1999 v Hungary	1–1
15 Nov 2000 v Italy	0–1
28 Feb 2001 v Spain	3–0
24 Mar 2001 v Finland	2–1
28 Mar 2001 v Albania	3–1
25 May 2001 v Mexico	4–0
6 Jun 2001 v Greece	2–0
10 Nov 2001 v Sweden	1–1
13 Feb 2002 v Holland	1–1
27 Mar 2002 v Italy	1–2
17 Apr 2002 v Paraguay	4–0
7 Jun 2002 v Argentina	1–0
12 Jun 2002 v Nigeria	0–0
15 Jun 2002 v Denmark	3–0
21 Jun 2002 v Brazil	1–2
7 Sep 2002 v Portugal	1–1
12 Oct 2002 v Slovakia	2–1
16 Oct 2002 v Macedonia	2–2
29 Mar 2003 v Liechtenstein	2–0
2 Apr 2003 v Turkey	2–0
20 Aug 2003 v Croatia	3–1
6 Sep 2003 v Macedonia	2–1
11 Oct 2003 v Turkey	0–0
16 Nov 2003 v Denmark	2–3
18 Feb 2004 v Portugal	1–1
31 Mar 2004 v Sweden	0–1
1 Jun 2004 v Japan	1–1
5 Jun 2004 v Iceland	6–1
18 Aug 2004 v Ukraine	3–0
9 Oct 2004 v Wales	2–0
13 Oct 2004 v Azerbaijan	1–0
17 Nov 2004 v Spain	0–1

1082. Paul Scholes
Midfielder
Born   Salford, 16 November 1974
Clubs   Manchester Utd

Caps 66	Result	Goals
24 May 1997 v South Africa	2–1	
4 Jun 1997 v Italy	2–0	1
10 Jun 1997 v Brazil	0–1	
10 Sep 1997 v Moldova	4–0	1
15 Nov 1997 v Cameroon	2–0	1
22 Apr 1998 v Portugal	3–0	
23 May 1998 v Saudi Arabia	0–0	
15 Jun 1998 v Tunisia	2–0	1

22 Jun 1998 v Romania	1–2	
26 Jun 1998 v Colombia	2–0	
30 Jun 1998 v Argentina	2–2	
5 Sep 1998 v Sweden	1–2	
10 Oct 1998 v Bulgaria	0–0	
14 Oct 1998 v Luxembourg	3–0	
10 Feb 1999 v France	0–2	
27 Mar 1999 v Poland	3–1	3
5 Jun 1999 v Sweden	0–0	
8 Sep 1999 v Poland	0–0	
13 Nov 1999 v Scotland	2–0	2
17 Nov 1999 v Scotland	0–1	
23 Feb 2000 v Argentina	0–0	
27 May 2000 v Brazil	1–1	
31 May 2000 v Ukraine	2–0	
3 Jun 2000 v Malta	2–1	
12 Jun 2000 v Portugal	2–3	1
17 Jun 2000 v Germany	1–0	
20 Jun 2000 v Romania	2–3	
2 Sep 2000 v France	1–1	
7 Oct 2000 v Germany	0–1	
11 Oct 2000 v Finland	0–0	
28 Feb 2001 v Spain	3–0	
24 Mar 2001 v Finland	2–1	
28 Mar 2001 v Albania	3–1	1
25 May 2001 v Mexico	4–0	1
6 Jun 2001 v Greece	2–0	1
15 Aug 2001 v Holland	0–2	
1 Sep 2001 v Germany	5–1	
5 Sep 2001 v Albania	2–0	
6 Oct 2001 v Greece	2–2	
10 Nov 2001 v Sweden	1–1	
13 Feb 2002 v Holland	1–1	
17 Apr 2002 v Paraguay	4–0	
21 May 2002 v South Korea	1–1	
26 May 2002 v Cameroon	2–2	
2 Jun 2002 v Sweden	1–1	
7 Jun 2002 v Argentina	1–0	
12 Jun 2002 v Nigeria	0–0	
15 Jun 2002 v Denmark	3–0	
21 Jun 2002 v Brazil	1–2	
12 Oct 2002 v Slovakia	2–1	
16 Oct 2002 v Macedonia	2–2	
12 Feb 2003 v Australia	1–3	
29 Mar 2003 v Liechtenstein	2–0	
2 Apr 2003 v Turkey	2–0	
22 May 2003 v South Africa	2–1	
3 Jun 2003 v Serbia	2–1	
11 Jun 2003 v Slovakia	2–1	
20 Aug 2003 v Croatia	3–1	
11 Oct 2003 v Turkey`	0–0	
18 Feb 2004 v Portugal	1–1	
1 Jun 2004 v Japan	1–1	
5 Jun 2004 v Iceland	6–1	
13 Jun 2004 v France	1–2	
17 Jun 2004 v Switzerland	3–0	
21 Jun 2004 v Croatia	4–2	1
24 Jun 2004 v Portugal	2–2	

1083. Rio Gavin Ferdinand
Central defender
Born Peckham, 8 November 1978
Clubs West Ham Utd; Bournemouth (on loan); Leeds Utd; Manchester Utd

Caps 44	*Result*	*Goals*
15 Nov 1997 v Cameroon	2–0	
25 Mar 1998 v Switzerland	1–1	
29 May 1998 v Belgium	0–0	
14 Oct 1998 v Luxembourg	3–0	
18 Nov 1998 v Czech Republic	2–0	
10 Feb 1999 v France	0–2	
28Apr 1999 v Hungary	1–1	
5 Jun 1999 v Sweden	0–0	
23 Feb 2000 v Argentina	0–0	
15 Nov 2000 v Italy	0–1	
28 Feb 2001 v Spain	3–0	

24 Mar 2001 v Finland	2–1	
28 Mar 2001 v Albania	3–1	
25 May 2001 v Mexico	4–0	
6 Jun 2001 v Greece	2–0	
1 Sep 2001 v Germany	5–1	
5 Sep 2001 v Albania	2–0	
6 Oct 2001 v Greece	2–2	
10 Nov 2001 v Sweden	1–1	
13 Feb 2002 v Holland	1–1	
21 May 2002 v South Korea	1–1	
26 May 2002 v Cameroon	2–2	
2 Jun 2002 v Sweden	1–1	
7 Jun 2002 v Argentina	1–0	
12 Jun 2002 v Nigeria	0–0	
15 Jun 2002 v Denmark	3–0	1
21 Jun 2002 v Brazil	1–2	
7 Sep 2002 v Portugal	1–1	
12 Feb 2003 v Australia	1–3	
29 Mar 2003 v Liechtenstein	2–0	
2 Apr 2003 v Turkey	2–0	
22 May 2003 v South Africa	2–1	
20 Aug 2003 v Croatia	3–1	
9 Oct 2004 v Wales	2–0	
13 Oct 2004 v Azerbaijan	1–0	
17 Nov 2004 v Spain	0–1	
26 Mar 2005 v N. Ireland	4–0	
30 Mar 2005 v Azerbaijan	2–0	
17 Aug 2005 v Denmark	1–4	
3 Sep 2005 v Wales	1–0	
7 Sep 2005 v N. Ireland	0–1	
8 Oct 2005 v Austria	1–0	
12 Oct 2005 v Poland	2–1	
12 Nov 2005 v Argentina	3–2	

1084. Christopher Roy Sutton
Forward
Born Nottingham, 10 March 1973
Clubs Norwich City, Blackburn Rovers; Chelsea; Glasgow Celtic

Caps 1	*Result*
15 Nov 1997 v Cameroon	2–0

1085. Dion Dublin
Forward
Born Leicester, 22 April 1969
Clubs Norwich City; Cambridge Utd; Manchester Utd; Coventry City; Aston Villa; Millwall (on loan); Leicester City

Caps 4	*Result*
11 Feb 1998 v Chile	0–2
27 May 1998 v Morocco	1–0
29 May 1998 v Belgium	0–0
18 Nov 1998 v Czech Republic	2–0

1086. Michael James Owen
Forward
Born Chester, 14 December 1979
Clubs Liverpool; Real Madrid; Newcastle Utd

Caps 75	*Result*	*Goals*
11 Feb 1998 v Chile	0–2	
25 Mar 1998 v Switzerland	1–1	
22 Apr 1998 v Portugal	3–0	
27 May 1998 v Morocco	1–0	1
29 May 1998 v Belgium	0–0	
15 Jun 1998 v Tunisia	2–0	
22 Jun 1998 v Romania	1–2	1
26 Jun 1998 v Colombia	2–0	
30 Jun 1998 v Argentina	2–2	1
5 Sep 1998 v Sweden	1–2	
10 Oct 1998 v Bulgaria	0–0	
14 Oct 1998 v Luxembourg	3–0	1
10 Feb 1999 v France	0–2	
4 Sep 1999 v Luxembourg	6–0	1
8 Sep 1999 v Poland	0–0	
10 Oct 1999 v Belgium	2–1	
13 Nov 1999 v Scotland	2–0	

17 Nov 1999 v Scotland	0–1	
27 May 2000 v Brazil	1–1	1
12 Jun 2000 v Portugal	2–3	
17 Jun 2000 v Germany	1–0	
20 Jun 2000 v Romania	2–3	1
2 Sep 2000 v France	1–1	1
7 Oct 2000 v Germany	0–1	
28 Feb 2001 v Spain	3–0	
24 Mar 2001 v Finland	2–1	1
28 Mar 2001 v Albania	3–1	1
25 May 2001 v Mexico	4–0	
6 Jun 2001 v Greece	2–0	
15 Aug 2001 v Holland	0–2	
1 Sep 2001 v Germany	5–1	3
5 Sep 2001 v Albania	2–0	1
27 Mar 2002 v Italy	1–2	
17 Apr 2002 v Paraguay	4–0	1
21 May 2002 v South Korea	1–1	1
26 May 2002 v Cameroon	2–2	
2 Jun 2002 v Sweden	1–1	
7 Jun 2002 v Argentina	1–0	
12 Jun 2002 v Nigeria	0–0	
15 Jun 2002 v Denmark	3–0	1
21 Jun 2002 v Brazil	1–2	1
7 Sep 2002 v Portugal	1–1	
12 Oct 2002 v Slovakia	2–1	1
16 Oct 2002 v Macedonia	2–2	
12 Feb 2003 v Australia	1–3	
29 Mar 2003 v Liechtenstein	2–0	1
2 Apr 2003 v Turkey	2–0	
22 May 2003 v South Africa	2–1	
3 Jun 2003 v Serbia	2–1	
11 Jun 2003 v Slovakia	2–1	2
20 Aug 2003 v Croatia	3–1	1
6 Sep 2003 v Macedonia	2–1	
10 Sep 2003 v Liechtenstein	2–0	1
18 Feb 2004 v Portugal	1–1	
1 Jun 2004 v Japan	1–1	1
5 Jun 2004 v Iceland	6–1	
13 Jun 2004 v France	1–2	
17 Jun 2004 v Switzerland	3–0	
21 Jun 2004 v Croatia	4–2	
24 Jun 2004 v Portugal	2–2	1
18 Aug 2004 v Ukraine	3–0	1
4 Sep 2004 v Austria	2–2	
8 Sep 2004 v Poland	2–1	
9 Oct 2004 v Wales	2–0	
13 Oct 2004 v Azerbaijan	1–0	1
17 Nov 2004 v Spain	0–1	
9 Feb 2005 v Holland	0–0	
26 Mar 2005 v N. Ireland	4–0	1
30 Mar 2005 v Azerbaijan	2–0	
31 May 2005 v Colombia	3–2	3
17 Aug 2005 v Denmark	1–4	
7 Sep 2005 v N. Ireland	0–1	
8 Oct 2005 v Austria	1–0	
12 Oct 2005 v Poland	2–1	1
12 Nov 2005 v Argentina	3–2	2

1087. Lee Andrew Hendrie
Midfielder
Born   Birmingham, 18 May 1977
Clubs Aston Villa

Caps	1	Result
	18 Nov 1998 v Czech Republic	2–0

1088. Raymond Parlour
Midfielder
Born   Romford, 7 March 1973
Clubs Arsenal; Middlesbrough

Caps	10	Result
	27 Mar 1999 v Poland	3–1
	5 Jun 1999 v Sweden	0–0
	9 Jun 1999 v Bulgaria	1–1
	4 Sep 1999 v Luxembourg	6–0
	17 Nov 1999 v Scotland	0–1

23 Feb 2000 v Argentina	0–0	
27 May 2000 v Brazil	1–1	
7 Oct 2000 v Germany	0–1	
11 Oct 2000 v Finland	0–0	
15 Nov 2000 v Italy	0–1	

1089. Timothy Alan Sherwood
Midfielder
Born   St Albans, 6 February 1969
Clubs Watford; Norwich City; Blackburn Rovers;
Tottenham Hotspur; Portsmouth; Coventry City

Caps	3	Result
	27 Mar 1999 v Poland	3–1
	28 Apr 1999 v Hungary	1–1
	5 Jun 1999 v Sweden	0–0

1090. Wesley Michael Brown
Defender
Born   Manchester, 13 October 1979
Clubs Manchester Utd

Caps	9	Result
	28 Apr 1999 v Hungary	1–1
	24 Mar 2001 v Finland	2–1
	28 Mar 2001 v Albania	3–1
	13 Feb 2002 v Holland	1–1
	21 May 2002 v South Korea	1–1
	26 May 2002 v Cameroon	2–2
	12 Feb 2003 v Australia	1–3
	9 Feb 2005 v Holland	0–0
	28 May 2005 v USA	2–1

1091. Michael Gray
Left back
Born   Sunderland, 3 August 1974
Clubs Sunderland; Glasgow Celtic; Blackburn Rovers;
Leeds Utd (on loan)

Caps	3	Result
	28 Apr 1999 v Hungary	1–1
	5 Jun 1999 v Sweden	0–0
	9 Jun 1999 v Bulgaria	0–0

1092. Kevin Mark Phillips
Forward
Born   Hitchin, 25 July 1973
Clubs Watford; Sunderland; Southampton; Aston Villa

Caps	8	Result
	28 Apr 1999 v Hungary	1–1
	10 Oct 1999 v Belgium	2–1
	23 Feb 2000 v Argentina	0–0
	27 May 2000 v Brazil	1–1
	3 Jun 2000 v Malta	2–1
	15 Nov 2000 v Italy	0–1
	10 Nov 2001 v Sweden	1–1
	13 Feb 2002 v Holland	1–1

1093. Emile William Ivanhoe Heskey
Forward
Born   Leicester, 11 January 1978
Clubs Leicester City; Liverpool; Birmingham City

Caps	43	Result	Goals
	28 Apr 1999 v Hungary	1–1	
	9 Jun 1999 v Bulgaria	1–1	
	10 Oct 1999 v Belgium	2–1	
	17 Nov 1999 v Scotland	0–1	
	23 Feb 2000 v Argentina	0–0	
	31 May 2000 v Ukraine	2–0	
	3 Jun 2000 v Malta	2–1	1
	12 Jun 2000 v Portugal	2–3	
	12 Jun 2000 v Romania	2–3	
	11 Oct 2000 v Finland	0–0	
	15 Nov 2000 v Italy	0–1	
	28 Feb 2001 v Spain	3–0	1
	24 Mar 2001 v Finland	2–1	
	28 Mar 2001 v Albania	3–1	
	25 May 2001 v Mexico	4–0	
	6 Jun 2001 v Greece	2–0	

1 Sep 2001 v Germany	5–1	1
5 Sep 2001 v Albania	2–0	
6 Oct 2001 v Greece	2–2	
10 Nov 2001 v Sweden	1–1	
13 Feb 2002 v Holland	1–1	
27 Mar 2002 v Italy	1–2	
21 May 2002 v South Korea	1–1	
26 May 2002 v Cameroon	2–2	
2 Jun 2002 v Sweden	1–1	
7 Jun 2002 v Argentina	1–0	
12 Jun 2002 v Nigeria	0–0	
15 Jun 2002 v Denmark	3–0	1
21 Jun 2002 v Brazil	1–2	
7 Sep 2002 v Portugal	1–1	
12 Oct 2002 v Slovakia	2–1	
29 Mar 2003 v Liechtenstein	2–0	
22 May 2003 v South Africa	2–1	1
3 Jun 2003 v Serbia	2–1	
20 Aug 2003 v Croatia	3–1	
6 Sep 2003 v Macedonia	2–1	
11 Oct 2003 v Turkey	0–0	
16 Nov 2003 v Denmark	2–3	
18 Feb 2004 v Portugal	1–1	
31 Mar 2004 v Sweden	0–1	
1 Jun 2004 v Japan	1–1	
5 Jun 2004 v Iceland	6–1	
13 Jun 2004 v France	1–2	

1094. James Lee Carragher
Defender
Born   Bootle, 28 January 1978
Clubs Liverpool

Caps	22	Result
	28 Apr 1999 v Hungary	1–1
	15 Nov 2000 v Italy	0–1
	25 May 2001 v Mexico	4–0
	15 Aug 2001 v Holland	0–2
	1 Sep 2001 v Germany	5–1
	5 Sep 2001 v Albania	2–0
	10 Nov 2001 v Sweden	1–1
	17 Apr 2002 v Paraguay	4–0
	3 Jun 2003 v Serbia	2–1
	18 Feb 2004 v Portugal	1–1
	31 Mar 2004 v Sweden	0–1
	5 Jun 2004 v Iceland	6–1
	18 Aug 2004 v Ukraine	3–0
	4 Sep 2004 v Austria	2–2
	8 Sep 2004 v Poland	2–1
	17 Nov 2004 v Spain	0–1
	9 Feb 2005 v Holland	0–0
	17 Aug 2005 v Denmark	1–4
	3 Sep 2005 v Wales	1–0
	7 Sep 2005 v N. Ireland	0–1
	8 Oct 2005 v Austria	1–0
	12 Oct 2005 v Poland	2–1

1095. Jonathan Simon Woodgate
Central defender
Born   Middlesbrough, 22 January 1980
Clubs Leeds Utd; Newcastle Utd; Real Madrid

Caps	4	Result
	9 Jun 1999 v Bulgaria	1–1
	7 Sep 2002 v Portugal	1–1
	12 Oct 2002 v Slovakia	2–1
	16 Oct 2002 v Macedonia	2–2

1096. Kieron Courtney Dyer
Midfielder
Born   Ipswich, 29 December 1978
Clubs Ipswich Town; Newcastle Utd

Caps	28	Result
	4 Sep 1999 v Luxembourg	6–0
	8 Sep 1999 v Poland	0–0
	10 Oct 1999 v Belgium	2–1
	23 Feb 2000 v Argentina	0–0
	31 May 2000 v Ukraine	2–0
	2 Sep 2000 v France	1–1

7 Oct 2000 v Germany	0–1	
15 Nov 2000 v Italy	0–1	
17 Apr 2002 v Paraguay	4–0	
2 Jun 2002 v Sweden	1–1	
15 Jun 2002 v Denmark	3–0	
21 Jun 2002 v Brazil	1–2	
12 Oct 2002 v Slovakia	2–1	
12 Feb 2003 v Australia	1–3	
29 Mar 2003 v Liechtenstein	2–0	
2 Apr 2003 v Turkey	2–0	
20 Aug 2003 v Croatia	3–1	
6 Sep 2003 v Macedonia	2–1	
11 Oct 2003 v Turkey	0–0	
18 Feb 2004 v Portugal	1–1	
1 Jun 2004 v Japan	1–1	
5 Jun 2004 v Iceland	6–1	
17 Jun 2004 v Switzerland	3–0	
18 Aug 2004 v Ukraine	3–0	
8 Sep 2004 v Poland	2–1	
9 Feb 2005 v Holland	0–0	
26 Mar 2005 v N. Ireland	4–0	
30 Mar 2005 v Azerbaijan	2–0	

1097. Stephen Andrew Guppy
Winger
Born   Winchester, 29 March 1969
Clubs Wycombe Wanderers; Newcastle Utd; Port Vale; Leicester City; Glasgow Celtic; Leeds Utd; Stoke City

Caps	1	Result
	10 Oct 1999 v Belgium	2–1

1098. Frank Lampard Jnr
Midfielder
Born   Romford, 20 June 1978
Clubs West Ham Utd; Swansea City (on loan); Chelsea

Caps	38	Result	Goals
	10 Oct 1999 v Belgium	2–1	
	28 Feb 2001 v Spain	3–0	
	15 Aug 2001 v Holland	0–2	
	10 Nov 2001 v Sweden	1–1	
	13 Feb 2002 v Holland	1–1	
	27 Mar 2002 v Italy	1–2	
	17 Apr 2002 v Paraguay	4–0	
	12 Feb 2003 v Australia	1–3	
	22 May 2003 v South Africa	2–1	
	3 Jun 2003 v Serbia	2–1	
	11 Jun 2003 v Slovakia	2–1	
	20 Aug 2003 v Croatia	3–1	1
	6 Sep 2003 v Macedonia	2–1	
	10 Sep 2003 v Liechtenstein	2–0	
	11 Oct 2003 v Turkey	0–0	
	16 Nov 2003 v Denmark	2–3	
	18 Feb 2004 v Portugal	1–1	
	1 Jun 2004 v Japan	1–1	
	5 Jun 2004 v Iceland	6–1	1
	13 Jun 2004 v France	1–2	1
	17 Jun 2004 v Switzerland	3–0	
	21 Jun 2004 v Croatia	4–2	1
	24 Jun 2004 v Portugal	2–2	1
	18 Aug 2004 v Ukraine	3–0	
	4 Sep 2004 v Austria	2–2	1
	8 Sep 2004 v Poland	2–1	
	9 Oct 2004 v Wales	2–0	1
	13 Oct 2004 v Azerbaijan	1–0	
	17 Nov 2004 v Spain	0–1	
	9 Feb 2005 v Holland	0–0	
	26 Mar 2005 v N. Ireland	4–0	1
	30 Mar 2005 v Azerbaijan	2–0	
	17 Aug 2005 v Denmark	1–4	
	3 Sep 2005 v Wales	1–0	
	7 Sep 2005 v N. Ireland	0–1	
	8 Oct 2005 v Austria	1–0	1
	12 Oct 2005 v Poland	2–1	1
	12 Nov 2005 v Argentina	3–2	

1099. Steven George Gerrard
Midfielder

Born Huyton, 30 May 1980
Clubs Liverpool

Caps	39	Result	Goals
	31 May 2000 v Ukraine	2–0	
	7 Oct 2000 v Germany	0–1	
	24 Mar 2001 v Finland	2–1	
	25 May 2001 v Mexico	4–0	
	6 Jun 2001 v Greece	2–0	
	1 Sep 2001 v Germany	5–1	1
	5 Sep 2001 v Albania	2–0	
	6 Oct 2001 v Greece	2–2	
	13 Feb 2002 v Holland	1–1	
	17 Apr 2002 v Paraguay	4–0	
	7 Sep 2002 v Portugal	1–1	
	12 Oct 2002 v Slovakia	2–1	
	16 Oct 2002 v Macedonia	2–2	1
	29 Mar 2003 v Liechtenstein	2–0	
	2 Apr 2003 v Turkey	2–0	
	22 May 2003 v South Africa	2–1	
	3 Jun 2003 v Serbia	2–1	1
	11 Jun 2003 v Slovakia	2–1	
	20 Aug 2003 v Croatia	3–1	
	10 Sep 2003 v Liechtenstein	2–0	
	11 Oct 2003 v Turkey	0–0	
	31 Mar 2004 v Sweden	0–1	
	1 Jun 2004 v Japan	1–1	
	5 Jun 2004 v Iceland	6–1	
	13 Jun 2004 v France	1–2	
	17 Jun 2004 v Switzerland	3–0	1
	21 Jun 2004 v Croatia	4–2	
	24 Jun 2004 v Portugal	2–2	
	18 Aug 2004 v Ukraine	3–0	
	4 Sep 2004 v Austria	2–2	1
	8 Sep 2004 v Poland	2–1	
	9 Feb 2005 v Holland	0–0	
	26 Mar 2005 v N. Ireland	4–0	
	30 Mar 2005 v Azerbaijan	1–0	
	17 Aug 2005 v Denmark	1–4	
	3 Sep 2005 v Wales	1–0	
	7 Sep 2005 v N. Ireland	0–1	
	8 Oct 2005 v Austria	1–0	
	12 Nov 2005 v Argentina	3–2	

1100. Gareth Barry
Defender

Born Hastings, 23 February 1981
Clubs Aston Villa

Caps	8	Result
	31 May 2000 v Ukraine	2–0
	3 Jun 2000 v Malta	2–1
	2 Sep 2000 v France	1–1
	7 Oct 2000 v Germany	0–1
	11 Oct 2000 v Finland	0–0
	15 Nov 2000 v Italy	0–1
	22 May 2003 v South Africa	2–1
	3 Jun 2003 v Serbia	2–1

1101. Richard Ian Wright
Goalkeeper

Born Ipswich, 5 November 1977
Clubs Ipswich Town; Arsenal; Everton

Caps	2	Result
	3 Jun 2000 v Malta	2–1
	15 Aug 2001 v Holland	0–2

1102. Seth Art Maurice Johnson
Midfielder

Born Birmingham, 12 March 1979
Clubs Crewe Alexandra; Derby County; Leeds Utd

Caps	1	Result
	15 Nov 2000 v Italy	0–1

1103. Christopher George Robin Powell
Left back

Born Lambeth, 8 September 1969
Clubs Crystal Palace; Aldershot (on loan); Southend Utd;
Derby County; Charlton Athletic; West Ham Utd

Caps	5	Result
	28 Feb 2001 v Spain	3–0
	24 Mar 2001 v Finland	2–1
	25 May 2001 v Mexico	4–0
	15 Aug 2001 v Holland	0–2
	13 Feb 2002 v Holland	1–1

1104. Michael John Ball
Defender

Born Liverpool, 2 October 1979
Clubs Everton; Glasgow Rangers

Caps	1	Result
	28 Feb 2001 v Spain	3–0

1105. Gavin Peter McCann
Midfielder

Born Blackpool, 10 January 1978
Clubs Everton; Sunderland; Aston Villa

Caps	1	Result
	28 Feb 2001 v Spain	3–0

1106. Ashley Cole
Left back

Born Stepney, 20 December 1980
Clubs Arsenal; Crystal Palace (on loan)

Caps	44	Result
	28 Mar 2001 v Albania	3–1
	25 May 2001 v Mexico	4–0
	6 Jun 2001 v Greece	2–0
	15 Aug 2001 v Holland	0–2
	1 Sep 2001 v Germany	5–1
	5 Sep 2001 v Albania	2–0
	6 Oct 2001 v Greece	2–2
	21 May 2002 v South Korea	1–1
	2 Jun 2002 v Sweden	1–1
	7 Jun 2002 v Argentina	1–0
	12 Jun 2002 v Nigeria	0–0
	15 Jun 2002 v Denmark	3–0
	21 Jun 2002 v Brazil	1–2
	7 Sep 2002 v Portugal	1–1
	12 Oct 2002 v Slovakia	2–1
	16 Oct 2002 v Macedonia	2–2
	12 Feb 2003 v Australia	1–3
	3 Jun 2003 v Serbia	2–1
	11 Jun 2003 v Slovakia	2–1
	20 Aug 2003 v Croatia	3–1
	6 Sep 2003 v Macedonia	2–1
	11 Oct 2003 v Turkey	0–0
	16 Nov 2003 v Denmark	2–3
	18 Feb 2004 v Portugal	1–1
	1 Jun 2004 v Japan	1–1
	5 Jun 2004 v Iceland	6–1
	13 Jun 2004 v France	1–2
	17 Jun 2004 v Switzerland	3–0
	21 Jun 2004 v Croatia	4–2
	24 Jun 2004 v Portugal	2–2
	18 Aug 2004 v Ukraine	3–0
	4 Sep 2004 v Austria	2–2
	8 Sep 2004 v Poland	2–1
	9 Oct 2004 v Wales	2–0
	13 Oct 2004 v Azerbaijan	1–0
	17 Nov 2004 v Spain	0–1
	9 Feb 2005 v Holland	0–0
	26 Mar 2005 v N. Ireland	4–0
	30 Mar 2005 v Azerbaijan	2–0
	28 May 2005 v USA	2–1
	31 May 2005 v Colombia	3–2
	17 Aug 2005 v Denmark	1–4
	3 Sep 2005 v Wales	1–0
	7 Sep 2005 v N. Ireland	0–1

1107. Michael Carrick
Midfielder
Born Wallsend, 28 July 1981
Clubs West Ham Utd; Swindon Town (on loan);
Birmingham City (on loan); Tottenham Hotspur

Caps	4	*Result*
	25 May 2001 v Mexico	4–0
	15 Aug 2001 v Holland	0–2
	28 May 2005 v USA	2–1
	31 May 2005 v Colombia	3–2

1108. Joseph John Cole
Midfielder
Born Islington, 8 November 1981
Clubs West Ham Utd; Chelsea

Caps	29	*Result*	*Goals*
	25 May 2001 v Mexico	4–0	
	15 Aug 2001 v Holland	0–2	
	27 Mar 2002 v Italy	1–2	
	17 Apr 2002 v Paraguay	4–0	
	21 May 2002 v South Korea	1–1	
	26 May 2002 v Cameroon	2–2	
	2 Jun 2002 v Sweden	1–1	
	7 Sep 2002 v Portugal	1–1	
	22 May 2003 v South Africa	2–1	
	3 Jun 2003 v Serbia	2–1	1
	20 Aug 2003 v Croatia	3–1	
	10 Sep 2003 v Liechtenstein	2–0	
	16 Nov 2003 v Denmark	2–3	1
	18 Feb 2004 v Portugal	1–1	
	31 Mar 2004 v Sweden	0–1	
	1 Jun 2004 v Japan	1–1	
	5 Jun 2004 v Iceland	6–1	
	4 Sep 2004 v Austria	2–2	
	13 Oct 2004 v Azerbaijan	1–0	
	26 Mar 2005 v N. Ireland	4–0	1
	30 Mar 2005 v Azerbaijan	2–0	
	28 May 2005 v USA	2–1	
	31 May 2005 v Colombia	3–2	
	17 Aug 2005 v Denmark	1–4	
	3 Sep 2005 v Wales	1–0	1
	7 Sep 2005 v N. Ireland	0–1	
	8 Oct 2005 v Austria	1–0	
	12 Oct 2005 v Poland	2–1	
	12 Nov 2005 v Argentina	3–2	

1109. Daniel John Mills
Right back
Born Norwich, 18 May 1977
Clubs Norwich City; Charlton Athletic; Leeds Utd;
Middlesbrough (on loan); Manchester City

Caps	19	*Result*
	25 May 2001 v Mexico	4–0
	15 Aug 2001 v Holland	0–2
	10 Nov 2001 v Sweden	1–1
	27 Mar 2002 v Italy	1–2
	17 Apr 2002 v Paraguay	4–0
	21 May 2002 v South Korea	1–1
	26 May 2002 v Cameroon	2–2
	2 Jun 2002 v Sweden	1–1
	7 Jun 2002 v Argentina	1–0
	12 Jun 2002 v Nigeria	0–0
	15 Jun 2002 v Denmark	3–0
	21 Jun 2002 v Brazil	1–2
	7 Sep 2002 v Portugal	1–1
	12 Feb 2003 v Australia	1–3
	22 May 2003 v South Africa	2–1
	3 Jun 2003 v Serbia	2–1
	11 Jun 2003 v Slovakia	2–1
	20 Aug 2003 v Croatia	3–1
	18 Feb 2004 v Portugal	1–1

1110. Alan Smith
Midfielder/Forward
Born Rothwell, 28 October 1980
Clubs Leeds Utd; Manchester Utd

Caps	15	*Result*	*Goals*
	25 May 2001 v Mexico	4–0	
	6 Jun 2001 v Greece	2–0	
	15 Aug 2001 v Holland	0–2	
	7 Sep 2002 v Portugal	1–1	1
	12 Oct 2002 v Slovakia	2–1	
	16 Oct 2002 v Macedonia	2–2	
	18 Feb 2004 v Portugal	1–1	
	31 Mar 2004 v Sweden	0–1	
	18 Aug 2004 v Ukraine	3–0	
	4 Sep 2004 v Austria	2–2	
	9 Oct 2004 v Wales	2–0	
	13 Oct 2004 v Azerbaijan	1–0	
	17 Nov 2004 v Spain	0–1	
	28 May 2005 v USA	2–1	
	31 May 2005 v Colombia	3–2	

1111. Owen Hargreaves
Midfielder
Born Calgary, Canada, 20 January 1981
Clubs Bayern Munich

Caps	29	*Result*
	15 Aug 2001 v Holland	0–2
	1 Sep 2001 v Germany	5–1
	27 Mar 2002 v Italy	1–2
	17 Apr 2002 v Paraguay	4–0
	21 May 2002 v South Korea	1–1
	26 May 2002 v Cameroon	2–2
	2 Jun 2002 v Sweden	1–1
	7 Jun 2002 v Argentina	1–0
	7 Sep 2002 v Portugal	1–1
	12 Oct 2002 v Slovakia	2–1
	12 Feb 2003 v Australia	1–3
	3 Jun 2003 v Serbia	2–1
	11 Jun 2003 v Slovakia	2–1
	6 Sep 2003 v Macedonia	2–1
	10 Sep 2003 v Liechtenstein	2–0
	18 Feb 2004 v Portugal	1–1
	31 Mar 2004 v Sweden	0–1
	1 Jun 2004 v Japan	1–1
	5 Jun 2004 v Iceland	6–1
	13 Jun 2004 v France	1–2
	17 Jun 2004 v Switzerland	3–0
	24 Jun 2004 v Portugal	2–2
	8 Sep 2004 v Poland	2–1
	9 Oct 2004 v Wales	2–0
	9 Feb 2005 v Holland	0–0
	26 Mar 2005 v N. Ireland	4–0
	17 Aug 2005 v Denmark	1–4
	3 Sep 2005 v Wales	1–0
	7 Sep 2005 v N. Ireland	0–1

1112. Trevor Lloyd Sinclair
Midfielder
Born Dulwich, 2 March 1973
Clubs Blackpool; Queen's Park Rangers; West Ham Utd;
Manchester City

Caps	12	*Result*
	10 Nov 2001 v Sweden	1–1
	27 Mar 2002 v Italy	1–2
	17 Apr 2002 v Paraguay	4–0
	21 May 2002 v South Korea	1–1
	26 May 2002 v Cameroon	2–2
	7 Jun 2002 v Argentina	1–0
	12 Jun 2002 v Nigeria	0–0
	15 Jun 2002 v Denmark	3–0
	21 Jun 2002 v Brazil	1–2
	7 Sep 2002 v Portugal	1–1
	22 May 2003 v South Africa	2–1
	20 Aug 2003 v Croatia	3–1

1113. Daniel Benjamin Murphy
Midfielder
Born Chester, 18 March 197?
Clubs Crewe Alexandra; Liverpool; Charlton Athletic

Caps 9	Result	Goals
10 Nov 2001 v Sweden	1–1	
27 Mar 2002 v Italy	1–2	
17 Apr 2002 v Paraguay	4–0	1
21 May 2002 v South Korea	1–1	
7 Sep 2002 v Portugal	1–1	
12 Feb 2003 v Australia	1–3	
29 Mar 2003 v Liechtenstein	2–0	
20 Aug 2003 v Croatia	3–1	
16 Nov 2003 v Denmark	2–3	

1114. Wayne Michael Bridge
Left back
Born Southampton, 5 August 1980
Clubs Southampton; Chelsea

Caps 21	Result
13 Feb 2002 v Holland	1–1
27 Mar 2002 v Italy	1–2
17 Apr 2002 v Paraguay	4–0
21 May 2002 v South Korea	1–1
26 May 2002 v Cameroon	2–2
7 Jun 2002 v Argentina	1–0
12 Jun 2002 v Nigeria	0–0
7 Sep 2002 v Portugal	1–1
16 Oct 2002 v Macedonia	2–2
29 Mar 2003 v Liechtenstein	2–0
2 Apr 2003 v Turkey	2–0
3 Jun 2003 v Serbia	2–1
20 Aug 2003 v Croatia	3–1
10 Sep 2003 v Liechtenstein	2–0
16 Nov 2003 v Denmark	2–3
18 Feb 2004 v Portugal	1–1
5 Jun 2004 v Iceland	6–1
4 Sep 2004 v Austria	2–2
7 Sep 2004 v Poland	2–1
17 Nov 2004 v Spain	0–1
12 Nov 2005 v Argentina	3–2

1115. Michael Ricketts
Forward
Born Birmingham, 4 December 1978
Clubs Walsall; Bolton Wanderers; Middlesbrough; Leeds Utd; Stoke City (on loan); Cardiff City (on loan)

Caps 1	Result
13 Feb 2002 v Holland	1–1

1116. Darius Vassell
Forward
Born Birmingham, 13 June 1980
Clubs Aston Villa; Manchester City

Caps 22	Result	Goals
13 Feb 2002 v Holland	1–1	1
27 Mar 2002 v Italy	1–2	
17 Apr 2002 v Paraguay	4–0	1
21 May 2002 v South Korea	1–1	
26 May 2002 v Cameroon	2–2	1
2 Jun 2002 v Sweden	1–1	
12 Jun 2002 v Nigeria	0–0	
21 Jun 2002 v Brazil	1–2	
16 Oct 2002 v Macedonia	2–2	
12 Feb 2003 v Australia	1–3	
2 Apr 2003 v Turkey	2–0	1
22 May 2003 v South Africa	2–1	
3 Jun 2003 v Serbia	2–1	
11 Jun 2003 v Slovakia	2–1	
11 Oct 2003 v Turkey	0–0	
31 Mar 2004 v Sweden	0–1	
1 Jun 2004 v Japan	1–1	
5 Jun 2004 v Iceland	6–1	2
13 Jun 2004 v France	1–2	
17 Jun 2004 v Switzerland	3–0	
21 Jun 2004 v Croatia	4–2	
24 Jun 2004 v Portugal	2–2	

1117. Ledley Brenton King
Defender
Born Stepney, 12 October 1980
Clubs Tottenham Hotspur

Caps 15	Result	Goals
27 Mar 2002 v Italy	1–2	
12 Feb 2003 v Australia	1–3	
18 Feb 2004 v Portugal	1–1	1
1 Jun 2004 v Japan	1–1	
5 Jun 2004 v Iceland	6–1	
13 Jun 2004 v France	1–2	
21 Jun 2004 v Croatia	4–2	
18 Aug 2004 v Ukraine	3–0	
4 Sep 2004 v Austria	2–2	
8 Sep 2004 v Poland	2–1	
9 Oct 2004 v Wales	2–0	
13 Oct 2004 v Azerbaijan	1–0	
8 Oct 2005 v Austria	1–0	
12 Oct 2005 v Poland	2–1	
12 Nov 2005 v Argentina	3–2	

1118. Lee David Bowyer
Midfielder
Born London, 3 January 1977
Clubs Charlton Athletic; Leeds Utd; West Ham Utd; Newcastle Utd

Caps 1	Result
7 Sep 2002 v Portugal	1–1

1119. David John Ian Dunn
Midfielder
Born Blackburn, 27 December 1979
Clubs Blackburn Rovers; Birmingham City

Caps 1	Result
7 Sep 2002 v Portugal	1–1

1120. James Scott Beattie
Forward
Born Lancaster, 27 February 1978
Clubs Blackburn Rovers; Southampton; Everton

Caps 5	Result
12 Feb 2003 v Australia	1–3
3 Jun 2003 v Serbia	2–
20 Aug 2003 v Croatia	3–1
10 Sep 2003 v Liechtenstein	2–0
16 Nov 2003 v Denmark	2–3

1121. Francis Jeffers
Forward
Born Liverpool, 25 January 1981
Clubs Everton; Arsenal; Charlton Athletic; Everton (on loan)

Caps 1	Result	Goals
12 Feb 2003 v Australia	1–3	1

1122. Jermaine Anthony Jenas
Midfielder
Born Nottingham, 18 February 1983
Clubs Nottingham Forest; Newcastle Utd; Tottenham Hotspur

Caps 14	Result
12 Feb 2003 v Australia	1–3
22 May 2003 v South Africa	2–1
3 Jun 2003 v Serbia	2–1
16 Nov 2003 v Denmark	2–3
18 Feb 2004 v Portugal	1–1
31 Mar 2004 v Sweden	0–1
18 Aug 2004 v Ukraine	3–0
13 Oct 2004 v Azerbaijan	1–0
17 Nov 2004 v Spain	0–1
9 Feb 2005 v Holland	0–0
28 May 2005 v USA	2–1
31 May 2005 v Colombia	3–2
17 Aug 2005 v Denmark	1–4
12 Oct 2005 v Poland	2–1

1123. Paul William Robinson
Goalkeeper
Born   Beverley, 15 October 1979
Clubs Leeds Utd; Tottenham Hotspur
Caps   18

	Result
12 Feb 2003 v Australia	1–3
22 May 2003 v South Africa	2–1
20 Aug 2003 v Croatia	3–1
16 Nov 2003 v Denmark	2–3
5 Jun 2004 v Iceland	6–1
8 Sep 2004 v Poland	2–1
9 Oct 2004 v Wales	2–0
13 Oct 2004 v Azerbaijan	1–0
17 Nov 2004 v Spain	0–1
9 Feb 2005 v Holland	0–0
26 Mar 2005 v N. Ireland	4–0
30 Mar 2005 v Azerbaijan	2–0
17 Aug 2005 v Denmark	1–4
3 Sep 2005 v Wales	1–0
7 Sep v N. Ireland	0–1
8 Oct 2005 v Austria	1–0
12 Oct 2005 v Poland	2–1
12 Nov 2005 v Argentina	3–2

1124. Wayne Rooney
Forward
Born   Croxteth, 24 October 1985
Clubs Everton; Manchester Utd
Caps   28

	Result	Goals
12 Feb 2003 v Australia	1–3	
29 Mar 2003 v Liechtenstein	2–0	
2 Apr 2003 v Turkey	2–0	
3 Jun 2003 v Serbia	2–1	
11 Jun 2003 v Slovakia	2–1	
6 Sep 2003 v Macedonia	2–1	1
10 Sep 2003 v Liechtenstein	2–0	1
11 Oct 2003 v Turkey	0–0	
16 Nov 2003 v Denmark	2–3	1
18 Feb 2004 v Portugal	1–1	
31 Mar 2004 v Sweden	0–1	
1 Jun 2004 v Japan	1–1	
5 Jun 2004 v Iceland	6–1	2
13 Jun 2004 v France	1–2	
17 Jun 2004 v Switzerland	3–0	2
21 Jun 2004 v Croatia	4–2	2
24 Jun 2004 v Portugal	2–2	
9 Oct 2004 v Wales	2–0	
13 Oct 2004 v Azerbaijan	1–0	
17 Nov 2004 v Spain	0–1	
9 Feb 2005 v Holland	0–0	
26 Mar 2005 v N. Ireland	4–0	
30 Mar 2005 v Azerbaijan	2–0	
17 Aug 2005 v Denmark	1–4	1
3 Sep 2005 v Wales	0–0	
7 Sep 2005 v N. Ireland	0–1	
12 Oct 2005 v Poland	2–1	
12 Nov 2005 v Argentina	3–2	1

1125. Paul Martyn Konchesky
Defender
Born   Barking, 15 May 1981
Clubs Charlton Athletic; Tottenham Hotspur (on loan), West Ham Utd
Caps   2

	Result
12 Feb 2003 v Australia	1–3
12 Nov 2005 v Argentina	3–2

1126. Matthew James Upson
Central defender
Born   Stowmarket, 18 April 1979
Clubs Luton Town; Arsenal; Nottingham Forest (on loan); Crystal Palace (on loan); Reading (on loan); Birmingham City
Caps   7

	Result
22 May 2003 v South Africa	2–1

	Result
3 Jun 2003 v Serbia	2–1
11 Jun 2003 v Slovakia	2–1
20 Aug 2003 v Croatia	3–1
10 Sep 2003 v Liechtenstein	2–0
16 Nov 2003 v Denmark	2–3
17 Nov 2004 v Spain	0–1

1127. John George Terry
Central defender
Born   Barking, 7 December 1980
Clubs Chelsea; Nottingham Forest (on loan)
Caps   21

	Result
3 Jun 2003 v Serbia	2–1
20 Aug 2003 v Croatia	3–1
6 Sep 2003 v Macedonia	2–1
10 Sep 2003 v Liechtenstein	2–0
11 Oct 2003 v Turkey	0–0
16 Nov 2003 v Denmark	2–3
31 Mar 2004 v Sweden	0–1
1 Jun 2004 v Japan	1–1
17 Jun 2004 v Switzerland	3–0
21 Jun 2004 v Croatia	4–2
24 Jun 2004 v Portugal	2–2
18 Aug 2004 v Ukraine	3–0
4 Sep 2004 v Austria	2–2
8 Sep 2004 v Poland	2–1
17 Nov 2004 v Spain	0–1
26 Mar 2005 v N. Ireland	4–0
30 Mar 2005 v Azerbaijan	2–0
17 Aug 2005 v Denmark	1–4
8 Oct 2005 v Austria	1–0
12 Oct 2005 v Poland	2–1
12 Nov 2005 v Argentina	3–2

1128. Glen McLeod Johnson
Defender
Born   London, 23 August 1984
Clubs West Ham Utd; Millwall (on loan); Chelsea
Caps   5

	Result
16 Nov 2003 v Denmark	2–3
18 Aug 2004 v Ukraine	3–0
28 May 2005 v USA	2–1
31 May 2005 v Colombia	3–2
17 Aug 2005 v Denmark	1–4

1129. Scott Matthew Parker
Midfielder
Born   Lambeth, 13 October 1980
Clubs Charlton Athletic; Norwich City (on loan); Chelsea; Newcastle Utd
Caps   2

	Result
16 Nov 2003 v Denmark	2–3
31 Mar 2004 v Sweden	0–1

 DID YOU KNOW...?

Wayne Rooney became the youngest England cap – aged 17 years and 111 days – in the 3–1 defeat by Australia at Upton Park in February 2003.

1130. Jermain Colin Defoe
Forward
Born   Beckton, 7 October 1982
Clubs West Ham Utd; Bournemouth (on loan); Tottenham Hotspur
Caps   15

	Result	Goals
31 Mar 2004 v Sweden	0–1	
5 Jun 2004 v Iceland	6–1	
18 Aug 2004 v Ukraine	3–0	
4 Sep 2004 v Austria	2–2	

8 Sep 2004 v Poland	2–1	1
9 Oct 2004 v Wales	2–0	
13 Oct 2004 v Azerbaijan	1–0	
17 Nov 2004 v Spain	0–1	
26 Mar 2005 v N. Ireland	4–0	
30 Mar 2004 v Azerbaijan	2–0	
28 May 2005 v USA	2–1	
31 May 2005 v Colombia	3–2	
17 Aug 2005 v Denmark	1–4	
3 Sep 2005 v Wales	0–0	
7 Sep 2005 v N. Ireland	0–1	

1131. Anthony Gardner
Defender

Born	Stone, 19 September 1980	
Clubs	Port Vale; Tottenham Hotspur	
Caps	1	*Result*
	31 Mar 2004 v Sweden	0–1

1132. Alan Thompson
Midfielder

Born	Newcastle, 22 December 1973	
Clubs	Newcastle Utd; Bolton Wanderers; Aston Villa; Glasgow Celtic	
Caps	1	*Result*
	31 Mar 2004 v Sweden	0–1

1133. Shaun Wright-Phillips
Midfielder/Forward

Born	Greenwich, 25 October 1981		
Clubs	Manchester City; Chelsea		
Caps	7	*Result*	*Goals*
	18 Aug 2004 v Ukraine	3–0	1
	13 Oct 2004 v Azerbaijan	1–0	
	17 Nov 2004 v Spain	0–1	
	9 Feb 2005 v Holland	0–0	
	3 Sep 2005 v Wales	0–0	
	7 Sep 2005 v N. Ireland	0–1	
	12 Oct 2005 v Poland	2–1	

1134. Stewart Downing
Midfielder

Born	Middlesbrough, 22 July 1984	
Clubs	Middlesbrough; Sunderland (on loan)	
Caps	1	*Result*
	9 Feb 2005 v Holland	0–0

1135. Andrew Johnson
Forward

Born	Bedford, 10 February 1981	
Clubs	Birmingham City; Crystal Palace	
Caps	2	*Result*
	9 Feb 2005 v Holland	0–0
	28 May 2005 v USA	2–1

1136. Kieran Edward Richardson
Midfielder

Born	Greenwich, 21 October 1984
Clubs	Manchester United; West Bromwich Albion (on loan)

Caps	4	*Result* *Goals*
	28 May 2005 v USA	2–1 2
	31 May 2005 v Colombia	3–2
	3 Sep 2005 v Wales	0–0
	8 Oct 2005 v Austria	1–0

1137. Zatyiah Knight
Defender

Born	Solihull, 2 May 1980	
Clubs	Peterborough Utd (on loan); Fulham	
Caps	2	*Result*
	28 May 2005 v USA	2–1
	31 May 2005 v Colombia	3–2

1138. Luke Paul Young
Defender

Born	Harlow, 19 July 1979	
Clubs	Tottenham Hotspur; Charlton Athletic	
Caps	7	*Result*
	28 May 2005 v USA	2–1
	31 May 2005 v Colombia	3–2
	3 Sep 2005 v Wales	0–0
	7 Sep 2005 v N. Ireland	0–1
	8 Oct 2005 v Austria	1–0
	12 Oct 2005 v Poland	2–1
	12 Nov 2005 v Argentina	3–2

1139. Peter James Crouch
Forward

Born	Macclesfield, 30 January 1981	
Clubs	Tottenham Hotspur; Queen's Park Rangers; Portsmouth; Aston Villa; Norwich City (on loan); Southampton; Liverpool	
Caps	4	*Result*
	31 May 2005 v Colombia	3–2
	8 Oct 2005 v Austria	1–0
	12 Oct 2005 v Poland	2–1
	12 Nov 2005 v Argentina	3–2

1140. Robert Paul Green
Goalkeeper

Born	Chertsey, 18 January 1980	
Clubs	Norwich City	
Caps	1	*Result*
	31 May 2005 v Colombia	3–2

⚽ **DID YOU KNOW...?**

Standing at a height of 6 feet 7 inches, Peter Crouch became England's tallest ever international when he made his debut against Colombia in New Jersey on 31 May 2005.

3 ENGLAND'S MANAGERS

EARLY DAYS: INTERNATIONAL SELECTION COMMITTEE

For England's first full international match in November 1872, the team was chosen by Charles Alcock, Secretary of the Football Association, from applications tendered by players, following the advertisement placed in *The Sportsman* newspaper. This allowed any footballer – all of whom were amateurs – to apply for a place in the national team. And thus applications came from sides such as the 1st Surrey Rifles (W. J. Maynard) and the Wanderers (Reginald de Courtney Welch), the FA Cup's first winners in 1872.

In the early years of the games against Scotland, clubs were asked to nominate players for the England side and then a series of trial matches would take place in order to select the final side. The trial system lasted until 1888 – the year the Football League began – when the Football Association found a typically British method for team selection by forming a committee.

The International Selection Committee (ISC) initially comprised seven members taken from the FA's board. At its most preposterous height in the 1950s, the Committee consisted of over thirty members. In general these men were administrators who had originally featured on the boards of football clubs and later acquired the status of County/Regional FA Representatives, before being elected to the FA board. The FA created many committees, which meant that the International Selection members also appeared on other Association committees.

The ISC operated in a quite absurd fashion. Their method was to consider each position on the team sheet and simply vote, by majority decision, on which person would play there. The problem was that these amateur selectors, who for the most part had never even played football, had no understanding as to whether the eleven chosen players could actually work well together as a team.

The Committee was very erratic and unpredictable in team choice and seemed oblivious to the merits of sticking with a settled side. There is also the suggestion that committee members showed less than impartial judgement, as certain selected players appeared to emanate from clubs who had members on the ISC. The proliferation of Third Division (South) players during the 1920s and 1930s provides clear evidence of this bias.

Furthermore, there is also a long list of players who only earned a single cap because either the match venue was the player's home ground and he was selected as the token clubman to attract the local support, or else his chairman, a member of the ISC, wanted to boost his club's income by boasting an England international.

A good example of the Committee's inconsistent selection policy is the case of Frank Osborne, a travel clerk by profession, who played amateur football with Bromley. The South African-born forward was signed by Fulham, who were then a rather mediocre Second Division club, and within a month of arriving at Craven Cottage, in October 1922, he had won the first of his four caps for England against Ireland. The three remaining caps were earned in May 1923, December 1924 and May 1926 respectively.

England's World Cup campaigns after the Second World War were also affected by the ISC. For example, the 1950 squad for Brazil was selected by just three men, one of whom, FA Chairman Arthur Drewry, was voted as 'member-in-charge', which meant that he made his team selection while out in Brazil. In 1954 seven ISC members chose the original squad of twenty-three, which the new chairman of the FA Mr H. Shentall and manager Walter Winterbottom managed to whittle down to seventeen. The FA then sent five members-in-charge for team selection in Switzerland. For the 1958 tournament, it took another seven members to vote for the preparation squad of forty players, and six (including five of the original seven) to select both the final twenty-two and the actual teams themselves. It is therefore not surprising that Walter Winterbottom had his work cut out.

Committees work by meetings and if any committee member is absent, an apology is read and the discussion continues with the business of the day. The upshot of this in the early days of English football was that different groups of men voted for different teams, while on tours, the members-in-charge changed each time. The shambolic organization and general overmanning destroyed any hope of continuity for England's national team.

Walter Winterbottom also had to fight against the committee mentality, though he did manage, at least, to offer his recommendations. However, it was not until Alf Ramsey was appointed in 1963, with the condition of autonomy over team affairs and choice of players, that the International Selection Committee was finally laid to rest.

WALTER WINTERBOTTOM (1946–62)

Walter Winterbottom was England's first Team Manager and the FA's Director of Coaching. The position of national Team Manager had been put forward and instigated by Stanley Rous, then FA Secretary, during the war, and Winterbottom was duly appointed in the first year of peacetime.

Winterbottom had been a centre half with Manchester United, but he had never quite attained international status. By profession he was a qualified PE teacher, and during the war had served his country in the RAF, rising to the rank of Wing Commander. Although Winterbottom lacked previous managerial experience, he gained a reputation of being both a good administrator and an outstanding coach. In his role of Director of Coaching he created and ran the FA's coaching courses, from which successful students gained the coveted FA Coaching Badge. Among Winterbottom's pupils were future England managers Ron Greenwood and Bobby Robson.

The role of Team Manager in Winterbottom's day differed considerably from the modern-day position. His role was essentially limited to that of a coach, because team selection still remained the prerogative of the FA's International Selection Committee. It was not until 1953 that the affable and scholarly Winterbottom was allowed to make any recommendations to the ISC.

Unfortunately for Winterbottom, he presided over three of the lowest moments in the history of English football when the team lost to the United States in 1950 and the Hungarians in 1953 and 1954. They also had a poor World Cup record under his management, winning just three out of fourteen games in four finals. However, Winterbottom did have the opportunity of working with the great English players of the forties, fifties and sixties. He helped to bring stability to the England set-up by introducing Schoolboy, Youth, Under-23 and 'B' international teams. Among the players under his charge were Billy Wright, Stanley Matthews, Tom Finney, Nat Lofthouse and Wilf Mannion, as well as future England bosses Alf Ramsey, Don Revie and Bobby Robson, who were selected during his leadership. Towards the end of his managership, Winterbottom also introduced four players who were to feature prominently in England's future success: Bobby Charlton, Jimmy Greaves, Bobby Moore and Ray Wilson.

The statistics suggest that Walter Winterbottom's England won the majority of the games they played, scoring nearly double the goals they conceded, but there was never any silverware to show for their success, nor any likelihood of it.

When he was defeated in a vote to become FA Secretary, to replace Stanley Rous, who was moving to FIFA after twenty-seven years, Winterbottom moved on, later becoming Director of the Sports Council and receiving a knighthood and CBE for his services to football. On paper his record as the first England manager doesn't look too outstanding, but successors Alf Ramsey and Ron Greenwood both believed him to be an influential figure on the tactical structure of the game.

ENGLAND RECORD:

P	W	D	L	F	A	SUCCESS RATE
139	78	33	28	383	196	68%

ALF RAMSEY (1963–74)

Alf Ramsey was not the FA's first choice for the job of England manager. The vacant post had first been offered to Jimmy Adamson, assistant coach to Walter Winterbottom, but he had declined the promotion. Ramsey chose to accept the job, however, and uttered a prophecy that he would win England the World Cup.

He had played his football with Southampton and Tottenham Hotspur, winning the Second Division title and the Football League Championship with the North London club in successive seasons in 1950 and 1951. He had also won thirty-two England caps, playing in the 1950 World Cup – where he experienced the shock 1–0 defeat by the United States – and, in his final match, England lost 6–3 to Hungary, which was the first time they had been defeated by non-British opposition at home. Ramsey scored England's third goal from the penalty spot.

The appointment of Alf Ramsey as England manager came on the back of his fantastic managerial success with Ipswich Town. He had guided the Suffolk club out of the Second Division as champions in 1961, and the following season led them to the top of Division One, to take a successive League title.

Ramsey's acceptance of the England job was on the condition that he have total control over team selection. His first official match in charge was in February 1963 – a European Championship first-round tie with France in Paris, which England lost 5–2. From that inauspicious start, Ramsey set about fulfilling his prophecy and duly took England to the 1966 World Cup Final, where the host nation beat West Germany 4–2 after extra time, with a hat-trick from Geoff Hurst and a goal by Martin Peters. The team of England '66 was dubbed the 'Wingless Wonders'.

Although he was an unemotional man in public – save for his 'animals' outburst after the Argentina game at Wembley in 1966 – Ramsey was passionate about football and England. He protected his players and was prepared to bear the brunt of any criticism and take ultimate blame for his players' mistakes. Ramsey never really hit it off with the press, though, and so, when things did go against him, there were no critics who would openly support him.

After their 1966 success, England reached the 1968 European Championship semi-final, where they were literally kicked out by a tough Yugoslavia side, losing 1–0. Two years later, the 1970 defence of the World Cup in Mexico had looked a realistic possibility until the quarter-final against West Germany, when the loss of goalkeeper Gordon Banks and the substitutional errors that followed allowed the Germans to win the game 3–2 after being two goals down.

Ramsey continued with his outmoded 4–3–3 formation and adopted a policy of expediency and functional tactics to achieve results, but in April 1972, another significant defeat by the Germans in the first leg of the European Championship quarter-final at Wembley left England with it all to do in Berlin. The second leg ended goalless with the result that Ramsey's tactical naivety was called into question. The failure to qualify for the 1974 World Cup Finals after an unlucky night of frustration against Poland in October 1973 brought the inevitable calls for his sacking, which the FA duly acted upon two matches later.

Having joined the board of Birmingham City after his England experience, Ramsey returned briefly to management in 1977 but, in his late fifties, he was afflicted with ill health and gave up the position after just six months. He later had a short spell as a consultant to Greek outfit Panathinaikos, before retiring to the modest house in Ipswich he had owned since the mid-1950s.

ENGLAND RECORD:

P	W	D	L	F	A	SUCCESS RATE
113	69	27	17	224	98	73%

JOE MERCER (1974)

Following Alf Ramsey's dismissal, the FA had to think very carefully about their next appointment for England's hot seat. For the interim period, meanwhile, a caretaker-manager was appointed – Joe Mercer – who was placed in charge for England's 1974 Home International Championship matches, the friendly against Argentina and the three-match end-of-season European tour behind the Iron Curtain.

As a player, Mercer lined up in the Football League Championship-winning teams of Everton (1939) and Arsenal (1948 and 1953). The cultured wing half also played in Arsenal's 1950 FA Cup Final triumph over Liverpool. Injury ended his playing days in 1955, whereupon he went into management with Sheffield United, then subsequently with Aston Villa, Manchester City and Coventry City. He guided Villa out of the Second Division in 1960 and achieved the same with Manchester City six years later. Under his leadership City also won the League Championship, FA Cup, League Cup and European Cup Winners' Cup, where the younger Malcolm Allison was Mercer's 'legs'.

After the sad and dismal ending to Ramsey's reign, Joe Mercer's arrival was a boost for the game's public image. His jovial character brought a smile to the face of English football. He led with cheerful informality and a genuine feeling for the players – even if he didn't always get their names right.

Mercer's seven-match spell saw England beat Wales and Northern Ireland, but Scotland proved too strong at Hampden Park. A Wembley friendly against Argentina finished 2–2, while visits to East Germany and Yugoslavia also ended all-square. Bulgaria were beaten by a goal from Frank Worthington, one of the flair players who responded well to Mercer's direction.

Joe Mercer never sought the post on a permanent basis, but his caretaker role proved invaluable to lightening the air before a new era under a different leader could begin. Following his England experience, Mercer served as a director at Coventry City from 1975 until 1981, and enjoyed a well-earned retirement in his native Merseyside until his death in 1990.

ENGLAND RECORD:

P	W	D	L	F	A	SUCCESS RATE
7	3	3	1	9	7	64%

DON REVIE (1974–7)

To the Football Association and to everyone else for that matter, Don Revie seemed the obvious choice for the new England manager. Since 1958, as player-manager and manager, he had built a formidable and successful club in the form of Leeds United, and was consequently deemed worthy of leading his country on the world stage.

Under Revie's guidance, Leeds had won promotion to the top flight as Second Division Champions in 1964, become Football League Champions twice in 1969 and 1974, and never been outside the top four since their promotion. In addition, the Yorkshire club had appeared in four FA Cup Finals (winning once in 1972), a Football League Cup Final (winners in 1968), European Fairs Cup Finals in 1968 and 1971 as winners, and losing finalists in the 1973 European Cup Winners' Cup competition – the most successful roll of achievement at that time. As a player, he had appeared for Leicester City, Hull City, Manchester City (with whom he won an FA Cup winners' medal in 1956) and Leeds United.

The Revie era was greeted with much optimism, but sadly ended in controversy, failure and remorse. Revie talked of full co-operation from the League clubs regarding player release, and ensured that fixtures scheduled before international matches were postponed. He adopted 'Land of Hope and Glory' as the team's anthem and ordered it to be sung before each of England's Wembley matches. His obsession with money persuaded him to believe that a wages increase (which he organized for the players) was the necessary incentive they needed to perform for England.

Revie was a scrupulous planner, to the point that dossiers were produced about England's opponents, drawing attention to their strengths and weaknesses. He allowed his players to engage in only bingo and carpet bowls as diversions from the pressures of international football. In all, Revie created a squad of confused and bemused players who slowly had their confidence eaten away.

The fact was that Revie used far too many players during his twenty-nine-match term of office. Of the fifty-two players he selected, over half of them were new caps, which clearly indicated that he was never really certain about his best team line-up.

Don Revie's England won just fourteen matches, including a 2–0 defeat of West Germany, the 5–1 thrashing of Scotland and a 5–0 victory over Cyprus, when Malcolm Macdonald scored all five goals. England failed to qualify for the 1976 European Championships, and on Revie's departure the side looked very unlikely to make it to Argentina for the 1978 World Cup.

In the summer of 1977, the *Daily Mail* broke the news that Revie had resigned. He had negotiated a lucrative contract with the United Arab Emirates while on a trip to see Finland, one of England's World Cup-qualifying opponents, while the England squad was in South America.

The FA imposed a ten-year ban on Revie for the manner in which he breached his contract after advocating the virtues of loyalty and commitment, but the High Court overturned the decision. Revie left an unfinished job and brought the confidence of the home side to its lowest ebb. The players had begun to hate playing at Wembley, added to which England faced an uphill struggle to qualify for the 1978 World Cup.

Revie died in May 1989, after a long battle against motor neurone disease, asking that his ashes be strewn over the Elland Road pitch.

ENGLAND RECORD:

P	W	D	L	F	A	SUCCESS RATE
29	14	8	7	49	25	62%

RON GREENWOOD (1977–82)

The thinking man's England manager, Ron Greenwood began his professional football career as a player with Chelsea, just after the Second World War. From Stamford Bridge he turned out for Bradford Park Avenue, Brentford, Chelsea (a second time – winning a League Championship medal in 1955) and Fulham.

Greenwood was far-sighted enough to see life after the end of his days as a player. He attended Walter Winterbottom's FA coaching course at Lilleshall to earn his FA Coaching badge and certificate, and through his diligence he became chief coach with the Middlesex FA and Sussex County FA, before becoming coach/manager for Eastbourne United, Oxford University, Walthamstow Avenue, Arsenal and West Ham United.

At Upton Park, Greenwood cultivated the skills of three young players who were to become instrumental in England's moment of glory in 1966 – Geoff Hurst, Bobby Moore and Martin Peters. Greenwood guided the Hammers to success in the FA Cup in 1964 and 1975, and in the European Cup Winners' Cup in 1965. Among his other achievements, Greenwood was in charge of the England Youth and Under-23 sides. He was also a member of FIFA's technical committee, and chairman of the League Secretaries and Managers Association.

Greenwood had previously been considered for the full England post as early as 1962–3, but back then the job went to Alf Ramsey. Eventually his success at club level was rewarded in August 1977, when he was appointed as caretaker-manager for England, before the post was made permanent later that year.

He improved football's image at home and created a coaching team that included Bobby Robson, Dave Sexton, Terry Venables, Don Howe, Howard Wilkinson, Brian Clough and Peter Taylor. He also re-introduced the 'B' international side. Although Greenwood failed in his immediate task of getting England to the 1978 World Cup Finals, he did go on to take the national side to the 1980 European Championships in Italy and the 1982 World Cup Finals in Spain. However, his bid to find consistency and a suitable tactical system brought an erratic run of results, which almost saw England eliminated from the latter competition, and caused Greenwood to consider retiring until the players, led by Ray Clemence, Kevin Keegan and Mick Mills, convinced him otherwise.

In Spain '82, despite not losing any of their five games, the England team was knocked out at the second-phase stage when a goalless draw with Spain in Madrid also brought Greenwood's tenure to an end. He had succeeded in putting England back on track, and taken the national side to two international tournament finals for the first time since 1970, and been the first England manager to progress beyond the World Cup qualification process since 1968.

Ron Greenwood became a director of Brighton and Hove Albion in 1983, maintaining some contact in retirement with the game he loved.

ENGLAND RECORD:

P	W	D	L	F	A	SUCCESS RATE
55	33	12	10	93	40	71%

BOBBY ROBSON (1982–90)

Bobby Robson was the natural successor to Ron Greenwood when he was promoted from manager of the 'B' squad. Like his predecessor, he had been influenced by Winterbottom's training course at Lilleshall and enlightened by the brilliance of the Hungarians in the 1950s. Robson, who played for both Fulham and West Bromwich Albion, had been an England international himself, making twenty appearances for his country, including seven caps at the 1958 and 1962 World Cup Finals.

His first sojourn into management was with the Vancouver Royals of Canada, which was a project shrouded in ridicule. The club enjoyed the services of two separate managers – the other was Ferenc Puskás – and, even more bizarrely, two sets of players. Fortunately, Fulham brought him back to England, and made him manager in January 1968, though he lasted less than a year before being removed by boardroom politics.

Unemployment followed until he applied for the vacancy of manager at Ipswich Town and was successful. As successor to Bill McGarry, Bobby Robson built up Ipswich Town into one of the nation's leading club sides in the seventies and early eighties. During this time they were the second most consistent club team behind Liverpool, and Robson led them to FA Cup glory in 1978 and UEFA Cup victory in 1981. It was also Robson who set up Ipswich's enviable youth scheme, which brought talented youngsters to the fore as First Division players, and was developed in reaction to the Suffolk club's inability to compete constantly in the transfer market.

Bobby Robson played a crucial role in catapulting a number of Ipswich players on to the international scene, including Terry Butcher, Kevin Beattie, Eric Gates, David Johnson, Mick Mills, Russell Osman, Brian Talbot, Trevor Whymark and Colin Viljoen for England, George Burley and John Wark for

Scotland, Allan Hunter for Northern Ireland, Les Tibbott for Wales and Brendan O'Callaghan for the Republic of Ireland.

Robson's eight turbulent years as national team manager began with England's failure to qualify for the 1984 European Championships in France, but success later followed as England reached the quarter-finals of the 1986 World Cup before falling victim to Diego Maradona's 'Hand of God'. There was more European disaster in the summer of 1988 during the European Championship Finals, when England slumped to straight defeats to the Republic of Ireland, Holland and the Soviet Union. This resulted in Robson becoming the first England manager to undergo 'trial by tabloid', one of the newspapers even offering its readers 'Robson Out' lapel badges.

Though pursued by Barcelona, who were eager to take him on as manager, he refused to give in to certain loudly expressed sections of public opinion, and instead persevered with the job in hand. Although Robson had already decided to step down after the 1990 World Cup Finals, in the event he bowed out on a high – the so near yet so far semi-final with West Germany, decided on penalties after a 1–1 extra-time scoreline.

Robson's reign had witnessed such unique talents as Gary Lineker and Paul Gascoigne grace the international stage, and it was no surprise when he later headed for Europe and found success first in Holland with PSV Eindhoven, then in Portugal with Sporting Lisbon and FC Porto, before Barcelona, the biggest club in the world, took him on as successor to Johann Cruyff. Knighted for his services to football, he later had a five-year spell as Newcastle United manager before being bounced out in August 2004.

For club and country, Bobby Robson always tried to strike the right balance between direct and possession football, while his enthusiasm, good humour and loyalty won him the deserved affection and respect of both players and fans.

ENGLAND RECORD:

P	W	D	L	F	A	SUCCESS RATE
95	47	30	18	154	60	65%

GRAHAM TAYLOR (1990–3)

Graham Taylor was the first manager for whom the FA had to pay a transfer fee, as he still had a year of his Aston Villa contract to run when the England job offer was made. Lawrie McMenemy, the former Southampton manager, was installed as his number two, but even with such an experienced hand on board and a track record with the youth, Under-21 and 'B' teams, Taylor's tenure was to be a troubled one.

The son of a sports journalist, Taylor had an undistinguished playing career as a fullback with Grimsby Town and Lincoln City before he was forced into early retirement by a hip injury. At the age of twenty-eight he took over the manager's job at Lincoln's Sincil Bank ground, where his meticulous planning helped the Imps win promotion to the Third Division. His qualities were spotted by Elton John, who took him to Watford, where Taylor overhauled the entire structure of the club, and transformed the Hornets' fortunes on the field by playing the 'long ball' game. Though it was certainly not pretty, Watford rose meteorically from the Fourth Division to the Second, where they spent two seasons before winning promotion to the top flight and finishing runners-up to Liverpool in their first season. In 1984, Taylor also guided the club to the FA Cup Final, where they lost 2–0 to Everton.

In 1987 he accepted the challenge of yet another rescue mission when he took over the reins at Aston Villa, who had just been relegated to the Second Division. Taylor ensured their return to the top flight the following season, and, in 1989–90, he steered them to second place behind Liverpool.

His three-and-a-half years in charge of the national team got off to a solid if somewhat unspectacular start, and it was to be a year before England tasted defeat – a record for any England manager. Under Taylor's leadership, the side reached the 1992 European Championship Finals in Sweden, thanks to a Gary Lineker-inspired draw in Poland, but the team's performance there was unsatisfactory – two 0–0 draws and a defeat. He also sparked a storm of criticism during England's 2–1 loss to Sweden when he decided that Lineker would take no further part in the game, despite the fact that the striker was still searching for the goal that would enable him to equal Bobby Charlton's goalscoring record.

The decision to take off a national treasure and replace him with Arsenal's Alan Smith marked the turning point in his relationship with both press and public. England slid from bad to worse over the next eighteen months and finally missed out on qualification for the 1994 World Cup after failing to beat either Holland or Norway at home or away. Even lowly San Marino managed to open the scoring against England after just nine seconds (the quickest goal ever in international football), thus underlining the feeling that Taylor's tactical chopping and changing had availed him little.

He had fallen on his own sword, though many disagreed with the tabloids' unjustifiable hate campaigns, one of the more bizarre of which involved printing a mocking caricature of him, complete with turnip-like features.

Following his eventual resignation in November 1993, Taylor then returned to the club scene whence he had come, managing Wolves first of all, and then both Watford and Aston Villa for a second time each.

ENGLAND RECORD:

P	W	D	L	F	A	SUCCESS RATE
38	18	13	7	62	32	64%

TERRY VENABLES (1994–6)

The England manager's job seemed tailor-made for Terry Venables – the only man to have represented England as a player at schoolboy, youth, amateur, Under-23 and full international level. Yet circumstances conspired to make his potentially the shortest permanent tenure on record, when he announced in January 1996 that he would not be leading England beyond the European Championships due to legal complications and allegations about his business interests.

Terry Venables's playing career spanned four London clubs from 1958 to 1976: Chelsea, Spurs, Queen's Park Rangers and Crystal Palace. During the early 1970s he went to secretarial college to learn how to type before co-writing a novel with Gordon Williams titled *They Used to Play on Grass*, as well as the TV detective series *Hazell*. He also designed a board game, and his early business interests included a company called Thingummywigs, which made wigs for women to wear over their curlers.

In the mid-1970s, Venables succeeded Malcolm Allison as manager of Crystal Palace at the age of thirty-three, and steered them from the Third Division to the First with a style that led many to believe the south London club would be the team of the 1980s. But by October 1980, Venables was on the move to west London, where he took charge of Queen's Park Rangers, a team that he even tried to buy. He guided the Loftus Road club into the UEFA Cup, as well as their first FA Cup Final in 1982, before Barcelona recognized his potential.

He arrived in Spain in May 1984 amidst great doubts about his ability to reverse the fortunes of the world's biggest club, but despite this climate of uncertainty, he showed he would not shirk from the challenge when he walked into the centre of the Nou Camp pitch, took the microphone and addressed the crowd in Catalan with a heavy cockney accent.

Dubbed by the British papers as 'El Tel', Venables was an instant success, guiding Barcelona to their first league title in eleven years and then to the 1986 European Cup Final, where they lost to Steaua Bucharest on penalties.

In 1987 he returned to Tottenham Hotspur as manager and led the team to an FA Cup win four years later. In 1993 he left White Hart Lane amid acrimonious exchanges with owner Alan Sugar, and it was the legal ramifications of this, plus libel suits against others who had pried into his business affairs, that were among the reasons he gave for leaving the England job.

From the moment of his 1994 appointment, his first dozen matches in charge of the national team brought only one defeat – against Brazil in the Umbro International Trophy – but saw seven matches drawn. With qualification for Euro '96 assured as hosts, he evolved a 'Christmas tree' formation with Alan Shearer the sole striker, even though this courted the wrath of the critics. Proving a difficult team to beat, England reached the semi-finals of Euro '96, only to end up losing on penalties to who else but their great German rivals.

A few months after quitting the international scene, he bought First Division Portsmouth for £1 and was later appointed coach of the Australian national team. Having had spells in charge of both Middlesbrough and Leeds United, Venables now concentrates on his role as a TV pundit.

ENGLAND RECORD:

P	W	D	L	F	A	SUCCESS RATE
23	12	9	2	35	13	72%

GLENN HODDLE (1996–9)

It was perhaps Glenn Hoddle's relative lack of success as an England player that gave him greater cause to succeed as the national team's manager – yet after thirty months in charge, the FA decided to terminate his contract.

He was one of the most gifted footballers ever to have played for Tottenham Hotspur. He represented England youth, the Under-21s and the 'B' team before scoring on his full international debut against Bulgaria in 1979. At the end of that season, he was named the PFA's 'Young Player of the Year'. He won FA Cup winners' medals in 1981 (when his free kick resulted in an equalizer), and 1982 (when he scored in both games), and he played for the losing team in 1987.

On leaving Spurs, Hoddle signed for French League club AS Monaco, helping them to the title in 1987–8, when he was voted the best foreign player in French football. Unfortunately, he was subsequently troubled by persistent knee injuries, which all but ended his career. In December 1990 he bought up his contract and returned to England to sign for Chelsea on a non-contract basis. Without playing a single game, he left in 1991 to embark on a career in management.

Succeeding Ossie Ardiles at Swindon Town, he took the club to promotion in 1992–3 via the play-offs, but then left the County Ground to manage Chelsea, in a player-manager capacity. Though he led them to the FA Cup Final in 1994, the Blues went down 4–0 to Manchester United.

Hoddle took over as manager of England in the summer of 1996, and, after achieving a momentous goalless draw against Italy in Rome in October 1997, the national team qualified for the 1998 World Cup Finals. However, the game was marred by scenes of violence on the terraces with baton-wielding police wading into a section of England fans.

In the 1998 World Cup Finals, England made a solid start by beating Tunisia 2–0, but a week later they lost 2–1 to Romania. Fortunately, a 2–0 victory over Colombia was enough to send them into the quarter-finals against Argentina. Reduced to ten men for seventy-three minutes following Beckham's sending-off, England held the Argentinians to a 2–2 draw after extra time. The game went to penalties, but with the score at 4–3 to Argentina, David Batty's spot-kick was saved, and England were out of the World Cup once again.

In an article in *The Times*, Glenn Hoddle's controversial comments regarding suggestions that people born disabled were paying for sins committed in a previous life provoked furious condemnation from sports bodies, church and government. Defending himself later on BBC's *Football Focus*, Hoddle said his remarks were 'misconstrued', 'misinterpreted' and 'misunderstood'. With the story dominating the front pages of virtually every newspaper as well as countless radio and television news bulletins, the FA decided to terminate his contract.

Hoddle later took charge of Southampton before returning to his beloved White Hart Lane in the hope of bringing success to his former club. This wasn't to be, however, and in September 2003 he was dismissed after a disappointing start to the season. At the time of writing he is manager of Wolverhampton Wanderers.

ENGLAND RECORD:

P	W	D	L	F	A	SUCCESS RATE
28	17	6	5	42	13	71%

HOWARD WILKINSON (1999 and 2000)

Howard Wilkinson was the FA's Technical Director when he was installed on a temporary basis to replace the departed Glenn Hoddle. He had a steady but unspectacular playing career with Sheffield Wednesday and Brighton and Hove Albion before joining Northern Premier League club Boston United as player-coach in 1971. He later gained a degree in Physical Education at Sheffield University and taught for two years.

After becoming FA regional coach in Sheffield, he was appointed manager of the England semi-professional side, and then the England Under-21 team in November 1982 when Ron Greenwood was in charge of the country's senior side. Prior to that, in January 1980 Wilkinson entered League football as coach to Notts County and played his part in getting the Midlands side promoted to Division One in 1980–1. He later succeeded Jimmy Sirrel as manager at Meadow Lane before taking over from Jack Charlton as manager of Sheffield Wednesday in June 1983. He guided the Owls back to Division One in his first season at Hillsborough, but later, sensing that Leeds United had greater potential, he took the chance to move to Elland Road.

In 1990, during his first full season in charge, Wilkinson led Leeds United back to the top flight as Second Division Champions. In the summer of 1990, Wilkinson was part of the England set-up, assessing likely opposition in the World Cup in Italy. Leeds finished fourth in their first season since returning to Division One, but won the League Championship in 1991–2, with Wilkinson being named Manager of the Year. Wilkinson, who was chairman of the Managers' Association, signed a new contract at Elland Road, but the FA were also given permission to speak to him and he was later appointed their technical director.

Following Hoddle's departure, he stepped into the limelight with his first press conference as England caretaker boss. His first game in charge in February 1999 saw England made to look ordinary by World Cup holders France, who beat the home side 2–0 at Wembley, inspired by Zinedine Zidane and the clinical finishing of Nicolas Anelka.

Wilkinson was also put in charge for England's World Cup qualifier against Finland in October 2000, following Keegan's shock resignation, but with Wilkinson playing striker Emile Heskey on the left wing, England's goalless draw in Helsinki certainly didn't mark the start of a bright new age. England were also unlucky, though, as Finland's keeper Antti Niemi should have been dismissed after five minutes for cynically upending Teddy Sheringham, while a shot from Ray Parlour a couple of minutes from time, which struck the crossbar but clearly crossed the line, was disallowed.

ENGLAND RECORD:

P	W	D	L	F	A
2	0	1	1	0	2

KEVIN KEEGAN (1999–2000)

Initially accepting the England managerial post for just four games, Kevin Keegan stated that he did not want to be considered for any time longer. He also vowed that supporters would see an improvement in the players' approach to singing the national anthem as well as in their performance on the pitch. However, within a couple of months, he surprised everyone by confirming his desire for the full-time role. 'It's time to stop playing games – I want the job.' Within days he was therefore unveiled as England's full-time coach.

Beginning his playing career with Scunthorpe United as an apprentice, Keegan joined Liverpool in May 1971, his all-action approach winning over the fans and making him the idol of the Kop. Brave, quick and inexhaustible, he shared an understanding with John Toshack that bordered on the telepathic. There were numerous high spots in his Liverpool career, his performance in the 1974 FA Cup Final against Newcastle, when he scored two goals, perhaps being one of his best. In June 1977, Keegan answered the call of continental football and joined SV Hamburg, having won three League Championship medals, two UEFA Cup medals, and European and FA Cup winners' medals during his six years at Anfield. His three years at Hamburg enhanced his game further, teaching him to overcome man-to-man marking.

Returning to England, he next joined Southampton and in his first season at The Dell, 1980–1, he netted twenty-six goals to make him the First Division's leading scorer and winner of the Golden Boot. Keegan, who won sixty-three caps for England, joined Newcastle United in 1982 and helped the Magpies win back their place in the top flight. He became a folk hero on Tyneside and later returned to St James' Park as manager, where, during the 1992–3 season, United won the First Division Championship, and they also went on to finish runners-up in the Premiership in 1996 and 1997.

Keegan later managed Fulham, whom he led to the Second Division title in 1999, before he took on the poisoned chalice of the England job. Indeed it was not too long before he offered Sweden 'a thousand thanks' for earning England a place in the 2000 European Championship play-offs, where they beat Scotland over two legs. Unfortunately, England's hopes in the European competition were ended when an 89th-minute penalty rashly conceded by Phil Neville gave Romania a 3–2 win, when England needed only a draw to advance into the quarter-finals against Italy.

In October 2000, Keegan stunned the nation by quitting his nineteen-month reign as England coach just minutes after his side lost depressingly 1–0 to Germany in a World Cup qualifier at Wembley. Leaving the pitch to a chorus of boos, he was immediately locked in discussion with FA officials, before emerging in front of the camera, close to tears, admitting, 'I have no complaints. I have not been quite good enough. I blame no one but myself.'

After a period of time away from the game, Keegan returned to management with Manchester City in May 2001, and in his first season in charge he led them into the Premiership as champions of the First Division. In March 2005, Keegan parted company with the Blues, to be replaced by former England favourite Stuart Pearce.

ENGLAND RECORD:

P	W	D	L	F	A	SUCCESS RATE
18	7	7	4	26	15	58%

PETER TAYLOR (2000)

Peter Taylor became England's caretaker coach in place of Howard Wilkinson – who ironically forced Taylor's departure from the Under-21 set-up the previous year – for the game against Italy in November 2000, which England ended up losing 1–0. Despite the scoreline, England gave an encouraging performance overall. Taylor's only match in charge also coincided with the appointment of David Beckham as England captain for the first time.

As a player, Peter Taylor started his career with his hometown club Southend United, where he stood out as a player of immense potential. In October 1973, he was transferred to Crystal Palace, rose to Under-23 status, and became one of the first Third Division players to appear in a full international for England. He represented his country four times in 1976.

A fast-raiding winger, Taylor joined Spurs in September 1976, but was hampered with injuries during his time at White Hart Lane. Four years later he moved to Orient, and had a loan spell with Oldham Athletic before entering non-League football with Maidstone United. He then helped out former Palace teammate Gerry Francis as a non-contract player with Exeter City before returning to Maidstone as player-manager.

A member of the England semi-professional team, he managed a number of non-League clubs before taking over the reins at Southend United. Since then he has managed Gillingham, whom he took into the First Division, and Leicester City, before taking charge of Brighton and Hove Albion. He led the Seagulls to the Second Division Championship before parting company with the Sussex club. At the time of writing, Taylor is manager of Hull City, having guided the Tigers into the Championship following two successive promotions.

ENGLAND RECORD:

P	W	D	L	F	A
1	0	0	1	0	1

SVEN-GÖRAN ERIKSSON (2001–6)

A knee injury brought an abrupt end to Sven-Göran Eriksson's undistinguished playing career as a defender for Swedish Second Division side Karlskoga.

In 1976 he was appointed coach of Swedish Third Division club Degefors, and within three years he had guided them to the top flight. After winning the UEFA Cup with IFK Gothenburg in 1982, he moved on to Portugal to join Benfica, where he won two League Championships and the domestic cup in two seasons.

Eriksson arrived in Italy in 1984–5 and joined AS Roma as manager, before moving to Fiorentina two seasons later. In 1989 he returned to Benfica and led the Portuguese team to the 1990 European Cup Final as well as the 1991 League title. He went back to Italy two years later to join Sampdoria, helping them win the Coppa Italia.

In 1996 a move to England was on the cards when he was named as the new manager of Blackburn Rovers, but the Swede was unable to join the north-west club until the summer of 1997 due to contractual obligations with Sampdoria. Ultimately, though, he was to change his mind, and instead took over at Lazio, where he was a great success. During his time there he led the Roman team to victory in the Coppa Italia twice, the Italian Super Cup, European Cup Winners' Cup and the UEFA Super Cup, and, in 2000, Lazio took the prestigious Serie A title for only the second time in their history.

In October 2000, Eriksson agreed a five-year contract to become the first foreign manager of the English national team from the following year. There were many who were angry at the appointment of a foreign coach, but given the influx of overseas managers into the Premiership in recent years, this surely was the next logical step. Perhaps a more valid criticism that could be levelled at Eriksson concerned his lack of knowledge of the English game.

In September 2001, after falling behind in Munich, an historic Michael Owen treble helped England devastate Germany with a stunning 5–1 win. Thousands of dejected home fans headed for the exits when Emile Heskey netted the fifth goal, and later, proud coach Eriksson was greeted with a round of applause in the press room.

At the 2002 World Cup, England skipper David Beckham wiped out four years of misery with a penalty winner, taking sweet revenge over Argentina. But despite Owen giving England the lead in the quarter-final against Brazil, Rivaldo equalized and Ronaldinho made it 2–1 before his sending-off.

In February 2003, during a friendly against Australia at Upton Park, Eriksson decided to try out a completely different side in each half, and ended up losing 3–1 to a team that England should have easily beaten. Off the field, the England coach admitted to meeting new Chelsea owner Roman Abramovich, which many at the time viewed with suspicion.

Following England's qualification for Euro 2004, Eriksson agreed to a two-year extension to his contract, but having reached the quarter-final of the European competition, England faced the hosts Portugal, and once again ended up losing in a penalty shoot-out. Having been plagued by revelations about his private life since moving to England, Eriksson faced yet another tabloid exposé when the *News of the World* reported that he had had a relationship with a secretary at the FA.

The 2004–5 season didn't get off to a good start for England, and following the 1–0 defeat in Northern Ireland, fans called for the manager's sacking. Fortunately, later wins over Austria and Poland helped to guarantee England's safe passage to the 2006 World Cup Finals, where, under Eriksson's leadership, hopes are high for a successful summer.

However, the FA announced in January 2006 that Eriksson would quit after the Finals in Germany, following an undercover journalist's accusation that the Swede had said he would be willing to manage Aston Villa if England won the World Cup. He is alleged to have been duped into believing that Villa would be bought by a wealthy Arab. Both Eriksson and the FA denied that these allegations led to the decision that he should relinquish his position as England boss.

ENGLAND RECORD:

P	W	D	L	F	A	SUCCESS RATE
59	34	15	10	111	57	70%

4 ENGLAND'S MATCHES

In addition to listing the date, opposition, team line-up, result and scorers for every England match since 1872, this section also contains match reports on twenty featured games.

1. 30 November 1872
v SCOTLAND . . . . Hamilton Crescent, Glasgow
Maynard . . . . 1st Surrey Rifles
Greenhalgh . . . . Notts County
Welch . . . . Wanderers
Maddison. . . . . Oxford University
Barker . . . . Hertfordshire Rangers
Brockbank . . . . Cambridge University
Clegg, J. C. . . . . Sheffield Wednesday
Smith, A. K. . . . . Oxford University
Ottaway. . . . . Oxford University
Chenery . . . . Crystal Palace
Morice . . . . Barnes FC
Result: 0–0

2. 8 March 1873
v SCOTLAND. . . . . Kennington Oval, London
Morten. . . . . Crystal Palace
Greenhalgh . . . . Notts County
Howell . . . . Wanderers
Goodwyn . . . . Royal Engineers
Vidal . . . . Oxford University
Von Donop. . . . . Royal Engineers
Chenery . . . . Crystal Palace
Clegg, W. E. . . . . Sheffield Wednesday
Bonsor . . . . Wanderers
Kenyon-Slaney . . . . Wanderers
Heron, H. . . . . Uxbridge
Result: 4–2
Scorers: Kenyon-Slaney (2), Bonsor, Chenery

3. 7 March 1874
v SCOTLAND . . . . Hamilton Crescent, Glasgow
Welch . . . . Harrow Chequers
Ogilvie . . . . Clapham Rovers
Stratford . . . . Wanderers
Ottaway. . . . . Oxford University
Birley. . . . . Oxford University
Wollaston. . . . . Wanderers
Kingsford . . . . Wanderers
Edwards. . . . . Shropshire Wanderers
Chenery . . . . Crystal Palace
Heron, H. . . . . Uxbridge
Owen. . . . . Sheffield FC
Result: 1–2
Scorer: Kingsford

4. 6 March 1875
v SCOTLAND. . . . . Kennington Oval, London
Carr . . . . Owlerton
Haygarth . . . . Swifts
Rawson, W. S. . . . . Oxford University
Birley. . . . . Wanderers
Von Donop. . . . . Royal Engineers
Wollaston. . . . . Wanderers
Alcock . . . . Wanderers
Rawson, H. E. . . . . Royal Engineers
Bonsor . . . . Wanderers
Heron, H. . . . . Wanderers
Geaves. . . . . Clapham Rovers
Result: 2–2
Scorers: Wollaston, Alcock

5. 4 March 1876
v SCOTLAND. . . . . Hamilton Crescent, Glasgow
Savage. . . . . Crystal Palace
Green. . . . . Wanderers
Field. . . . . Clapham Rovers
Bambridge, E. H. . . . . Swifts
Jarrett . . . . Cambridge University
Heron, H. . . . . Wanderers
Cursham, A. W. . . . . Notts County
Heron, F. . . . . Wanderers
Smith, C. E. . . . . Crystal Palace
Buchanan. . . . . Clapham Rovers
Maynard . . . . 1st Surrey Rifles
Result: 0–3

6. 3 March 1877
v SCOTLAND. . . . . Kennington Oval, London
Betts . . . . Old Harrovians
Lindsay . . . . Wanderers
Bury. . . . . Cambridge University
Rawson, W. S. . . . . Oxford University
Jarrett . . . . Cambridge University
Wollaston. . . . . Wanderers
Cursham, A. W. . . . . Notts County
Lyttelton, A. . . . . Cambridge University
Wingfield-Stratford. . . . . . . Royal Engineers
Bain. . . . . Oxford University
Mosforth . . . . Sheffield Wednesday
Result: 1–3
Scorer: A. Lyttelton

7. 2 March 1878
v SCOTLAND. . . . . 1st Hampden Park, Glasgow
Warner. . . . . Upton Park
Lyttelton, E. . . . . Cambridge University
Hunter . . . . Sheffield Heeley
Bailey. . . . . Clapham Rovers
Jarrett . . . . Cambridge University
Cursham, A. W. . . . . Notts County
Fairclough . . . . Old Foresters
Wace . . . . Wanderers
Wylie . . . . Wanderers
Heron, H. . . . . Wanderers
Mosforth . . . . Sheffield Albion
Result: 2–7
Scorers: Wylie, A. W. Cursham

8. 18 January 1879
v WALES. . . . . Kennington Oval, London
Anderson . . . . Old Etonians
Bury. . . . . Old Etonians
Wilson . . . . Oxford University
Bailey. . . . . Clapham Rovers
Clegg, W. E. . . . . Sheffield Albion
Parry . . . . Old Carthusians
Sorby . . . . Thursday Wanderers
Cursham, A. W. . . . . Notts County
Wace . . . . Wanderers
Mosforth . . . . Sheffield Albion
Whitfeld. . . . . Old Etonians
Result: 2–1
Scorers: Sorby, Whitfeld

9. 5 April 1879
v SCOTLAND . . . . Kennington Oval, London
Birkett . . . . Clapham Rovers
Morse . . . . Notts County
Christian . . . . Old Etonians
Bailey . . . . Clapham Rovers
Prinsep . . . . Clapham Rovers
Hills . . . . Old Harrovians
Goodyer . . . . Nottingham Forest
Wace . . . . Wanderers
Sparks . . . . Hertfordshire Rangers
Bambridge, E. C. . . . . Swifts
Mosforth . . . . Sheffield Albion
Result: 5–4
Scorers: Mosforth, E. C. Bambridge (2), Goodyer, Bailey

10. 13 March 1880
v SCOTLAND . . . . 1st Hampden Park,
Glasgow
Swepstone . . . . Pilgrims
Brindle . . . . Darwen
Luntley . . . . Nottingham Forest
Bailey . . . . Clapham Rovers
Hunter . . . . Sheffield Heeley
Wollaston . . . . Wanderers
Bastard . . . . Upton Park
Sparks . . . . Clapham Rovers
Widdowson . . . . Nottingham Forest
Mosforth . . . . Sheffield Albion
Bambridge, E. C. . . . . Swifts
Result: 4–5
Scorers: Mosforth, E. C. Bambridge (2), Sparks

11. 15 March 1880
v WALES . . . . Racecourse Ground,
Wrexham
Sands . . . . Nottingham Forest
Brindle . . . . Darwen
Luntley . . . . Nottingham Forest
Hunter . . . . Sheffield Heeley
Hargreaves, F. W. . . . . Blackburn Rovers
Marshall . . . . Darwen
Mitchell . . . . Upton Park
Sparks . . . . Clapham Rovers
Cursham, H. A. . . . . Notts County
Johnson . . . . Saltley College
Mosforth . . . . Sheffield Albion
Result: 3–2
Scorers: Sparks (2), Brindle

12. 26 February 1881
v WALES . . . . Alexandra Meadows,
Blackburn
Hawtrey . . . . Old Etonians
Harvey . . . . Wednesbury Strollers
Bambridge, A. L. . . . . Swifts
Hunter . . . . Sheffield Heeley
Hargreaves, F. W. . . . . Blackburn Rovers
Marshall . . . . Darwen
Rostron . . . . Darwen
Brown, J. . . . . Blackburn Rovers
Tait . . . . Birmingham Excelsior
Hargreaves, J. . . . . Blackburn Rovers
Mosforth . . . . Sheffield Wednesday
Result: 0–1

13. 26 March 1881
v SCOTLAND . . . . Kennington Oval, London
Hawtrey . . . . Old Etonians
Field . . . . Clapham Rovers
Wilson . . . . Oxford University
Bailey . . . . Clapham Rovers
Hunter . . . . Sheffield Heeley
Holden . . . . Wednesbury Old Athletic
Rostron . . . . Darwen

Macaulay . . . . Cambridge University
Mitchell . . . . Upton Park
Bambridge, E. C. . . . . Swifts
Hargreaves, J. . . . . Blackburn Rovers
Result: 1–6
Scorer: E.C. Bambridge

14. 18 February 1882
v IRELAND . . . . Bloomfield, Belfast
Rawlinson . . . . Cambridge University
Dobson, A. . . . . Notts County
Greenwood . . . . Blackburn Rovers
Hargreaves, F. W. . . . . Blackburn Rovers
King . . . . Oxford University
Bambridge, E. C. . . . . Swifts
Barnet . . . . Royal Engineers
Brown, A. . . . . Aston Villa
Brown, J. . . . . Blackburn Rovers
Vaughton . . . . Aston Villa
Cursham, H. A. . . . . Notts County
Result: 13–0
Scorers: Vaughton (5), A. Brown (4), J. Brown (2), H. A.
Cursham, E. C. Bambridge

15. 11 March 1882
v SCOTLAND . . . . 1st Hampden Park,
Glasgow
Swepstone . . . . Pilgrims
Greenwood . . . . Blackburn Rovers
Jones, A. . . . . Walsall Town Swifts
Bailey . . . . Clapham Rovers
Hunter . . . . Sheffield Heeley
Cursham, H. A. . . . . Notts County
Parry . . . . Old Carthusians
Brown, A. . . . . Aston Villa
Vaughton . . . . Aston Villa
Mosforth . . . . Sheffield Wednesday
Bambridge, E. C. . . . . Swifts
Result: 1–5
Scorer: Vaughton

⚽ **DID YOU KNOW...?**

The only instance of three brothers playing for
England occurred when Arthur, Edward and Ernest
Bambridge shared twenty-two appearances
between 1876 and 1887. Although the three never
appeared on the same teamsheet, Arthur and
Edward played together twice in 1883 and 1884.

16. 13 March 1882
v WALES . . . . Racecourse Ground,
Wrexham
Swepstone . . . . Pilgrims
Hunter . . . . Sheffield Heeley
Jones, A. . . . . Walsall Town Swifts
Bailey . . . . Clapham Rovers
Bambridge, E. C. . . . . Swifts
Parry . . . . Old Carthusians
Cursham, H. A. . . . . Notts County
Parr . . . . Oxford University
Brown, A. . . . . Aston Villa
Vaughton . . . . Aston Villa
Mosforth . . . . Sheffield Wednesday
Result: 3–5
Scorers: Mosforth, Parry, H. A. Cursham

17. 3 February 1883
v WALES . . . . Kennington Oval, London
Swepstone . . . . Pilgrims
Paravicini . . . . Cambridge University
Russell . . . . Royal Engineers
Bailey . . . . Clapham Rovers
Macrae . . . . Notts County
Cursham, A. W. . . . . Notts County
Bambridge, A. L. . . . . Swifts
Mitchell . . . . Upton Park
Goodhart . . . . Old Etonians
Cursham, H. A. . . . . Notts County
Bambridge, E. C. . . . . Swifts
Result: 5–0
Scorers: Mitchell (3), A. W. Cursham, E. C. Bambridge

18. 24 February 1883
v IRELAND . . . . Aigburth Park CCG, Liverpool
Swepstone . . . . Pilgrims
Paravicini . . . . Cambridge University
Moore . . . . Notts County
Hudson . . . . Sheffield Wednesday
Macrae . . . . Notts County
Whateley . . . . Aston Villa
Pawson . . . . Cambridge University
Goodhart . . . . Old Etonians
Dunn . . . . Cambridge University
Cobbold . . . . Cambridge University
Cursham, H. A. . . . . Notts County
Result: 7–0
Scorers: Cobbold (2), Dunn (2), Whateley (2), Pawson

19. 10 March 1883
v SCOTLAND . . . . Bramall Lane, Sheffield
Swepstone . . . . Pilgrims
Paravicini . . . . Cambridge University
Jones, A. . . . . Great Lever
Bailey . . . . Clapham Rovers
Macrae . . . . Notts County
Mitchell . . . . Upton Park
Whateley . . . . Aston Villa
Goodhart . . . . Old Etonians
Cursham, A. W. . . . . Notts County
Cobbold . . . . Cambridge University
Cursham, H. A. . . . . Notts County
Result: 2–3
Scorers: Mitchell, Cobbold

20. 25 February 1884
v IRELAND . . . . Ballynafeigh Park, Belfast
Rose . . . . Swifts
Dobson, A. . . . . Notts County
Beverley . . . . Blackburn Rovers
Bailey . . . . Clapham Rovers
Macrae . . . . Notts County
Johnson . . . . Stoke
Holden . . . . Wednesbury Old Athletic
Bambridge, A. L. . . . . Swifts
Dunn . . . . Cambridge University
Bambridge, E. C. . . . . Swifts
Cursham, H. A. . . . . Notts County
Result: 8–1
Scorers: Johnson (2), E. C. Bambridge (2), H. A. Cursham (3), A. L. Bambridge

21. 15 March 1884
v SCOTLAND . . . . 1st Cathkin Park, Glasgow
Rose . . . . Swifts
Dobson, A. . . . . Notts County
Beverley . . . . Blackburn Rovers
Bailey . . . . Clapham Rovers
Macrae . . . . Notts County
Wilson, C. P. . . . . Hendon
Bromley-Davenport . . . . . . Oxford University
Gunn . . . . Notts County
Bambridge, E. C. . . . . Swifts

Vaughton . . . . Aston Villa
Holden . . . . Wednesbury Old Athletic
Result: 0–1

22. 17 March 1884
v WALES . . . . Racecourse Ground, Wrexham
Rose . . . . Swifts
Dobson, A. . . . . Notts County
Beverley . . . . Blackburn Rovers
Bailey . . . . Clapham Rovers
Forrest . . . . Blackburn Rovers
Wilson, C. P. . . . . Hendon
Bromley-Davenport . . . . . . Oxford University
Gunn . . . . Notts County
Bambridge, E. C. . . . . Swifts
Vaughton . . . . Aston Villa
Holden . . . . Wednesbury Old Athletic
Result: 4–0
Scorers: Bromley-Davenport (2), Gunn, Bailey

23. 28 February 1885
v IRELAND . . . . Whalley Range, Manchester
Arthur . . . . Blackburn Rovers
Walters, P. M. Oxford University
Walters, A. M. . . . . Cambridge University
Bailey . . . . Clapham Rovers
Forrest . . . . Blackburn Rovers
Lofthouse . . . . Blackburn Rovers
Spilsbury . . . . Cambridge University
Brown, J. . . . . Blackburn Rovers
Pawson . . . . Swifts
Cobbold . . . . Cambridge University
Bambridge, E. C. . . . . Swifts
Result: 4–0
Scorers: E. C. Bambridge, Spilsbury, Brown, Lofthouse

24. 14 March 1885
v WALES . . . . Leamington Road, Blackburn
Arthur . . . . Blackburn Rovers
Moore . . . . Notts County
Ward . . . . Blackburn Olympic
Bailey . . . . Clapham Rovers
Forrest . . . . Blackburn Rovers
Lofthouse . . . . Blackburn Rovers
Davenport . . . . Bolton Wanderers
Brown, J. . . . . Blackburn Rovers
Mitchell . . . . Upton Park
Dixon . . . . Notts County
Bambridge, E. C. . . . . Swifts
Result: 1–1
Scorer: Mitchell

25. 21 March 1885
v SCOTLAND . . . . Kennington Oval, London
Arthur . . . . Blackburn Rovers
Walters, P. M. . . . . Oxford University
Walters, A. M. . . . . Cambridge University
Bailey . . . . Clapham Rovers
Forrest . . . . Blackburn Rovers
Amos . . . . Old Carthusians
Brown, J. . . . . Blackburn Rovers
Lofthouse . . . . Blackburn Rovers
Danks . . . . Nottingham Forest
Bambridge, E. C. . . . . Swifts
Cobbold . . . . Cambridge University
Result: 1–1
Scorer: E. C. Bambridge

26. 13 March 1886
v IRELAND . . . . Ballynafeigh Park, Belfast
Rose . . . . Preston North End
Walters, P. M. . . . . Old Carthusians
Baugh . . . . Stafford Road
Shutt . . . . Stoke
Squire . . . . Cambridge University

Dobson, C. . . . . Notts County
Leighton. . . . . Nottingham Forest
Dewhurst. . . . . Preston North End
Lindley . . . . Cambridge University
Spilsbury . . . . Cambridge University
Pike . . . . Cambridge University
Result: 6–1
Scorers: Spilsbury (4), Dewhurst, Lindley

27. 29 March 1886
v WALES. . . . . Racecourse Ground,
Wrexham
Arthur . . . . Blackburn Rovers
Squire . . . . Cambridge University
Walters, P. M. . . . . Old Carthusians
Bailey. . . . . Clapham Rovers
Amos . . . . Old Carthusians
Forrest . . . . Blackburn Rovers
Dewhurst . . . . Preston North End
Brann. . . . . Swifts
Lindley . . . . Cambridge University
Cobbold . . . . Cambridge University
Bambridge, E. C. . . . . Swifts
Result: 3–1
Scorers: Dewhurst, E. C. Bambridge, Lindley

28. 31 March 1886
v SCOTLAND . . . . 2nd Hampden Park, Glasgow
Arthur . . . . Blackburn Rovers
Walters, A. M. . . . . Cambridge University
Walters, P. M. . . . . Old Carthusians
Bailey. . . . . Clapham Rovers
Squire . . . . Cambridge University
Forrest . . . . Blackburn Rovers
Cobbold . . . . Cambridge University
Bambridge, E. C. . . . . Swifts
Lindley . . . . Cambridge University
Spilsbury . . . . Cambridge University
Brann. . . . . Swifts
Result: 1–1
Scorer: Lindley

29. 5 February 1887
v IRELAND . . . . Bramall Lane, Sheffield
Arthur . . . . Blackburn Rovers
Howarth, R. . . . . Preston North End
Mason . . . . Wolverhampton Wanderers
Haworth, G. . . . . Accrington
Brayshaw . . . . Sheffield Wednesday
Forrest . . . . Blackburn Rovers
Sayer . . . . Stoke
Dewhurst . . . . Preston North End
Lindley . . . . Cambridge University
Cobbold . . . . Old Carthusians
Bambridge, E. C. . . . . Swifts
Result: 7–0
Scorers: Cobbold (2), Lindley (3), Dewhurst (2)

30. 26 February 1887
v WALES. . . . . Kennington Oval, London
Arthur . . . . Blackburn Rovers
Walters, P. M. . . . . Old Carthusians
Walters, A. M. . . . . Cambridge University
Haworth, G. . . . . Accrington
Bailey. . . . . Clapham Rovers
Forrest . . . . Blackburn Rovers
Lofthouse. . . . . Blackburn Rovers
Dewhurst . . . . Preston North End
Lindley . . . . Cambridge University
Cobbold . . . . Old Carthusians
Bambridge, E. C. . . . . Swifts
Result: 4–0
Scorers: Cobbold (2), Lindley (2)

31. 19 March 1887
v SCOTLAND . . . . Leamington Road, Blackburn
Roberts . . . . West Bromwich Albion

Walters, A. M. . . . . Cambridge University
Walters, P. M. . . . . Old Carthusians
Bailey. . . . . Clapham Rovers
Haworth, G. . . . . Accrington
Forrest . . . . Blackburn Rovers
Bambridge, E. C. . . . . Swifts
Cobbold . . . . Old Carthusians
Lofthouse. . . . . Blackburn Rovers
Dewhurst . . . . Preston North End
Lindley . . . . Cambridge University
Result: 2–3
Scorers: Dewhurst, Lindley

32. 4 February 1888
v WALES. . . . . Nantwich Road, Crewe
Moon. . . . . Old Westminsters
Howarth, R. . . . . Preston North End
Mason . . . . Wolverhampton Wanderers
Saunders . . . . Swifts
Allen, H. . . . . Wolverhampton Wanderers
Holden-White. . . . . Corinthians
Woodhall . . . . West Bromwich Albion
Goodall . . . . Preston North End
Lindley . . . . Cambridge University
Dewhurst . . . . Preston North End
Hodgetts . . . . Aston Villa
Result: 5–1
Scorers: Dewhurst (2), Woodhall, Goodall, Lindley

33. 17 March 1888
v SCOTLAND . . . . 2nd Hampden Park, Glasgow
Moon. . . . . Old Westminsters
Howarth, R. . . . . Preston North End
Walters, P. M. . . . . Old Carthusians
Allen, H. . . . . Wolverhampton Wanderers
Haworth, G. . . . . Accrington
Holden-White. . . . . Corinthians
Woodhall . . . . West Bromwich Albion
Goodall . . . . Preston North End
Lindley . . . . Cambridge University
Hodgetts . . . . Aston Villa
Dewhurst . . . . Preston North End
Result: 5–0
Scorers: Lindley, Hodgetts, Dewhurst (2), Goodall

34. 31 March 1888
v IRELAND . . . . Ballynafeigh Park, Belfast
Roberts . . . . West Bromwich Albion
Aldridge. . . . . West Bromwich Albion
Walters, P. M. . . . . Old Carthusians
Holmes . . . . Preston North End
Allen, H. . . . . Wolverhampton Wanderers
Shelton, C. . . . . Notts Rangers
Bassett. . . . . West Bromwich Albion
Dewhurst . . . . Preston North End
Lindley . . . . Cambridge University
Allen, A. . . . . Aston Villa
Hodgetts . . . . Aston Villa
Result: 5–1
Scorers: Dewhurst, A. Allen (3), Lindley

35. 23 February 1889
v WALES. . . . . Victoria Ground, Stoke
Moon. . . . . Old Westminsters
Walters, A. M. . . . . Old Carthusians
Walters, P. M. . . . . Old Carthusians
Fletcher . . . . Wolverhampton Wanderers
Lowder . . . . Wolverhampton Wanderers
Betts . . . . Sheffield Wednesday
Bassett. . . . . West Bromwich Albion
Goodall . . . . Preston North End
Southworth . . . . Blackburn Rovers
Dewhurst . . . . Preston North End
Townley . . . . Blackburn Rovers
Result: 4–1
Scorers: Bassett, Goodall, Southworth, Dewhurst

36. 2 March 1889
v IRELAND . . . . Goodison Park, Everton
Rowley. . . . . Stoke
Clare . . . . Stoke
Aldridge. . . . . Walsall Town Swifts
Wreford-Brown . . . . Oxford University
Weir. . . . . Bolton Wanderers
Shelton, A. . . . . Notts County
Lofthouse. . . . . Accrington
Burton . . . . Nottingham Forest
Brodie . . . . Wolverhampton Wanderers
Daft. . . . . Notts County
Yates . . . . Burnley
Result: 6–1
Scorers: Weir, Yates (3), Lofthouse, Brodie

37. 13 April 1889
v SCOTLAND. . . . . Kennington Oval, London
Moon. . . . . Old Westminsters
Walters, A. M.. . . . . Old Carthusians
Walters, P. M. . . . . Old Carthusians
Hammond . . . . Oxford University
Allen, H.. . . . . Wolverhampton Wanderers
Forrest . . . . Blackburn Rovers
Brodie . . . . Wolverhampton Wanderers
Goodall . . . . Preston North End
Bassett. . . . . West Bromwich Albion
Weir. . . . . Bolton Wanderers
Lindley. . . . . Nottingham Forest
Result: 2–3
Scorers: Bassett, Weir

38. 15 March 1890
v WALES. . . . . Racecourse Ground,
                                 Wrexham
Moon. . . . . Old Westminsters
Walters, A. M.. . . . . Old Carthusians
Walters, P. M. . . . . Old Carthusians
Fletcher . . . . Wolverhampton Wanderers
Holt . . . . Everton
Shelton, A. . . . . Notts County
Bassett. . . . . West Bromwich Albion
Currey . . . . Oxford University
Lindley. . . . . Nottingham Forest
Daft. . . . . Notts County
Wood. . . . . Wolverhampton Wanderers
Result: 3–1
Scorers: Currey (2), Lindley

39. 15 March 1890
v IRELAND . . . . Ballynafeigh Park, Belfast
Roberts . . . . West Bromwich Albion
Baugh . . . . Wolverhampton Wanderers
Mason . . . . Wolverhampton Wanderers
Barton . . . . Blackburn Rovers
Perry, C. . . . . West Bromwich Albion
Forrest . . . . Blackburn Rovers
Lofthouse. . . . . Blackburn Rovers
Davenport . . . . Bolton Wanderers
Geary. . . . . Everton
Walton. . . . . Blackburn Rovers
Townley . . . . Blackburn Rovers
Result: 9–1
Scorers: Townley (2), Davenport (2), Geary (3), Lofthouse, Barton

⚽ **DID YOU KNOW...?**

England played two internationals on the same day in 1890. One team beat Wales 3–1 in Wrexham on 15 March, while another side playing Ireland won 9–1 in Belfast.

40. 5 April 1890
v SCOTLAND. . . . . 2nd Hampden Park, Glasgow
Moon. . . . . Old Westminsters
Walters, A. M.. . . . . Old Carthusians
Walters, P. M. . . . . Old Carthusians
Haworth, G. . . . . Accrington
Allen, H.. . . . . Wolverhampton Wanderers
Shelton, A. . . . . Notts County
Bassett. . . . . West Bromwich Albion
Currey . . . . Oxford University
Lindley. . . . . Nottingham Forest
Wood. . . . . Wolverhampton Wanderers
Daft. . . . . Notts County
Result: 1–1
Scorer: Wood

41. 7 March 1891
v WALES. . . . . Newcastle Road,
                                 Sunderland
Wilkinson. . . . . Oxford University
Porteous. . . . . Sunderland
Jackson . . . . Oxford University
Smith, A. . . . . Nottingham Forest
Holt . . . . Everton
Shelton, A. . . . . Notts County
Brann. . . . . Swifts
Goodall . . . . Derby County
Southworth . . . . Blackburn Rovers
Milward . . . . Everton
Chadwick. . . . . Everton
Result: 4–1
Scorers: Goodall, Southworth, Chadwick, Milward

42. 7 March 1891
v IRELAND . . . . Molineux, Wolverhampton
Rose . . . . Wolverhampton Wanderers
Marsden . . . . Darwen
Underwood . . . . Stoke
Bayliss . . . . West Bromwich Albion
Perry, C. . . . . West Bromwich Albion
Brodie . . . . Wolverhampton Wanderers
Bassett. . . . . West Bromwich Albion
Cotterill . . . . Cambridge University
Lindley. . . . . Nottingham Forest
Henfrey . . . . Cambridge University
Daft. . . . . Notts County
Result: 6–1
Scorers: Cotterill, Daft, Henfrey, Lindley (2), Bassett

43. 6 April 1891
v SCOTLAND. . . . . Ewood Park, Blackburn
Moon. . . . . Old Westminsters
Howarth, R. . . . . Preston North End
Holmes . . . . Preston North End
Smith, A. . . . . Nottingham Forest
Holt . . . . Everton
Shelton, A. . . . . Notts County
Bassett. . . . . West Bromwich Albion
Goodall . . . . Derby County
Geary. . . . . Everton
Chadwick. . . . . Everton
Milward . . . . Everton
Result: 2–1
Scorers: Goodall, Chadwick

44. 5 March 1892
v WALES. . . . . Racecourse Ground,
                                 Wrexham
Toone. . . . . Notts County
Dunn . . . . Old Etonians
Lilley . . . . Sheffield United
Hossack . . . . Corinthians
Winckworth . . . . Old Westminsters
Kinsey . . . . Wolverhampton Wanderers
Gosling . . . . Old Etonians

Cotterill . . . . Old Brightonians
Henfrey . . . . Corinthians
Schofield . . . . Stoke
Sandilands . . . . Old Westminsters
Result: 2–0
Scorers: Henfrey, Sandilands

45. 5 March 1892
v IRELAND . . . . Solitude Ground, Belfast
Rowley. . . . . Stoke
Underwood . . . . Stoke
Clare . . . . Stoke
Cox . . . . Derby County
Holt . . . . Everton
Whitham . . . . Sheffield United
Athersmith . . . . Aston Villa
Pearson . . . . Crewe Alexandra
Devey . . . . Aston Villa
Daft . . . . Notts County
Hodgetts . . . . Aston Villa
Result: 2–0
Scorer: Daft (2)

46. 2 April 1892
v SCOTLAND. . . . . Ibrox Park, Glasgow
Toone. . . . . Notts County
Dunn . . . . Old Etonians
Holmes . . . . Preston North End
Holt . . . . Everton
Reynolds . . . . West Bromwich Albion
Shelton, A. . . . . Notts County
Bassett. . . . . West Bromwich Albion
Goodall . . . . Derby County
Chadwick. . . . . Everton
Hodgetts . . . . Aston Villa
Southworth . . . . Blackburn Rovers
Result: 4–1
Scorers: Southworth, Goodall (2), Chadwick

47. 25 February 1893
v IRELAND . . . . Perry Barr, Birmingham
Charsley. . . . . Small Heath
Harrison . . . . Old Westminsters
Pelly. . . . . Old Foresters
Smith, A. . . . . Nottingham Forest
Winckworth . . . . Old Westminsters
Cooper. . . . . Cambridge University
Topham, R. . . . . Wolverhampton Wanderers
Smith, G. O. . . . . Oxford University
Cotterill . . . . Old Brightonians
Gilliat. . . . . Old Carthusians
Sandilands . . . . Old Westminsters
Result: 6–1
Scorers: Sandilands, Gilliat (3), Winckworth, G. O. Smith

48. 13 March 1893
v WALES. . . . . Victoria Ground, Stoke
Sutcliffe . . . . Bolton Wanderers
Clare . . . . Stoke
Holmes . . . . Preston North End
Reynolds . . . . West Bromwich Albion
Perry, C. . . . . West Bromwich Albion
Turner . . . . Bolton Wanderers
Bassett. . . . . West Bromwich Albion
Whitehead . . . . Accrington
Goodall . . . . Derby County
Schofield . . . . Stoke
Spiksley . . . . Sheffield Wednesday
Result: 6–0
Scorers: Spiksley (2), Goodall, Bassett, Schofield, Reynolds

49. 1 April 1893
v SCOTLAND . . . . Athletic Ground, Richmond
Gay . . . . Cambridge University
Harrison . . . . Old Westminsters

Holmes . . . . Preston North End
Reynolds . . . . West Bromwich Albion
Holt . . . . Everton
Kinsey . . . . Wolverhampton Wanderers
Bassett. . . . . West Bromwich Albion
Gosling . . . . Old Etonians
Cotterill . . . . Old Brightonians
Chadwick. . . . . Everton
Spiksley . . . . Sheffield Wednesday
Result: 5–2
Scorers: Spiksley (2), Gosling, Cotterill, Reynolds

50. 1 March 1894
v IRELAND . . . . Solitude Ground, Belfast
Reader. . . . . West Bromwich Albion
Howarth, R. . . . . Everton
Holmes . . . . Preston North End
Reynolds . . . . Aston Villa
Holt . . . . Everton
Crabtree. . . . . Burnley
Chippendale. . . . . Blackburn Rovers
Whitehead . . . . Blackburn Rovers
Devey . . . . Aston Villa
Hodgetts . . . . Aston Villa
Spiksley . . . . Sheffield Wednesday
Result: 2–2
Scorers: Devey, Spiksley

51. 12 March 1894
v WALES. . . . . Racecourse Ground, Wrexham
Gay . . . . Old Brightonians
Lodge . . . . Cambridge University
Pelly. . . . . Old Foresters
Hossack . . . . Corinthians
Wreford-Brown . . . . Old Carthusians
Topham, A. G. . . . . Casuals
Topham, R. . . . . Casuals
Gosling . . . . Old Etonians
Smith, G. O. . . . . Oxford University
Veitch . . . . Old Westminsters
Sandilands . . . . Old Westminsters
Result: 5–1
Scorers: Veitch (3), Gosling, o.g.

52. 7 April 1894
v SCOTLAND. . . . . Glasgow
Gay . . . . Old Brightonians
Clare . . . . Stoke
Pelly. . . . . Old Foresters
Reynolds . . . . Aston Villa
Holt . . . . Everton
Needham. . . . . Sheffield United
Bassett. . . . . West Bromwich Albion
Smith, G. O. . . . . Oxford University
Goodall . . . . Derby County
Chadwick. . . . . Everton
Spiksley . . . . Sheffield Wednesday
Result: 2–2
Scorers: Goodall, Reynolds

53. 9 March 1895
v IRELAND . . . . Derbyshire CCC, Derby
Sutcliffe . . . . Bolton Wanderers
Crabtree. . . . . Burnley
Holmes . . . . Preston North End
Howell. . . . . Sheffield United
Crawshaw . . . . Sheffield Wednesday
Turner . . . . Stoke
Bassett. . . . . West Bromwich Albion
Bloomer. . . . . Derby County
Goodall . . . . Derby County
Becton . . . . Preston North End
Schofield . . . . Stoke
Result: 9–0
Scorers: Bloomer (2), Goodall (2), Bassett, Howell, Becton (2), o.g.

DID YOU KNOW...?

The last full England team made up of eleven amateurs drew 1–1 against Wales at Queen's Club, Kensington, on 18 March 1895.

54. 18 March 1895
v WALES . . . . Queen's Club, Kensington
Raikes . . . . Oxford University
Lodge . . . . Cambridge University
Oakley . . . . Oxford University
Henfrey . . . . Corinthians
Wreford-Brown . . . . Old Carthusians
Barker . . . . Casuals
Stanbrough . . . . Old Carthusians
Dewhurst, G. . . . . Liverpool Ramblers
Smith, G. O. . . . . Oxford University
Gosling . . . . Old Etonians
Sandilands . . . . Old Westminsters
Result: 1–1
Scorer: G. O. Smith

55. 6 April 1895
v SCOTLAND . . . . Goodison Park, Everton
Sutcliffe . . . . Bolton Wanderers
Crabtree . . . . Burnley
Lodge . . . . Cambridge University
Needham . . . . Sheffield United
Holt . . . . Everton
Reynolds . . . . Aston Villa
Gosling . . . . Old Etonians
Smith, S. . . . . Aston Villa
Goodall . . . . Derby County
Bassett . . . . West Bromwich Albion
Bloomer . . . . Derby County
Result: 3–0
Scorers: Bloomer, S. Smith, o.g.

56. 7 March 1896
v IRELAND . . . . Solitude Ground, Belfast
Raikes . . . . Oxford University
Lodge . . . . Corinthians
Oakley . . . . Oxford University
Crabtree . . . . Aston Villa
Crawshaw . . . . Sheffield Wednesday
Kinsey . . . . Derby County
Bassett . . . . West Bromwich Albion
Bloomer . . . . Derby County
Smith, G. O. . . . . Oxford University
Chadwick . . . . Everton
Spiksley . . . . Sheffield Wednesday
Result: 2–0
Scorers: Bloomer, G. O. Smith

57. 16 March 1896
v WALES . . . . Cardiff Arms Park
Raikes . . . . Oxford University
Oakley . . . . Oxford University
Crabtree . . . . Aston Villa
Henfrey . . . . Corinthians
Crawshaw . . . . Sheffield Wednesday
Kinsey . . . . Derby County
Bassett . . . . West Bromwich Albion
Bloomer . . . . Derby County
Smith, G. O. . . . . Oxford University
Goodall . . . . Derby County
Sandilands . . . . Old Westminsters
Result: 9–1
Scorer: Bloomer (5), G. O. Smith (2), Goodall, Bassett

58. 4 April 1896
v SCOTLAND . . . . Celtic Park, Glasgow
Raikes . . . . Oxford University
Lodge . . . . Corinthians

Oakley . . . . Oxford University
Crabtree . . . . Aston Villa
Crawshaw . . . . Sheffield Wednesday
Henfrey . . . . Corinthians
Goodall . . . . Derby County
Bassett . . . . West Bromwich Albion
Smith, G. O. . . . . Oxford University
Wood . . . . Wolverhampton Wanderers
Burnup . . . . Cambridge University
Result: 1–2
Scorer: Bassett

59. 20 February 1897
v IRELAND . . . . Trent Bridge, Nottingham
Robinson . . . . Derby County
Oakley . . . . Corinthians
Williams . . . . West Bromwich Albion
Middleditch . . . . Corinthians
Crawshaw . . . . Sheffield Wednesday
Needham . . . . Sheffield United
Athersmith . . . . Aston Villa
Bloomer . . . . Derby County
Smith, G. O. . . . . Old Carthusians
Wheldon . . . . Aston Villa
Bradshaw . . . . Liverpool
Result: 6–0
Scorers: Bloomer (2), Wheldon (3), Athersmith

60. 29 March 1897
v WALES . . . . Bramall Lane, Sheffield
Foulke . . . . Sheffield United
Oakley . . . . Corinthians
Spencer . . . . Aston Villa
Reynolds . . . . Aston Villa
Crawshaw . . . . Sheffield Wednesday
Needham . . . . Sheffield United
Athersmith . . . . Aston Villa
Bloomer . . . . Derby County
Smith, G. O. . . . . Old Carthusians
Becton . . . . Liverpool
Milward . . . . Everton
Result: 4–0
Scorers: Bloomer, Needham, Milward (2)

61. 3 April 1897
v SCOTLAND . . . . Crystal Palace, London
Robinson . . . . Derby County
Oakley . . . . Corinthians
Spencer . . . . Aston Villa
Reynolds . . . . Aston Villa
Crawshaw . . . . Sheffield Wednesday
Needham . . . . Sheffield United
Athersmith . . . . Aston Villa
Bloomer . . . . Derby County
Smith, G. O. . . . . Old Carthusians
Chadwick . . . . Everton
Milward . . . . Everton
Result: 1–2
Scorer: Bloomer

62. 5 March 1898
v IRELAND . . . . Solitude Ground, Belfast
Robinson . . . . New Brighton Tower
Oakley . . . . Corinthians
Williams . . . . West Bromwich Albion
Forman, Frank . . . . Nottingham Forest
Morren . . . . Sheffield United
Turner . . . . Derby County
Athersmith . . . . Aston Villa
Richards . . . . Nottingham Forest
Smith, G. O. . . . . Old Carthusians
Garfield . . . . West Bromwich Albion
Wheldon . . . . Aston Villa
Result: 3–2
Scorers: Morren, Athersmith, G. O. Smith

63. 28 March 1898
v WALES . . . . Racecourse Ground, Wrexham

Robinson . . . . New Brighton Tower
Oakley . . . . Corinthians
Williams . . . . West Bromwich Albion
Perry, T . . . . West Bromwich Albion
Booth, T, ... Blackburn Rovers
Needham . . . . Sheffield United
Athersmith . . . . Aston Villa
Goodall . . . . Derby County
Smith, G. O. . . . . Old Carthusians
Wheldon . . . . Aston Villa
Spiksley . . . . Sheffield Wednesday
Result: 3–0
Scorers: G. O. Smith, Wheldon (2)

64. 2 April 1898
v SCOTLAND . . . . Celtic Park, Glasgow
Robinson . . . . New Brighton Tower
Oakley . . . . Corinthians
Williams . . . . West Bromwich Albion
Wreford-Brown . . . . Old Carthusians
Forman, Frank . . . . Nottingham Forest
Needham . . . . Sheffield United
Athersmith . . . . Aston Villa
Bloomer . . . . Derby County
Smith, G. O. . . . . Old Carthusians
Wheldon . . . . Aston Villa
Spiksley . . . . Sheffield Wednesday
Result: 3–1
Scorers: Bloomer (2), Wheldon

65. 18 February 1899
v IRELAND . . . . Roker Park, Sunderland
Hillman . . . . Burnley
Bach . . . . Sunderland
Williams . . . . West Bromwich Albion
Forman, Frank . . . . Nottingham Forest
Crabtree . . . . Aston Villa
Needham . . . . Sheffield United
Athersmith . . . . Aston Villa
Bloomer . . . . Derby County
Smith, G. O. . . . . Corinthians
Settle . . . . Bury
Forman, Fred . . . . Nottingham Forest
Result: 13–2
Scorers: Frank Forman, Bloomer (2), Athersmith, Settle (3), G. O. Smith (4), Fred Forman (2)

66. 20 March 1899
v WALES . . . . Ashton Gate, Bristol
Robinson . . . . Southampton
Thickett . . . . Sheffield United
Williams . . . . West Bromwich Albion
Needham . . . . Sheffield United
Crabtree . . . . Aston Villa
Forman, Frank . . . . Nottingham Forest
Athersmith . . . . Aston Villa
Bloomer . . . . Derby County
Smith, G. O. . . . . Corinthians
Settle . . . . Bury
Forman, Fred . . . . Nottingham Forest
Result: 4–0
Scorers: Bloomer (2), Fred Forman, Needham

67. 8 April 1899
v SCOTLAND . . . . Villa Park, Birmingham
Robinson . . . . Southampton
Thickett . . . . Sheffield United
Howell . . . . Liverpool
Needham . . . . Sheffield United
Crabtree . . . . Aston Villa
Forman, Frank . . . . Nottingham Forest
Athersmith . . . . Aston Villa
Bloomer . . . . Derby County
Smith, G. O. . . . . Corinthians
Settle . . . . Bury
Forman, Fred . . . . Nottingham Forest
Result: 2–1
Scorers: G. O. Smith, Settle

68. 17 March 1900
v IRELAND . . . . Lansdowne Road, Dublin
Robinson . . . . Southampton
Oakley . . . . Corinthians
Crabtree . . . . Aston Villa
Johnson . . . . Sheffield United
Holt . . . . Reading
Needham . . . . Sheffield United
Turner, A. . . . . Southampton
Cunliffe . . . . Portsmouth
Smith, G. O. . . . . Corinthians
Sagar . . . . Bury
Priest . . . . Sheffield United
Result: 2–0
Scorers: Johnson, Sagar

69. 26 March 1900
v WALES . . . . Cardiff Arms Park
Robinson . . . . Southampton
Spencer . . . . Aston Villa
Oakley . . . . Corinthians
Johnson . . . . Sheffield United
Chadwick, A. . . . . Southampton
Crabtree . . . . Aston Villa
Athersmith . . . . Aston Villa
Foster . . . . Oxford University
Smith, G. O. . . . . Corinthians
Wilson . . . . Corinthians
Spouncer . . . . Nottingham Forest
Result: 1–1
Scorer: Wilson

70. 7 April 1900
v SCOTLAND . . . . Celtic Park, Glasgow
Robinson . . . . Southampton
Oakley . . . . Corinthians
Crabtree . . . . Aston Villa
Johnson . . . . Sheffield United
Chadwick, A. . . . . Southampton
Needham . . . . Sheffield United
Athersmith . . . . Aston Villa
Bloomer . . . . Derby County
Smith, G. O. . . . . Corinthians
Wilson . . . . Corinthians
Plant . . . . Bury
Result: 1–4
Scorer: Bloomer

 DID YOU KNOW...?

England's best run without defeat lasted from March 1890 until March 1896, when they went twenty games without losing a match.

71. 9 March 1901
v IRELAND . . . . The Dell, Southampton
Robinson . . . . Southampton
Fry . . . . Corinthians
Oakley . . . . Corinthians
Jones, W. . . . . Bristol City
Crawshaw . . . . Sheffield Wednesday
Needham . . . . Sheffield United
Turner, A. . . . . Southampton
Foster . . . . Corinthians
Hedley . . . . Sheffield United
Banks . . . . Millwall Athletic
Cox . . . . Liverpool
Result: 3–0
Scorers: Foster (2), Crawshaw

72. 18 March 1901
v WALES. . . . . St James' Park, Newcastle
Kingsley . . . . Newcastle United
Crabtree. . . . . Aston Villa
Oakley . . . . Corinthians
Wilkes . . . . Aston Villa
Bannister . . . . Burnley
Needham. . . . . Sheffield United
Bennett . . . . Sheffield United
Bloomer. . . . . Derby County
Beats . . . . Wolverhampton Wanderers
Foster. . . . . Corinthians
Corbett, B. . . . . Corinthians
Result: 6–0
Scorers: Bloomer (4), Foster, Needham (pen.)

73. 30 March 1901
v SCOTLAND. . . . . Crystal Palace, London
Sutcliffe . . . . Bolton Wanderers
Iremonger . . . . Nottingham Forest
Oakley . . . . Corinthians
Wilkes . . . . Aston Villa
Forman, Frank . . . . Nottingham Forest
Needham. . . . . Sheffield United
Bennett . . . . Sheffield United
Bloomer. . . . . Derby County
Smith, G. O. . . . . Corinthians
Foster. . . . . Corinthians
Blackburn. . . . . Blackburn Rovers
Result: 2–2
Scorers: Bloomer, Blackburn

74. 3 March 1902
v WALES. . . . . Racecourse Ground,
 Wrexham
George. . . . . Aston Villa
Crompton. . . . . Blackburn Rovers
Crabtree. . . . . Aston Villa
Wilkes . . . . Aston Villa
Abbott . . . . Everton
Needham. . . . . Sheffield United
Hogg . . . . Sunderland
Bloomer. . . . . Derby County
Sagar. . . . . Bury
Foster. . . . . Corinthians
Lipsham . . . . Sheffield United
Result: 0–0

75. 22 March 1902
v IRELAND . . . . Balmoral Showgrounds,
 Belfast
George. . . . . Aston Villa
Crompton. . . . . Blackburn Rovers
Iremonger . . . . Nottingham Forest
Wilkes . . . . Aston Villa
Bannister . . . . Bolton Wanderers
Forman, Frank . . . . Nottingham Forest
Hogg . . . . Sunderland
Bloomer. . . . . Derby County
Calvey . . . . Nottingham Forest
Settle. . . . . Everton
Blackburn. . . . . Blackburn Rovers
Result: 1–0
Scorer: Settle

76. 3 May 1902
v SCOTLAND. . . . . Villa Park, Birmingham
George. . . . . Aston Villa
Crompton. . . . . Blackburn Rovers
Molyneux. . . . . Southampton
Wilkes . . . . Aston Villa
Forman, Frank . . . . Nottingham Forest
Houlker . . . . Blackburn Rovers
Hogg . . . . Sunderland
Bloomer. . . . . Derby County
Beats . . . . Wolverhampton Wanderers

Settle . . . . Everton
Cox . . . . Liverpool
Result: 2–2
Scorers: Wilkes, Settle

77. 14 February 1903
v IRELAND . . . . Molineux, Wolverhampton
Baddeley . . . . Wolverhampton Wanderers
Spencer . . . . Aston Villa
Molyneux. . . . . Southampton
Johnson . . . . Sheffield United
Holford . . . . Stoke
Hadley . . . . West Bromwich Albion
Davis, H. . . . . Sheffield Wednesday
Sharp. . . . . Everton
Woodward . . . . Tottenham Hotspur
Settle . . . . Everton
Lockett. . . . . Stoke
Result: 4–0
Scorers: Sharp, Davis, Woodward (2)

78. 2 March 1903
v WALES. . . . . Fratton Park, Portsmouth
Sutcliffe . . . . Millwall Athletic
Crompton. . . . . Blackburn Rovers
Molyneux. . . . . Southampton
Johnson . . . . Sheffield United
Forman, Frank . . . . Nottingham Forest
Houlker . . . . Portsmouth
Davis, H. . . . . Sheffield Wednesday
Garratty . . . . Aston Villa
Woodward . . . . Tottenham Hotspur
Bache . . . . Aston Villa
Corbett, R. . . . . Old Malvernians
Result: 2–1
Scorers: Bache, Woodward

79. 14 April 1903
v SCOTLAND. . . . . Bramall Lane, Sheffield
Baddeley . . . . Wolverhampton Wanderers
Crompton. . . . . Blackburn Rovers
Molyneux. . . . . Southampton
Johnson . . . . Sheffield United
Booth, T. . . . . Everton
Houlker . . . . Portsmouth
Davis, H. . . . . Sheffield Wednesday
Humphreys. . . . . Notts County
Woodward . . . . Tottenham Hotspur
Capes . . . . Stoke
Cox . . . . Liverpool
Result: 1–2
Scorer: Woodward

80. 29 February 1904
v WALES. . . . . Racecourse Ground,
 Wrexham
Baddeley . . . . Wolverhampton Wanderers
Crompton. . . . . Blackburn Rovers
Burgess . . . . Manchester City
Lee . . . . Southampton
Crawshaw . . . . Sheffield Wednesday
Ruddlesdin. . . . . Sheffield Wednesday
Brawn . . . . Aston Villa
Common . . . . Sheffield United
Brown, A. . . . . Sheffield United
Bache . . . . Aston Villa
Davis, G. . . . . Derby County
Result: 2–2
Scorers: Common, Bache

81. 12 March 1904
v IRELAND . . . . Solitude Ground, Belfast
Baddeley . . . . Wolverhampton Wanderers
Crompton. . . . . Blackburn Rovers
Burgess . . . . Manchester City
Ruddlesdin. . . . . Sheffield Wednesday

Crawshaw . . . . Sheffield Wednesday
Leake . . . . Aston Villa
Brawn . . . . Aston Villa
Common . . . . Sheffield United
Woodward . . . . Tottenham Hotspur
Bache . . . . Aston Villa
Davis, G. . . . . Derby County
Result: 3–1
Scorers: Common, Bache, Davis

82. 9 April 1904

v SCOTLAND . . . . Celtic Park, Glasgow
Baddeley . . . . Wolverhampton Wanderers
Crompton . . . . Blackburn Rovers
Burgess . . . . Manchester City
Wolstenholme . . . . Everton
Wilkinson . . . . Sheffield United
Leake . . . . Aston Villa
Rutherford . . . . Newcastle United
Bloomer . . . . Derby County
Woodward . . . . Tottenham Hotspur
Harris . . . . Cambridge University
Blackburn . . . . Blackburn Rovers
Result: 1–0
Scorer: Bloomer

83. 25 February 1905

v IRELAND . . . . Ayresome Park,
 Middlesbrough
Williamson . . . . Middlesbrough
Balmer . . . . Everton
Carr . . . . Newcastle United
Wolstenholme . . . . Blackburn Rovers
Roberts . . . . Manchester United
Leake . . . . Aston Villa
Bond . . . . Preston North End
Bloomer . . . . Derby County
Woodward . . . . Tottenham Hotspur
Harris . . . . Old Westminsters
Booth, F. . . . . Manchester City
Result: 1–1
Scorer: Bloomer

84. 27 March 1905

v WALES . . . . Anfield, Liverpool
Linacre . . . . Nottingham Forest
Spencer . . . . Aston Villa
Smith, H. . . . . Reading
Wolstenholme . . . . Blackburn Rovers
Roberts . . . . Manchester United
Leake . . . . Aston Villa
Bond . . . . Preston North End
Bloomer . . . . Derby County
Woodward . . . . Tottenham Hotspur
Harris . . . . Old Westminsters
Hardman . . . . Everton
Result: 3–1
Scorers: Woodward (2), Harris

85. 1 April 1905

v SCOTLAND . . . . Crystal Palace, London
Linacre . . . . Nottingham Forest
Spencer . . . . Aston Villa
Smith, H. . . . . Reading
Ruddlesdin . . . . Sheffield Wednesday
Roberts . . . . Manchester United
Leake . . . . Aston Villa
Sharp . . . . Everton
Bloomer . . . . Derby County
Woodward . . . . Tottenham Hotspur
Bache . . . . Aston Villa
Bridgett . . . . Sunderland
Result: 1–0
Scorer: Bache

86. 17 February 1906

v IRELAND . . . . Solitude Ground, Belfast
Ashcroft . . . . Woolwich Arsenal
Crompton . . . . Blackburn Rovers
Smith, H. . . . . Reading
Warren . . . . Derby County
Veitch . . . . Newcastle United
Houlker . . . . Southampton
Bond . . . . Preston North End
Day . . . . Old Malvernians
Brown, A. . . . . Sheffield United
Harris . . . . Old Westminsters
Gosnell . . . . Newcastle United
Result: 5–0
Scorers: Bond (2), Day, Harris, Brown

87. 19 March 1906

v WALES . . . . Cardiff Arms Park
Ashcroft . . . . Woolwich Arsenal
Crompton . . . . Blackburn Rovers
Smith, H. . . . . Reading
Warren . . . . Derby County
Veitch . . . . Newcastle United
Houlker . . . . Southampton
Bond . . . . Preston North End
Day . . . . Old Malvernians
Common . . . . Middlesbrough
Harris . . . . Old Westminsters
Wright . . . . Cambridge University
Result: 1–0
Scorer: Day

88. 7 April 1906

v SCOTLAND . . . . Hampden Park, Glasgow
Ashcroft . . . . Woolwich Arsenal
Crompton . . . . Blackburn Rovers
Burgess . . . . Manchester City
Warren . . . . Derby County
Veitch . . . . Newcastle United
Makepeace . . . . Everton
Bond . . . . Preston North End
Day . . . . Old Malvernians
Shepherd . . . . Bolton Wanderers
Harris . . . . Old Westminsters
Conlin . . . . Bradford City
Result: 1–2
Scorer: Shepherd

 DID YOU KNOW...?

When England met Scotland at Crystal Palace on
1 April 1905, the visitors were wearing Lord
Rosebery's racing colours of primrose and white
hoops.

89. 16 February 1907

v IRELAND . . . . Goodison Park, Everton
Hardy . . . . Liverpool
Crompton . . . . Blackburn Rovers
Carr . . . . Newcastle United
Warren . . . . Derby County
Wedlock . . . . Bristol City
Hawkes . . . . Luton Town
Rutherford . . . . Newcastle United
Coleman . . . . Woolwich Arsenal
Hilsdon . . . . Chelsea
Bache . . . . Aston Villa
Hardman . . . . Everton
Result: 1–0
Scorer: Hardman

90. 18 March 1907
v WALES . . . . Craven Cottage, Fulham
Hardy. . . . . Liverpool
Crompton. . . . . Blackburn Rovers
Pennington. . . . . West Bromwich Albion
Warren. . . . . Derby County
Wedlock. . . . . Bristol City
Veitch . . . . Newcastle United
Rutherford . . . . Newcastle United
Bloomer. . . . . Middlesbrough
Thornley. . . . . Manchester City
Stewart . . . . Sheffield Wednesday
Wall . . . . Manchester United
Result: 1–1
Scorer: Stewart

91. 6 April 1907
v SCOTLAND. . . . . St James' Park, Newcastle
Hardy. . . . . Liverpool
Crompton. . . . . Blackburn Rovers
Pennington. . . . . West Bromwich Albion
Warren. . . . . Derby County
Wedlock. . . . . Bristol City
Veitch . . . . Newcastle United
Rutherford . . . . Newcastle United
Bloomer. . . . . Middlesbrough
Woodward . . . . Tottenham Hotspur
Stewart . . . . Sheffield Wednesday
Hardman . . . . Everton
Result: 1–1
Scorer: Bloomer

92. 15 February 1908
v IRELAND . . . . Solitude Ground, Belfast
Maskrey. . . . . Derby County
Crompton. . . . . Blackburn Rovers
Pennington. . . . . West Bromwich Albion
Warren. . . . . Derby County
Wedlock. . . . . Bristol City
Lintott . . . . Queen's Park Rangers
Rutherford . . . . Newcastle United
Woodward . . . . Tottenham Hotspur
Hilsdon . . . . Chelsea
Windridge . . . . Chelsea
Hardman . . . . Manchester United
Result: 3–1
Scorers: Woodward, Hilsdon (2)

93. 16 March 1908
v WALES. . . . . Racecourse Ground,
Wrexham
Bailey. . . . . Leicester Fosse
Crompton. . . . . Blackburn Rovers
Pennington. . . . . West Bromwich Albion
Warren. . . . . Derby County
Wedlock. . . . . Bristol City
Lintott . . . . Queen's Park Rangers
Rutherford . . . . Newcastle United
Woodward . . . . Tottenham Hotspur
Hilsdon . . . . Chelsea
Windridge . . . . Chelsea
Hardman . . . . Everton
Result: 7–1
Scorers: Wedlock, Windridge, Hilsdon (2), Woodward (3)

94. 4 April 1908
v SCOTLAND. . . . . Hampden Park, Glasgow
Hardy. . . . . Liverpool
Crompton. . . . . Blackburn Rovers
Pennington. . . . . West Bromwich Albion
Warren. . . . . Derby County
Wedlock. . . . . Bristol City
Lintott . . . . Queen's Park Rangers
Rutherford . . . . Newcastle United
Woodward . . . . Tottenham Hotspur

Hilsdon . . . . Chelsea
Windridge . . . . Chelsea
Bridgett . . . . Sunderland
Result: 1–1
Scorer: Windridge

95. 6 June 1908
v AUSTRIA . . . . Vienna
Bailey. . . . . Leicester Fosse
Crompton. . . . . Blackburn Rovers
Corbett, W. . . . . Birmingham
Warren. . . . . Derby County
Wedlock. . . . . Bristol City
Hawkes . . . . Luton Town
Rutherford . . . . Newcastle United
Woodward . . . . Tottenham Hotspur
Hilsdon . . . . Chelsea
Windridge . . . . Chelsea
Bridgett . . . . Sunderland
Result: 6–1
Scorers: Hilsdon (2), Windridge (2), Bridgett, Woodward

96. 8 June 1908
v AUSTRIA . . . . Vienna
Bailey. . . . . Leicester Fosse
Crompton. . . . . Blackburn Rovers
Pennington. . . . . West Bromwich Albion
Warren. . . . . Derby County
Wedlock. . . . . Bristol City
Hawkes . . . . Luton Town
Rutherford . . . . Newcastle United
Woodward . . . . Tottenham Hotspur
Bradshaw. . . . . Sheffield Wednesday
Windridge . . . . Chelsea
Bridgett . . . . Sunderland
Result: 11–1
Scorers: Woodward (4), Bradshaw (3), Bridgett, Warren,
Rutherford, Windridge

⚽ **DID YOU KNOW...?**

In 1908, the England team enjoyed a great success
on their first overseas tour. In the space of eight
days in June they beat Austria 6–1 and 11–1,
Hungary 7–0 and Bohemia 4–0.

97. 10 June 1908
v HUNGARY . . . . Budapest
Bailey. . . . . Leicester Fosse
Crompton. . . . . Blackburn Rovers
Corbett, W. . . . . Birmingham
Warren. . . . . Derby County
Wedlock. . . . . Bristol City
Hawkes . . . . Luton Town
Rutherford . . . . Newcastle United
Woodward . . . . Tottenham Hotspur
Hilsdon . . . . Chelsea
Windridge . . . . Chelsea
Bridgett . . . . Sunderland
Result: 7–0
Scorers: Hilsdon (4), Windridge, Woodward, Rutherford

98. 13 June 1908
v BOHEMIA . . . . Prague
Bailey. . . . . Leicester Fosse
Crompton. . . . . Blackburn Rovers
Corbett, W. . . . . Birmingham
Warren. . . . . Derby County
Wedlock. . . . . Bristol City

Hawkes . . . . Luton Town
Rutherford . . . . Newcastle United
Woodward . . . . Tottenham Hotspur
Hilsdon . . . . Chelsea
Windridge . . . . Chelsea
Bridgett . . . . Sunderland
Result: 4–0
Scorers: Hilsdon (2 – 1 pen.), Windridge, Rutherford

99. 13 February 1909
v IRELAND . . . . Valley Parade, Bradford
Hardy. . . . . Liverpool
Crompton. . . . . Blackburn Rovers
Cottle. . . . . Bristol City
Warren. . . . . Chelsea
Wedlock. . . . . Bristol City
Lintott . . . . Bradford City
Berry . . . . Oxford United
Woodward . . . . Tottenham Hotspur
Hilsdon . . . . Chelsea
Windridge . . . . Chelsea
Bridgett . . . . Sunderland
Result: 4–0
Scorers: Hilsdon (2 – 1 pen.), Woodward (2)

100. 15 March 1909
v WALES. . . . . City Ground, Nottingham
Hardy. . . . . Liverpool
Crompton. . . . . Blackburn Rovers
Pennington. . . . . West Bromwich Albion
Warren. . . . . Chelsea
Wedlock. . . . . Bristol City
Veitch . . . . Newcastle United
Pentland . . . . Middlesbrough
Woodward . . . . Tottenham Hotspur
Freeman. . . . . Everton
Holley . . . . Sunderland
Bridgett . . . . Sunderland
Result: 2–0
Scorers: Holley, Freeman

101. 3 April 1909
v SCOTLAND. . . . . Crystal Palace, London
Hardy. . . . . Liverpool
Crompton. . . . . Blackburn Rovers
Pennington. . . . . West Bromwich Albion
Warren. . . . . Chelsea
Wedlock. . . . . Bristol City
Lintott . . . . Bradford City
Pentland . . . . Middlesbrough
Fleming . . . . Swindon Town
Freeman. . . . . Everton
Holley . . . . Sunderland
Wall. . . . . Manchester United
Result: 2–0
Scorers: Wall (2)

102. 29 May 1909
v HUNGARY . . . . Budapest
Hardy. . . . . Liverpool
Crompton. . . . . Blackburn Rovers
Pennington. . . . . West Bromwich Albion
Warren. . . . . Chelsea
Wedlock. . . . . Bristol City
Lintott . . . . Bradford City
Pentland . . . . Middlesbrough
Fleming . . . . Swindon Town
Woodward . . . . Tottenham Hotspur
Holley . . . . Sunderland
Bridgett . . . . Sunderland
Result: 4–2
Scorers: Woodward (2), Fleming, Bridgett

103. 31 May 1909
v HUNGARY . . . . Budapest
Hardy. . . . . Liverpool

Crompton. . . . . Blackburn Rovers
Pennington. . . . . West Bromwich Albion
Warren. . . . . Chelsea
Wedlock. . . . . Bristol City
Lintott . . . . Bradford City
Pentland . . . . Middlesbrough
Fleming . . . . Swindon Town
Woodward . . . . Tottenham Hotspur
Holley . . . . Sunderland
Bridgett . . . . Sunderland
Result: 8–2
Scorers: Woodward (4), Fleming (2), Holley (2)

104. 1 June 1909
v AUSTRIA . . . . Vienna
Hardy. . . . . Liverpool
Crompton. . . . . Blackburn Rovers
Pennington. . . . . West Bromwich Albion
Warren. . . . . Chelsea
Wedlock. . . . . Bristol City
Richards. . . . . Derby County
Pentland . . . . Middlesbrough
Halse . . . . Manchester United
Woodward . . . . Tottenham Hotspur
Holley . . . . Sunderland
Bridgett . . . . Sunderland
Result: 8–1
Scorers: Woodward (3), Warren, Halse (2), Holley (2)

105. 12 February 1910
v IRELAND . . . . Solitude Ground, Belfast
Hardy. . . . . Liverpool
Morley. . . . . Notts County
Cowell . . . . Blackburn Rovers
Ducat . . . . Woolwich Arsenal
Wedlock. . . . . Bristol City
Bradshaw, W. . . . . Blackburn Rovers
Bond . . . . Bradford City
Fleming . . . . Swindon Town
Woodward . . . . Chelsea
Bache . . . . Aston Villa
Hall . . . . Aston Villa
Result: 1–1
Scorer: Fleming

106. 14 March 1910
v WALES. . . . . Cardiff Arms Park
Hardy. . . . . Liverpool
Crompton. . . . . Blackburn Rovers
Pennington. . . . . West Bromwich Albion
Ducat. . . . . Woolwich Arsenal
Wedlock. . . . . Bristol City
Bradshaw, W. . . . . Blackburn Rovers
Bond . . . . Bradford City
Fleming . . . . Swindon Town
Parkinson. . . . . Liverpool
Holley . . . . Sunderland
Wall. . . . . Manchester United
Result: 1–0
Scorer: Ducat

107. 2 April 1910
v SCOTLAND. . . . . Hampden Park, Glasgow
Hardy. . . . . Liverpool
Crompton. . . . . Blackburn Rovers
Pennington. . . . . West Bromwich Albion
Ducat. . . . . Woolwich Arsenal
Wedlock. . . . . Bristol City
Makepeace . . . . Everton
Bond . . . . Bradford City
Hibbert. . . . . Bury
Parkinson. . . . . Liverpool
Hardinge . . . . Sheffield United
Wall. . . . . Manchester United
Result: 0–2

108. **11 February 1911**
v IRELAND . . . . Baseball Ground, Derby
Williamson . . . . Middlesbrough
Crompton. . . . . Blackburn Rovers
Pennington. . . . . West Bromwich Albion
Warren . . . . Chelsea
Wedlock . . . . Bristol City
Sturgess . . . . Sheffield United
Simpson . . . . Blackburn Rovers
Fleming . . . . Swindon Town
Shepherd . . . . Newcastle United
Woodger . . . . Oldham Athletic
Evans . . . . Sheffield United
Result: 2–1
Scorers: Shepherd, Evans

109. **13 March 1911**
v WALES . . . . The Den, Millwall
Williamson . . . . Middlesbrough
Crompton. . . . . Blackburn Rovers
Pennington. . . . . West Bromwich Albion
Warren. . . . . Chelsea
Wedlock . . . . Bristol City
Hunt . . . . Leyton Orient
Simpson . . . . Blackburn Rovers
Fleming . . . . Swindon Town
Webb . . . . West Ham United
Woodward . . . . Chelsea
Evans . . . . Sheffield United
Result: 3–0
Scorers: Woodward (2), Webb

110. **1 April 1911**
v SCOTLAND . . . . Goodison Park, Everton
Williamson . . . . Middlesbrough
Crompton. . . . . Blackburn Rovers
Pennington. . . . . West Bromwich Albion
Warren. . . . . Chelsea
Wedlock . . . . Bristol City
Hunt . . . . Leyton Orient
Simpson . . . . Blackburn Rovers
Stewart . . . . Newcastle United
Webb . . . . West Ham United
Bache . . . . Aston Villa
Evans . . . . Sheffield United
Result: 1–1
Scorer: Stewart

111. **10 February 1912**
v IRELAND . . . . Dalymount Park, Dublin
Hardy . . . . Liverpool
Crompton. . . . . Blackburn Rovers
Pennington. . . . . West Bromwich Albion
Brittleton . . . . Sheffield Wednesday
Wedlock . . . . Bristol City
Bradshaw, W. . . . . Blackburn Rovers
Simpson . . . . Blackburn Rovers
Fleming . . . . Swindon Town
Freeman . . . . Burnley
Holley . . . . Sunderland
Mordue . . . . Sunderland
Result: 6–1
Scorers: Fleming (3), Freeman, Holley, Simpson

112. **11 March 1912**
v WALES . . . . Racecourse Ground,
Wrexham
Williamson . . . . Middlesbrough
Crompton. . . . . Blackburn Rovers
Pennington . . . . West Bromwich Albion
Brittleton . . . . Sheffield Wednesday
Wedlock . . . . Bristol City
Makepeace . . . . Everton
Simpson . . . . Blackburn Rovers
Jefferis . . . . Everton
Freeman . . . . Burnley

Holley . . . . Sunderland
Evans . . . . Sheffield United
Result: 2–0
Scorers: Holley, Freeman

113. **23 March 1912**
v SCOTLAND . . . . Hampden Park, Glasgow
Williamson . . . . Middlesbrough
Crompton. . . . . Blackburn Rovers
Pennington. . . . . West Bromwich Albion
Brittleton . . . . Sheffield Wednesday
Wedlock . . . . Bristol City
Makepeace . . . . Everton
Simpson . . . . Blackburn Rovers
Jefferis . . . . Everton
Freeman . . . . Burnley
Holley . . . . Sunderland
Wall . . . . Manchester United
Result: 1–1
Scorer: Holley

114. **15 February 1913**
v IRELAND . . . . Belfast
Williamson . . . . Middlesbrough
Crompton. . . . . Blackburn Rovers
Benson. . . . . Sheffield United
Cuggy . . . . Sunderland
Boyle . . . . Burnley
Utley . . . . Barnsley
Mordue . . . . Sunderland
Buchan . . . . Sunderland
Elliott. . . . . Middlesbrough
Smith, Joe . . . . Bolton Wanderers
Wall . . . . Manchester United
Result: 1–2
Scorer: Buchan

115. **17 March 1913**
v WALES . . . . Ashton Gate, Bristol
Scattergood . . . . Derby County
Crompton. . . . . Blackburn Rovers
Pennington. . . . . West Bromwich Albion
Moffatt . . . . Oldham Athletic
McCall . . . . Preston North End
Bradshaw, W. . . . . Blackburn Rovers
Wallace . . . . Aston Villa
Fleming . . . . Swindon Town
Hampton . . . . Aston Villa
Latheron . . . . Blackburn Rovers
Hodkinson . . . . Blackburn Rovers
Result: 4–3
Scorers: Fleming, McCall, Latheron, Hampton

116. **5 April 1913**
v SCOTLAND . . . . Stamford Bridge, Chelsea
Hardy . . . . Aston Villa
Crompton. . . . . Blackburn Rovers
Pennington. . . . . West Bromwich Albion
Brittleton . . . . Sheffield Wednesday
McCall . . . . Preston North End
Watson, W. . . . . Burnley
Simpson . . . . Blackburn Rovers
Fleming . . . . Swindon Town
Hampton . . . . Aston Villa
Holley . . . . Sunderland
Hodkinson . . . . Blackburn Rovers
Result: 1–0
Scorer: Hampton

117. **14 February 1914**
v IRELAND . . . . Ayresome Park,
Middlesbrough
Hardy . . . . Aston Villa
Crompton. . . . . Blackburn Rovers
Pennington. . . . . West Bromwich Albion
Cuggy . . . . Sunderland

Buckley . . . . Derby County
Watson, W. . . . . Burnley
Wallace . . . . Aston Villa
Shea . . . . Blackburn Rovers
Elliott. . . . . Middlesbrough
Latheron . . . . Blackburn Rovers
Martin . . . . Sunderland
Result: 0–3

118. 16 March 1914
v WALES. . . . . Ninian Park, Cardiff
Hardy. . . . . Aston Villa
Crompton. . . . . Blackburn Rovers
Colclough. . . . . Crystal Palace
Brittleton . . . . Sheffield Wednesday
Wedlock. . . . . Bristol City
McNeal . . . . West Bromwich Albion
Simpson. . . . . Blackburn Rovers
Shea . . . . Blackburn Rovers
Hampton . . . . Aston Villa
Smith, Joe . . . . Bolton Wanderers
Mosscrop. . . . . Burnley
Result: 2–0
Scorers: Joe Smith, Wedlock

119. 4 April 1914
v SCOTLAND. . . . . Hampden Park, Glasgow
Hardy. . . . . Aston Villa
Crompton. . . . . Blackburn Rovers
Pennington. . . . . West Bromwich Albion
Sturgess. . . . . Sheffield United
McCall . . . . Preston North End
McNeal . . . . West Bromwich Albion
Walden . . . . Tottenham Hotspur
Fleming . . . . Swindon Town
Hampton . . . . Aston Villa
Smith, Joe . . . . Bolton Wanderers
Mosscrop. . . . . Burnley
Result: 1–3
Scorer: Fleming

120. 25 October 1919
v IRELAND . . . . Belfast
Hardy. . . . . Aston Villa
Smith, Joseph. . . . . West Bromwich Albion
Knight . . . . Portsmouth
Bagshaw . . . . Derby County
Bowser . . . . West Bromwich Albion
Watson, W. . . . . Burnley
Turnbull . . . . Bradford Park Avenue
Carr . . . . Middlesbrough
Cock . . . . Huddersfield Town
Smith, Joe . . . . Bolton Wanderers
Hodkinson . . . . Blackburn Rovers
Result: 1–1
Scorer: Cock

121. 15 March 1920
v WALES. . . . . Highbury Stadium, Arsenal
Hardy. . . . . Aston Villa
Clay . . . . Tottenham Hotspur
Pennington. . . . . West Bromwich Albion
Ducat. . . . . Aston Villa
Barson . . . . Aston Villa
Grimsdell . . . . Tottenham Hotspur
Chedgzoy. . . . . Everton
Buchan . . . . Sunderland
Elliott. . . . . Middlesbrough
Smith, Joe . . . . Bolton Wanderers
Quantrill. . . . . Derby County
Result: 1–2
Scorer: Buchan

122. 10 April 1920
v SCOTLAND. . . . . Hillsborough, Sheffield
Hardy. . . . . Aston Villa

Longworth . . . . Liverpool
Pennington. . . . . West Bromwich Albion
Ducat. . . . . Aston Villa
McCall . . . . Preston North End
Grimsdell . . . . Tottenham Hotspur
Wallace . . . . Aston Villa
Kelly. . . . . Burnley
Cock . . . . Chelsea
Morris . . . . West Bromwich Albion
Quantrill. . . . . Derby County
Result: 5–4
Scorers: Kelly (2), Cock, Morris, Quantrill

123. 23 October 1920
v IRELAND . . . . Roker Park, Sunderland
Mew . . . . Manchester United
Downs . . . . Everton
Bullock, F. . . . . Huddersfield Town
Ducat. . . . . Aston Villa
McCall . . . . Preston North End
Grimsdell . . . . Tottenham Hotspur
Chedgzoy. . . . . Everton
Kelly. . . . . Burnley
Walker . . . . Aston Villa
Morris . . . . West Bromwich Albion
Quantrill. . . . . Derby County
Result: 2–0
Scorers: Kelly, Walker

124. 14 March 1921
v WALES. . . . . Ninian Park, Cardiff
Coleman . . . . Dulwich Hamlet
Cresswell . . . . South Shields
Silcock . . . . Manchester United
Bamber . . . . Liverpool
Wilson . . . . Sheffield Wednesday
Bromilow . . . . Liverpool
Chedgzoy. . . . . Everton
Kelly. . . . . Burnley
Buchan . . . . Sunderland
Chambers. . . . . Liverpool
Quantrill. . . . . Derby County
Result: 0–0

125. 19 April 1921
v SCOTLAND . . . . Hampden Park, Glasgow
Gough . . . . Sheffield United
Smart. . . . . Aston Villa
Silcock . . . . Manchester United
Smith, B. . . . . Tottenham Hotspur
Wilson . . . . Sheffield Wednesday
Grimsdell . . . . Tottenham Hotspur
Chedgzoy. . . . . Everton
Kelly. . . . . Burnley
Chambers. . . . . Liverpool
Bliss. . . . . Tottenham Hotspur
Dimmock . . . . Tottenham Hotspur
Result: 0–3

126. 21 May 1921
v BELGIUM . . . . Brussels
Baker, H. . . . . Everton
Fort . . . . Millwall Athletic
Longworth . . . . Liverpool
Read . . . . Tufnell Park
Wilson . . . . Sheffield Wednesday
Barton . . . . Birmingham
Rawlings . . . . Preston North End
Seed . . . . Tottenham Hotspur
Buchan . . . . Sunderland
Chambers. . . . . Liverpool
Harrison. . . . . Everton
Result: 2–0
Scorers: Buchan, Chambers

127. 22 October 1921
v IRELAND . . . . Belfast
Dawson . . . . Burnley
Clay . . . . Tottenham Hotspur
Lucas . . . . Liverpool
Moss . . . . Aston Villa
Wilson . . . . Sheffield Wednesday
Barton . . . . Birmingham
Chedgzoy . . . . Everton
Kirton . . . . Aston Villa
Simms . . . . Luton Town
Walker . . . . Aston Villa
Harrison . . . . Everton
Result: 1–1
Scorer: Kirton

128. 13 March 1922
v WALES . . . . Anfield, Liverpool
Davison . . . . Sheffield Wednesday
Clay . . . . Tottenham Hotspur
Titmuss . . . . Southampton
Smith, B. . . . . Tottenham Hotspur
Woosnam . . . . Manchester City
Bromilow . . . . Liverpool
Walden . . . . Tottenham Hotspur
Kelly . . . . Burnley
Rawlings, W. . . . . Southampton
Walker . . . . Aston Villa
Smith, W. H. . . . . Huddersfield Town
Result: 1–0
Scorer: Kelly

129. 8 April 1922
v SCOTLAND . . . . Villa Park, Birmingham
Dawson . . . . Burnley
Clay . . . . Tottenham Hotspur
Wadsworth . . . . Huddersfield Town
Moss . . . . Aston Villa
Wilson . . . . Sheffield Wednesday
Bromilow . . . . Liverpool
York . . . . Aston Villa
Kelly . . . . Burnley
Rawlings, W. . . . . Southampton
Walker . . . . Aston Villa
Smith, W. H. . . . . Huddersfield Town
Result: 0–1

130. 21 October 1922
v IRELAND . . . . The Hawthorns, West
. . . . Bromwich
Taylor . . . . Huddersfield Town
Smith, Joseph . . . . West Bromwich Albion
Harrow . . . . Chelsea
Moss . . . . Aston Villa
Wilson . . . . Sheffield Wednesday
Grimsdell . . . . Tottenham Hotspur
Mercer . . . . Sheffield United
Seed . . . . Tottenham Hotspur
Osborne . . . . Fulham
Chambers . . . . Liverpool
Williams . . . . Clapton Orient
Result: 2–0
Scorer: Chambers (2)

131. 5 March 1923
v WALES . . . . Ninian Park, Cardiff
Taylor . . . . Huddersfield Town
Longworth . . . . Liverpool
Titmuss . . . . Southampton
Magee . . . . West Bromwich Albion
Wilson . . . . Sheffield Wednesday
Grimsdell . . . . Tottenham Hotspur
Carr . . . . Middlesbrough
Seed . . . . Tottenham Hotspur
Watson . . . . West Ham United

Chambers . . . . Liverpool
Williams . . . . Clapton Orient
Result: 2–2
Scorers: Chambers, Watson

132. 19 March 1923
v BELGIUM . . . . Highbury Stadium, Arsenal
Taylor . . . . Huddersfield Town
Longworth . . . . Liverpool
Wadsworth . . . . Huddersfield Town
Kean . . . . Sheffield Wednesday
Wilson . . . . Sheffield Wednesday
Bromilow . . . . Liverpool
Mercer . . . . Sheffield United
Seed . . . . Tottenham Hotspur
Bullock, N. . . . . Bury
Chambers . . . . Liverpool
Hegan . . . . Corinthians
Result: 6–1
Scorers: Hegan (2), Chambers, Seed, Mercer, N. Bullock

133. 14 April 1923
v SCOTLAND . . . . Hampden Park, Glasgow
Taylor . . . . Huddersfield Town
Longworth . . . . Liverpool
Wadsworth . . . . Huddersfield Town
Kean . . . . Sheffield Wednesday
Wilson . . . . Sheffield Wednesday
Tresadern . . . . West Ham United
Chedgzoy . . . . Everton
Kelly . . . . Burnley
Watson, V. . . . . West Ham United
Chambers . . . . Liverpool
Tunstall . . . . Sheffield United
Result: 2–2
Scorers: Kelly, V. Watson

134. 10 May 1923
v FRANCE . . . . Paris
Alderson . . . . Crystal Palace
Cresswell . . . . Sunderland
Jones, H. . . . . Nottingham Forest
Plum . . . . Charlton Athletic
Seddon . . . . Bolton Wanderers
Barton . . . . Birmingham
Osborne, F. . . . . Fulham
Buchan . . . . Sunderland
Creek . . . . Corinthians
Hartley . . . . Oxford City
Hegan . . . . Corinthians
Result: 4–1
Scorers: Hegan (2), Buchan, Creek

135. 21 May 1923
v SWEDEN . . . . Stockholm
Williamson . . . . Arsenal
Ashurst . . . . Notts County
Harrow . . . . Chelsea
Patchitt . . . . Corinthians
Seddon . . . . Bolton Wanderers
Tresadern . . . . West Ham United
Thornewell . . . . Derby County
Moore, J. . . . . Derby County
Bedford . . . . Blackpool
Walker . . . . Aston Villa
Urwin . . . . Middlesbrough
Result: 4–2
Scorers: Walker (2), J. Moore, Thornewell

136. 24 May 1923
v SWEDEN . . . . Stockholm
Williamson . . . . Arsenal
Ashurst . . . . Notts County
Silcock . . . . Manchester United
Magee . . . . West Bromwich Albion

Seddon . . . . Bolton Wanderers
Patchitt . . . . Corinthians
Thornewell . . . . Derby County
Moore, W. . . . . West Ham United
Walker . . . . Aston Villa
Miller . . . . Charlton Athletic
Urwin . . . . Middlesbrough
Result: 3–1
Scorers: W. Moore (2), Miller

137. 20 October 1923
v N. IRELAND . . . . Windsor Park, Belfast
Taylor . . . . Huddersfield Town
Bower . . . . Corinthians
Wadsworth . . . . Huddersfield Town
Pantling . . . . Sheffield United
Wilson . . . . Sheffield Wednesday
Meehan . . . . Chelsea
Hegan . . . . Corinthians
Kelly . . . . Burnley
Bradford . . . . Birmingham
Chambers . . . . Liverpool
Tunstall . . . . Sheffield United
Result: 1–2
Scorer: Bradford

138. 1 November 1923
v BELGIUM . . . . Antwerp
Hufton . . . . West Ham United
Cresswell . . . . Sunderland
Bower . . . . Corinthians
Moss . . . . Aston Villa
Seddon . . . . Bolton Wanderers
Barton . . . . Birmingham
Hegan . . . . Corinthians
Brown, W. . . . . West Ham United
Roberts, W. . . . . Preston North End
Doggart . . . . Corinthians
Urwin . . . . Middlesbrough
Result: 2–2
Scorers: W. Brown, W. Roberts

139. 3 March 1924
v WALES . . . . Ewood Park, Blackburn
Sewell . . . . Blackburn Rovers
Smart . . . . Aston Villa
Mort . . . . Aston Villa
Kean . . . . Sheffield Wednesday
Wilson . . . . Sheffield Wednesday
Barton . . . . Birmingham
Chedgzoy . . . . Everton
Jack . . . . Bolton Wanderers
Roberts, W. . . . . Preston North End
Stephenson, C. . . . . Huddersfield Town
Tunstall . . . . Sheffield United
Result: 1–2
Scorer: W. Roberts

140. 12 April 1924
v SCOTLAND . . . . Wembley Stadium
Taylor . . . . Huddersfield Town
Smart . . . . Aston Villa
Wadsworth . . . . Huddersfield Town
Moss . . . . Aston Villa
Spencer . . . . Newcastle United
Barton . . . . Birmingham
Butler, W. . . . . Bolton Wanderers
Jack . . . . Bolton Wanderers
Buchan . . . . Sunderland
Walker . . . . Aston Villa
Tunstall . . . . Sheffield United
Result: 1–1
Scorer: Walker

 DID YOU KNOW...?

The first international to be played at Wembley was a 1–1 draw between England and Scotland that took place on 12 April 1924.

141. 17 May 1924
v FRANCE . . . . Paris
Taylor . . . . Huddersfield Town
Lucas . . . . Liverpool
Mort . . . . Aston Villa
Ewer . . . . Casuals
Wilson . . . . Sheffield Wednesday
Blackburn . . . . Aston Villa
Thornewell . . . . Derby County
Earle . . . . Clapton Orient
Gibbins . . . . Clapton Orient
Storer . . . . Derby County
Tunstall . . . . Sheffield United
Result: 3–1
Scorers: Gibbins (2), Storer

142. 22 October 1924
v N. IRELAND . . . . Goodison Park, Everton
Mitchell . . . . Manchester City
Cresswell . . . . Sunderland
Wadsworth . . . . Huddersfield Town
Kean . . . . Sheffield Wednesday
Healless . . . . Blackburn Rovers
Barton . . . . Birmingham
Chedgzoy . . . . Everton
Kelly . . . . Burnley
Bedford . . . . Derby County
Walker . . . . Aston Villa
Tunstall . . . . Sheffield United
Result: 3–1
Scorers: Kelly, Bedford, Walker

143. 8 December 1924
v BELGIUM . . . . The Hawthorns, West
Bromwich
Hardy, H. . . . . Stockport County
Ashurst . . . . Notts County
Bower . . . . Corinthians
Magee . . . . West Bromwich Albion
Butler, J. . . . . Arsenal
Ewer . . . . Casuals
Osborne, F. . . . . Tottenham Hotspur
Roberts, F. . . . . Manchester City
Bradford . . . . Birmingham
Walker . . . . Aston Villa
Dorrell . . . . Aston Villa
Result: 4–0
Scorers: Bradford (2), Walker (2)

144. 29 February 1925
v WALES . . . . Vetch Field, Swansea
Pym . . . . Bolton Wanderers
Ashurst . . . . Notts County
Bower . . . . Corinthians
Hill, J. H. . . . . Burnley
Spencer . . . . Newcastle United
Graham . . . . Millwall Athletic
Kelly . . . . Burnley
Roberts, F. . . . . Manchester City
Cook . . . . Brighton & Hove Albion
Walker . . . . Aston Villa
Dorrell . . . . Aston Villa
Result: 2–1
Scorers: F. Roberts (2)

145. 4 April 1925

v SCOTLAND . . . . Hampden Park, Glasgow
Pym . . . . Bolton Wanderers
Ashurst . . . . Notts County
Wadsworth . . . . Huddersfield Town
Magee . . . . West Bromwich Albion
Townrow . . . . Clapton Orient
Graham . . . . Millwall Athletic
Kelly . . . . Burnley
Seed . . . . Tottenham Hotspur
Roberts, F. . . . . Manchester City
Walker . . . . Aston Villa
Tunstall . . . . Sheffield United
Result: 0–2

146. 21 May 1925

v FRANCE . . . . Paris
Fox . . . . Millwall Athletic
Parker . . . . Southampton
Felton . . . . Sheffield Wednesday
Magee . . . . West Bromwich Albion
Bryant . . . . Clapton Orient
Green. . . . . Sheffield United
Thornewell . . . . Derby County
Roberts, F. . . . . Manchester City
Gibbins . . . . Clapton Orient
Walker . . . . Aston Villa
Dorrell . . . . Aston Villa
Result: 3–2
Scorers: Gibbins, Dorrell, o.g.

147. 24 October 1925

v N. IRELAND . . . . Windsor Park, Belfast
Baker, H. . . . . Chelsea
Smart. . . . . Aston Villa
Hudspeth . . . . Newcastle United
Kean . . . . Sheffield Wednesday
Armitage . . . . Charlton Athletic
Bromilow . . . . Liverpool
Austin . . . . Manchester City
Puddefoot . . . . Blackburn Rovers
Ashton . . . . Corinthians
Walker . . . . Aston Villa
Dorrell . . . . Aston Villa
Result: 0–0

148. 1 March 1926

v WALES . . . . Selhurst Park, London
Pym . . . . Bolton Wanderers
Cresswell . . . . Sunderland
Wadsworth . . . . Huddersfield Town
Edwards. . . . . Leeds United
Townrow . . . . Clapton Orient
Green. . . . . Sheffield United
Urwin. . . . . Newcastle United
Kelly. . . . . Sunderland
Bullock, N. . . . . Bury
Walker . . . . Aston Villa
Dimmock . . . . Tottenham Hotspur
Result: 1–3
Scorer: Walker

149. 17 April 1926

v SCOTLAND . . . . Old Trafford, Manchester
Taylor. . . . . Huddersfield Town
Goodall . . . . Huddersfield Town
Mort . . . . Aston Villa
Edwards. . . . . Leeds United
Hill, J. H. . . . . Burnley
Green. . . . . Sheffield United
York. . . . . Aston Villa
Puddefoot . . . . Blackburn Rovers
Harper . . . . Blackburn Rovers
Walker . . . . Aston Villa
Ruffell . . . . West Ham United
Result: 0–1

150. 24 May 1926

v BELGIUM . . . . Antwerp
Ashmore . . . . West Bromwich Albion
Lucas . . . . Liverpool
Hill, R. H. . . . . Millwall Athletic
Kean . . . . Sheffield Wednesday
Cowan. . . . . Manchester City
Green. . . . . Sheffield United
Spence . . . . Manchester United
Carter, J. H. . . . . West Bromwich Albion
Osborne, F. . . . . Tottenham Hotspur
Johnson . . . . Manchester City
Dimmock . . . . Tottenham Hotspur
Result: 5–3
Scorers: Osborne (3), Carter, Johnson

151. 20 October 1926

v N. IRELAND . . . . Anfield, Liverpool
McInroy . . . . Sunderland
Cresswell . . . . Sunderland
Wadsworth . . . . Huddersfield Town
Edwards. . . . . Leeds United
Hill, J. H. . . . . Burnley
Green. . . . . Sheffield United
Spence . . . . Manchester United
Brown, G. . . . . Huddersfield Town
Bullock, N. . . . . Bury
Walker . . . . Aston Villa
Ruffell . . . . West Ham United
Result: 3–3
Scorers: G. Brown, Spence, N. Bullock

152. 12 February 1927

v WALES . . . . Racecourse Ground,
                                    Wrexham
Brown, J. . . . . Sheffield Wednesday
Bower . . . . Corinthians
Waterfield . . . . Burnley
Edwards. . . . . Leeds United
Seddon . . . . Bolton Wanderers
Green. . . . . Sheffield United
Pease . . . . Middlesbrough
Brown, G. . . . . Huddersfield Town
Dean . . . . Everton
Walker . . . . Aston Villa
Page . . . . Burnley
Result: 3–3
Scorers: Dean (2), Walker

153. 2 April 1927

v SCOTLAND . . . . Hampden Park, Glasgow
Brown, J. . . . . Sheffield Wednesday
Goodall . . . . Huddersfield Town
Jones, H. . . . . Blackburn Rovers
Edwards. . . . . Leeds United
Hill, J. H. . . . . Burnley
Bishop . . . . Leicester City
Hulme . . . . Arsenal
Brown, G. . . . . Huddersfield Town
Dean . . . . Everton
Rigby . . . . Blackburn Rovers
Page . . . . Burnley
Result: 2–1
Scorers: Dean (2)

154. 11 May 1927

v BELGIUM . . . . Brussels
Brown, J. . . . . Sheffield Wednesday
Goodall . . . . Huddersfield Town
Jones, H. . . . . Blackburn Rovers
Edwards. . . . . Leeds United
Hill, J. H. . . . . Burnley
Bishop . . . . Leicester City
Hulme . . . . Arsenal
Brown, G. . . . . Huddersfield Town

Dean . . . . Everton
Rigby . . . . Blackburn Rovers
Page . . . . Burnley
Result: 9–1
Scorers: Dean (3), G. Brown (2), Rigby (2), Page, Hulme

155. 21 May 1927
v LUXEMBOURG . . . . Luxembourg
Brown, J. . . . . Sheffield Wednesday
Goodall . . . . Huddersfield Town
Jones, H. . . . . Blackburn Rovers
Edwards. . . . . Leeds United
Kean . . . . Sheffield Wednesday
Bishop . . . . Leicester City
Kelly. . . . . Huddersfield Town
Brown, G. . . . . Huddersfield Town
Dean . . . . Everton
Rigby . . . . Blackburn Rovers
Page . . . . Burnley
Result: 5–2
Scorers: Dean (3), Kelly, Bishop

156. 26 May 1927
v FRANCE . . . . Paris
Brown, J. . . . . Sheffield Wednesday
Goodall . . . . Huddersfield Town
Jones, H. . . . . Blackburn Rovers
Edwards. . . . . Leeds United
Hill, J. H. . . . . Burnley
Bishop . . . . Leicester City
Hulme . . . . Arsenal
Brown, G. . . . . Huddersfield Town
Dean . . . . Everton
Rigby . . . . Blackburn Rovers
Page . . . . Burnley
Result: 6–0
Scorers: Dean (2), G. Brown (2), Rigby, o.g.

157. 22 October 1927
v N. IRELAND . . . . Windsor Park, Belfast
Hufton . . . . West Ham United
Cooper. . . . . Derby County
Jones, H. . . . . Blackburn Rovers
Nuttall . . . . Bolton Wanderers
Hill, J. H. . . . . Burnley
Storer. . . . . Derby County
Hulme . . . . Arsenal
Earle . . . . West Ham United
Dean . . . . Everton
Ball . . . . Bury
Page . . . . Burnley
Result: 0–2

158. 28 November 1927
v WALES . . . . Turf Moor, Burnley
Tremelling . . . . Birmingham
Goodall . . . . Huddersfield Town
Osborne, R. . . . . Leicester City
Baker, A. . . . . Arsenal
Hill, J. H. . . . . Burnley
Nuttall . . . . Bolton Wanderers
Hulme . . . . Arsenal
Brown, G. . . . . Huddersfield Town
Dean . . . . Everton
Rigby . . . . Blackburn Rovers
Page . . . . Burnley
Result: 1–2
Scorer: o.g.

159. 31 March 1928
v SCOTLAND. . . . . Wembley Stadium
Hufton . . . . West Ham United
Goodall . . . . Huddersfield Town
Jones, H. . . . . Blackburn Rovers
Edwards. . . . . Leeds United

Wilson, T. . . . . Huddersfield Town
Healless . . . . Blackburn Rovers
Hulme . . . . Arsenal
Kelly. . . . . Huddersfield Town
Dean . . . . Everton
Bradford. . . . . Birmingham
Smith, W. H. . . . . Huddersfield Town
Result: 1–5
Scorer: Kelly

160. 17 May 1928
v FRANCE . . . . Paris
Olney. . . . . Aston Villa
Goodall . . . . Huddersfield Town
Blenkinsop . . . . Sheffield Wednesday
Edwards. . . . . Leeds United
Matthews, V. . . . . Sheffield United
Green. . . . . Sheffield United
Bruton . . . . Burnley
Jack . . . . Bolton Wanderers
Dean . . . . Everton
Stephenson, G. . . . . Derby County
Barry . . . . Leicester City
Result: 5–1
Scorers: G. Stephenson (2), Dean (2), Jack

161. 19 May 1928
v BELGIUM . . . . Antwerp
Olney. . . . . Aston Villa
Goodall . . . . Huddersfield Town
Blenkinsop . . . . Sheffield Wednesday
Edwards. . . . . Leeds United
Matthews, V. . . . . Sheffield United
Green. . . . . Sheffield United
Bruton . . . . Burnley
Jack . . . . Bolton Wanderers
Dean . . . . Everton
Stephenson, G. . . . . Derby County
Barry . . . . Leicester City
Result: 3–1
Scorers: Dean (2), V. Matthews

162. 22 October 1928
v N. IRELAND . . . . Goodison Park, Everton
Hacking . . . . Oldham Athletic
Cooper. . . . . Derby County
Blenkinsop . . . . Sheffield Wednesday
Edwards. . . . . Leeds United
Barrett. . . . . West Ham United
Campbell . . . . Blackburn Rovers
Hulme . . . . Arsenal
Hine. . . . . Leicester City
Dean . . . . Everton
Bradford. . . . . Birmingham
Ruffell . . . . West Ham United
Result: 2–1
Scorers: Hulme, Dean

163. 17 November 1928
v WALES. . . . . Vetch Field, Swansea
Hacking . . . . Oldham Athletic
Cooper. . . . . Derby County
Blenkinsop . . . . Sheffield Wednesday
Edwards. . . . . Leeds United
Hart. . . . . Leeds United
Campbell . . . . Blackburn Rovers
Hulme . . . . Arsenal
Hine. . . . . Leicester City
Dean . . . . Everton
Bradford. . . . . Birmingham
Ruffell . . . . West Ham United
Result: 3–2
Scorers: Hulme (2), Hine

164. 13 April 1929
v SCOTLAND . . . . Hampden Park, Glasgow
Hacking . . . . Oldham Athletic
Cooper. . . . . Derby County
Blenkinsop . . . . Sheffield Wednesday
Edwards. . . . . Leeds United
Seddon . . . . Bolton Wanderers
Nuttall . . . . Bolton Wanderers
Bruton . . . . Burnley
Brown, G. . . . . Huddersfield Town
Dean . . . . Everton
Wainscoat . . . . Leeds United
Ruffell . . . . West Ham United
Result: 0–1

165. 9 May 1929
v FRANCE . . . . Paris
Hufton . . . . West Ham United
Blenkinsop . . . . Sheffield Wednesday
Cooper. . . . . Derby County
Kean . . . . Bolton Wanderers
Hill, J. H. . . . . Newcastle United
Peacock . . . . Middlesbrough
Adcock. . . . . Leicester City
Kail . . . . Dulwich Hamlet
Camsell . . . . Middlesbrough
Bradford. . . . . Birmingham
Barry . . . . Leicester City
Result: 4–1
Scorers: Kail (2), Camsell (2)

166. 11 May 1929
v BELGIUM . . . . Brussels
Hufton . . . . West Ham United
Cooper. . . . . Derby County
Blenkinsop . . . . Sheffield Wednesday
Oliver. . . . . Fulham
Hill, J. H. . . . . Newcastle United
Peacock . . . . Middlesbrough
Adcock. . . . . Leicester City
Kail . . . . Dulwich Hamlet
Camsell . . . . Middlesbrough
Carter, J. H. . . . . West Bromwich Albion
Barry . . . . Leicester City
Result: 5–1
Scorers: Camsell (4), J. H. Carter

167. 15 May 1929
v SPAIN . . . . Madrid
Hufton . . . . West Ham United
Cooper. . . . . Derby County
Blenkinsop . . . . Sheffield Wednesday
Kean . . . . Bolton Wanderers
Hill, J. H. . . . . Newcastle United
Peacock . . . . Middlesbrough
Adcock. . . . . Leicester City
Kail . . . . Dulwich Hamlet
Bradford. . . . . Birmingham
Carter, J. H. . . . . West Bromwich Albion
Barry . . . . Leicester City
Result: 3–4
Scorers: J. H. Carter (2), Bradford

168. 19 October 1929
v N. IRELAND . . . . Windsor Park, Belfast
Brown, J. . . . . Sheffield Wednesday
Cresswell . . . . Everton
Blenkinsop . . . . Sheffield Wednesday
Edwards. . . . . Leeds United
Hart. . . . . Leeds United
Barrett, A. . . . . Fulham
Adcock. . . . . Leicester City
Hine. . . . . Leicester City
Camsell . . . . Middlesbrough
Bradford. . . . . Birmingham

Brook. . . . . Manchester City
Result: 3–0
Scorers: Camsell (2), Hine (pen.)

169. 20 November 1929
v WALES. . . . . Stamford Bridge, Chelsea
Hibbs. . . . . Birmingham
Smart. . . . . Aston Villa
Blenkinsop . . . . Sheffield Wednesday
Edwards. . . . . Leeds United
Hart. . . . . Leeds United
Marsden . . . . Sheffield Wednesday
Adcock. . . . . Leicester City
Hine. . . . . Leicester City
Camsell . . . . Middlesbrough
Johnson . . . . Manchester City
Ruffell . . . . West Ham United
Result: 6–0
Scorers: Adcock, Camsell (3), Johnson (2)

170. 5 April 1930
v SCOTLAND . . . . Wembley Stadium
Hibbs. . . . . Birmingham
Goodall . . . . Huddersfield Town
Blenkinsop . . . . Sheffield Wednesday
Strange . . . . Sheffield Wednesday
Webster . . . . Middlesbrough
Marsden . . . . Sheffield Wednesday
Crooks . . . . Derby County
Jack . . . . Arsenal
Watson, V. . . . . West Ham United
Bradford. . . . . Birmingham
Rimmer . . . . Sheffield Wednesday
Result: 5–2
Scorers: Jack, Watson (2), Rimmer (2)

171. 10 May 1930
v GERMANY . . . . Berlin
Hibbs. . . . . Birmingham
Goodall . . . . Huddersfield Town
Blenkinsop . . . . Sheffield Wednesday
Strange . . . . Sheffield Wednesday
Webster . . . . Middlesbrough
Marsden . . . . Sheffield Wednesday
Crooks . . . . Derby County
Jack . . . . Arsenal
Watson, V. . . . . West Ham United
Bradford . . . . Birmingham
Rimmer . . . . Sheffield Wednesday
Result: 3–3
Scorers: Bradford (2), Jack

172. 14 May 1930
v AUSTRIA . . . . Vienna
Hibbs. . . . . Birmingham
Goodall . . . . Huddersfield Town
Blenkinsop . . . . Sheffield Wednesday
Strange . . . . Sheffield Wednesday
Webster . . . . Middlesbrough
Cowan . . . . Manchester City
Crooks . . . . Derby County
Jack . . . . Arsenal
Watson, V. . . . . West Ham United
Bradford. . . . . Birmingham
Rimmer . . . . Sheffield Wednesday
Result: 0–0

173. 20 October 1930
v N. IRELAND . . . . Bramall Lane, Sheffield
Hibbs. . . . . Birmingham
Goodall . . . . Huddersfield Town
Blenkinsop . . . . Sheffield Wednesday
Strange . . . . Sheffield Wednesday
Leach. . . . . Sheffield Wednesday
Campbell . . . . Huddersfield Town

Crooks . . . . Derby County
Hodgson . . . . Liverpool
Hampson . . . . Blackpool
Burgess . . . . Sheffield Wednesday
Houghton. . . . . Aston Villa
Result: 5–1
Scorers: Burgess (2), Crooks, Hampson, Houghton

174. 22 November 1930
v WALES. . . . . Racecourse Ground,
                                   Wrexham
Hibbs. . . . . Birmingham
Goodall . . . . Huddersfield Town
Blenkinsop. . . . . Sheffield Wednesday
Strange . . . . Sheffield Wednesday
Leach . . . . Sheffield Wednesday
Campbell . . . . Huddersfield Town
Crooks . . . . Derby County
Hodgson . . . . Liverpool
Hampson . . . . Blackpool
Bradford. . . . . Birmingham
Houghton. . . . . Aston Villa
Result: 4–0
Scorers: Hodgson, Hampson (2), Bradford

175. 28 March 1931
v SCOTLAND. . . . . Hampden Park, Glasgow
Hibbs. . . . . Birmingham
Goodall . . . . Huddersfield Town
Blenkinsop. . . . . Sheffield Wednesday
Strange . . . . Sheffield Wednesday
Roberts, Herbert . . . . Arsenal
Campbell . . . . Huddersfield Town
Crooks . . . . Derby County
Hodgson . . . . Liverpool
Dean . . . . Everton
Burgess . . . . Sheffield Wednesday
Crawford . . . . Chelsea
Result: 0–2

176. 14 May 1931
v FRANCE. . . . . Paris
Turner . . . . Huddersfield Town
Cooper. . . . . Derby County
Blenkinsop. . . . . Sheffield Wednesday
Strange . . . . Sheffield Wednesday
Graham, T. . . . . Nottingham Forest
Tate . . . . Aston Villa
Crooks . . . . Derby County
Stephenson . . . . Sheffield Wednesday
Waring. . . . . Aston Villa
Burgess . . . . Sheffield Wednesday
Houghton. . . . . Aston Villa
Result: 2–5
Scorers: Crooks, Waring

177. 16 May 1931
v BELGIUM. . . . . Brussels
Turner . . . . Huddersfield Town
Goodall . . . . Huddersfield Town
Blenkinsop. . . . . Sheffield Wednesday
Strange . . . . Sheffield Wednesday
Cowan . . . . Manchester City
Tate . . . . Aston Villa
Crooks . . . . Derby County
Roberts, Henry . . . . Millwall
Waring. . . . . Aston Villa
Burgess . . . . Sheffield Wednesday
Houghton. . . . . Aston Villa
Result: 4–1
Scorers: Houghton, Burgess (2), H. Roberts

178. 17 October 1931
v N. IRELAND . . . . Windsor Park, Belfast
Hibbs. . . . . Birmingham

Goodall . . . . Huddersfield Town
Blenkinsop. . . . . Sheffield Wednesday
Strange . . . . Sheffield Wednesday
Graham, T. . . . . Nottingham Forest
Campbell . . . . Huddersfield Town
Crooks . . . . Derby County
Smith, J. W.. . . . . Portsmouth
Waring. . . . . Aston Villa
Hine. . . . . Leicester City
Houghton. . . . . Aston Villa
Result: 6–2
Scorers: Waring (2), Houghton (2), Hine, J. W. Smith

179. 18 November 1931
v WALES. . . . . Anfield, Liverpool
Hibbs. . . . . Birmingham
Cooper. . . . . Derby County
Blenkinsop. . . . . Sheffield Wednesday
Strange . . . . Sheffield Wednesday
Gee . . . . Everton
Campbell . . . . Huddersfield Town
Crooks . . . . Derby County
Smith, J. W.. . . . . Portsmouth
Waring. . . . . Aston Villa
Hine. . . . . Leicester City
Bastin . . . . Arsenal
Result: 3–1
Scorers: J. W. Smith, Crooks, Hine

180. 9 December 1931
v SPAIN . . . . Highbury Stadium, Arsenal
Hibbs. . . . . Birmingham
Cooper. . . . . Derby County
Blenkinsop. . . . . Sheffield Wednesday
Strange . . . . Sheffield Wednesday
Gee . . . . Everton
Campbell . . . . Huddersfield Town
Crooks . . . . Derby County
Smith, J. W.. . . . . Portsmouth
Dean . . . . Everton
Johnson . . . . Everton
Rimmer . . . . Sheffield Wednesday
Result: 7–1
Scorers: J. W. Smith (2), Johnson (2), Crooks (2), Dean

 DID YOU KNOW...?

England avenged a 4–3 defeat against Spain in
Madrid in May 1929 with a 7–1 demolition of the
Spanish side at Highbury on 9 December 1931.
Ricardo Zamora, the Spanish goalkeeper, was so
shell-shocked that he was reduced to tears before
the match had finished.

181. 9 April 1932
v SCOTLAND . . . . Wembley Stadium
Pearson . . . . West Bromwich Albion
Shaw . . . . West Bromwich Albion
Blenkinsop. . . . . Sheffield Wednesday
Strange . . . . Sheffield Wednesday
O'Dowd . . . . Chelsea
Weaver . . . . Newcastle United
Crooks . . . . Derby County
Barclay. . . . . Sheffield United
Waring. . . . . Aston Villa
Johnson . . . . Everton
Houghton. . . . . Aston Villa
Result: 3–0
Scorers: Waring, Crooks, Barclay

182. 17 October 1932
v N. IRELAND . . . . Bloomfield Road, Blackpool
Hibbs . . . . Birmingham
Goodall . . . . Huddersfield Town
Blenkinsop . . . . Sheffield Wednesday
Strange . . . . Sheffield Wednesday
O'Dowd . . . . Chelsea
Weaver . . . . Newcastle United
Crooks . . . . Derby County
Barclay . . . . Sheffield United
Dean . . . . Everton
Johnson . . . . Everton
Cunliffe, A. . . . . Blackburn Rovers
Result: 1–0
Scorer: Barclay

183. 16 November 1932
v WALES . . . . Racecourse Ground, Wrexham
Hibbs . . . . Birmingham
Goodall . . . . Huddersfield Town
Blenkinsop . . . . Sheffield Wednesday
Stoker . . . . Birmingham
Young . . . . Huddersfield Town
Tate . . . . Aston Villa
Crooks . . . . Derby County
Jack . . . . Arsenal
Brown, G. . . . . Aston Villa
Sandford . . . . West Bromwich Albion
Cunliffe, A. . . . . Blackburn Rovers
Result: 0–0

184. 7 December 1932
v AUSTRIA . . . . Stamford Bridge, Chelsea
Hibbs . . . . Birmingham
Goodall . . . . Huddersfield Town
Blenkinsop . . . . Sheffield Wednesday
Strange . . . . Sheffield Wednesday
Hart . . . . Leeds United
Keen . . . . Derby County
Crooks . . . . Derby County
Jack . . . . Arsenal
Hampson . . . . Blackpool
Walker . . . . Aston Villa
Houghton . . . . Aston Villa
Result: 4–3
Scorers: Hampson (2), Houghton, Crooks

185. 1 April 1933
v SCOTLAND . . . . Hampden Park, Glasgow
Hibbs . . . . Birmingham
Cooper . . . . Derby County
Blenkinsop . . . . Sheffield Wednesday
Strange . . . . Sheffield Wednesday
Hart . . . . Leeds United
Weaver . . . . Newcastle United
Hulme . . . . Arsenal
Starling . . . . Sheffield Wednesday
Hunt . . . . Tottenham Hotspur
Pickering . . . . Sheffield United
Arnold . . . . Fulham
Result: 1–2
Scorer: Hunt

186. 13 May 1933
v ITALY . . . . Rome
Hibbs . . . . Birmingham
Goodall . . . . Huddersfield Town
Hapgood . . . . Arsenal
Strange . . . . Sheffield Wednesday
White . . . . Everton
Copping . . . . Leeds United
Geldard . . . . Everton
Richardson, J. . . . . Newcastle United
Hunt . . . . Tottenham Hotspur
Furness . . . . Leeds United
Bastin . . . . Arsenal
Result: 1–1
Scorer: Bastin

FEATURED MATCH

7 DECEMBER 1932

ENGLAND 4 AUSTRIA 3 – STAMFORD BRIDGE

A couple of decades before the Hungarians came to Wembley to teach England a most unforgettable lesson, Austria sent their 'Wunderteam' to Chelsea's Stamford Bridge ground, hoping to become the first foreign side to overturn the England team on their home soil. Spain, who had beaten England 4–3 in Madrid in May 1929, came to Highbury two years later and were defeated 7–1, so if nothing else, England were certainly a formidable force with the home crowd behind them.

Jimmy Hampson's early opening goal seemed to be the cue for the Austrian team to roll over, but despite Hampson adding a second on 27 minutes, the Austrians had regained their composure. Just before half-time, Vogl completely miskicked in front of a gaping net, a time when a goal might have proved psychologically vital. However, early in the second half, right-winger Zischek reduced the deficit with a shot that England goalkeeper Harry Hibbs got his hands to, but couldn't keep out. The red-shirted Austrians began to play with a new confidence, but against the run of play Eric Houghton's free kick rebounded off the visitors' wall to give England a 3–1 advantage with thirteen minutes still to go.

Following a period of sustained pressure, Austrian centre forward Matthias Sindelar's 80th-minute goal initially offered Austria renewed hope, but an outstanding long-range drive from Derby County winger Sammy Crooks two minutes later increased England's chances of hanging on for a win. The tenacious Austrians finally got the luck they deserved when Zischek scored his second and the visitors' third goal after obstruction at a corner kick.

At the final whistle the result was the expected home win, but what had not been anticipated was Austria's superb passing game, and had they been able to convert some of their numerous chances as well, the events of November 1953 might not have been quite as historic for Hungary (see page 193).

187. 20 May 1933
v SWITZERLAND . . . . Berne
Hibbs . . . . Birmingham
Goodall . . . . Huddersfield Town
Hapgood . . . . Arsenal
Strange . . . . Sheffield Wednesday
O'Dowd . . . . Chelsea
Copping . . . . Leeds United
Geldard . . . . Everton
Richardson, J. . . . . Newcastle United
Hunt . . . . Tottenham Hotspur
Bastin . . . . Arsenal
Brook . . . . Manchester City
Result: 4–0
Scorers: Bastin (2), J. Richardson (2)

188. 14 October 1933
v N. IRELAND . . . . Windsor Park, Belfast
Hibbs . . . . Birmingham
Goodall . . . . Huddersfield Town
Hapgood . . . . Arsenal
Strange . . . . Sheffield Wednesday
Allen . . . . Portsmouth
Copping . . . . Leeds United

Crooks . . . . Derby County
Grosvenor . . . . Birmingham City
Bowers . . . . Derby County
Bastin . . . . Arsenal
Brook . . . . Manchester City
Result: 3–0
Scorers: Brook, Grosvenor, Bowers

189. 15 November 1933
v WALES . . . . St James' Park, Newcastle
Hibbs . . . . Birmingham
Goodall . . . . Huddersfield Town
Hapgood . . . . Arsenal
Strange . . . . Sheffield Wednesday
Allen . . . . Portsmouth
Copping . . . . Leeds United
Crooks . . . . Derby County
Grosvenor . . . . Birmingham City
Bowers . . . . Derby County
Bastin . . . . Arsenal
Brook . . . . Manchester City
Result: 1–2
Scorer: Brook

190. 6 December 1933
v FRANCE . . . . White Hart Lane, Tottenham
Hibbs . . . . Birmingham
Goodall . . . . Huddersfield Town
Fairhurst . . . . Newcastle United
Strange . . . . Sheffield Wednesday
Rowe . . . . Tottenham Hotspur
Copping . . . . Leeds United
Crooks . . . . Derby County
Grosvenor . . . . Birmingham
Camsell . . . . Middlesbrough
Hall . . . . Tottenham Hotspur
Brook . . . . Manchester City
Result: 4–1
Scorers: Camsell (2), Brook, Grosvenor

191. 14 April 1934
v SCOTLAND . . . . Wembley Stadium
Moss . . . . Arsenal
Cooper . . . . Derby County
Hapgood . . . . Arsenal
Stoker . . . . Birmingham
Hart . . . . Leeds United
Copping . . . . Leeds United
Crooks . . . . Derby County
Carter H. S. . . . . Sunderland
Bowers . . . . Derby County
Bastin . . . . Arsenal
Brook . . . . Manchester City
Result: 3–0
Scorers: Brook, Bastin, Bowers

192. 10 May 1934
v HUNGARY . . . . Budapest
Moss . . . . Arsenal
Cooper . . . . Derby County
Hapgood . . . . Arsenal
Stoker . . . . Birmingham
Hart . . . . Leeds United
Burrows . . . . Sheffield Wednesday
Crooks . . . . Derby County
Carter, H. S. . . . . Sunderland
Tilson . . . . Manchester City
Bastin . . . . Arsenal
Brook . . . . Manchester City
Result: 1–2
Scorer: Tilson

193. 16 May 1934
v CZECHOSLOVAKIA . . . . Prague
Moss . . . . Arsenal
Cooper . . . . Derby County
Hapgood . . . . Arsenal
Gardner . . . . Aston Villa

Hart . . . . Leeds United
Burrows . . . . Sheffield Wednesday
Crooks . . . . Derby County
Beresford . . . . Aston Villa
Tilson . . . . Manchester City
Bastin . . . . Arsenal
Brook . . . . Manchester City
Result: 1–2
Scorer: Tilson

194. 29 September 1934
v WALES . . . . Ninian Park, Cardiff
Hibbs . . . . Birmingham
Cooper . . . . Derby County
Hapgood . . . . Arsenal
Britton . . . . Everton
Barker . . . . Derby County
Bray . . . . Manchester City
Matthews, S. . . . . Stoke City
Bowden . . . . Arsenal
Tilson . . . . Manchester City
Westwood . . . . Bolton Wanderers
Brook . . . . Manchester City
Result: 4–0
Scorers: Tilson (2), Brook, S. Matthews

195. 14 November 1934
v ITALY . . . . Highbury Stadium, Arsenal
Moss . . . . Arsenal
Male . . . . Arsenal
Hapgood . . . . Arsenal
Britton . . . . Everton
Barker . . . . Derby County
Copping . . . . Arsenal
Matthews, S. . . . . Stoke City
Bowden . . . . Arsenal
Drake . . . . Arsenal
Bastin . . . . Arsenal
Brook . . . . Manchester City
Result: 3–2
Scorers: Brook (2), Drake

 FEATURED MATCH

14 NOVEMBER 1934

ENGLAND 3 ITALY 2 – HIGHBURY STADIUM

Seven of Arsenal's League Championship-winning side featured in the England team for the match against the 1934 World Cup winners, Italy. The Gunners had won the Football League title twice in successive years and were on their way to a hat-trick in 1934–35. Italy, for their part, had lifted the Jules Rimet Trophy on home territory earlier in the year, beating Czechoslovakia 2–1 after extra time in the final. The fact that England had yet to enter the World Cup meant they had a point to prove.

The opening minute saw Manchester City's Eric Brook miss a penalty when Carlo Ceresoli produced a vital save – the Italian goalkeeper making amends for bringing down Ted Drake. Two minutes later Italy lost the services of Luis Monti, who broke a bone in his foot after an accidental clash with Drake, and it was this incident that sparked a match of unrelenting violence. Apparently, Monti had to have a cloth pushed in his mouth to stop the screams of pain as he was taken away to hospital. The Italians were convinced the injury to their star player was deliberate and they responded with a wave of ugly challenges, including a punch to Drake's chin early on that laid the Arsenal player out on his back. ➡

After eight minutes Brook did find the net for the first of his two goals: Everton's Cliff Britton, who was making his England debut, sent in a free kick for Brook to head home, and shortly afterwards Brook scored again with a left-foot shot that was good enough to beat Ceresoli. An attack down the right flank ended in Drake hooking the ball into the net for the third goal.

This being the era of no substitutes, the World Cup winners had to play most of the match with just ten men, but despite England's player advantage, the home side conceded two goals both scored by Giuseppe Meazza; the first created by the skill of Enrique Guaita, and the second from Attilio Ferraris's free kick.

Though Italy had been allowed back into the match and could have almost snatched a draw, England held on to win the game that entered football folklore as the 'Battle of Highbury', while maintaining their own unbeaten home record. Perhaps if the visitors had been at full strength, the end result would have been somewhat different.

196. 6 February 1935

v N. IRELAND . . . . Goodison Park, Everton
Hibbs . . . . Birmingham
Male . . . . Arsenal
Hapgood . . . . Arsenal
Britton . . . . Everton
Barker . . . . Derby County
Copping . . . . Arsenal
Crooks . . . . Derby County
Bestall . . . . Grimsby Town
Drake . . . . Arsenal
Bastin . . . . Arsenal
Brook . . . . Manchester City
Result: 2–1
Scorers: Bastin (2)

197. 6 April 1935

v SCOTLAND . . . . Hampden Park, Glasgow
Hibbs . . . . Birmingham
Male . . . . Arsenal
Hapgood . . . . Arsenal
Britton . . . . Everton
Barker . . . . Derby County
Alsford . . . . Tottenham Hotspur
Geldard . . . . Everton
Bastin . . . . Arsenal
Gurney . . . . Sunderland
Westwood . . . . Bolton Wanderers
Brook . . . . Manchester City
Result: 0–2

198. 18 May 1935

v HOLLAND . . . . Amsterdam
Hibbs . . . . Birmingham
Male . . . . Arsenal
Hapgood . . . . Arsenal
Gardner . . . . Aston Villa
Barker . . . . Derby County
Burrows . . . . Sheffield Wednesday
Worrall . . . . Portsmouth
Eastham . . . . Bolton Wanderers
Richardson, W. . . . . West Bromwich Albion
Westwood . . . . Bolton Wanderers
Boyes . . . . West Bromwich Albion
Result: 1–0
Scorer: Worrall

199. 19 October 1935

v N IRELAND . . . . Windsor Park, Belfast
Sagar . . . . Everton
Male . . . . Arsenal
Hapgood . . . . Arsenal
Smith, S. . . . . Leicester City
Barker . . . . Derby County
Bray . . . . Manchester City
Birkett . . . . Middlesbrough
Bowden . . . . Arsenal
Tilson . . . . Manchester City
Westwood . . . . Bolton Wanderers
Brook . . . . Manchester City
Result: 3–1
Scorers: Tilson (2), Brook

200. 4 December 1935

v GERMANY . . . . White Hart Lane, Tottenham
Hibbs . . . . Birmingham
Male . . . . Arsenal
Hapgood . . . . Arsenal
Crayston . . . . Arsenal
Barker . . . . Derby County
Bray . . . . Manchester City
Matthews, S. . . . . Stoke City
Carter, H. S. . . . . Sunderland
Camsell . . . . Middlesbrough
Westwood . . . . Bolton Wanderers
Bastin . . . . Arsenal
Result: 3–0
Scorers: Camsell (2), Bastin

201. 5 February 1936

v WALES . . . . Molineux, Wolverhampton
Hibbs . . . . Birmingham
Male . . . . Arsenal
Hapgood . . . . Arsenal
Crayston . . . . Arsenal
Barker . . . . Derby County
Bray . . . . Manchester City
Crooks . . . . Derby County
Bowden . . . . Arsenal
Drake . . . . Arsenal
Bastin . . . . Arsenal
Brook . . . . Manchester City
Result: 1–2
Scorer: Bowden

202. 4 April 1936

v SCOTLAND . . . . Wembley Stadium
Sagar . . . . Everton
Male . . . . Arsenal
Hapgood . . . . Arsenal
Crayston . . . . Arsenal
Barker . . . . Derby County
Bray . . . . Manchester City
Crooks . . . . Derby County
Barclay . . . . Sheffield United
Camsell . . . . Middlesbrough
Bastin . . . . Arsenal
Brook . . . . Manchester City
Result: 1–1
Scorer: Camsell

⚽ DID YOU KNOW...?

Arsenal AFC supplied a record seven men to the England team against Italy at Highbury on 14 November 1934. They were Frank Moss, George Male, Eddie Hapgood, Wilf Copping, Ray Bowden, Ted Drake and Cliff Bastin. In addition, Arsenal's Tom Whittaker was England's trainer.

203. 6 May 1936
v AUSTRIA . . . . Vienna
Sagar . . . . Everton
Male . . . . Arsenal
Hapgood . . . . Arsenal
Crayston . . . . Arsenal
Barker . . . . Derby County
Copping . . . . Arsenal
Spence . . . . Chelsea
Bowden . . . . Arsenal
Camsell . . . . Middlesbrough
Bastin . . . . Arsenal
Hobbis . . . . Charlton Athletic
Result: 1–2
Scorer: Camsell

204. 9 May 1936
v BELGIUM . . . . Brussels
Sagar . . . . Everton
Male . . . . Arsenal
Hapgood . . . . Arsenal
Crayston . . . . Arsenal
Joy . . . . Casuals
Copping . . . . Arsenal
Spence . . . . Chelsea
Barkas . . . . Manchester City
Camsell . . . . Middlesbrough
Cunliffe, J. . . . . Everton
Hobbis . . . . Charlton Athletic
Result: 2–3
Scorers: Camsell, Hobbis

205. 17 October 1936
v WALES . . . . Ninian Park, Cardiff
Holdcroft . . . . Preston North End
Sproston . . . . Leeds United
Catlin . . . . Sheffield Wednesday
Smalley . . . . Wolverhampton Wanderers
Barker . . . . Derby County
Keen . . . . Derby County
Crooks . . . . Derby County
Scott . . . . Brentford
Steele . . . . Stoke City
Westwood . . . . Bolton Wanderers
Bastin . . . . Arsenal
Result: 1–2
Scorer: Bastin

206. 18 November 1936
v N. IRELAND . . . . Victoria Ground, Stoke
Holdcroft . . . . Preston North End
Male . . . . Arsenal
Catlin . . . . Sheffield Wednesday
Britton . . . . Everton
Gee . . . . Everton
Keen . . . . Derby County
Worrall . . . . Portsmouth
Carter, H. S. . . . . Sunderland
Steele . . . . Stoke City
Bastin . . . . Arsenal
Johnson, J. . . . . Stoke City
Result: 3–1
Scorer: H. S. Carter, Bastin, Worrall

207. 2 December 1936
v HUNGARY . . . . Highbury Stadium, Arsenal
Tweedy . . . . Grimsby Town
Male . . . . Arsenal
Catlin . . . . Sheffield Wednesday
Britton . . . . Everton
Young . . . . Huddersfield Town
Keen . . . . Derby County
Crooks . . . . Derby County
Bowden . . . . Arsenal
Drake . . . . Arsenal
Carter, H. S. . . . . Sunderland
Brook . . . . Manchester City
Result: 6–2
Scorers: Drake (3), H. S. Carter, Brook, Britton

DID YOU KNOW...?

The game between Scotland and England at Hampden Park in 1937 attracted not only the biggest attendance for a British international, but also the greatest for any game in Britain. It was played on 17 April 1937, and although the official attendance was given as 149,547, it is estimated a further 10,000 got into the ground without paying.

208. 17 April 1937
v SCOTLAND . . . . Hampden Park, Glasgow
Woodley . . . . Chelsea
Male . . . . Arsenal
Barkas . . . . Manchester City
Britton . . . . Everton
Young . . . . Huddersfield Town
Bray . . . . Manchester City
Matthews, S. . . . . Stoke City
Carter, H. S. . . . . Sunderland
Steele . . . . Stoke City
Starling . . . . Aston Villa
Johnson J . . . . Stoke City
Result: 1–3
Scorer: Steele

209. 14 May 1937
v NORWAY . . . . Oslo
Woodley . . . . Chelsea
Male . . . . Arsenal
Catlin . . . . Sheffield Wednesday
Britton . . . . Everton
Young . . . . Huddersfield Town
Copping . . . . Arsenal
Kirchen . . . . Arsenal
Galley . . . . Wolverhampton Wanderers
Steele . . . . Stoke City
Goulden . . . . West Ham United
Johnson, J. . . . . Stoke City
Result: 6–0
Scorers: Steele (2), Kirchen, Galley, Goulden, o.g.

210. 17 May 1937
v SWEDEN . . . . Solna
Woodley . . . . Chelsea
Male . . . . Arsenal
Catlin . . . . Sheffield Wednesday
Britton . . . . Everton
Young . . . . Huddersfield Town
Copping . . . . Arsenal
Kirchen . . . . Arsenal
Galley . . . . Wolverhampton Wanderers
Steele . . . . Stoke City
Goulden . . . . West Ham United
Johnson, J. . . . . Stoke City
Result: 4–0
Scorers: Steele (3), J. Johnson

211. 20 May 1937
v FINLAND . . . . Helsinki
Woodley . . . . Chelsea
Male . . . . Arsenal
Hapgood . . . . Arsenal
Willingham . . . . Huddersfield Town
Betmead . . . . Grimsby Town
Copping . . . . Arsenal
Kirchen . . . . Arsenal
Robinson . . . . Sheffield Wednesday
Payne . . . . Luton Town
Steele . . . . Stoke City
Johnson, J. . . . . Stoke City
Result: 8–0
Scorers: Payne (2), Steele (2), Kirchen, J. Johnson,
   Willingham, Robinson

212. 23 October 1937

v N. IRELAND . . . . Windsor Park, Belfast
Woodley . . . . Chelsea
Sproston . . . . Leeds United
Barkas . . . . Manchester City
Crayston . . . . Arsenal
Cullis . . . . Wolverhampton Wanderers
Copping . . . . Arsenal
Geldard . . . . Everton
Hall . . . . Tottenham Hotspur
Mills . . . . Chelsea
Goulden . . . . West Ham United
Brook . . . . Manchester City
Result: 5–1
Scorers: Mills (3), Hall, Brook

FEATURED MATCH

14 MAY 1938

GERMANY 3 ENGLAND 6 – OLYMPIC STADIUM, BERLIN

The indelible memory of this game was in the pre-match arrangements when, as a mark of diplomatic respect to their hosts, the England players gave the Nazi salute during the British national anthem. The match itself proved to be one of England's finest displays and was played before a crowd of approximately 115,000, including Nazi politicians Rudolf Hess, Joseph Goebbels and Joachim von Ribbentrop.

Arsenal's Cliff Bastin put England into the lead after sixteen minutes, but Rudi Gellesch scored a 20th-minute equalizer. England, however, quickly re-established their authority, and, six minutes later, Jackie Robinson side-footed home from close range following a needless corner given away by the German defence. England's two debutants then combined to get the visitors' third goal: Don Welsh of Charlton Athletic played a probing pass into the path of Aston Villa's Frank Broome, who dutifully collected his first goal for his country. Stanley Matthews then added to the score most skilfully, trapping a high ball and evading the attention of three German defenders before beating keeper Hans Jakob with a low shot. The home side pulled a goal back on the stroke of half-time after Vic Woodley failed to hold a tame strike and Jupp Gauchel pounced, which left the Germans four goals to two down by the break.

The second half was only minutes old when Robinson helped to regain England's three-goal advantage with a rising drive that took Jakob completely by surprise. Broome almost extended England's lead further when he broke clear of Reinhold Münzenberg, but his shot was directed straight at the keeper. In the 77th minute, Hans Pesser scored a third goal for the Germans, taking advantage of a moment of confusion between Woodley and Bert Sproston, but there was never any hope of the home side drawing level, let alone winning. England completed the rout in spectacular style with Len Goulden, winning his sixth cap, driving the ball home off the underside of the crossbar from well outside the penalty area – in fact, the power of the shot ripped the net from the crossbar!

The German team had been unable to match their vociferous supporters' expectations and England had taken advantage in what was to be one of their last dozen internationals before the outbreak of the Second World War.

213. 17 November 1937

v WALES . . . . Ayresome Park,
 Middlesbrough
Woodley . . . . Chelsea
Sproston . . . . Leeds United
Barkas . . . . Manchester City
Crayston . . . . Arsenal
Cullis . . . . Wolverhampton Wanderers
Copping . . . . Arsenal
Matthews, S. . . . . Stoke City
Hall . . . . Tottenham Hotspur
Mills . . . . Chelsea
Goulden . . . . West Ham United
Brook . . . . Manchester City
Result: 2–1
Scorers: S. Matthews, Hall

214. 1 December 1937

v CZECHOSLOVAKIA . . . . White Hart Lane
Woodley . . . . Chelsea
Sproston . . . . Leeds United
Barkas . . . . Manchester City
Crayston . . . . Arsenal
Cullis . . . . Wolverhampton Wanderers
Copping . . . . Arsenal
Matthews, S. . . . . Stoke City
Hall . . . . Tottenham Hotspur
Mills . . . . Chelsea
Goulden . . . . West Ham United
Morton . . . . West Ham United
Result: 5–4
Scorers: S. Matthews (3), Morton, Crayston

215. 9 April 1938

v SCOTLAND . . . . Wembley Stadium
Woodley . . . . Chelsea
Sproston . . . . Leeds United
Hapgood . . . . Arsenal
Willingham . . . . Huddersfield Town
Cullis . . . . Wolverhampton Wanderers
Copping . . . . Arsenal
Matthews, S. . . . . Stoke City
Hall . . . . Tottenham Hotspur
Fenton . . . . Middlesbrough
Stephenson, J. . . . . Leeds United
Bastin . . . . Arsenal
Result: 0–1

216. 14 May 1938

v GERMANY . . . . Berlin
Woodley . . . . Chelsea
Sproston . . . . Leeds United
Hapgood . . . . Arsenal
Willingham . . . . Huddersfield Town
Young . . . . Huddersfield Town
Welsh . . . . Charlton Athletic
Matthews, S. . . . . Stoke City
Robinson . . . . Sheffield Wednesday
Broome . . . . Aston Villa
Goulden . . . . West Ham United
Bastin . . . . Arsenal
Result: 6–3
Scorers: Bastin, Robinson (2), Broome, S. Matthews, Goulden

217. 21 May 1938

v SWITZERLAND . . . . Zurich
Woodley . . . . Chelsea
Sproston . . . . Leeds United
Hapgood . . . . Arsenal
Willingham . . . . Huddersfield Town
Young . . . . Huddersfield Town
Welsh . . . . Charlton Athletic
Matthews, S. . . . . Stoke City
Robinson . . . . Sheffield Wednesday
Broome . . . . Aston Villa

Goulden . . . . West Ham United
Bastin . . . . Arsenal
Result: 1–2
Scorer: Bastin (pen.)

218. 26 May 1938
v FRANCE . . . . Paris
Woodley . . . . Chelsea
Sproston . . . . Leeds United
Hapgood . . . . Arsenal
Willingham . . . . Huddersfield Town
Young . . . . Huddersfield Town
Cullis . . . . Wolverhampton Wanderers
Broome . . . . Aston Villa
Matthews, S. . . . . Stoke City
Drake . . . . Arsenal
Goulden . . . . West Ham United
Bastin . . . . Arsenal
Result: 4–2
Scorers: Drake (2), Broome, Bastin (pen.)

219. 22 October 1938
v WALES . . . . Ninian Park, Cardiff
Woodley . . . . Chelsea
Sproston . . . . Tottenham Hotspur
Hapgood . . . . Arsenal
Willingham . . . . Huddersfield Town
Young . . . . Huddersfield Town
Copping . . . . Arsenal
Matthews, S. . . . . Stoke City
Robinson . . . . Sheffield Wednesday
Lawton . . . . Everton
Goulden . . . . West Ham United
Boyes . . . . Everton
Result: 2–4
Scorers: Lawton (pen.), S. Matthews

220. 26 October 1938
v FIFA . . . . Highbury Stadium, Arsenal
Woodley . . . . Chelsea
Sproston . . . . Tottenham Hotspur
Hapgood . . . . Arsenal
Willingham . . . . Huddersfield Town
Cullis . . . . Wolverhampton Wanderers
Copping . . . . Arsenal
Matthews, S. . . . . Stoke City
Hall . . . . Tottenham Hotspur
Lawton . . . . Everton
Goulden . . . . West Ham United
Boyes . . . . Everton
Result: 3–0
Scorers: Lawton, Hall, Goulden

221. 9 November 1938
v NORWAY . . . . St James' Park, Newcastle
Woodley . . . . Chelsea
Sproston . . . . Tottenham Hotspur
Hapgood . . . . Arsenal
Willingham . . . . Huddersfield Town
Cullis . . . . Wolverhampton Wanderers
Wright, D. . . . . Newcastle United
Matthews, S. . . . . Stoke City
Broome . . . . Aston Villa
Lawton . . . . Everton
Dix . . . . Derby County
Smith, J. R. . . . . Millwall
Result: 4–0
Scorers: J. R. Smith (2), Dix, Lawton

222. 16 November 1938
v N. IRELAND . . . . Old Trafford, Manchester
Woodley . . . . Chelsea
Morris . . . . Wolverhampton Wanderers
Hapgood . . . . Arsenal
Willingham . . . . Huddersfield Town

Cullis . . . . Wolverhampton Wanderers
Mercer . . . . Everton
Matthews, S. . . . . Stoke City
Hall . . . . Tottenham Hotspur
Lawton . . . . Everton
Stephenson, J. . . . . Leeds United
Smith, J. R. . . . . Millwall
Result: 7–0
Scorers: Hall (5), Lawton, S. Matthews

223. 15 April 1939
v SCOTLAND . . . . Hampden Park, Glasgow
Woodley . . . . Chelsea
Morris . . . . Wolverhampton Wanderers
Hapgood . . . . Arsenal
Willingham . . . . Huddersfield Town
Cullis . . . . Wolverhampton Wanderers
Mercer . . . . Everton
Matthews, S. . . . . Stoke City
Hall . . . . Tottenham Hotspur
Lawton . . . . Everton
Goulden . . . . West Ham United
Beasley . . . . Huddersfield Town
Result: 2–1
Scorers: Beasley, Lawton

224. 13 May 1939
v ITALY . . . . Milan
Woodley . . . . Chelsea
Male . . . . Arsenal
Hapgood . . . . Arsenal
Willingham . . . . Huddersfield Town
Cullis . . . . Wolverhampton Wanderers
Mercer . . . . Everton
Matthews, S. . . . . Stoke City
Hall . . . . Tottenham Hotspur
Lawton . . . . Everton
Goulden . . . . West Ham United
Broome . . . . Aston Villa
Result: 2–2
Scorers: Lawton, Hall

225. 18 May 1939
v YUGOSLAVIA . . . . Belgrade
Woodley . . . . Chelsea
Male . . . . Arsenal
Hapgood . . . . Arsenal
Willingham . . . . Huddersfield Town
Cullis . . . . Wolverhampton Wanderers
Mercer . . . . Everton
Matthews, S. . . . . Stoke City
Hall . . . . Tottenham Hotspur
Lawton . . . . Everton
Goulden . . . . West Ham United
Broome . . . . Aston Villa
Result: 1–2
Scorers: Broome

226. 24 May 1939
v ROMANIA . . . . Bucharest
Woodley . . . . Chelsea
Male . . . . Arsenal
Morris . . . . Wolverhampton Wanderers
Mercer . . . . Everton
Cullis . . . . Wolverhampton Wanderers
Copping . . . . Arsenal
Smith, L. G. . . . . Brentford
Welsh . . . . Charlton Athletic
Lawton . . . . Everton
Goulden . . . . West Ham United
Broome . . . . Aston Villa
Result: 2–0
Scorers: Goulden, Welsh

227. 28 September 1946
v N. IRELAND . . . . Windsor Park, Belfast
Swift . . . . Manchester City
Scott . . . . Arsenal
Hardwick . . . . Middlesbrough
Wright, W. . . . . Wolverhampton Wanderers
Franklin . . . . Stoke City
Cockburn . . . . Manchester United
Finney . . . . Preston North End
Carter, H. S. . . . . Derby County
Lawton . . . . Chelsea
Mannion . . . . Middlesbrough
Langton . . . . Blackburn Rovers
Result: 7–2
Scorers: H. S. Carter, Finney, Mannion (3), Lawton, Langton

228. 30 September 1946
v EIRE . . . . Dalymount Park, Dublin
Swift . . . . Manchester City
Scott . . . . Arsenal
Hardwick . . . . Middlesbrough
Wright, W. . . . . Wolverhampton Wanderers
Franklin . . . . Stoke City
Cockburn . . . . Manchester United
Finney . . . . Preston North End
Carter, H. S. . . . . Derby County
Lawton . . . . Chelsea
Mannion . . . . Middlesbrough
Langton . . . . Blackburn Rovers
Result: 1–0
Scorer: Finney

229. 19 October 1946
v WALES . . . . Maine Road, Manchester
Swift . . . . Manchester City
Scott . . . . Arsenal
Hardwick . . . . Middlesbrough
Wright, W. . . . . Wolverhampton Wanderers
Franklin . . . . Stoke City
Cockburn . . . . Manchester United
Finney . . . . Preston North End
Carter, H. S. . . . . Derby County
Lawton . . . . Chelsea
Mannion . . . . Middlesbrough
Langton . . . . Blackburn Rovers
Result: 3–0
Scorers: Mannion (2), Lawton

230. 27 November 1946
v HOLLAND . . . . Leeds Road, Huddersfield
Swift . . . . Manchester City
Scott . . . . Arsenal
Hardwick . . . . Middlesbrough
Wright, W. . . . . Wolverhampton Wanderers
Franklin . . . . Stoke City
Johnston . . . . Blackpool
Finney . . . . Preston North End
Carter, H. S. . . . . Derby County
Lawton . . . . Chelsea
Mannion . . . . Middlesbrough
Langton . . . . Blackburn Rovers
Result: 8–2
Scorers: Lawton (4), H. S. Carter (2), Mannion, Finney

231. 12 April 1947
v SCOTLAND . . . . Wembley Stadium
Swift . . . . Manchester City
Scott . . . . Arsenal
Hardwick . . . . Middlesbrough
Wright, W. . . . . Wolverhampton Wanderers
Franklin . . . . Stoke City
Johnston . . . . Blackpool
Matthews, S. . . . . Stoke City
Carter, H. S. . . . . Derby County
Lawton . . . . Chelsea
Mannion . . . . Middlesbrough
Mullen . . . . Wolverhampton Wanderers
Result: 1–1
Scorer: H. S. Carter

232. 3 May 1947
v FRANCE . . . . Highbury Stadium, Arsenal
Swift . . . . Manchester City
Scott . . . . Arsenal
Hardwick . . . . Middlesbrough
Wright, W. . . . . Wolverhampton Wanderers
Franklin . . . . Stoke City
Lowe . . . . Aston Villa
Finney . . . . Preston North End
Carter, H. S. . . . . Derby County
Lawton . . . . Chelsea
Mannion . . . . Middlesbrough
Langton . . . . Blackburn Rovers
Result: 3–0
Scorers: Finney, Mannion, H. S. Carter

233. 18 May 1947
v SWITZERLAND . . . . Zurich
Swift . . . . Manchester City
Scott . . . . Arsenal
Hardwick . . . . Middlesbrough
Wright, W. . . . . Wolverhampton Wanderers
Franklin . . . . Stoke City
Lowe . . . . Aston Villa
Matthews, S. . . . . Blackpool
Carter, H. S. . . . . Derby County
Lawton . . . . Chelsea
Mannion . . . . Middlesbrough
Langton . . . . Blackburn Rovers
Result: 0–1

234. 27 May 1947
v PORTUGAL . . . . Lisbon
Swift . . . . Manchester City
Scott . . . . Arsenal
Hardwick . . . . Middlesbrough
Wright, W. . . . . Wolverhampton Wanderers
Franklin . . . . Stoke City
Lowe . . . . Aston Villa
Matthews, S. . . . . Blackpool
Mortensen . . . . Blackpool
Lawton . . . . Chelsea
Mannion . . . . Middlesbrough
Finney . . . . Preston North End
Result: 10–0
Scorers: Lawton (4), Mortensen (4), Finney, S. Matthews

235. 21 September 1947
v BELGIUM . . . . Brussels
Swift . . . . Manchester City
Scott . . . . Arsenal
Hardwick . . . . Middlesbrough
Ward . . . . Derby County
Franklin . . . . Stoke City
Wright, W. . . . . Wolverhampton Wanderers
Matthews, S. . . . . Blackpool
Mortensen . . . . Blackpool
Lawton . . . . Chelsea
Mannion . . . . Middlesbrough
Finney . . . . Preston North End
Result: 5–2
Scorers: Lawton (2), Mortensen, Finney (2)

236. 18 October 1947
v WALES . . . . Ninian Park, Cardiff
Swift . . . . Manchester City
Scott . . . . Arsenal
Hardwick . . . . Middlesbrough
Taylor, P. . . . . Liverpool
Franklin . . . . Stoke City
Wright, W. . . . . Wolverhampton Wanderers

FEATURED MATCH

27 MAY 1947

PORTUGAL 0 ENGLAND 10 – NATIONAL STADIUM, LISBON

How best to utilize two world-class right-wingers: that was the problem England solved in Lisbon in May 1947 to the agony of the home side. Both Stanley Matthews and Tom Finney were superb ball players with magical swerves, but since the end of the Second World War, the less charismatic Finney had had the edge over his great rival. Now profiting from the fact that Finney was naturally left-footed, England chose him to play outside-left with Matthews on the right flank. With the rest of the England forward line comprising Stan Mortensen, Tommy Lawton and Wilf Mannion, there was very little the Portuguese could do to stop the onslaught.

Within the first couple of minutes both Mortensen and Lawton had smashed goals past the Portuguese goalkeeper Joao Azevedo, even though the ball they were playing with had been switched. Before the match it was agreed that the customary full-size ball would be used, but somehow, the smaller, lighter, Portuguese ball was introduced. Later in the game the rules were bent even further when the Portuguese goalkeeper and then right-back Alvaro Cardoso were both substituted in an attempt to stop the rout.

The change in the type of ball used clearly made little difference, and certainly gave no advantage to the home side. Lawton got England's third goal and then Finney scored a remarkable fourth: taking control of the ball near the halfway line he beat one man and then another, before reaching the goal line. As he turned to strike, a third defender came at him, only to be beaten as well. Finney then shot past the keeper from the narrowest of angles.

Lawton increased his tally to four on the hour-mark, having completed his hat-trick just before the break; Mortensen got another three and finally Matthews scored one of his rare goals to help the total to double figures. It was little wonder that the unhappy Portuguese team missed the official banquet that night, while the victorious England side, dubbed the 'Lions of Lisbon' on their return home, justly savoured their momentous win.

Matthews, S. . . . . Blackpool
Mortensen . . . . Blackpool
Lawton . . . . Chelsea
Mannion . . . . Middlesbrough
Finney . . . . Preston North End
Result: 3–0
Scorers: Finney, Mortensen, Lawton

237. 5 November 1947
v N. IRELAND . . . . Goodison Park, Everton
Swift . . . . Manchester City
Scott . . . . Arsenal
Hardwick . . . . Middlesbrough
Taylor, P. . . . . Liverpool
Franklin . . . . Stoke City
Wright, W. . . . . Wolverhampton Wanderers
Matthews, S. . . . . Blackpool
Mortensen . . . . Blackpool
Lawton . . . . Chelsea
Mannion . . . . Middlesbrough
Finney . . . . Preston North End
Result: 2–2
Scorers: Mannion, Lawton

238. 19 November 1947
v SWEDEN . . . . Highbury Stadium, Arsenal
Swift . . . . Manchester City
Scott . . . . Arsenal
Hardwick . . . . Middlesbrough
Taylor, P. . . . . Liverpool
Franklin . . . . Stoke City
Wright, W. . . . . Wolverhampton Wanderers
Finney . . . . Preston North End
Mortensen . . . . Blackpool
Lawton . . . . Notts County
Mannion . . . . Middlesbrough
Langton . . . . Blackburn Rovers
Result: 4–2
Scorers: Mortensen (3), Lawton (pen.)

239. 10 April 1948
v SCOTLAND . . . . Hampden Park, Glasgow
Swift . . . . Manchester City
Scott . . . . Arsenal
Hardwick . . . . Middlesbrough
Wright, W. . . . . Wolverhampton Wanderers
Franklin . . . . Stoke City
Cockburn . . . . Manchester United
Matthews, S. . . . . Blackpool
Mortensen . . . . Blackpool
Lawton . . . . Notts County
Pearson . . . . Manchester United
Finney . . . . Preston North End
Result: 2–0
Scorers: Mortensen, Finney

240. 16 May 1948
v ITALY . . . . Turin
Swift . . . . Manchester City
Scott . . . . Arsenal
Howe, J. . . . . Derby County
Wright, W. . . . . Wolverhampton Wanderers
Franklin . . . . Stoke City
Cockburn . . . . Manchester United
Matthews, S. . . . . Blackpool
Mortensen . . . . Blackpool
Lawton . . . . Notts County
Mannion . . . . Middlesbrough
Finney . . . . Preston North End
Result: 4–0
Scorers: Mortensen, Finney (2), Lawton

FEATURED MATCH

16 MAY 1948

ITALY 0 ENGLAND 4 – MUNICIPAL STADIUM, TURIN

In complete contrast to the 'Battle of Highbury' in 1934, Italy behaved impeccably in defeat at Turin, even though it was a match they might have won and one that they never deserved to lose so heavily. It was played in the era when the Italians based their side on the great Torino team, seven of whom were on the pitch that day, which was to perish in a plane crash tragedy the following year.

England gained the upper hand early on with a magnificent goal by Stan Mortensen. Stanley Matthews sent the ball through to his Blackpool teammate, who set off on a prodigious run towards the Italian defence. Because the angle to goal was so acute, everyone thought he would cross to Lawton, but instead he pivoted and sent an astonishing shot past Valerio Bacigalupo into the near top corner. →

The Italians responded by putting England under a great deal of pressure and it was only superb goalkeeping by the giant Frank Swift that kept them at bay. Despite the immense Italian effort, it was England who scored again after twenty-four minutes and once more it was Matthews who sent Mortensen away past Giuseppe Grezar and Carlo Parola to the goal line. This time Mortensen did pull the ball back and Lawton's drive put England two up at half-time.

Early in the second half, Swift, England's first goalkeeping captain, made yet another remarkable save from a bewildered Guglielmo Gabetto and finally England got back on top. Matthews mesmerized Alberto Eliani, Mannion moved the ball sweetly and Tom Finney capped two sweeping movements with fine goals. Yet despite the score, it was a game in which Italy played just as well as England and, if it were not for Mortensen and Swift, could so easily have ended in an Italian victory.

241. 26 September 1948
v DENMARK . . . . Copenhagen
Swift . . . . Manchester City
Scott . . . . Arsenal
Aston. . . . . Manchester United
Wright, W. . . . . Wolverhampton Wanderers
Franklin . . . . Stoke City
Cockburn . . . . Manchester United
Matthews, S. . . . . Blackpool
Hagan . . . . Sheffield United
Lawton . . . . Notts County
Shackleton . . . . Sunderland
Langton . . . . Preston North End
Result: 0–0

242. 9 October 1948
v N. IRELAND . . . . Windsor Park, Belfast
Swift . . . . Manchester City
Scott . . . . Arsenal
Howe, J. . . . . Derby County
Wright, W. . . . . Wolverhampton Wanderers
Franklin . . . . Stoke City
Cockburn . . . . Manchester United
Matthews, S. . . . . Blackpool
Mortensen . . . . Blackpool
Milburn . . . . Newcastle United
Pearson . . . . Manchester United
Finney . . . . Preston North End
Result: 6–2
Scorers: Mortensen (3), Milburn, S. Matthews, Pearson

243. 10 November 1948
v WALES. . . . . Villa Park, Birmingham
Swift . . . . Manchester City
Scott . . . . Arsenal
Aston. . . . . Manchester United
Ward . . . . Derby County
Franklin . . . . Stoke City
Wright, W. . . . . Wolverhampton Wanderers
Matthews . . . . Blackpool
Mortensen . . . . Blackpool
Milburn . . . . Newcastle United
Shackleton . . . . Sunderland
Finney . . . . Newcastle United
Result: 1–0
Scorer: Finney

244. 2 December 1948
v SWITZERLAND . . . . Highbury Stadium, Arsenal
Ditchburn. . . . . Tottenham Hotspur
Ramsey . . . . Southampton
Aston. . . . . Manchester United
Wright, W. . . . . Wolverhampton Wanderers
Franklin . . . . Stoke City
Cockburn . . . . Manchester United
Matthews . . . . Blackpool
Rowley. . . . . Manchester United
Milburn . . . . Newcastle United
Haines . . . . West Bromwich Albion
Hancocks . . . . Wolverhampton Wanderers
Result: 6–0
Scorers: Haines (2), Hancocks (2), Milburn, Rowley

245. 9 April 1949
v SCOTLAND. . . . . Wembley Stadium
Swift . . . . Manchester City
Aston. . . . . Manchester United
Howe, J. . . . . Derby County
Wright, W. . . . . Wolverhampton Wanderers
Franklin . . . . Stoke City
Cockburn . . . . Manchester United
Matthews, S. . . . . Blackpool
Mortensen . . . . Blackpool
Milburn . . . . Newcastle United
Pearson . . . . Manchester United
Finney . . . . Preston North End
Result: 1–3
Scorer: Milburn

246. 13 May 1949
v SWEDEN . . . . Solna
Ditchburn. . . . . Tottenham Hotspur
Shimwell . . . . Blackpool
Aston. . . . . Manchester United
Wright, W. . . . . Wolverhampton Wanderers
Franklin . . . . Stoke City
Cockburn . . . . Manchester United
Finney . . . . Preston North End
Mortensen . . . . Blackpool
Bentley . . . . Chelsea
Rowley. . . . . Manchester United
Langton . . . . Preston North End
Result: 1–3
Scorer: Finney

247. 18 May 1949
v NORWAY . . . . Oslo
Swift . . . . Manchester City
Ellerington . . . . Southampton
Aston. . . . . Manchester United
Wright, W. . . . . Wolverhampton Wanderers
Franklin . . . . Stoke City
Dickinson. . . . . Portsmouth
Finney . . . . Preston North End
Morris, J. . . . . Derby County
Mortensen . . . . Blackpool
Mannion . . . . Middlesbrough
Mullen . . . . Wolverhampton Wanderers
Result: 4–1
Scorers: J. Morris, Finney, Mullen, o.g.

248. 22 May 1949
v FRANCE . . . . Paris
Williams. . . . . Wolverhampton Wanderers
Ellerington . . . . Southampton
Aston. . . . . Manchester United
Wright, W. . . . . Wolverhampton Wanderers
Franklin . . . . Stoke City
Dickinson. . . . . Portsmouth
Finney . . . . Preston North End
Morris, J. . . . . Derby County

Rowley. . . . . Manchester United
Mannion . . . . Middlesbrough
Mullen. . . . . Wolverhampton Wanderers
Result: 3–1
Scorers: J. Morris (2), W. Wright

249. 21 September 1949
v EIRE. . . . . Goodison Park, Everton
Williams. . . . . Wolverhampton Wanderers
Mozley. . . . . Derby County
Aston. . . . . Manchester United
Wright, W. . . . . Wolverhampton Wanderers
Franklin . . . . Stoke City
Dickinson. . . . . Portsmouth
Harris. . . . . Portsmouth
Morris, J. . . . . Derby County
Pye . . . . Wolverhampton Wanderers
Mannion . . . . Middlesbrough
Finney . . . . Preston North End
Result: 0–2

250. 15 October 1949
v WALES. . . . . Ninian Park, Cardiff
Williams. . . . . Wolverhampton Wanderers
Mozley. . . . . Derby County
Aston. . . . . Manchester United
Wright, W. . . . . Wolverhampton Wanderers
Franklin . . . . Stoke City
Dickinson. . . . . Portsmouth
Finney . . . . Preston North End
Mortensen . . . . Blackpool
Milburn . . . . Newcastle United
Shackleton. . . . . Sunderland
Hancocks. . . . . Wolverhampton Wanderers
Result: 4–1
Scorers: Milburn (3), Mortensen

251. 16 November 1949
v N. IRELAND . . . . Manchester, Maine Road
Streten. . . . . Luton Town
Mozley. . . . . Derby County
Aston. . . . . Manchester United
Watson, W.. . . . . Sunderland
Franklin . . . . Stoke City
Wright, W. . . . . Wolverhampton Wanderers
Finney . . . . Preston North End
Mortensen . . . . Blackpool
Rowley. . . . . Manchester United
Pearson . . . . Manchester United
Froggatt, J. . . . . Portsmouth
Result: 9–2
Scorers: Rowley (4), Mortensen (2), Pearson (2), J. Froggatt

252. 30 November 1949
v ITALY. . . . . White Hart Lane, Tottenham
Williams. . . . . Wolverhampton Wanderers
Ramsey . . . . Tottenham Hotspur
Aston. . . . . Manchester United
Watson, W.. . . . . Sunderland
Franklin . . . . Stoke City
Wright, W. . . . . Wolverhampton Wanderers
Finney . . . . Preston North End
Mortensen . . . . Blackpool
Rowley. . . . . Manchester United
Pearson . . . . Manchester United
Froggatt, J. . . . . Portsmouth
Result: 2–0
Scorers: Rowley, W. Wright

253. 15 April 1950
v SCOTLAND. . . . . Hampden Park, Glasgow
Williams. . . . . Wolverhampton Wanderers
Ramsey . . . . Tottenham Hotspur

Aston. . . . . Manchester United
Wright, W. . . . . Wolverhampton Wanderers
Franklin . . . . Stoke City
Dickinson. . . . . Portsmouth
Finney . . . . Preston North End
Mannion . . . . Middlesbrough
Mortensen . . . . Blackpool
Bentley . . . . Chelsea
Langton . . . . Bolton Wanderers
Result: 1–0
Scorer: Bentley

254. 14 May 1950
v PORTUGAL. . . . . Lisbon
Williams. . . . . Wolverhampton Wanderers
Ramsey . . . . Tottenham Hotspur
Aston. . . . . Manchester United
Wright, W. . . . . Wolverhampton Wanderers
Jones, W. H. . . . . Liverpool
Dickinson. . . . . Portsmouth
Milburn . . . . Newcastle United
Mortensen . . . . Blackpool
Bentley . . . . Chelsea
Mannion . . . . Middlesbrough
Finney . . . . Preston North End
Result: 5–3
Scorers: Finney (4 – 2 pens), Mortensen

255. 18 May 1950
v BELGIUM. . . . . Brussels
Williams. . . . . Wolverhampton Wanderers
Ramsey . . . . Tottenham Hotspur
Aston. . . . . Manchester United
Wright, W. . . . . Wolverhampton Wanderers
Jones, W. H. . . . . Liverpool
Dickinson. . . . . Portsmouth
Milburn* . . . . Newcastle United
Mortensen . . . . Blackpool
Bentley . . . . Chelsea
Mannion . . . . Middlesbrough
Finney . . . . Preston North End
Sub: *Mullen. . . . . Wolverhampton Wanderers
Result: 4–1
Scorers: Mullen, Mortensen, Mannion, Bentley

 DID YOU KNOW...?

Stan Mortensen scored England's first ever goal in the World Cup Finals when he headed home against Chile in June 1950 at Brazil's Maracanã Stadium.

256. 25 June 1950
v CHILE. . . . . Rio de Janeiro
Williams. . . . . Wolverhampton Wanderers
Ramsey . . . . Tottenham Hotspur
Aston. . . . . Manchester United
Wright, W. . . . . Wolverhampton Wanderers
Hughes . . . . Liverpool
Dickinson. . . . . Portsmouth
Finney . . . . Preston North End
Mannion . . . . Middlesbrough
Bentley . . . . Chelsea
Mortensen . . . . Blackpool
Mullen. . . . . Wolverhampton Wanderers
Result: 2–0
Scorers: Mortensen, Mannion

257. 29 June 1950
v USA . . . . Belo Horizonte
Williams . . . . Wolverhampton Wanderers
Ramsey . . . . Tottenham Hotspur
Aston . . . . Manchester United
Wright, W. . . . . Wolverhampton Wanderers
Hughes . . . . Liverpool
Dickinson . . . . Portsmouth
Finney . . . . Preston North End
Mannion . . . . Middlesbrough
Bentley . . . . Chelsea
Mortensen . . . . Blackpool
Mullen . . . . Wolverhampton Wanderers
Result: 0–1

258. 2 July 1950
v SPAIN . . . . Rio de Janeiro
Williams . . . . Wolverhampton Wanderers
Ramsey . . . . Tottenham Hotspur
Eckersley . . . . Blackburn Rovers
Wright, W. . . . . Wolverhampton Wanderers
Hughes . . . . Liverpool
Dickinson . . . . Portsmouth
Matthews, S. . . . . Blackpool
Mortensen . . . . Blackpool
Milburn . . . . Newcastle United
Baily . . . . Tottenham Hotspur
Finney . . . . Preston North End
Result: 0–1

259. 7 October 1950
v N. IRELAND . . . . Windsor Park, Belfast
Williams . . . . Wolverhampton Wanderers
Ramsey . . . . Tottenham Hotspur
Aston . . . . Manchester United
Wright, W. . . . . Wolverhampton Wanderers
Chilton . . . . Manchester United
Dickinson . . . . Portsmouth
Matthews, S. . . . . Blackpool
Mannion . . . . Middlesbrough
Lee . . . . Derby County
Baily . . . . Tottenham Hotspur
Langton . . . . Bolton Wanderers
Result: 4–1
Scorers: Baily (2), Lee, W. Wright

260. 15 November 1950
v WALES . . . . Roker Park, Sunderland
Williams . . . . Wolverhampton Wanderers
Ramsey . . . . Tottenham Hotspur
Smith, L. . . . . Arsenal
Watson . . . . Sunderland
Compton . . . . Arsenal
Dickinson . . . . Portsmouth
Finney . . . . Preston North End
Mannion . . . . Middlesbrough
Milburn . . . . Newcastle United
Baily . . . . Tottenham Hotspur
Medley . . . . Tottenham Hotspur
Result: 4–2
Scorers: Baily (2), Mannion, Milburn

261. 22 November 1950
v YUGOSLAVIA . . . . Highbury Stadium, Arsenal
Williams . . . . Wolverhampton Wanderers
Ramsey . . . . Tottenham Hotspur
Eckersley . . . . Blackburn Rovers
Watson . . . . Sunderland
Compton . . . . Arsenal
Dickinson . . . . Portsmouth
Hancocks . . . . Wolverhampton Wanderers
Mannion . . . . Middlesbrough
Lofthouse . . . . Bolton Wanderers
Baily . . . . Tottenham Hotspur
Medley . . . . Tottenham Hotspur
Result: 2–2
Scorers: Lofthouse (2)

 FEATURED MATCH

29 JUNE 1950

ENGLAND 0 USA 1 – BELO HORIZONTE

England went into the 1950 World Cup Finals as one of the favourites to lift the Jules Rimet Trophy, while the USA entered the competition with the strict intention of trying to keep the scores down to a respectable level. Therefore, the event that occurred at Belo Horizonte in Brazil was the first real instance of World Cup giant-killing.

Despite the absence of Stanley Matthews, the presence of Mortensen, Finney and Mannion should have been enough to guarantee a flood of goals against the American part-timers. The US captain Eddie McIlvenny – a Scot like their manager Bill Jeffrey – had gone to the States after being given a free transfer by Third Division Wrexham and he was thought to be their outstanding player!

Thus, the game that should have provided mere shooting practice for England only emphasized how inaccurate that shooting was, when a shot was made at all. Too often an extra pass was attempted in error, the woodwork was struck twice, a Mullen header was cleared from a position seemingly a yard behind the goal line, but equally the Americans did defend valiantly. For these reasons and more besides, England were unable to register even a single goal on that fateful day in 1950, unlike the Americans, who scored with a Gaetjens header from their only real chance of the game – in stark contrast to the many wasted by the England players.

True, the bumpy pitch with the spectators crowded in close didn't help matters. True, the England players were tired after a busy domestic season. True, they were ill-prepared, and even scornful of their austere manager, Walter Winterbottom, but regardless of these circumstances, the undeniable fact was that England had lost. They had recorded one of the most surprising results of the nation's footballing annals and the name of Belo Horizonte went down in history as the little mining town that played host to England's first ever soccer disaster.

262. 14 April 1951
v SCOTLAND . . . . Wembley Stadium
Williams . . . . Wolverhampton Wanderers
Ramsey . . . . Tottenham Hotspur
Eckersley . . . . Blackburn Rovers
Johnston . . . . Blackpool
Froggatt, J. . . . . Portsmouth
Wright, W. . . . . Wolverhampton Wanderers
Matthews . . . . Blackpool
Mannion . . . . Middlesbrough
Mortensen . . . . Blackpool
Hassall . . . . Huddersfield Town
Finney . . . . Preston North End
Result: 2–3
Scorers: Hassall, Finney

263. 9 May 1951
v ARGENTINA . . . . Wembley Stadium
Williams . . . . Wolverhampton Wanderers
Ramsey . . . . Tottenham Hotspur
Eckersley . . . . Blackburn Rovers
Wright, W. . . . . Wolverhampton Wanderers
Taylor, J. . . . . Fulham

Cockburn . . . . Manchester United
Finney . . . . Preston North End
Mortensen . . . . Blackpool
Milburn . . . . Newcastle United
Hassall . . . . Huddersfield Town
Metcalfe . . . . Huddersfield Town
Result: 2–1
Scorers: Mortensen, Milburn

264. 19 May 1951
v PORTUGAL . . . . Goodison Park, Everton
Williams . . . . Wolverhampton Wanderers
Ramsey . . . . Tottenham Hotspur
Eckersley . . . . Blackburn Rovers
Nicholson . . . . Tottenham Hotspur
Taylor, J. . . . . Fulham
Cockburn . . . . Manchester United
Finney . . . . Preston North End
Pearson . . . . Manchester United
Milburn . . . . Newcastle United
Hassall . . . . Huddersfield Town
Metcalfe . . . . Huddersfield Town
Result: 5–2
Scorers: Nicholson, Milburn (2), Finney, Hassall

265. 3 October 1951
v FRANCE . . . . Highbury Stadium, Arsenal
Williams . . . . Wolverhampton Wanderers
Ramsey . . . . Tottenham Hotspur
Willis . . . . Tottenham Hotspur
Wright, W. . . . . Wolverhampton Wanderers
Chilton . . . . Manchester United
Cockburn . . . . Manchester United
Finney . . . . Preston North End
Mannion . . . . Middlesbrough
Milburn . . . . Newcastle United
Hassall . . . . Huddersfield Town
Medley . . . . Tottenham Hotspur
Result: 2–2
Scorers: o.g., Medley

266. 20 October 1951
v WALES . . . . Ninian Park, Cardiff
Williams . . . . Wolverhampton Wanderers
Ramsey . . . . Tottenham Hotspur
Smith, L. . . . . Arsenal
Wright, W. . . . . Wolverhampton Wanderers
Barrass . . . . Bolton Wanderers
Dickinson . . . . Portsmouth
Finney . . . . Preston North End
Thompson . . . . Aston Villa
Lofthouse . . . . Bolton Wanderers
Baily . . . . Tottenham Hotspur
Medley . . . . Tottenham Hotspur
Result: 1–1
Scorer: Baily

267. 14 November 1951
v N. IRELAND . . . . Villa Park, Birmingham
Merrick . . . . Birmingham City
Ramsey . . . . Tottenham Hotspur
Smith, L. . . . . Arsenal
Wright, W. . . . . Wolverhampton Wanderers
Barrass . . . . Bolton Wanderers
Dickinson . . . . Portsmouth
Finney . . . . Preston North End
Sewell . . . . Sheffield Wednesday
Lofthouse . . . . Bolton Wanderers
Phillips . . . . Portsmouth
Medley . . . . Tottenham Hotspur
Result: 2–0
Scorers: Lofthouse (2)

268. 28 November 1951
v AUSTRIA . . . . Wembley Stadium
Merrick . . . . Birmingham City
Ramsey . . . . Tottenham Hotspur

Eckersley . . . . Blackburn Rovers
Wright, W. . . . . Wolverhampton Wanderers
Froggatt, J. . . . . Portsmouth
Dickinson . . . . Portsmouth
Milton . . . . Arsenal
Broadis . . . . Manchester City
Lofthouse . . . . Bolton Wanderers
Baily . . . . Tottenham Hotspur
Medley . . . . Tottenham Hotspur
Result: 2–2
Scorers: Ramsey (pen.), Lofthouse

269. 5 April 1952
v SCOTLAND . . . . Hampden Park, Glasgow
Merrick . . . . Birmingham City
Ramsey . . . . Tottenham Hotspur
Garrett . . . . Blackpool
Wright, W. . . . . Wolverhampton Wanderers
Froggatt, J. . . . . Portsmouth
Dickinson . . . . Portsmouth
Finney . . . . Preston North End
Broadis . . . . Manchester City
Lofthouse . . . . Bolton Wanderers
Pearson . . . . Manchester United
Rowley . . . . Manchester United
Result: 2–1
Scorers: Pearson (2)

270. 18 May 1952
v ITALY . . . . Florence
Merrick . . . . Birmingham City
Ramsey . . . . Tottenham Hotspur
Garrett . . . . Blackpool
Wright, W. . . . . Wolverhampton Wanderers
Froggatt, J. . . . . Portsmouth
Dickinson . . . . Portsmouth
Finney . . . . Preston North End
Broadis . . . . Manchester City
Lofthouse . . . . Bolton Wanderers
Pearson . . . . Manchester United
Elliott . . . . Burnley
Result: 1–1
Scorer: Broadis

271. 25 May 1952
v AUSTRIA . . . . Vienna
Merrick . . . . Birmingham City
Ramsey . . . . Tottenham Hotspur
Eckersley . . . . Blackburn Rovers
Wright, W. . . . . Wolverhampton Wanderers
Froggatt, J. . . . . Portsmouth
Dickinson . . . . Portsmouth
Finney . . . . Preston North End
Sewell . . . . Sheffield Wednesday
Lofthouse . . . . Bolton Wanderers
Baily . . . . Tottenham Hotspur
Elliott . . . . Burnley
Result: 3–2
Scorers: Lofthouse (2), Sewell

272. 28 May 1952
v SWITZERLAND . . . . Zurich
Merrick . . . . Birmingham City
Ramsey . . . . Tottenham Hotspur
Eckersley . . . . Blackburn Rovers
Wright, W. . . . . Wolverhampton Wanderers
Froggatt, J. . . . . Portsmouth
Dickinson . . . . Portsmouth
Allen, R. . . . . West Bromwich Albion
Sewell . . . . Sheffield Wednesday
Lofthouse . . . . Bolton Wanderers
Baily . . . . Tottenham Hotspur
Finney . . . . Preston North End
Result: 3–0
Scorers: Sewell, Lofthouse (2)

273. 4 October 1952
v N. IRELAND . . . . Windsor Park, Belfast
Merrick . . . . Birmingham City
Ramsey . . . . Tottenham Hotspur
Eckersley . . . . Blackburn Rovers
Wright, W. . . . . Wolverhampton Wanderers
Froggatt, J. . . . . Portsmouth
Dickinson. . . . . Portsmouth
Finney . . . . Preston North End
Sewell . . . . Sheffield Wednesday
Lofthouse. . . . . Bolton Wanderers
Baily . . . . Tottenham Hotspur
Elliott. . . . . Burnley
Result: 2–2
Scorers: Lofthouse, Elliott

274. 12 November 1952
v WALES. . . . . Wembley Stadium
Merrick . . . . Birmingham City
Ramsey . . . . Tottenham Hotspur
Smith, L. . . . . Arsenal
Wright, W. . . . . Wolverhampton Wanderers
Froggatt, J. . . . . Portsmouth
Dickinson . . . . Portsmouth
Finney . . . . Preston North End
Froggatt, R. . . . . Sheffield Wednesday
Lofthouse. . . . . Bolton Wanderers
Bentley . . . . Chelsea
Elliott. . . . . Burnley
Result: 5–2
Scorers: Finney, Lofthouse (2), J. Froggatt, Bentley

275. 26 November 1952
v BELGIUM. . . . . Wembley Stadium
Merrick . . . . Birmingham City
Ramsey . . . . Tottenham Hotspur
Smith, L. . . . . Arsenal
Wright, W. . . . . Wolverhampton Wanderers
Froggatt, J. . . . . Portsmouth
Dickinson . . . . Portsmouth
Finney . . . . Preston North End
Bentley . . . . Chelsea
Lofthouse. . . . . Bolton Wanderers
Froggatt, R. . . . . Sheffield Wednesday
Elliott. . . . . Burnley
Result: 5–0
Scorers: Elliott (2), Lofthouse (2), R. Froggatt

276. 18 April 1953
v SCOTLAND. . . . . Wembley Stadium
Merrick . . . . Birmingham City
Ramsey . . . . Tottenham Hotspur
Smith, L. . . . . Arsenal
Wright, W. . . . . Wolverhampton Wanderers
Barrass. . . . . Bolton Wanderers
Dickinson. . . . . Portsmouth
Finney . . . . Preston North End
Broadis . . . . Manchester City
Lofthouse. . . . . Bolton Wanderers
Froggatt, R. . . . . Sheffield Wednesday
Froggatt, J. . . . . Portsmouth
Result: 2–2
Scorers: Broadis (2)

277. 17 May 1953
v ARGENTINA. . . . . Buenos Aires
Merrick . . . . Birmingham City
Ramsey . . . . Tottenham Hotspur
Eckersley . . . . Blackburn Rovers
Wright, W. . . . . Wolverhampton Wanderers
Johnston . . . . Blackpool
Dickinson. . . . . Portsmouth
Finney . . . . Preston North End
Broadis . . . . Manchester City
Lofthouse. . . . . Bolton Wanderers
Taylor, T. . . . . Manchester United
Berry . . . . Manchester United
Result: 0–0 (abandoned after 22 minutes)

> ⚽ **DID YOU KNOW...?**
>
> England's shortest match took place in Buenos Aires against Argentina on 17 May 1953. The game was abandoned after twenty-two minutes with the score at 0–0, when a monsoon struck and a burst of torrential rain made the pitch unplayable. The match against the Republic of Ireland on 15 February 1995, which was abandoned due to crowd trouble, lasted for twenty-seven minutes.

278. 24 May 1953
v CHILE. . . . . Santiago
Merrick . . . . Birmingham City
Ramsey . . . . Tottenham Hotspur
Eckersley . . . . Blackburn Rovers
Wright, W. . . . . Wolverhampton Wanderers
Johnston . . . . Blackpool
Dickinson. . . . . Portsmouth
Finney . . . . Preston North End
Broadis . . . . Manchester City
Lofthouse. . . . . Bolton Wanderers
Taylor, T. . . . . Manchester United
Berry . . . . Manchester United
Result: 2–1
Scorers: Taylor, Lofthouse

279. 31 May 1953
v URUGUAY . . . . Montevideo
Merrick . . . . Birmingham City
Ramsey . . . . Tottenham Hotspur
Eckersley . . . . Blackburn Rovers
Wright, W. . . . . Wolverhampton Wanderers
Johnston . . . . Blackpool
Dickinson . . . . Portsmouth
Finney . . . . Preston North End
Broadis . . . . Manchester City
Lofthouse. . . . . Bolton Wanderers
Taylor, T. . . . . Manchester United
Berry . . . . Manchester United
Result: 1–2
Scorer: Taylor

280. 8 June 1953
v USA. . . . . New York City
Ditchburn. . . . . Tottenham Hotspur
Ramsey . . . . Tottenham Hotspur
Eckersley . . . . Blackburn Rovers
Wright, W. . . . . Wolverhampton Wanderers
Johnston . . . . Blackpool
Dickinson. . . . . Portsmouth
Finney . . . . Preston North End
Broadis . . . . Manchester City
Lofthouse. . . . . Bolton Wanderers
Froggatt, R. . . . . Sheffield Wednesday
Froggatt, J. . . . . Portsmouth
Result: 6–3
Scorers: Broadis, Finney (2), Lofthouse (2), R. Froggatt

281. 10 October 1953
v WALES. . . . . Ninian Park, Cardiff
Merrick . . . . Birmingham City
Garrett. . . . . Blackpool
Eckersley . . . . Blackburn Rovers
Wright, W. . . . . Wolverhampton Wanderers
Johnston . . . . Blackpool
Dickinson. . . . . Portsmouth
Finney . . . . Preston North End
Quixall . . . . Sheffield Wednesday
Lofthouse. . . . . Bolton Wanderers
Wilshaw. . . . . Wolverhampton Wanderers
Mullen. . . . . Wolverhampton Wanderers
Result: 4–1
Scorers: Wilshaw (2), Lofthouse (2)

Ray Clemence (*above*) wore the number-one shirt 61 times during his 11-year England career until November 1983.

England's greatest goalkeepers:

World Cup-winning Gordon Banks (*above*) played in 73 internationals between 1963 and 1972.

Peter Shilton (*below*) is England's longest-serving goalkeeper, having made 125 international appearances in a career spanning almost 20 years.

Between November 1988 and October 2002, David Seaman (*below*) was awarded a total of 75 caps as England goalkeeper.

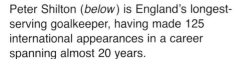

Alf Ramsey (*below*) took charge of England football matters in 1963, leading his side to victory in the 1966 World Cup Final and to the quarter-final of the 1970 World Cup.

England's managers through the ages:

In 1946 Walter Winterbottom (*above*) became England's first team manager, and led the national side for 139 games.

Ron Greenwood (*below*) was next in line after Revie, and during 55 games in charge, he led England to the European Championships in 1980, as well as the 1982 World Cup Finals.

After Joe Mercer had taken temporary control for seven games, former Leeds United manager Don Revie (*above*) took over from 1974 until 1977.

Below: Bobby Robson's eight-year tenure as England coach, which began in 1982, included highlights such as reaching the 1990 World Cup semi-final.

Above: Though Graham Taylor's England side remained undefeated in his first year as manager, when the team's promising start faded the press became ruthlessly critical, and he resigned in November 1993.

Under Terry Venables (*below*), England lost only twice in 23 matches. The team also reached the semi-final of the 1996 European Championships, but were beaten by Germany on penalties.

After Glenn Hoddle's reign as England manager (1996–9), Kevin Keegan (*above*) coached the national team for just 18 matches before resigning in October 2000.

14 June 1970: In the quarter-final of the 1970 World Cup in Mexico, England lost 3–2 to West Germany. (*Above*) Franz Beckenbauer is pictured on the ball close to England's Alan Mullery.

17 October 1973: The 1–1 draw against Poland in the qualifying round of the 1974 World Cup meant that England failed to qualify for the finals in Germany. (*Below*) Roy McFarland is seen retrieving the ball from a distraught Norman Hunter following the defensive error that led to the Poles' opening goal.

16 June 1982: The first score in England's 3–1 defeat of France was the World Cup's fastest ever goal. It was fired home by Bryan Robson (*right, pictured celebrating*) after 27 seconds.

22 June 1986: Diego Maradona hit the headlines with his infamous 'hand of God' goal during England's 2–1 defeat by Argentina in the 1986 World Cup quarter-final.

4 July 1990: After England crashed out of the 1990 World Cup semi-final against Germany on penalties, an emotional Paul Gascoigne left the field, accompanied by teammate Terry Butcher.

30 June 1998: During an incident-packed World Cup second-round match against Argentina, Michael Owen (*pictured left with Juan-Sebastián Verón*) scored a fantastic goal, David Beckham was sent off, and the England team once again crashed out of a major competition on penalties.

1 September 2001: England enjoyed a surprise 5–1 triumph over Germany in Munich. With a Michael Owen hat-trick and goals from Steven Gerrard and Emile Heskey (*pictured above in the number-nine shirt, celebrating his goal*), England recorded their biggest away-win against Germany in modern times.

21 June 2002: England lost 2–1 to Brazil in the 2002 World Cup quarter-final thanks in no small part to the genius of striker Ronaldinho. Keeper David Seaman (*right*) misjudged the flight of a second-half free kick, only to watch the ball float deftly over his shoulder.

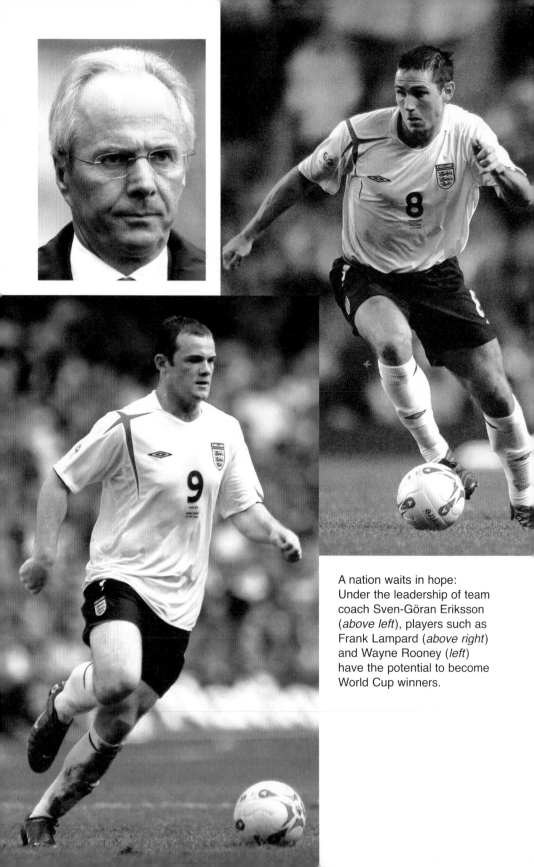

A nation waits in hope: Under the leadership of team coach Sven-Göran Eriksson (*above left*), players such as Frank Lampard (*above right*) and Wayne Rooney (*left*) have the potential to become World Cup winners.

282. 21 October 1953
v REST OF EUROPE . . . . Wembley Stadium
  Merrick . . . . Birmingham City
  Ramsey . . . . Tottenham Hotspur
  Eckersley . . . . Blackburn Rovers
  Wright, W. . . . . Wolverhampton Wanderers
  Ufton . . . . Charlton Athletic
  Dickinson . . . . Portsmouth
  Matthews, S. . . . . Blackpool
  Mortensen . . . . Blackpool
  Lofthouse . . . . Bolton Wanderers
  Quixall . . . . Sheffield Wednesday
  Mullen . . . . Wolverhampton Wanderers
Result: 4–4
Scorers: Mullen (2), Mortensen, Ramsey (pen.)

283. 11 November 1953
v N. IRELAND . . . . Goodison Park, Everton
  Merrick . . . . Birmingham City
  Rickaby . . . . West Bromwich Albion
  Eckersley . . . . Blackburn Rovers
  Wright, W. . . . . Wolverhampton Wanderers
  Johnston . . . . Blackpool
  Dickinson . . . . Portsmouth
  Matthews, S. . . . . Blackpool
  Quixall . . . . Sheffield Wednesday
  Lofthouse . . . . Bolton Wanderers
  Hassall . . . . Bolton Wanderers
  Mullen . . . . Wolverhampton Wanderers
Result: 3–1
Scorers: Hassall (2), Lofthouse

⚽ DID YOU KNOW...?

On the day that England were beaten 6–3 at Wembley by Hungary in November 1953, police were initially bemused by the number of pigeons flying out of the ground before kick-off, until they realized that the birds were being used to send tickets to people outside the ground who had been unable to obtain them!

284. 25 November 1953
v HUNGARY . . . . Wembley Stadium
  Merrick . . . . Birmingham City
  Ramsey . . . . Tottenham Hotspur
  Eckersley . . . . Blackburn Rovers
  Wright, W. . . . . Wolverhampton Wanderers
  Johnston . . . . Blackpool
  Dickinson . . . . Portsmouth
  Matthews, S. . . . . Blackpool
  Taylor, E. . . . . Blackpool
  Mortensen . . . . Blackpool
  Sewell . . . . Sheffield Wednesday
  Robb . . . . Tottenham Hotspur
Result: 3–6
Scorers: Sewell, Mortensen, Ramsey (pen.)

285. 3 April 1954
v SCOTLAND . . . . Hampden Park, Glasgow
  Merrick . . . . Birmingham City
  Staniforth . . . . Huddersfield Town
  Byrne, R. . . . . Manchester United
  Wright, W. . . . . Wolverhampton Wanderers
  Clarke . . . . Tottenham Hotspur
  Dickinson . . . . Portsmouth
  Finney . . . . Preston North End
  Broadis . . . . Newcastle United
  Allen, R. . . . . West Bromwich Albion
  Nicholls . . . . West Bromwich Albion
  Mullen . . . . Wolverhampton Wanderers
Result: 4–2
Scorers: Broadis, Nicholls, R. Allen, Mullen

FEATURED MATCH

25 NOVEMBER 1953

ENGLAND 3 HUNGARY 6 – WEMBLEY STADIUM

England's first home defeat by foreign opposition, apart from Eire's largely forgotten 2–0 win at Goodison Park four years earlier, was achieved by perhaps the finest team the world had ever seen. The speedy, fluent, confident Hungarians gave a display that would have shattered any top-class side. England, who were ill-prepared and possibly over-confident after so many invincible years, were not in the same league, but they didn't play badly, and their first two goals were brilliantly taken. The problem was that the Hungarians were so good; indeed their margin could have been greater had they not slowed their pace in the last half-hour, after building up a 6–2 lead.

It took only a single minute for the visitors to breach the England defence. József Bozsik, József Zakariás and Nándor Hidegkuti all combined through the centre of the field culminating in Hidegkuti dummying a defender and releasing a swift rising shot past keeper Gil Merrick. Hidegkuti also had the ball in the net a second time after a fine move involving Zoltan Czibor and Ferenc Puskás, but this time he was ruled offside. John Sewell in his fifth international levelled the scores with his third goal for England.

England goalscoring parity with Hungary was not to last long before the opposition launched a determined onslaught. Puskás released Czibor down the left wing after twenty minutes, who hit the ball towards Sándor Kocsis to flick on for Hidegkuti to score from close range. The third goal emanated from the right flank: Czibor beat Bill Eckersley and pulled back a diagonal pass for Puskás to score with a left-foot shot just inside the near post. Three minutes later Puskás struck again as he diverted Bozsik's free kick past Merrick with his head.

Mortensen helped to reduce the deficit for the home side with his last goal for England, before Bozsik added his own name to the scoresheet by pouncing on a rebound from Merrick's save from Czibor's header. Hidegkuti completed his hat-trick with a volley from Puskás's lingering lob. Minutes later England got a third goal from an Alf Ramsey penalty after Mortensen had been brought down in the box, but the undeniable truth was that the national team had been soundly beaten on home soil to rampant foreign opposition. The five Hungarian forwards had provided ample proof that there was more than enough talent and ability to challenge the pride of England's footballing nation.

286. 16 May 1954
v YUGOSLAVIA . . . . Belgrade
  Merrick . . . . Birmingham City
  Staniforth . . . . Huddersfield Town
  Byrne, R. . . . . Manchester United
  Wright, W. . . . . Wolverhampton Wanderers
  Owen . . . . Luton Town
  Dickinson . . . . Portsmouth
  Finney . . . . Preston North End
  Broadis . . . . Newcastle United
  Allen, R. . . . . West Bromwich Albion
  Nicholls . . . . West Bromwich Albion
  Mullen . . . . Wolverhampton Wanderers
Result: 0–1

287. 23 May 1954

v HUNGARY . . . . Budapest
Merrick . . . . Birmingham City
Staniforth. . . . . Huddersfield Town
Byrne, R. . . . . Manchester United
Wright, W. . . . . Wolverhampton Wanderers
Owen. . . . . Luton Town
Dickinson. . . . . Portsmouth
Harris, P.. . . . . Portsmouth
Sewell . . . . Sheffield Wednesday
Jezzard. . . . . Fulham
Broadis . . . . Newcastle United
Finney . . . . Preston North End
Result: 1–7
Scorer: Broadis

288. 17 June 1954

v BELGIUM . . . . Basle
Merrick . . . . Birmingham City
Staniforth. . . . . Huddersfield Town
Byrne, R. . . . . Manchester United
Wright, W. . . . . Wolverhampton Wanderers
Owen. . . . . Luton Town
Dickinson . . . . Portsmouth
Matthews, S. . . . . Blackpool
Broadis . . . . Newcastle United
Lofthouse. . . . . Bolton Wanderers
Taylor, T. . . . . Manchester United
Finney . . . . Preston North End
Result: 4–4
Scorers: Broadis (2), Lofthouse (2)

289. 20 June 1954

v SWITZERLAND . . . . Berne
Merrick . . . . Birmingham City
Staniforth. . . . . Huddersfield Town
Byrne, R. . . . . Manchester United
McGarry. . . . . Huddersfield Town
Wright, W. . . . . Wolverhampton Wanderers
Dickinson . . . . Portsmouth
Finney . . . . Preston North End
Broadis . . . . Newcastle United
Taylor, T. . . . . Manchester United
Wilshaw. . . . . Wolverhampton Wanderers
Mullen. . . . . Wolverhampton Wanderers
Result: 2–0
Scorers: Wilshaw, Mullen

290. 26 June 1954

v URUGUAY . . . . Basle
Merrick . . . . Birmingham City
Staniforth. . . . . Huddersfield Town
Byrne, R. . . . . Manchester United
McGarry. . . . . Huddersfield Town
Wright, W. . . . . Wolverhampton Wanderers
Dickinson . . . . Portsmouth
Matthews, S. . . . . Blackpool
Broadis . . . . Newcastle United
Lofthouse. . . . . Bolton Wanderers
Wilshaw. . . . . Wolverhampton Wanderers
Finney . . . . Preston North End
Result: 2–4
Scorers: Lofthouse, Finney

291. 2 October 1954

v N. IRELAND . . . . Windsor Park, Belfast
Wood. . . . . Manchester United
Foulkes . . . . Manchester United
Byrne, R. . . . . Manchester United
Wheeler . . . . Bolton Wanderers
Wright, W. . . . . Wolverhampton Wanderers
Barlow. . . . . West Bromwich Albion
Matthews, S. . . . . Blackpool
Revie . . . . Manchester City
Lofthouse. . . . . Bolton Wanderers

Haynes. . . . . Fulham
Pilkington . . . . Burnley
Result: 2–0
Scorers: Haynes, Revie

292. 10 November 1954

v WALES. . . . . Wembley Stadium
Wood. . . . . Manchester United
Staniforth. . . . . Huddersfield Town
Byrne, R. . . . . Manchester United
Phillips. . . . . Portsmouth
Wright, W. . . . . Wolverhampton Wanderers
Slater. . . . . Wolverhampton Wanderers
Matthews, S. . . . . Blackpool
Bentley . . . . Chelsea
Allen, R. . . . . West Bromwich Albion
Shackleton . . . . Sunderland
Blunstone. . . . . Chelsea
Result: 3–2
Scorers: Bentley (3)

293. 1 December 1954

v WEST GERMANY . . . . Wembley Stadium
Williams. . . . . Wolverhampton Wanderers
Staniforth. . . . . Huddersfield Town
Byrne, R. . . . . Manchester United
Phillips. . . . . Portsmouth
Wright, W. . . . . Wolverhampton Wanderers
Slater. . . . . Wolverhampton Wanderers
Matthews, S. . . . . Blackpool
Bentley . . . . Chelsea
Allen, R. . . . . West Bromwich Albion
Shackleton . . . . Sunderland
Finney . . . . Preston North End
Result: 3–1
Scorers: Bentley, R. Allen, Shackleton

294. 2 April 1955

v SCOTLAND. . . . . Wembley Stadium
Williams. . . . . Wolverhampton Wanderers
Meadows. . . . . Manchester City
Byrne, R. . . . . Manchester United
Armstrong . . . . Chelsea
Wright, W. . . . . Wolverhampton Wanderers
Edwards. . . . . Manchester United
Matthews, S. . . . . Blackpool
Revie . . . . Manchester City
Lofthouse. . . . . Bolton Wanderers
Wilshaw. . . . . Wolverhampton Wanderers
Blunstone. . . . . Chelsea
Result: 7–2
Scorers: Wilshaw (4), Lofthouse (2), Revie

295. 15 May 1955

v FRANCE. . . . . Paris
Williams. . . . . Wolverhampton Wanderers
Sillett. . . . . Chelsea
Byrne, R. . . . . Manchester United
Flowers . . . . Wolverhampton Wanderers
Wright, W. . . . . Wolverhampton Wanderers
Edwards. . . . . Manchester United
Matthews, S. . . . . Blackpool
Revie . . . . Manchester City
Lofthouse. . . . . Bolton Wanderers
Wilshaw. . . . . Wolverhampton Wanderers
Blunstone. . . . . Chelsea
Result: 0–1

296. 18 May 1955

v SPAIN . . . . Madrid
Williams. . . . . Wolverhampton Wanderers
Sillett. . . . . Chelsea
Byrne, R. . . . . Manchester United
Dickinson . . . . Portsmouth
Wright, W. . . . . Wolverhampton Wanderers

Edwards. . . . . Manchester United
Matthews, S. . . . . Blackpool
Bentley . . . . Chelsea
Lofthouse. . . . . Bolton Wanderers
Quixall. . . . . Sheffield Wednesday
Wilshaw. . . . . Wolverhampton Wanderers
Result: 1–1
Scorer: Bentley

297. 22 May 1955
v PORTUGAL. . . . . Oporto
Williams. . . . . Wolverhampton Wanderers
Sillett. . . . . Chelsea
Byrne, R. . . . . Manchester United
Dickinson. . . . . Portsmouth
Wright, W. . . . . Wolverhampton Wanderers
Edwards. . . . . Manchester United
Matthews, S. . . . . Blackpool
Bentley . . . . Chelsea
Lofthouse*. . . . . Bolton Wanderers
Wilshaw. . . . . Wolverhampton Wanderers
Blunstone. . . . . Chelsea
Sub: *Quixall. . . . . Sheffield Wednesday
Result: 1–3
Scorer: Bentley

298. 2 October 1955
v DENMARK . . . . Copenhagen
Baynham . . . . Luton Town
Hall . . . . Birmingham City
Byrne, R. . . . . Manchester United
McGarry. . . . . Huddersfield Town
Wright, W. . . . . Wolverhampton Wanderers
Dickinson. . . . . Portsmouth
Milburn . . . . Newcastle United
Revie . . . . Manchester City
Lofthouse. . . . . Bolton Wanderers
Bradford. . . . . Bristol Rovers
Finney . . . . Preston North End
Result: 5–1
Scorers: Revie (2 – 1 pen.), Lofthouse (2), Bradford

299. 22 October 1955
v WALES. . . . . Ninian Park, Cardiff
Williams. . . . . Wolverhampton Wanderers
Hall . . . . Birmingham City
Byrne, R. . . . . Manchester United
McGarry. . . . . Huddersfield Town
Wright, W. . . . . Wolverhampton Wanderers
Dickinson. . . . . Portsmouth
Matthews, S. . . . . Blackpool
Revie . . . . Manchester City
Lofthouse. . . . . Bolton Wanderers
Wilshaw. . . . . Wolverhampton Wanderers
Finney . . . . Preston North End
Result: 1–2
Scorer: o.g.

300. 2 November 1955
v N. IRELAND . . . . Wembley Stadium
Baynham . . . . Luton Town
Hall . . . . Birmingham City
Byrne, R. . . . . Manchester United
Clayton . . . . Blackburn Rovers
Wright, W. . . . . Wolverhampton Wanderers
Dickinson. . . . . Portsmouth
Finney . . . . Preston North End
Haynes. . . . . Fulham
Jezzard. . . . . Fulham
Wilshaw. . . . . Wolverhampton Wanderers
Perry . . . . Blackpool
Result: 3–0
Scorers: Wilshaw (2), Finney

 DID YOU KNOW...?

The first Wembley match played under floodlights
was England v Spain on 30 November 1955. On a
foggy afternoon, the stadium was lit up after 73
minutes of the game, which England won 4–1. The
first complete match under lights took place on the
evening of 20 November 1963; England beat
Northern Ireland 8–3.

301. 30 November 1955
v SPAIN . . . . Wembley Stadium
Baynham . . . . Luton Town
Hall . . . . Birmingham City
Byrne, R. . . . . Manchester United
Clayton . . . . Blackburn Rovers
Wright, W. . . . . Wolverhampton Wanderers
Dickinson. . . . . Portsmouth
Finney . . . . Preston North End
Atyeo. . . . . Bristol City
Lofthouse. . . . . Bolton Wanderers
Haynes. . . . . Fulham
Perry . . . . Blackpool
Result: 4–1
Scorers: Atyeo, Perry (2), Finney

302. 14 April 1956
v SCOTLAND. . . . . Hampden Park, Glasgow
Matthews, R. . . . . Coventry City
Hall . . . . Birmingham City
Byrne, R. . . . . Manchester United
Dickinson. . . . . Portsmouth
Wright, W. . . . . Wolverhampton Wanderers
Edwards. . . . . Manchester United
Finney . . . . Preston North End
Taylor, T. . . . . Manchester United
Lofthouse. . . . . Bolton Wanderers
Haynes. . . . . Fulham
Perry . . . . Blackpool
Result: 1–1
Scorer: Haynes

303. 9 May 1956
v BRAZIL. . . . . Wembley Stadium
Matthews, R. . . . . Coventry City
Hall . . . . Birmingham City
Byrne, R. . . . . Manchester United
Clayton . . . . Blackburn Rovers
Wright, W. . . . . Wolverhampton Wanderers
Edwards. . . . . Manchester United
Matthews, S. . . . . Blackpool
Atyeo. . . . . Bristol City
Taylor, T. . . . . Manchester United
Haynes. . . . . Fulham
Grainger. . . . . Sheffield United
Result: 4–2
Scorers: T. Taylor (2), Grainger (2)

304. 16 May 1956
v SWEDEN . . . . Solna
Matthews, R. . . . . Coventry City
Hall . . . . Birmingham City
Byrne, R. . . . . Manchester United
Clayton . . . . Blackburn Rovers
Wright, W. . . . . Wolverhampton Wanderers
Edwards. . . . . Manchester United
Berry . . . . Manchester United
Atyeo. . . . . Bristol City
Taylor, T. . . . . Manchester United
Haynes. . . . . Fulham
Grainger. . . . . Sheffield United
Result: 0–0

305. 20 May 1956
v FINLAND . . . . Helsinki
  Wood. . . . . Manchester United
  Hall . . . . Birmingham City
  Byrne, R. . . . . Manchester United
  Clayton . . . . Blackburn Rovers
  Wright, W. . . . . Wolverhampton Wanderers
  Edwards. . . . . Manchester United
  Astall . . . . Birmingham City
  Haynes. . . . . Fulham
  Taylor, T.* . . . . Manchester United
  Wilshaw. . . . . Wolverhampton Wanderers
  Grainger. . . . . Sheffield United
Sub: *Lofthouse. . . . . Bolton Wanderers
Result: 5–1
Scorers: Wilshaw, Haynes, Astall, Lofthouse (2)

306. 26 May 1956
v WEST GERMANY . . . . Berlin
  Matthews, R. . . . . Coventry City
  Hall . . . . Birmingham City
  Byrne, R. . . . . Manchester United
  Clayton . . . . Blackburn Rovers
  Wright, W. . . . . Wolverhampton Wanderers
  Edwards. . . . . Manchester United
  Astall . . . . Birmingham City
  Haynes. . . . . Fulham
  Taylor, T. . . . . Manchester United
  Wilshaw. . . . . Wolverhampton Wanderers
  Grainger. . . . . Sheffield United
Result: 3–1
Scorers: Edwards, Grainger, Haynes

307. 6 October 1956
v N. IRELAND . . . . Windsor Park, Belfast
  Matthews, R. . . . . Coventry City
  Hall . . . . Birmingham City
  Byrne, R. . . . . Manchester United
  Clayton . . . . Blackburn Rovers
  Wright, W. . . . . Wolverhampton Wanderers
  Edwards. . . . . Manchester United
  Matthews, S. . . . . Blackpool
  Revie . . . . Manchester City
  Taylor, T. . . . . Manchester United
  Wilshaw. . . . . Wolverhampton Wanderers
  Grainger. . . . . Sheffield United
Result: 1–1
Scorer: S. Matthews

308. 14 November 1956
v WALES. . . . . Wembley Stadium
  Ditchburn. . . . . Tottenham Hotspur
  Hall . . . . Birmingham City
  Byrne, R. . . . . Manchester United
  Clayton . . . . Blackburn Rovers
  Wright, W. . . . . Wolverhampton Wanderers
  Dickinson. . . . . Portsmouth
  Matthews, S. . . . . Blackpool
  Brooks . . . . Tottenham Hotspur
  Finney . . . . Preston North End
  Haynes. . . . . Fulham
  Grainger. . . . . Sheffield United
Result: 3–1
Scorers: Haynes, Brooks, Finney

309. 28 November 1956
v YUGOSLAVIA . . . . Wembley Stadium
  Ditchburn. . . . . Tottenham Hotspur
  Hall . . . . Birmingham City
  Byrne, R. . . . . Manchester United
  Clayton . . . . Blackburn Rovers
  Wright, W. . . . . Wolverhampton Wanderers
  Dickinson. . . . . Portsmouth
  Matthews, S. . . . . Blackpool
  Brooks . . . . Tottenham Hotspur

  Finney . . . . Preston North End
  Haynes*. . . . . Fulham
  Blunstone. . . . . Chelsea
Sub: *Taylor, T. . . . . Manchester United
Result: 3–0
Scorers: Brooks, T. Taylor (2)

310. 5 December 1956
v DENMARK . . . . Molineux, Wolverhampton
  Ditchburn. . . . . Tottenham Hotspur
  Hall . . . . Birmingham City
  Byrne, R. . . . . Manchester United
  Clayton . . . . Blackburn Rovers
  Wright, W. . . . . Wolverhampton Wanderers
  Dickinson. . . . . Portsmouth
  Matthews, S. . . . . Blackpool
  Brooks . . . . Tottenham Hotspur
  Taylor, T. . . . . Manchester United
  Edwards. . . . . Manchester United
  Finney . . . . Preston North End
Result: 5–2
Scorers: T. Taylor (3), Edwards (2)

311. 6 April 1957
v SCOTLAND . . . . Wembley Stadium
  Hodgkinson . . . . Sheffield United
  Hall . . . . Birmingham City
  Byrne, R. . . . . Manchester United
  Clayton . . . . Blackburn Rovers
  Wright, W. . . . . Wolverhampton Wanderers
  Edwards. . . . . Manchester United
  Matthews, S. . . . . Blackpool
  Thompson, T. . . . . Preston North End
  Finney . . . . Preston North End
  Kevan. . . . . West Bromwich Albion
  Grainger. . . . . Sunderland
Result: 2–1
Scorers: Kevan, Edwards

312. 8 May 1957
v EIRE. . . . . Wembley Stadium
  Hodgkinson . . . . Sheffield United
  Hall . . . . Birmingham City
  Byrne, R. . . . . Manchester United
  Clayton . . . . Blackburn Rovers
  Wright, W. . . . . Wolverhampton Wanderers
  Edwards. . . . . Manchester United
  Matthews, S. . . . . Blackpool
  Atyeo. . . . . Bristol City
  Taylor, T. . . . . Manchester United
  Haynes. . . . . Fulham
  Finney . . . . Preston North End
Result: 5–1
Scorers: T. Taylor (3), Atyeo (2)

313. 15 May 1957
v DENMARK . . . . Copenhagen
  Hodgkinson . . . . Sheffield United
  Hall . . . . Birmingham City
  Byrne, R. . . . . Manchester United
  Clayton . . . . Blackburn Rovers
  Wright, W. . . . . Wolverhampton Wanderers
  Edwards. . . . . Manchester United
  Matthews, S. . . . . Blackpool
  Atyeo. . . . . Bristol City
  Taylor, T. . . . . Manchester United
  Haynes. . . . . Fulham
  Finney . . . . Preston North End
Result: 4–1
Scorers: Haynes, T. Taylor (2), Atyeo

314. 19 May 1957
v EIRE. . . . . Dalymount Park, Dublin
  Hodgkinson . . . . Sheffield United
  Hall . . . . Birmingham City

Byrne, R. . . . . Manchester United
Clayton . . . . Blackburn Rovers
Wright, W. . . . . Wolverhampton Wanderers
Edwards. . . . . Manchester United
Finney . . . . Preston North End
Atyeo. . . . . Bristol City
Taylor, T. . . . . Manchester United
Haynes. . . . . Fulham
Pegg . . . . Manchester United
Result: 1–1
Scorer: Atyeo

315. 19 October 1957
v WALES. . . . . Ninian Park, Cardiff
Hopkinson . . . . Bolton Wanderers
Howe. . . . . West Bromwich Albion
Byrne, R. . . . . Manchester United
Clayton . . . . Blackburn Rovers
Wright, W. . . . . Wolverhampton Wanderers
Edwards. . . . . Manchester United
Douglas . . . . Blackburn Rovers
Kevan. . . . . West Bromwich Albion
Taylor, T. . . . . Manchester United
Haynes. . . . . Fulham
Finney . . . . Preston North End
Result: 4–0
Scorers: o.g., Haynes (2), Finney

316. 6 November 1957
v N. IRELAND . . . . Wembley Stadium
Hopkinson . . . . Bolton Wanderers
Howe. . . . . West Bromwich Albion
Byrne, R. . . . . Manchester United
Clayton . . . . Blackburn Rovers
Wright, W. . . . . Wolverhampton Wanderers
Edwards. . . . . Manchester United
Douglas . . . . Blackburn Rovers
Kevan. . . . . West Bromwich Albion
Taylor, T. . . . . Manchester United
Haynes. . . . . Fulham
A'Court . . . . Liverpool
Result: 2–3
Scorers: A'Court, Edwards

317. 27 November 1957
v FRANCE. . . . . Wembley Stadium
Hopkinson . . . . Bolton Wanderers
Howe. . . . . West Bromwich Albion
Byrne, R. . . . . Manchester United
Clayton . . . . Blackburn Rovers
Wright, W. . . . . Wolverhampton Wanderers
Edwards. . . . . Manchester United
Douglas . . . . Blackburn Rovers
Robson . . . . West Bromwich Albion
Taylor, T. . . . . Manchester United
Haynes. . . . . Fulham
Finney . . . . Preston North End
Result: 4–0
Scorers: T. Taylor (2), Robson (2)

318. 19 April 1958
v SCOTLAND . . . . Hampden Park, Glasgow
Hopkinson . . . . Bolton Wanderers
Howe. . . . . West Bromwich Albion
Langley . . . . Fulham
Clayton . . . . Blackburn Rovers
Wright, W. . . . . Wolverhampton Wanderers
Slater. . . . . Wolverhampton Wanderers
Douglas . . . . Blackburn Rovers
Charlton, R. . . . . Manchester United
Kevan. . . . . West Bromwich Albion
Haynes. . . . . Fulham
Finney . . . . Preston North End
Result: 4–0
Scorers: Douglas, Kevan (2), R. Charlton

319. 7 May 1958
v PORTUGAL. . . . . Wembley Stadium
Hopkinson . . . . Bolton Wanderers
Howe. . . . . West Bromwich Albion
Langley . . . . Fulham
Clayton . . . . Blackburn Rovers
Wright, W. . . . . Wolverhampton Wanderers
Slater. . . . . Wolverhampton Wanderers
Douglas . . . . Blackburn Rovers
Charlton, R. . . . . Manchester United
Kevan. . . . . West Bromwich Albion
Haynes. . . . . Fulham
Finney . . . . Preston North End
Result: 2–1
Scorers: R. Charlton (2)

320. 11 May 1958
v YUGOSLAVIA . . . . Belgrade
Hopkinson . . . . Bolton Wanderers
Howe. . . . . West Bromwich Albion
Langley . . . . Fulham
Clayton . . . . Blackburn Rovers
Wright, W. . . . . Wolverhampton Wanderers
Slater. . . . . Wolverhampton Wanderers
Douglas . . . . Blackburn Rovers
Charlton, R. . . . . Manchester United
Kevan. . . . . West Bromwich Albion
Haynes. . . . . Fulham
Finney . . . . Preston North End
Result: 0–5

321. 18 May 1958
v SOVIET UNION . . . . Moscow
McDonald . . . . Burnley
Howe. . . . . West Bromwich Albion
Banks. . . . . Bolton Wanderers
Clamp . . . . Wolverhampton Wanderers
Wright, W. . . . . Wolverhampton Wanderers
Slater. . . . . Wolverhampton Wanderers
Douglas . . . . Blackburn Rovers
Robson . . . . West Bromwich Albion
Kevan. . . . . West Bromwich Albion
Haynes. . . . . Fulham
Finney . . . . Preston North End
Result: 1–1
Scorer: Kevan

322. 8 June 1958
v SOVIET UNION . . . . Gothenburg
McDonald . . . . Burnley
Howe. . . . . West Bromwich Albion
Banks. . . . . Bolton Wanderers
Clamp . . . . Wolverhampton Wanderers
Wright, W. . . . . Wolverhampton Wanderers
Slater. . . . . Wolverhampton Wanderers
Douglas . . . . Blackburn Rovers
Robson . . . . West Bromwich Albion
Kevan. . . . . West Bromwich Albion
Haynes. . . . . Fulham
Finney . . . . Preston North End
Result: 2–2
Scorers: Kevan, Finney (pen.)

323. 11 June 1958
v BRAZIL. . . . . Gothenburg
McDonald . . . . Burnley
Howe. . . . . West Bromwich Albion
Banks. . . . . Bolton Wanderers
Clamp . . . . Wolverhampton Wanderers
Wright, W. . . . . Wolverhampton Wanderers
Slater. . . . . Wolverhampton Wanderers
Douglas . . . . Blackburn Rovers
Robson . . . . West Bromwich Albion
Kevan. . . . . West Bromwich Albion
Haynes. . . . . Fulham
A'Court . . . . Liverpool
Result: 0–0

324. 15 June 1958
v AUSTRIA . . . . Boras
McDonald . . . . Burnley
Howe. . . . . West Bromwich Albion
Banks. . . . . Bolton Wanderers
Clamp . . . . Wolverhampton Wanderers
Wright, W. . . . . Wolverhampton Wanderers
Slater. . . . . Wolverhampton Wanderers
Douglas . . . . Blackburn Rovers
Robson . . . . West Bromwich Albion
Kevan. . . . . West Bromwich Albion
Haynes. . . . . Fulham
A'Court . . . . Liverpool
Result: 2–2
Scorers: Haynes, Kevan

325. 17 June 1958
v SOVIET UNION . . . . Gothenburg
McDonald . . . . Burnley
Howe. . . . . West Bromwich Albion
Banks. . . . . Bolton Wanderers
Clayton . . . . Blackburn Rovers
Wright, W. . . . . Wolverhampton Wanderers
Slater. . . . . Wolverhampton Wanderers
Brabrook . . . . Chelsea
Broadbent . . . . Wolverhampton Wanderers
Kevan. . . . . West Bromwich Albion
Haynes. . . . . Fulham
A'Court . . . . Liverpool
Result: 0–1

326. 4 October 1958
v N. IRELAND . . . . Windsor Park, Belfast
McDonald . . . . Burnley
Howe. . . . . West Bromwich Albion
Banks. . . . . Bolton Wanderers
Clayton . . . . Blackburn Rovers
Wright, W. . . . . Wolverhampton Wanderers
McGuinness. . . . . Manchester United
Brabrook . . . . Chelsea
Broadbent . . . . Wolverhampton Wanderers
Charlton, R. . . . . Manchester United
Haynes. . . . . Fulham
Finney . . . . Preston North End
Result: 3–3
Scorers: R. Charlton (2), Finney

327. 22 October 1958
v SOVIET UNION . . . . Wembley Stadium
McDonald . . . . Burnley
Howe. . . . . West Bromwich Albion
Shaw . . . . Sheffield United
Clayton . . . . Blackburn Rovers
Wright, W. . . . . Wolverhampton Wanderers
Slater. . . . . Wolverhampton Wanderers
Douglas . . . . Blackburn Rovers
Charlton, R. . . . . Manchester United
Lofthouse. . . . . Bolton Wanderers
Haynes. . . . . Fulham
Finney . . . . Preston North End
Result: 5–0
Scorers: Haynes (3), Lofthouse, R. Charlton (pen.)

328. 26 November 1958
v WALES. . . . . Villa Park, Birmingham
McDonald . . . . Burnley
Howe. . . . . West Bromwich Albion
Shaw . . . . Sheffield United
Clayton . . . . Blackburn Rovers
Wright, W. . . . . Wolverhampton Wanderers
Flowers . . . . Wolverhampton Wanderers
Clapton . . . . Arsenal
Charlton, R. . . . . Manchester United
Lofthouse. . . . . Bolton Wanderers
Broadbent . . . . Wolverhampton Wanderers

A'Court . . . . Liverpool
Result: 2–2
Scorers: Broadbent (2)

329. 11 April 1959
v SCOTLAND. . . . . Wembley Stadium
Hopkinson . . . . Bolton Wanderers
Howe. . . . . West Bromwich Albion
Shaw . . . . Sheffield United
Clayton . . . . Blackburn Rovers
Wright, W. . . . . Wolverhampton Wanderers
Flowers . . . . Wolverhampton Wanderers
Douglas . . . . Blackburn Rovers
Broadbent . . . . Wolverhampton Wanderers
Charlton, R. . . . . Manchester United
Haynes. . . . . Fulham
Holden. . . . . Bolton Wanderers
Result: 1–0
Scorer: R. Charlton

330. 6 May 1959
v ITALY . . . . Wembley Stadium
Hopkinson . . . . Bolton Wanderers
Howe. . . . . West Bromwich Albion
Shaw . . . . Sheffield United
Clayton . . . . Blackburn Rovers
Wright, W. . . . . Wolverhampton Wanderers
Flowers . . . . Wolverhampton Wanderers
Bradley . . . . Manchester United
Broadbent . . . . Wolverhampton Wanderers
Charlton, R. . . . . Manchester United
Haynes. . . . . Fulham
Holden. . . . . Bolton Wanderers
Result: 2–2
Scorers: R. Charlton, Bradley

331. 13 May 1959
v BRAZIL. . . . . Rio de Janeiro
Hopkinson . . . . Bolton Wanderers
Howe. . . . . West Bromwich Albion
Armfield. . . . . Blackpool
Clayton . . . . Blackburn Rovers
Wright, W. . . . . Wolverhampton Wanderers
Flowers . . . . Wolverhampton Wanderers
Deeley . . . . Wolverhampton Wanderers
Broadbent . . . . Wolverhampton Wanderers
Charlton, R. . . . . Manchester United
Haynes. . . . . Fulham
Holden. . . . . Bolton Wanderers
Result: 0–2

332. 17 May 1959
v PERU . . . . Lima
Hopkinson . . . . Bolton Wanderers
Howe. . . . . West Bromwich Albion
Armfield. . . . . Blackpool
Clayton . . . . Blackburn Rovers
Wright, W. . . . . Wolverhampton Wanderers
Flowers . . . . Wolverhampton Wanderers
Deeley . . . . Wolverhampton Wanderers
Greaves . . . . Chelsea
Charlton, R. . . . . Manchester United
Haynes. . . . . Fulham
Holden. . . . . Bolton Wanderers
Result: 1–4
Scorer: Greaves

333. 24 May 1959
v MEXICO. . . . . Mexico City
Hopkinson . . . . Bolton Wanderers
Howe. . . . . West Bromwich Albion
Armfield. . . . . Blackpool
Clayton . . . . Blackburn Rovers
Wright, W. . . . . Wolverhampton Wanderers
McGuinness* . . . . Manchester United

Holden** . . . . Bolton Wanderers
Greaves . . . . Chelsea
Kevan. . . . . West Bromwich Albion
Haynes. . . . . Fulham
Charlton, R. . . . . Manchester United
Subs: *Flowers . . . . Wolverhampton Wanderers
**Bradley . . . . Manchester United
Result: 1–2
Scorer: Kevan

334. 28 May 1959
v USA. . . . . Los Angeles
Hopkinson . . . . Bolton Wanderers
Howe. . . . . West Bromwich Albion
Armfield. . . . . Blackpool
Clayton . . . . Blackburn Rovers
Wright, W. . . . . Wolverhampton Wanderers
Flowers . . . . Wolverhampton Wanderers
Bradley . . . . Manchester United
Greaves . . . . Chelsea
Kevan. . . . . West Bromwich Albion
Haynes. . . . . Fulham
Charlton, R. . . . . Manchester United
Result: 8–1
Scorers: R. Charlton (3 – 1 pen.), Flowers (2), Bradley,
Kevan, Haynes

335. 17 October 1959
v WALES. . . . . Ninian Park, Cardiff
Hopkinson . . . . Bolton Wanderers
Howe. . . . . West Bromwich Albion
Allen, A. . . . . Stoke City
Clayton . . . . Blackburn Rovers
Smith, T. . . . . Birmingham City
Flowers . . . . Wolverhampton Wanderers
Connelly. . . . . Burnley
Greaves . . . . Chelsea
Clough. . . . . Middlesbrough
Holliday . . . . Middlesbrough
Charlton, R. . . . . Manchester United
Result: 1–1
Scorer: Greaves

336. 28 October 1959
v SWEDEN . . . . Wembley Stadium
Hopkinson . . . . Bolton Wanderers
Howe. . . . . West Bromwich Albion
Allen, A. . . . . Stoke City
Clayton . . . . Blackburn Rovers
Smith, T. . . . . Birmingham City
Flowers . . . . Wolverhampton Wanderers
Connelly. . . . . Burnley
Greaves . . . . Chelsea
Clough. . . . . Middlesbrough
Holliday . . . . Middlesbrough
Charlton, R. . . . . Manchester United
Result: 2–3
Scorers: Connelly, R. Charlton

337. 18 November 1959
v N. IRELAND . . . . Wembley Stadium
Springett . . . . Sheffield Wednesday
Howe. . . . . West Bromwich Albion
Allen, A. . . . . Stoke City
Clayton . . . . Blackburn Rovers
Brown . . . . West Ham United
Flowers . . . . Wolverhampton Wanderers
Connelly. . . . . Burnley
Haynes. . . . . Fulham
Baker. . . . . Hibernian
Parry . . . . Bolton Wanderers
Holliday . . . . Middlesbrough
Result: 2–1
Scorers: Baker, Parry

338. 19 April 1960
v SCOTLAND. . . . . Hampden Park, Glasgow
Springett . . . . Sheffield Wednesday
Armfield. . . . . Blackpool
Wilson . . . . Huddersfield Town
Clayton . . . . Blackburn Rovers
Slater. . . . . Wolverhampton Wanderers
Flowers . . . . Wolverhampton Wanderers
Connelly. . . . . Burnley
Broadbent . . . . Wolverhampton Wanderers
Baker. . . . . Hibernian
Parry . . . . Bolton Wanderers
Charlton, R. . . . . Manchester United
Result: 1–1
Scorer: R. Charlton (pen.)

339. 11 May 1960
v YUGOSLAVIA . . . . Wembley Stadium
Springett . . . . Sheffield Wednesday
Armfield. . . . . Blackpool
Wilson . . . . Huddersfield Town
Clayton . . . . Blackburn Rovers
Swan . . . . Sheffield Wednesday
Flowers . . . . Wolverhampton Wanderers
Douglas . . . . Blackburn Rovers
Haynes. . . . . Fulham
Baker. . . . . Hibernian
Greaves . . . . Chelsea
Charlton, R. . . . . Manchester United
Result: 3–3
Scorers: Douglas, Greaves, Haynes

340. 15 May 1960
v SPAIN . . . . Madrid
Springett . . . . Sheffield Wednesday
Armfield. . . . . Blackpool
Wilson . . . . Huddersfield Town
Robson . . . . West Bromwich Albion
Swan . . . . Sheffield Wednesday
Flowers . . . . Wolverhampton Wanderers
Brabrook . . . . Chelsea
Haynes. . . . . Fulham
Baker. . . . . Hibernian
Greaves . . . . Chelsea
Charlton, R. . . . . Manchester United
Result: 0–3

341. 22 May 1960
v HUNGARY . . . . Budapest
Springett . . . . Sheffield Wednesday
Armfield. . . . . Blackpool
Wilson . . . . Huddersfield Town
Robson . . . . West Bromwich Albion
Swan . . . . Sheffield Wednesday
Flowers . . . . Wolverhampton Wanderers
Douglas . . . . Blackburn Rovers
Haynes. . . . . Fulham
Baker. . . . . Hibernian
Viollet . . . . Manchester United
Charlton, R. . . . . Manchester United
Result: 0–2

342. 8 October 1960
v N. IRELAND . . . . Belfast
Springett . . . . Sheffield Wednesday
Armfield. . . . . Blackpool
McNeil. . . . . Middlesbrough
Robson . . . . West Bromwich Albion
Swan . . . . Sheffield Wednesday
Flowers . . . . Wolverhampton Wanderers
Douglas . . . . Blackburn Rovers
Greaves . . . . Chelsea
Smith, R. . . . . Tottenham Hotspur
Haynes. . . . . Fulham
Charlton, R. . . . . Manchester United
Result: 5–2
Scorers: Smith, Greaves (2), R. Charlton, Douglas

343. 19 October 1960
v LUXEMBOURG . . . . Luxembourg
Springett . . . . Sheffield Wednesday
Armfield. . . . . Blackpool
McNeil . . . . Middlesbrough
Robson . . . . West Bromwich Albion
Swan . . . . Sheffield Wednesday
Flowers . . . . Wolverhampton Wanderers
Douglas . . . . Blackburn Rovers
Greaves . . . . Chelsea
Smith, R. . . . . Tottenham Hotspur
Haynes. . . . . Fulham
Charlton, R. . . . . Manchester United
Result: 9–0
Scorers: Greaves (3), R. Charlton (3), R. Smith (2), Haynes

344. 26 October 1960
v SPAIN . . . . Wembley Stadium
Springett . . . . Sheffield Wednesday
Armfield. . . . . Blackpool
McNeil . . . . Middlesbrough
Robson . . . . West Bromwich Albion
Swan . . . . Sheffield Wednesday
Flowers . . . . Wolverhampton Wanderers
Douglas . . . . Blackburn Rovers
Greaves . . . . Chelsea
Smith, R. . . . . Tottenham Hotspur
Haynes. . . . . Fulham
Charlton, R. . . . . Manchester United
Result: 4–2
Scorers: Greaves, Douglas, R. Smith (2)

345. 23 November 1960
v WALES. . . . . Wembley Stadium
Hodgkinson . . . . Sheffield United
Armfield. . . . . Blackpool
McNeil . . . . Middlesbrough
Robson . . . . West Bromwich Albion
Swan . . . . Sheffield Wednesday
Flowers . . . . Wolverhampton Wanderers
Douglas . . . . Blackburn Rovers
Greaves . . . . Chelsea
Smith, R. . . . . Tottenham Hotspur
Haynes. . . . . Fulham
Charlton, R. . . . . Manchester United
Result: 5–1
Scorers: Greaves (2), R. Charlton, R. Smith, Haynes

346. 15 April 1961
v SCOTLAND. . . . . Wembley Stadium
Springett . . . . Sheffield Wednesday
Armfield. . . . . Blackpool
McNeil . . . . Middlesbrough
Robson . . . . West Bromwich Albion
Swan . . . . Sheffield Wednesday
Flowers . . . . Wolverhampton Wanderers
Douglas . . . . Blackburn Rovers
Greaves . . . . Chelsea
Smith, R. . . . . Tottenham Hotspur
Haynes. . . . . Fulham
Charlton, R. . . . . Manchester United
Result: 9–3
Scorers: Robson, Greaves (3), Douglas, R. Smith (2),
Haynes (2)

347. 10 May 1961
v MEXICO. . . . . Wembley Stadium
Springett . . . . Sheffield Wednesday
Armfield. . . . . Blackpool
McNeil . . . . Middlesbrough
Robson . . . . West Bromwich Albion
Swan . . . . Sheffield Wednesday
Flowers . . . . Wolverhampton Wanderers
Douglas . . . . Blackburn Rovers
Kevan. . . . . West Bromwich Albion

Hitchens. . . . . Aston Villa
Haynes. . . . . Fulham
Charlton, R. . . . . Manchester United
Result: 8–0
Scorers: Hitchens, R. Charlton (3), Douglas (2), Robson,
Flowers (pen.)

 FEATURED MATCH

15 APRIL 1961

ENGLAND 9 SCOTLAND 3 – WEMBLEY STADIUM

Her Majesty Queen Elizabeth II was present at Wembley Stadium to witness her first 'Auld Enemy' clash on this day, and it would seem that the attendance of the ruling monarch inspired England to the highest ever score and also the highest ever aggregate score that this confrontation has produced throughout its history.

Winterbottom's policy of making as few changes as possible had resulted in a fine season for England: this occasion would mark their fifth successive victory. England's lethal 4–2–4 formation began the rout in the ninth minute with Bobby Robson opening the scoring. Ten minutes later, Jimmy Greaves scored two goals within sixty seconds, taking his international tally for the season into double figures. Later in the match he would complete his hat-trick.

Shortly after half-time, Scotland temporarily got back into the game with goals from Dave Mackay and Davie Wilson, but this merely gave the Scots a false glimmer of hope. Bryan Douglas in the 56th minute quickly re-established a two-goal lead for England. Bobby Smith, who featured in Tottenham's double-winning side and who scored in the FA Cup Final against Leicester City, scored two goals, as did the very talented Johnny Haynes. Among the last six goals (including Greaves's third), the Scots scraped a third consolation goal.

Frank Haffey, Scotland's goalkeeper, left the field in tears after his country's record defeat. It was not surprising because the Celtic keeper – called in because of injuries to two other players – had had a nightmare match. At least four of England's goals were attributable to his errors. Yet for all Haffey's generosity, England's display was a remarkable one, full of pace, skill and a continuing hunger for goals. The England players had shown themselves to be deserving British champions, displaying brilliant attacking flair that simply outclassed the opposition.

England hit the back of the net forty-five times in nine matches that season, including the 8–0 thrashing of Mexico at Wembley in the following game, in which Bobby Charlton netted a hat-trick.

348. 21 May 1961
v PORTUGAL. . . . . Lisbon
Springett . . . . Sheffield Wednesday
Armfield. . . . . Blackpool
McNeil . . . . Middlesbrough
Robson . . . . West Bromwich Albion
Swan . . . . Sheffield Wednesday
Flowers . . . . Wolverhampton Wanderers
Douglas . . . . Blackburn Rovers

Greaves . . . . Chelsea
Smith, R. . . . . Tottenham Hotspur
Haynes. . . . . Fulham
Charlton, R. . . . . Manchester United
Result: 1–1
Scorer: Flowers

349. 24 May 1961
v ITALY . . . . Rome
Springett . . . . Sheffield Wednesday
Armfield. . . . . Blackpool
McNeil . . . . Middlesbrough
Robson . . . . West Bromwich Albion
Swan . . . . Sheffield Wednesday
Flowers . . . . Wolverhampton Wanderers
Douglas . . . . Blackburn Rovers
Greaves . . . . Chelsea
Hitchens. . . . . Aston Villa
Haynes. . . . . Fulham
Charlton, R. . . . . Manchester United
Result: 3–2
Scorers: Hitchens (2), Greaves

350. 27 May 1961
v AUSTRIA . . . . Vienna
Springett . . . . Sheffield Wednesday
Armfield. . . . . Blackpool
Angus . . . . Burnley
Miller. . . . . Burnley
Swan . . . . Sheffield Wednesday
Flowers . . . . Wolverhampton Wanderers
Douglas . . . . Blackburn Rovers
Greaves . . . . Chelsea
Hitchens. . . . . Aston Villa
Haynes. . . . . Fulham
Charlton, R. . . . . Manchester United
Result: 1–3
Scorer: Greaves

351. 28 September 1961
v LUXEMBOURG . . . . Highbury Stadium, Arsenal
Springett . . . . Sheffield Wednesday
Armfield. . . . . Blackpool
McNeil . . . . Middlesbrough
Robson . . . . West Bromwich Albion
Swan . . . . Sheffield Wednesday
Flowers . . . . Wolverhampton Wanderers
Douglas . . . . Blackburn Rovers
Fantham. . . . . Sheffield Wednesday
Pointer. . . . . Burnley
Viollet . . . . Manchester United
Charlton, R. . . . . Manchester United
Result: 4–1
Scorers: Pointer, Viollet, R. Charlton (2)

352. 14 October 1961
v WALES. . . . . Ninian Park, Cardiff
Springett . . . . Sheffield Wednesday
Armfield. . . . . Blackpool
Wilson . . . . Huddersfield Town
Robson . . . . West Bromwich Albion
Swan . . . . Sheffield Wednesday
Flowers . . . . Wolverhampton Wanderers
Connelly. . . . . Burnley
Douglas . . . . Blackburn Rovers
Pointer. . . . . Burnley
Haynes. . . . . Fulham
Charlton, R. . . . . Manchester United
Result: 1–1
Scorer: Douglas

353. 25 October 1961
v PORTUGAL. . . . . Wembley Stadium
Springett . . . . Sheffield Wednesday
Armfield. . . . . Blackpool

Wilson . . . . Huddersfield Town
Robson . . . . West Bromwich Albion
Swan . . . . Sheffield Wednesday
Flowers . . . . Wolverhampton Wanderers
Connelly. . . . . Burnley
Douglas . . . . Blackburn Rovers
Pointer. . . . . Burnley
Haynes. . . . . Fulham
Charlton, R. . . . . Manchester United
Result: 2–0
Scorers: Pointer, Connelly

354. 22 November 1961
v N. IRELAND . . . . Wembley Stadium
Springett . . . . Sheffield Wednesday
Armfield. . . . . Blackpool
Wilson . . . . Huddersfield Town
Robson . . . . West Bromwich Albion
Swan . . . . Sheffield Wednesday
Flowers . . . . Wolverhampton Wanderers
Douglas . . . . Blackburn Rovers
Byrne, J. . . . . Crystal Palace
Crawford . . . . Ipswich Town
Haynes. . . . . Fulham
Charlton, R. . . . . Manchester United
Result: 1–1
Scorer: R. Charlton

355. 4 April 1962
v AUSTRIA . . . . Wembley Stadium
Springett . . . . Sheffield Wednesday
Armfield. . . . . Blackpool
Wilson . . . . Huddersfield Town
Anderson . . . . Sunderland
Swan . . . . Sheffield Wednesday
Flowers . . . . Wolverhampton Wanderers
Connelly. . . . . Burnley
Hunt . . . . Liverpool
Crawford . . . . Ipswich Town
Haynes. . . . . Fulham
Charlton, R. . . . . Manchester United
Result: 3–1
Scorers: Crawford, Flowers (pen.), Hunt

356. 14 April 1962
v SCOTLAND. . . . . Hampden Park, Glasgow
Springett . . . . Sheffield Wednesday
Armfield. . . . . Blackpool
Wilson . . . . Huddersfield Town
Anderson . . . . Sunderland
Swan . . . . Sheffield Wednesday
Flowers . . . . Wolverhampton Wanderers
Douglas . . . . Blackburn Rovers
Greaves . . . . Tottenham Hotspur
Smith, R. . . . . Tottenham Hotspur
Haynes. . . . . Fulham
Charlton, R. . . . . Manchester United
Result: 0–2

357. 9 May 1962
v SWITZERLAND . . . . Wembley Stadium
Springett . . . . Sheffield Wednesday
Armfield. . . . . Blackpool
Wilson . . . . Huddersfield Town
Robson . . . . West Bromwich Albion
Swan . . . . Sheffield Wednesday
Flowers . . . . Wolverhampton Wanderers
Connelly. . . . . Burnley
Greaves . . . . Tottenham Hotspur
Hitchens. . . . . Inter Milan
Haynes. . . . . Fulham
Charlton, R. . . . . Manchester United
Result: 3–1
Scorers: Flowers, Hitchens, Connelly

358. 20 May 1962
v PERU . . . . Lima
Springett . . . . Sheffield Wednesday
Armfield. . . . . Blackpool
Wilson . . . . Huddersfield Town
Moore . . . . West Ham United
Norman . . . . Tottenham Hotspur
Flowers . . . . Wolverhampton Wanderers
Douglas . . . . Blackburn Rovers
Greaves . . . . Tottenham Hotspur
Hitchens. . . . . Inter Milan
Haynes. . . . . Fulham
Charlton, R. . . . . Manchester United
Result: 4–0
Scorers: Flowers (pen.), Greaves (3)

359. 31 May 1962
v HUNGARY . . . . Rancagua
Springett . . . . Sheffield Wednesday
Armfield. . . . . Blackpool
Wilson . . . . Huddersfield Town
Moore . . . . West Ham United
Norman . . . . Tottenham Hotspur
Flowers . . . . Wolverhampton Wanderers
Douglas . . . . Blackburn Rovers
Greaves . . . . Tottenham Hotspur
Hitchens. . . . . Inter Milan
Haynes. . . . . Fulham
Charlton, R. . . . . Manchester United
Result: 1–2
Scorer: Flowers (pen.)

360. 2 June 1962
v ARGENTINA. . . . . Rancagua
Springett . . . . Sheffield Wednesday
Armfield. . . . . Blackpool
Wilson . . . . Huddersfield Town
Moore . . . . West Ham United
Norman . . . . Tottenham Hotspur
Flowers . . . . Wolverhampton Wanderers
Douglas . . . . Blackburn Rovers
Greaves . . . . Tottenham Hotspur
Peacock . . . . Middlesbrough
Haynes. . . . . Fulham
Charlton, R. . . . . Manchester United
Result: 3–1
Scorers: Flowers (pen.), R. Charlton, Greaves

361. 7 June 1962
v BULGARIA . . . . Rancagua
Springett . . . . Sheffield Wednesday
Armfield. . . . . Blackpool
Wilson . . . . Huddersfield Town
Moore . . . . West Ham United
Norman . . . . Tottenham Hotspur
Flowers . . . . Wolverhampton Wanderers
Douglas . . . . Blackburn Rovers
Greaves . . . . Tottenham Hotspur
Peacock . . . . Middlesbrough
Haynes. . . . . Fulham
Charlton, R. . . . . Manchester United
Result: 0–0

⚽ **DID YOU KNOW...?**

England's 0–0 draw with Bulgaria in the final
Group IV game of the 1962 World Cup was billed
as 'the most boring match of the tournament' by
watching journalists.

362. 10 June 1962
v BRAZIL. . . . . Viña del Mar
Springett . . . . Sheffield Wednesday
Armfield. . . . . Blackpool
Wilson . . . . Huddersfield Town
Moore . . . . West Ham United
Norman . . . . Tottenham Hotspur
Flowers . . . . Wolverhampton Wanderers
Douglas . . . . Blackburn Rovers
Greaves . . . . Tottenham Hotspur
Hitchens. . . . . Inter Milan
Haynes. . . . . Fulham
Charlton, R. . . . . Manchester United
Result: 1–3
Scorer: Hitchens

363. 3 October 1962
v FRANCE. . . . . Hillsborough, Sheffield
Springett . . . . Sheffield Wednesday
Armfield. . . . . Blackpool
Wilson . . . . Huddersfield Town
Moore . . . . West Ham United
Norman . . . . Tottenham Hotspur
Flowers . . . . Wolverhampton Wanderers
Hellawell . . . . Birmingham City
Crowe . . . . Wolverhampton Wanderers
Charnley . . . . Blackpool
Greaves . . . . Tottenham Hotspur
Hinton . . . . Wolverhampton Wanderers
Result: 1–1
Scorer: Flowers (pen.)

364. 20 October 1962
v N. IRELAND . . . . Windsor Park, Belfast
Springett . . . . Sheffield Wednesday
Armfield. . . . . Blackpool
Wilson . . . . Huddersfield Town
Moore . . . . West Ham United
Labone. . . . . Everton
Flowers . . . . Wolverhampton Wanderers
Hellawell . . . . Birmingham City
Hill. . . . . Bolton Wanderers
Peacock . . . . Middlesbrough
Greaves . . . . Tottenham Hotspur
O'Grady . . . . Huddersfield Town
Result: 3–1
Scorers: Greaves, O'Grady (2)

365. 21 November 1962
v WALES. . . . . Wembley Stadium
Springett . . . . Sheffield Wednesday
Armfield. . . . . Blackpool
Shaw . . . . Sheffield United
Moore . . . . West Ham United
Labone. . . . . Everton
Flowers . . . . Wolverhampton Wanderers
Connelly. . . . . Burnley
Hill. . . . . Bolton Wanderers
Peacock . . . . Middlesbrough
Greaves . . . . Tottenham Hotspur
Tambling . . . . Chelsea
Result: 4–0
Scorers: Connelly, Peacock (2), Greaves

366. 27 February 1963
v FRANCE. . . . . Paris
Springett . . . . Sheffield Wednesday
Armfield. . . . . Blackpool
Henry. . . . . Tottenham Hotspur
Moore . . . . West Ham United
Labone. . . . . Everton
Flowers . . . . Wolverhampton Wanderers
Connelly. . . . . Burnley
Tambling . . . . Chelsea

Smith, R. . . . . Tottenham Hotspur
Greaves . . . . Tottenham Hotspur
Charlton, R. . . . . Manchester United
Result: 2–5
Scorers: R. Smith, Tambling

367. 6 April 1963
v SCOTLAND . . . . Wembley Stadium
Banks. . . . . Leicester City
Armfield. . . . . Blackpool
Byrne, G. . . . . Liverpool
Moore . . . . West Ham United
Norman . . . . Tottenham Hotspur
Flowers . . . . Wolverhampton Wanderers
Douglas . . . . Blackburn Rovers
Melia . . . . Liverpool
Smith, R. . . . . Tottenham Hotspur
Greaves . . . . Tottenham Hotspur
Charlton, R. . . . . Manchester United
Result: 1–2
Scorer: Douglas

368. 8 May 1963
v BRAZIL. . . . . Wembley Stadium
Banks. . . . . Leicester City
Armfield . . . . Blackpool
Wilson . . . . Huddersfield Town
Milne . . . . Liverpool
Norman . . . . Tottenham Hotspur
Moore . . . . West Ham United
Douglas . . . . Blackburn Rovers
Greaves . . . . Tottenham Hotspur
Smith, R. . . . . Tottenham Hotspur
Eastham. . . . . Arsenal
Charlton, R. . . . . Manchester United
Result: 1–1
Scorer: Douglas

369. 20 May 1963
v CZECHOSLOVAKIA . . . . Bratislava
Banks. . . . . Leicester City
Shellito . . . . Chelsea
Wilson . . . . Huddersfield Town
Milne . . . . Liverpool
Norman . . . . Tottenham Hotspur
Moore . . . . West Ham United
Paine . . . . Southampton
Greaves . . . . Tottenham Hotspur
Smith, R. . . . . Tottenham Hotspur
Eastham. . . . . Arsenal
Charlton, R. . . . . Manchester United
Result: 4–2
Scorers: Greaves (2), R. Smith, R. Charlton

370. 2 June 1963
v EAST GERMANY . . . . Leipzig
Banks. . . . . Leicester City
Armfield. . . . . Blackpool
Wilson . . . . Huddersfield Town
Milne . . . . Liverpool
Norman . . . . Tottenham Hotspur
Moore . . . . West Ham United
Paine . . . . Southampton
Hunt . . . . Liverpool
Smith, R. . . . . Tottenham Hotspur
Eastham. . . . . Arsenal
Charlton, R. . . . . Manchester United
Result: 2–1
Scorers: Hunt, R. Charlton

371. 5 June 1963
v SWITZERLAND . . . . Basle
Springett . . . . Sheffield Wednesday
Armfield. . . . . Blackpool

Wilson . . . . Huddersfield Town
Kay . . . . Everton
Moore . . . . West Ham United
Flowers . . . . Wolverhampton Wanderers
Douglas . . . . Blackburn Rovers
Greaves . . . . Tottenham Hotspur
Byrne, J. . . . . West Ham United
Melia . . . . Liverpool
Charlton, R. . . . . Manchester United
Result: 8–1
Scorers: R. Charlton (3), Byrne (2), Douglas, Kay, Melia

372. 12 October 1963
v WALES. . . . . Ninian Park, Cardiff
Banks. . . . . Leicester City
Armfield. . . . . Blackpool
Wilson . . . . Huddersfield Town
Milne . . . . Liverpool
Norman . . . . Tottenham Hotspur
Moore . . . . West Ham United
Paine . . . . Southampton
Greaves . . . . Tottenham Hotspur
Smith, R. . . . . Tottenham Hotspur
Eastham. . . . . Arsenal
Charlton, R. . . . . Manchester United
Result: 4–0
Scorers: R. Smith (2), Greaves, R. Charlton

373. 23 October 1963
v REST OF THE WORLD . . . . . Wembley Stadium
Banks. . . . . Leicester City
Armfield. . . . . Blackpool
Wilson . . . . Huddersfield Town
Milne . . . . Liverpool
Norman . . . . Tottenham Hotspur
Moore . . . . West Ham United
Paine . . . . Southampton
Greaves . . . . Tottenham Hotspur
Smith, R. . . . . Tottenham Hotspur
Eastham. . . . . Arsenal
Charlton, R. . . . . Manchester United
Result: 2–1
Scorers: Paine, Greaves

374. 20 November 1963
v N. IRELAND . . . . Wembley Stadium
Banks. . . . . Leicester City
Armfield. . . . . Blackpool
Thomson . . . . Wolverhampton Wanderers
Milne . . . . Liverpool
Norman . . . . Tottenham Hotspur
Moore . . . . West Ham United
Paine . . . . Southampton
Greaves . . . . Tottenham Hotspur
Smith, R. . . . . Tottenham Hotspur
Eastham. . . . . Arsenal
Charlton, R. . . . . Manchester United
Result: 8–3
Scorers: Greaves (4), Paine (3), Smith

375. 11 April 1964
v SCOTLAND . . . . Hampden Park, Glasgow
Banks. . . . . Leicester City
Armfield. . . . . Blackpool
Wilson . . . . Huddersfield Town
Milne . . . . Liverpool
Norman . . . . Tottenham Hotspur
Moore . . . . West Ham United
Paine . . . . Southampton
Hunt . . . . Liverpool
Byrne, J. . . . . West Ham United
Eastham. . . . . Arsenal
Charlton, R. . . . . Manchester United
Result: 0–1

376. 6 May 1964
v URUGUAY . . . . Wembley Stadium
Banks. . . . . Leicester City
Cohen . . . . Fulham
Wilson . . . . Huddersfield Town
Milne. . . . . Liverpool
Norman . . . . Tottenham Hotspur
Moore . . . . West Ham United
Paine . . . . Southampton
Greaves . . . . Tottenham Hotspur
Byrne, J. . . . . West Ham United
Eastham. . . . . Arsenal
Charlton, R. . . . . Manchester United
Result: 2–1
Scorers: Byrne (2)

377. 17 May 1964
v PORTUGAL. . . . . Lisbon
Banks. . . . . Leicester City
Cohen . . . . Fulham
Wilson . . . . Huddersfield Town
Milne. . . . . Liverpool
Norman . . . . Tottenham Hotspur
Moore . . . . West Ham United
Thompson . . . . Liverpool
Greaves . . . . Tottenham Hotspur
Byrne, J. . . . . West Ham United
Eastham. . . . . Arsenal
Charlton, R. . . . . Manchester United
Result: 4–3
Scorers: Byrne (3), R. Charlton

378. 24 May 1964
v EIRE. . . . . Dalymount Park, Dublin
Waiters . . . . Blackpool
Cohen . . . . Fulham
Wilson . . . . Huddersfield Town
Milne. . . . . Liverpool
Flowers . . . . Wolverhampton Wanderers
Moore . . . . West Ham United
Thompson . . . . Liverpool
Greaves . . . . Tottenham Hotspur
Byrne, J. . . . . West Ham United
Eastham. . . . . Arsenal
Charlton, R. . . . . Manchester United
Result: 3–1
Scorers: Eastham, J. Byrne, Greaves

379. 27 May 1964
v USA. . . . . New York City
Banks. . . . . Leicester City
Cohen . . . . Fulham
Thomson . . . . Wolverhampton Wanderers
Bailey. . . . . Wolverhampton Wanderers
Norman . . . . Tottenham Hotspur
Flowers . . . . Wolverhampton Wanderers
Paine . . . . Southampton
Hunt . . . . Liverpool
Pickering . . . . Everton
Eastham* . . . . Arsenal
Thompson . . . . Liverpool
Sub: *Charlton, R. . . . . Manchester United
Result: 10–0
Scorers: Hunt (4), Pickering (3), Paine (2), R. Charlton

380. 30 May 1964
v BRAZIL. . . . . Rio de Janeiro
Waiters . . . . Blackpool
Cohen . . . . Fulham
Wilson . . . . Huddersfield Town
Milne. . . . . Liverpool
Norman . . . . Tottenham Hotspur
Moore . . . . West Ham United
Thompson . . . . Liverpool
Greaves . . . . Tottenham Hotspur
Byrne, J. . . . . West Ham United

Eastham. . . . . Arsenal
Charlton, R. . . . . Manchester United
Result: 1–5
Scorer: Greaves

381. 4 June 1964
v PORTUGAL. . . . . São Paulo
Banks. . . . . Leicester City
Thomson . . . . Wolverhampton Wanderers
Wilson . . . . Huddersfield Town
Flowers . . . . Wolverhampton Wanderers
Norman . . . . Tottenham Hotspur
Moore . . . . West Ham United
Paine . . . . Southampton
Greaves . . . . Tottenham Hotspur
Byrne, J. . . . . West Ham United
Hunt . . . . Liverpool
Thompson . . . . Liverpool
Result: 1–1
Scorer: Hunt

382. 6 June 1964
v ARGENTINA. . . . . Rio de Janeiro
Banks. . . . . Leicester City
Thomson . . . . Wolverhampton Wanderers
Wilson . . . . Huddersfield Town
Milne. . . . . Liverpool
Norman . . . . Tottenham Hotspur
Moore . . . . West Ham United
Thompson . . . . Liverpool
Greaves . . . . Tottenham Hotspur
Byrne, J. . . . . West Ham United
Eastham. . . . . Arsenal
Charlton, R. . . . . Manchester United
Result: 0–1

383. 3 October 1964
v N. IRELAND . . . . Windsor Park, Belfast
Banks. . . . . Leicester City
Cohen . . . . Fulham
Thomson . . . . Wolverhampton Wanderers
Milne. . . . . Liverpool
Norman . . . . Tottenham Hotspur
Moore . . . . West Ham United
Paine . . . . Southampton
Greaves . . . . Tottenham Hotspur
Pickering . . . . Everton
Charlton, R. . . . . Manchester United
Thompson . . . . Liverpool
Result: 4–3
Scorers: Pickering, Greaves (3)

384. 21 October 1964
v BELGIUM. . . . . Wembley Stadium
Waiters . . . . Blackpool
Cohen . . . . Fulham
Thomson . . . . Wolverhampton Wanderers
Milne. . . . . Liverpool
Norman . . . . Tottenham Hotspur
Moore . . . . West Ham United
Thompson . . . . Liverpool
Greaves . . . . Tottenham Hotspur
Pickering . . . . Everton
Venables . . . . Chelsea
Hinton . . . . Nottingham Forest
Result: 2–2
Scorers: Pickering, Hinton

385. 18 November 1964
v WALES. . . . . Wembley Stadium
Waiters . . . . Blackpool
Cohen . . . . Fulham
Thomson . . . . Wolverhampton Wanderers
Bailey. . . . . Wolverhampton Wanderers
Flowers . . . . Wolverhampton Wanderers
Young . . . . Sheffield Wednesday

Thompson . . . . Liverpool
Hunt . . . . Liverpool
Wignall . . . . Nottingham Forest
Byrne, J. . . . . West Ham United
Hinton . . . . Nottingham Forest
Result: 2–1
Scorers: Wignall (2)

386. 9 December 1964
v HOLLAND . . . . Amsterdam
Waiters . . . . Blackpool
Cohen . . . . Fulham
Thomson . . . . Wolverhampton Wanderers
Mullery . . . . Tottenham Hotspur
Norman . . . . Tottenham Hotspur
Flowers . . . . Wolverhampton Wanderers
Thompson . . . . Liverpool
Greaves . . . . Tottenham Hotspur
Wignall . . . . Nottingham Forest
Venables . . . . Chelsea
Charlton, R. . . . . Manchester United
Result: 1–1
Scorer: Greaves

387. 10 April 1965
v SCOTLAND . . . . Wembley Stadium
Banks. . . . . Leicester City
Cohen . . . . Fulham
Wilson . . . . Everton
Stiles . . . . Manchester United
Charlton, J. . . . . Leeds United
Moore . . . . West Ham United
Thompson . . . . Liverpool
Greaves . . . . Tottenham Hotspur
Bridges . . . . Chelsea
Byrne, J. . . . . West Ham United
Charlton, R. . . . . Manchester United
Result: 2–2
Scorers: R. Charlton, Greaves

388. 5 May 1965
v HUNGARY . . . . Wembley Stadium
Banks. . . . . Leicester City
Cohen . . . . Fulham
Wilson . . . . Everton
Stiles . . . . Manchester United
Charlton, J. . . . . Leeds United
Moore . . . . West Ham United
Paine . . . . Southampton
Greaves . . . . Tottenham Hotspur
Bridges . . . . Chelsea
Eastham. . . . . Arsenal
Connelly. . . . . Manchester United
Result: 1–0
Scorer: Greaves

389. 9 May 1965
v YUGOSLAVIA . . . . Belgrade
Banks. . . . . Leicester City
Cohen . . . . Fulham
Wilson . . . . Everton
Stiles . . . . Manchester United
Charlton, J. . . . . Leeds United
Moore . . . . West Ham United
Paine . . . . Southampton
Greaves . . . . Tottenham Hotspur
Bridges . . . . Chelsea
Ball . . . . Blackpool
Connelly. . . . . Manchester United
Result: 1–1
Scorer: Bridges

390. 12 May 1965
v WEST GERMANY . . . . Nuremberg
Banks. . . . . Leicester City
Cohen . . . . Fulham

Wilson . . . . Everton
Flowers . . . . Wolverhampton Wanderers
Charlton, J. . . . . Leeds United
Moore . . . . West Ham United
Paine . . . . Southampton
Ball . . . . Blackpool
Jones . . . . Leeds United
Eastham. . . . . Arsenal
Temple. . . . . Everton
Result: 1–0
Scorer: Paine

391. 16 May 1965
v SWEDEN . . . . Gothenburg
Banks. . . . . Leicester City
Cohen . . . . Fulham
Wilson . . . . Everton
Stiles . . . . Manchester United
Charlton, J. . . . . Leeds United
Moore . . . . West Ham United
Paine . . . . Southampton
Ball . . . . Blackpool
Jones . . . . Leeds United
Eastham. . . . . Arsenal
Connelly. . . . . Manchester United
Result: 2–1
Scorers: Ball, Connelly

392. 2 October 1965
v WALES. . . . . Ninian Park, Cardiff
Springett . . . . Sheffield Wednesday
Cohen . . . . Fulham
Wilson . . . . Everton
Stiles . . . . Manchester United
Charlton, J. . . . . Leeds United
Moore . . . . West Ham United
Paine . . . . Southampton
Greaves . . . . Tottenham Hotspur
Peacock . . . . Leeds United
Charlton, R. . . . . Manchester United
Connelly. . . . . Manchester United
Result: 0–0

393. 20 October 1965
v AUSTRIA . . . . Wembley Stadium
Springett . . . . Sheffield Wednesday
Cohen . . . . Fulham
Wilson . . . . Everton
Stiles . . . . Manchester United
Charlton, J. . . . . Leeds United
Moore . . . . West Ham United
Paine . . . . Southampton
Greaves . . . . Tottenham Hotspur
Bridges . . . . Chelsea
Charlton, R. . . . . Manchester United
Connelly. . . . . Manchester United
Result: 2–3
Scorers: R. Charlton, Connelly

394. 10 November 1965
v N. IRELAND . . . . Wembley Stadium
Banks. . . . . Leicester City
Cohen . . . . Fulham
Wilson . . . . Everton
Stiles . . . . Manchester United
Charlton, J. . . . . Leeds United
Moore . . . . West Ham United
Thompson . . . . Liverpool
Baker . . . . Arsenal
Peacock . . . . Leeds United
Charlton, R. . . . . Manchester United
Connelly. . . . . Manchester United
Result: 2–1
Scorers: Baker, Peacock

395. 8 December 1965
v SPAIN . . . . Madrid
Banks. . . . . Leicester City
Cohen . . . . Fulham
Wilson . . . . Everton
Stiles . . . . Manchester United
Charlton, J. . . . . Leeds United
Moore . . . . West Ham United
Ball . . . . Blackpool
Hunt . . . . Liverpool
Baker* . . . . Arsenal
Eastham. . . . . Arsenal
Charlton, R. . . . . Manchester United
Sub: *Hunter . . . . Leeds United
Result: 2–0
Scorers: Baker, Hunt

396. 5 January 1966
v POLAND . . . . Goodison Park, Everton
Banks. . . . . Leicester City
Cohen . . . . Fulham
Wilson . . . . Everton
Stiles . . . . Manchester United
Charlton, J. . . . . Leeds United
Moore . . . . West Ham United
Ball . . . . Blackpool
Hunt . . . . Liverpool
Baker. . . . . Arsenal
Eastham. . . . . Arsenal
Harris. . . . . Burnley
Result: 1–1
Scorer: Moore

397. 23 February 1966
v WEST GERMANY . . . . Wembley Stadium
Banks. . . . . Leicester City
Cohen . . . . Fulham
Newton* . . . . Blackburn Rovers
Moore . . . . West Ham United
Charlton, J. . . . . Leeds United
Hunter . . . . Leeds United
Ball . . . . Blackpool
Hunt . . . . Liverpool
Stiles . . . . Manchester United
Hurst . . . . West Ham United
Charlton, R. . . . . Manchester United
Sub: *Wilson . . . . Everton
Result: 1–0
Scorer: Stiles

398. 2 April 1966
v SCOTLAND. . . . . Hampden Park, Glasgow
Banks. . . . . Leicester City
Cohen . . . . Fulham
Newton . . . . Blackburn Rovers
Stiles . . . . Manchester United
Charlton, J. . . . . Leeds United
Moore . . . . West Ham United
Ball . . . . Blackpool
Hunt . . . . Liverpool
Charlton, R. . . . . Manchester United
Hurst . . . . West Ham United
Connelly. . . . . Manchester United
Result: 4–3
Scorers: Hurst, Hunt (2), R. Charlton

 DID YOU KNOW...?

The most famous dog in football is Pickles, who was responsible for finding the missing Jules Rimet World Cup trophy, a week after it had been stolen from Westminster Central Hall in March 1966.

 DID YOU KNOW...?

In the 1966 World Cup, on 11 July, the opening match between England and Uruguay at Wembley was nearly called off by the Hungarian referee Istvan Zsolt when he found that seven England players had left their identity cards in the hotel. A police motorcyclist had to be despatched to retrieve them.

399. 4 May 1966
v YUGOSLAVIA . . . . Wembley Stadium
Banks. . . . . Leicester City
Armfield. . . . . Blackpool
Wilson . . . . Everton
Peters . . . . West Ham United
Charlton, J. . . . . Leeds United
Hunter . . . . Leeds United
Paine . . . . Southampton
Greaves . . . . Tottenham Hotspur
Charlton, R. . . . . Manchester United
Hurst . . . . West Ham United
Tambling . . . . Chelsea
Result: 2–0
Scorers: Greaves, R. Charlton

400. 26 June 1966
v FINLAND . . . . Helsinki
Banks. . . . . Leicester City
Armfield. . . . . Blackpool
Wilson . . . . Everton
Peters . . . . West Ham United
Charlton, J. . . . . Leeds United
Hunter . . . . Leeds United
Callaghan . . . . Liverpool
Hunt . . . . Liverpool
Charlton, R. . . . . Manchester United
Hurst . . . . West Ham United
Ball . . . . Blackpool
Result: 3–0
Scorers: Peters, Hunt, J. Charlton

401. 29 June 1966
v NORWAY . . . . Oslo
Springett . . . . Sheffield Wednesday
Cohen . . . . Fulham
Byrne, G. . . . . Liverpool
Stiles . . . . Manchester United
Flowers . . . . Wolverhampton Wanderers
Moore . . . . West Ham United
Paine . . . . Southampton
Greaves . . . . Tottenham Hotspur
Charlton, R. . . . . Manchester United
Hunt . . . . Liverpool
Connelly. . . . . Manchester United
Result: 6–1
Scorers: Greaves (4), Connelly, Moore

402. 3 July 1966
v DENMARK . . . . Copenhagen
Bonetti. . . . . Chelsea
Cohen . . . . Fulham
Wilson . . . . Everton
Stiles . . . . Manchester United
Charlton, J. . . . . Leeds United
Moore . . . . West Ham United
Ball . . . . Blackpool
Greaves . . . . Tottenham Hotspur
Hurst . . . . West Ham United
Eastham. . . . . Arsenal
Connelly. . . . . Manchester United
Result: 2–0
Scorers: J. Charlton, Eastham

403. 5 July 1966
v POLAND . . . . Chorzów
Banks. . . . . Leicester City
Cohen . . . . Fulham
Wilson . . . . Everton
Stiles . . . . Manchester United
Charlton, J. . . . . Leeds
Moore . . . . West Ham United
Ball . . . . Blackpool
Greaves . . . . Tottenham Hotspur
Charlton, R. . . . . Manchester United
Hunt . . . . Liverpool
Peters . . . . West Ham United
Result: 1–0
Scorer: Hunt

404. 11 July 1966
v URUGUAY . . . . Wembley Stadium
Banks. . . . . Leicester City
Cohen . . . . Fulham
Wilson . . . . Everton
Stiles . . . . Manchester United
Charlton, J. . . . . Leeds United
Moore . . . . West Ham United
Ball . . . . Blackpool
Greaves . . . . Tottenham Hotspur
Charlton, R. . . . . Manchester United
Hunt . . . . Liverpool
Connelly. . . . . Manchester United
Result: 0–0

405. 16 July 1966
v MEXICO. . . . . Wembley Stadium
Banks. . . . . Leicester City
Cohen . . . . Fulham
Wilson . . . . Everton
Stiles . . . . Manchester United
Charlton, J. . . . . Leeds United
Moore . . . . West Ham United
Paine . . . . Southampton
Greaves . . . . Tottenham Hotspur
Charlton, R. . . . . Manchester United
Hunt . . . . Liverpool
Peters . . . . West Ham United
Result: 2–0
Scorers: R. Charlton, Hunt

406. 20 July 1966
v FRANCE. . . . . Wembley Stadium
Banks. . . . . Leicester City
Cohen . . . . Fulham
Wilson . . . . Everton
Stiles . . . . Manchester United
Charlton, J. . . . . Leeds United
Moore . . . . West Ham United
Callaghan . . . . Liverpool
Greaves . . . . Tottenham Hotspur
Charlton, R. . . . . Manchester United
Hunt . . . . Liverpool
Peters . . . . West Ham United
Result: 2–0
Scorers: Hunt (2)

407. 23 July 1966
v ARGENTINA. . . . . Wembley Stadium

Banks. . . . . Leicester City
Cohen . . . . Fulham
Wilson . . . . Everton
Stiles . . . . Manchester United
Charlton, J. . . . . Leeds United
Moore . . . . West Ham United
Ball . . . . Blackpool
Hunt . . . . Liverpool
Charlton, R. . . . . Manchester United
Hurst . . . . West Ham United
Peters . . . . West Ham United
Result: 1–0
Scorer: Hurst

 FEATURED MATCH

23 JULY 1966

ENGLAND 1 ARGENTINA 0 – WEMBLEY STADIUM

Having qualified for the knockout stages of the World Cup, England faced Argentina, whom FIFA had censured for episodes of 'unethical tackling', which occurred in their group match against the Germans. Nobby Stiles had also been publicly warned, but Alf Ramsey significantly kept faith with the Manchester United player despite diplomatic pressure from the Football Association.

Sadly, this particular match would not be remembered for the level of football played on the field, but rather for the fact that Argentina, quite inexplicably, adopted a cynical approach throughout the entire game, with brutal body-checking and tripping the order of the day. In the opening third of the game, Antonio Rattin, the Argentinian captain, maintained a constant stream of verbal abuse and harassment towards the German referee, Rudolf Kreitlein, and also found time to get himself booked for a foul on Bobby Charlton.

In the 35th minute, Kreitein booked Luis Artime, and such were the animated protests of Rattin in response to his countryman's caution, the referee's patience at last broke and he had no alternative but to send the Argentine captain off the field. For the next eight minutes, pandemonium reigned as Argentina remonstrated with officials and almost walked off en masse. Rattin stood on the touchline hoping, vainly, to return to the game, but it was not to be and the match restarted with Argentina down to ten men.

Despite the player advantage, England could not dominate the opposition, who showed much resilience and skill. However, it was England who were to progress through to the semi-finals with a single goal scored with thirteen minutes still to play. Ray Wilson, earning his 49th cap, hit the ball down the left flank for Martin Peters, whose cross to the near post was met by Hurst, and it was his glancing header that produced the only goal of the match.

At the final whistle, Alf Ramsey physically separated his players from the Argentines and prevented them from exchanging shirts. As a consequence of their unsporting behaviour that day, Argentina received the maximum FIFA fine of 1,000 Swiss francs and Rattin received a four-match ban. England had displayed fine discipline and restraint in the face of the most crude adversity, while Argentina would return home complaining of discrimination against their players.

408. 26 July 1966
v PORTUGAL. . . . . Wembley Stadium
  Banks. . . . . Leicester City
  Cohen . . . . Fulham
  Wilson . . . . Everton
  Stiles . . . . Manchester United
  Charlton, J. . . . . Leeds United
  Moore . . . . West Ham United
  Ball . . . . Blackpool
  Hunt . . . . Liverpool
  Charlton, R. . . . . Manchester United
  Hurst . . . . West Ham United
  Peters . . . . West Ham United
Result: 2–1
Scorers: R. Charlton (2)

 DID YOU KNOW...?

The first World Cup tournament mascot was devised
for England '66. Named World Cup Willie, it was a
proud looking lion dressed in a Union Jack and
undoubtedly helped England win the trophy . . .

409. 30 July 1966
v WEST GERMANY . . . . Wembley Stadium
  Banks. . . . . Leicester City
  Cohen . . . . Fulham
  Wilson . . . . Everton
  Stiles . . . . Manchester United
  Charlton, J. . . . . Leeds United
  Moore . . . . West Ham United
  Ball . . . . Blackpool
  Hunt . . . . Liverpool
  Charlton, R. . . . . Manchester United
  Hurst . . . . West Ham United
  Peters . . . . West Ham United
Result: 4–2 (a.e.t.)
Scorers: Hurst (3), Peters

410. 22 October 1966
v N. IRELAND . . . . Belfast
  Banks. . . . . Leicester City
  Cohen . . . . Fulham
  Wilson . . . . Everton
  Stiles . . . . Manchester United
  Charlton, J. . . . . Leeds United
  Moore . . . . West Ham United
  Ball . . . . Everton
  Hunt . . . . Liverpool
  Charlton, R. . . . . Manchester United
  Hurst . . . . West Ham United
  Peters . . . . West Ham United
Result: 2–0
Scorers: Hunt, Peters

411. 2 November 1966
v CZECHOSLOVAKIA . . . . Wembley Stadium
  Banks. . . . . Leicester City
  Cohen . . . . Fulham
  Wilson . . . . Everton
  Stiles . . . . Manchester United
  Charlton, J. . . . . Leeds United
  Moore . . . . West Ham United
  Ball . . . . Everton
  Hunt . . . . Liverpool
  Charlton, R. . . . . Manchester United
  Hurst . . . . West Ham United
  Peters . . . . West Ham United
Result: 0–0

 FEATURED MATCH

30 JULY 1966

**ENGLAND 4 WEST GERMANY 2 (after
extra time) – WEMBLEY STADIUM**

England became the fifth country to win the Jules
Rimet Trophy, which they achieved in a match of
compelling drama and engrossing football.

It was a tentative start by the two teams as the
importance of the occasion sank in, but after twelve
minutes, England went behind for the first time in
the tournament. Siggi Held centred, Ray Wilson mist-
imed his headed clearance and the ball fell to
Helmut Haller, who fired past Gordon Banks.
Fortunately, the lead only lasted six minutes, to the
relief and delight of most of the 93,000 Wembley
crowd. Wolfgang Overath fouled Bobby Moore, who
quickly got to his feet to take the resulting free kick.
The England captain played the ball forward for
Hurst, his West Ham teammate, who headed low
past goalkeeper Hans Tilkowski. Inspired by the goal,
England began to take a firm grip of the proceedings
and held control until just before half-time when the
Germans got back into the game.

The second half opened at a more sedate pace as
a downpour fell on Wembley, but England found
time to take the lead from a corner after Tilkowski
had carried Alan Ball's shot over the byline. Ball took
the corner, which was not fully cleared, and Hurst's
shot cannoned off Horst Hoettges into the air and
Martin Peters volleyed home his first goal of the
competition with only twelve minutes left to play.
Less than a minute remained on the clock when Jack
Charlton was harshly adjudged to have fouled Uwe
Seeler on the edge of the box. Lothar Emmerich
struck his kick into the wall and the ball was
deflected across the goal, possibly encouraged by
the hand of Karl-Heinz Schnellinger. The ball reached
Wolfgang Weber at the far post and his shot beat the
reach of both Banks and Wilson: it was now 2–2.

In the first period of extra time, Stiles sent the ball
into space for the ever-running Ball to chase. The
Blackpool player got to the byline and crossed for
Hurst to lash out. The ball went over Tilkowski's head
and crashed against the underside of the bar and
bounced to the floor and away from goal. Referee
Gottfried Dienst of Switzerland consulted his Soviet
linesman and awarded the goal. Even now, almost
forty years to the day, no one is really sure if the
whole of the ball did cross the line.

Immediately, Seeler almost levelled the scores,
but failed to make contact with Held's header. Moore
took the loose ball and played a beautiful long pass
for the running Hurst to chest down and run towards
goal. The West Ham man realized the space he was
in and unleashed a powerful shot for his worthy hat-
trick. England were crowned world champions after
a pulsating final tie, bringing a brilliant climax to
World Cup '66 for the host nation.

412. 16 November 1966
v WALES. . . . . Wembley Stadium
  Banks. . . . . Leicester City
  Cohen . . . . Fulham
  Wilson . . . . Everton
  Stiles . . . . Manchester United

Charlton, J. . . . . Leeds United
Moore . . . . West Ham United
Ball . . . . Everton
Hunt . . . . Liverpool
Charlton, R. . . . . Manchester United
Hurst . . . . West Ham United
Peters . . . . West Ham United
Result: 5–1
Scorers: Hurst (2), R. Charlton, J. Charlton, o.g.

413. 15 April 1967
v SCOTLAND. . . . . Wembley Stadium
Banks. . . . . Leicester City
Cohen . . . . Fulham
Wilson . . . . Everton
Stiles . . . . Manchester United
Charlton, J. . . . . Leeds United
Moore . . . . West Ham United
Ball . . . . Everton
Greaves . . . . Tottenham Hotspur
Charlton, R. . . . . Manchester United
Hurst . . . . West Ham United
Peters . . . . West Ham United
Result: 2–3
Scorers: J. Charlton, Hurst

414. 24 May 1967
v SPAIN . . . . Wembley Stadium
Bonetti. . . . . Chelsea
Cohen . . . . Fulham
Newton . . . . Blackburn Rovers
Mullery . . . . Tottenham Hotspur
Labone. . . . . Everton
Moore . . . . West Ham United
Ball . . . . Everton
Greaves . . . . Tottenham Hotspur
Hurst . . . . West Ham United
Hunt . . . . Liverpool
Hollins . . . . Chelsea
Result: 2–0
Scorers: Greaves, Hunt

415. 27 May 1967
v AUSTRIA . . . . Vienna
Bonetti. . . . . Chelsea
Newton . . . . Blackburn Rovers
Wilson . . . . Everton
Mullery . . . . Tottenham Hotspur
Labone. . . . . Everton
Moore . . . . West Ham United
Ball . . . . Everton
Greaves . . . . Tottenham Hotspur
Hurst . . . . West Ham United
Hunt . . . . Liverpool
Hunter . . . . Leeds United
Result: 1–0
Scorer: Ball

416. 21 October 1967
v WALES. . . . . Ninian Park, Cardiff
Banks. . . . . Stoke City
Cohen . . . . Fulham
Newton . . . . Blackburn Rovers
Mullery . . . . Tottenham Hotspur
Charlton, J. . . . . Leeds United
Moore . . . . West Ham United
Ball . . . . Everton
Hunt . . . . Liverpool
Charlton, R. . . . . Manchester United
Hurst . . . . West Ham United
Peters . . . . West Ham United
Result: 3–0
Scorers: Peters, R. Charlton, Ball (pen.)

417. 22 November 1967
v N. IRELAND . . . . Wembley Stadium
Banks. . . . . Stoke City

Cohen . . . . Fulham
Wilson . . . . Everton
Mullery . . . . Tottenham Hotspur
Sadler . . . . Manchester United
Moore . . . . West Ham United
Thompson . . . . Liverpool
Hunt . . . . Liverpool
Charlton, R. . . . . Manchester United
Hurst . . . . West Ham United
Peters . . . . West Ham United
Result: 2–0
Scorers: Hurst, R. Charlton

418. 6 December 1967
v SOVIET UNION . . . . Wembley Stadium
Banks. . . . . Stoke City
Knowles. . . . . Tottenham Hotspur
Wilson . . . . Everton
Mullery . . . . Tottenham Hotspur
Sadler . . . . Manchester United
Moore . . . . West Ham United
Ball . . . . Everton
Hunt . . . . Liverpool
Charlton, R. . . . . Manchester United
Hurst . . . . West Ham United
Peters . . . . West Ham United
Result: 2–2
Scorers: Ball, Peters

419. 24 February 1968
v SCOTLAND. . . . . Hampden Park, Glasgow
Banks. . . . . Stoke City
Newton . . . . Blackburn Rovers
Wilson . . . . Everton
Mullery . . . . Tottenham Hotspur
Labone. . . . . Everton
Moore . . . . West Ham United
Ball . . . . Everton
Hurst . . . . West Ham United
Summerbee . . . . Manchester City
Charlton, R. . . . . Manchester United
Peters . . . . West Ham United
Result: 1–1
Scorer: Peters

420. 3 April 1968
v SPAIN . . . . Wembley Stadium
Banks. . . . . Stoke City
Knowles. . . . . Tottenham Hotspur
Wilson . . . . Everton
Mullery . . . . Tottenham Hotspur
Charlton, J. . . . . Leeds United
Moore . . . . West Ham United
Ball . . . . Everton
Hunt . . . . Liverpool
Summerbee . . . . Manchester City
Charlton, R. . . . . Manchester United
Peters . . . . West Ham United
Result: 1–0
Scorer: R. Charlton

421. 8 May 1968
v SPAIN . . . . Madrid
Bonetti. . . . . Chelsea
Newton . . . . Blackburn Rovers
Wilson . . . . Everton
Mullery . . . . Tottenham Hotspur
Labone. . . . . Everton
Moore . . . . West Ham United
Ball . . . . Everton
Peters . . . . West Ham United
Charlton, R. . . . . Manchester United
Hunt . . . . Liverpool
Hunter . . . . Leeds United
Result: 2–1
Scorers: Peters, Hunter

422. 22 May 1968
v SWEDEN .... Wembley Stadium
Stepney .... Manchester United
Newton .... Blackburn Rovers
Knowles............. Tottenham Hotspur
Mullery .... Tottenham Hotspur
Labone............... Everton
Moore .... West Ham United
Bell .... Manchester City
Peters .... West Ham United
Charlton, R.* .... Manchester United
Hunt .... Liverpool
Hunter .... Leeds United
Sub: *Hurst .... West Ham United
Result: 3–1
Scorers: Peters, R. Charlton, Hunt

423. 1 June 1968
v WEST GERMANY .... Hanover
Banks................. Stoke City
Newton .... Blackburn Rovers
Knowles............. Tottenham Hotspur
Hunter .... Leeds United
Labone............... Everton
Moore .... West Ham United
Ball .... Everton
Bell .... Manchester City
Summerbee .... Manchester City
Hurst .... West Ham United
Thompson .... Liverpool
Result: 0–1

424. 5 June 1968
v YUGOSLAVIA .... Florence
Banks................. Stoke City
Newton .... Blackburn Rovers
Wilson .... Everton
Mullery .... Tottenham Hotspur
Labone............... Everton
Moore .... West Ham United
Ball .... Everton
Peters .... West Ham United
Charlton, R. .... Manchester United
Hunt .... Liverpool
Hunter .... Leeds United
Result: 0–1

425. 8 June 1968
v SOVIET UNION .... Rome
Banks................. Stoke City
Wright, T. .... Everton
Wilson .... Everton
Stiles .... Manchester United
Labone............... Everton
Moore .... West Ham United
Hunter .... Leeds United
Hunt .... Liverpool
Charlton, R. .... Manchester United
Hurst .... West Ham United
Peters .... West Ham United
Result: 2–0
Scorers: R. Charlton, Hurst

426. 6 November 1968
v ROMANIA .... Bucharest
Banks................. Stoke City
Wright, T.* .... Everton
Newton .... Blackburn Rovers
Mullery .... Tottenham Hotspur
Labone............... Everton
Moore .... West Ham United
Ball .... Everton
Hunt .... Liverpool
Charlton, R. .... Manchester United
Hurst .... West Ham United
Peters .... West Ham United
Sub: *McNab............ Arsenal
Result: 0–0

427. 11 December 1968
v BULGARIA .... Wembley Stadium
West .... Everton
Newton* .... Blackburn Rovers
McNab............... Arsenal
Mullery .... Tottenham Hotspur
Labone............... Everton
Moore .... West Ham United
Lee .... Manchester City
Bell .... Manchester City
Charlton, R. .... Manchester United
Hurst .... West Ham United
Peters .... West Ham United
Sub: *Reaney .... Leeds United
Result: 1–1
Scorer: Hurst

428. 15 January 1969
v ROMANIA .... Wembley Stadium
Banks................. Stoke City
Wright, T. .... Everton
McNab............... Arsenal
Stiles .... Manchester United
Charlton, J. .... Leeds United
Hunter .... Leeds United
Radford .... Arsenal
Hunt .... Liverpool
Charlton, R. .... Manchester United
Hurst .... West Ham United
Ball .... Everton
Result: 1–1
Scorer: J. Charlton

429. 12 March 1969
v FRANCE............... Wembley Stadium
Banks................. Stoke City
Newton .... Blackburn Rovers
Cooper............... Leeds United
Mullery .... Tottenham Hotspur
Charlton, J. .... Leeds United
Moore .... West Ham United
Lee .... Manchester City
Bell .... Manchester City
Hurst .... West Ham United
Peters .... West Ham United
O'Grady.............. Leeds United
Result: 5–0
Scorers: Hurst (3 – 2 pens), O'Grady, Lee

430. 3 May 1969
v N. IRELAND .... Belfast
Banks................. Stoke City
Newton .... Blackburn Rovers
McNab............... Arsenal
Mullery .... Tottenham Hotspur
Labone............... Everton
Moore .... West Ham United
Ball .... Everton
Lee .... Manchester City
Charlton, R. .... Manchester United
Hurst .... West Ham United
Peters .... West Ham United
Result: 3–1
Scorers: Peters, Lee, Hurst (pen.)

431. 7 May 1969
v WALES............... Wembley Stadium
West .... Everton
Newton .... Blackburn Rovers
Cooper............... Leeds United
Moore .... West Ham United
Charlton, J. .... Leeds United
Hunter .... Leeds United
Lee .... Manchester City
Bell .... Manchester City
Astle .... West Bromwich Albion

Charlton, R. . . . . Manchester United
Ball . . . . Everton
Result: 2–1
Scorers: R. Charlton, Lee

432. 10 May 1969
v SCOTLAND. . . . . Wembley Stadium
Banks. . . . . Stoke City
Newton . . . . Blackburn Rovers
Cooper. . . . . Leeds United
Mullery . . . . Tottenham Hotspur
Labone. . . . . Everton
Moore . . . . West Ham United
Lee . . . . Manchester City
Ball . . . . Everton
Charlton, R. . . . . Manchester United
Hurst . . . . West Ham United
Peters . . . . West Ham United
Result: 4–1
Scorers: Peters (2), Hurst (2 – 1 pen.)

433. 1 June 1969
v MEXICO. . . . . Mexico City
West . . . . Everton
Newton* . . . . Blackburn Rovers
Cooper. . . . . Leeds United
Mullery . . . . Tottenham Hotspur
Labone. . . . . Everton
Moore . . . . West Ham United
Lee . . . . Manchester City
Ball . . . . Everton
Charlton, R. . . . . Manchester United
Hurst . . . . West Ham United
Peters . . . . West Ham United
Sub: *Wright, T. . . . . Everton
Result: 0–0

434. 8 June 1969
v URUGUAY . . . . Montevideo
Banks. . . . . Stoke City
Wright, T. . . . . Everton
Newton . . . . Blackburn Rovers
Mullery . . . . Tottenham Hotspur
Labone. . . . . Everton
Moore . . . . West Ham United
Lee . . . . Manchester City
Bell . . . . Manchester City
Hurst . . . . West Ham United
Ball . . . . Everton
Peters . . . . West Ham United
Result: 2–1
Scorers: Lee, Hurst

435. 12 June 1969
v BRAZIL. . . . . Rio de Janeiro
Banks. . . . . Stoke City
Wright, T. . . . . Everton
Newton . . . . Blackburn Rovers
Mullery . . . . Tottenham Hotspur
Labone. . . . . Everton
Moore . . . . West Ham United
Ball . . . . Everton
Bell . . . . Manchester City
Charlton, R. . . . . Manchester United
Hurst . . . . West Ham United
Peters . . . . West Ham United
Result: 1–2
Scorer: Bell

436. 5 November 1969
v HOLLAND . . . . Amsterdam
Bonetti. . . . . Chelsea
Wright, T. . . . . Everton
Hughes . . . . Liverpool
Mullery . . . . Tottenham Hotspur
Charlton, J. . . . . Leeds United

Moore . . . . West Ham United
Lee* . . . . Manchester City
Bell . . . . Manchester City
Charlton, R. . . . . Manchester United
Hurst . . . . West Ham United
Peters . . . . West Ham United
Sub: *Thompson . . . . Liverpool
Result: 1–0
Scorer: Bell

437. 10 December 1969
v PORTUGAL. . . . . Wembley Stadium
Bonetti. . . . . Chelsea
Reaney. . . . . Leeds United
Hughes . . . . Liverpool
Mullery . . . . Tottenham Hotspur
Charlton, J. . . . . Leeds United
Moore . . . . West Ham United
Lee . . . . Manchester City
Bell* . . . . Manchester City
Astle . . . . West Bromwich Albion
Charlton, R. . . . . Manchester United
Ball . . . . Everton
Sub: *Peters . . . . West Ham United
Result: 1–0
Scorer: J. Charlton

438. 14 January 1970
v HOLLAND . . . . Wembley Stadium
Banks. . . . . Stoke City
Newton . . . . Everton
Cooper. . . . . Leeds United
Peters . . . . West Ham United
Charlton, J. . . . . Leeds United
Hunter . . . . Leeds United
Lee* . . . . Manchester City
Bell . . . . Manchester City
Jones** . . . . Leeds United
Charlton, R. . . . . Manchester United
Storey-Moore . . . . Nottingham Forest
Subs: *Mullery. . . . . Tottenham Hotspur
**Hurst . . . . West Ham United
Result: 0–0

439. 25 February 1970
v BELGIUM. . . . . Brussels
Banks. . . . . Stoke City
Wright, T. . . . . Everton
Cooper. . . . . Leeds United
Hughes . . . . Liverpool
Labone. . . . . Everton
Moore . . . . West Ham United
Lee . . . . Manchester City
Ball . . . . Everton
Osgood . . . . Chelsea
Hurst . . . . West Ham United
Peters . . . . West Ham United
Result: 3–1
Scorers: Ball (2), Hurst

440. 18 April 1970
v WALES. . . . . Ninian Park, Cardiff
Banks. . . . . Stoke City
Wright, T. . . . . Everton
Hughes . . . . Liverpool
Mullery . . . . Tottenham Hotspur
Labone. . . . . Everton
Moore . . . . West Ham United
Lee . . . . Manchester City
Ball . . . . Everton
Charlton, R. . . . . Manchester United
Hurst . . . . West Ham United
Peters . . . . Tottenham Hotspur
Result: 1–1
Scorer: Lee

441. 21 April 1970

v N. IRELAND . . . . Wembley Stadium
Banks . . . . Stoke City
Newton* . . . . Everton
Hughes . . . . Liverpool
Mullery . . . . Tottenham Hotspur
Moore . . . . West Ham United
Stiles . . . . Manchester United
Coates . . . . Burnley
Kidd . . . . Manchester United
Charlton, R . . . . Manchester United
Hurst . . . . West Ham United
Peters . . . . Tottenham Hotspur
Sub: *Bell . . . . Manchester City
Result: 3–1
Scorers: Peters, Hurst, R. Charlton

442. 25 April 1970

v SCOTLAND . . . . Hampden Park, Glasgow
Banks . . . . Stoke City
Newton . . . . Everton
Hughes . . . . Liverpool
Stiles . . . . Manchester United
Labone . . . . Everton
Moore . . . . West Ham United
Thompson* . . . . Liverpool
Ball . . . . Everton
Astle . . . . West Bromwich Albion
Hurst . . . . West Ham United
Peters . . . . Tottenham Hotspur
Sub: *Mullery . . . . Tottenham Hotspur
Result: 0–0

443. 20 May 1970

v COLOMBIA . . . . Bogotá
Banks . . . . Stoke City
Newton . . . . Everton
Cooper . . . . Leeds United
Mullery . . . . Tottenham Hotspur
Labone . . . . Everton
Moore . . . . West Ham United
Lee . . . . Manchester City
Ball . . . . Everton
Charlton, R . . . . Manchester United
Hurst . . . . West Ham United
Peters . . . . Tottenham Hotspur
Result: 4–0
Scorers: Peters (2), R. Charlton, Ball

444. 24 May 1970

v ECUADOR . . . . Quito
Banks . . . . Stoke City
Newton . . . . Everton
Cooper . . . . Leeds United
Mullery . . . . Tottenham Hotspur
Labone . . . . Everton
Moore . . . . West Ham United
Lee* . . . . Manchester City
Ball . . . . Everton
Charlton, R.** . . . . Manchester United
Hurst . . . . West Ham United
Peters . . . . Tottenham Hotspur
Subs: *Kidd . . . . Manchester United
**Sadler . . . . Manchester United
Result: 2–0
Scorers: Lee, Kidd

445. 2 June 1970

v ROMANIA . . . . Guadalajara
Banks . . . . Stoke City
Newton* . . . . Everton
Cooper . . . . Leeds United
Mullery . . . . Tottenham Hotspur
Labone . . . . Everton
Moore . . . . West Ham United
Lee** . . . . Manchester City

Ball . . . . Everton
Charlton, R . . . . Manchester United
Hurst . . . . West Ham United
Peters . . . . Tottenham Hotspur
Subs: *Wright, T. . . . . Everton
**Osgood . . . . Chelsea
Result: 1–0
Scorer: Hurst

 FEATURED MATCH

14 JUNE 1970

ENGLAND 2 WEST GERMANY 3 – LEÓN, MEXICO

England's quarter-final place had been secured courtesy of two 1–0 victories over Romania and Czechoslovakia. Their second place in Group 3 meant that they faced the winners of Group 4, West Germany, the nation they had beaten in the final of the 1966 World Cup. Disconcertingly, England had lost Gordon Banks with a mysterious illness and therefore Chelsea's Peter Bonetti was brought in to deputize.

England began in tremendous and confident form, and took complete control of the tie. The inevitable England goal arrived on the half-hour: Alan Mullery, who had a splendid tournament, began the move and dashed half the length of the field to finish it off. Despite the attentions of Berti Vogts, Mullery met Keith Newton's cross from eight yards out to score. England went further ahead five minutes after the break. Newton, receiving Hurst's pass, once more centred, this time for Peters to get on the scoresheet. England it seemed were on their way to the semi-finals.

In the 68th minute, however, an innocuous move ended in West Germany pulling a goal back. Franz Beckenbauer put in a shot that was blocked by Franny Lee, but he followed up to fire in another shot that did not appear dangerous. Bonetti, unfortunately, dived late and awkwardly – the ball went under him and into the net. England opted to play possession football to conserve their energy and, as planned, Ramsey took off Charlton and Ball. One consequence of Charlton's substitution was that it released Beckenbauer more into open play, but his replacement Colin Bell soon set up Hurst, whose shot hit the upright. In response a strike from Gerd Müller brought a fine save from Bonetti.

Then, with just eight minutes remaining, the Germans clawed their way level. Brian Labone failed to clear properly and this allowed Karl-Heinz Schnellinger to return a high cross, which Uwe Seeler headed past Bonetti, who perhaps should have come off his line.

The match went into extra time, but unlike four years previously it was West Germany who would prove to be the stronger. It was Müller who claimed the winner in acrobatic fashion, severely punishing Labone, who was guilty of ball watching.

England's reign as World Champions had ended, and so had the international careers of Bobby Charlton and Peter Bonetti, after 106 and 7 appearances respectively.

446. **7 June 1970**
v BRAZIL. . . . . Guadalajara
  Banks. . . . . Stoke City
  Wright, T. . . . . Everton
  Cooper. . . . . Leeds United
  Mullery . . . . Tottenham Hotspur
  Labone. . . . . Everton
  Moore . . . . West Ham United
  Lee* . . . . Manchester City
  Ball . . . . Everton
  Charlton, R.** . . . . Manchester United
  Hurst . . . . West Ham United
  Peters . . . . Tottenham Hotspur
  Subs: *Astle . . . . West Bromwich Albion
  **Bell . . . . Manchester City
  Result: 0–1

447. **11 June 1970**
v CZECHOSLOVAKIA . . . . . . Guadalajara
  Banks. . . . . Stoke City
  Newton . . . . Everton
  Cooper. . . . . Leeds United
  Mullery . . . . Tottenham Hotspur
  Charlton, J. . . . . Leeds United
  Moore . . . . West Ham United
  Bell . . . . Manchester City
  Charlton, R.* . . . . Manchester United
  Astle** . . . . West Bromwich Albion
  Clarke . . . . Leeds United
  Peters . . . . Tottenham Hotspur
  Subs: *Ball . . . . Everton
  **Osgood . . . . Chelsea
  Result: 1–0
  Scorer: Clarke (pen.)

448. **14 June 1970**
v WEST GERMANY . . . . León
  Bonetti. . . . . Chelsea
  Newton . . . . Everton
  Cooper. . . . . Leeds United
  Mullery . . . . Tottenham Hotspur
  Labone. . . . . Everton
  Moore . . . . West Ham United
  Lee . . . . Manchester City
  Ball . . . . Everton
  Charlton, R.* . . . . Manchester United
  Hurst . . . . West Ham United
  Peters**. . . . . Tottenham Hotspur
  Subs: *Bell . . . . Manchester City
  **Hunter. . . . . Leeds United
  Result: 2–3 (a.e.t.)
  Scorers: Mullery, Peters

449. **25 November 1970**
v EAST GERMANY . . . . Wembley Stadium
  Shilton. . . . . Leicester City
  Hughes . . . . Liverpool
  Cooper. . . . . Leeds United
  Mullery . . . . Tottenham Hotspur
  Sadler . . . . Manchester United
  Moore . . . . West Ham United
  Lee . . . . Manchester City
  Ball . . . . Everton
  Hurst . . . . West Ham United
  Clarke . . . . Leeds United
  Peters . . . . Tottenham Hotspur
  Result: 3–1
  Scorers: Peters, Lee, Clarke

450. **3 February 1971**
v MALTA. . . . . Gzira
  Banks. . . . . Stoke City
  Reaney. . . . . Leeds United
  Hughes . . . . Liverpool
  Mullery . . . . Tottenham Hotspur

  McFarland . . . . Derby County
  Hunter . . . . Leeds United
  Ball . . . . Everton
  Chivers. . . . . Tottenham Hotspur
  Royle . . . . Everton
  Harvey . . . . Everton
  Peters . . . . Tottenham Hotspur
  Result: 1–0
  Scorer: Peters

451. **21 April 1971**
v GREECE . . . . Wembley Stadium
  Banks. . . . . Stoke City
  Storey . . . . Arsenal
  Hughes . . . . Liverpool
  Mullery . . . . Tottenham Hotspur
  McFarland . . . . Derby County
  Moore . . . . West Ham United
  Lee . . . . Manchester City
  Ball* . . . . Everton
  Chivers. . . . . Tottenham Hotspur
  Hurst . . . . West Ham United
  Peters . . . . Tottenham Hotspur
  Sub: *Coates. . . . . Burnley
  Result: 3–0
  Scorers: Chivers, Hurst, Lee

452. **12 May 1971**
v MALTA. . . . . Wembley Stadium
  Banks. . . . . Stoke City
  Lawler . . . . Liverpool
  Cooper. . . . . Leeds United
  Hughes . . . . Liverpool
  McFarland . . . . Derby County
  Moore . . . . West Ham United
  Lee . . . . Manchester City
  Coates . . . . Tottenham Hotspur
  Chivers. . . . . Tottenham Hotspur
  Clarke . . . . Leeds United
  Peters*. . . . . Tottenham Hotspur
  Sub: *Ball . . . . Everton
  Result: 5–0
  Scorers: Chivers (2), Lee, Clarke (pen.), Lawler

 DID YOU KNOW...?

When England played Malta on 12 May 1971 at
Wembley in the Nations Cup, the England goalkeeper Gordon Banks did not receive the ball
directly from a Maltese player once during the
match, which England won 5–0.

453. **15 May 1971**
v N. IRELAND . . . . Windsor Park, Belfast
  Banks. . . . . Stoke City
  Madeley. . . . . Leeds United
  Cooper. . . . . Leeds United
  Storey . . . . Arsenal
  McFarland . . . . Derby County
  Moore . . . . West Ham United
  Lee . . . . Manchester City
  Ball . . . . Everton
  Chivers. . . . . Tottenham Hotspur
  Clarke . . . . Leeds United
  Peters . . . . Tottenham Hotspur
  Result: 1–0
  Scorer: Clarke

454. 19 May 1971
v WALES . . . . Wembley Stadium
Shilton . . . . Leicester City
Lawler . . . . Liverpool
Cooper . . . . Leeds United
Smith, T. . . . . Liverpool
Lloyd . . . . Liverpool
Hughes . . . . Liverpool
Lee . . . . Manchester City
Brown* . . . . West Bromwich Albion
Hurst . . . . West Ham United
Coates . . . . Tottenham Hotspur
Peters . . . . Tottenham Hotspur
Sub: *Clarke . . . . Leeds United
Result: 0–0

455. 22 May 1971
v SCOTLAND . . . . Wembley Stadium
Banks . . . . Stoke City
Lawler . . . . Liverpool
Cooper . . . . Leeds United
Storey . . . . Arsenal
McFarland . . . . Derby County
Moore . . . . West Ham United
Lee* . . . . Manchester City
Ball . . . . Everton
Chivers . . . . Tottenham Hotspur
Hurst . . . . West Ham United
Peters . . . . Tottenham Hotspur
Sub: *Clarke . . . . Leeds United
Result: 3–1
Scorers: Peters, Chivers (2)

456. 13 October 1971
v SWITZERLAND . . . . Basle
Banks . . . . Stoke City
Lawler . . . . Liverpool
Cooper . . . . Leeds United
Mullery . . . . Tottenham Hotspur
McFarland . . . . Derby County
Moore . . . . West Ham United
Lee . . . . Manchester City
Madeley . . . . Leeds United
Chivers . . . . Tottenham Hotspur
Hurst* . . . . West Ham United
Peters . . . . Tottenham Hotspur
Sub: *Radford . . . . Arsenal
Result: 3–2
Scorers: Hurst, Chivers, o.g.

457. 10 November 1971
v SWITZERLAND . . . . Wembley Stadium
Shilton . . . . Leicester City
Madeley . . . . Leeds United
Cooper . . . . Leeds United
Storey . . . . Arsenal
Lloyd . . . . Liverpool
Moore . . . . West Ham United
Summerbee* . . . . Manchester City
Ball . . . . Everton
Hurst . . . . West Ham United
Lee** . . . . Manchester City
Hughes . . . . Liverpool
Subs: *Chivers . . . . Tottenham Hotspur
**Marsh . . . . Queen's Park Rangers
Result: 1–1
Scorer: Summerbee

458. 1 December 1971
v GREECE . . . . Piraes
Banks . . . . Stoke City
Madeley . . . . Leeds United
Hughes . . . . Liverpool
Bell . . . . Manchester City
McFarland . . . . Derby County

Moore . . . . West Ham United
Lee . . . . Manchester City
Ball . . . . Everton
Chivers . . . . Tottenham Hotspur
Hurst . . . . West Ham United
Peters . . . . Tottenham Hotspur
Result: 2–0
Scorers: Hurst, Chivers

459. 29 April 1972
v WEST GERMANY . . . . Wembley Stadium
Banks . . . . Stoke City
Madeley . . . . Leeds United
Hughes . . . . Liverpool
Bell . . . . Manchester City
Moore . . . . West Ham United
Hunter . . . . Leeds United
Lee . . . . Manchester City
Ball . . . . Arsenal
Chivers . . . . Tottenham Hotspur
Hurst* . . . . West Ham United
Peters . . . . Tottenham Hotspur
Sub: *Marsh . . . . Manchester City
Result: 1–3
Scorer: Lee

460. 13 May 1972
v WEST GERMANY . . . . Berlin
Banks . . . . Stoke City
Madeley . . . . Leeds United
Hughes . . . . Liverpool
Storey . . . . Arsenal
McFarland . . . . Derby County
Moore . . . . West Ham United
Ball . . . . Arsenal
Bell . . . . Manchester City
Chivers . . . . Tottenham Hotspur
Marsh* . . . . Manchester City
Hunter** . . . . Leeds United
Subs: *Summerbee . . . . Manchester City
**Peters . . . . Tottenham Hotspur
Result: 0–0

461. 20 May 1972
v WALES . . . . Ninian Park, Cardiff
Banks . . . . Stoke City
Madeley . . . . Leeds United
Hughes . . . . Liverpool
Storey . . . . Arsenal
McFarland . . . . Derby County
Moore . . . . West Ham United
Summerbee . . . . Manchester City
Bell . . . . Manchester City
Macdonald . . . . Newcastle United
Marsh . . . . Manchester City
Hunter . . . . Leeds United
Result: 3–0
Scorers: Hughes, Bell, Marsh

462. 23 May 1972
v N. IRELAND . . . . Wembley Stadium
Shilton . . . . Leicester City
Todd . . . . Derby County
Hughes . . . . Liverpool
Storey . . . . Arsenal
Lloyd . . . . Liverpool
Hunter . . . . Leeds United
Summerbee . . . . Manchester City
Bell . . . . Manchester City
Macdonald* . . . . Newcastle United
Marsh . . . . Manchester City
Currie** . . . . Sheffield United
Subs: *Chivers . . . . Tottenham Hotspur
**Peters . . . . Tottenham Hotspur
Result: 0–1

463. 27 May 1972
v SCOTLAND............ Hampden Park, Glasgow
Banks.............. Stoke City
Madeley.............. Leeds United
Hughes .... Liverpool
Storey .... Arsenal
McFarland .... Derby County
Moore .... West Ham United
Ball .... Arsenal
Bell .... Manchester City
Chivers............... Tottenham Hotspur
Marsh* .... Manchester City
Hunter .... Leeds United
Sub: *Macdonald.......... Newcastle United
Result: 1–0
Scorer: Ball

464. 11 October 1972
v YUGOSLAVIA.......... Wembley Stadium
Shilton .... Leicester City
Mills .... Ipswich Town
Lampard .... West Ham United
Storey .... Arsenal
Blockley.............. Arsenal
Moore .... West Ham United
Ball .... Arsenal
Channon .... Southampton
Royle .... Everton
Bell .... Manchester City
Marsh .... Manchester City
Result: 1–1
Scorer: Royle

465. 15 November 1972
v WALES............... Ninian Park, Cardiff
Clemence............. Liverpool
Storey .... Arsenal
Hughes .... Liverpool
Hunter............... Leeds United
McFarland .... Derby County
Moore .... West Ham United
Keegan .... Liverpool
Bell .... Manchester City
Chivers............... Tottenham Hotspur
Marsh .... Manchester City
Ball .... Arsenal
Result: 1–0
Scorer: Bell

466. 24 January 1973
v WALES............... Wembley Stadium
Clemence............. Liverpool
Storey .... Arsenal
Hughes .... Liverpool
Hunter............... Leeds United
McFarland .... Derby County
Moore .... West Ham United
Keegan .... Liverpool
Bell .... Manchester City
Chivers............... Tottenham Hotspur
Marsh .... Manchester City
Ball .... Arsenal
Result: 1–1
Scorer: Hunter

467. 14 February 1973
v SCOTLAND............ Hampden Park, Glasgow
Shilton .... Leicester City
Storey .... Arsenal
Hughes .... Liverpool
Bell .... Manchester City
Madeley.............. Leeds United
Moore .... West Ham United
Ball .... Arsenal
Channon .... Southampton
Chivers............... Tottenham Hotspur
Clarke .... Leeds United
Peters .... Tottenham Hotspur

Result: 5–0
Scorers: o.g., Clarke (2), Channon, Chivers

468. 12 May 1973
v N. IRELAND .... Goodison Park, Everton
Shilton .... Leicester City
Storey .... Arsenal
Nish.................. Derby County
Bell .... Manchester City
McFarland .... Derby County
Moore .... West Ham United
Ball .... Arsenal
Channon .... Southampton
Chivers............... Tottenham Hotspur
Richards.............. Wolverhampton Wanderers
Peters .... Tottenham Hotspur
Result: 2–1
Scorers: Chivers (2)

 DID YOU KNOW...?

On 12 May 1973, when England played Northern Ireland at Goodison Park, the game was officially classed as a home match for the Irish. The venue had been switched from Belfast for security reasons.

469. 15 May 1973
v WALES............... Wembley Stadium
Shilton .... Leicester City
Storey .... Arsenal
Hughes .... Liverpool
Bell .... Manchester City
McFarland .... Derby County
Moore .... West Ham United
Ball .... Arsenal
Channon .... Southampton
Chivers............... Tottenham Hotspur
Clarke .... Leeds United
Peters .... Tottenham Hotspur
Result: 3–0
Scorers: Chivers, Channon, Peters

470. 19 May 1973
v SCOTLAND............ Wembley Stadium
Shilton .... Leicester City
Storey .... Arsenal
Hughes .... Liverpool
Bell .... Manchester City
McFarland .... Derby County
Moore .... West Ham United
Ball .... Arsenal
Channon .... Southampton
Chivers............... Tottenham Hotspur
Clarke .... Leeds United
Peters .... Tottenham Hotspur
Result: 1–0
Scorer: Peters

471. 27 May 1973
v CZECHOSLOVAKIA .... Prague
Shilton .... Leicester City
Madeley.............. Leeds United
Storey .... Arsenal
Bell .... Manchester City
McFarland .... Derby County
Moore .... West Ham United
Ball .... Arsenal
Channon .... Southampton
Chivers............... Tottenham Hotspur
Clarke .... Leeds United
Peters .... Tottenham Hotspur
Result: 1–1
Scorer: Clarke

472. 6 June 1973
v POLAND . . . . Chorzów
Shilton . . . . Leicester City
Madeley. . . . . Leeds United
Hughes . . . . Liverpool
Storey . . . . Arsenal
McFarland . . . . Derby County
Moore . . . . West Ham United
Ball . . . . Arsenal
Bell . . . . Manchester City
Chivers. . . . . Tottenham Hotspur
Clarke . . . . Leeds United
Peters . . . . Tottenham Hotspur
Result: 0–2

473. 10 June 1973
v SOVIET UNION . . . . Moscow
Shilton . . . . Leicester City
Madeley. . . . . Leeds United
Hughes . . . . Liverpool
Storey . . . . Arsenal
McFarland . . . . Derby County
Moore . . . . West Ham United
Currie. . . . . Sheffield United
Channon* . . . . Southampton
Chivers. . . . . Tottenham Hotspur
Clarke** . . . . Leeds United
Peters*** . . . . Tottenham Hotspur
Subs: *Summerbee . . . . Manchester City
**Macdonald. . . . . Newcastle United
***Hunter . . . . Leeds United
Result: 2–1
Scorers: Chivers, o.g.

474. 14 June 1973
v ITALY . . . . Turin
Shilton . . . . Leicester City
Madeley. . . . . Leeds United
Hughes . . . . Liverpool
Storey . . . . Arsenal
McFarland . . . . Derby County
Moore . . . . West Ham United
Currie. . . . . Sheffield United
Channon . . . . Southampton
Chivers. . . . . Tottenham Hotspur
Clarke . . . . Leeds United
Peters . . . . Tottenham Hotspur
Result: 0–2

475. 26 September 1973
v AUSTRIA . . . . Wembley Stadium
Shilton . . . . Leicester City
Madeley. . . . . Leeds United
Hughes . . . . Liverpool
Bell . . . . Manchester City
McFarland . . . . Derby County
Hunter . . . . Leeds United
Currie. . . . . Sheffield United
Channon . . . . Southampton
Chivers. . . . . Tottenham Hotspur
Clarke . . . . Leeds United
Peters . . . . Tottenham Hotspur
Result: 7–0
Scorers: Channon (2), Clarke (2), Chivers, Currie, Bell

476. 17 October 1973
v POLAND . . . . Wembley Stadium
Shilton . . . . Leicester City
Madeley. . . . . Leeds United
Hughes . . . . Liverpool
Bell . . . . Manchester City
McFarland . . . . Derby County
Hunter . . . . Leeds United
Currie. . . . . Sheffield United
Channon . . . . Southampton
Chivers* . . . . Tottenham Hotspur

Clarke . . . . Leeds United
Peters . . . . Tottenham Hotspur
Sub: *Hector . . . . Derby County
Result: 1–1
Scorer: Clarke (pen.)

 FEATURED MATCH

17 OCTOBER 1973

ENGLAND 1 POLAND 1 – WEMBLEY STADIUM

By the last game of the qualifying rounds for the 1974 World Cup, after recording a win, a draw and a defeat in earlier matches against group competitors Wales and Poland, for the first time England faced the daunting prospect of failing to reach the finals. The successful 4–3–3 formation that had worked during the 1966 World Cup remained firmly embedded in Sir Alf Ramsey's mind as the functional system for getting results, but continuing with this strategy was no longer proving effective, and the press and public had become increasingly perplexed at his negative attitude and tactics.

In June 1973, when England played in Poland, the team not only lost 2–0, but also had Alan Ball sent off. Thus the task was obvious for the Poles' visit to Wembley – England had to win. Four weeks earlier, the England team had thrashed Austria 7–0, and so Ramsey kept faith with the same starting line-up.

In the event, England dictated the match and indeed should have won, but on the night it seemed that luck was very much against them and they were punished by the Poles for just one bad error. Numerous goalscoring opportunities were created by the home side, but the ball just would not go into the net. England hit the woodwork twice, the ball was cleared off the line four times; Colin Bell, Martin Chivers and Martin Peters all missed open goals, and Jan Tomaszewski, the Polish goalkeeper whom Brian Clough dubbed a 'clown', kept the ball out by both conventional and fortuitous means. Over the ninety minutes, England had won twenty-six corners to Poland's two – a statistic that truly reflected England's domination of the match.

Against all odds, it was Poland who took the lead in the 55th minute, due mainly to a poor error of judgement by Leeds United's Norman Hunter. Instead of kicking the ball into touch, Hunter rashly attempted to dribble round the Polish winger Grzegorz Lato and ended up losing possession needlessly. Lato raced away and launched a diagonal cross for Jan Domarski. His right-foot shot went through Emlyn Hughes's legs, under Shilton's dive and straight into the back of the net. Poland's lead lasted only eight minutes, however, as Adam Musial was deemed guilty of a foul on Peters in the box, and Allan Clarke converted the penalty awarded by referee Vital Loraux.

After Bobby Moore had pleaded with Ramsey to put on a left-sided player, debutant Kevin Hector was catapulted on to the field with just two minutes remaining. Hector nearly achieved immortality as England frantically chased a second goal: another corner and Hector headed goalward, but the ball was once again cleared off the line and Clarke stabbed the rebound wide. A win proved to be agonizingly out of reach for England – their World Cup hopes cruelly dashed.

477. 14 November 1973
v ITALY . . . . Wembley Stadium
Shilton . . . . Leicester City
Madeley . . . . Leeds United
Hughes . . . . Liverpool
Bell . . . . Manchester City
McFarland . . . . Derby County
Moore . . . . West Ham United
Currie . . . . Sheffield United
Channon . . . . Southampton
Osgood . . . . Chelsea
Clarke* . . . . Leeds United
Peters . . . . Tottenham Hotspur
Sub: *Hector . . . . Derby County
Result: 0–1

478. 3 April 1974
v PORTUGAL . . . . Lisbon
Parkes . . . . Queen's Park Rangers
Nish . . . . Derby County
Pejic . . . . Stoke City
Dobson . . . . Burnley
Watson, D. V. . . . . Sunderland
Todd . . . . Derby County
Bowles . . . . Queen's Park Rangers
Channon . . . . Southampton
Macdonald* . . . . Newcastle United
Brooking . . . . West Ham United
Peters . . . . Tottenham Hotspur
Sub: *Ball . . . . Arsenal
Result: 0–0

479. 11 May 1974
v WALES . . . . Ninian Park, Cardiff
Shilton . . . . Leicester City
Nish . . . . Derby County
Pejic . . . . Stoke City
Hughes . . . . Liverpool
McFarland . . . . Derby County
Todd . . . . Derby County
Keegan . . . . Liverpool
Bell . . . . Manchester City
Weller . . . . Leicester City
Bowles . . . . Queen's Park Rangers
Channon . . . . Southampton
Result: 2–0
Scorers: Bowles, Keegan

480. 15 May 1974
v N. IRELAND . . . . Wembley Stadium
Shilton . . . . Leicester City
Nish . . . . Derby County
Pejic . . . . Stoke City
Hughes . . . . Liverpool
McFarland* . . . . Derby County
Todd . . . . Derby County
Keegan . . . . Liverpool
Bell . . . . Manchester City
Channon . . . . Southampton
Bowles** . . . . Queen's Park Rangers
Weller . . . . Leicester City
Subs: *Hunter . . . . Leeds United
**Worthington . . . . Leicester City
Result: 1–0
Scorer: Weller

481. 18 May 1974
v SCOTLAND . . . . Hampden Park, Glasgow
Shilton . . . . Leicester City
Nish . . . . Derby County
Pejic . . . . Stoke City
Hughes . . . . Liverpool
Hunter* . . . . Leeds United
Todd . . . . Derby County

Channon . . . . Southampton
Bell . . . . Manchester City
Worthington** . . . . Leicester City
Weller . . . . Leicester City
Peters . . . . Tottenham Hotspur
Subs: *Watson, D. V. . . . . Sunderland
**Macdonald . . . . Newcastle United
Result: 0–2

482. 22 May 1974
v ARGENTINA . . . . Wembley Stadium
Shilton . . . . Leicester City
Hughes . . . . Liverpool
Lindsay . . . . Liverpool
Todd . . . . Derby County
Watson, D. V. . . . . Sunderland
Bell . . . . Manchester City
Keegan . . . . Liverpool
Channon . . . . Southampton
Worthington . . . . Leicester City
Weller . . . . Leicester City
Brooking . . . . West Ham United
Result: 2–2
Scorers: Channon, Worthington

483. 29 May 1974
v EAST GERMANY . . . . Leipzig
Clemence . . . . Liverpool
Hughes . . . . Liverpool
Lindsay . . . . Liverpool
Todd . . . . Derby County
Watson, D. V. . . . . Sunderland
Dobson . . . . Burnley
Keegan . . . . Liverpool
Channon . . . . Southampton
Worthington . . . . Leicester City
Bell . . . . Manchester City
Brooking . . . . West Ham United
Result: 1–1
Scorer: Channon

484. 1 June 1974
v BULGARIA . . . . Sofia
Clemence . . . . Liverpool
Hughes . . . . Liverpool
Lindsay . . . . Liverpool
Todd . . . . Derby County
Watson, D. V. . . . . Sunderland
Dobson . . . . Burnley
Keegan . . . . Liverpool
Channon . . . . Southampton
Worthington . . . . Leicester City
Bell . . . . Manchester City
Brooking . . . . West Ham United
Result: 1–0
Scorer: Worthington

485. 5 June 1974
v YUGOSLAVIA . . . . Belgrade
Clemence . . . . Liverpool
Hughes . . . . Liverpool
Lindsay . . . . Liverpool
Todd . . . . Derby County
Watson, D. V. . . . . Sunderland
Dobson . . . . Burnley
Keegan . . . . Liverpool
Channon . . . . Southampton
Worthington* . . . . Leicester City
Bell . . . . Manchester City
Brooking . . . . West Ham United
Sub: *Macdonald . . . . Newcastle United
Result: 2–2
Scorers: Channon, Keegan

486. 30 October 1974
v CZECHOSLOVAKIA . . . . Wembley Stadium
Clemence . . . . Liverpool
Madeley . . . . Leeds United
Hughes . . . . Liverpool
Dobson* . . . . Everton
Watson, D. V. . . . . Sunderland
Hunter . . . . Leeds United
Francis, G. . . . . Queen's Park Rangers
Bell . . . . Manchester City
Worthington** . . . . Leicester City
Channon . . . . Southampton
Keegan . . . . Liverpool
Subs: *Brooking . . . . West Ham United
**Thomas . . . . Queen's Park Rangers
Result: 3–0
Scorers: Channon, Bell (2)

487. 20 November 1974
v PORTUGAL . . . . Wembley Stadium
Clemence . . . . Liverpool
Madeley . . . . Leeds United
Cooper* . . . . Leeds United
Bell . . . . Manchester City
Watson, D. V. . . . . Sunderland
Hughes . . . . Liverpool
Francis, G. . . . . Queen's Park Rangers
Channon . . . . Southampton
Clarke** . . . . Leeds United
Brooking . . . . West Ham United
Thomas . . . . Queen's Park Rangers
Subs: *Todd . . . . Derby County
**Worthington . . . . Leicester City
Result: 0–0

488. 12 March 1975
v WEST GERMANY . . . . Wembley Stadium
Clemence . . . . Liverpool
Whitworth . . . . Leicester City
Gillard . . . . Queen's Park Rangers
Bell . . . . Manchester City
Watson, D.V. . . . . Sunderland
Todd . . . . Derby County
Ball . . . . Arsenal
Channon . . . . Southampton
Macdonald . . . . Newcastle United
Hudson . . . . Stoke City
Keegan . . . . Liverpool
Result: 2–0
Scorers: Bell, Macdonald

⚽ **DID YOU KNOW...?**

When England beat West Germany 2–0 on 12
March 1975, it was the 100th international held at
Wembley Stadium.

489. 16 April 1975
v CYPRUS . . . . Wembley Stadium
Shilton . . . . Stoke City
Madeley . . . . Leeds United
Beattie . . . . Ipswich Town
Bell . . . . Manchester City
Watson, D. V. . . . . Sunderland
Todd . . . . Derby County
Ball . . . . Arsenal
Channon* . . . . Southampton
Macdonald . . . . Newcastle United
Hudson . . . . Stoke City
Keegan . . . . Liverpool
Sub: *Thomas . . . . Queen's Park Rangers

Result: 5–0
Scorers: Macdonald (5)

490. 11 May 1975
v CYPRUS . . . . Limassol
Clemence . . . . Liverpool
Whitworth . . . . Leicester City
Beattie* . . . . Ipswich Town
Bell . . . . Manchester City
Watson, D. V. . . . . Sunderland
Todd . . . . Derby County
Ball . . . . Arsenal
Channon . . . . Southampton
Macdonald . . . . Newcastle United
Keegan** . . . . Liverpool
Thomas . . . . Queen's Park Rangers
Subs: *Hughes . . . . Liverpool
**Tueart . . . . Manchester City
Result: 1–0
Scorer: Keegan

491. 17 May 1975
v N. IRELAND . . . . Windsor Park, Belfast
Clemence . . . . Liverpool
Whitworth . . . . Leicester City
Hughes . . . . Liverpool
Bell . . . . Manchester City
Watson, D. V. . . . . Sunderland
Todd . . . . Derby County
Ball . . . . Arsenal
Viljoen . . . . Ipswich Town
Macdonald* . . . . Newcastle United
Keegan . . . . Liverpool
Tueart . . . . Manchester City
Sub: *Channon . . . . Southampton
Result: 0–0

492. 21 May 1975
v WALES . . . . Wembley Stadium
Clemence . . . . Liverpool
Whitworth . . . . Leicester City
Gillard . . . . Queen's Park Rangers
Francis, G. . . . . Queen's Park Rangers
Watson, D. V. . . . . Sunderland
Todd . . . . Derby County
Ball . . . . Arsenal
Channon* . . . . Southampton
Johnson . . . . Ipswich Town
Viljoen . . . . Ipswich Town
Thomas . . . . Queen's Park Rangers
Sub: *Little . . . . Aston Villa
Result: 2–2
Scorers: Johnson (2)

493. 24 May 1975
v SCOTLAND . . . . Wembley Stadium
Clemence . . . . Liverpool
Whitworth . . . . Leicester City
Beattie . . . . Ipswich Town
Bell . . . . Manchester City
Watson, D. V. . . . . Sunderland
Todd . . . . Derby County
Ball . . . . Arsenal
Channon . . . . Southampton
Johnson . . . . Ipswich Town
Francis, G. . . . . Queen's Park Rangers
Keegan* . . . . Liverpool
Sub: *Thomas . . . . Queen's Park Rangers
Result: 5–1
Scorers: G. Francis (2), Beattie, Bell, Johnson

494. 3 September 1975
v SWITZERLAND . . . . Basle
Clemence . . . . Liverpool
Whitworth . . . . Leicester City
Beattie . . . . Ipswich Town

Todd . . . . Derby County
Watson, D. V. . . . . Manchester City
Francis, G. . . . . Queen's Park Rangers
Bell . . . . Manchester City
Channon . . . . Southampton
Johnson* . . . . Ipswich Town
Currie. . . . . Sheffield United
Keegan . . . . Liverpool
Sub: *Macdonald. . . . . Newcastle United
Result: 2–1
Scorers: Keegan, Channon

495. 30 October 1975

v CZECHOSLOVAKIA . . . . Bratislava
Clemence. . . . . Liverpool
Madeley. . . . . Leeds United
Gillard . . . . Queen's Park Rangers
Todd . . . . Derby County
McFarland* . . . . Derby County
Francis, G. . . . . Queen's Park Rangers
Bell . . . . Manchester City
Channon** . . . . Southampton
Macdonald. . . . . Newcastle United
Clarke . . . . Leeds United
Keegan . . . . Liverpool
Subs: *Watson, D. V. . . . . Manchester City
**Thomas . . . . Queen's Park Rangers
Result: 1–2
Scorer: Channon

496. 19 November 1975

v PORTUGAL. . . . . Lisbon
Clemence. . . . . Liverpool
Whitworth . . . . Leicester City
Beattie. . . . . Ipswich Town
Madeley*. . . . . Leeds United
Watson, D. V. . . . . Manchester City
Todd . . . . Derby County
Keegan . . . . Liverpool
Channon . . . . Southampton
Macdonald** . . . . Newcastle United
Francis, G. . . . . Queen's Park Rangers
Brooking . . . . West Ham United
Subs: *Thomas . . . . Queen's Park Rangers
**Clarke . . . . Leeds United
Result: 1–1
Scorer: Channon

497. 24 March 1976

v WALES. . . . . Racecourse Ground,
Wrexham
Clemence. . . . . Liverpool
Cherry* . . . . Leeds United
Neal. . . . . Liverpool
Mills . . . . Ipswich Town
Thompson . . . . Liverpool
Doyle. . . . . Manchester City
Keegan . . . . Liverpool
Channon** . . . . Southampton
Boyer. . . . . Norwich City
Brooking . . . . West Ham United
Kennedy, R. . . . . Liverpool
Subs: *Clement . . . . Queen's Park Rangers
**Taylor. . . . . Crystal Palace
Result: 2–1
Scorers: Kennedy, Taylor

498. 8 May 1976

v WALES. . . . . Ninian Park, Cardiff
Clemence. . . . . Liverpool
Clement. . . . . Queen's Park Rangers
Mills . . . . Ipswich Town
Thompson . . . . Liverpool
Greenhoff, B. . . . . Manchester United
Kennedy, R. . . . . Liverpool
Keegan . . . . Liverpool

Francis, G. . . . . Queen's Park Rangers
Pearson . . . . Manchester United
Towers. . . . . Sunderland
Taylor. . . . . Crystal Palace
Result: 1–0
Scorer: Taylor

499. 11 May 1976

v N. IRELAND . . . . Wembley Stadium
Clemence. . . . . Liverpool
Todd . . . . Derby County
Mills . . . . Ipswich Town
Thompson . . . . Liverpool
Greenhoff, B. . . . . Manchester United
Kennedy, R. . . . . Liverpool
Keegan*. . . . . Liverpool
Channon . . . . Southampton
Pearson . . . . Manchester United
Francis, G. . . . . Queen's Park Rangers
Taylor**. . . . . Crystal Palace
Subs: *Royle . . . . Manchester City
**Towers. . . . . Sunderland
Result: 4–0
Scorers: G. Francis, Channon (2 – 1 pen.), Pearson

500. 15 May 1976

v SCOTLAND. . . . . Hampden Park, Glasgow
Clemence. . . . . Liverpool
Todd . . . . Derby County
Mills . . . . Ipswich Town
Thompson . . . . Liverpool
McFarland* . . . . Derby County
Kennedy, R. . . . . Liverpool
Keegan . . . . Liverpool
Channon . . . . Southampton
Pearson** . . . . Manchester United
Francis, G. . . . . Queen's Park Rangers
Taylor. . . . . Crystal Palace
Subs: *Doyle . . . . Manchester City
**Cherry . . . . Leeds United
Result: 1–2
Scorer: Channon

501. 23 May 1976

v BRAZIL. . . . . Los Angeles
Clemence. . . . . Liverpool
Todd . . . . Derby County
Mills . . . . Ipswich Town
Thompson . . . . Liverpool
Doyle. . . . . Manchester City
Cherry . . . . Leeds United
Keegan . . . . Liverpool
Channon . . . . Southampton
Pearson . . . . Manchester United
Brooking . . . . West Ham United
Francis, G. . . . . Queen's Park Rangers
Result: 0–1

502. 28 May 1976

v ITALY. . . . . New York City
Rimmer* . . . . Arsenal
Clement. . . . . Queen's Park Rangers
Neal. . . . . Liverpool
Doyle. . . . . Manchester City
Thompson . . . . Liverpool
Towers. . . . . Sunderland
Wilkins. . . . . Chelsea
Channon . . . . Southampton
Royle . . . . Manchester City
Brooking . . . . West Ham United
Hill**. . . . . Manchester United
Subs: *Corrigan . . . . Manchester City
**Mills . . . . Ipswich Town
Result: 3–2
Scorers: Channon (2), Thompson

503. **13 June 1976**
v FINLAND . . . . Helsinki
Clemence. . . . . Liverpool
Todd . . . . Derby County
Mills . . . . Ipswich Town
Thompson . . . . Liverpool
Madeley. . . . . Leeds United
Cherry . . . . Leeds United
Francis, G. . . . . Queen's Park Rangers
Channon . . . . Southampton
Pearson . . . . Manchester United
Brooking . . . . West Ham United
Keegan . . . . Liverpool
Result: 4–1
Scorers: Pearson, Keegan (2), Channon

504. **8 September 1976**
v EIRE. . . . . Wembley Stadium
Clemence. . . . . Liverpool
Todd . . . . Derby County
Cherry . . . . Leeds United
Greenhoff, B. . . . . Manchester United
McFarland . . . . Derby County
Madeley. . . . . Leeds United
Keegan . . . . Liverpool
Wilkins. . . . . Chelsea
Pearson . . . . Manchester United
Brooking . . . . West Ham United
George* . . . . Derby County
Sub: *Hill. . . . . Manchester United
Result: 1–1
Scorer: Pearson

505. **13 October 1976**
v FINLAND . . . . Wembley Stadium
Clemence. . . . . Liverpool
Todd . . . . Derby County
Beattie. . . . . Ipswich Town
Thompson . . . . Liverpool
Greenhoff, B. . . . . Manchester United
Wilkins. . . . . Chelsea
Keegan . . . . Liverpool
Channon . . . . Southampton
Royle . . . . Manchester City
Brooking* . . . . West Ham United
Tueart** . . . . Manchester City
Subs: *Mills. . . . . Ipswich Town
**Hill. . . . . Manchester United
Result: 2–1
Scorers: Tueart, Royle

506. **17 November 1976**
v ITALY. . . . . Rome
Clemence. . . . . Liverpool
Clement* . . . . Queen's Park Rangers
Mills . . . . Ipswich Town
Greenhoff, B. . . . . Manchester United
McFarland . . . . Derby County
Hughes . . . . Liverpool
Keegan . . . . Liverpool
Channon . . . . Southampton
Bowles. . . . . Queen's Park Rangers
Cherry . . . . Leeds United
Brooking . . . . West Ham United
Sub: *Beattie. . . . . Ipswich Town
Result: 0–2

507. **9 February 1977**
v HOLLAND . . . . Wembley Stadium
Clemence. . . . . Liverpool
Clement. . . . . Queen's Park Rangers
Beattie. . . . . Ipswich Town
Doyle. . . . . Manchester City
Watson, D. V. . . . . Manchester City
Madeley*. . . . . Leeds United
Keegan . . . . Liverpool

Francis, T. . . . . Birmingham City
Greenhoff, B.** . . . . Manchester United
Bowles. . . . . Queen's Park Rangers
Brooking . . . . West Ham United
Subs: *Pearson . . . . Manchester United
**Todd . . . . Derby County
Result: 0–2

508. **30 March 1977**
v LUXEMBOURG . . . . Wembley Stadium
Clemence. . . . . Liverpool
Gidman . . . . Aston Villa
Cherry . . . . Leeds United
Kennedy, R. . . . . Liverpool
Watson, D. V. . . . . Manchester City
Hughes . . . . Liverpool
Keegan . . . . Liverpool
Channon . . . . Southampton
Royle* . . . . Manchester City
Francis, T. . . . . Birmingham City
Hill. . . . . Manchester United
Sub: *Mariner . . . . Ipswich Town
Result: 5–0
Scorers: Keegan, T. Francis, Kennedy, Channon (2 – 1 pen.)

509. **28 May 1977**
v N. IRELAND . . . . Windsor Park, Belfast
Shilton . . . . Stoke City
Cherry . . . . Leeds United
Mills . . . . Ipswich Town
Greenhoff, B. . . . . Manchester United
Watson, D. V. . . . . Manchester City
Todd . . . . Derby County
Wilkins* . . . . Chelsea
Channon . . . . Southampton
Mariner . . . . Ipswich Town
Brooking . . . . West Ham United
Tueart . . . . Manchester City
Sub: *Talbot . . . . Ipswich Town
Result: 2–1
Scorers: Channon, Tueart

510. **31 May 1977**
v WALES. . . . . Wembley Stadium
Shilton . . . . Stoke City
Neal. . . . . Liverpool
Mills . . . . Ipswich Town
Greenhoff, B. . . . . Manchester United
Watson, D. V. . . . . Manchester City
Hughes . . . . Liverpool
Keegan . . . . SV Hamburg
Channon . . . . Southampton
Pearson . . . . Manchester United
Brooking* . . . . West Ham United
Kennedy, R. . . . . Liverpool
Sub: *Tueart . . . . Manchester City
Result: 0–1

511. **4 June 1977**
v SCOTLAND. . . . . Wembley Stadium
Clemence. . . . . Liverpool
Neal. . . . . Liverpool
Mills . . . . Ipswich Town
Greenhoff, B.* . . . . Manchester United
Watson, D. V. . . . . Manchester City
Hughes . . . . Liverpool
Francis, T. . . . . Birmingham City
Channon . . . . Southampton
Pearson . . . . Manchester United
Talbot . . . . Ipswich Town
Kennedy, R.** . . . . Liverpool
Subs: *Cherry . . . . Leeds United
**Tueart . . . . Manchester City
Result: 1–2
Scorer: Channon (pen.)

512. 8 June 1977
v BRAZIL. . . . . Rio de Janeiro
    Clemence. . . . . Liverpool
    Neal. . . . . Liverpool
    Cherry . . . . Leeds United
    Greenhoff, B. . . . . Manchester United
    Watson, D. V. . . . . Manchester City
    Hughes . . . . Liverpool
    Keegan . . . . SV Hamburg
    Francis, T. . . . . Birmingham City
    Pearson* . . . . Manchester United
    Wilkins** . . . . Chelsea
    Talbot . . . . Ipswich Town
Subs: *Channon . . . . Southampton
    **Kennedy, R. . . . . Liverpool
Result: 0–0

513. 12 June 1977
v ARGENTINA. . . . . Buenos Aires
    Clemence. . . . . Liverpool
    Neal. . . . . Liverpool
    Cherry . . . . Leeds United
    Greenhoff, B.* . . . . Manchester United
    Watson, D. V. . . . . Manchester City
    Hughes . . . . Liverpool
    Keegan . . . . SV Hamburg
    Channon . . . . Southampton
    Pearson . . . . Manchester United
    Wilkins. . . . . Chelsea
    Talbot . . . . Ipswich Town
Sub: *Kennedy, R. . . . . Liverpool
Result: 1–1
Scorer: Pearson

514. 15 June 1977
v URUGUAY . . . . Montevideo
    Clemence. . . . . Liverpool
    Neal. . . . . Liverpool
    Cherry . . . . Leeds United
    Greenhoff, B. . . . . Manchester United
    Watson, D. V. . . . . Manchester City
    Hughes . . . . Liverpool
    Keegan . . . . SV Hamburg
    Channon . . . . Manchester City
    Pearson . . . . Manchester United
    Wilkins. . . . . Chelsea
    Talbot . . . . Ipswich Town
Result: 0–0

515. 7 September 1977
v SWITZERLAND . . . . Wembley Stadium
    Clemence. . . . . Liverpool
    Neal. . . . . Liverpool
    Cherry . . . . Leeds United
    McDermott. . . . . Liverpool
    Watson, D. V. . . . . Manchester City
    Hughes . . . . Liverpool
    Keegan . . . . SV Hamburg
    Channon* . . . . Manchester City
    Francis, T. . . . . Birmingham City
    Kennedy, R. . . . . Liverpool
    Callaghan** . . . . Liverpool
Subs: *Hill. . . . . Manchester United
    **Wilkins. . . . . Chelsea
Result: 0–0

516. 12 October 1977
v LUXEMBOURG . . . . Luxembourg
    Clemence. . . . . Liverpool
    Cherry . . . . Leeds United
    Hughes . . . . Liverpool
    Watson, D. V.* . . . . Manchester City
    Kennedy, R. . . . . Liverpool
    Callaghan, I.. . . . . Liverpool
    McDermott** . . . . Liverpool
    Wilkins. . . . . Chelsea

    Mariner . . . . Ipswich Town
    Francis, T. . . . . Birmingham City
    Hill. . . . . Manchester United
Subs: *Beattie . . . . Ipswich Town
    **Whymark . . . . Ipswich Town
Result: 2–0
Scorers: R. Kennedy, Mariner

517. 16 November 1977
v ITALY . . . . Wembley Stadium
    Clemence. . . . . Liverpool
    Neal. . . . . Liverpool
    Cherry . . . . Leeds United
    Wilkins. . . . . Chelsea
    Watson, D.V.. . . . . Manchester City
    Hughes . . . . Liverpool
    Keegan* . . . . SV Hamburg
    Coppell . . . . Manchester United
    Latchford** . . . . Everton
    Brooking . . . . West Ham United
    Barnes, P. . . . . Manchester City
Subs: *Francis, T. . . . . Birmingham City
    **Pearson . . . . Manchester United
Result: 2–0
Scorers: Keegan, Brooking

518. 22 February 1978
v WEST GERMANY . . . . Munich
    Clemence. . . . . Liverpool
    Neal. . . . . Liverpool
    Mills . . . . Ipswich Town
    Wilkins. . . . . Chelsea
    Watson, D. V. . . . . Manchester City
    Hughes . . . . Liverpool
    Keegan* . . . . SV Hamburg
    Coppell . . . . Manchester United
    Pearson . . . . Manchester United
    Brooking . . . . West Ham United
    Barnes, P. . . . . Manchester City
Sub: *Francis, T. . . . . Birmingham City
Result: 1–2
Scorer: Pearson

519. 19 April 1978
v BRAZIL. . . . . Wembley Stadium
    Corrigan. . . . . Manchester City
    Mills . . . . Ipswich Town
    Cherry . . . . Leeds United
    Greenhoff, B. . . . . Manchester United
    Watson, D. V. . . . . Manchester City
    Currie. . . . . Leeds United
    Keegan . . . . SV Hamburg
    Coppell . . . . Manchester United
    Latchford . . . . Everton
    Francis, T. . . . . Birmingham City
    Barnes, P. . . . . Manchester City
Result: 1–1
Scorer: Keegan

520. 13 May 1978
v WALES. . . . . Ninian Park, Cardiff
    Shilton . . . . Nottingham Forest
    Mills . . . . Ipswich Town
    Cherry* . . . . Leeds United
    Greenhoff, B. . . . . Manchester United
    Watson, D. V. . . . . Manchester City
    Wilkins. . . . . Chelsea
    Coppell . . . . Manchester United
    Francis, T. . . . . Birmingham City
    Latchford** . . . . Everton
    Brooking . . . . West Ham United
    Barnes, P. . . . . Manchester City
Subs: *Currie. . . . . Leeds United
    **Mariner . . . . Ipswich Town
Result: 3–1
Scorer: Latchford, Currie, P. Barnes

521. 16 May 1978
v N. IRELAND . . . . Wembley Stadium
Clemence. . . . . Liverpool
Neal. . . . . Liverpool
Mills . . . . Ipswich Town
Greenhoff, B. . . . . Manchester United
Watson, D. V. . . . . Manchester City
Hughes . . . . Liverpool
Coppell . . . . Manchester United
Wilkins. . . . . Chelsea
Pearson . . . . Manchester United
Currie. . . . . Leeds United
Woodcock . . . . Nottingham Forest
Result: 1–0
Scorer: Neal

522. 20 May 1978
v SCOTLAND. . . . . Hampden Park, Glasgow
Clemence. . . . . Liverpool
Neal. . . . . Liverpool
Mills . . . . Ipswich Town
Wilkins. . . . . Chelsea
Watson, D. V. . . . . Manchester City
Hughes* . . . . Liverpool
Coppell . . . . Manchester United
Currie. . . . . Leeds United
Mariner** . . . . Ipswich Town
Francis, T. . . . . Birmingham City
Barnes, P. . . . . Manchester City
Subs: *Greenhoff. . . . . Manchester United
**Brooking . . . . West Ham United
Result: 1–0
Scorer: Coppell

523. 24 May 1978
v HUNGARY . . . . Wembley Stadium
Shilton. . . . . Nottingham Forest
Neal. . . . . Liverpool
Mills . . . . Ipswich Town
Wilkins. . . . . Chelsea
Watson, D. V.* . . . . Manchester City
Hughes . . . . Liverpool
Keegan . . . . SV Hamburg
Coppell** . . . . Manchester United
Francis, T. . . . . Birmingham City
Brooking . . . . West Ham United
Barnes, P. . . . . Manchester City
Subs: *Greenhoff. . . . . Manchester United
**Currie. . . . . Leeds United
Result: 4–1
Scorers: P. Barnes, Neal (pen.), T. Francis, Currie

524. 20 September 1978
v DENMARK . . . . Copenhagen
Clemence. . . . . Liverpool
Neal. . . . . Liverpool
Mills . . . . Ipswich Town
Wilkins. . . . . Chelsea
Watson, D. V. . . . . Manchester City
Hughes . . . . Liverpool
Keegan . . . . SV Hamburg
Coppell . . . . Manchester United
Latchford . . . . Everton
Brooking . . . . West Ham United
Barnes, P. . . . . Manchester City
Result: 4–3
Scorers: Keegan (2), Neal, Latchford

525. 25 October 1978
v EIRE. . . . . Lansdowne Road, Dublin
Clemence. . . . . Liverpool
Neal. . . . . Liverpool
Mills . . . . Ipswich Town
Wilkins. . . . . Chelsea

Watson, D. V.* . . . . Manchester City
Hughes . . . . Liverpool
Keegan . . . . SV Hamburg
Coppell . . . . Manchester United
Latchford . . . . Everton
Brooking . . . . West Ham United
Barnes, P.** . . . . Manchester City
Subs: *Thompson . . . . Liverpool
**Woodcock . . . . Nottingham Forest
Result: 1–1
Scorer: Latchford

526. 29 November 1978
v CZECHOSLOVAKIA . . . . . . Wembley Stadium
Shilton. . . . . Nottingham Forest
Anderson . . . . Nottingham Forest
Cherry . . . . Leeds United
Thompson . . . . Liverpool
Watson, D. V. . . . . Manchester City
Wilkins. . . . . Chelsea
Keegan . . . . SV Hamburg
Coppell . . . . Manchester United
Woodcock* . . . . Nottingham Forest
Currie. . . . . Leeds United
Barnes, P. . . . . Manchester City
Sub: *Latchford . . . . Everton
Result: 1–0
Scorer: Coppell

527. 7 February 1979
v N. IRELAND . . . . Wembley Stadium
Clemence. . . . . Liverpool
Neal. . . . . Liverpool
Mills . . . . Ipswich Town
Currie. . . . . Leeds United
Watson, D. V. . . . . Manchester City
Hughes . . . . Liverpool
Keegan . . . . SV Hamburg
Coppell . . . . Manchester United
Latchford . . . . Everton
Brooking . . . . West Ham United
Barnes, P. . . . . Manchester City
Result: 4–0
Scorers: Keegan, Latchford (2), D. V. Watson

528. 19 May 1979
v N. IRELAND . . . . Windsor Park, Belfast
Clemence. . . . . Liverpool
Neal. . . . . Liverpool
Mills . . . . Ipswich Town
Thompson . . . . Liverpool
Watson, D. V. . . . . Manchester City
Currie. . . . . Leeds United
Coppell . . . . Manchester United
Wilkins. . . . . Chelsea
Latchford . . . . Everton
McDermott. . . . . Liverpool
Barnes, P. . . . . Manchester City
Result: 2–0
Scorers: D. V. Watson, Coppell

529. 23 May 1979
v WALES. . . . . Wembley Stadium
Corrigan. . . . . Manchester City
Cherry . . . . Leeds United
Sansom . . . . Crystal Palace
Currie. . . . . Leeds United
Watson, D. V. . . . . Manchester City
Hughes . . . . Liverpool
Keegan* . . . . SV Hamburg
Wilkins**. . . . . Chelsea
Latchford . . . . Everton
McDermott. . . . . Liverpool
Cunningham . . . . West Bromwich Albion

Subs: *Coppell. . . . . Manchester United
**Brooking . . . . West Ham United
Result: 0–0

530. 26 May 1979
v SCOTLAND. . . . . Wembley Stadium
Clemence. . . . . Liverpool
Neal. . . . . Liverpool
Mills . . . . Ipswich Town
Thompson . . . . Liverpool
Watson, D. V. . . . . Manchester City
Wilkins. . . . . Chelsea
Coppell . . . . Manchester United
Keegan . . . . SV Hamburg
Latchford . . . . Everton
Brooking . . . . West Ham United
Barnes, P. . . . . Manchester City
Result: 3–1
Scorers: P. Barnes, Coppell, Keegan

531. 6 June 1979
v BULGARIA . . . . Sofia
Clemence. . . . . Liverpool
Neal. . . . . Liverpool
Mills . . . . Ipswich Town
Thompson . . . . Liverpool
Watson, D. V. . . . . Manchester City
Wilkins. . . . . Chelsea
Keegan . . . . SV Hamburg
Coppell . . . . Manchester United
Latchford* . . . . Everton
Brooking . . . . West Ham United
Barnes, P.** . . . . Manchester City
Subs: *Francis, T. . . . . Nottingham Forest
**Woodcock . . . . Nottingham Forest
Result: 3–0
Scorers: Keegan, D. V. Watson, P. Barnes

532. 10 June 1979
v SWEDEN . . . . Solna
Shilton . . . . Nottingham Forest
Anderson . . . . Nottingham Forest
Cherry . . . . Leeds United
McDermott* . . . . Liverpool
Watson, D. V.** . . . . Manchester City
Hughes . . . . Liverpool
Keegan . . . . SV Hamburg
Currie*** . . . . Leeds United
Francis, T. . . . . Nottingham Forest
Woodcock . . . . Nottingham Forest
Cunningham . . . . West Bromwich Albion
Subs: *Wilkins. . . . . Chelsea
**Thompson . . . . Liverpool
***Brooking . . . . West Ham United
Result: 0–0

533. 13 June 1979
v AUSTRIA . . . . Vienna
Shilton* . . . . Nottingham Forest
Neal. . . . . Liverpool
Mills . . . . Ipswich Town
Thompson . . . . Liverpool
Watson, D. V. . . . . Manchester City
Wilkins. . . . . Chelsea
Keegan . . . . SV Hamburg
Coppell . . . . Manchester United
Latchford** . . . . Everton
Brooking . . . . West Ham United
Barnes, P.*** . . . . Manchester City
Subs: *Clemence . . . . Liverpool
**Francis, T. . . . . Nottingham Forest
***Cunningham . . . . West Bromwich Albion
Result: 3–4
Scorers: Keegan, Coppell, Wilkins

534. 9 September 1979
v DENMARK . . . . Wembley Stadium
Clemence. . . . . Liverpool
Neal. . . . . Liverpool
Mills . . . . Ipswich Town
Thompson . . . . Liverpool
Watson, D. V. . . . . Werder Bremen
Wilkins. . . . . Manchester United
McDermott. . . . . Liverpool
Coppell . . . . Manchester United
Keegan . . . . SV Hamburg
Brooking . . . . West Ham United
Barnes, P. . . . . West Bromwich Albion
Result: 1–0
Scorer: Keegan

535. 17 October 1979
v N. IRELAND . . . . Windsor Park, Belfast
Shilton . . . . Nottingham Forest
Neal. . . . . Liverpool
Mills . . . . Ipswich Town
Thompson . . . . Liverpool
Watson, D. V. . . . . Southampton
Wilkins. . . . . Manchester United
Keegan . . . . SV Hamburg
Coppell . . . . Manchester United
Francis, T. . . . . Nottingham Forest
Brooking* . . . . West Ham United
Woodcock . . . . Nottingham Forest
Sub: *McDermott . . . . Liverpool
Result: 5–1
Scorers: T. Francis (2), o.g., Woodcock (2)

536. 22 November 1979
v BULGARIA . . . . Wembley Stadium
Clemence. . . . . Liverpool
Anderson . . . . Nottingham Forest
Sansom . . . . Crystal Palace
Thompson . . . . Liverpool
Watson, D. V. . . . . Southampton
Wilkins. . . . . Manchester United
Reeves. . . . . Norwich City
Hoddle. . . . . Tottenham Hotspur
Francis, T. . . . . Nottingham Forest
Kennedy, R. . . . . Liverpool
Woodcock . . . . FC Cologne
Result: 2–0
Scorers: D. V. Watson, Hoddle

 DID YOU KNOW...?

The first match ever to be postponed at Wembley was the England–Bulgaria game of 21 November 1979. Owing to a heavy fog, the match was played the following day.

537. 6 February 1980
v EIRE. . . . . Wembley Stadium
Clemence. . . . . Liverpool
Cherry . . . . Leeds United
Sansom . . . . Crystal Palace
Thompson . . . . Liverpool
Watson, D. V. . . . . Southampton
Robson . . . . West Bromwich Albion
Keegan . . . . SV Hamburg
McDermott. . . . . Liverpool
Johnson* . . . . Liverpool
Woodcock . . . . FC Cologne
Cunningham . . . . Real Madrid
Sub: *Coppell . . . . Manchester United
Result: 2–0
Scorers: Keegan (2)

538. 26 March 1980
v SPAIN . . . . Barcelona
Shilton. . . . . Nottingham Forest
Neal*. . . . . Liverpool
Mills . . . . Ipswich Town
Thompson . . . . Liverpool
Watson, D. V. . . . . Southampton
Wilkins. . . . . Manchester United
Keegan . . . . SV Hamburg
Coppell . . . . Manchester United
Francis, T.** . . . . Nottingham Forest
Kennedy, R. . . . . Liverpool
Woodcock . . . . FC Cologne
Subs: *Hughes. . . . . Wolverhampton Wanderers
**Cunningham . . . . Real Madrid
Result: 2–0
Scorers: Woodcock, T. Francis

539. 13 May 1980
v ARGENTINA. . . . . Wembley Stadium
Clemence. . . . . Liverpool
Neal*. . . . . Liverpool
Sansom . . . . Crystal Palace
Thompson . . . . Liverpool
Watson, D. V. . . . . Southampton
Wilkins. . . . . Manchester United
Keegan . . . . SV Hamburg
Coppell . . . . Manchester United
Johnson** . . . . Liverpool
Woodcock . . . . FC Cologne
Kennedy, R.*** . . . . Liverpool
Subs: *Cherry . . . . Leeds United
**Birtles . . . . Nottingham Forest
***Brooking . . . . West Ham United
Result: 3–1
Scorers: Johnson (2), Keegan

540. 17 May 1980
v WALES. . . . . Racecourse Ground,
Wrexham
Clemence. . . . . Liverpool
Neal*. . . . . Liverpool
Cherry . . . . Leeds United
Thompson . . . . Liverpool
Lloyd** . . . . Nottingham Forest
Hoddle. . . . . Tottenham Hotspur
Brooking . . . . West Ham United
Kennedy, R. . . . . Liverpool
Coppell . . . . Manchester United
Mariner . . . . Ipswich Town
Barnes, P. . . . . West Bromwich Albion
Subs: *Sansom . . . . Crystal Palace
**Wilkins. . . . . Manchester United
Result: 1–4
Scorer: Mariner

⚽ **DID YOU KNOW...?**

During the 1979–80 season, England rejected an
invitation to play in a special tournament in
Uruguay featuring all the countries that had won
the World Cup.

541. 20 May 1980
v N. IRELAND . . . . Wembley Stadium
Corrigan. . . . . Manchester City
Cherry . . . . Leeds United
Sansom . . . . Crystal Palace
Brooking . . . . West Ham United
Watson, D. V. . . . . Southampton
Hughes . . . . Wolverhampton Wanderers

McDermott. . . . . Liverpool
Wilkins. . . . . Manchester United
Johnson . . . . Liverpool
Reeves* . . . . Manchester City
Devonshire. . . . . West Ham United
Sub: *Mariner . . . . Ipswich Town
Result: 1–1
Scorer: Johnson

542. 24 May 1980
v SCOTLAND. . . . . Hampden Park, Glasgow
Clemence. . . . . Liverpool
Cherry . . . . Leeds United
Sansom . . . . Crystal Palace
Thompson . . . . Liverpool
Watson, D. V. . . . . Southampton
Wilkins. . . . . Manchester United
Coppell . . . . Manchester United
McDermott. . . . . Liverpool
Johnson . . . . Liverpool
Mariner* . . . . Ipswich Town
Brooking . . . . West Ham United
Sub: *Hughes . . . . Wolverhampton Wanderers
Result: 2–0
Scorers: Brooking, Coppell

543. 31 May 1980
v AUSTRALIA . . . . Sydney
Corrigan. . . . . Manchester City
Cherry . . . . Leeds United
Lampard . . . . West Ham United
Talbot . . . . Arsenal
Osman. . . . . Ipswich Town
Butcher . . . . Ipswich Town
Robson* . . . . West Bromwich Albion
Sunderland**. . . . . Arsenal
Mariner . . . . Ipswich Town
Hoddle. . . . . Tottenham Hotspur
Armstrong*** . . . . Middlesbrough
Subs: *Greenhoff. . . . . Leeds United
**Ward . . . . Brighton & Hove Albion
***Devonshire. . . . . West Ham United
Result: 2–1
Scorers: Hoddle, Mariner

544. 12 June 1980
v BELGIUM. . . . . Turin
Clemence. . . . . Liverpool
Neal. . . . . Liverpool
Sansom . . . . Crystal Palace
Thompson . . . . Liverpool
Watson, D. V. . . . . Southampton
Wilkins. . . . . Manchester United
Keegan . . . . SV Hamburg
Coppell* . . . . Manchester United
Johnson** . . . . Liverpool
Brooking . . . . West Ham United
Woodcock . . . . FC Cologne
Subs: *McDermott. . . . . Liverpool
**Kennedy. . . . . Liverpool
Result: 1–1
Scorer: Wilkins

545. 15 June 1980
v ITALY. . . . . Turin
Shilton. . . . . Nottingham Forest
Neal. . . . . Liverpool
Sansom . . . . Crystal Palace
Thompson . . . . Liverpool
Watson, D. V. . . . . Southampton
Wilkins. . . . . Manchester United
Keegan . . . . SV Hamburg
Coppell . . . . Manchester United
Birtles* . . . . Nottingham Forest
Kennedy, R. . . . . Liverpool
Woodcock . . . . FC Cologne

Sub: *Mariner . . . . Ipswich Town
Result: 0–1

546. **18 June 1980**
v SPAIN . . . . Naples
Clemence. . . . . Liverpool
Anderson* . . . . Nottingham Forest
Mills . . . . Ipswich Town
Thompson . . . . Liverpool
Watson, D. V. . . . . Southampton
Wilkins. . . . . Manchester United
Keegan . . . . SV Hamburg
McDermott. . . . . Liverpool
Woodcock . . . . FC Cologne
Brooking . . . . West Ham United
Hoddle**. . . . . Tottenham Hotspur
Subs: *Cherry . . . . Leeds United
**Mariner . . . . Ipswich Town
Result: 2–1
Scorers: Brooking, Woodcock

547. **10 September 1980**
v NORWAY . . . . Wembley Stadium
Shilton. . . . . Nottingham Forest
Anderson . . . . Nottingham Forest
Sansom . . . . Arsenal
Thompson . . . . Liverpool
Watson, D. V. . . . . Southampton
Robson . . . . West Bromwich Albion
Gates. . . . . Ipswich Town
McDermott. . . . . Liverpool
Mariner . . . . Ipswich Town
Woodcock . . . . FC Cologne
Rix. . . . . Arsenal
Result: 4–0
Scorers: McDermott (2 – 1 pen.), Woodcock, Mariner

548. **15 October 1980**
v ROMANIA . . . . Bucharest
Clemence. . . . . Liverpool
Neal. . . . . Liverpool
Sansom . . . . Arsenal
Thompson . . . . Liverpool
Watson, D. V. . . . . Southampton
Robson . . . . West Bromwich Albion
Rix. . . . . Arsenal
McDermott. . . . . Liverpool
Birtles* . . . . Nottingham Forest
Woodcock . . . . FC Cologne
Gates** . . . . Ipswich Town
Subs: *Cunningham. . . . . . . Real Madrid
**Coppell . . . . Manchester United
Result: 1–2
Scorer: Woodcock

549. **19 November 1980**
v SWITZERLAND . . . . Wembley Stadium
Shilton. . . . . Nottingham Forest
Neal. . . . . Liverpool
Sansom . . . . Arsenal
Robson . . . . West Bromwich Albion
Watson, D. V. . . . . Southampton
Mills . . . . Ipswich Town
Coppell . . . . Manchester United
McDermott. . . . . Liverpool
Mariner . . . . Ipswich Town
Brooking* . . . . West Ham United
Woodcock . . . . FC Cologne
Sub: *Rix. . . . . Arsenal
Result: 2–1
Scorers: Mariner, o.g.

550. **25 March 1981**
v SPAIN . . . . Wembley Stadium
Clemence. . . . . Liverpool
Neal. . . . . Liverpool

Sansom . . . . Arsenal
Robson . . . . West Bromwich Albion
Osman. . . . . Ipswich Town
Butcher . . . . Ipswich Town
Keegan . . . . Southampton
Francis, T.* . . . . Nottingham Forest
Mariner . . . . Ipswich Town
Brooking** . . . . West Ham United
Hoddle. . . . . Tottenham Hotspur
Subs: *Barnes, P. . . . . West Bromwich Albion
**Wilkins. . . . . Manchester United
Result: 1–2
Scorer: Hoddle

551. **29 April 1981**
v ROMANIA . . . . Wembley Stadium
Shilton. . . . . Nottingham Forest
Anderson . . . . Nottingham Forest
Sansom . . . . Arsenal
Robson . . . . West Bromwich Albion
Watson, D. V. . . . . Southampton
Osman. . . . . Ipswich Town
Wilkins. . . . . Manchester United
Brooking* . . . . West Ham United
Coppell . . . . Manchester United
Francis, T. . . . . Nottingham Forest
Woodcock . . . . FC Cologne
Sub: *McDermott . . . . Liverpool
Result: 0–0

552. **12 May 1981**
v BRAZIL. . . . . Wembley Stadium
Clemence. . . . . Liverpool
Neal. . . . . Liverpool
Sansom . . . . Arsenal
Robson . . . . West Bromwich Albion
Martin . . . . West Ham United
Wilkins. . . . . Manchester United
Coppell . . . . Manchester United
McDermott. . . . . Liverpool
Withe. . . . . Aston Villa
Rix. . . . . Arsenal
Barnes, P. . . . . West Bromwich Albion
Result: 0–1

553. **20 May 1981**
v WALES. . . . . Wembley Stadium
Corrigan. . . . . Manchester City
Anderson . . . . Nottingham Forest
Sansom . . . . Arsenal
Robson . . . . West Bromwich Albion
Watson, D. V. . . . . Southampton
Wilkins. . . . . Manchester United
Coppell . . . . Manchester United
Hoddle. . . . . Tottenham Hotspur
Withe*. . . . . Aston Villa
Rix. . . . . Arsenal
Barnes, P. . . . . West Bromwich Albion
Sub: *Woodcock . . . . FC Cologne
Result: 0–0

554. **23 May 1981**
v SCOTLAND. . . . . Wembley Stadium
Corrigan. . . . . Manchester City
Anderson . . . . Nottingham Forest
Sansom . . . . Arsenal
Wilkins. . . . . Manchester United
Watson, D. V.* . . . . Southampton
Robson . . . . West Bromwich Albion
Coppell . . . . Manchester United
Hoddle. . . . . Tottenham Hotspur
Withe. . . . . Aston Villa
Woodcock** . . . . FC Cologne
Rix. . . . . Arsenal
Subs: *Martin . . . . West Ham United
**Francis . . . . Nottingham Forest
Result: 0–1

555. 30 May 1981
v SWITZERLAND . . . . Basle
Clemence . . . . Liverpool
Mills . . . . Ipswich Town
Sansom . . . . Arsenal
Wilkins . . . . Manchester United
Watson, D. V.* . . . . Southampton
Osman . . . . Ipswich Town
Coppell . . . . Manchester United
Keegan . . . . Southampton
Mariner . . . . Ipswich Town
Francis, T.** . . . . Nottingham Forest
Robson . . . . West Bromwich Albion
Subs: *Barnes, P. . . . . West Bromwich Albion
**McDermott . . . . Liverpool
Result: 1–2
Scorer: McDermott

556. 6 June 1981
v HUNGARY . . . . Budapest
Clemence . . . . Liverpool
Neal . . . . Liverpool
Mills . . . . Ipswich Town
Thompson . . . . Liverpool
Watson, D. V. . . . . Southampton
Robson . . . . West Bromwich Albion
Keegan . . . . Southampton
Coppell . . . . Manchester United
Mariner . . . . Ipswich Town
Brooking* . . . . West Ham United
McDermott . . . . Liverpool
Sub: *Wilkins . . . . Manchester United
Result: 3–1
Scorers: Brooking (2), Keegan (pen.)

557. 9 September 1981
v NORWAY . . . . Oslo
Clemence . . . . Tottenham Hotspur
Neal . . . . Liverpool
Mills . . . . Ipswich Town
Thompson . . . . Liverpool
Osman . . . . Ipswich Town
Robson . . . . West Bromwich Albion
Keegan . . . . Southampton
Francis, T. . . . . Manchester City
Mariner* . . . . Ipswich Town
Hoddle** . . . . Tottenham Hotspur
McDermott . . . . Liverpool
Subs: *Withe . . . . Aston Villa
**Barnes, P. . . . . Leeds United
Result: 1–2
Scorer: Robson

558. 18 November 1981
v HUNGARY . . . . Wembley Stadium
Shilton . . . . Nottingham Forest
Neal . . . . Liverpool
Mills . . . . Ipswich Town
Thompson . . . . Liverpool
Martin . . . . West Ham United
Robson . . . . Manchester United
Keegan . . . . Southampton
Coppell* . . . . Manchester United
Mariner . . . . Ipswich Town
Brooking . . . . West Ham United
McDermott . . . . Liverpool
Sub: *Morley . . . . Aston Villa
Result: 1–0
Scorer: Mariner

559. 23 February 1982
v N. IRELAND . . . . Wembley Stadium
Clemence . . . . Tottenham Hotspur
Anderson . . . . Nottingham Forest
Sansom . . . . Arsenal
Wilkins . . . . Manchester United

Watson, D. V. . . . . Stoke City
Foster . . . . Brighton & Hove Albion
Keegan . . . . Southampton
Robson . . . . Manchester United
Francis, T.* . . . . Manchester City
Hoddle . . . . Tottenham Hotspur
Morley** . . . . Aston Villa
Subs: *Regis . . . . West Bromwich Albion
**Woodcock . . . . FC Cologne
Result: 4–0
Scorers: Robson, Keegan, Hoddle, Wilkins

560. 27 April 1982
v WALES . . . . Ninian Park, Cardiff
Corrigan . . . . Manchester City
Neal . . . . Liverpool
Sansom . . . . Arsenal
Thompson . . . . Liverpool
Butcher . . . . Ipswich Town
Robson . . . . Manchester United
Wilkins . . . . Manchester United
Francis, T.* . . . . Manchester City
Withe . . . . Aston Villa
Hoddle** . . . . Tottenham Hotspur
Morley . . . . Aston Villa
Subs: *Regis . . . . West Bromwich Albion
**McDermott . . . . Liverpool
Result: 1–0
Scorer: T. Francis

561. 25 May 1982
v HOLLAND . . . . Wembley Stadium
Shilton . . . . Nottingham Forest
Neal . . . . Liverpool
Sansom . . . . Arsenal
Thompson . . . . Liverpool
Foster . . . . Brighton & Hove Albion
Robson . . . . Manchester United
Wilkins . . . . Manchester United
Devonshire* . . . . West Ham United
Mariner** . . . . Ipswich Town
McDermott . . . . Liverpool
Woodcock . . . . FC Cologne
Subs: *Rix . . . . Arsenal
**Barnes, P. . . . . Leeds United
Result: 2–0
Scorers: Mariner, Woodcock

562. 29 May 1982
v SCOTLAND . . . . Hampden Park, Glasgow
Shilton . . . . Nottingham Forest
Mills . . . . Ipswich Town
Sansom . . . . Arsenal
Thompson . . . . Liverpool
Butcher . . . . Ipswich Town
Robson . . . . Manchester United
Keegan* . . . . Southampton
Coppell . . . . Manchester United
Mariner** . . . . Ipswich Town
Brooking . . . . West Ham United
Wilkins . . . . Manchester United
Subs: *McDermott . . . . Liverpool
**Francis . . . . Manchester City
Result: 1–0
Scorer: Mariner

563. 2 June 1982
v ICELAND . . . . Reykjavik
Corrigan . . . . Manchester City
Anderson . . . . Nottingham Forest
Neal . . . . Liverpool
Watson, D. V. . . . . Stoke City
Osman . . . . Ipswich Town
McDermott . . . . Liverpool
Hoddle . . . . Tottenham Hotspur
Devonshire* . . . . West Ham United

Withe.................. Aston Villa
Regis**.............. West Bromwich Albion
Morley................ Aston Villa
Subs: *Perryman.......... Tottenham Hotspur
**Goddard............. West Ham United
Result: 1–1
Scorer: Goddard

564. 3 June 1982
v FINLAND.............. Helsinki
Clemence.............. Tottenham Hotspur
Mills.................. Ipswich Town
Sansom................ Arsenal
Thompson.............. Liverpool
Martin................ West Ham United
Robson*............... Manchester United
Keegan................ Southampton
Coppell**............. Manchester United
Mariner............... Ipswich Town
Brooking***........... West Ham United
Wilkins............... Manchester United
Subs: *Rix................ Arsenal
**Francis............. Manchester City
***Woodcock........... FC Cologne
Result: 4–1
Scorers: Robson (2), Mariner (2)

565. 16 June 1982
v FRANCE............... Bilbao
Shilton............... Nottingham Forest
Mills................. Ipswich Town
Sansom*............... Arsenal
Thompson.............. Liverpool
Butcher............... Ipswich Town
Robson................ Manchester United
Coppell............... Manchester United
Francis, T............ Manchester City
Mariner............... Ipswich Town
Rix................... Arsenal
Wilkins............... Manchester United
Sub: *Neal.............. Liverpool
Result: 3–1
Scorers: Robson (2), Mariner

566. 20 June 1982
v CZECHOSLOVAKIA...... Bilbao
Shilton............... Nottingham Forest
Mills................. Ipswich Town
Sansom................ Arsenal
Thompson.............. Liverpool
Butcher............... Ipswich Town
Robson*............... Manchester United
Coppell............... Manchester United
Francis, T............ Manchester City
Mariner............... Ipswich Town
Rix................... Arsenal
Wilkins............... Manchester United
Sub: *Hoddle........... Tottenham Hotspur
Result: 2–0
Scorers: T. Francis, o.g.

567. 25 June 1982
v KUWAIT.............. Bilbao
Shilton............... Nottingham Forest
Neal.................. Liverpool
Mills................. Ipswich Town
Thompson.............. Liverpool
Foster................ Brighton & Hove Albion
Hoddle................ Tottenham Hotspur
Coppell............... Manchester United
Francis, T............ Manchester City
Mariner............... Ipswich Town
Rix................... Arsenal
Wilkins............... Manchester United
Result: 1–0
Scorer: T. Francis

 FEATURED MATCH

16 JUNE 1982

FRANCE 1 ENGLAND 3 – BILBAO, SPAIN

After missing out on World Cup qualification in two consecutive tournaments, England's eventual return in 1982 was received with welcome relief at home and abroad. In their first match against France, they made an instant impact by scoring the World Cup's quickest ever goal.

Red-shirted England won a throw-in straight from the kick-off. Steve Coppell threw it long into the French penalty area, where Terry Butcher at the near post headed back for Manchester United's Bryan Robson to run in and score with an outstretched left foot after just twenty-seven seconds. It was a superb start for England, who had arrived in Spain following a seven-match unbeaten run. In the 24th minute, however, the French drew level. Jean-François Larios intercepted Trevor Francis's midfield pass and laid it off to Alain Giresse. He hit a long pass forward for Gérard Soler, who had caught out the English defence with his run, and he advanced to strike a low shot past Peter Shilton.

Patrick Battiston for France plus Phil Thompson and Coppell for England also went close with other first-half chances, while Butcher was booked for upending France's scorer Soler just before the break.

Manager Ron Greenwood then made a tactical switch at half-time which would tip the balance in England's favour. Graham Rix was asked to drop deeper in midfield, in order to enable the release of Robson and Ray Wilkins to go forward. Consequently, England were able to come out and create more chances: Francis had a shot blocked by Jean-Luc Ettori, the French goalkeeper, and Wilkins hit the rebound over the bar, while Coppell put in a volley that Ettori saved down by his post, and Rix set up Francis for a shot that was inches off target.

In the 67th minute, after sustained pressure, England reclaimed their well-earned lead when Francis glided a cross into the penalty area, where Robson, once again, raced in to score with a flying header. Seven minutes from time, England sealed the win with a third goal. Rix hit a high cross to the far post for Wilkins, who passed the ball to Francis to shoot. The shot was deflected off Marius Trésor and ran on to Ipswich Town's Paul Mariner, who duly scored his eleventh England goal in twenty-two games.

England played out the game comfortably in possession. Both Mariner and Rix could have added to the score and increased the margin of victory, but their shots were respectively saved and wide.

568. 29 June 1982
v WEST GERMANY........ Madrid
Shilton............... Nottingham Forest
Mills................. Ipswich Town
Sansom................ Arsenal
Thompson.............. Liverpool
Butcher............... Ipswich Town
Robson................ Manchester United
Coppell............... Manchester United
Francis, T.*.......... Manchester City
Mariner............... Ipswich Town
Rix................... Arsenal
Wilkins............... Manchester United
Sub: *Woodcock......... FC Cologne
Result: 0–0

569. 5 July 1982
v SPAIN . . . . Madrid
Shilton . . . . Nottingham Forest
Mills . . . . Ipswich Town
Sansom . . . . Arsenal
Thompson . . . . Liverpool
Butcher . . . . Ipswich Town
Robson . . . . Manchester United
Rix* . . . . Arsenal
Francis, T. . . . . Manchester City
Mariner . . . . Ipswich Town
Woodcock** . . . . FC Cologne
Wilkins . . . . Manchester United
Subs: *Brooking . . . . West Ham United
**Keegan . . . . Southampton
Result: 0–0

570. 22 September 1982
v DENMARK . . . . Copenhagen
Shilton . . . . Southampton
Neal . . . . Liverpool
Sansom . . . . Arsenal
Wilkins . . . . Manchester United
Osman . . . . Ipswich Town
Butcher . . . . Ipswich Town
Morley* . . . . Aston Villa
Robson . . . . Manchester United
Mariner . . . . Ipswich Town
Francis, T. . . . . Sampdoria
Rix . . . . Arsenal
Sub: *Hill, R. . . . . Luton Town
Result: 2–2
Scorers: T. Francis (2)

571. 13 October 1982
v WEST GERMANY . . . . Wembley Stadium
Shilton . . . . Southampton
Mabbutt . . . . Tottenham Hotspur
Sansom . . . . Arsenal
Thompson . . . . Liverpool
Butcher . . . . Ipswich Town
Wilkins . . . . Manchester United
Hill, R. . . . . Luton Town
Regis* . . . . West Bromwich Albion
Mariner** . . . . Ipswich Town
Armstrong*** . . . . Southampton
Devonshire . . . . West Ham United
Subs: *Blissett . . . . Watford
**Woodcock . . . . Arsenal
***Rix . . . . Arsenal
Result: 1–2
Scorer: Woodcock

572. 17 November 1982
v GREECE . . . . Thessalonika
Shilton . . . . Southampton
Neal . . . . Liverpool
Sansom . . . . Arsenal
Thompson . . . . Liverpool
Martin . . . . West Ham United
Robson . . . . Manchester United
Lee . . . . Liverpool
Mabbutt . . . . Tottenham Hotspur
Mariner . . . . Ipswich Town
Woodcock . . . . Arsenal
Morley . . . . Aston Villa
Result: 3–0
Scorers: Woodcock (2), Lee

573. 15 December 1982
v LUXEMBOURG . . . . Wembley Stadium
Clemence . . . . Tottenham Hotspur
Neal . . . . Liverpool
Sansom . . . . Arsenal
Martin . . . . West Ham United
Butcher . . . . Ipswich Town

Robson . . . . Manchester United
Lee . . . . Liverpool
Mabbutt* . . . . Tottenham Hotspur
Blissett . . . . Watford
Coppell** . . . . Manchester United
Woodcock . . . . Arsenal
Subs: *Hoddle . . . . Tottenham Hotspur
**Chamberlain . . . . Stoke City
Result: 9–0
Scorers: Blissett (3), Woodcock, Coppell, Hoddle, o.g.,
Chamberlain, Neal

574. 23 February 1983
v WALES . . . . Wembley Stadium
Shilton . . . . Southampton
Neal . . . . Liverpool
Statham . . . . West Bromwich Albion
Lee . . . . Liverpool
Martin . . . . West Ham United
Butcher . . . . Ipswich Town
Mabbutt . . . . Tottenham Hotspur
Blissett . . . . Watford
Mariner . . . . Ipswich Town
Cowans . . . . Aston Villa
Devonshire . . . . West Ham United
Result: 2–1
Scorers: Butcher, Neal (pen.)

575. 30 March 1983
v GREECE . . . . Wembley Stadium
Shilton . . . . Southampton
Neal . . . . Liverpool
Sansom . . . . Arsenal
Lee . . . . Liverpool
Martin . . . . West Ham United
Butcher . . . . Ipswich Town
Coppell . . . . Manchester United
Mabbutt . . . . Tottenham Hotspur
Francis, T. . . . . Sampdoria
Woodcock* . . . . Arsenal
Devonshire** . . . . West Ham United
Subs: *Blissett . . . . Watford
**Rix . . . . Arsenal
Result: 0–0

576. 27 April 1983
v HUNGARY . . . . Wembley Stadium
Shilton . . . . Southampton
Neal . . . . Liverpool
Sansom . . . . Arsenal
Lee . . . . Liverpool
Martin . . . . West Ham United
Butcher . . . . Ipswich Town
Mabbutt . . . . Tottenham Hotspur
Francis, T. . . . . Sampdoria
Withe . . . . Aston Villa
Blissett . . . . Watford
Cowans . . . . Aston Villa
Result: 2–0
Scorers: T. Francis, Withe

577. 28 May 1983
v N. IRELAND . . . . Windsor Park, Belfast
Shilton . . . . Southampton
Neal . . . . Liverpool
Sansom . . . . Arsenal
Hoddle . . . . Tottenham Hotspur
Roberts . . . . Tottenham Hotspur
Butcher . . . . Ipswich Town
Mabbutt . . . . Tottenham Hotspur
Francis, T. . . . . Sampdoria
Withe . . . . Aston Villa
Blissett* . . . . Watford
Cowans . . . . Aston Villa
Sub: *Barnes, J. . . . . Watford
Result: 0–0

578. 1 June 1983

v SCOTLAND . . . . Wembley Stadium
Shilton . . . . Southampton
Neal . . . . Liverpool
Sansom . . . . Arsenal
Lee . . . . Liverpool
Roberts . . . . Tottenham Hotspur
Butcher . . . . Ipswich Town
Robson* . . . . Manchester United
Francis, T. . . . . Sampdoria
Withe** . . . . Aston Villa
Hoddle . . . . Tottenham Hotspur
Cowans . . . . Aston Villa
Subs: *Mabbutt . . . . Tottenham Hotspur
**Blissett . . . . Watford
Result: 2–0
Scorers: Robson, Cowans

579. 12 June 1983

v AUSTRALIA . . . . Sydney
Shilton . . . . Southampton
Thomas . . . . Coventry City
Statham* . . . . West Bromwich Albion
Williams . . . . Southampton
Osman . . . . Ipswich Town
Butcher . . . . Ipswich Town
Barham . . . . Norwich City
Gregory . . . . Queen's Park Rangers
Blissett** . . . . Watford
Francis, T. . . . . Sampdoria
Cowans . . . . Aston Villa
Subs: *Barnes, J. . . . . Watford
**Walsh . . . . Luton Town
Result: 0–0

580. 15 June 1983

v AUSTRALIA . . . . Brisbane
Shilton . . . . Southampton
Neal . . . . Liverpool
Statham* . . . . West Bromwich Albion
Barham . . . . Norwich City
Osman . . . . Ipswich Town
Butcher . . . . Ipswich Town
Gregory . . . . Queen's Park Rangers
Francis, T. . . . . Sampdoria
Walsh . . . . Luton Town
Cowans . . . . Aston Villa
Barnes, J. . . . . Watford
Sub: *Williams . . . . Southampton
Result: 1–0
Scorer: Walsh

581. 19 June 1983

v AUSTRALIA . . . . Melbourne
Shilton* . . . . Southampton
Neal** . . . . Liverpool
Pickering . . . . Sunderland
Osman . . . . Ipswich Town
Butcher . . . . Ipswich Town
Lee . . . . Liverpool
Gregory . . . . Queen's Park Rangers
Cowans . . . . Aston Villa
Francis, T. . . . . Sampdoria
Walsh*** . . . . Luton Town
Barnes, J. . . . . Watford
Subs: *Spink . . . . Aston Villa
**Thomas . . . . Coventry City
***Blissett . . . . Watford
Result: 1–1
Scorer: T. Francis

582. 21 September 1983

v DENMARK . . . . Wembley Stadium
Shilton . . . . Southampton
Neal . . . . Liverpool
Sansom . . . . Arsenal
Lee* . . . . Liverpool

Osman . . . . Ipswich Town
Butcher . . . . Ipswich Town
Wilkins . . . . Manchester United
Gregory . . . . Queen's Park Rangers
Mariner . . . . Ipswich Town
Francis, T. . . . . Sampdoria
Barnes, J.** . . . . Watford
Subs: *Chamberlain . . . . Stoke City
**Blissett . . . . AC Milan
Result: 0–1

583. 12 October 1983

v HUNGARY . . . . Budapest
Shilton . . . . Southampton
Gregory . . . . Queen's Park Rangers
Sansom . . . . Arsenal
Butcher . . . . Ipswich Town
Martin . . . . West Ham United
Lee . . . . Liverpool
Robson . . . . Manchester United
Hoddle . . . . Tottenham Hotspur
Mariner . . . . Ipswich Town
Mabbutt . . . . Tottenham Hotspur
Blissett* . . . . AC Milan
Sub: *Withe . . . . Aston Villa
Result: 3–0
Scorers: Hoddle, Lee, Mariner

584. 16 November 1983

v LUXEMBOURG . . . . Luxembourg
Clemence . . . . Liverpool
Duxbury . . . . Manchester United
Sansom . . . . Arsenal
Lee . . . . Liverpool
Martin . . . . West Ham United
Butcher . . . . Ipswich Town
Robson . . . . Manchester United
Hoddle . . . . Tottenham Hotspur
Mariner . . . . Ipswich Town
Woodcock* . . . . Arsenal
Devonshire . . . . West Ham United
Sub: *Barnes, J. . . . . Watford
Result: 4–0
Scorers: Robson (2), Mariner, Butcher

585. 29 February 1984

v FRANCE . . . . Paris
Shilton . . . . Southampton
Duxbury . . . . Manchester United
Sansom . . . . Arsenal
Lee* . . . . Liverpool
Roberts . . . . Tottenham Hotspur
Butcher . . . . Ipswich Town
Robson . . . . Manchester United
Stein** . . . . Luton Town
Walsh . . . . Liverpool
Hoddle . . . . Tottenham Hotspur
Williams . . . . Southampton
Sub: *Barnes, J. . . . . Watford
**Woodcock . . . . Arsenal
Result: 0–2

586. 4 April 1984

v N. IRELAND . . . . Wembley Stadium
Shilton . . . . Southampton
Anderson . . . . Nottingham Forest
Kennedy, A. . . . . Liverpool
Lee . . . . Liverpool
Roberts . . . . Tottenham Hotspur
Butcher . . . . Ipswich Town
Robson . . . . Manchester United
Wilkins . . . . Manchester United
Francis, T. . . . . Sampdoria
Woodcock . . . . Arsenal
Rix . . . . Arsenal
Result: 1–0
Scorer: Woodcock

587. 2 May 1984
v WALES . . . . Racecourse Ground,
Wrexham
Shilton . . . . Southampton
Duxbury . . . . Manchester United
Kennedy, A. . . . . Liverpool
Lee . . . . Liverpool
Martin* . . . . West Ham United
Wright, M. . . . . Southampton
Gregory . . . . Queen's Park Rangers
Wilkins. . . . . Manchester United
Walsh . . . . Luton Town
Woodcock . . . . Arsenal
Armstrong** . . . . Southampton
Subs: *Fenwick . . . . Queen's Park Rangers
**Blissett. . . . . AC Milan
Result: 0–1

 FEATURED MATCH

10 JUNE 1984

BRAZIL 0 ENGLAND 2 – MARACANÃ STADIUM, RIO DE JANEIRO

England came to the home of Brazilian football, the famed Maracanã Stadium in Rio, to teach the host nation a lesson in a friendly that would be remembered as one of England's all-time outstanding performances on foreign soil.

Described by one newspaper as coming 'from a different planet', Brazil faced an England side staunch in defence and bold in attack. Manager Bobby Robson had gambled by playing two young wingers in Watford's John Barnes and Mark Chamberlain of Stoke City, and it was the former player who became the hero of the hour. Barnes, playing in only his tenth international, had attacked the Brazilian defence a number of times during the early stages of the game, but it was his solo run just before half-time, comprising a mazy dribble that took him across the field from his left-wing berth, which opened many people's eyes. Beating defender after defender, quiet gasps of appreciation could be heard as Barnes eventually found himself one-on-one with keeper Roberto Costa. To the relief of all the England fans, he made no mistake with the scoring opportunity.

During the second half the Watford winger also ensured that England didn't let their advantage slip, putting in a decisive cross – after a Ray Wilkins and Tony Woodcock combination – for centre forward Mark Hateley to nod decisively home in the 62nd minute. If Barnes had taken a leaf out of Brazil's coaching manual for his first effort, then England's second key strike was a typical Football League goal.

The Brazilians came back strongly, but the England defence, featuring an outstanding performance from Norwich City's Dave Watson on his international debut, held firm. Although the home side was missing one or two key players, this fact detracted not one bit from a thrilling England win. As Bobby Robson explained: 'It was an unbelievable performance. We were under pressure for the first twenty minutes, but held firm before going on to win. It was one of the most important moments in my life.'

588. 26 May 1984
v SCOTLAND . . . . Hampden Park, Glasgow
Shilton . . . . Southampton
Duxbury . . . . Manchester United
Sansom . . . . Arsenal
Wilkins. . . . . Manchester United
Roberts . . . . Tottenham Hotspur
Fenwick . . . . Queen's Park Rangers
Chamberlain*. . . . . Stoke City
Robson . . . . Manchester United
Woodcock** . . . . Arsenal
Blissett. . . . . AC Milan
Barnes, J. . . . . Watford
Subs: *Hunt. . . . . West Bromwich Albion
**Lineker. . . . . Leicester City
Result: 1–1
Scorer: Woodcock

589. 2 June 1984
v SOVIET UNION . . . . Wembley Stadium
Shilton . . . . Southampton
Duxbury . . . . Manchester United
Sansom . . . . Arsenal
Wilkins. . . . . Manchester United
Roberts . . . . Tottenham Hotspur
Fenwick . . . . Queen's Park Rangers
Chamberlain . . . . Stoke City
Robson . . . . Manchester United
Francis, T.* . . . . Sampdoria
Blissett. . . . . AC Milan
Barnes, J.** . . . . Watford
Subs: *Hateley. . . . . Portsmouth
**Hunt . . . . West Bromwich Albion
Result: 0–2

590. 10 June 1984
v BRAZIL. . . . . Rio de Janeiro
Shilton . . . . Southampton
Duxbury . . . . Manchester United
Sansom . . . . Arsenal
Wilkins. . . . . Manchester United
Watson, D. . . . . Norwich City
Fenwick . . . . Queen's Park Rangers
Robson . . . . Manchester United
Chamberlain . . . . Stoke City
Hateley . . . . Portsmouth
Woodcock* . . . . Arsenal
Barnes, J. . . . . Watford
Sub: *Allen, C. . . . . Queen's Park Rangers
Result: 2–0
Scorers: J. Barnes, Hateley

591. 13 June 1984
v URUGUAY . . . . Montevideo
Shilton . . . . Southampton
Duxbury . . . . Manchester United
Sansom . . . . Arsenal
Wilkins. . . . . Manchester United
Watson, D. . . . . Norwich City
Fenwick . . . . Queen's Park Rangers
Robson . . . . Manchester United
Chamberlain*. . . . . Stoke City
Hateley . . . . Portsmouth
Allen, C. . . . . Queen's Park Rangers
Barnes, J. . . . . Watford
Sub: *Woodcock . . . . Arsenal
Result: 0–2

592. 17 June 1984
v CHILE. . . . . Santiago
Shilton . . . . Southampton
Duxbury . . . . Manchester United
Sansom . . . . Arsenal
Wilkins. . . . . Manchester United
Watson, D. . . . . Norwich City

Fenwick . . . . Queen's Park Rangers
Robson . . . . Manchester United
Chamberlain* . . . . Stoke City
Hateley . . . . Portsmouth
Allen, C. . . . . Queen's Park Rangers
Barnes, J. . . . . Watford
Sub: *Lee . . . . Liverpool
Result: 0–0

593. 12 September 1984
v EAST GERMANY . . . . Wembley Stadium
Shilton . . . . Southampton
Duxbury . . . . Manchester United
Sansom . . . . Arsenal
Williams . . . . Southampton
Wright, M. . . . . Southampton
Butcher . . . . Ipswich Town
Robson . . . . Manchester United
Wilkins . . . . AC Milan
Mariner* . . . . Arsenal
Woodcock** . . . . Arsenal
Barnes, J. . . . . Watford
Subs: *Hateley . . . . AC Milan
**Francis . . . . Sampdoria
Result: 1–0
Scorer: Robson

594. 17 October 1984
v FINLAND . . . . Wembley Stadium
Shilton . . . . Southampton
Duxbury* . . . . Manchester United
Sansom . . . . Arsenal
Williams . . . . Southampton
Wright, M. . . . . Southampton
Butcher . . . . Ipswich Town
Robson** . . . . Manchester United
Wilkins . . . . AC Milan
Hateley . . . . AC Milan
Woodcock . . . . Arsenal
Barnes, J. . . . . Watford
Subs: *Stevens, G. A. . . . . . . Tottenham Hotspur
**Chamberlain . . . . Stoke City
Result: 5–0
Scorers: Hateley (2), Woodcock, Robson, Sansom

595. 14 November 1984
v TURKEY . . . . Istanbul
Shilton . . . . Southampton
Anderson . . . . Arsenal
Sansom . . . . Arsenal
Williams* . . . . Southampton
Wright, M. . . . . Southampton
Butcher . . . . Ipswich Town
Robson . . . . Manchester United
Wilkins . . . . AC Milan
Withe** . . . . Aston Villa
Woodcock . . . . Arsenal
Barnes, J. . . . . Watford
Subs: *Stevens, G. A. . . . . . . Tottenham Hotspur
**Francis . . . . Sampdoria
Result: 8–0
Scorers: Robson (3), Woodcock (2), J. Barnes (2),
Anderson

596. 27 February 1985
v N. IRELAND . . . . Windsor Park, Belfast
Shilton . . . . Southampton
Anderson . . . . Arsenal
Sansom . . . . Arsenal
Wilkins . . . . AC Milan
Martin . . . . West Ham United
Butcher . . . . Ipswich Town
Steven . . . . Everton
Stevens, G. A. . . . . Tottenham Hotspur
Hateley . . . . AC Milan

Woodcock* . . . . Arsenal
Barnes, J. . . . . Watford
Sub: *Francis . . . . Sampdoria
Result: 1–0
Scorer: Hateley

597. 26 March 1985
v EIRE . . . . Wembley Stadium
Bailey . . . . Manchester United
Anderson . . . . Arsenal
Sansom . . . . Arsenal
Steven . . . . Everton
Wright, M. . . . . Southampton
Butcher . . . . Ipswich Town
Robson* . . . . Manchester United
Wilkins . . . . AC Milan
Hateley** . . . . AC Milan
Lineker . . . . Leicester City
Waddle . . . . Newcastle United
Subs: *Hoddle . . . . Tottenham Hotspur
**Davenport . . . . Nottingham Forest
Result: 2–1
Scorers: Steven, Lineker

598. 1 May 1985
v ROMANIA . . . . Bucharest
Shilton . . . . Southampton
Anderson . . . . Arsenal
Sansom . . . . Arsenal
Steven . . . . Everton
Wright, M. . . . . Southampton
Butcher . . . . Ipswich Town
Robson . . . . Manchester United
Wilkins . . . . AC Milan
Mariner* . . . . Arsenal
Francis, T. . . . . Sampdoria
Barnes** . . . . Watford
Subs: *Lineker . . . . Leicester City
**Waddle . . . . Newcastle United
Result: 0–0

599. 22 May 1985
v FINLAND . . . . Helsinki
Shilton . . . . Southampton
Anderson . . . . Arsenal
Sansom . . . . Arsenal
Steven* . . . . Everton
Fenwick . . . . Queen's Park Rangers
Butcher . . . . Ipswich Town
Robson . . . . Manchester United
Wilkins . . . . AC Milan
Hateley . . . . AC Milan
Francis, T. . . . . Sampdoria
Barnes, J. . . . . Watford
Sub: *Waddle . . . . Newcastle United
Result: 1–1
Scorer: Hateley

600. 25 May 1985
v SCOTLAND . . . . Hampden Park, Glasgow
Shilton . . . . Southampton
Anderson . . . . Arsenal
Sansom . . . . Arsenal
Hoddle* . . . . Tottenham Hotspur
Fenwick . . . . Queen's Park Rangers
Butcher . . . . Ipswich Town
Robson . . . . Manchester United
Wilkins . . . . AC Milan
Hateley . . . . AC Milan
Francis, T. . . . . Sampdoria
Barnes, J.** . . . . Watford
Subs: *Lineker . . . . Leicester City
**Waddle . . . . Newcastle United
Result: 0–1

601. 6 June 1985

v ITALY	Mexico City
Shilton	Southampton
Stevens, M. G.	Everton
Sansom	Arsenal
Steven*	Everton
Wright, M.	Southampton
Butcher	Ipswich Town
Robson	Manchester United
Wilkins	AC Milan
Hateley	AC Milan
Francis, T.**	Sampdoria
Waddle***	Newcastle United
Subs: *Hoddle	Tottenham Hotspur
**Lineker	Leicester City
***Barnes, J.	Watford

Result: 1–2
Scorer: Hateley

602. 9 June 1985

v MEXICO	Mexico City
Bailey	Manchester United
Anderson	Arsenal
Sansom*	Arsenal
Hoddle*	Tottenham Hotspur
Fenwick	Queen's Park Rangers
Watson, D.	Norwich City
Robson	Manchester United
Wilkins**	AC Milan
Hateley	AC Milan
Francis, T.	Sampdoria
Barnes, J.***	Watford
Subs: *Dixon	Chelsea
**Reid	Everton
***Waddle	Newcastle United

Result: 0–1

603. 12 June 1985

v WEST GERMANY	Mexico City
Shilton	Southampton
Stevens, M. G.	Everton
Sansom	Arsenal
Hoddle	Tottenham Hotspur
Wright, M.	Southampton
Butcher	Ipswich Town
Robson*	Manchester United
Reid	Everton
Dixon	Chelsea
Lineker**	Leicester City
Waddle	Newcastle United
Subs: *Bracewell	Everton
**Barnes, J.	Watford

Result: 3–0
Scorers: Robson, Dixon (2)

604. 16 June 1985

v USA	Los Angeles
Woods	Norwich City
Anderson	Arsenal
Sansom*	Arsenal
Hoddle**	Tottenham Hotspur
Fenwick	Queen's Park Rangers
Butcher	Ipswich Town
Robson***	Manchester United
Bracewell	Everton
Dixon	Chelsea
Lineker	Leicester City
Waddle****	Newcastle United
Subs: *Watson, D.	Norwich City
**Steven	Everton
***Reid	Everton
****Barnes, J.	Watford

Result: 5–0
Scorers: Lineker (2), Dixon (2), Steven

605. 11 September 1985

v ROMANIA	Wembley Stadium
Shilton	Southampton
Stevens, M. G.	Everton
Sansom	Arsenal
Fenwick	Queen's Park Rangers
Wright, M.	Southampton
Hoddle	Tottenham Hotspur
Robson	Manchester United
Reid	Everton
Hateley	AC Milan
Lineker*	Everton
Waddle**	Tottenham Hotspur
Subs: *Woodcock	Arsenal
**Barnes, J.	Watford

Result: 1–1
Scorer: Hoddle

606. 16 October 1985

v TURKEY	Wembley Stadium
Shilton	Southampton
Stevens, M. G.	Everton
Sansom	Arsenal
Hoddle	Tottenham Hotspur
Wright, M.	Southampton
Fenwick	Queen's Park Rangers
Robson*	Manchester United
Wilkins	AC Milan
Hateley**	AC Milan
Lineker	Everton
Waddle	Tottenham Hotspur
Subs: *Steven	Everton
**Woodcock	Arsenal

Result: 5–0
Scorers: Waddle, Lineker (3), Robson

607. 13 November 1985

v N. IRELAND	Wembley Stadium
Shilton	Southampton
Stevens, M. G.	Everton
Sansom	Arsenal
Wilkins	AC Milan
Wright, M.	Southampton
Fenwick	Queen's Park Rangers
Bracewell	Everton
Lineker	Everton
Dixon	Chelsea
Hoddle	Tottenham Hotspur
Waddle	Tottenham Hotspur

Result: 0–0

608. 29 January 1986

v EGYPT	Cairo
Shilton*	Southampton
Stevens, M. G.	Everton
Sansom	Arsenal
Cowans	Bari
Wright, M.	Southampton
Fenwick	Queen's Park Rangers
Steven**	Everton
Wilkins	AC Milan
Hateley	AC Milan
Lineker***	Everton
Wallace, D.	Southampton
Subs: *Woods	Norwich City
**Hill	Luton Town
***Beardsley	Newcastle United

Result: 4–0
Scorers: Steven, o.g., Wallace, Cowans

609. 26 February 1986

v ISRAEL	Tel Aviv
Shilton*	Southampton
Stevens, M. G.	Everton
Sansom	Arsenal
Wilkins	AC Milan
Butcher	Ipswich Town
Martin	West Ham United
Robson	Manchester United
Hoddle	Tottenham Hotspur
Dixon**	Chelsea

Beardsley . . . . Newcastle United
Waddle*** . . . . Tottenham Hotspur
Subs: *Woods . . . . Norwich City
   **Woodcock . . . . Arsenal
   ***Barnes, J. . . . . Watford
Result: 2–1
Scorer: Robson (2 – 1 pen.)

610. 26 March 1986
v SOVIET UNION . . . . Tbilisi
Shilton . . . . Southampton
Anderson . . . . Arsenal
Sansom . . . . Arsenal
Wilkins . . . . AC Milan
Wright, M. . . . . Southampton
Butcher . . . . Ipswich Town
Hoddle . . . . Tottenham Hotspur
Cowans* . . . . Bari
Lineker . . . . Everton
Beardsley . . . . Newcastle United
Waddle** . . . . Tottenham Hotspur
Subs: *Hodge . . . . Aston Villa
   **Steven . . . . Everton
Result: 1–0
Scorer: Waddle

611. 23 April 1986
v SCOTLAND . . . . Wembley Stadium
Shilton . . . . Southampton
Stevens, M. G. . . . . Everton
Sansom . . . . Arsenal
Hoddle . . . . Tottenham Hotspur
Watson, D. . . . . Norwich City
Butcher . . . . Ipswich Town
Wilkins* . . . . AC Milan
Hodge** . . . . Aston Villa
Hateley . . . . AC Milan
Francis, T. . . . . Sampdoria
Waddle . . . . Tottenham Hotspur
Subs: *Reid . . . . Everton
   **Stevens, G. A. . . . . Tottenham Hotspur
Result: 2–1
Scorers: Butcher, Hoddle

612. 17 May 1986
v MEXICO . . . . Los Angeles
Shilton . . . . Southampton
Anderson . . . . Arsenal
Sansom . . . . Arsenal
Hoddle . . . . Tottenham Hotspur
Fenwick . . . . Queen's Park Rangers
Butcher . . . . Ipswich Town
Robson* . . . . Manchester United
Wilkins** . . . . AC Milan
Hateley*** . . . . AC Milan
Beardsley . . . . Newcastle United
Waddle**** . . . . Tottenham Hotspur
Subs: *Stevens, G. A. . . . . Tottenham Hotspur
   **Steven . . . . Everton
   ***Dixon . . . . Chelsea
   ****Barnes, J. . . . . Watford
Result: 3–0
Scorers: Hateley (2), Beardsley

613. 24 May 1986
v CANADA . . . . Burnaby
Shilton* . . . . Southampton
Stevens, M. G. . . . . Everton
Sansom . . . . Arsenal
Hoddle . . . . Tottenham Hotspur
Martin . . . . West Ham United
Butcher . . . . Ipswich Town
Hodge . . . . Aston Villa
Wilkins** . . . . AC Milan
Hateley . . . . AC Milan
Lineker*** . . . . Everton
Waddle**** . . . . Tottenham Hotspur

Subs: *Woods . . . . Norwich City
   **Reid . . . . Everton
   ***Beardsley . . . . Newcastle United
   ****Barnes, J. . . . . Watford
Result: 1–0
Scorer: Hateley

614. 3 June 1986
v PORTUGAL . . . . Monterrey
Shilton . . . . Southampton
Stevens, M. G. . . . . Everton
Sansom . . . . Arsenal
Hoddle . . . . Tottenham Hotspur
Fenwick . . . . Queen's Park Rangers
Butcher . . . . Ipswich Town
Robson* . . . . Manchester United
Wilkins . . . . AC Milan
Hateley . . . . AC Milan
Lineker . . . . Everton
Waddle** . . . . Tottenham Hotspur
Subs: *Hodge . . . . Aston Villa
   **Beardsley . . . . Newcastle United
Result: 0–1

615. 6 June 1986
v MOROCCO . . . . Monterrey
Shilton . . . . Southampton
Stevens, M. G. . . . . Everton
Sansom . . . . Arsenal
Hoddle . . . . Tottenham Hotspur
Fenwick . . . . Queen's Park Rangers
Butcher . . . . Ipswich Town
Robson* . . . . Manchester United
Wilkins . . . . AC Milan
Hateley** . . . . AC Milan
Lineker . . . . Everton
Waddle . . . . Tottenham Hotspur
Subs: *Hodge . . . . Aston Villa
   **Stevens, G. A. . . . . Tottenham Hotspur
Result: 0–0

616. 11 June 1986
v POLAND . . . . Monterrey
Shilton . . . . Southampton
Stevens, M. G. . . . . Everton
Sansom . . . . Arsenal
Hoddle . . . . Tottenham Hotspur
Fenwick . . . . Queen's Park Rangers
Butcher . . . . Ipswich Town
Hodge . . . . Aston Villa
Reid . . . . Everton
Beardsley* . . . . Newcastle United
Lineker** . . . . Everton
Steven . . . . Everton
Subs: *Waddle . . . . Tottenham Hotspur
   **Dixon . . . . Chelsea
Result: 3–0
Scorers: Lineker (3)

 FEATURED MATCH

11 JUNE 1986

ENGLAND 3 POLAND 0 – MONTERREY, MEXICO

After qualifying easily for the 1986 World Cup Finals, England found the tournament to be an unmitigated disaster. After losing 1–0 to Portugal in their first match, they later lost the services of Bryan Robson in the game against Morocco, when, as feared, he dislocated his harnessed shoulder on the

→

hard Mexican pitch. To further aggravate the situation, Ray Wilkins was sent off just before half-time. Fortunately, England's ten men gallantly held out for a goalless draw.

Once again England found themselves desperately needing to win their last group match if they wished to remain in the competition. The fact that their opponents were Poland brought echoes of 1973 flooding back. In addition to the enforced absences of Robson and Wilkins, Bobby Robson also dropped Mark Hateley and Chris Waddle from the starting line-up. The 4–3–3 system was abandoned in favour of a loose four-man midfield of Trevor Steven, Glenn Hoddle, Peter Reid and Steve Hodge, with Peter Beardsley partnering Gary Lineker up front.

In the first half England outclassed Poland, and unlike previous games the domination was reflected in the scoreline with a virtuoso performance from Gary Lineker, who netted a hat-trick. After eight minutes, a five-man move started by Hoddle in his own half ended with Lineker scoring from close range. On the quarter-hour mark, Beardsley and Hodge created an opening down the left flank. The Aston Villa man hit a high cross that Lineker met with a half-volley, giving Polish keeper Jozef Mlynarczyk no chance to save it. Hodge also planted the ball in the back of the net himself, but was adjudged to have received it in an offside position. Twenty minutes after his second goal Lineker completed his hat-trick when a Trevor Steven corner from the left beat everyone except Lineker, who duly put away the easiest of opportunities.

England's brilliant first-half performance was sufficient to guarantee them qualification to the second round. Gary Lineker regarded his hat-trick and all-round performance as his best for England; indeed the whole team had played magnificently. Fortune had smiled on England, and the loss of Robson and Wilkins had turned an underperforming England side into one displaying attacking flair and fighting spirit.

617. 18 June 1986

v PARAGUAY............ Mexico City
Shilton................ Southampton
Stevens, M. G. .... Everton
Sansom .... Arsenal
Hoddle................ Tottenham Hotspur
Martin .... West Ham United
Butcher .... Ipswich Town
Hodge .... Aston Villa
Reid*................. Everton
Beardsley**........... Newcastle United
Lineker............... Everton
Steven .... Everton
Subs: *Stevens, G. A. .... Tottenham Hotspur
**Hateley .... AC Milan
Result: 3–0
Scorers: Lineker (2), Beardsley

 DID YOU KNOW...?

The most famous piece of cheating took place when Diego Maradona fisted a ball into the net against England in the quarter-finals of the 1986 World Cup in June 1986. After the match, Maradona said the goal had been scored by 'the Hand of God and the head of Diego' ...

618. 22 June 1986

v ARGENTINA........... Mexico City
Shilton................ Southampton
Stevens, M. G. .... Everton
Sansom .... Arsenal
Hoddle................ Tottenham Hotspur
Fenwick .... Queen's Park Rangers
Butcher .... Ipswich Town
Hodge .... Aston Villa
Reid*................. Everton
Beardsley............. Newcastle United
Lineker............... Everton
Steven**.............. Everton
Subs: *Waddle........... Tottenham Hotspur
**Barnes, J. .... Watford
Result: 1–2
Scorer: Lineker

619. 10 September 1986

v SWEDEN .... Stockholm
Shilton................ Southampton
Anderson.............. Arsenal
Sansom .... Arsenal
Steven*............... Everton
Martin .... West Ham United
Butcher .... Glasgow Rangers
Hodge .... Aston Villa
Wilkins............... AC Milan
Dixon................. Chelsea
Hoddle................ Tottenham Hotspur
Barnes, J.**........... Watford
Subs: *Cottee .... West Ham United
**Waddle .... Tottenham Hotspur
Result: 0–1

620. 15 October 1986

v N. IRELAND .... Wembley Stadium
Shilton................ Southampton
Anderson.............. Arsenal
Sansom .... Arsenal
Hoddle................ Tottenham Hotspur
Watson .... Everton
Butcher .... Glasgow Rangers
Robson .... Manchester United
Hodge .... Aston Villa
Beardsley*............ Newcastle United
Lineker............... Barcelona
Waddle .... Tottenham Hotspur
Sub: *Cottee .... West Ham United
Result: 3–0
Scorers: Lineker (2), Waddle

621. 12 November 1986

v YUGOSLAVIA.......... Wembley Stadium
Woods................ Glasgow Rangers
Anderson.............. Arsenal
Sansom .... Arsenal
Hoddle................ Tottenham Hotspur
Wright, M............. Southampton
Butcher .... Glasgow Rangers
Mabbutt.............. Tottenham Hotspur
Hodge*............... Aston Villa
Beardsley............. Newcastle United
Lineker............... Barcelona
Waddle**............. Tottenham Hotspur
Subs: *Wilkins........... AC Milan
**Steven .... Everton
Result: 2–0
Scorers: Mabbutt, Anderson

622. 18 February 1987

v SPAIN .... Madrid
Shilton*.............. Southampton
Anderson.............. Arsenal
Sansom .... Arsenal
Hoddle................ Tottenham Hotspur

FEATURED MATCH

22 JUNE 1986

ENGLAND 1 ARGENTINA 2 – AZTECA STADIUM, MEXICO CITY

The Azteca Stadium in Mexico City, with a full house of more than 100,000 fans, can justifiably be described as one of world football's hotbeds. The quarter-final clash with Diego Maradona and his Argentinian teammates would prove to be the ultimate test of England's character. The fixture carried plenty of history, most of it unhappy. Feelings were still running high after the Falklands War, and sporting and diplomatic ties between the two countries remained severed. In footballing terms, memories were still fresh of England's 1–0 controversial win in the 1966 quarter-finals, when Rattin's sending-off prompted South American allegations of a European conspiracy.

Bobby Robson's team selection showed caution. Unlike the Brazil game two years previously, the aim on this occasion was clearly to stop the Argentinians from playing. Though Terry Fenwick was soon in the book for a foul on Maradona, the first half passed without incident. Five minutes after the restart Maradona played an inadvertent one-two off England's Steve Hodge, and although Shilton looked favourite to punch clear as the ball ballooned up into the air, it was the South American whose hand made contact and produced the 'Hand of God' goal that would go down in history.

England refused to let their heads drop, but another solo effort from Maradona, ironically rivalling John Barnes's 1984 wonder goal in brilliance, doubled the Argentinians' lead minutes later. In desperation Robson threw on his wingers Waddle and Barnes, and the gamble almost paid off as England responded with verve to the 2–0 deficit. Barnes was the inspiration behind England's fightback, delivering a perfect cross for Lineker to score from close range ten minutes from time. Moments later the Watford winger set up the chance of an identical second, which Lineker came within a whisker of converting. But it was to be England's last attack of the World Cup and they left the field with their heads held high, having battled the eventual champions as best they could before being ultimately thwarted by a dubious act of divine intervention . . .

Adams	Arsenal
Butcher	Glasgow Rangers
Robson	Manchester United
Hodge	Tottenham Hotspur
Beardsley	Newcastle United
Lineker	Barcelona
Waddle**	Tottenham Hotspur
Subs: *Woods	Glasgow Rangers
**Steven	Everton

Result: 4–2
Scorers: Lineker (4)

623. 1 April 1987

v N. IRELAND	Windsor Park, Belfast
Shilton*	Southampton
Anderson	Arsenal
Sansom	Arsenal
Mabbutt	Tottenham Hotspur
Wright, M.	Southampton
Butcher	Glasgow Rangers
Robson	Manchester United
Hodge	Tottenham Hotspur
Beardsley	Newcastle United
Lineker	Barcelona
Waddle	Tottenham Hotspur
Sub: *Woods	Glasgow Rangers

Result: 2–0
Scorers: Robson, Waddle

624. 29 April 1987

v TURKEY	Izmir
Woods	Glasgow Rangers
Anderson	Arsenal
Sansom	Arsenal
Hoddle	Tottenham Hotspur
Adams	Arsenal
Mabbutt	Tottenham Hotspur
Robson	Manchester United
Hodge*	Tottenham Hotspur
Allen, C.**	Tottenham Hotspur
Lineker	Barcelona
Waddle	Tottenham Hotspur
Subs: *Barnes, J.	Watford
**Hateley	AC Milan

Result: 0–0

625. 19 May 1987

v BRAZIL	Wembley Stadium
Shilton	Southampton
Stevens, M. G.	Everton
Pearce	Nottingham Forest
Reid	Everton
Adams	Arsenal
Butcher	Glasgow Rangers
Robson	Manchester United
Barnes, J.	Watford
Beardsley	Newcastle United
Lineker*	Barcelona
Waddle	Tottenham Hotspur
Sub: *Hateley	AC Milan

Result: 1–1
Scorer: Lineker

626. 23 May 1987

v SCOTLAND	Hampden Park, Glasgow
Woods	Glasgow Rangers
Stevens, M. G.	Everton
Pearce	Nottingham Forest
Hoddle	Tottenham Hotspur
Wright, M.	Southampton
Butcher	Glasgow Rangers
Robson	Manchester United
Hodge	Tottenham Hotspur
Hateley	AC Milan
Beardsley	Newcastle United
Waddle	Tottenham Hotspur

Result: 0–0

627. 9 September 1987

v WEST GERMANY	Düsseldorf
Shilton	Derby County
Anderson	Manchester United
Sansom*	Arsenal
Hoddle**	Monaco
Adams	Arsenal
Mabbutt	Tottenham Hotspur
Reid	Everton
Barnes, J.	Liverpool
Beardsley	Liverpool
Lineker	Barcelona
Waddle***	Tottenham Hotspur
Subs: *Pearce	Nottingham Forest
**Webb	Nottingham Forest
***Hateley	Monaco

Result: 1–3
Scorer: Lineker

628. 14 October 1987
v TURKEY . . . . Wembley Stadium
Shilton . . . . Derby County
Stevens, M. G. . . . . Everton
Sansom . . . . Arsenal
Steven* . . . . Everton
Adams . . . . Arsenal
Butcher . . . . Glasgow Rangers
Robson . . . . Manchester United
Webb . . . . Nottingham Forest
Beardsley** . . . . Liverpool
Lineker . . . . Barcelona
Barnes, J. . . . . Liverpool
Sub: *Hoddle . . . . Monaco
**Regis . . . . Coventry City
Result: 8–0
Scorers: Lineker (3), J. Barnes (2), Robson, Beardsley, Webb

629. 11 November 1987
v YUGOSLAVIA . . . . Belgrade
Shilton . . . . Derby County
Stevens, M. G. . . . . Everton
Sansom . . . . Arsenal
Steven . . . . Everton
Adams . . . . Arsenal
Butcher . . . . Glasgow Rangers
Robson* . . . . Manchester United
Webb** . . . . Nottingham Forest
Beardsley . . . . Liverpool
Lineker . . . . Barcelona
Barnes, J. . . . . Liverpool
Subs: *Reid . . . . Everton
**Hoddle . . . . Monaco
Result: 4–1
Scorers: Beardsley, Barnes, Robson, Adams

630. 17 February 1988
v ISRAEL . . . . Tel Aviv
Woods . . . . Glasgow Rangers
Stevens, M. G. . . . . Everton
Pearce . . . . Nottingham Forest
Webb . . . . Nottingham Forest
Watson, D. . . . . Everton
Wright, M.* . . . . Derby County
Allen, C.** . . . . Tottenham Hotspur
McMahon . . . . Liverpool
Beardsley . . . . Liverpool
Barnes . . . . Liverpool
Waddle . . . . Tottenham Hotspur
Subs: *Fenwick . . . . Tottenham Hotspur
**Harford . . . . Luton Town
Result: 0–0

631. 23 March 1988
v HOLLAND . . . . Wembley Stadium
Shilton . . . . Derby County
Stevens, M. G. . . . . Everton
Sansom . . . . Arsenal
Steven . . . . Everton
Adams . . . . Arsenal
Watson, D.* . . . . Everton
Robson . . . . Manchester United
Webb** . . . . Nottingham Forest
Beardsley*** . . . . Liverpool
Lineker . . . . Barcelona
Barnes, J. . . . . Liverpool
Subs: *Wright, M. . . . . Derby County
**Hoddle . . . . Monaco
***Hateley . . . . Monaco
Result: 2–2
Scorers: Lineker, Adams

632. 27 April 1988
v HUNGARY . . . . Budapest
Woods . . . . Glasgow Rangers
Anderson . . . . Manchester United
Pearce* . . . . Nottingham Forest

Steven . . . . Everton
Adams . . . . Arsenal
Pallister . . . . Middlesbrough
Robson . . . . Manchester United
McMahon . . . . Liverpool
Beardsley** . . . . Liverpool
Lineker*** . . . . Barcelona
Waddle**** . . . . Tottenham Hotspur
Subs: *Stevens, M. G. . . . . . . Everton
**Hateley . . . . Monaco
***Cottee . . . . West Ham United
****Hoddle . . . . Monaco
Result: 0–0

633. 21 May 1988
v SCOTLAND . . . . Wembley Stadium
Shilton . . . . Derby County
Stevens, M. G. . . . . Everton
Sansom . . . . Arsenal
Webb . . . . Nottingham Forest
Watson, D. . . . . Everton
Adams . . . . Arsenal
Robson . . . . Manchester United
Steven* . . . . Everton
Beardsley . . . . Liverpool
Lineker . . . . Barcelona
Barnes, J. . . . . Liverpool
Sub: *Waddle . . . . Tottenham Hotspur
Result: 1–0
Scorer: Beardsley

634. 24 May 1988
v COLOMBIA . . . . Wembley Stadium
Shilton . . . . Derby County
Anderson . . . . Manchester United
Sansom . . . . Arsenal
McMahon . . . . Liverpool
Wright, M. . . . . Derby County
Adams . . . . Arsenal
Robson . . . . Manchester United
Waddle* . . . . Tottenham Hotspur
Beardsley . . . . Liverpool
Lineker . . . . Barcelona
Barnes, J.** . . . . Liverpool
Subs: *Hoddle . . . . Monaco
**Hateley . . . . Monaco
Result: 1–1
Scorer: Lineker

635. 28 May 1988
v SWITZERLAND . . . . Lausanne
Shilton* . . . . Derby County
Stevens, M. G. . . . . Everton
Sansom . . . . Arsenal
Steven** . . . . Everton
Wright, M. . . . . Derby County
Adams*** . . . . Arsenal
Robson**** . . . . Manchester United
Webb . . . . Nottingham Forest
Beardsley . . . . Liverpool
Lineker . . . . Barcelona
Barnes, J. . . . . Liverpool
Subs: *Woods . . . . Glasgow Rangers
**Waddle . . . . Tottenham Hotspur
***Watson, D. . . . . Everton
****Reid . . . . Everton
Result: 1–0
Scorer: Lineker

636. 12 June 1988
v EIRE . . . . Stuttgart
Shilton . . . . Derby County
Stevens, M. G. . . . . Everton
Sansom . . . . Arsenal
Webb* . . . . Nottingham Forest
Adams . . . . Arsenal
Wright, M. . . . . Derby County

Robson . . . . Manchester United
Beardsley** . . . . Liverpool
Lineker. . . . . Barcelona
Barnes, J. . . . . Liverpool
Waddle . . . . Tottenham Hotspur
Subs: *Hoddle . . . . Monaco
**Hateley . . . . Monaco
Result: 0–1

637. 15 June 1988
v HOLLAND . . . . Düsseldorf
Shilton . . . . Derby County
Stevens, M. G. . . . . Everton
Sansom . . . . Arsenal
Adams . . . . Arsenal
Wright, M. . . . . Derby County
Steven* . . . . Everton
Robson . . . . Manchester United
Hoddle . . . . Monaco
Beardsley** . . . . Liverpool
Lineker. . . . . Barcelona
Barnes, J. . . . . Liverpool
Subs: *Waddle. . . . . Tottenham Hotspur
**Hateley . . . . Monaco
Result: 1–3
Scorer: Robson

638. 18 June 1988
v SOVIET UNION . . . . Frankfurt
Woods . . . . Glasgow Rangers
Stevens, M. G. . . . . Everton
Sansom . . . . Arsenal
Watson, D. . . . . Everton
Adams . . . . Arsenal
Hoddle . . . . Monaco
Robson . . . . Manchester United
McMahon* . . . . Liverpool
Lineker** . . . . Barcelona
Steven . . . . Everton
Barnes, J. . . . . Liverpool
Sub: *Webb. . . . . Nottingham Forest
**Hateley . . . . Monaco
Result: 1–3
Scorer: Adams

639. 14 September 1988
v DENMARK . . . . Wembley Stadium
Shilton* . . . . Derby County
Stevens, M. G. . . . . Glasgow Rangers
Pearce . . . . Nottingham Forest
Rocastle. . . . . Arsenal
Adams** . . . . Arsenal
Butcher . . . . Glasgow Rangers
Robson . . . . Manchester United
Webb. . . . . Nottingham Forest
Harford*** . . . . Luton Town
Beardsley**** . . . . Liverpool
Hodge . . . . Nottingham Forest
Subs: *Woods . . . . Glasgow Rangers
**Walker . . . . Nottingham Forest
***Cottee . . . . Everton
****Gascoigne . . . . Tottenham Hotspur
Result: 1–0
Scorer: Webb

640. 19 October 1988
v SWEDEN . . . . Wembley Stadium
Shilton. . . . . Derby County
Stevens, M. G. . . . . Glasgow Rangers
Pearce . . . . Nottingham Forest
Webb. . . . . Nottingham Forest
Adams* . . . . Arsenal
Butcher . . . . Glasgow Rangers
Robson . . . . Manchester United
Beardsley . . . . Liverpool
Waddle . . . . Tottenham Hotspur
Lineker. . . . . Barcelona

Barnes, J.** . . . . Liverpool
Subs: *Walker . . . . Nottingham Forest
**Cottee . . . . Everton
Result: 0–0

641. 16 November 1988
v SAUDI ARABIA . . . . Riyadh
Seaman . . . . Queen's Park Rangers
Sterland . . . . Sheffield Wednesday
Pearce . . . . Nottingham Forest
Thomas* . . . . Arsenal
Adams . . . . Arsenal
Pallister . . . . Middlesbrough
Robson . . . . Manchester United
Rocastle . . . . Arsenal
Beardsley** . . . . Liverpool
Lineker. . . . . Barcelona
Waddle*** . . . . Tottenham Hotspur
Subs: *Gascoigne . . . . Tottenham Hotspur
**Smith, A. . . . . Arsenal
***Marwood. . . . . Arsenal
Result: 1–1
Scorer: Adams

642. 8 February 1989
v GREECE . . . . Athens
Shilton . . . . Derby County
Stevens, M. G. . . . . Glasgow Rangers
Pearce . . . . Nottingham Forest
Walker . . . . Nottingham Forest
Butcher . . . . Glasgow Rangers
Robson . . . . Manchester United
Rocastle . . . . Arsenal
Webb. . . . . Nottingham Forest
Smith, A.* . . . . Arsenal
Lineker. . . . . Barcelona
Barnes, J . . . . Liverpool
Sub: *Beardsley . . . . Liverpool
Result: 2–1
Scorers: Barnes, Robson

643. 8 March 1989
v ALBANIA . . . . Tirana
Shilton . . . . Derby County
Stevens, M. G. . . . . Glasgow Rangers
Pearce . . . . Nottingham Forest
Rocastle. . . . . Arsenal
Walker . . . . Nottingham Forest
Butcher . . . . Glasgow Rangers
Robson . . . . Manchester United
Webb. . . . . Nottingham Forest
Barnes, J. . . . . Liverpool
Lineker* . . . . Barcelona
Waddle** . . . . Tottenham Hotspur
Subs: *Smith, A. . . . . Arsenal
**Beardsley . . . . Liverpool
Result: 2–0
Scorers: J. Barnes, Robson

644. 26 April 1989
v ALBANIA . . . . Wembley Stadium
Shilton . . . . Derby County
Stevens, M. G.* . . . . Glasgow Rangers
Pearce . . . . Nottingham Forest
Webb. . . . . Nottingham Forest
Walker . . . . Nottingham Forest
Butcher . . . . Glasgow Rangers
Robson . . . . Manchester United
Rocastle** . . . . Arsenal
Beardsley . . . . Liverpool
Lineker. . . . . Barcelona
Waddle . . . . Tottenham Hotspur
Subs: *Parker. . . . . Queen's Park Rangers
**Gascoigne . . . . Tottenham Hotspur
Result: 5–0
Scorers: Lineker, Beardsley (2), Waddle, Gascoigne

645. 23 May 1989
v CHILE . . . . Wembley Stadium
Shilton . . . . Derby County
Parker . . . . Queen's Park Rangers
Pearce . . . . Nottingham Forest
Webb . . . . Nottingham Forest
Walker . . . . Nottingham Forest
Butcher . . . . Glasgow Rangers
Robson . . . . Manchester United
Gascoigne . . . . Tottenham Hotspur
Clough . . . . Nottingham Forest
Fashanu* . . . . Wimbledon
Waddle . . . . Tottenham Hotspur
Sub: *Cottee . . . . Everton
Result: 0–0

⚽ **DID YOU KNOW...?**

The lowest crowd ever to watch an England game
at Wembley turned up for the friendly game against
Chile in May 1989, when just 15,628 watched
England play out a goalless draw. The attendance
had been affected by a tube strike.

646. 27 May 1989
v SCOTLAND . . . . Hampden Park, Glasgow
Shilton . . . . Derby County
Stevens, M. G. . . . . Glasgow Rangers
Pearce . . . . Nottingham Forest
Steven . . . . Everton
Walker . . . . Nottingham Forest
Butcher . . . . Glasgow Rangers
Robson . . . . Manchester United
Waddle . . . . Tottenham Hotspur
Fashanu* . . . . Wimbledon
Cottee** . . . . Everton
Webb . . . . Nottingham Forest
Subs: *Bull . . . . Wolverhampton Wanderers
**Gascoigne . . . . Tottenham Hotspur
Result: 2–0
Scorers: Waddle, Bull

647. 3 June 1989
v POLAND . . . . Wembley Stadium
Shilton . . . . Derby County
Stevens, M. G. . . . . Glasgow Rangers
Pearce . . . . Nottingham Forest
Webb . . . . Nottingham Forest
Walker . . . . Nottingham Forest
Butcher . . . . Glasgow Rangers
Robson . . . . Manchester United
Waddle* . . . . Tottenham Hotspur
Beardsley** . . . . Liverpool
Lineker . . . . Barcelona
Barnes, J. . . . . Liverpool
Subs: *Rocastle . . . . Arsenal
**Smith, A. . . . . Arsenal
Result: 3–0
Scorers: Lineker, J. Barnes, Webb

648. 7 June 1989
v DENMARK . . . . Copenhagen
Shilton* . . . . Derby County
Parker . . . . Queen's Park Rangers
Pearce . . . . Nottingham Forest
Webb** . . . . Nottingham Forest
Walker . . . . Nottingham Forest
Butcher . . . . Glasgow Rangers
Robson . . . . Manchester United
Rocastle . . . . Arsenal

Beardsley*** . . . . Liverpool
Lineker . . . . Barcelona
Barnes, J.**** . . . . Liverpool
Subs: *Seaman . . . . Queen's Park Rangers
**McMahon . . . . Liverpool
***Bull . . . . Wolverhampton Wanderers
****Waddle . . . . Tottenham Hotspur
Result: 1–1
Scorer: Lineker

649. 6 September 1989
v SWEDEN . . . . Solna
Shilton . . . . Derby County
Stevens, M. G. . . . . Glasgow Rangers
Pearce . . . . Nottingham Forest
Walker . . . . Nottingham Forest
Butcher . . . . Glasgow Rangers
McMahon . . . . Liverpool
Waddle . . . . Marseille
Webb* . . . . Manchester United
Beardsley . . . . Liverpool
Lineker . . . . Tottenham Hotspur
Barnes, J.** . . . . Liverpool
Subs: *Gascoigne . . . . Tottenham Hotspur
**Rocastle . . . . Arsenal
Result: 0–0

650. 11 October 1989
v POLAND . . . . Chorzów
Shilton . . . . Derby County
Stevens, M. G. . . . . Glasgow Rangers
Pearce . . . . Nottingham Forest
McMahon . . . . Liverpool
Walker . . . . Nottingham Forest
Butcher . . . . Glasgow Rangers
Robson . . . . Manchester United
Rocastle . . . . Arsenal
Beardsley . . . . Liverpool
Lineker . . . . Tottenham Hotspur
Waddle . . . . Marseille
Result: 0–0

651. 15 November 1989
v ITALY . . . . Wembley Stadium
Shilton* . . . . Derby County
Stevens, M. G. . . . . Glasgow Rangers
Pearce** . . . . Nottingham Forest
McMahon*** . . . . Liverpool
Walker . . . . Nottingham Forest
Butcher . . . . Glasgow Rangers
Robson**** . . . . Manchester United
Waddle . . . . Marseille
Beardsley***** . . . . Liverpool
Lineker . . . . Tottenham Hotspur
Barnes, J. . . . . Liverpool
Subs: *Beasant . . . . Chelsea
**Winterburn . . . . Arsenal
***Hodge . . . . Nottingham Forest
****Phelan . . . . Manchester United
*****Platt . . . . Aston Villa
Result: 0–0

652. 13 December 1989
v YUGOSLAVIA . . . . Wembley Stadium
Shilton* . . . . Derby County
Parker . . . . Queen's Park Rangers
Pearce** . . . . Nottingham Forest
Thomas*** . . . . Arsenal
Walker . . . . Nottingham Forest
Butcher . . . . Glasgow Rangers
Robson**** . . . . Manchester United
Rocastle***** . . . . Arsenal
Bull . . . . Wolverhampton Wanderers
Lineker . . . . Tottenham Hotspur
Waddle . . . . Marseille
Subs: *Beasant . . . . Chelsea

**Dorigo . . . . Chelsea
***Platt . . . . Aston Villa
****McMahon . . . . Liverpool
*****Hodge . . . . Nottingham Forest
Result: 2–1
Scorers: Robson (2)

653. 28 March 1990
v BRAZIL . . . . Wembley Stadium
Shilton* . . . . Derby County
Stevens, M. G. . . . . Glasgow Rangers
Pearce . . . . Nottingham Forest
McMahon . . . . Liverpool
Walker . . . . Nottingham Forest
Butcher . . . . Glasgow Rangers
Platt . . . . Aston Villa
Waddle . . . . Marseille
Beardsley** . . . . Liverpool
Lineker . . . . Tottenham Hotspur
Barnes, J. . . . . Liverpool
Subs: *Woods . . . . Glasgow Rangers
**Gascoigne . . . . Tottenham Hotspur
Result: 1–0
Scorer: Lineker

 DID YOU KNOW...?

The first full-house all-seated international at Wembley was on 28 March 1990, for England v Brazil (1–0), when a capacity 80,000 crowd paid record British receipts of £1,200,000.

654. 25 April 1990
v CZECHOSLOVAKIA . . . . Wembley Stadium
Shilton* . . . . Derby County
Dixon . . . . Arsenal
Pearce** . . . . Nottingham Forest
Steven . . . . Glasgow Rangers
Walker*** . . . . Nottingham Forest
Butcher . . . . Glasgow Rangers
Robson**** . . . . Manchester United
Gascoigne . . . . Tottenham Hotspur
Bull . . . . Wolverhampton Wanderers
Lineker . . . . Tottenham Hotspur
Hodge . . . . Nottingham Forest
Subs: *Seaman . . . . Queen's Park Rangers
**Dorigo . . . . Chelsea
***Wright, M. . . . . Derby County
****McMahon . . . . Liverpool
Result: 4–2
Scorers: Bull (2), Pearce, Gascoigne

655. 15 May 1990
v DENMARK . . . . Wembley Stadium
Shilton* . . . . Derby County
Stevens, M. G. . . . . Glasgow Rangers
Pearce** . . . . Nottingham Forest
McMahon*** . . . . Liverpool
Walker . . . . Nottingham Forest
Butcher . . . . Glasgow Rangers
Hodge . . . . Nottingham Forest
Gascoigne . . . . Tottenham Hotspur
Waddle**** . . . . Marseille
Lineker***** . . . . Tottenham Hotspur
Barnes, J. . . . . Liverpool
Subs: *Woods . . . . Glasgow Rangers
**Dorigo . . . . Chelsea
***Platt . . . . Aston Villa
****Rocastle . . . . Arsenal

*****Bull . . . . Wolverhampton Wanderers
Result: 1–0
Scorer: Lineker

656. 22 May 1990
v URUGUAY . . . . Wembley Stadium
Shilton . . . . Derby County
Parker . . . . Queen's Park Rangers
Pearce . . . . Nottingham Forest
Hodge* . . . . Nottingham Forest
Walker . . . . Nottingham Forest
Butcher . . . . Glasgow Rangers
Robson . . . . Manchester United
Gascoigne . . . . Tottenham Hotspur
Waddle . . . . Marseille
Lineker** . . . . Tottenham Hotspur
Barnes, J. . . . . Liverpool
Subs: *Beardsley . . . . Liverpool
**Bull . . . . Wolverhampton Wanderers
Result: 1–2
Scorer: J. Barnes

657. 2 June 1990
v TUNISIA . . . . Tunis
Shilton . . . . Derby County
Stevens, M. G. . . . . Glasgow Rangers
Pearce . . . . Nottingham Forest
Hodge* . . . . Nottingham Forest
Walker . . . . Nottingham Forest
Butcher** . . . . Glasgow Rangers
Robson . . . . Manchester United
Gascoigne . . . . Tottenham Hotspur
Waddle*** . . . . Marseille
Lineker**** . . . . Tottenham Hotspur
Barnes, J. . . . . Liverpool
Subs: *Beardsley . . . . Liverpool
**Wright, M. . . . . Derby County
***Platt . . . . Aston Villa
****Bull . . . . Wolverhampton Wanderers
Result: 1–1
Scorer: Bull

658. 11 June 1990
v EIRE . . . . Cagliari
Shilton . . . . Derby County
Stevens, M. G. . . . . Glasgow Rangers
Pearce . . . . Nottingham Forest
Walker . . . . Nottingham Forest
Butcher . . . . Glasgow Rangers
Robson . . . . Manchester United
Waddle . . . . Marseille
Gascoigne . . . . Tottenham Hotspur
Barnes, J. . . . . Liverpool
Lineker* . . . . Tottenham Hotspur
Beardsley** . . . . Liverpool
Subs: *Bull . . . . Wolverhampton Wanderers
**McMahon . . . . Liverpool
Result: 1–1
Scorer: Lineker

659. 16 June 1990
v HOLLAND . . . . Cagliari
Shilton . . . . Derby County
Parker . . . . Queen's Park Rangers
Pearce . . . . Nottingham Forest
Wright, M. . . . . Derby County
Butcher . . . . Glasgow Rangers
Walker . . . . Nottingham Forest
Robson* . . . . Manchester United
Gascoigne . . . . Tottenham Hotspur
Waddle** . . . . Marseille
Lineker . . . . Tottenham Hotspur
Barnes, J. . . . . Liverpool
Subs: *Platt . . . . Aston Villa
**Bull . . . . Wolverhampton Wanderers
Result: 0–0

FEATURED MATCH

1 JULY 1990

ENGLAND 3 CAMEROON 2 (after extra time) – NAPLES, ITALY

England matched their achievement of four years earlier by once again reaching the World Cup quarter-finals. This time their opponents were Cameroon, a team that had already beaten reigning champions Argentina in the curtain-raiser, despite having two players sent off. They had lit up the group stages with their exciting brand of attacking and unpredictable football, and in thirty-eight-year-old Roger Milla, they could also boast one of the oldest but deadliest strikers in the tournament.

England took the lead on twenty-five minutes, when David Platt headed home a Stuart Pearce cross past Thomas N'Kono. Cameroon then responded by mounting a sustained assault on Shilton's goal and fifteen minutes after the break, equalized from the penalty spot following Gascoigne's foul on Milla. Minutes later Eugene Ekeke added a second with a delightful chip and the traffic was all one-way towards Shilton's net. Bobby Robson abandoned the sweeper system as England reverted to instinct in a frantic bid to avoid one of the greatest upsets in their history.

The excitement was far from over and another penalty decision, earned and converted by Gary Lineker, pulled England back from the abyss with just eight minutes remaining. Extra time saw the issuing of the game's third penalty – and again the Spurs striker was equal to the task, despite the pressure. He hadn't had much practice, England having waited four years since their last spot-kick was awarded, but his success set up a semi-final against old enemy, West Germany.

In the semi-final, with the score after extra time remaining at 1–1, Lineker again converted a spot-kick as the first player in the penalty shoot-out, but Stuart Pearce and Chris Waddle both failed to hit the target, consigning Bobby Robson's team to the third-place play-off fixture with host nation Italy, which they went on to lose 2–1.

660. 21 June 1990
v EGYPT . . . . Cagliari
Shilton . . . . Derby County
Parker . . . . Queen's Park Rangers
Pearce . . . . Nottingham Forest
Gascoigne . . . . Tottenham Hotspur
Walker . . . . Nottingham Forest
Wright, M. . . . . Derby County
McMahon . . . . Liverpool
Waddle* . . . . Marseille
Bull** . . . . Wolverhampton Wanderers
Lineker. . . . . Tottenham Hotspur
Barnes, J. . . . . Liverpool
Subs: *Platt . . . . Aston Villa
**Beardsley . . . . Liverpool
Result: 1–0
Scorer: Wright

661. 26 June 1990
v BELGIUM . . . . Bologna
Shilton . . . . Derby County

Parker . . . . Queen's Park Rangers
Pearce . . . . Nottingham Forest
Wright, M. . . . . Derby County
Walker . . . . Nottingham Forest
Butcher . . . . Glasgow Rangers
McMahon* . . . . Liverpool
Waddle . . . . Marseille
Gascoigne . . . . Tottenham Hotspur
Lineker. . . . . Tottenham Hotspur
Barnes, J.** . . . . Liverpool
Subs: *Platt . . . . Aston Villa
**Bull . . . . Wolverhampton Wanderers
Result: 1–0 (a.e.t.)
Scorer: Platt

662. 1 July 1990
v CAMEROON . . . . Naples
Shilton . . . . Derby County
Parker . . . . Queen's Park Rangers
Pearce . . . . Nottingham Forest
Wright, M. . . . . Derby County
Walker . . . . Nottingham Forest
Butcher* . . . . Glasgow Rangers
Platt. . . . . Aston Villa
Waddle . . . . Marseille
Gascoigne . . . . Tottenham Hotspur
Lineker. . . . . Tottenham Hotspur
Barnes, J.** . . . . Liverpool
Subs: *Steven . . . . Glasgow Rangers
**Beardsley . . . . Liverpool
Result: 3–2 (a.e.t.)
Scorers: Platt, Lineker (2 pens)

663. 4 July 1990
v WEST GERMANY . . . . Turin
Shilton . . . . Derby County
Parker . . . . Queen's Park Rangers
Pearce . . . . Nottingham Forest
Walker . . . . Nottingham Forest
Butcher* . . . . Glasgow Rangers
Wright, M. . . . . Derby County
Platt. . . . . Aston Villa
Gascoigne . . . . Tottenham Hotspur
Beardsley . . . . Liverpool
Lineker. . . . . Tottenham Hotspur
Waddle . . . . Marseille
Sub: *Steven . . . . Glasgow Rangers
Result: 1–1 (a.e.t.)
Scorer: Lineker
West Germany won 4–3 on penalties

664. 7 July 1990
v ITALY . . . . Bari
Shilton . . . . Derby County
Stevens, M. G. . . . . Glasgow Rangers
Dorigo . . . . Chelsea
Walker . . . . Nottingham Forest
Parker . . . . Queen's Park Rangers
Wright, M. . . . . Derby County
Platt. . . . . Aston Villa
McMahon* . . . . Liverpool
Beardsley . . . . Liverpool
Lineker. . . . . Tottenham Hotspur
Steven** . . . . Glasgow Rangers
Subs: *Webb . . . . Manchester United
**Waddle . . . . Marseille
Result: 1–2
Scorer: Platt

665. 12 September 1990
v HUNGARY . . . . Wembley Stadium
Woods . . . . Glasgow Rangers
Dixon . . . . Arsenal
Pearce* . . . . Nottingham Forest
Parker . . . . Queen's Park Rangers

Walker . . . . Nottingham Forest
Wright, M. . . . . Derby County
Platt. . . . . Aston Villa
Gascoigne . . . . Tottenham Hotspur
Bull** . . . . Wolverhampton Wanderers
Lineker. . . . . Tottenham Hotspur
Barnes, J. . . . . Liverpool
Subs: *Dorigo . . . . Chelsea
   **Waddle . . . . Marseille
Result: 1–0
Scorer: Lineker

666. 17 October 1990
v POLAND . . . . Wembley Stadium
Woods . . . . Glasgow Rangers
Dixon. . . . . Arsenal
Pearce . . . . Nottingham Forest
Parker . . . . Queen's Park Rangers
Walker . . . . Nottingham Forest
Wright, M. . . . . Derby County
Platt. . . . . Aston Villa
Gascoigne . . . . Tottenham Hotspur
Bull* . . . . Wolverhampton Wanderers
Lineker**. . . . . Tottenham Hotspur
Barnes, J. . . . . Liverpool
Subs: *Waddle. . . . . Marseille
   **Beardsley. . . . . Liverpool
Result: 2–0
Scorers: Lineker (pen.), Beardsley

667. 14 November 1990
v EIRE. . . . . Lansdowne Road, Dublin
Woods . . . . Glasgow Rangers
Dixon. . . . . Arsenal
Pearce . . . . Nottingham Forest
Adams. . . . . Arsenal
Walker . . . . Nottingham Forest
Wright, M. . . . . Derby County
Platt. . . . . Aston Villa
Cowans . . . . Aston Villa
Beardsley. . . . . Liverpool
Lineker. . . . . Tottenham Hotspur
McMahon . . . . Liverpool
Result: 1–1
Scorer: Platt

668. 6 February 1991
v CAMEROON. . . . . Wembley Stadium
Seaman . . . . Arsenal
Dixon. . . . . Arsenal
Pearce . . . . Nottingham Forest
Steven . . . . Glasgow Rangers
Walker . . . . Nottingham Forest
Wright, M. . . . . Derby County
Robson* . . . . Manchester United
Gascoigne** . . . . Tottenham Hotspur
Wright, I. . . . . Crystal Palace
Lineker. . . . . Tottenham Hotspur
Barnes, J. . . . . Liverpool
Subs: *Pallister . . . . Manchester United
   **Hodge . . . . Nottingham Forest
Result: 2–0
Scorers: Lineker (2 – 1 pen.)

669. 27 March 1991
v EIRE. . . . . Wembley Stadium
Seaman . . . . Arsenal
Dixon. . . . . Arsenal
Pearce . . . . Nottingham Forest
Adams*. . . . . Arsenal
Walker . . . . Nottingham Forest
Wright, M. . . . . Derby County
Robson . . . . Manchester United
Platt. . . . . Aston Villa
Beardsley. . . . . Liverpool
Lineker**. . . . . Tottenham Hotspur

Barnes . . . . Liverpool
Subs: *Sharpe . . . . Manchester United
   **Wright, I. . . . . Crystal Palace
Result: 1–1
Scorer: Dixon

670. 1 May 1991
v TURKEY . . . . Izmir
Seaman . . . . Arsenal
Dixon. . . . . Arsenal
Pearce . . . . Nottingham Forest
Wise . . . . Chelsea
Walker . . . . Nottingham Forest
Pallister . . . . Manchester United
Platt. . . . . Aston Villa
Thomas* . . . . Crystal Palace
Smith, A. . . . . Arsenal
Lineker. . . . . Tottenham Hotspur
Barnes, J. . . . . Liverpool
Sub: *Hodge . . . . Nottingham Forest
Result: 1–0
Scorer: Wise

671. 21 May 1991
v SOVIET UNION. . . . . Wembley Stadium
Woods . . . . Glasgow Rangers
Stevens, M. G. . . . . Glasgow Rangers
Dorigo . . . . Chelsea
Wise* . . . . Chelsea
Parker . . . . Queen's Park Rangers
Wright, M.** . . . . Derby County
Platt. . . . . Aston Villa
Thomas . . . . Crystal Palace
Smith, A. . . . . Arsenal
Wright, I. . . . . Crystal Palace
Barnes, J. . . . . Liverpool
Subs: *Batty . . . . Leeds United
   **Beardsley. . . . . Liverpool
Result: 3–1
Scorers: Smith, Platt (2 – 1 pen.)

672. 25 May 1991
v ARGENTINA. . . . . Wembley Stadium
Seaman . . . . Arsenal
Dixon. . . . . Arsenal
Pearce . . . . Nottingham Forest
Batty . . . . Leeds United
Walker . . . . Nottingham Forest
Wright, M. . . . . Derby County
Platt. . . . . Aston Villa
Thomas . . . . Crystal Palace
Smith, A. . . . . Arsenal
Lineker. . . . . Tottenham Hotspur
Barnes, J.* . . . . Liverpool
Sub: *Clough. . . . . Nottingham Forest
Result: 2–2
Scorers: Lineker, Platt

673. 1 June 1991
v AUSTRALIA . . . . Sydney
Woods . . . . Glasgow Rangers
Parker . . . . Queen's Park Rangers
Pearce . . . . Nottingham Forest
Batty . . . . Leeds United
Walker . . . . Nottingham Forest
Wright, M. . . . . Derby County
Platt. . . . . Aston Villa
Thomas . . . . Crystal Palace
Clough. . . . . Nottingham Forest
Lineker*. . . . . Tottenham Hotspur
Hirst**. . . . . Sheffield Wednesday
Subs: *Wise . . . . Chelsea
   **Salako . . . . Crystal Palace
Result: 1–0
Scorer: o.g.

674. 3 June 1991
v NEW ZEALAND . . . . Auckland
Woods . . . . Glasgow Rangers
Parker . . . . Queen's Park Rangers
Pearce . . . . Nottingham Forest
Batty* . . . . Leeds United
Walker . . . . Nottingham Forest
Barrett . . . . Oldham Athletic
Platt . . . . Aston Villa
Thomas . . . . Crystal Palace
Wise . . . . Chelsea
Lineker . . . . Tottenham Hotspur
Walters** . . . . Glasgow Rangers
Subs: *Deane . . . . Sheffield United
**Salako . . . . Crystal Palace
Result: 1–0
Scorer: Lineker

675. 8 June 1991
v NEW ZEALAND . . . . Wellington
Woods . . . . Glasgow Rangers
Charles . . . . Nottingham Forest
Pearce . . . . Nottingham Forest
Wise . . . . Chelsea
Walker . . . . Nottingham Forest
Wright, M. . . . . Derby County
Platt . . . . Aston Villa
Thomas . . . . Crystal Palace
Deane* . . . . Sheffield United
Wright, I. . . . . Crystal Palace
Salako . . . . Crystal Palace
Sub: *Hirst . . . . Sheffield Wednesday
Result: 2–0
Scorers: Pearce, Hirst

676. 12 June 1991
v MALAYSIA . . . . Kuala Lumpur
Woods . . . . Glasgow Rangers
Charles . . . . Nottingham Forest
Pearce . . . . Nottingham Forest
Batty . . . . Leeds United
Walker . . . . Nottingham Forest
Wright, M. . . . . Derby County
Platt . . . . Aston Villa
Thomas . . . . Crystal Palace
Clough . . . . Nottingham Forest
Lineker . . . . Tottenham Hotspur
Salako . . . . Crystal Palace
Result: 4–2
Scorers: Lineker (4)

677. 11 September 1991
v GERMANY . . . . Wembley Stadium
Woods . . . . Sheffield Wednesday
Dixon . . . . Arsenal
Dorigo . . . . Leeds United
Batty . . . . Leeds United
Pallister . . . . Manchester United
Parker . . . . Manchester United
Platt . . . . Bari
Steven* . . . . Marseille
Smith, A. . . . . Arsenal
Lineker . . . . Tottenham Hotspur
Salako** . . . . Crystal Palace
Subs: *Merson . . . . Arsenal
**Stewart . . . . Tottenham Hotspur
Result: 0–1

678. 16 October 1991
v TURKEY . . . . Wembley Stadium
Woods . . . . Sheffield Wednesday
Dixon . . . . Arsenal
Pearce . . . . Nottingham Forest
Batty . . . . Leeds United
Walker . . . . Nottingham Forest
Mabbutt . . . . Tottenham Hotspur

Robson . . . . Manchester United
Platt . . . . Bari
Smith, A. . . . . Arsenal
Lineker . . . . Tottenham Hotspur
Waddle . . . . Marseille
Result: 1–0
Scorer: A. Smith

679. 13 November 1991
v POLAND . . . . Poznan
Woods . . . . Sheffield Wednesday
Dixon . . . . Arsenal
Pearce . . . . Nottingham Forest
Gray* . . . . Crystal Palace
Walker . . . . Nottingham Forest
Mabbutt . . . . Tottenham Hotspur
Platt . . . . Bari
Thomas . . . . Crystal Palace
Rocastle . . . . Arsenal
Lineker . . . . Tottenham Hotspur
Sinton** . . . . Queen's Park Rangers
Subs: *Smith, A. . . . . Arsenal
**Daley . . . . Aston Villa
Result: 1–1
Scorer: Lineker

680. 19 February 1992
v FRANCE . . . . Wembley Stadium
Woods . . . . Sheffield Wednesday
Jones . . . . Liverpool
Pearce . . . . Nottingham Forest
Keown . . . . Everton
Wright, M. . . . . Liverpool
Walker . . . . Nottingham Forest
Webb . . . . Manchester United
Thomas . . . . Crystal Palace
Clough . . . . Nottingham Forest
Shearer . . . . Southampton
Hirst* . . . . Sheffield Wednesday
Sub: *Lineker . . . . Tottenham Hotspur
Result: 2–0
Scorers: Shearer, Lineker

681. 25 March 1992
v CZECHOSLOVAKIA . . . . Prague
Seaman . . . . Arsenal
Keown . . . . Everton
Pearce . . . . Nottingham Forest
Rocastle* . . . . Arsenal
Walker . . . . Nottingham Forest
Mabbutt** . . . . Tottenham Hotspur
Platt . . . . Bari
Merson . . . . Arsenal
Clough*** . . . . Nottingham Forest
Hateley . . . . Glasgow Rangers
Barnes, J.**** . . . . Liverpool
Subs: *Dixon . . . . Arsenal
**Lineker . . . . Tottenham Hotspur
***Stewart . . . . Tottenham Hotspur
****Dorigo . . . . Leeds United
Result: 2–2
Scorers: Merson, Keown

682. 29 April 1992
v CIS . . . . Moscow
Woods* . . . . Sheffield Wednesday
Stevens, M. G. . . . . Glasgow Rangers
Sinton** . . . . Queen's Park Rangers
Walker . . . . Nottingham Forest
Keown . . . . Everton
Steven*** . . . . Marseille
Platt . . . . Bari
Palmer . . . . Sheffield Wednesday
Daley . . . . Aston Villa
Lineker . . . . Tottenham Hotspur
Shearer**** . . . . Southampton

Subs: *Martyn . . . . Crystal Palace
**Curle . . . . Manchester City
***Stewart . . . . Tottenham Hotspur
****Clough . . . . Nottingham Forest
Result: 2–2
Scorers: Lineker, Steven

683. 12 May 1992
v HUNGARY . . . . Budapest
Martyn* . . . . Crystal Palace
Stevens, M. G. . . . . Glasgow Rangers
Dorigo . . . . Leeds United
Curle** . . . . Manchester City
Walker . . . . Nottingham Forest
Keown . . . . Everton
Webb*** . . . . Manchester United
Palmer . . . . Sheffield Wednesday
Merson**** . . . . Arsenal
Lineker . . . . Tottenham Hotspur
Daley***** . . . . Aston Villa
Subs: *Seaman . . . . Arsenal
**Sinton . . . . Queen's Park Rangers
***Batty . . . . Leeds United
****Smith, A. . . . . Arsenal
*****Wright, I. . . . . Arsenal
Result: 1–0
Scorer: Webb

684. 17 May 1992
v BRAZIL . . . . Wembley Stadium
Woods . . . . Sheffield Wednesday
Stevens, M. G. . . . . Glasgow Rangers
Dorigo* . . . . Leeds United
Palmer . . . . Sheffield Wednesday
Walker . . . . Nottingham Forest
Keown . . . . Everton
Daley** . . . . Aston Villa
Steven*** . . . . Marseille
Platt. . . . . Bari
Lineker . . . . Tottenham Hotspur
Sinton**** . . . . Queen's Park Rangers
Subs: *Pearce . . . . Nottingham Forest
**Merson . . . . Arsenal
***Rocastle . . . . Arsenal
****Webb . . . . Manchester United
Result: 1–1
Scorer: Platt

685. 3 June 1992
v FINLAND . . . . Helsinki
Woods . . . . Sheffield Wednesday
Stevens, M. G.* . . . . Glasgow Rangers
Pearce . . . . Nottingham Forest
Keown . . . . Everton
Walker . . . . Nottingham Forest
Wright, M. . . . . Liverpool
Platt. . . . . Bari
Steven** . . . . Marseille
Webb. . . . . Manchester United
Lineker . . . . Tottenham Hotspur
Barnes, J.*** . . . . Liverpool
Subs: *Palmer . . . . Sheffield Wednesday
**Daley . . . . Aston Villa
***Merson . . . . Arsenal
Result: 2–1
Scorers: Platt (2)

686. 11 June 1992
v DENMARK . . . . Malmö
Woods . . . . Sheffield Wednesday
Curle* . . . . Manchester City
Pearce . . . . Nottingham Forest
Keown . . . . Everton
Walker . . . . Nottingham Forest
Steven . . . . Marseille
Platt. . . . . Bari

Merson** . . . . Arsenal
Smith, A. . . . . Arsenal
Lineker . . . . Tottenham Hotspur
Palmer . . . . Sheffield Wednesday
Subs: *Daley . . . . Aston Villa
**Webb. . . . . Manchester United
Result: 0–0

687. 14 June 1992
v FRANCE . . . . Malmö
Woods . . . . Sheffield Wednesday
Sinton . . . . Queen's Park Rangers
Pearce . . . . Nottingham Forest
Keown . . . . Everton
Walker . . . . Nottingham Forest
Palmer . . . . Sheffield Wednesday
Platt. . . . . Bari
Batty . . . . Leeds United
Shearer . . . . Southampton
Lineker . . . . Tottenham Hotspur
Steven . . . . Marseille
Result: 0–0

688. 17 June 1992
v SWEDEN . . . . Solna
Woods . . . . Sheffield Wednesday
Batty . . . . Leeds United
Pearce . . . . Nottingham Forest
Keown . . . . Everton
Walker . . . . Nottingham Forest
Palmer . . . . Sheffield Wednesday
Daley . . . . Aston Villa
Webb. . . . . Manchester United
Platt. . . . . Bari
Lineker* . . . . Tottenham Hotspur
Sinton** . . . . Queen's Park Rangers
Subs: *Smith, A. . . . . Arsenal
**Merson . . . . Arsenal
Result: 1–2
Scorer: Platt

689. 9 September 1992
v SPAIN . . . . Santander
Woods . . . . Sheffield Wednesday
Dixon* . . . . Arsenal
Pearce . . . . Nottingham Forest
Ince . . . . Manchester United
Walker . . . . Sampdoria
Wright, M. . . . . Liverpool
White** . . . . Manchester City
Platt. . . . . Juventus
Clough . . . . Nottingham Forest
Shearer . . . . Blackburn Rovers
Sinton*** . . . . Queen's Park Rangers
Subs: *Bardsley**** . . . . . . Queen's Park Rangers
**Merson . . . . Arsenal
***Deane . . . . Sheffield United
****Palmer . . . . Sheffield Wednesday
Result: 0–1

690. 14 October 1992
v NORWAY . . . . Wembley Stadium
Woods . . . . Sheffield Wednesday
Dixon* . . . . Arsenal
Pearce . . . . Nottingham Forest
Batty . . . . Leeds United
Walker . . . . Sampdoria
Adams . . . . Arsenal
Platt. . . . . Juventus
Gascoigne . . . . Lazio
Shearer . . . . Blackburn Rovers
Wright, I.** . . . . Arsenal
Ince . . . . Manchester United
Subs: *Palmer . . . . Sheffield Wednesday
**Merson . . . . Arsenal
Result: 1–1
Scorer: Platt

691. 18 November 1992

v TURKEY . . . . Wembley Stadium
Woods . . . . Sheffield Wednesday
Dixon . . . . Arsenal
Pearce . . . . Nottingham Forest
Palmer . . . . Sheffield Wednesday
Walker . . . . Sampdoria
Adams . . . . Arsenal
Platt . . . . Juventus
Gascoigne . . . . Lazio
Shearer . . . . Blackburn Rovers
Wright, I. . . . . Arsenal
Ince . . . . Manchester United
Result: 4–0
Scorers: Gascoigne (2), Shearer, Pearce

692. 17 February 1993

v SAN MARINO . . . . Wembley Stadium
Woods . . . . Sheffield Wednesday
Dixon . . . . Arsenal
Dorigo . . . . Leeds United
Palmer . . . . Sheffield Wednesday
Walker . . . . Sampdoria
Adams . . . . Arsenal
Platt . . . . Juventus
Gascoigne . . . . Lazio
Ferdinand, L. . . . . Queen's Park Rangers
Barnes, J. . . . . Liverpool
Batty . . . . Leeds United
Result: 6–0
Scorers: Platt (4), Palmer, L. Ferdinand

693. 31 March 1993

v TURKEY . . . . Izmir
Woods . . . . Sheffield Wednesday
Dixon* . . . . Arsenal
Sinton . . . . Queen's Park Rangers
Palmer . . . . Sheffield Wednesday
Walker . . . . Sampdoria
Adams . . . . Arsenal
Platt . . . . Juventus
Gascoigne . . . . Lazio
Barnes, J. . . . . Liverpool
Wright, I.** . . . . Arsenal
Ince . . . . Manchester United
Subs: *Clough . . . . Nottingham Forest
**Sharpe . . . . Manchester United
Result: 2–0
Scorers: Platt, Gascoigne

694. 28 April 1993

v HOLLAND . . . . Wembley Stadium
Woods . . . . Sheffield Wednesday
Dixon . . . . Arsenal
Keown . . . . Arsenal
Palmer . . . . Sheffield Wednesday
Walker . . . . Sampdoria
Adams . . . . Arsenal
Platt . . . . Juventus
Gascoigne* . . . . Lazio
Ferdinand, L. . . . . Queen's Park Rangers
Barnes, J. . . . . Liverpool
Ince . . . . Manchester United
Sub: *Merson . . . . Arsenal
Result: 2–2
Scorers: J. Barnes, Platt

695. 29 May 1993

v POLAND . . . . Chorzów
Woods . . . . Sheffield Wednesday
Bardsley . . . . Queen's Park Rangers
Dorigo . . . . Leeds United
Palmer* . . . . Sheffield Wednesday
Walker . . . . Sampdoria
Adams . . . . Arsenal

Platt . . . . Juventus
Gascoigne** . . . . Lazio
Sheringham . . . . Tottenham Hotspur
Barnes, J. . . . . Liverpool
Ince . . . . Manchester United
Subs: *Wright, I. . . . . Arsenal
**Clough . . . . Nottingham Forest
Result: 1–1
Scorer: I. Wright

696. 2 June 1993

v NORWAY . . . . Oslo
Woods . . . . Sheffield Wednesday
Dixon . . . . Arsenal
Pallister . . . . Manchester United
Walker* . . . . Sampdoria
Adams . . . . Arsenal
Sharpe . . . . Manchester United
Platt . . . . Juventus
Palmer . . . . Sheffield Wednesday
Ferdinand, L. . . . . Queen's Park Rangers
Gascoigne . . . . Lazio
Sheringham** . . . . Tottenham Hotspur
Subs: *Clough . . . . Nottingham Forest
**Wright, I. . . . . Arsenal
Result: 0–2

697. 9 June 1993

v USA . . . . Boston
Woods . . . . Sheffield Wednesday
Dixon . . . . Arsenal
Dorigo . . . . Leeds United
Batty . . . . Leeds United
Pallister . . . . Manchester United
Palmer* . . . . Sheffield Wednesday
Ince . . . . Manchester United
Clough . . . . Nottingham Forest
Ferdinand, L.** . . . . Queen's Park Rangers
Barnes, J. . . . . Liverpool
Sharpe . . . . Manchester United
Subs: *Walker . . . . Sampdoria
**Wright, I. . . . . Arsenal
Result: 0–2

698. 13 June 1993

v BRAZIL . . . . Washington, DC
Flowers . . . . Southampton
Barrett . . . . Aston Villa
Dorigo . . . . Leeds United
Batty* . . . . Leeds United
Pallister . . . . Manchester United
Walker . . . . Sampdoria
Ince** . . . . Manchester United
Clough*** . . . . Nottingham Forest
Wright, I. . . . . Arsenal
Sinton . . . . Queen's Park Rangers
Sharpe . . . . Manchester United
Subs: *Platt . . . . Juventus
**Palmer . . . . Sheffield Wednesday
***Merson . . . . Arsenal
Result: 1–1
Scorer: Platt

699. 19 June 1993

v GERMANY . . . . Detroit
Martyn . . . . Crystal Palace
Barrett . . . . Aston Villa
Sinton . . . . Queen's Park Rangers
Walker . . . . Sampdoria
Pallister* . . . . Manchester United
Sharpe** . . . . Manchester United
Platt . . . . Juventus
Ince . . . . Manchester United
Merson . . . . Arsenal
Clough*** . . . . Nottingham Forest

Barnes, J. . . . . Liverpool
Subs: *Keown . . . . Arsenal
   **Winterburn. . . . . Arsenal
   ***Wright, I. . . . . Arsenal
Result: 1–2
Scorer: Platt

700. 8 September 1993
v POLAND . . . . Wembley Stadium
Seaman . . . . Arsenal
Jones . . . . Liverpool
Pearce . . . . Nottingham Forest
Ince . . . . Manchester United
Pallister . . . . Manchester United
Adams . . . . Arsenal
Platt. . . . . Sampdoria
Gascoigne . . . . Lazio
Ferdinand, L. . . . . Queen's Park Rangers
Wright, I. . . . . Arsenal
Sharpe. . . . . Manchester United
Result: 3–0
Scorer: L. Ferdinand, Gascoigne, Pearce

701. 13 October 1993
v HOLLAND . . . . Rotterdam
Seaman . . . . Arsenal
Parker . . . . Manchester United
Dorigo . . . . Leeds United
Palmer* . . . . Sheffield Wednesday
Adams . . . . Arsenal
Pallister . . . . Manchester United
Platt. . . . . Sampdoria
Ince . . . . Manchester United
Shearer . . . . Blackburn Rovers
Merson** . . . . Arsenal
Sharpe. . . . . Manchester United
Subs: *Sinton . . . . Sheffield Wednesday
   **Wright, I. . . . . Arsenal
Result: 0–2

702. 17 November 1993
v SAN MARINO. . . . . Bologna
Seaman . . . . Arsenal
Dixon. . . . . Arsenal
Pearce. . . . . Nottingham Forest
Ince . . . . Manchester United
Walker. . . . . Sheffield Wednesday
Pallister . . . . Manchester United
Ripley . . . . Blackburn Rovers
Wright, I. . . . . Arsenal
Ferdinand, L. . . . . Queen's Park Rangers
Platt. . . . . Sampdoria
Sinton . . . . Sheffield Wednesday
Result: 7–1
Scorers: Ince (2), I. Wright (4), L. Ferdinand

703. 9 March 1994
v DENMARK . . . . Wembley Stadium
Seaman . . . . Arsenal
Parker . . . . Manchester United
Adams . . . . Arsenal
Pallister . . . . Manchester United
Le Saux . . . . Blackburn Rovers
Anderton . . . . Tottenham Hotspur
Platt. . . . . Sampdoria
Ince* . . . . Manchester United
Gascoigne** . . . . Lazio
Beardsley. . . . . Newcastle United
Shearer . . . . Blackburn Rovers
Subs: *Batty . . . . Blackburn Rovers
   **Le Tissier . . . . Southampton
Result: 1–0
Scorer: Platt

704. 17 May 1994
v GREECE . . . . Wembley Stadium
Flowers . . . . Blackburn Rovers
Jones* . . . . Liverpool
Adams . . . . Arsenal
Bould. . . . . Arsenal
Le Saux . . . . Blackburn Rovers
Anderton** . . . . Tottenham Hotspur
Richardson. . . . . Aston Villa
Merson . . . . Arsenal
Beardsley*** . . . . Newcastle United
Platt. . . . . Sampdoria
Shearer . . . . Blackburn Rovers
Subs: *Pearce . . . . Nottingham Forest
   **Le Tissier . . . . Southampton
   ***Wright, I. . . . . Arsenal
Result: 5–0
Scorers: Anderton, Beardsley, Platt (2 – 1 pen.), Shearer

705. 22 May 1994
v NORWAY . . . . Wembley Stadium
Seaman . . . . Arsenal
Jones . . . . Liverpool
Bould. . . . . Arsenal
Adams . . . . Arsenal
Le Saux . . . . Blackburn Rovers
Anderton* . . . . Tottenham Hotspur
Ince** . . . . Manchester United
Wise . . . . Chelsea
Platt. . . . . Sampdoria
Beardsley. . . . . Newcastle United
Shearer . . . . Blackburn Rovers
Subs: *Le Tissier . . . . Southampton
   **Wright, I. . . . . Arsenal
Result: 0–0

706. 7 September 1994
v USA. . . . . Wembley Stadium
Seaman . . . . Arsenal
Jones . . . . Liverpool
Adams . . . . Arsenal
Pallister . . . . Manchester United
Le Saux . . . . Blackburn Rovers
Venison . . . . Newcastle United
Anderton . . . . Tottenham Hotspur
Barnes, J. . . . . Liverpool
Platt. . . . . Sampdoria
Sheringham* . . . . Tottenham Hotspur
Shearer** . . . . Blackburn Rovers
Subs: *Ferdinand, L. . . . . Queen's Park Rangers
   **Wright, I. . . . . Arsenal
Result: 2–0
Scorers: Shearer (2)

707. 12 October 1994
v ROMANIA . . . . Wembley Stadium
Seaman* . . . . Arsenal
Jones* . . . . Liverpool
Adams . . . . Arsenal
Pallister . . . . Manchester United
Le Saux . . . . Blackburn Rovers
Ince . . . . Manchester United
Lee** . . . . Newcastle United
Barnes, J. . . . . Liverpool
Le Tissier . . . . Southampton
Wright, I.*** . . . . Arsenal
Shearer . . . . Blackburn Rovers
Subs: *Pearce . . . . Nottingham Forest
   **Wise . . . . Chelsea
   ***Sheringham . . . . Tottenham Hotspur
Result: 1–1
Scorer: Lee

708. 16 November 1994
v NIGERIA . . . . Wembley Stadium
Flowers . . . . Blackburn Rovers
Jones . . . . Liverpool
Ruddock. . . . . Liverpool
Howey . . . . Newcastle United
Le Saux . . . . Blackburn Rovers
Wise . . . . Chelsea
Lee* . . . . Newcastle United
Platt. . . . . Sampdoria
Barnes, J. . . . . Liverpool
Beardsley** . . . . Newcastle United
Shearer*** . . . . Blackburn Rovers
Subs: *McManaman . . . . . . Liverpool
**Le Tissier . . . . Southampton
***Sheringham . . . . Tottenham Hotspur
Result: 1–0
Scorer: Platt

709. 15 February 1995
v EIRE. . . . . Lansdowne Road, Dublin
Seaman . . . . Arsenal
Barton . . . . Wimbledon
Adams . . . . Arsenal
Pallister . . . . Manchester United
Le Saux . . . . Blackburn Rovers
Ince . . . . Manchester United
Anderton . . . . Tottenham Hotspur
Platt. . . . . Sampdoria
Beardsley . . . . Newcastle United
Le Tissier . . . . Southampton
Shearer . . . . Blackburn Rovers
Result: 0–1 (abandoned after 27 mins)

710. 29 March 1995
v URUGUAY . . . . Wembley Stadium
Flowers . . . . Blackburn Rovers
Jones . . . . Liverpool
Adams . . . . Arsenal
Pallister . . . . Manchester United
Le Saux* . . . . Blackburn Rovers
Venison . . . . Newcastle United
Platt. . . . . Sampdoria
Anderton . . . . Tottenham Hotspur
Barnes, J. . . . . Liverpool
Sheringham** . . . . Tottenham Hotspur
Beardsley*** . . . . Newcastle United
Subs: *McManaman . . . . . . Liverpool
**Cole, Andy . . . . Manchester United
***Barmby . . . . Tottenham Hotspur
Result: 0–0

711. 3 June 1995
v JAPAN . . . . Wembley Stadium
Flowers . . . . Blackburn Rovers
Neville, G. . . . . Manchester United
Scales . . . . Liverpool
Unsworth . . . . Everton
Pearce . . . . Nottingham Forest
Batty* . . . . Blackburn Rovers
Anderton . . . . Tottenham Hotspur
Platt. . . . . Sampdoria
Beardsley** . . . . Newcastle United
Collymore*** . . . . Nottingham Forest
Shearer . . . . Blackburn Rovers
Subs: *Gascoigne . . . . Lazio
**McManaman . . . . Liverpool
***Sheringham . . . . Tottenham Hotspur
Result: 2–1
Scorers: Anderton, Platt (pen.)

712. 8 June 1995
v SWEDEN . . . . Elland Road, Leeds
Flowers . . . . Blackburn Rovers

Barton . . . . Newcastle United
Cooper. . . . . Nottingham Forest
Pallister* . . . . Manchester United
Le Saux . . . . Blackburn Rovers
Anderton . . . . Tottenham Hotspur
Barnes,J.** . . . . Liverpool
Platt. . . . . Sampdoria
Beardsley*** . . . . Newcastle United
Sheringham . . . . Tottenham Hotspur
Shearer . . . . Blackburn Rovers
Subs: *Scales. . . . . Liverpool
**Gascoigne . . . . Lazio
***Barmby . . . . Tottenham Hotspur
Result: 3–3
Scorers: Sheringham, Platt, Anderton

713. 11 June 1995
v BRAZIL. . . . . Wembley Stadium
Flowers . . . . Blackburn Rovers
Neville, G. . . . . Manchester United
Scales* . . . . Liverpool
Cooper. . . . . Nottingham Forest
Pearce . . . . Nottingham Forest
Anderton . . . . Tottenham Hotspur
Platt. . . . . Sampdoria
Batty** . . . . Blackburn Rovers
Le Saux . . . . Blackburn Rovers
Sheringham*** . . . . Tottenham Hotspur
Shearer . . . . Blackburn Rovers
Subs: *Barton . . . . Newcastle United
**Gascoigne . . . . Lazio
***Collymore. . . . . Nottingham Forest
Result: 1–3
Scorer: Le Saux

714. 6 September 1995
v COLOMBIA . . . . Wembley Stadium
Seaman . . . . Arsenal
Neville, G. . . . . Manchester United
Le Saux . . . . Blackburn Rovers
Howey . . . . Newcastle United
Adams . . . . Arsenal
Redknapp* . . . . Liverpool
Gascoigne** . . . . Glasgow Rangers
Wise . . . . Chelsea
McManaman . . . . Liverpool
Barmby . . . . Middlesbrough
Shearer*** . . . . Blackburn Rovers
Subs: *Lee . . . . Newcastle United
**Barnes, J. . . . . Liverpool
***Sheringham . . . . Tottenham Hotspur
Result: 0–0

715. 11 October 1995
v NORWAY . . . . Oslo
Seaman . . . . Arsenal
Neville, G. . . . . Manchester United
Adams . . . . Arsenal
Pallister . . . . Manchester United
Pearce . . . . Nottingham Forest
Wise* . . . . Chelsea
Redknapp. . . . . Liverpool
Lee . . . . Newcastle United
Barmby** . . . . Middlesbrough
McManaman . . . . Liverpool
Shearer . . . . Blackburn Rovers
Subs: *Stone . . . . Nottingham Forest
**Sheringham . . . . Tottenham Hotspur
Result: 0–0

716. 15 November 1995
v SWITZERLAND . . . . Wembley Stadium
Seaman . . . . Arsenal
Neville, G. . . . . Manchester United

Pearce . . . . Nottingham Forest
Adams . . . . Arsenal
Pallister . . . . Manchester United
Lee . . . . Newcastle United
Redknapp* . . . . Liverpool
Gascoigne . . . . Glasgow Rangers
McManaman . . . . Liverpool
Sheringham . . . . Tottenham Hotspur
Shearer . . . . Blackburn Rovers
Sub: *Stone . . . . Nottingham Forest
Result: 3–1
Scorers: Pearce, Sheringham, Stone

717. 12 December 1995
v PORTUGAL . . . . Wembley Stadium
Seaman . . . . Arsenal
Neville, G. . . . . Manchester United
Pearce* . . . . Nottingham Forest
Stone . . . . Nottingham Forest
Howey . . . . Newcastle United
Adams . . . . Arsenal
Barmby** . . . . Middlesbrough
Gascoigne . . . . Glasgow Rangers
Shearer . . . . Blackburn Rovers
Ferdinand, L.*** . . . . Newcastle United
Wise**** . . . . Chelsea
Subs: *Le Saux . . . . Blackburn Rovers
**McManaman . . . . Liverpool
***Beardsley . . . . Newcastle United
****Southgate . . . . Aston Villa
Result: 1–1
Scorer: Stone

718. 27 March 1996
v BULGARIA . . . . Wembley Stadium
Seaman . . . . Arsenal
Neville, G. . . . . Manchester United
Pearce . . . . Nottingham Forest
Ince . . . . Inter Milan
Southgate . . . . Aston Villa
Howey . . . . Newcastle United
McManaman . . . . Liverpool
Gascoigne* . . . . Glasgow Rangers
Ferdinand, L.** . . . . Newcastle United
Sheringham*** . . . . Tottenham Hotspur
Stone . . . . Nottingham Forest
Subs: *Lee . . . . Newcastle United
**Platt . . . . Arsenal
***Fowler . . . . Liverpool
Result: 1–0
Scorer: L. Ferdinand

719. 24 April 1996
v CROATIA . . . . Wembley Stadium
Seaman . . . . Arsenal
Neville, G. . . . . Manchester United
Pearce . . . . Nottingham Forest
Ince . . . . Inter Milan
Wright, M. . . . . Liverpool
McManaman . . . . Liverpool
Platt . . . . Arsenal
Gascoigne . . . . Glasgow Rangers
Fowler . . . . Liverpool
Sheringham . . . . Tottenham Hotspur
Stone . . . . Nottingham Forest
Result: 0–0

720. 18 May 1996
v HUNGARY . . . . Wembley Stadium
Seaman* . . . . Arsenal
Neville, G. . . . . Manchester United
Pearce . . . . Nottingham Forest
Wright, M.** . . . . Liverpool
Anderton . . . . Tottenham Hotspur

Ince*** . . . . Inter Milan
Wilcox . . . . Blackburn Rovers
Ferdinand, L.**** . . . . Newcastle United
Lee . . . . Newcastle United
Platt***** . . . . Arsenal
Sheringham . . . . Tottenham Hotspur
Subs: *Walker . . . . Tottenham Hotspur
**Southgate . . . . Aston Villa
***Campbell . . . . Tottenham Hotspur
****Shearer . . . . Blackburn Rovers
*****Wise . . . . Chelsea
Result: 3–0
Scorers: Anderton (2), Platt

721. 23 May 1996
v CHINA . . . . Beijing
Flowers* . . . . Blackburn Rovers
Neville, G. . . . . Manchester United
Neville, P. . . . . Manchester United
Redknapp . . . . Liverpool
Adams** . . . . Arsenal
Southgate . . . . Aston Villa
Barmby*** . . . . Middlesbrough
Gascoigne . . . . Glasgow Rangers
Shearer**** . . . . Blackburn Rovers
McManaman***** . . . . . Liverpool
Anderton . . . . Tottenham Hotspur
Subs: *Walker . . . . Tottenham Hotspur
**Ehiogu . . . . Aston Villa
***Beardsley . . . . Newcastle United
****Fowler . . . . Liverpool
*****Stone . . . . Nottingham Forest
Result: 3–0
Scorers: Barmby (2), Gascoigne

722. 8 June 1996
v SWITZERLAND . . . . Wembley Stadium
Seaman . . . . Arsenal
Neville, G. . . . . Manchester United
Pearce . . . . Nottingham Forest
Ince . . . . Inter Milan
Adams . . . . Arsenal
Southgate . . . . Aston Villa
Gascoigne* . . . . Glasgow Rangers
Shearer . . . . Blackburn Rovers
Sheringham** . . . . Tottenham Hotspur
Anderton . . . . Tottenham Hotspur
McManaman*** . . . . Liverpool
Subs: *Platt . . . . Arsenal
**Barmby . . . . Middlesbrough
***Stone . . . . Nottingham Forest
Result: 1–1
Scorer: Shearer

723. 15 June 1996
v SCOTLAND . . . . Wembley Stadium
Seaman . . . . Arsenal
Neville, G. . . . . Manchester United
Pearce* . . . . Nottingham Forest
Ince** . . . . Inter Milan
Adams . . . . Arsenal
Southgate . . . . Aston Villa
Gascoigne . . . . Glasgow Rangers
Shearer . . . . Blackburn Rovers
Sheringham . . . . Tottenham Hotspur
Anderton . . . . Tottenham Hotspur
McManaman . . . . Liverpool
Subs: *Redknapp*** . . . . Liverpool
**Stone . . . . Nottingham Forest
***Campbell . . . . Tottenham Hotspur
Result: 2–0
Scorers: Shearer, Gascoigne

724. 18 June 1996
v HOLLAND .... Wembley Stadium
Seaman .... Arsenal
Neville, G. .... Manchester United
Adams................ Arsenal
Southgate .... Aston Villa
Pearce .... Nottingham Forest
Gascoigne .... Glasgow Rangers
Ince* .... Inter Milan
McManaman .... Liverpool
Shearer** .... Blackburn Rovers
Anderton .... Tottenham Hotspur
Sheringham*** .... Tottenham Hotspur
Subs: *Platt............. Arsenal
**Barmby .... Middlesbrough
***Fowler .... Liverpool
Result: 4–1
Scorers: Shearer (2 – 1 pen.), Sheringham (2)

725. 22 June 1996
v SPAIN .... Wembley Stadium
Seaman .... Arsenal
Neville, G. .... Manchester United
Pearce .... Nottingham Forest
Adams................ Arsenal
Southgate .... Aston Villa
Platt................. Arsenal
Gascoigne .... Glasgow Rangers
Shearer .... Blackburn Rovers
Sheringham* .... Tottenham Hotspur
Anderton** .... Tottenham Hotspur
McManaman*** .... Liverpool
Subs: *Stone .... Nottingham Forest
**Fowler .... Liverpool
***Barmby .... Middlesbrough
Result: 0–0 (a.e.t.)
England won 4–2 on penalties

726. 26 June 1996
v GERMANY .... Wembley Stadium
Seaman .... Arsenal
Pearce .... Nottingham Forest
Ince.................. Inter Milan
Adams................ Arsenal
Southgate .... Aston Villa
Platt................. Arsenal
Gascoigne .... Glasgow Rangers
Shearer .... Blackburn Rovers
Sheringham .... Tottenham Hotspur
Anderton .... Tottenham Hotspur
McManaman .... Liverpool
Result: 1–1 (a.e.t.)
Scorer: Shearer
Germany won 6–5 on penalties

727. 1 September 1996
v MOLDOVA .... Kishinev
Seaman .... Arsenal
Neville, G. .... Manchester United
Pearce .... Nottingham Forest
Southgate .... Aston Villa
Pallister .... Manchester United
Hinchcliffe .... Everton
Barmby* .... Middlesbrough
Ince.................. Inter Milan
Shearer .... Newcastle United
Gascoigne** .... Glasgow Rangers
Beckham .... Manchester United
Subs: *Le Tissier .... Southampton
**Batty .... Newcastle United
Result: 3–0
Scorers: Barmby, Gascoigne, Shearer

728. 9 October 1996
v POLAND .... Wembley Stadium
Seaman .... Arsenal
Neville, G. .... Manchester United
Pearce .... Nottingham Forest
Southgate* .... Aston Villa
Ince.................. Inter Milan
Hinchcliffe .... Everton
McManaman .... Liverpool
Gascoigne .... Glasgow Rangers
Shearer .... Newcastle United
Ferdinand, L. .... Newcastle United
Beckham .... Manchester United
Sub: *Pallister .... Manchester United
Result: 2–1
Scorers: Shearer (2)

729. 9 November 1996
v GEORGIA............. Tbilisi
Seaman .... Arsenal
Campbell .... Tottenham Hotspur
Hinchcliffe .... Everton
Batty .... Newcastle United
Southgate .... Aston Villa
Adams................ Arsenal
Beckham .... Manchester United
Gascoigne .... Glasgow Rangers
Ferdinand, L.* .... Newcastle United
Sheringham .... Tottenham Hotspur
Ince.................. Inter Milan
Sub: *Wright, I. .... Arsenal
Result: 2–0
Scorers: L. Ferdinand, Sheringham

730. 12 February 1997
v ITALY .... Wembley Stadium
Walker .... Tottenham Hotspur
Neville, G. .... Manchester United
Pearce .... Nottingham Forest
Ince.................. Inter Milan
Campbell .... Tottenham Hotspur
Batty* .... Newcastle United
McManaman** .... Liverpool
Le Tissier*** .... Southampton
Shearer .... Newcastle United
Beckham .... Manchester United
Le Saux .... Blackburn Rovers
Subs: *Wright, I. .... Arsenal
**Merson .... Arsenal
***Ferdinand, L. .... Newcastle United
Result: 0–1

731. 29 March 1997
v MEXICO.............. Wembley Stadium
James .... Liverpool
Pearce .... Nottingham Forest
Keown .... Arsenal
Southgate .... Aston Villa
Ince.................. Inter Milan
Lee .... Newcastle United
Batty* .... Newcastle United
Le Saux .... Blackburn Rovers
Fowler .... Liverpool
Sheringham** .... Tottenham Hotspur
McManaman*** .... Liverpool
Subs: *Redknapp.......... Liverpool
**Wright, I. .... Arsenal
***Butt .... Manchester United
Result: 2–0
Scorers: Sheringham (pen.), Fowler

732. 30 April 1997
v GEORGIA . . . . Wembley Stadium
  Seaman . . . . Arsenal
  Neville, G. . . . . Manchester United
  Le Saux . . . . Blackburn Rovers
  Batty . . . . Newcastle United
  Campbell . . . . Tottenham Hotspur
  Adams* . . . . Arsenal
  Lee . . . . Newcastle United
  Ince** . . . . Inter Milan
  Shearer . . . . Newcastle United
  Sheringham . . . . Tottenham Hotspur
  Beckham . . . . Manchester United
  Subs: *Southgate. . . . . Aston Villa
  **Redknapp. . . . . Liverpool
  Result: 2–0
  Scorers: Sheringham, Shearer

733. 24 May 1997
v SOUTH AFRICA . . . . Old Trafford, Manchester
  Martyn. . . . . Leeds United
  Neville, P. . . . . Manchester United
  Pearce . . . . Nottingham Forest
  Keown . . . . Arsenal
  Southgate . . . . Aston Villa
  Le Saux* . . . . Blackburn Rovers
  Redknapp**. . . . . Liverpool
  Gascoigne*** . . . . Glasgow Rangers
  Wright, I. . . . . Arsenal
  Sheringham**** . . . . Tottenham Hotspur
  Lee***** . . . . Newcastle United
  Subs: *Beckham . . . . Manchester United
  **Batty . . . . Newcastle United
  ***Campbell . . . . Tottenham Hotspur
  ****Scholes . . . . Manchester United
  *****Butt . . . . Manchester United
  Result: 2–1
  Scorers: Lee, I. Wright

734. 31 May 1997
v POLAND . . . . Chorzów
  Seaman . . . . Arsenal
  Neville, G. . . . . Manchester United
  Le Saux . . . . Blackburn Rovers
  Southgate . . . . Aston Villa
  Campbell . . . . Tottenham Hotspur
  Ince . . . . Inter Milan
  Lee . . . . Newcastle United
  Gascoigne* . . . . Glasgow Rangers
  Shearer . . . . Newcastle United
  Sheringham . . . . Tottenham Hotspur
  Beckham** . . . . Manchester United
  Subs: *Batty . . . . Newcastle United
  **Neville, P. . . . . Manchester United
  Result: 2–0
  Scorers: Shearer, Sheringham

735. 4 June 1997
v ITALY . . . . Nantes
  Flowers . . . . Blackburn Rovers
  Neville, P. . . . . Manchester United
  Pearce . . . . Nottingham Forest
  Keown . . . . Arsenal
  Southgate . . . . Aston Villa
  Le Saux* . . . . Blackburn Rovers
  Scholes . . . . Manchester United
  Ince . . . . Inter Milan
  Wright, I.** . . . . Arsenal
  Sheringham*** . . . . Tottenham Hotspur
  Beckham . . . . Manchester United
  Subs: *Neville, G. . . . . Manchester United
  **Cole, Andy . . . . Manchester United
  ***Gascoigne . . . . Glasgow Rangers
  Result: 2–0
  Scorers: I. Wright, Scholes

736. 7 June 1997
v FRANCE . . . . Montpellier
  Seaman . . . . Arsenal
  Neville, G. . . . . Manchester United
  Neville, P. . . . . Manchester United
  Batty* . . . . Newcastle United
  Southgate . . . . Aston Villa
  Campbell . . . . Tottenham Hotspur
  Beckham** . . . . Manchester United
  Gascoigne . . . . Glasgow Rangers
  Shearer . . . . Newcastle United
  Wright, I.*** . . . . Arsenal
  Le Saux . . . . Blackburn Rovers
  Subs: *Ince . . . . Inter Milan
  **Lee . . . . Newcastle United
  ***Sheringham . . . . Tottenham Hotspur
  Result: 1–0
  Scorer: Shearer

737. 10 June 1997
v BRAZIL . . . . Paris
  Seaman . . . . Arsenal
  Neville, P. . . . . Manchester United
  Le Saux . . . . Blackburn Rovers
  Keown* . . . . Arsenal
  Southgate . . . . Aston Villa
  Campbell . . . . Tottenham Hotspur
  Scholes** . . . . Manchester United
  Gascoigne . . . . Glasgow Rangers
  Shearer . . . . Newcastle United
  Sheringham*** . . . . Tottenham Hotspur
  Ince . . . . Inter Milan
  Subs: *Neville, G. . . . . Manchester United
  **Lee . . . . Newcastle United
  ***Wright, I. . . . . Arsenal
  Result: 0–1

738. 10 September 1997
v MOLDOVA . . . . Wembley Stadium
  Seaman . . . . Arsenal
  Neville, G. . . . . Manchester United
  Neville, P. . . . . Manchester United
  Batty . . . . Newcastle United
  Campbell . . . . Tottenham Hotspur
  Southgate . . . . Aston Villa
  Beckham* . . . . Manchester United
  Gascoigne . . . . Glasgow Rangers
  Wright, I. . . . . Arsenal
  Ferdinand, L.** . . . . Tottenham Hotspur
  Scholes . . . . Manchester United
  Subs: *Ripley*** . . . . Blackburn Rovers
  **Collymore . . . . Aston Villa
  ***Butt . . . . Manchester United
  Result: 4–0
  Scorers: Scholes, I. Wright (2), Gascoigne

739. 11 October 1997
v ITALY . . . . Rome
  Seaman . . . . Arsenal
  Campbell . . . . Tottenham Hotspur
  Le Saux . . . . Chelsea
  Southgate . . . . Aston Villa
  Adams . . . . Arsenal
  Batty . . . . Newcastle United
  Beckham . . . . Manchester United
  Gascoigne* . . . . Glasgow Rangers
  Wright, I. . . . . Arsenal
  Sheringham . . . . Manchester United
  Ince . . . . Liverpool
  Sub: *Butt . . . . Manchester United
  Result: 0–0

740. 15 November 1997
v CAMEROON............ Wembley Stadium
Martyn................ Leeds United
Southgate*............ Aston Villa
Hinchcliffe............ Everton
Ince.................. Liverpool
Campbell.............. Tottenham Hotspur
Neville, P............. Manchester United
Beckham.............. Manchester United
Gascoigne**.......... Glasgow Rangers
Fowler................ Liverpool
Scholes***............ Manchester United
McManaman........... Liverpool
Subs: *Ferdinand, R........ West Ham United
**Lee.............. Newcastle United
***Sutton............ Blackburn Rovers
Result: 2–0
Scorers: Scholes, Fowler

741. 11 February 1998
v CHILE................ Wembley Stadium
Martyn................ Leeds United
Neville, G............. Manchester United
Neville, P.*........... Manchester United
Batty**.............. Newcastle United
Adams................ Arsenal
Campbell.............. Tottenham Hotspur
Lee .... Newcastle United
Butt................. Manchester United
Dublin................ Coventry City
Sheringham***........ Manchester United
Owen................. Liverpool
Subs: *Le Saux........... Chelsea
**Ince.............. Liverpool
***Shearer........... Newcastle United
Result: 0–2

742. 25 March 1998
v SWITZERLAND .... Berne
Flowers .... Blackburn Rovers
Lee .... Newcastle United
Hinchcliffe............ Sheffield Wednesday
Keown................ Arsenal
Ferdinand, R.......... West Ham United
Southgate............ Aston Villa
McManaman........... Liverpool
Ince.................. Liverpool
Shearer.............. Newcastle United
Merson*.............. Middlesbrough
Owen**............... Liverpool
Subs: *Batty............. Newcastle United
**Sheringham.......... Manchester United
Result: 1–1
Scorer: Merson

743. 22 April 1998
v PORTUGAL............ Wembley Stadium
Seaman............... Arsenal
Neville, G.*........... Manchester United
Le Saux............... Chelsea
Ince.................. Liverpool
Adams................ Arsenal
Campbell.............. Tottenham Hotspur
Beckham**............ Manchester United
Batty................ Newcastle United
Shearer.............. Newcastle United
Sheringham***........ Manchester United
Scholes .... Manchester United
Subs: *Neville ,P.......... Manchester United
**Merson............ Middlesbrough
***Owen............. Liverpool
Result: 3–0
Scorers: Shearer (2), Sheringham

744. 23 May 1998
v SAUDI ARABIA......... Wembley Stadium
Seaman............... Arsenal
Neville, G............. Manchester United
Hinchcliffe*........... Sheffield Wednesday
Batty................ Newcastle United
Adams................ Arsenal
Southgate .... Aston Villa
Anderton............. Tottenham Hotspur
Beckham**............ Manchester United
Shearer***........... Newcastle United
Sheringham****....... Manchester United
Scholes .... Manchester United
Subs: *Neville, P.......... Manchester United
**Gascoigne.......... Middlesbrough
***Ferdinand, L........ Tottenham Hotspur
****Wright, I.......... Arsenal
Result: 0–0

745. 27 May 1998
v MOROCCO............ Casablanca
Flowers .... Blackburn Rovers
Le Saux............... Chelsea
Keown................ Arsenal
Southgate .... Aston Villa
Campbell.............. Tottenham Hotspur
Anderton............. Tottenham Hotspur
Ince.................. Liverpool
Dublin*............... Coventry City
Wright, I.**........... Arsenal
Gascoigne .... Middlesbrough
McManaman........... Liverpool
Subs: *Ferdinand, L........ Tottenham Hotspur
**Owen............. Liverpool
Result: 1–0
Scorer: Owen

746. 29 May 1998
v BELGIUM............. Casablanca
Martyn................ Leeds United
Neville, G.*........... Manchester United
Le Saux............... Chelsea
Keown................ Arsenal
Campbell**............ Tottenham Hotspur
Neville, P.***.......... Manchester United
Lee .... Newcastle United
Gascoigne****........ Middlesbrough
Ferdinand, L........... Tottenham Hotspur
Merson .... Middlesbrough
Butt................. Manchester United
Subs: *Owen............. Liverpool
**Dublin............ Coventry City
***Ferdinand, R........ West Ham United
****Beckham.......... Manchester United
Result: 0–0
Belgium won 4–3 in a special penalty shootout

747. 15 June 1998
v TUNISIA.............. Marseille
Seaman............... Arsenal
Southgate .... Aston Villa
Adams................ Arsenal
Campbell.............. Tottenham Hotspur
Le Saux .... Chelsea
Anderton............. Tottenham Hotspur
Batty................ Newcastle United
Scholes .... Manchester United
Ince.................. Liverpool
Sheringham*.......... Manchester United
Shearer.............. Newcastle United
Sub: *Owen............. Liverpool
Result: 2–0
Scorers: Shearer, Scholes

748. 22 June 1998
v ROMANIA . . . . Toulouse
Seaman . . . . Arsenal
Neville, G. . . . . Manchester United
Adams . . . . Arsenal
Campbell . . . . Tottenham Hotspur
Le Saux . . . . Chelsea
Anderton* . . . . Tottenham Hotspur
Ince** . . . . Liverpool
Scholes . . . . Manchester United
Batty . . . . Newcastle United
Sheringham . . . . Manchester United
Shearer . . . . Newcastle United
Subs: *Beckham . . . . Manchester United
**Owen . . . . Liverpool
Result: 1–2
Scorer: Owen

749. 26 June 1998
v COLOMBIA . . . . Lens
Seaman . . . . Arsenal
Neville, G. . . . . Manchester United
Adams . . . . Arsenal
Campbell . . . . Tottenham Hotspur
Le Saux . . . . Chelsea
Anderton* . . . . Tottenham Hotspur
Beckham . . . . Manchester United
Ince** . . . . Liverpool
Scholes*** . . . . Manchester United
Owen . . . . Liverpool
Shearer . . . . Newcastle United
Subs: *Lee . . . . Newcastle United
**Batty . . . . Newcastle United
***McManaman . . . . Liverpool
Result: 2–0
Scorers: Anderton, Beckham

750. 30 June 1998
v ARGENTINA . . . . Saint-Etienne
Seaman . . . . Arsenal
Neville, G. . . . . Manchester United
Adams . . . . Arsenal
Campbell . . . . Tottenham Hotspur
Le Saux* . . . . Chelsea
Anderton** . . . . Tottenham Hotspur
Beckham . . . . Manchester United
Ince . . . . Liverpool
Scholes*** . . . . Manchester United
Owen . . . . Liverpool
Shearer . . . . Newcastle United
Subs: *Southgate . . . . Aston Villa
**Batty . . . . Newcastle United
***Merson . . . . Middlesbrough
Result: 2–2 (a.e.t.)
Scorers: Shearer, Owen
Argentina won 4–3 on penalties

751. 5 September 1998
v SWEDEN . . . . Solna
Seaman . . . . Arsenal
Anderton* . . . . Tottenham Hotspur
Le Saux . . . . Chelsea
Southgate . . . . Aston Villa
Adams . . . . Arsenal
Campbell** . . . . Tottenham Hotspur
Redknapp . . . . Liverpool
Ince . . . . Liverpool
Shearer . . . . Newcastle United
Owen . . . . Liverpool
Scholes*** . . . . Manchester United
Subs: *Lee . . . . Newcastle United
**Merson . . . . Middlesbrough
***Sheringham . . . . Manchester United
Result: 1–2
Scorer: Shearer

752. 10 October 1998
v BULGARIA . . . . Wembley Stadium
Seaman . . . . Arsenal
Neville, G. . . . . Manchester United
Hinchcliffe* . . . . Sheffield Wednesday
Southgate . . . . Aston Villa
Campbell . . . . Tottenham Hotspur
Anderton** . . . . Tottenham Hotspur
Lee . . . . Newcastle United
Scholes*** . . . . Manchester United
Shearer . . . . Newcastle United
Owen . . . . Liverpool
Redknapp . . . . Liverpool
Subs: *Le Saux . . . . Chelsea
**Batty . . . . Newcastle United
***Sheringham . . . . Manchester United
Result: 0–0

753. 14 October 1998
v LUXEMBOURG . . . . Luxembourg
Seaman . . . . Arsenal
Neville, P. . . . . Manchester United
Southgate . . . . Aston Villa
Ferdinand, R. . . . . West Ham United
Campbell . . . . Tottenham Hotspur
Batty . . . . Newcastle United
Anderton* . . . . Tottenham Hotspur
Beckham . . . . Manchester United
Shearer . . . . Newcastle United
Owen . . . . Liverpool
Scholes** . . . . Manchester United
Subs: *Lee . . . . Newcastle United
**Wright, I. . . . . West Ham United
Result: 3–0
Scorers: Owen, Shearer (pen.), Southgate

754. 18 November 1998
v CZECH REPUBLIC . . . . Wembley Stadium
Martyn . . . . Leeds United
Anderton . . . . Tottenham Hotspur
Le Saux . . . . Chelsea
Keown . . . . Arsenal
Ferdinand, R. . . . . West Ham United
Campbell . . . . Tottenham Hotspur
Beckham . . . . Manchester United
Butt . . . . Manchester United
Dublin . . . . Aston Villa
Wright, I.* . . . . West Ham United
Merson** . . . . Aston Villa
Subs: *Fowler . . . . Liverpool
**Hendrie . . . . Aston Villa
Result: 2–0
Scorers: Anderton, Merson

755. 10 February 1999
v FRANCE . . . . Wembley Stadium
Seaman* . . . . Arsenal
Dixon** . . . . Arsenal
Le Saux . . . . Chelsea
Keown*** . . . . Arsenal
Adams . . . . Arsenal
Redknapp**** . . . . Liverpool
Beckham . . . . Manchester United
Ince . . . . Liverpool
Shearer . . . . Newcastle United
Owen***** . . . . Liverpool
Anderton . . . . Tottenham Hotspur
Subs: *Martyn . . . . Leeds United
**Ferdinand, R. . . . . West Ham United
***Wilcox . . . . Blackburn Rovers
****Scholes . . . . Manchester United
*****Cole, Andy . . . . Manchester United
Result: 0–2

756. 27 March 1999
v POLAND . . . . Wembley Stadium
Seaman . . . . Arsenal
Neville, G. . . . . Manchester United
Le Saux . . . . Chelsea
Sherwood. . . . . Tottenham Hotspur
Keown . . . . Arsenal
Campbell . . . . Tottenham Hotspur
Beckham* . . . . Manchester United
Scholes** . . . . Manchester United
Shearer . . . . Newcastle United
Cole, Andy . . . . Manchester United
McManaman*** . . . . Liverpool
Subs: *Neville, P. . . . . Manchester United
**Redknapp. . . . . Liverpool
***Parlour. . . . . Arsenal
Result: 3–1
Scorers: Scholes (3)

757. 28 April 1999
v HUNGARY . . . . Budapest
Seaman . . . . Arsenal
Brown* . . . . Manchester United
Neville, P. . . . . Manchester United
Keown . . . . Arsenal
Ferdinand, R.** . . . . West Ham United
Batty . . . . Leeds United
McManaman*** . . . . Liverpool
Sherwood. . . . . Tottenham Hotspur
Shearer . . . . Newcastle United
Phillips**** . . . . Sunderland
Butt . . . . Manchester United
Subs: *Gray. . . . . Sunderland
**Carragher. . . . . Liverpool
***Redknapp. . . . . Liverpool
****Heskey . . . . Leicester City
Result: 1–1
Scorer: Shearer (pen.)

758. 5 June 1999
v SWEDEN . . . . Wembley Stadium
Seaman . . . . Arsenal
Neville, P. . . . . Manchester United
Le Saux* . . . . Chelsea
Batty . . . . Leeds United
Keown** . . . . Arsenal
Campbell . . . . Tottenham Hotspur
Beckham*** . . . . Manchester United
Sherwood. . . . . Tottenham Hotspur
Shearer . . . . Newcastle United
Cole, Andy . . . . Manchester United
Scholes . . . . Manchester United
Subs: *Gray. . . . . Sunderland
**Ferdinand, R. . . . . West Ham United
***Parlour. . . . . Arsenal
Result: 0–0

759. 9 June 1999
v BULGARIA . . . . Sofia
Seaman . . . . Arsenal
Neville, P. . . . . Manchester United
Gray. . . . . Sunderland
Southgate . . . . Aston Villa
Woodgate* . . . . Leeds United
Campbell . . . . Tottenham Hotspur
Redknapp. . . . . Liverpool
Batty . . . . Leeds United
Shearer . . . . Newcastle United
Fowler** . . . . Liverpool
Sheringham . . . . Manchester United
Subs: *Parlour . . . . Arsenal
**Heskey. . . . . Leicester City
Result: 1–1
Scorer: Shearer

760. 4 September 1999
v LUXEMBOURG. . . . . Wembley Stadium
Martyn. . . . . Leeds United
Dyer*. . . . . Newcastle United
Pearce . . . . West Ham United
Batty . . . . Leeds United
Keown . . . . Arsenal
Adams** . . . . Arsenal
Parlour. . . . . Arsenal
Beckham*** . . . . Manchester United
Shearer . . . . Newcastle United
Fowler . . . . Liverpool
McManaman . . . . Real Madrid
Subs: *Neville, G.. . . . . Manchester United
**Neville, P. . . . . Manchester United
***Owen. . . . . Liverpool
Result: 6–0
Scorers: Shearer (3 – 1 pen.), McManaman (2), Owen

761. 8 September 1999
v POLAND . . . . Warsaw
Martyn. . . . . Leeds United
Neville, G.* . . . . Manchester United
Pearce . . . . West Ham United
Batty . . . . Leeds United
Keown . . . . Arsenal
Adams . . . . Arsenal
Beckham . . . . Manchester United
Scholes . . . . Manchester United
Shearer . . . . Newcastle United
Fowler** . . . . Liverpool
McManaman*** . . . . Real Madrid
Subs: *Neville, P. . . . . Manchester United
**Owen . . . . Liverpool
***Dyer. . . . . Newcastle United
Result: 0–0

762. 10 October 1999
v BELGIUM. . . . . Stadium of Light,
                                 Sunderland
Seaman* . . . . Arsenal
Dyer**. . . . . Newcastle United
Guppy . . . . Leicester City
Keown . . . . Arsenal
Adams . . . . Arsenal
Southgate . . . . Aston Villa
Lampard*** . . . . West Ham United
Redknapp. . . . . Liverpool
Shearer**** . . . . Newcastle United
Phillips***** . . . . Sunderland
Ince . . . . Middlesbrough
Subs: *Martyn . . . . Leeds United
**Neville, P. . . . . Manchester United
***Wise . . . . Chelsea
****Heskey . . . . Leicester City
*****Owen. . . . . Liverpool
Result: 2–1
Scorers: Shearer, Redknapp

763. 13 November 1999
v SCOTLAND. . . . . Hampden Park, Glasgow
Seaman . . . . Arsenal
Campbell . . . . Tottenham Hotspur
Neville, P. . . . . Manchester United
Redknapp. . . . . Liverpool
Keown . . . . Arsenal
Adams . . . . Arsenal
Beckham . . . . Manchester United
Scholes . . . . Manchester United
Shearer . . . . Newcastle United
Owen* . . . . Liverpool
Ince . . . . Middlesbrough
Sub: *Cole, Andy . . . . Manchester United
Result: 2–0
Scorers: Scholes (2)

764. 17 November 1999
v SCOTLAND . . . . Wembley Stadium
  Seaman . . . . Arsenal
  Campbell . . . . Tottenham Hotspur
  Neville, P. . . . . Manchester United
  Ince . . . . Middlesbrough
  Southgate . . . . Aston Villa
  Adams . . . . Arsenal
  Beckham . . . . Manchester United
  Redknapp. . . . . Liverpool
  Shearer . . . . Newcastle United
  Owen* . . . . Liverpool
  Scholes** . . . . Manchester United
Subs: *Heskey . . . . Leicester City
  **Parlour . . . . Arsenal
Result: 0–1

765. 23 February 2000
v ARGENTINA . . . . Wembley Stadium
  Seaman . . . . Arsenal
  Dyer* . . . . Newcastle United
  Wilcox . . . . Leeds United
  Southgate . . . . Aston Villa
  Keown** . . . . Arsenal
  Campbell . . . . Tottenham Hotspur
  Beckham*** . . . . Manchester United
  Scholes . . . . Manchester United
  Shearer**** . . . . Newcastle United
  Heskey***** . . . . Leicester City
  Wise . . . . Chelsea
Subs: *Neville, P. . . . . Manchester United
  **Ferdinand. R. . . . . West Ham United
  ***Parlour . . . . Arsenal
  ****Phillips . . . . Sunderland
  *****Cole, Andy . . . . Manchester United
Result: 0–0

766. 27 May 2000
v BRAZIL . . . . Wembley Stadium
  Seaman . . . . Arsenal
  Neville, G. . . . . Manchester United
  Neville, P. . . . . Manchester United
  Ince* . . . . Middlesbrough
  Keown . . . . Arsenal
  Campbell . . . . Tottenham Hotspur
  Beckham . . . . Manchester United
  Scholes . . . . Manchester United
  Shearer** . . . . Newcastle United
  Owen**** . . . . Liverpool
  Wise . . . . Chelsea
Subs: *Parlour*** . . . . Arsenal
  **Fowler . . . . Liverpool
  ***Barmby . . . . Everton
  ****Phillips . . . . Sunderland
Result: 1–1
Scorer: Owen

767. 31 May 2000
v UKRAINE . . . . Wembley Stadium
  Martyn. . . . . Leeds United
  Neville, P.* . . . . Manchester United
  Southgate . . . . Aston Villa
  Adams. . . . . Arsenal
  Gerrard** . . . . Liverpool
  Campbell . . . . Tottenham Hotspur
  Beckham . . . . Manchester United
  Scholes*** . . . . Manchester United
  Shearer . . . . Newcastle United
  Fowler**** . . . . Liverpool
  McManaman . . . . Real Madrid
Subs: *Barry . . . . Aston Villa
  **Dyer. . . . . Newcastle United
  ***Barmby . . . . Everton
  ****Heskey . . . . Liverpool
Result: 2–0
Scorers: Fowler, Adams

768. 3 June 2000
v MALTA . . . . Valetta
  Wright . . . . Ipswich Town
  Neville, G. . . . . Manchester United
  Neville, P. . . . . Manchester United
  Wise* . . . . Chelsea
  Keown** . . . . Arsenal
  Campbell . . . . Tottenham Hotspur
  Beckham*** . . . . Manchester United
  Barmby . . . . Everton
  Shearer**** . . . . Newcastle United
  Phillips***** . . . . Sunderland
  Scholes****** . . . . Manchester United
Subs: *Ince . . . . Middlesbrough
  **Southgate . . . . Aston Villa
  ***Barry . . . . Aston Villa
  ****Heskey . . . . Liverpool
  *****Fowler . . . . Liverpool
  ******McManaman . . . . . Real Madrid
Result: 2–1
Scorers: Keown, Heskey

769. 12 June 2000
v PORTUGAL . . . . Eindhoven
  Seaman . . . . Arsenal
  Neville, G. . . . . Manchester United
  Neville, P. . . . . Manchester United
  Ince . . . . Middlesbrough
  Campbell . . . . Tottenham Hotspur
  Adams* . . . . Arsenal
  Beckham . . . . Manchester United
  Scholes . . . . Manchester United
  Shearer . . . . Newcastle United
  Owen** . . . . Liverpool
  McManaman*** . . . . Real Madrid
Subs: *Keown . . . . Arsenal
  **Heskey . . . . Liverpool
  ***Wise . . . . Chelsea
Result: 2–3
Scorers: Scholes, McManaman

770. 17 June 2000
v GERMANY . . . . Charleroi
  Seaman . . . . Arsenal
  Neville, G. . . . . Manchester United
  Neville, P. . . . . Manchester United
  Ince . . . . Middlesbrough
  Keown . . . . Arsenal
  Campbell . . . . Tottenham Hotspur
  Beckham . . . . Manchester United
  Scholes* . . . . Manchester United
  Shearer . . . . Newcastle United
  Owen** . . . . Liverpool
  Wise . . . . Chelsea
Subs: *Barmby . . . . Everton
  **Gerrard . . . . Liverpool
Result: 1–0
Scorer: Shearer

771. 20 June 2000
v ROMANIA . . . . Charleroi
  Martyn. . . . . Leeds United
  Neville, G. . . . . Manchester United
  Neville, P . . . . Manchester United
  Ince . . . . Middlesbrough
  Keown . . . . Arsenal
  Campbell . . . . Tottenham Hotspur
  Beckham . . . . Manchester United
  Scholes* . . . . Manchester United
  Shearer . . . . Newcastle United
  Owen** . . . . Liverpool
  Wise*** . . . . Chelsea
Subs: *Southgate. . . . . Aston Villa
  **Heskey . . . . Liverpool
  ***Barmby . . . . Everton
Result: 2–3
Scorers: Shearer (pen.), Owen

772. 2 September 2000
v FRANCE . . . . Paris
Seaman . . . . Arsenal
Campbell . . . . Tottenham Hotspur
Barry . . . . Aston Villa
Anderton* . . . . Tottenham Hotspur
Keown . . . . Arsenal
Adams** . . . . Arsenal
Beckham . . . . Manchester United
Barmby*** . . . . Liverpool
Cole, Andy . . . . Manchester United
Scholes**** . . . . Manchester United
Wise . . . . Chelsea
Subs: *Dyer . . . . Newcastle United
**Southgate . . . . Aston Villa
***McManaman . . . . Real Madrid
****Owen . . . . Liverpool
Result: 1–1
Scorer: Owen

773. 7 October 2000
v GERMANY . . . . Wembley Stadium
Seaman . . . . Arsenal
Neville, G.* . . . . Manchester United
Le Saux** . . . . Chelsea
Southgate . . . . Aston Villa
Keown . . . . Arsenal
Adams . . . . Arsenal
Beckham*** . . . . Manchester United
Barmby . . . . Liverpool
Cole, Andy . . . . Manchester United
Owen . . . . Liverpool
Scholes . . . . Manchester United
Subs: *Dyer . . . . Newcastle United
**Barry . . . . Aston Villa
***Parlour . . . . Arsenal
Result: 0–1

774. 11 October 2000
v FINLAND . . . . Helsinki
Seaman . . . . Arsenal
Neville, P. . . . . Manchester United
Barry* . . . . Aston Villa
Southgate . . . . Aston Villa
Keown . . . . Arsenal
Wise . . . . Chelsea
Parlour . . . . Arsenal
Scholes . . . . Manchester United
Cole, Andy . . . . Manchester United
Sheringham** . . . . Manchester United
Heskey . . . . Liverpool
Subs: *Brown . . . . Manchester United
**McManaman . . . . Real Madrid
Result: 0–0

775. 15 November 2000
v ITALY . . . . Turin
James . . . . Aston Villa
Parlour* . . . . Arsenal
Barry** . . . . Aston Villa
Neville, G. . . . . Manchester United
Ferdinand, R. . . . . West Ham United
Southgate . . . . Aston Villa
Beckham . . . . Manchester United
Butt*** . . . . Manchester United
Dyer**** . . . . Newcastle United
Barmby . . . . Liverpool
Heskey***** . . . . Liverpool
Subs: *Anderton . . . . Tottenham Hotspur
**Johnson, S. . . . . Derby County
***Carragher . . . . Liverpool
****Fowler . . . . Liverpool
*****Phillips . . . . Sunderland
Result: 0–1

⚽ **DID YOU KNOW...?**

Since Wembley Stadium closed in October 2000,
England have played home fixtures at fourteen club
grounds – Manchester United, Aston Villa,
Newcastle United, Liverpool, Manchester City, Derby
County, Tottenham Hotspur, Leeds United,
Southampton, West Ham United, Sunderland,
Leicester City, Middlesbrough and Ipswich Town.

776. 28 February 2001
v SPAIN . . . . Villa Park, Birmingham
James* . . . . Aston Villa
Neville, P.** . . . . Manchester United
Powell*** . . . . Charlton Athletic
Butt**** . . . . Manchester United
Campbell . . . . Tottenham Hotspur
Ferdinand, R.***** . . . . . . Leeds United
Beckham****** . . . . Manchester United
Scholes******* . . . . Manchester United
Cole, Andy . . . . Manchester United
Owen . . . . Liverpool
Barmby . . . . Liverpool
Subs: *Martyn . . . . Leeds United
**Neville, G. . . . . Manchester United
***Ball . . . . Everton
****McCann . . . . Sunderland
*****Ehiogu . . . . Middlesbrough
******Heskey . . . . Liverpool
*******Lampard . . . . West Ham United
Result: 3–0
Scorers: Barmby, Heskey, Ehiogu

777. 24 March 2001
v FINLAND . . . . Anfield, Liverpool
Seaman . . . . Arsenal
Neville, G. . . . . Manchester United
Powell . . . . Charlton Athletic
Ferdinand, R. . . . . Leeds United
Campbell . . . . Tottenham Hotspur
Scholes . . . . Manchester United
Beckham . . . . Manchester United
Gerrard . . . . Liverpool
Cole, Andy* . . . . Manchester United
Owen** . . . . Liverpool
McManaman*** . . . . Real Madrid
Subs: *Fowler . . . . Liverpool
**Butt . . . . Manchester United
***Heskey . . . . Liverpool
Result: 2–1
Scorers: Owen, Beckham

778. 28 March 2001
v ALBANIA . . . . Tirana
Seaman . . . . Arsenal
Neville, G. . . . . Manchester United
Cole, Ashley . . . . Arsenal
Ferdinand, R. . . . . Leeds United
Campbell* . . . . Tottenham Hotspur
Butt . . . . Manchester United
Beckham . . . . Manchester United
Scholes . . . . Manchester United
Cole, Andy . . . . Manchester United
Owen** . . . . Liverpool
McManaman*** . . . . Real Madrid
Subs: *Brown . . . . Manchester United
**Sheringham . . . . Manchester United
***Heskey . . . . Liverpool
Result: 3–1
Scorers: Owen, Scholes, Andy Cole

779. 25 May 2001

v MEXICO	Pride Park, Derby
Martyn*	Leeds United
Neville, P.	Manchester United
Cole, Ashley**	Arsenal
Gerrard***	Liverpool
Keown****	Arsenal
Ferdinand, R.*****	Leeds United
Beckham******	Manchester United
Scholes+	Manchester United
Fowler++	Liverpool
Owen+++	Liverpool
Heskey++++	Liverpool
Subs: *James	Aston Villa
**Powell	Charlton Athletic
***Carrick	West Ham United
****Southgate	Aston Villa
*****Carragher	Liverpool
******Cole, J.	West Ham United
+Butt	Manchester United
++Sheringham	Manchester United
+++Smith	Leeds United
++++Mills	Leeds United

Result: 4–0
Scorers: Scholes, Fowler, Beckham, Sheringham

780. 6 June 2001

v GREECE	Athens
Seaman	Arsenal
Neville, P.	Manchester United
Cole, Ashley	Arsenal
Gerrard	Liverpool
Keown	Arsenal
Ferdinand, R.	Leeds United
Beckham	Manchester United
Scholes*	Manchester United
Fowler**	Liverpool
Owen	Liverpool
Heskey***	Liverpool
Subs: *Butt	Manchester United
**Smith	Leeds United
***McManaman	Real Madrid

Result: 2–0
Scorers: Scholes, Beckham

781. 15 August 2001

v HOLLAND	White Hart Lane, Tottenham
Martyn*	Leeds United
Neville, G.**	Manchester United
Cole, Ashley***	Arsenal
Carragher	Liverpool
Brown****	Manchester United
Keown*****	Arsenal
Beckham******	Manchester United
Scholes+	Manchester United
Cole, Andy++	Manchester United
Fowler+++	Liverpool
Hargreaves++++	Bayern Munich
Subs: *James+++++	West Ham United
**Mills	Leeds United
***Powell	Charlton Athletic
****Southgate	Middlesbrough
*****Ehiogu	Middlesbrough
******Lampard	Chelsea
+Carrick	West Ham United
++Smith	Leeds United
+++Owen	Liverpool
++++Barmby	Liverpool
+++++Wright, R.	Arsenal

Result: 0–2

782. 1 September 2001

v GERMANY	Munich
Seaman	Arsenal
Neville, G.	Manchester United

Cole, Ashley	Arsenal
Gerrard*	Liverpool
Ferdinand, R.	Leeds United
Campbell	Arsenal
Beckham	Manchester United
Scholes**	Manchester United
Heskey	Liverpool
Owen	Liverpool
Barmby***	Liverpool
Subs: *Hargreaves	Bayern Munich
**Carragher	Liverpool
***McManaman	Real Madrid

Result: 5–1
Scorers: Owen (3), Gerrard, Heskey

 FEATURED MATCH

1 SEPTEMBER 2001

GERMANY 1 ENGLAND 5 – OLYMPIC STADIUM, MUNICH

England's victory over Germany in Munich was not only historic, but also the most astonishing victory ever recorded by the national football team.

In routing opponents whose record in major competitions has long been embarrassingly superior, the English players rose to a thrilling level of penetrative excellence as they put an array of discouraging statistics to flight. Germany had suffered just one previous defeat in sixty World Cup qualifying games and had not conceded a goal in a serious engagement at the Olympic Stadium for sixteen years. Yet in this encounter, they surrendered three to Michael Owen alone.

Initially, though, it was the Germans who took an early lead when Carsten Jancker fired past David Seaman in the sixth minute, which gave their supporters false hope that their team's habit of invincibility on home soil would be sustained. England struck back swiftly when Michael Owen equalized a few minutes later. It was the first of an impressive hat-trick which was almost matched in impact by a single glorious strike from his Anfield teammate, Steven Gerrard, who controlled the ball on his chest all of 25 yards out, before drilling a low right-foot shot at extraordinary velocity into the furthest corner of Oliver Kahn's goal. This timely score in first-half stoppage time gave England a 2–1 lead at the break.

Just three minutes after the restart, Owen's extreme alertness put England further ahead, and his third followed in the 66th minute. When another Liverpool player, Emile Heskey, completed the rout in the 74th minute, it was all over for Germany, and thousands of dejected home fans headed for the exits.

Sven-Göran Eriksson was greeted with a round of applause in the press room after the game, and back home the result sparked a carnival atmosphere throughout towns and cities the length and breadth of the country. England's first win in Germany since 1965, and their biggest margin of victory over the Germans in modern times, put them in the driving seat for automatic World Cup qualification.

783. 5 September 2001
v ALBANIA . . . . St James' Park, Newcastle
Seaman . . . . Arsenal
Neville, G. . . . . Manchester United
Cole, Ashley . . . . Arsenal
Gerrard* . . . . Liverpool
Ferdinand, R. . . . . Leeds United
Campbell . . . . Arsenal
Beckham . . . . Manchester United
Scholes . . . . Manchester United
Heskey** . . . . Liverpool
Owen. . . . . Liverpool
Barmby*** . . . . Liverpool
Subs: *Carragher. . . . . Liverpool
**Fowler . . . . Liverpool
***McManaman . . . . Real Madrid
Result: 2–0
Scorers: Owen, Fowler

784. 6 October 2001
v GREECE . . . . Old Trafford, Manchester
Martyn. . . . . Leeds United
Neville, G. . . . . Manchester United
Cole, Ashley* . . . . Arsenal
Gerrard . . . . Liverpool
Ferdinand, R. . . . . Leeds United
Keown . . . . Arsenal
Beckham . . . . Manchester United
Scholes . . . . Manchester United
Fowler** . . . . Liverpool
Heskey. . . . . Liverpool
Barmby*** . . . . Liverpool
Subs: *McManaman . . . . Real Madrid
**Sheringham . . . . Tottenham Hotspur
***Cole, Andy . . . . Manchester United
Result: 2–2
Scorers: Sheringham, Beckham

785. 10 November 2001
v SWEDEN . . . . Old Trafford, Manchester
Martyn. . . . . Leeds United
Neville, G.* . . . . Manchester United
Carragher** . . . . Liverpool
Butt*** . . . . Manchester United
Ferdinand, R. . . . . Leeds United
Southgate . . . . Middlesbrough
Beckham . . . . Manchester United
Scholes**** . . . . Manchester United
Heskey***** . . . . Liverpool
Phillips+ . . . . Sunderland
Sinclair++ . . . . West Ham United
Subs: *Mills. . . . . Leeds United
**Neville, P. . . . . Manchester United
***Murphy . . . . Liverpool
****Lampard. . . . . Chelsea
*****Sheringham . . . . Tottenham Hotspur
+Anderton . . . . Tottenham Hotspur
++Fowler. . . . . Liverpool
Result: 1–1
Scorer: Beckham (pen.)

786. 13 February 2002
v HOLLAND . . . . Amsterdam
Martyn* . . . . Leeds United
Neville, G.** . . . . Manchester United
Campbell*** . . . . Arsenal
Ferdinand, R. . . . . Leeds United
Bridge**** . . . . Southampton
Gerrard***** . . . . Liverpool
Beckham . . . . Manchester United
Scholes+ . . . . Manchester United
Heskey. . . . . Liverpool
Vassell++. . . . . Aston Villa
Ricketts+++. . . . . Bolton Wanderers
Subs: *James. . . . . West Ham United
**Neville, P. . . . . Manchester United
***Southgate . . . . Middlesbrough

****Powell . . . . Charlton Athletic
*****Butt. . . . . Manchester United
+Cole, J. . . . . West Ham United
++Lampard . . . . Chelsea
+++Phillips . . . . Sunderland
Result: 1–1
Scorer: Vassell

787. 27 March 2002
v ITALY . . . . Elland Road, Leeds
Martyn* . . . . Leeds United
Mills** . . . . Leeds United
Campbell*** . . . . Arsenal
Southgate**** . . . . Middlesbrough
Bridge***** . . . . Southampton
Lampard******. . . . . Chelsea
Beckham+ . . . . Manchester United
Butt++. . . . . Manchester United
Sinclair+++ . . . . West Ham United
Owen++++ . . . . Liverpool
Heskey+++++. . . . . Liverpool
Subs: *James. . . . . West Ham United
**Neville, P . . . . Manchester United
***King. . . . . Tottenham Hotspur
****Ehiogu . . . . Middlesbrough
*****Neville, G. . . . . Manchester United
******Cole, J. . . . . West Ham United
+Murphy . . . . Liverpool
++Hargreaves . . . . Bayern Munich
+++Sheringham. . . . . Tottenham Hotspur
++++Fowler . . . . Leeds United
+++++Vassell . . . . Aston Villa
Result: 1–2
Scorer: Fowler

788. 17 April 2002
v PARAGUAY. . . . . Anfield, Liverpool
Seaman . . . . Arsenal
Neville, G.* . . . . Manchester United
Keown** . . . . Arsenal
Southgate*** . . . . Middlesbrough
Bridge**** . . . . Southampton
Butt***** . . . . Manchester United
Gerrard+ . . . . Liverpool
Scholes++ . . . . Manchester United
Dyer+++ . . . . Newcastle United
Owen++++ . . . . Liverpool
Vassell+++++ . . . . Aston Villa
Subs: *Carragher. . . . . Liverpool
**Mills . . . . Leeds United
***Sheringham . . . . Tottenham Hotspur
****Neville, P. . . . . Manchester United
*****Cole, J. . . . . West Ham United
+Sinclair . . . . West Ham United
++Fowler. . . . . Leeds United
+++Murphy. . . . . Liverpool
++++Hargreaves . . . . Bayern Munich
+++++Lampard. . . . . Chelsea
Result: 4–0
Scorers: Owen, Murphy, Vassell, o.g.

789. 21 May 2002
v SOUTH KOREA . . . . Seogwipo
Martyn* . . . . Leeds United
Mills** . . . . Leeds United
Cole, Ashley*** . . . . Arsenal
Murphy**** . . . . Liverpool
Ferdinand, R.***** . . . . . . Leeds United
Campbell+. . . . . Arsenal
Hargreaves. . . . . Bayern Munich
Scholes++ . . . . Manchester United
Vassell . . . . Aston Villa
Owen+++ . . . . Liverpool
Heskey. . . . . Liverpool
Subs: *James. . . . . West Ham United
**Brown . . . . Manchester United
***Bridge . . . . Southampton

****Cole, J. . . . . West Ham United
*****Southgate . . . . Middlesbrough
+Keown . . . . Arsenal
++Sinclair . . . . West Ham United
+++Sheringham. . . . . Tottenham Hotspur
Result: 1–1
Scorer: Owen

790. 26 May 2002

v CAMEROON. . . . . Kobe
Martyn* . . . . Leeds United
Brown . . . . Manchester United
Bridge . . . . Southampton
Hargreaves. . . . . Bayern Munich
Ferdinand, R.** . . . . Leeds United
Campbell*** . . . . Arsenal
Cole, J. . . . . West Ham United
Scholes**** . . . . Manchester United
Heskey***** . . . . Liverpool
Owen+ . . . . Liverpool
Vassell++. . . . . Aston Villa
Subs: *James. . . . . West Ham United
**Keown . . . . Arsenal
***Southgate . . . . Middlesbrough
****Mills . . . . Leeds United
*****Sinclair. . . . . West Ham United
+Sheringham . . . . Tottenham Hotspur
++Fowler. . . . . Leeds United
Result: 2–2
Scorers: Vassell, Fowler

791. 2 June 2002

v SWEDEN . . . . Saitama
Seaman . . . . Arsenal
Mills . . . . Leeds United
Cole, Ashley . . . . Arsenal
Hargreaves. . . . . Bayern Munich
Ferdinand, R. . . . . Leeds United
Campbell . . . . Arsenal
Beckham* . . . . Manchester United
Scholes . . . . Manchester United
Vassell** . . . . Aston Villa
Owen. . . . . Liverpool
Heskey. . . . . Liverpool
Subs: *Dyer . . . . Newcastle United
**Cole, J. . . . . West Ham United
Result: 1–1
Scorer: Campbell

792. 7 June 2002

v ARGENTINA. . . . . Sapporo
Seaman . . . . Arsenal
Mills . . . . Leeds United
Cole, Ashley . . . . Arsenal
Hargreaves*. . . . . Bayern Munich
Ferdinand, R. . . . . Leeds United
Campbell . . . . Arsenal
Beckham . . . . Manchester United
Scholes . . . . Manchester United
Butt. . . . . Manchester United
Owen**. . . . . Liverpool
Heskey*** . . . . Liverpool
Subs: *Sinclair. . . . . West Ham United
**Bridge . . . . Southampton
***Sheringham . . . . Tottenham Hotspur
Result: 1–0
Scorer: Beckham (pen.)

793. 12 June 2002

v NIGERIA . . . . Osaka
Seaman . . . . Arsenal
Mills . . . . Leeds United
Cole, Ashley* . . . . Arsenal
Sinclair. . . . . West Ham United
Ferdinand, R. . . . . Leeds United
Campbell . . . . Arsenal
Beckham . . . . Manchester United

Scholes . . . . Manchester United
Butt. . . . . Manchester United
Owen**. . . . . Liverpool
Heskey*** . . . . Liverpool
Subs: *Bridge . . . . Southampton
**Vassell . . . . Aston Villa
***Sheringham . . . . Tottenham Hotspur
Result: 0–0

794. 15 June 2002

v DENMARK . . . . Niigata
Seaman . . . . Arsenal
Mills . . . . Leeds United
Cole, Ashley . . . . Arsenal
Sinclair. . . . . West Ham United
Ferdinand, R. . . . . Leeds United
Campbell . . . . Arsenal
Beckham . . . . Manchester United
Scholes* . . . . Manchester United
Butt. . . . . Manchester United
Owen**. . . . . Liverpool
Heskey*** . . . . Liverpool
Subs: *Dyer . . . . Newcastle United
**Fowler . . . . Leeds United
***Sheringham . . . . Tottenham Hotspur
Result: 3–0
Scorers: R. Ferdinand, Owen, Heskey

795. 21 June 2002

v BRAZIL. . . . . Shizuoka
Seaman . . . . Arsenal
Mills . . . . Leeds United
Cole, Ashley* . . . . Arsenal
Sinclair**. . . . . West Ham United
Ferdinand, R. . . . . Leeds United
Campbell . . . . Arsenal
Beckham . . . . Manchester United
Scholes . . . . Manchester United
Butt. . . . . Manchester United
Heskey. . . . . Liverpool
Owen*** . . . . Liverpool
Subs: *Sheringham . . . . Tottenham Hotspur
**Dyer. . . . . Newcastle United
***Vassell . . . . Aston Villa
Result: 1–2
Scorer: Owen

 FEATURED MATCH

21 JUNE 2002

ENGLAND 1 BRAZIL 2 – SHIZUOKA

Despite playing against a team reduced to ten men, England did not manage a shot on target in the last half hour of this World Cup quarter-final. It was not due to lack of effort, even if the team's increasing tiredness may have made it look like that at times, but rather their problem was a lapse into familiar bad habits, long balls, a stretched midfield and the lack of strong leadership.

England took the lead in the 23rd minute, when, following neat footwork from Scholes to play himself out of trouble, Emile Heskey clipped the ball forward in search of Michael Owen, who had isolated Lucio. The defender should have tried to let the ball run past him or simply hacked away the danger, but in attempting to take the ball down on his thigh, he played the

→

perfect assist for Owen. The England striker only had Marcos to beat and he accomplished it with ease as the keeper went down early and Owen lifted his shot into the gaping net.

The belief that England could snatch and grab victory grew stronger as the first half wore on, even though David Seaman needed treatment on his back following an awkward fall. However, it was during first-half stoppage time that notions of an historic triumph began to ebb away. England's midfield was stranded up the pitch as Brazil launched a counter-attack through Ronaldinho. First he beat Ashley Cole, then he drew the rest of the England defence towards him before sweeping the ball out to Rivaldo, who made no mistake in stroking home his fifth goal of the tournament with a first-time shot.

An equalizer so close to the end of the first period made it an uncomfortable half-time, and five minutes after the restart, Scholes gave away a free kick that was to knock England out of the tournament and reduce David Seaman to tears. As Ronaldinho's deceptively flighted free kick floated towards him, the England keeper back-pedalled, his right arm flapping like that of a drowning man, but there was nothing he could do to stop its inevitable journey to the back of the net.

In the 57th minute, the Mexican referee harshly dismissed Ronaldinho for a far from vicious tackle on Danny Mills, and it was then that Roberto Carlos, Cafu and Rivaldo – who made blatant attempts to get England players booked or sent off – demonstrated their class by retaining possession while England, despite their efforts, could not take advantage against the determined ten-man opposition.

796. 7 September 2002
v PORTUGAL. . . . . Villa Park, Birmingham
James . . . . West Ham United
Mills* . . . . Leeds United
Cole, Ashley** . . . . Arsenal
Gerrard*** . . . . Liverpool
Ferdinand, R.**** . . . . . . Manchester United
Southgate . . . . Middlesbrough
Bowyer***** . . . . Leeds United
Butt+. . . . . Manchester United
Smith. . . . . Leeds United
Owen++ . . . . Liverpool
Heskey. . . . . Liverpool
Subs: *Bridge . . . . Southampton
**Hargreaves. . . . . Bayern Munich
***Dunn . . . . Blackburn Rovers
****Woodgate . . . . Leeds United
*****Sinclair. . . . . West Ham United
+Murphy . . . . Liverpool
++Cole, J. . . . . West Ham United
Result: 1–1
Scorer: Smith

797. 12 October 2002
v SLOVAKIA . . . . Bratislava
Seaman . . . . Arsenal
Neville, G. . . . . Manchester United
Cole, Ashley . . . . Arsenal
Gerrard* . . . . Liverpool
Southgate . . . . Middlesbrough
Woodgate . . . . Leeds United
Beckham . . . . Manchester United
Scholes . . . . Manchester United
Heskey** . . . . Liverpool
Owen*** . . . . Liverpool
Butt. . . . . Manchester United

Subs: *Dyer. . . . . Newcastle United
**Smith. . . . . Leeds United
***Hargreaves. . . . . Bayern Munich
Result: 2–1
Scorers: Beckham, Owen

798. 16 October 2002
v MACEDONIA . . . . St Mary's, Southampton
Seaman . . . . Arsenal
Neville, G. . . . . Manchester United
Cole, Ashley . . . . Arsenal
Gerrard* . . . . Liverpool
Woodgate . . . . Leeds United
Campbell . . . . Arsenal
Beckham . . . . Manchester United
Scholes . . . . Manchester United
Smith. . . . . Leeds United
Owen. . . . . Liverpool
Bridge** . . . . Southampton
Subs: *Butt. . . . . Manchester United
**Vassell . . . . Aston Villa
Result: 2–2
Scorers: Beckham, Gerrard

799. 12 February 2003
v AUSTRALIA . . . . Upton Park, West Ham
James* . . . . West Ham United
Neville, G.** . . . . Manchester United
Cole, Ashley*** . . . . Arsenal
Lampard****. . . . . Chelsea
Ferdinand, R.***** . . . . . Manchester United
Campbell****** . . . . Arsenal
Beckham+. . . . . Manchester United
Scholes++ . . . . Manchester United
Beattie+++ . . . . Southampton
Owen++++ . . . . Liverpool
Dyer+++++. . . . . Newcastle United
Subs: *Robinson . . . . Leeds United
**Mills . . . . Leeds United
***Konchesky . . . . Charlton Athletic
****Murphy . . . . Liverpool
*****Brown . . . . Manchester United
******King. . . . . Tottenham Hotspur
+Hargreaves . . . . Bayern Munich
++Jenas. . . . . Newcastle United
+++Jeffers. . . . . Arsenal
++++Rooney. . . . . Everton
+++++Vassell . . . . Aston Villa
Result: 1–3
Scorer: Jeffers

800. 29 March 2003
v LIECHTENSTEIN . . . . Vaduz
James . . . . West Ham United
Neville, G. . . . . Manchester United
Bridge . . . . Southampton
Gerrard* . . . . Liverpool
Ferdinand, R. . . . . Manchester United
Southgate . . . . Middlesbrough
Beckham** . . . . Manchester United
Scholes . . . . Manchester United
Heskey*** . . . . Liverpool
Owen. . . . . Liverpool
Dyer. . . . . Newcastle United
Subs: *Butt . . . . Manchester United
**Murphy . . . . Liverpool
***Rooney . . . . Everton
Result: 2–0
Scorers: Owen, Beckham

801. 2 April 2003
v TURKEY. . . . . Stadium of Light, Sunderland
James . . . . West Ham United
Neville, G. . . . . Manchester United
Bridge . . . . Southampton
Gerrard . . . . Liverpool

Ferdinand, R. . . . . Manchester United
Campbell . . . . Arsenal
Beckham . . . . Manchester United
Scholes . . . . Manchester United
Rooney* . . . . Everton
Owen** . . . . Liverpool
Butt . . . . Manchester United
Subs: *Dyer . . . . Newcastle United
**Vassell . . . . Aston Villa
Result: 2–0
Scorers: Vassell, Beckham (pen.)

802. 22 May 2003
v SOUTH AFRICA . . . . Durban
James* . . . . West Ham United
Mills . . . . Leeds United
Neville, P. . . . . Manchester United
Gerrard** . . . . Liverpool
Ferdinand, R.*** . . . . Manchester United
Southgate . . . . Middlesbrough
Beckham**** . . . . Manchester United
Scholes***** . . . . Manchester United
Heskey+ . . . . Liverpool
Owen . . . . Liverpool
Sinclair++ . . . . West Ham United
Subs: *Robinson . . . . Leeds United
**Barry . . . . Aston Villa
***Upson . . . . Birmingham City
****Jenas . . . . Newcastle United
*****Cole, J. . . . . West Ham United
+Vassell . . . . Aston Villa
++Lampard . . . . Chelsea
Result: 2–1
Scorers: Southgate, Heskey

803. 3 June 2003
v SERBIA & MONTENEGRO . . Walkers Stadium, Leicester
James . . . . West Ham United
Mills* . . . . Leeds United
Cole, Ashley** . . . . Arsenal
Gerrard*** . . . . Liverpool
Upson**** . . . . Birmingham City
Southgate***** . . . . Middlesbrough
Lampard+ . . . . Chelsea
Scholes++ . . . . Manchester United
Heskey+++ . . . . Liverpool
Owen++++ . . . . Liverpool
Neville, P.+++++ . . . . Manchester United
Subs: *Carragher . . . . Liverpool
**Bridge . . . . Southampton
***Jenas . . . . Newcastle United
****Barry . . . . Aston Villa
*****Terry . . . . Chelsea
+Cole, J. . . . . West Ham United
++Hargreaves . . . . Bayern Munich
+++Vassell . . . . Aston Villa
++++Rooney . . . . Everton
+++++Beattie . . . . Southampton
Result: 2–1
Scorers: Gerrard, J. Cole

804. 11 June 2003
v SLOVAKIA . . . . Riverside Stadium,
Middlesbrough
James . . . . West Ham United
Mills* . . . . Leeds United
Cole, Ashley . . . . Arsenal
Gerrard . . . . Liverpool
Upson . . . . Birmingham City
Southgate . . . . Middlesbrough
Lampard . . . . Chelsea
Scholes . . . . Manchester United
Rooney** . . . . Everton
Owen . . . . Liverpool
Neville, P. . . . . Manchester United
Subs: *Hargreaves . . . . Bayern Munich
**Vassell . . . . Aston Villa

Result: 2–1
Scorers: Owen (2 – 1 pen.)

805. 20 August 2003
v CROATIA . . . . Portman Road, Ipswich
James* . . . . West Ham United
Neville, P.** . . . . Manchester United
Cole, Ashley*** . . . . Arsenal
Gerrard**** . . . . Liverpool
Ferdinand, R.***** . . . . . . Manchester United
Terry . . . . Chelsea
Beckham+ . . . . Real Madrid
Scholes++ . . . . Manchester United
Heskey+++ . . . . Liverpool
Owen++++ . . . . Liverpool
Butt+++++ . . . . Manchester United
Subs: *Robinson . . . . Leeds United
**Mills . . . . Leeds United
***Upson . . . . Birmingham City
****Murphy . . . . Liverpool
*****Bridge . . . . Chelsea
+Cole, J. . . . . Chelsea
++Dyer . . . . Newcastle United
+++Beattie . . . . Southampton
++++Sinclair . . . . Manchester City
+++++Lampard . . . . Chelsea
Result: 3–1
Scorers: Beckham (pen.), Owen, Lampard

806. 6 September 2003
v MACEDONIA . . . . Skopje
James . . . . West Ham United
Neville, G. . . . . Manchester United
Cole, Ashley . . . . Arsenal
Hargreaves . . . . Bayern Munich
Terry . . . . Chelsea
Campbell . . . . Arsenal
Beckham . . . . Real Madrid
Lampard* . . . . Chelsea
Rooney** . . . . Everton
Owen*** . . . . Liverpool
Butt . . . . Manchester United
Subs: *Heskey . . . . Liverpool
**Neville, P. . . . . Manchester United
***Dyer . . . . Newcastle United
Result: 2–1
Scorers: Rooney, Beckham (pen.)

807. 10 September 2003
v LIECHTENSTEIN . . . . Old Trafford, Manchester
James . . . . West Ham United
Neville, G. . . . . Manchester United
Bridge . . . . Chelsea
Gerrard* . . . . Liverpool
Terry . . . . Chelsea
Upson . . . . Birmingham City
Beckham** . . . . Real Madrid
Lampard . . . . Chelsea
Rooney*** . . . . Everton
Owen . . . . Liverpool
Beattie . . . . Southampton
Subs: *Hargreaves . . . . Bayern Munich
**Neville, P. . . . . Manchester United
***Cole, J. . . . . Chelsea
Result: 2–0
Scorers: Owen, Rooney

⚽ **DID YOU KNOW...?**

England played indoors for the first time when they
beat Argentina 1–0 in the World Cup at the Sapporo
Dome, Japan, on 7 June 2002.

808. 11 October 2003

v TURKEY . . . . Istanbul
James . . . . West Ham United
Neville, G. . . . . Manchester United
Cole, Ashley . . . . Arsenal
Gerrard . . . . Liverpool
Terry . . . . Chelsea
Campbell . . . . Arsenal
Beckham . . . . Real Madrid
Scholes* . . . . Manchester United
Rooney** . . . . Everton
Heskey*** . . . . Liverpool
Butt . . . . Manchester United
Subs: *Lampard. . . . . Chelsea
**Dyer. . . . . Newcastle United
***Vassell . . . . Aston Villa
Result: 0–0

809. 16 November 2003

v DENMARK . . . . Old Trafford, Manchester
James* . . . . West Ham United
Neville, G.** . . . . Manchester United
Cole, Ashley*** . . . . Arsenal
Butt**** . . . . Manchester United
Terry . . . . Chelsea
Upson . . . . Birmingham City
Beckham***** . . . . Real Madrid
Lampard . . . . Chelsea
Rooney+ . . . . Everton
Heskey++ . . . . Liverpool
Cole, J.+++ . . . . Chelsea
Subs: *Robinson . . . . Leeds United
**Johnson, G. . . . . Chelsea
***Bridge . . . . Chelsea
****Neville, P. . . . . Manchester United
*****Jenas . . . . Newcastle United
+Parker . . . . Charlton Athletic
++Beattie . . . . Southampton
+++Murphy. . . . . Liverpool
Result: 2–3
Scorers: Rooney, J. Cole

810. 18 February 2004

v PORTUGAL. . . . . Faro Loulé
James . . . . Manchester City
Neville, P.* . . . . Manchester United
Cole, Ashley** . . . . Arsenal
Butt*** . . . . Manchester United
King. . . . . Tottenham Hotspur
Southgate . . . . Middlesbrough
Beckham**** . . . . Real Madrid
Scholes++ . . . . Manchester United
Rooney+++ . . . . Everton
Owen++++ . . . . Liverpool
Lampard+++++. . . . . Chelsea
Subs: *Mills. . . . . Leeds United
**Bridge+ . . . . Chelsea
***Carragher. . . . . Liverpool
****Jenas . . . . Newcastle United
+Hargreaves . . . . Bayern Munich
++Dyer . . . . Newcastle United
+++Smith . . . . Leeds United
++++Heskey . . . . Liverpool
+++++Cole, J. . . . . Chelsea
Result: 1–1
Scorer: King

811. 31 March 2004

v SWEDEN . . . . Gothenburg
James . . . . Manchester City
Carragher. . . . . Liverpool
Neville, P. . . . . Manchester United
Gerrard* . . . . Liverpool
Terry** . . . . Chelsea
Woodgate*** . . . . Newcastle United
Hargreaves**** . . . . Bayern Munich
Butt***** . . . . Manchester United

Rooney+ . . . . Everton
Vassell++. . . . . Aston Villa
Thompson+++. . . . . Glasgow Celtic
Subs: *Cole, J. . . . . Chelsea
**Southgate . . . . Middlesbrough
***Gardner . . . . Tottenham Hotspur
****Jenas . . . . Newcastle United
*****Parker . . . . Chelsea
+Heskey. . . . . Liverpool
++Defoe . . . . Tottenham Hotspur
+++Smith . . . . Leeds United
Result: 0–1

812. 1 June 2004

v JAPAN . . . . City of Manchester Stadium
James . . . . Manchester City
Neville, G.* . . . . Manchester United
Cole, Ashley . . . . Arsenal
Gerrard** . . . . Liverpool
Terry*** . . . . Chelsea
Campbell . . . . Arsenal
Beckham**** . . . . Real Madrid
Scholes***** . . . . Manchester United
Rooney+ . . . . Everton
Owen++ . . . . Liverpool
Lampard+++ . . . . Chelsea
Subs: *Neville, P. . . . . Manchester United
**Hargreaves. . . . . Bayern Munich
***King. . . . . Tottenham Hotspur
****Cole, J. . . . . Chelsea
*****Dyer. . . . . Newcastle United
+Heskey. . . . . Birmingham City
++Vassell. . . . . Aston Villa
+++Butt . . . . Manchester United
Result: 1–1
Scorer: Owen

813. 5 June 2004

v ICELAND . . . . City of Manchester Stadium
Robinson* . . . . Tottenham Hotspur
Neville, G.** . . . . Manchester United
Cole, Ashley*** . . . . Arsenal
Gerrard**** . . . . Liverpool
Carragher***** . . . . Liverpool
Campbell+. . . . . Arsenal
Beckham++. . . . . Real Madrid
Scholes+++ . . . . Manchester United
Rooney++++ . . . . Everton
Owen+++++. . . . . Liverpool
Lampard++++++ . . . . Chelsea
Subs: *Walker . . . . Leicester City
**Neville, P. . . . . Manchester United
***Bridge . . . . Chelsea
****Cole, J. . . . . Chelsea
*****Defoe . . . . Tottenham Hotspur
+King . . . . Tottenham Hotspur
++Hargreaves . . . . Bayern Munich
+++Butt . . . . Manchester United
++++Vassell . . . . Aston Villa
+++++Heskey . . . . Birmingham City
++++++Dyer . . . . Newcastle United
Result: 6–1
Scorers: Lampard, Rooney (2), Vassell (2), Bridge

814. 13 June 2004

v FRANCE. . . . . Lisbon
James . . . . Manchester City
Neville, G. . . . . Manchester United
Cole, Ashley . . . . Arsenal
Gerrard . . . . Liverpool
Campbell . . . . Arsenal
King. . . . . Tottenham Hotspur
Beckham . . . . Real Madrid
Scholes* . . . . Manchester United
Rooney** . . . . Everton
Owen*** . . . . Liverpool
Lampard . . . . Chelsea

Subs: *Hargreaves . . . . Bayern Munich
**Heskey . . . . Birmingham City
***Vassell . . . . Aston Villa
Result: 1–2
Scorer: Lampard

815. 17 June 2004
v SWITZERLAND . . . . Coimbra
James . . . . Manchester City
Neville, G. . . . . Manchester United
Cole, Ashley . . . . Arsenal
Gerrard . . . . Liverpool
Terry . . . . Chelsea
Campbell . . . . Arsenal
Beckham . . . . Real Madrid
Scholes* . . . . Manchester United
Rooney** . . . . Everton
Owen*** . . . . Liverpool
Lampard . . . . Chelsea
Subs: *Hargreaves . . . . Bayern Munich
**Dyer . . . . Newcastle United
***Vassell . . . . Aston Villa
Result: 3–0
Scorers: Rooney (2), Gerrard

816. 21 June 2004
v CROATIA . . . . Lisbon
James . . . . Manchester City
Neville, G. . . . . Manchester United
Cole, Ashley . . . . Arsenal
Gerrard . . . . Liverpool
Terry . . . . Chelsea
Campbell . . . . Arsenal
Beckham . . . . Real Madrid
Scholes* . . . . Manchester United
Rooney** . . . . Everton
Owen . . . . Liverpool
Lampard*** . . . . Chelsea
Subs: *King . . . . Tottenham Hotspur
**Vassell . . . . Aston Villa
***Neville, P. . . . . Manchester United
Result: 4–2
Scorers: Scholes, Rooney (2), Lampard

817. 24 June 2004
v PORTUGAL . . . . Lisbon
James . . . . Manchester City
Neville, G. . . . . Manchester United
Cole, Ashley . . . . Arsenal
Gerrard* . . . . Liverpool
Terry . . . . Chelsea
Campbell . . . . Arsenal
Beckham . . . . Real Madrid
Scholes** . . . . Manchester United
Rooney*** . . . . Everton
Owen . . . . Liverpool
Lampard . . . . Chelsea
Subs: *Hargreaves . . . . Bayern Munich
**Neville, P. . . . . Manchester United
***Vassell . . . . Aston Villa
Result: 2–2
Scorers: Owen, Lampard
Portugal won 6–5 on penalties

818. 18 August 2004
v UKRAINE . . . . St James' Park, Newcastle
James . . . . Manchester City
Neville, G.* . . . . Manchester United
Cole, Ashley** . . . . Arsenal
Gerrard*** . . . . Liverpool
Terry . . . . Chelsea
King . . . . Tottenham Hotspur
Beckham . . . . Real Madrid
Lampard**** . . . . Chelsea
Smith***** . . . . Manchester United
Owen . . . . Real Madrid
Butt****** . . . . Newcastle United
Subs: *Johnson, G. . . . . Chelsea

**Carragher . . . . Liverpool
***Dyer . . . . Newcastle United
****Jenas . . . . Newcastle United
*****Defoe . . . . Tottenham Hotspur
******Wright-Phillips . . . . Manchester City
Result: 3–0
Scorers: Beckham, Owen, Wright-Phillips

819. 4 September 2004
v AUSTRIA . . . . Vienna
James . . . . Manchester City
Neville, G. . . . . Manchester United
Cole, Ashley . . . . Arsenal
Gerrard* . . . . Liverpool
Terry . . . . Chelsea
King . . . . Tottenham Hotspur
Beckham . . . . Real Madrid
Lampard . . . . Chelsea
Smith** . . . . Manchester United
Owen . . . . Real Madrid
Bridge*** . . . . Chelsea
Subs: *Carragher . . . . Liverpool
**Defoe . . . . Tottenham Hotspur
***Cole, J. . . . . Chelsea
Result: 2–2
Scorers: Lampard, Gerrard

820. 8 September 2004
v POLAND . . . . Chorzów
Robinson . . . . Tottenham Hotspur
Neville, G.* . . . . Manchester United
Cole, Ashley . . . . Arsenal
Gerrard . . . . Liverpool
Terry . . . . Chelsea
King . . . . Tottenham Hotspur
Beckham** . . . . Real Madrid
Lampard . . . . Chelsea
Defoe*** . . . . Tottenham Hotspur
Owen . . . . Real Madrid
Bridge . . . . Chelsea
Subs: *Carragher . . . . Liverpool
**Hargreaves . . . . Bayern Munich
***Dyer . . . . Newcastle United
Result: 2–1
Scorers: Defoe, o.g.

821. 9 October 2004
v WALES . . . . Old Trafford, Manchester
Robinson . . . . Tottenham Hotspur
Neville, G. . . . . Manchester United
Cole, Ashley . . . . Arsenal
Butt . . . . Newcastle United
Ferdinand, R. . . . . Manchester United
Campbell . . . . Arsenal
Beckham* . . . . Real Madrid
Lampard . . . . Chelsea
Rooney** . . . . Manchester United
Owen . . . . Real Madrid
Defoe*** . . . . Tottenham Hotspur
Subs: *Hargreaves . . . . Bayern Munich
**King . . . . Tottenham Hotspur
***Smith . . . . Manchester United
Result: 2–0
Scorers: Lampard, Beckham

⚽ **DID YOU KNOW...?**

The most substitutions made by an England manager in a match is eleven: Sven-Göran Eriksson made eleven changes at half-time against Holland in August 2001, then switched the same number of players against Italy in March 2002, and repeated this tactic for a third time against Australia in February 2003, when the entire England team was substituted after the break.

822. 13 October 2004
v AZERBAIJAN . . . . Baku
Robinson . . . . Tottenham Hotspur
Neville, G. . . . . Manchester United
Cole, Ashley . . . . Arsenal
Butt . . . . Newcastle United
Ferdinand, R. . . . . Manchester United
Campbell . . . . Arsenal
Jenas* . . . . Newcastle United
Lampard . . . . Chelsea
Rooney** . . . . Manchester United
Owen. . . . . Real Madrid
Defoe*** . . . . Tottenham Hotspur
Subs: *Wright-Phillips . . . . . Manchester City
**Cole, J. . . . . Chelsea
***Smith . . . . Manchester United
Result: 1–0
Scorer: Owen

823. 17 November 2004
v SPAIN . . . . Madrid
Robinson . . . . Tottenham Hotspur
Neville, G. . . . . Manchester United
Cole, Ashley* . . . . Arsenal
Butt . . . . Newcastle United
Ferdinand, R.** . . . . Manchester United
Terry*** . . . . Chelsea
Beckham**** . . . . Real Madrid
Lampard***** . . . . Chelsea
Rooney****** . . . . Manchester United
Owen. . . . . Real Madrid
Bridge . . . . Chelsea
Subs: *Defoe . . . . Tottenham Hotspur
**Carragher. . . . . Liverpool
***Upson . . . . Birmingham City
****Wright-Phillips . . . . . . Manchester City
*****Jenas . . . . Newcastle United
******Smith . . . . Manchester United
Result: 0–1

824. 9 February 2005
v HOLLAND . . . . Villa Park, Birmingham
Robinson . . . . Tottenham Hotspur
Neville, G. . . . . Manchester United
Cole, Ashley . . . . Arsenal
Gerrard* . . . . Liverpool
Carragher. . . . . Liverpool
Brown . . . . Manchester United
Beckham** . . . . Real Madrid
Lampard*** . . . . Chelsea
Rooney**** . . . . Manchester United
Owen. . . . . Real Madrid
Wright-Phillips***** . . . . . Manchester City
Subs: *Jenas . . . . Newcastle United
**Dyer. . . . . Newcastle United
***Hargreaves. . . . . Bayern Munich
****Johnson, A.. . . . . Crystal Palace
*****Downing . . . . Middlesbrough
Result: 0–0

825. 26 March 2005
v N. IRELAND . . . . Old Trafford, Manchester
Robinson . . . . Tottenham Hotspur
Neville, G. . . . . Manchester United
Cole, Ashley . . . . Arsenal
Gerrard* . . . . Liverpool
Ferdinand, R. . . . . Manchester United
Terry . . . . Chelsea
Beckham** . . . . Real Madrid
Lampard . . . . Chelsea
Rooney*** . . . . Manchester United
Owen. . . . . Real Madrid
Cole, J. . . . . Chelsea
Subs: *Hargreaves . . . . Bayern Munich
**Dyer. . . . . Newcastle United

***Defoe . . . . Tottenham Hotspur
Result: 4–0
Scorers: J. Cole, Owen, o.g., Lampard

826. 30 March 2005
v AZERBAIJAN . . . . St James' Park, Newcastle
Robinson . . . . Tottenham Hotspur
Neville, G. . . . . Manchester United
Cole, Ashley . . . . Arsenal
Gerrard . . . . Liverpool
Ferdinand, R.* . . . . Manchester United
Terry . . . . Chelsea
Beckham** . . . . Real Madrid
Lampard . . . . Chelsea
Owen. . . . . Real Madrid
Rooney*** . . . . Manchester United
Cole, J. . . . . Chelsea
Subs: *King . . . . Tottenham Hotspur
**Defoe. . . . . Tottenham Hotspur
***Dyer. . . . . Newcastle United
Result: 2–0
Scorers: Gerrard, Beckham

827. 28 May 2005
v USA. . . . . Chicago
James . . . . Manchester City
Johnson, G. . . . . Chelsea
Cole, Ashley* . . . . Arsenal
Carrick. . . . . Tottenham Hotspur
Brown . . . . Manchester United
Campbell** . . . . Arsenal
Jenas . . . . Newcastle United
Richardson*** . . . . Manchester United
Smith . . . . Manchester United
Johnson, A.**** . . . . Crystal Palace
Cole, J. . . . . Chelsea
Subs: *Defoe . . . . Tottenham Hotspur
**Knight . . . . Fulham
***Neville, P. . . . . Manchester United
****Young . . . . Charlton Athletic
Result: 2–1
Scorers: Richardson (2)

828. 31 May 2005
v COLOMBIA . . . . New Jersey
James* . . . . Manchester City
Neville, P. . . . . Manchester United
Cole, Ashley . . . . Arsenal
Carrick. . . . . Tottenham Hotspur
Johnson, G. . . . . Chelsea
Knight . . . . Fulham
Beckham** . . . . Real Madrid
Jenas . . . . Newcastle United
Crouch*** . . . . Southampton
Owen**** . . . . Real Madrid
Cole, J.***** . . . . Chelsea
Subs: *Green. . . . . Norwich City
**Richardson . . . . Manchester United
***Defoe . . . . Tottenham Hotspur
****Smith . . . . Manchester United
*****Young . . . . Charlton Athletic
Result: 3–2
Scorers: Owen (3)

829. 17 August 2005
v DENMARK . . . . Copenhagen
Robinson* . . . . Tottenham Hotspur
Neville, G.** . . . . Manchester United
Cole, Ashley . . . . Arsenal
Gerrard*** . . . . Liverpool
Terry**** . . . . Chelsea
Ferdinand, R. . . . . Manchester United
Beckham . . . . Real Madrid
Lampard***** . . . . Chelsea
Rooney . . . . Manchester United

Defoe****** . . . . Tottenham Hotspur
Cole, J. . . . . Chelsea
Subs: *James. . . . . Manchester City
**Johnson, G. . . . . Chelsea
***Jenas . . . . Tottenham Hotspur
****Carragher. . . . . Liverpool
*****Hargreaves. . . . . . . Bayern Munich
******Owen. . . . . Real Madrid
Result: 1–4
Scorer: Rooney

830. 3 September 2005
v WALES. . . . . Millennium Stadium, Cardiff
Robinson . . . . Tottenham Hotspur
Young . . . . Charlton Athletic
Cole, Ashley . . . . Arsenal
Gerrard* . . . . Liverpool
Ferdinand, R. . . . . Manchester United
Carragher. . . . . Liverpool
Beckham . . . . Real Madrid
Lampard . . . . Chelsea
Rooney . . . . Manchester United
Wright-Phillips** . . . . Chelsea
Cole, J.*** . . . . Chelsea
Subs: *Richardson . . . . Manchester United
**Defoe. . . . . Tottenham Hotspur
***Hargreaves. . . . . Bayern Munich
Result: 1–0
Scorer: J. Cole

831. 7 September 2005
v N. IRELAND . . . . Windsor Park, Belfast
Robinson . . . . Tottenham Hotspur
Young . . . . Charlton Athletic
Cole, Ashley . . . . Arsenal
Gerrard* . . . . Liverpool
Ferdinand, R. . . . . Manchester United
Carragher. . . . . Liverpool
Beckham . . . . Real Madrid
Lampard** . . . . Chelsea
Rooney . . . . Manchester United
Owen. . . . . Newcastle United
Wright-Phillips*** . . . . . . Chelsea
Subs: *Defoe . . . . Tottenham Hotspur
**Hargreaves. . . . . Bayern Munich
***Cole, J. . . . . Chelsea
Result: 0–1

832. 8 October 2005
v AUSTRIA . . . . Old Trafford, Manchester
Robinson . . . . Tottenham Hotspur
Young . . . . Charlton Athletic
Carragher. . . . . Liverpool
Gerrard . . . . Liverpool
Terry . . . . Chelsea
Campbell* . . . . Arsenal
Beckham . . . . Real Madrid
Lampard . . . . Chelsea
Crouch. . . . . Liverpool
Owen** . . . . Newcastle United
Cole, J.*** . . . . Chelsea
Subs: *Ferdinand, R. . . . . Manchester United
**Richardson . . . . Manchester United
***King. . . . . Tottenham Hotspur
Result: 1–0
Scorers: Lampard (pen.)

833. 12 October 2005
v POLAND . . . . Old Trafford, Manchester
Robinson . . . . Tottenham Hotspur
Young . . . . Charlton Athletic
Carragher. . . . . Liverpool
King. . . . . Tottenham Hotspur
Ferdinand, R. . . . . Manchester United
Terry . . . . Chelsea

Wright-Phillips* . . . . Chelsea
Lampard . . . . Chelsea
Rooney** . . . . Manchester United
Owen. . . . . Newcastle United
Cole, J.*** . . . . Chelsea
Subs: *Crouch . . . . Liverpool
**Jenas . . . . Tottenham Hotspur
***Smith . . . . Manchester United
Result: 2–1
Scorers: Owen, Lampard

834. 12 November 2005
v ARGENTINA. . . . . Geneva
Robinson . . . . Tottenham Hotspur
Young* . . . . Charlton Athletic
Bridge** . . . . Chelsea
Gerrard . . . . Liverpool
Ferdinand, R. . . . . Manchester United
Terry . . . . Chelsea
Beckham . . . . Real Madrid
Lampard . . . . Chelsea
Rooney . . . . Manchester United
Owen. . . . . Newcastle United
King*** . . . . Tottenham Hotspur
Subs: *Crouch . . . . Liverpool
**Konchesky . . . . West Ham United
***Cole, J. . . . . Chelsea
Result: 3–2
Scorers: Rooney, Owen (2)

FEATURED MATCH

12 NOVEMBER 2005

ENGLAND 3 ARGENTINA 2 – GENEVA

Wayne Rooney had the rest of the football world quaking in fear after his stunning masterclass sent Argentina crashing to defeat in Geneva. The Manchester United player dispelled any fears that England will not be among the big guns in the 2006 World Cup finals in Germany by scoring one goal, playing his part in another, hitting the woodwork and leaving one of the top defences in the world on its knees.

The twenty-year-old thought he had opened the scoring after half an hour, with an exquisite flick over advancing Argentine keeper Roberto Abbondanzieri, but his effort struck a post. Hernan Crespo put the South American side ahead four minutes later, but Rooney refused to keep quiet and latched on to David Beckham's header to equalize in the 39th minute.

Argentina regained the lead through Walter Samuel eight minutes into the second-half, but Rooney was at the heart of every good move produced by an England team unrecognizable from the one humiliated by Northern Ireland earlier in the season. He set up Steven Gerrard to supply the cross for Michael Owen to level the scores in the 86th minute, before the Newcastle United frontman pounced again in injury time, nipping in ahead of Peter Crouch at the near-post to score the winner, and so cap an extraordinary game of football.

It was a marvellous match – indeed a contest worthy of the World Cup Final itself – and one that produced an England performance that certainly raised hopes of a successful 2006 World Cup run in Germany.

5 TAKING ON THE WORLD
England's World Cup Performances

WORLD CUP 1950

QUALIFYING ROUNDS

15 October 1949 – WALES v ENGLAND at Ninian Park, Cardiff
Half-time – 0–3: Mortensen (0–1), Milburn (0–2), Milburn (0–3)
Full-time – 1–4: Milburn (0–4), Griffiths (1–4)
Wales: Sidlow; Barnes; Sherwood; Paul; T. G. Jones; Burgess; Griffiths; Lucas; Ford; Scrine; Edwards.
England: Williams; Mozley; Aston; Wright; Franklin; Dickinson; Finney; Mortensen; Milburn; Shackleton; Hancocks.

16 November 1949 – ENGLAND v NORTHERN IRELAND at Maine Road, Manchester
Half-time – 4–0: Rowley (1–0), Froggatt (2–0), Pearson (3–0), Mortensen (4–0)
Full-time – 9–2: Rowley (5–0), Mortensen (6–0), Smyth (6–1), Rowley (7–1), Rowley (8–1), Pearson (9–1), Brennan (9–2)
England: Streten; Mozley; Aston; Watson; Franklin; Wright; Finney; Mortensen; Rowley; Pearson; Froggatt.
Northern Ireland: Kelly; Feeney; McMichael; Bowler; Vernon; McCabe; Cochrane; Smyth; Brennan; Tully; McKenna.

15 April 1950 – SCOTLAND v ENGLAND at Hampden Park, Glasgow
Half-time – 0–0
Full-time – 0–1: Bentley (0–1)
Scotland: Cowan; Young; Cox; McColl; Woodburn; Forbes; Waddell; Moir; Bauld; Steel; Liddell.
England: Williams; Ramsey; Aston; Wright; Franklin; Dickinson; Finney; Mannion; Mortensen; Bentley; Langton.

Other group results:
Northern Ireland 2 Scotland 8; Scotland 2 Wales 0; Wales 0 Northern Ireland 0.

British Qualifying Zone

	P	W	D	L	F	A	Pts
ENGLAND	3	3	0	0	14	3	6
Scotland	3	2	0	1	10	3	4
Northern Ireland	3	0	1	2	4	17	1
Wales	3	0	1	2	1	6	1

Scotland should also have qualified, but the Scottish FA declined because they had finished second.

1950 WORLD CUP FINALS

Hosts   Brazil
Holders Italy

Group B England (seeded) / Spain / Chile / USA

England Squad

Goalkeepers		*Age*	*Caps*
Bert Williams	Wolverhampton Wanderers	28	7
Ted Ditchburn	Tottenham Hotspur	28	2

Fullbacks			
Jack Aston	Manchester United	28	14
Alf Ramsey	Tottenham Hotspur	30	5
Laurie Scott	Arsenal	33	17
Bill Eckersley	Blackburn Rovers	23	0

Halfbacks			
Billy Wright	Wolverhampton Wanderers	26	29
Laurie Hughes	Liverpool	24	0
Jimmy Dickinson	Portsmouth	25	7
Bill Nicholson	Tottenham Hotspur	31	0
Willie Watson	Sunderland	30	2
Henry Cockburn	Manchester United	27	10
Jim Taylor	Fulham	32	0

Forwards			
Jackie Milburn	Newcastle United	26	7
Stan Mortensen	Blackpool	29	18
Roy Bentley	Chelsea	27	4
Wilf Mannion	Middlesbrough	32	19
Tom Finney	Preston North End	28	25
Eddie Baily	Tottenham Hotspur	23	0
Jimmy Mullen	Wolverhampton Wanderers	27	4
Stanley Matthews	Blackpool	35	30

Manager	Walter Winterbottom
Average age	28.2 years
Average experience	9.5 caps

Group B

25 June 1950 – CHILE v ENGLAND at Rio de Janeiro
Half-time – 0–1: Mortensen (0–1)
Full-time – 0–2: Mannion (0–2)
Chile: Livingstone; Farias; Roldán; Alvarez; Busquets; Carvalho; Mayanes; Cremaschi; Robledo; Muñoz; Diaz.
England: Williams; Ramsey; Aston; Wright; Hughes; Dickinson; Finney; Mannion; Bentley; Mortensen; Mullen.

29 June 1950 – USA v ENGLAND at Belo Horizonte
Half-time – 1–0: Gaetjens (1–0)
Full-time – 1–0

USA: Borghi; Keough; Maca; McIlvenny; Colombo; Bahr; Wallace; Pariani;
  J. Souza; Gaetjens; E. Souza.
England: Williams; Ramsey; Aston; Wright; Hughes; Dickinson; Finney;
  Mannion; Bentley; Mortensen; Mullen.

2 July 1950 – SPAIN v ENGLAND at Rio de Janeiro
Half-time – 0–0
Full-time – 1–0: Zarra (1–0)
Spain: Ramallets; Alonzo; Parra; Gonzalvo II; Gonzalvo III; Puchades; Basora;
  Igoa; Zarra; Panizo; Gainza.
England: Williams; Ramsey; Eckersley; Wright; Hughes; Dickinson; Matthews;
  Mortensen; Milburn; Baily; Finney.

Other group results:
Spain 3 USA 1; Spain 2 Chile 0; Chile 5 USA 2.

Group B final table

	P	W	D	L	F	A	Pts
Spain	3	3	0	0	6	1	6
ENGLAND	3	1	0	2	2	2	2
Chile	3	1	0	2	5	6	2
USA	3	1	0	2	4	8	2

WORLD CUP 1954

QUALIFYING ROUNDS

10 October 1953 – WALES v ENGLAND at Ninian Park, Cardiff
Half-time – 1–1: Allchurch (1–0), Wilshaw (1–1)
Full-time – 1–4: Wilshaw (1–2), Lofthouse (1–3), Lofthouse (1–4)
Wales: Howells; Barnes; Sherwood; Paul; Daniel; Burgess; Foulkes; R. Davies;
  Charles; I. Allchurch; Clarke.
England: Merrick; Garrett; Eckersley; Wright; Johnston; Dickinson; Finney;
  Quixall; Lofthouse; Wilshaw; Mullen.

**11 November 1953 – ENGLAND v NORTHERN IRELAND at Goodison
Park, Liverpool**
Half-time – 1–0: Hassall (1–0)
Full-time – 3–1: McMorran (1–1), Hassall (2–1), Lofthouse (3–1)
England: Merrick; Rickaby; Eckersley; Wright; Johnston; Dickinson; Matthews;
  Quixall; Lofthouse; Hassall; Mullen.
Northern Ireland: Smyth; Graham; McMichael; Blanchflower; Dickson; Cush;
  Bingham; McIlroy; Simpson; McMorran; Lockhart.

3 April 1954 – SCOTLAND v ENGLAND at Hampden Park, Glasgow
Half-time – 1–1: Brown (1–0), Broadis (1–1)
Full-time – 2–4: Nicholls (1–2), Allen (1–3), Mullen (1–4), Ormond (2–4)
Scotland: Farm; Haughney; Cox; Evans; Brennan; Aitken; McKenzie;
  Johnstone; Henderson; Brown; Ormond.
England: Merrick; Stainforth; Byrne; Wright; Clarke; Dickinson; Finney;
  Broadis; Allen; Nicholls; Mullen.

Other group results:
Northern Ireland 1 Scotland 3; Scotland 3 Wales 3; Wales 1 Northern Ireland 2.

British Qualifying Zone

	P	W	D	L	F	A	Pts
ENGLAND	3	3	0	0	11	4	6
Scotland	3	1	1	1	8	8	3
Northern Ireland	3	1	0	2	4	7	2
Wales	3	0	1	2	5	9	1

1954 WORLD CUP FINALS

Hosts   Switzerland
Holders   Uruguay

Group D   England (seeded) / Italy (seeded) / Belgium / Switzerland

England Squad

Goalkeepers		*Age*	*Caps*
Gil Merrick	Birmingham City	32	20
Ted Burgin	Sheffield United	26	0
Fullbacks			
Ron Staniforth	Huddersfield Town	30	3
Roger Byrne	Manchester United	24	3
Ken Green	Birmingham City	30	0
Halfbacks			
Billy Wright	Wolverhampton Wanderers	30	58
Sid Owen	Luton Town	31	2
Jimmy Dickinson	Portsmouth	29	35
Bill McGarry	Huddersfield Town	27	0
Forwards			
Stanley Matthews	Blackpool	39	36
Ivor Broadis	Newcastle United	31	11
Nat Lofthouse	Bolton Wanderers	28	19
Tommy Taylor	Manchester United	22	3
Tom Finney	Preston North End	32	49
Albert Quixall	Sheffield Wednesday	20	3
Dennis Wilshaw	Wolverhampton Wanderers	28	1
Jimmy Mullen	Wolverhampton Wanderers	31	11

Manager	Walter Winterbottom
Average age	28.8 years
Average experience	14.9 caps

Group D

17 June 1954 – BELGIUM v ENGLAND at Basle
Half-time – 1–2: Anoul (1–0), Broadis (1–1), Lofthouse (1–2)
Full-time – 3–3: Broadis (1–3), Anoul (2–3), Coppens (3–3)
After extra time – 4–4: Lofthouse (3–4), Dickinson o.g. (4–4)
Belgium: Gernaey; Dries; van Brandt; Huysmans; Carre; Mees; Mermans;
   Houf; Coppens; Anoul; van Dem Bosch.

England: Merrick; Staniforth; Byrne; Wright; Owen; Dickinson; Matthews; Broadis; Lofthouse; Taylor; Finney.

20 June 1954 – SWITZERLAND v ENGLAND at Berne
Half-time – 0–1: Mullen (0–1)
Full-time – 0–2: Wilshaw (0–2)
Switzerland: Parlier; Neury; Bocquet; Kernen; Eggiman; Bigler; Antenen; Vonlanthen; Meier; Ballaman; Fatton.
England: Merrick; Staniforth; Byrne; McGarry; Wright; Dickinson; Finney; Broadis; Taylor; Wilshaw; Mullen.

Other group results:
Switzerland 2 Italy 1; Italy 4 Belgium 1.

Group D final table

	P	W	D	L	F	A	Pts
ENGLAND	2	1	1	0	6	4	3
Italy	2	1	0	1	5	3	2
Switzerland	2	1	0	1	2	3	2
Belgium	2	0	1	1	5	8	1

Play-off   Switzerland 4 Italy 1

QUARTER-FINAL

26 June 1954 – URUGUAY v ENGLAND at Basle
Half-time – 2–1: Borges (1–0), Lofthouse (1–1), Varela (2–1)
Full-time – 4–2: Schiaffino (3–1), Finney (3–2), Ambrois (4–2)
Uruguay: Maspoli; Santamaria; Martinez; Andrade; Varela; Cruz; Abbadie; Ambrois; Miguez; Schiaffino; Borges.
England: Merrick; Staniforth; Byrne; McGarry; Wright; Dickinson; Matthews; Broadis; Lofthouse; Wilshaw; Finney.

WORLD CUP 1958

QUALIFYING ROUNDS

5 December 1956 – ENGLAND v DENMARK at Molineux, Wolverhampton
Half-time – 2–1: Taylor (1–0), Taylor (2–0), O. Nielsen (2–1)
Full-time – 5–2: Taylor (3–1), O. Nielsen (3–2), Edwards (4–2), Edwards (5–2)
England: Ditchburn; Hall; Byrne; Clayton; Wright; Dickinson; Matthews; Brooks; Taylor; Edwards; Finney.
Denmark: Drengsgaard; Larsen; V. Nielsen; F. Nielsen; O. Hansen; Olesen; J. Hansen; Petersen; O. Nielsen; Jensen; P. Hansen.

8 May 1957 – ENGLAND v EIRE at Wembley
Half-time – 4–0: Taylor (1–0). Taylor (2–0), Atyeo (3–0), Taylor (4–0)
Full-time – 5–1: Curtis (4–1), Atyeo (5–1)
England: Hodgkinson; Hall; Byrne; Clayton; Wright; Edwards; Matthews; Atyeo; Taylor; Haynes; Finney.
Eire: Kelly; Donovan; Cantwell; Farrell; Mackey; Saward; Ringstead; Whelan; Curtis; Fitzsimons; Haverty.

15 May 1957 – DENMARK v ENGLAND at Copenhagen
Half-time – 1–1: J. Jensen (1–0), Haynes (1–1)
Full-time – 1–4: Taylor (1–2), Atyeo (1–3), Taylor (1–4)
Denmark: Drengsgaard; Amdisen; V. Nielsen; F. Nielsen; O. Hansen; J. Olesen; J. Hansen; J. Jensen; E. Jensen; A. Jensen; P. Hansen.
England: Hodgkinson; Hall; Byrne; Clayton; Wright; Edwards; Matthews; Atyeo; Taylor; Haynes; Finney.

19 May 1957 – EIRE v ENGLAND at Dublin
Half-time – 1–0: Ringstead (1–0)
Full-time – 1–1: Atyeo (1–1)
Eire: Godwin; Dunne; Cantwell; Nolan; Hurley; Saward; Ringstead; Whelan; Curtis; Fitzsimons; Haverty.
England: Hodgkinson; Hall; Byrne; Clayton; Wright; Edwards; Finney; Atyeo; Taylor; Haynes; Pegg.

Other group results:
Eire 2 Denmark 1; Denmark 0 Eire 2.

World Cup Qualifying Zone

	P	W	D	L	F	A	Pts
ENGLAND	4	3	1	0	15	5	7
Eire	4	2	1	1	6	7	5
Denmark	4	0	0	4	4	13	0

1958 WORLD CUP FINALS

Hosts   Sweden
Holders   West Germany

Group D   England / Brazil / Soviet Union / Austria

England Squad

Goalkeepers		*Age*	*Caps*
Colin McDonald	Burnley	27	1
Eddie Hopkinson	Bolton Wanderers	22	6
Fullbacks			
Don Howe	West Bromwich Albion	22	7
Tommy Banks	Bolton Wanderers	28	1
Peter Sillett	Chelsea	25	3
Centre halves			
Billy Wright	Wolverhampton Wanderers	34	91
Maurice Norman	Tottenham Hotspur	24	0
Wing halves			
Ronnie Clayton	Blackburn Rovers	23	20
Eddie Clamp	Wolverhampton Wanderers	24	1
Bill Slater	Wolverhampton Wanderers	31	6
Bobby Robson	West Bromwich Albion	25	2
Wingers			
Tom Finney	Preston North End	36	73
Bryan Douglas	Blackburn Rovers	23	7

| Peter Brabrook | Chelsea | 20 | 0 |
| Alan A'Court | Liverpool | 23 | 1 |

Forwards
Bobby Charlton	Manchester United	20	3
Derek Kevan	West Bromwich Albion	23	7
Bobby Smith	Tottenham Hotspur	25	0
Johnny Haynes	Fulham	23	20
Peter Broadbent	Wolverhampton Wanderers	25	0

Manager	Walter Winterbottom
Average age	25.2 years
Average experience	12.5 caps

Group D

8 June 1958 – SOVIET UNION v ENGLAND at Gothenburg
Half-time – 1–0: Simonian (1–0)
Full-time – 2–2: A. Ivanov (2–0), Kevan (2–1), Finney pen. (2–2)
Soviet Union: Yashin; Kesarev; Kuznetsov; Voinov; Krijevski; Tsarev; A. Ivanov;
V. Ivanov; Simonian; Salnikov; Ilyin.
England: McDonald; Howe; Banks; Clamp; Wright; Slater; Douglas; Robson;
Kevan; Haynes; Finney.

11 June 1958 – BRAZIL v ENGLAND at Gothenburg
Half-time – 0–0
Full-time – 0–0
Brazil: Gilmar; De Sordi; N. Santos; Dino; Bellini; Orlando; Joel; Didi; Mazzola;
Vava; Zagallo.
England: McDonald; Howe; Banks; Clamp; Wright; Slater; Douglas; Robson;
Kevan; Haynes; A'Court.

15 June 1958 – AUSTRIA v ENGLAND at Boras
Half-time – 1–0: Koller (1–0)
Full-time – 2–2: Haynes (1–1), Koerner (2–1), Kevan (2–2)
Austria: Szanwald; Kollmann; Swoboda; Hanappi; Happell; Koller; E. Kozlicek;
P. Kozlicek; Busek; Koerner; Senekowitsch.
England: McDonald; Howe; Banks; Clamp; Wright; Slater; Douglas; Robson;
Kevan; Haynes; A'Court.

Other group results:
Brazil 3 Austria 0; Soviet Union 2 Austria 0; Brazil 2 Soviet Union 0.

Group D final table
	P	W	D	L	F	A	Pts
Brazil	3	2	1	0	5	0	5
ENGLAND	3	1	1	1	4	4	3
Soviet Union	3	1	1	1	4	4	3
Austria	3	0	1	2	2	7	1

Group D play-off

17 June 1958 – Soviet Union v ENGLAND at Gothenburg
Half-time – 0–0
Full-time – 1–0: Ilyin (1–0)*

Soviet Union: Yashin; Kesarev; Kuznetsov; Voinov; Krijevski; Tsarev; Apoukhtin; V. Ivanov; Simonian; Falin; Ilyin.

England: McDonald; Howe; Banks; Clayton; Wright; Slater; Brabrook; Broadbent; Kevan; Haynes; A'Court.

*Soviet Union qualified with Brazil

WORLD CUP 1962

QUALIFYING ROUNDS

19 October 1960 – LUXEMBOURG v ENGLAND at Luxembourg
Half-time – 0–4: Greaves (0–1), R. Charlton (0–2), Smith (0–3), Greaves (0–4)
Full-time – 0–9: R. Charlton (0–5), Greaves (0–6), R. Charlton (0–7), Haynes (0–8), Smith (0–9)
Luxembourg: Stendeback; Brenner; Hoffmann; Merti; Brosius; Jann; Schmidt; Cirelli; May; Konter; Bauer.
England: Springett; Armfield; McNeil; Robson; Swan; Flowers; Douglas; Greaves; Smith; Haynes; R. Charlton.

21 May 1961 – PORTUGAL v ENGLAND at Lisbon
Half-time – 0–0
Full-time – 1–1: Aguas (1–0), Flowers (1–1)
Portugal: Pereira; Lino; Hilario; Mendes; Germano; Cruz; Augusto; Sanatan; Aguas; Coluna; Cavern.
England: Springett; Armfield; McNeil; Robson; Swan; Flowers; Douglas; Greaves; Smith; Haynes; R. Charlton.

28 September 1961 – ENGLAND v LUXEMBOURG at Highbury
Half-time – 3–0: Pointer (1–0), Viollet (2–0), R. Charlton (3–0)
Full-time – 4–1: Dimmer (3–1), R. Charlton (4–1)
England: Springett; Armfield; McNeil; Robson; Swan; Flowers; Douglas; Fantham; Pointer; Viollet; R. Charlton.
Luxembourg: Stendeback; Brenner; Hoffmann; Merti; Brosius; Jann; Schmidt; Cirelli; Dimmer; Konter; Bauer.

25 October 1961 – ENGLAND v PORTUGAL at Wembley
Half-time – 2–0: Connelly (1–0), Pointer (2–0)
Full-time – 2–0
England: Springett; Armfield; Wilson; Robson; Swan; Flowers; Connelly; Douglas; Pointer; Haynes; R. Charlton.
Portugal: Pereira; Lino; Hilario; Perides; Soares; Vicente; Yuaca; Eusebio; Aguas; Coluna; Cavern.

Other group results:
Portugal 6 Luxembourg 0; Luxembourg 4 Portugal 2.

World Cup Qualifying Zone

	P	W	D	L	F	A	Pts
ENGLAND	4	3	1	0	16	2	7
Portugal	4	1	1	2	9	7	3
Luxembourg	4	1	0	3	5	21	2

1962 WORLD CUP FINALS

Hosts   Chile
Holders   Brazil

England Squad

Goalkeepers		*Age*	*Caps*
Ron Springett	Sheffield Wednesday	26	21
Alan Hodgkinson	Sheffield United	25	5
Fullbacks			
Jimmy Armfield	Blackpool	26	25
Ray Wilson	Huddersfield Town	27	11
Don Howe	West Bromwich Albion	26	23
Centre backs			
Peter Swan	Sheffield Wednesday	25	19
Ron Flowers	Wolverhampton Wanderers	27	32
Maurice Norman	Tottenham Hotspur	28	1
Midfield			
Bobby Robson	West Bromwich Albion	29	20
Stan Anderson	Sunderland	28	2
Bobby Moore	West Ham United	21	1
Johnny Haynes	Fulham	27	52
George Eastham	Arsenal	25	0
Forwards			
Bryan Douglas	Blackburn Rovers	27	29
Jimmy Greaves	Tottenham Hotspur	22	18
Gerry Hitchens	Inter Milan	24	5
Bobby Charlton	Manchester United	24	35
John Connelly	Burnley	23	8
Roger Hunt	Liverpool	23	1
Alan Peacock	Middlesbrough	24	0

Manager	Walter Winterbottom
Average age	25.4 years
Average experience	15.4 caps

Group D

31 May 1962 – HUNGARY v ENGLAND at Rancagua
Half-time – 1–0: Tichy (1–0)
Full-time – 2–1: Flowers pen. (1–1), Albert (2–1)
Hungary: Grosics; Matrái; Sárosi; Solymosi; Mészöly; Sipos; Sándor; Rakosi;
   Albert; Tichy; Fenyvesi.
England: Springett; Armfield; Wilson; Moore; Norman; Flowers; Douglas;
   Greaves; Hitchens; Haynes; R. Charlton.

2 June 1962 – ARGENTINA v ENGLAND at Rancagua
Half-time – 0–2: Flowers pen. (0–1), R. Charlton (0–2)
Full-time – 1–3: Greaves (0–3), Sanfilippo (1–3)
Argentina: Roma; Navarro; Paez; Cap; Marzolini; Sacchi; Rattin; Oleniak; Sosa;
   Sanfilippo; Belen.

England: Springett; Armfield; Wilson; Moore; Norman; Flowers; Douglas; Greaves; Peacock; Haynes; R. Charlton.

7 June 1962 – BULGARIA v ENGLAND at Rancagua
Half-time – 0–0
Full-time – 0–0
Bulgaria: Naidenov; Pentchev; Jetchev; D. Kostov; Dimitrov; Kovachev; A. Kostov; Velitchkov; Sokolov; Kolev; Dermendzhiev.
England: Springett; Armfield; Wilson; Moore; Norman; Flowers; Douglas; Greaves; Peacock; Haynes; R. Charlton.

Other group results
Argentina 1 Bulgaria 0; Hungary 6 Bulgaria 1; Argentina 0 Hungary 0.

Group D final table

	P	W	D	L	F	A	Pts
Hungary	3	2	1	0	8	2	5
ENGLAND	3	1	1	1	4	3	3
Argentina	3	1	1	1	2	3	3
Bulgaria	3	0	1	2	1	7	1

QUARTER-FINAL

10 June 1962 – BRAZIL v ENGLAND at Vina del Mar
Half-time – 1–1: Garrincha (1–0), Hitchens (1–1)
Full-time – 3–1: Vavá (2–1), Garrincha (3–1)
Brazil: Gilmar; D. Santos; N. Santos; Zito; Mauro; Zózimo; Garrincha; Didi; Vavá; Amarildo; Zagallo.
England: Springett; Armfield; Wilson; Moore; Norman; Flowers; Douglas; Greaves; Hitchens; Haynes; R. Charlton.

WORLD CUP 1966

Hosts   England
Holders   Brazil

England Squad

Goalkeepers		*Age*	*Caps*
Gordon Banks	Leicester City	28	27
Ron Springett	Sheffield Wednesday	30	33
Peter Bonetti	Chelsea	24	1
Fullbacks			
George Cohen	Fulham	26	24
Ray Wilson	Everton	31	45
Jimmy Armfield	Blackpool	30	43
Gerry Byrne	Liverpool	28	2
Central defence			
Jack Charlton	Leeds United	30	16
Bobby Moore	West Ham United	24	41
Ron Flowers	Wolverhampton Wanderers	31	49
Norman Hunter	Leeds United	22	4

Midfield

Nobby Stiles	Manchester United	24	14
Alan Ball	Blackpool	21	10
Martin Peters	West Ham United	22	3
George Eastham	Arsenal	29	19

Wingers

Terry Paine	Southampton	27	18
John Connelly	Manchester United	27	19
Ian Callaghan	Liverpool	24	1

Forwards

Bobby Charlton	Manchester United	28	68
Jimmy Greaves	Tottenham Hotspur	26	51
Roger Hunt	Liverpool	27	13
Geoff Hurst	West Ham United	24	5

Manager	Alf Ramsey
Average age	26.5 years
Average experience	23 caps

Group A

11 July 1966 – ENGLAND v URUGUAY at Wembley
Half-time – 0–0
Full-time – 0–0
England: Banks; Cohen; Wilson; Stiles; J. Charlton; Moore; Ball; Greaves;
  R. Charlton; Hunt; Connelly.
Uruguay: Mazurkiewicz; Troche; Manicera; Goncalvez; Caetano; Cortes;
  Rocha; Perez; Ubinas; Viera; Silva.

16 July 1966 – ENGLAND v MEXICO at Wembley
Half-time – 1–0: R. Charlton (1–0)
Full-time – 2–0: Hunt (2–0)
England: Banks; Cohen; Wilson; Stiles; J. Charlton; Moore; Paine; Greaves;
  R. Charlton; Hunt; Peters.
Mexico: Calderon; Chaires; Pena; Del Muro; Jauregui; Diaz; Padilla; Nunez;
  Borja; Reyes; Hernandez.

20 July 1966 – ENGLAND v FRANCE at Wembley
Half-time – 1–0: Hunt (1–0)
Full-time – 2–0: Hunt (2–0)
England: Banks; Cohen; Wilson; Stiles; J. Charlton; Moore; Callaghan; Greaves;
  R. Charlton; Hunt; Peters.
France: Aubour; Djorkaeff; Artelesa; Budzinski; Bosquier; Bonnel; Herbin;
  Simon; Herbet; Gondet; Hausser.

Other group results:
France 1 Mexico 1; Uruguay 2 France 1; Mexico 0 Uruguay 0.

Group A final table

	P	W	D	L	F	A	Pts
ENGLAND	3	2	1	0	4	0	5
Uruguay	3	1	2	0	2	1	4
Mexico	3	0	2	1	1	3	2
France	3	0	1	2	2	5	1

QUARTER-FINAL

23 July 1966 – ENGLAND v ARGENTINA at Wembley
Half-time – 0–0
Full-time – 1–0: Hurst (1–0)
England: Banks; Cohen; Wilson; Stiles; J. Charlton; Moore; Ball; Hurst;
    R. Charlton; Hunt; Peters.
Argentina: Roma; Ferreiro; Perfumo; Albrecht; Marzolini; Rattin; Solari;
    González; Artime; Onega; Más.

SEMI-FINAL

26 July 1966 – ENGLAND v PORTUGAL at Wembley
Half-time 1–0: R. Charlton (1–0)
Full-time – 2–1: R. Charlton (2–0), Eusebio pen. (2–1)
England: Banks; Cohen; Wilson; Stiles; J. Charlton; Moore; Ball; Hurst;
    R. Charlton; Hunt; Peters.
Portugal: Pereira; Festa; Baptista; Carlos; Hilario; Graca; Coluna; Augusto;
    Eusebio; Torres; Simóes.

FINAL

30 July 1966 – ENGLAND v WEST GERMANY at Wembley
Half-time – 1–1: Haller (0–1), Hurst (1–1)
Full-time – 2–2: Peters (2–1), Weber (2–2)
Extra-time – 4–2: Hurst (3–2), Hurst (4–2)
England: Banks; Cohen; Wilson; Stiles; J. Charlton; Moore; Ball; Hurst;
    R. Charlton; Hunt; Peters.
West Germany: Tilkowski; Höttges; Schulz; Weber; Schnellinger; Haller;
    Beckenbauer; Seeler; Held; Overath; Emmerich.

WORLD CUP 1970

Hosts   Mexico
Holders   England

England Squad

Goalkeepers		*Age*	*Caps*
Gordon Banks	Stoke City	32	59
Peter Bonetti	Chelsea	28	6
Alex Stepney	Manchester United	25	1
Fullbacks			
Keith Newton	Everton	28	24
Terry Cooper	Leeds United	24	8
Tommy Wright	Everton	25	9
Central defence			
Brian Labone	Everton	30	23
Bobby Moore	West Ham United	29	80
Jack Charlton	Leeds United	34	34
Norman Hunter	Leeds United	26	13

Midfield

Emlyn Hughes	Liverpool	22	6
Alan Mullery	Tottenham Hotspur	28	27
Alan Ball	Everton	25	41
Bobby Charlton	Manchester United	32	102
Nobby Stiles	Manchester United	28	28
Colin Bell	Manchester City	24	11
Martin Peters	Tottenham Hotspur	26	38

Forwards

Francis Lee	Manchester City	26	14
Geoff Hurst	West Ham United	28	38
Peter Osgood	Chelsea	23	1
Allan Clarke	Leeds United	23	0
Jeff Astle	West Bromwich Albion	28	3

Manager	Alf Ramsey
Average age	27 years
Average experience	25.7 caps

Group C

2 June 1970 – ROMANIA v ENGLAND at Guadalajara
Half-time – 0–0
Full-time – 0–1: Hurst (0–1)
Romania: Adamache; Satmareanu; Lupescu; Dinu; Mocanu; Dumitru; Nunweiller; Dembrowski; Tataru (Neagu); Dumitrache; Lucescu.
England: Banks; Newton (Wright); Cooper; Mullery; Labone; Moore; Lee (Osgood); Ball; R. Charlton; Hurst; Peters.

7 June 1970 – BRAZIL v ENGLAND at Guadalajara
Half-time – 0–0
Full-time – 1–0: Jairzinho (1–0)
Brazil: Felix; Carlos Alberto; Brito; Piazza; Everaldo; Paulo Cesar; Clodoaldo; Rivelino; Jairzinho; Tostao (Roberto); Pele.
England: Banks; Wright; Cooper; Mullery; Labone; Moore; Lee (Astle); Ball; R. Charlton (Bell); Hurst; Peters.

11 June 1970 – CZECHOSLOVAKIA v ENGLAND at Guadalajara
Half-time – 0–0
Full-time – 0–1: Clarke (0–1)
Czechoslovakia: Viktor; Dobias; Migas; Hagara; Hrivnak; Pollak; Kuna; Capkovic (Joki); Petras; Adamec; F. Vesely.
England: Banks; Newton; Cooper; Mullery; J. Charlton; Moore; Bell; R. Charlton (Ball); Astle (Osgood); Clarke; Peters.

Other group results:
Brazil 4 Czechoslovakia 1; Czechoslovakia 1 Romania 2; Romania 2 Brazil 3.

Group C final table

	P	W	D	L	F	A	Pts
Brazil	3	3	0	0	8	3	6
ENGLAND	3	2	0	1	2	1	4
Romania	3	1	0	2	4	5	2
Czechoslovakia	3	0	0	3	2	7	0

QUARTER-FINAL

14 June 1970 – WEST GERMANY v ENGLAND at León
Half-time – 0–1: Mullery (0–1)
Full-time – 2–2: Peters (0–2), Beckenbauer (1–2), Seeler (2–2)
After extra time – 3–2: Müller (3–2)
West Germany: Maier; Höttges (Schulz); Schnellinger; Fichtel; Vogts;
    Beckenbauer; Overath; Libuda (Grabowski); Seeler; Müller; Löhr.
England: Bonetti; Newton; Cooper; Mullery; Labone; Moore; Lee; Ball;
    R. Charlton (Bell); Hurst; Peters (Hunter).

WORLD CUP 1974

QUALIFYING ROUNDS

15 November 1972 – WALES v ENGLAND at Ninian Park, Cardiff
Half-time – 0–1: Bell (0–1)
Full-time – 0–1
Wales: Sprake; Rodrigues (Reece); Thomas; Hennessey; England; Hockey;
    Phillips; Mahoney; W. Davies; Toshack; James.
England: Clemence; Storey; Hughes; Hunter; McFarland; Moore; Keegan;
    Chivers; Marsh; Bell; Ball.

24 January 1973 – ENGLAND v WALES at Wembley
Half-time – 1–1: Toshack (0–1), Hunter (1–1)
Full-time – 1–1
England: Clemence; Storey; Hughes; Hunter; McFarland; Moore; Keegan; Bell;
    Chivers; Marsh; Ball.
Wales: Sprake; Rodrigues (Page); Thomas; Hockey; England; Roberts; Evans;
    Mahoney; Toshack; Yorath; James.

6 June 1973 – POLAND v ENGLAND at Chorzów
Half-time – 1–0: Gadocha (1–0)
Full-time – 2–0: Lubanski (2–0)
Poland: Tomaszewski; Rzesny; Gorgon; Musial; Bulzacki; Kraska; Banas;
    Cmikiewicz; Deyna; Lubanski (Domarski); Gadocha.
England: Shilton; Madeley; Hughes; Storey; McFarland; Moore; Ball; Bell;
    Chivers; Clarke; Peters.

17 October 1973 – ENGLAND v POLAND at Wembley
Half-time – 0–0
Full-time – 1–1: Domarski (0–1), Clarke pen. (1–1)
England: Shilton; Madeley; Hughes; Bell; McFarland; Hunter; Currie;
    Channon; Chivers (Hector); Clarke; Peters.
Poland: Tomaszewski; Szymanowski; Gorgon; Musial; Bulzacki; Kasperczak;
    Lato; Cmikiewicz; Deyna; Domarski; Gadocha.

Other group results:
Wales 2 Poland 0; Poland 3 Wales 0.

World Cup Qualifying Zone

	P	W	D	L	F	A	Pts
Poland	4	2	1	1	6	3	5
ENGLAND	4	1	2	1	3	4	4
Wales	4	1	1	2	3	5	3

WORLD CUP 1978

QUALIFYING ROUNDS

13 June 1976 – FINLAND v ENGLAND at Helsinki
Half-time – 1–2: Pearson (0–1), Paatelainen (1–1), Keegan (1–2)
Full-time – 1–4: Channon (1–3), Keegan (1–4)
Finland: Enckelman; Vihtila; Makynen; Tolsa; Ranta; Jantunen; Suomalainen (Pyykko); E. Heiskanen; A. Heiskanen; Rissanen; Paatelainen.
England: Clemence; Todd; Mills; Thompson; Madeley; Cherry; Keegan; Channon; Pearson; Brooking; G. Francis.

13 October 1976 – ENGLAND v FINLAND at Wembley
Half-time – 1–0: Tueart (1–0)
Full-time – 2–1: Nieminen (1–1), Royle (2–1)
England: Clemence; Todd; Beattie; Thompson; Greenhoff; Wilkins; Keegan; Channon; Royle; Brooking (Mills); Tueart (Hill).
Finland: Enckelman; Heikkinen; Vihtila; Makynen; Ranta; E. Heiskanen; Pyykko; Toivola; Nieminen; A. Heiskanen; Paatelainen.

17 November 1976 – ITALY v ENGLAND at Rome
Half-time – 1–0: Antognoni (1–0)
Full-time – 2–0: Bettega (2–0)
Italy: Zoff; Cuccureddu; Facchetti; Gentile; Tardelli; Causio; Benetti; Antognoni; Capello; Graziani; Bettega.
England: Clemence; Clement (Beattie); Mills; Greenhoff; McFarland; Hughes; Keegan; Channon; Bowles; Cherry; Brooking.

30 March 1977 – ENGLAND v LUXEMBOURG at Wembley
Half-time – 1–0: Keegan (1–0)
Full-time – 5–0: Francis (2–0), Kennedy (3–0), Channon (4–0), Channon pen. (5–0)
England: Clemence; Gidman; Cherry; Kennedy; Watson; Hughes; Keegan; Channon; Royle (Mariner); T. Francis; Hill.
Luxembourg: Zender; Fandel; Margue; Mond; Pilot; Zuang; Di Domenico; Dresch; Braun; Philipp; Dussier.

12 October 1977 – LUXEMBOURG v ENGLAND at Luxembourg
Half-time – 0–1: Kennedy (0–1)
Full-time – 0–2: Mariner (0–2)
Luxembourg: Moes; Barthel; Fandel (Zangerle); Mond; Rohmann; Zuang; Michaux; Philipp; Dussier; Monacelli; Braun (Di Domenico).
England: Clemence; Cherry; Watson (Beattie); Hughes; Kennedy; Callaghan; McDermott (Whymark); Wilkins; T. Francis; Mariner; Hill.

16 November 1977 – ENGLAND v ITALY at Wembley
Half-time – 1–0: Keegan (1–0)
Full-time – 2–0: Brooking (2–0)
England: Clemence; Neal; Cherry; Wilkins; Watson; Hughes; Keegan
  (T. Francis); Coppell; Latchford (Pearson); Brooking; P. Barnes.
Italy: Zoff; Tardelli; Mozzini; Facchetti (Cuccureddu); Gentile; Zaccarelli;
  Benetti; Antognoni; Causio; Graziani (Sala); Bettega.

Other group results:
Finland 7 Luxembourg 0; Luxembourg 1 Italy 4; Finland 0 Italy 3;
Luxembourg 0; Finland 1; Italy 3 Luxembourg 0.

World Cup Qualifying Zone

	P	W	D	L	F	A	Pts
Italy	6	5	0	1	18	4	10
ENGLAND	6	5	0	1	15	4	10
Finland	6	2	0	4	11	16	4
Luxembourg	6	0	0	6	2	22	0

WORLD CUP 1982

QUALIFYING ROUNDS

10 September 1980 – ENGLAND v NORWAY at Wembley
Half-time – 1–0: McDermott (1–0)
Full-time – 4–0: Woodcock (2–0), McDermott pen. (3–0), Mariner (4–0)
England: Shilton; Anderson; Sansom; Thompson; Watson; Robson; Gates;
  McDermott; Mariner; Woodcock; Rix.
Norway: T. Jacobsen; Berntsen; Kordahl; Aas; Grondalen; Albertsen; Hareide;
  Dokken; Larsen-Okland; P. Jacobsen; Erlandsen (Ottesen).

15 October 1980 – ROMANIA v ENGLAND at Bucharest
Half-time – 1–0: Raducanu (1–0)
Full-time – 2–1: Woodcock (1–1), Iordanescu pen. (2–1)
Romania: Iordache; Negrila; Munteanu; Sames; Stefanescu; Beldeanu; Crisan;
  Iordanescu; Camataru; Ticleanu; Raducanu.
England: Clemence; Neal; Sansom; Thompson; Watson; Robson; Rix;
  McDermott; Birtles (Cunningham); Woodcock; Gates (Coppell).

19 November 1980 – ENGLAND v SWITZERLAND at Wembley
Half-time – 2–0: Tanner o.g. (1–0), Mariner (2–0)
Full-time – 2–1: Pfister (2–1)
England: Shilton; Neal; Sansom; Robson; Watson; Mills; Coppell; McDermott;
  Mariner; Brooking (Rix); Woodcock.
Switzerland: Burgener; Wehrli; H. Hermann; Lüdi; Geiger; Barberis; Pfister;
  Tanner (Egli); Schönenberger (Marti); Elsener; Botteron.

29 April 1981 – ENGLAND v ROMANIA at Wembley
Half-time – 0–0
Full-time – 0–0
England: Shilton; Anderson; Sansom; Robson; Watson; Osman; Wilkins;
  Brooking (McDermott); Coppell; T. Francis; Woodcock.

Romania: Iordache; Negrila; Munteanu; Sames; Stefanescu; Beldeanu; Crisan; Iordanescu; Camataru; Stoica; Balaci.

30 May 1981 – SWITZERLAND v ENGLAND at Basle
Half-time – 2–0: Schweiller (1–0), Sulser (2–0)
Full-time – 2–1: McDermott (2–1)
Switzerland: Burgener; H. Hermann (Weber); Lüdi; Egli; Zappa; Wehrli; Scheiwiler; Botteron; Sulser; Barberis; Elsener (Maissen).
England: Clemence; Mills; Sansom; Wilkins; Watson (P. Barnes); Osman; Keegan; Coppell; Mariner; Robson; Francis (McDermott).

6 June 1981 – HUNGARY v ENGLAND at Budapest
Half-time – 1–1: Brooking (0–1), Garaba (1–1)
Full-time – 1–3: Brooking (1–2), Keegan pen. (1–3)
Hungary: Katzirz; Martos; Balint; Varga; Muller (Komjati); Garaba; Fazekas (Bodonyi); Nyilasi; Kiss; Mucha; Torocsik.
England: Clemence; Neal; Mills; Thompson; Watson; Robson; Keegan; Coppell; Mariner; Brooking (Wilkins); McDermott.

9 September 1981 – NORWAY v ENGLAND at Oslo
Half-time – 2–1: Robson (0–1), Albertsen (1–1), Thoresen (2–1)
Full-time – 2–1
Norway: Antonsen; Berntsen; Hareide; Aas; Grondalen; Albertsen; Giske; Thoresen; Larsen-Okland (Pedersen); Jacobsen; Lund (Dokken).
England: Clemence; Neal; Mills; Thompson; Osman; Robson; Keegan; T. Francis; Mariner (Withe); Hoddle (P. Barnes); McDermott.

18 November 1981 – ENGLAND v HUNGARY at Wembley
Half-time – 1–0: Mariner (1–0)
Full-time – 1–0
England: Shilton; Neal; Mills; Thompson; Martin; Robson; Keegan; Coppell (Morley); Mariner; Brooking; McDermott.
Hungary: Meszaros; Martos; Balint; Toth; Muller; Garaba; Fazekas; Csapo; Torocsik; Kiss; Sallai.

Other group results:
Norway 1 Romania 1; Switzerland 1 Norway 2; Switzerland 2 Hungary 2; Hungary 1 Romania 0; Norway 1 Hungary 2; Romania 1 Norway 0; Norway 1 Switzerland 1; Romania 0 Hungary 0; Romania 1 Switzerland 2; Hungary 3 Switzerland 0; Hungary 4 Switzerland 1; Switzerland 0 Romania 0.

World Cup Qualifying Zone

	P	W	D	L	F	A	Pts
Hungary	8	4	2	2	13	8	10
ENGLAND	8	4	1	3	13	8	9
Romania	8	2	4	2	5	5	8
Switzerland	8	2	3	3	9	12	7
Norway	8	2	2	4	8	15	6

1982 WORLD CUP FINALS

Hosts   Spain
Holders   Argentina

England Squad

Goalkeepers		*Age*	*Caps*
Ray Clemence	Tottenham Hotspur	33	59
Joe Corrigan	Manchester City	33	9
Peter Shilton	Nottingham Forest	32	37

Fullbacks			
Viv Anderson	Nottingham Forest	25	10
Mick Mills	Ipswich Town	33	37
Phil Neal	Liverpool	31	37
Kenny Sansom	Arsenal	23	23

Central defence			
Terry Butcher	Ipswich Town	23	4
Steve Foster	Brighton & Hove Albion	24	2
Phil Thompson	Liverpool	28	35

Midfield			
Trevor Brooking	West Ham United	33	46
Steve Coppell	Manchester United	26	36
Glenn Hoddle	Tottenham Hotspur	24	11
Ray Wilkins	Manchester United	25	47
Graham Rix	Arsenal	24	8
Bryan Robson	Manchester United	25	19
Terry McDermott	Liverpool	30	25

Forwards			
Kevin Keegan	Southampton	31	62
Paul Mariner	Ipswich Town	29	21
Peter Withe	Aston Villa	30	6
Tony Woodcock	Arsenal	26	22
Trevor Francis	Manchester City	28	27

Manager	Ron Greenwood		
Average age	28 years		
Average experience	26.5 caps		

Group D

16 June 1982 – FRANCE v ENGLAND at Bilbao
Half-time – 1–1: Robson (0–1), Soler (1–1)
Full-time – 1–3: Robson (1–2), Mariner (1–3)
France: Ettori; Battiston; Lopez; Tresor; Bossis; Girard; Giresse; Larios
(Tigana); Rocheteau (Six); Platini; Soler.
England: Shilton; Mills; Thompson; Butcher; Sansom (Neal); Coppell; Wilkins;
Robson; Rix; T. Francis; Mariner.

20 June 1982 – CZECHOSLOVAKIA v ENGLAND at Bilbao
Half-time – 0–0
Full-time – 0–2: T. Francis (0–1), Barmos o.g. (0–2)
Czechoslovakia: Seman (Stromsik); Barmos; Fiala; Vojacek; Radimec; Jurkemik;
Chaloupka; Berger; Janecka (Masny); Vizek; Nehoda.
England: Shilton; Mills; Thompson; Butcher; Sansom; Coppell; Wilkins;
Robson (Hoddle); Rix; T. Francis; Mariner.

25 June 1982 – KUWAIT v ENGLAND at Bilbao
Half-time – 0–1: T. Francis (0–1)
Full-time – 0–1
Kuwait: Al-Tarabulsi; Naeem Saed; M. Mubarek; Al-Mubraek (Al-Shemmari); Mayoof; Al-Buloushi; Al-Suwaayed; Al-Houti; Marzouq; Al-Dakhil; Al-Anbari.
England: Shilton; Neal; Thompson; Foster; Mills; Coppell; Wilkins; Hoddle; Rix; T. Francis; Mariner.

Other group results:
Czechoslovakia 1 Kuwait 1; France 4 Kuwait 1; France 1 Czechoslovakia 1.

Group D final table

	P	W	D	L	F	A	Pts
ENGLAND	3	3	0	0	6	1	6
France	3	1	1	1	6	5	3
Czechoslovakia	3	0	2	1	2	4	2
Kuwait	3	0	1	2	2	6	1

Group 2

29 June 1982 – WEST GERMANY v ENGLAND at Madrid
Half-time – 0–0
Full-time – 0–0
West Germany: Schumacher; Kaltz; K-H. Förster; Stielike; Briegel; B. Förster; Dremmler; Müller (Fischer); Breitner; Rummenigge; Reinders (Littbarski).
England: Shilton; Mills; Thompson; Butcher; Sansom; Coppell; Wilkins; Robson; Rix; T. Francis (Woodcock); Mariner.

5 July 1982 – SPAIN v ENGLAND at Madrid
Half-time – 0–0
Full-time – 0–0
Spain: Arconada; Urquiaga; Tendillo (Maceda); Alesanco; Gordillo; Alonso; Camacho; Zamora; Saura (Uralde); Satrustegui; Santillana.
England: Shilton; Mills; Butcher; Thompson; Sansom; Wilkins; Robson; Rix (Brooking); T. Francis; Mariner; Woodcock (Keegan).

Other group result:
West Germany 2 Spain 1.

Group 2 final table

	P	W	D	L	F	A	Pts
West Germany	2	1	1	0	2	1	3
ENGLAND	2	0	2	0	0	0	2
Spain	2	0	1	1	1	2	1

WORLD CUP 1986

QUALIFYING ROUND

17 October 1984 – ENGLAND v FINLAND at Wembley
Half-time – 2–0: Hateley (1–0), Woodcock (2–0)
Full-time – 5–0: Hateley (3–0), Robson (4–0), Sansom (5–0)

England: Shilton; Duxbury (G. A. Stevens); Sansom; Williams; M. Wright;
   Butcher; Robson (Chamberlain); Wilkins; Hateley; Woodcock; J. Barnes.
Finland: Huttunen; Pekonen; Kymalainen; Lahtinen; Petaja; Haaskivi
   (Turunen); Houtsonen; Ukkonen; Ikalainen; Rautiainen; Valvee (Hjelm).

14 November 1984 – TURKEY v ENGLAND at Istanbul
Half-time – 0–3: Robson (0–1), Woodcock (0–2), Robson (0–3)
Full-time – 0–8: J. Barnes (0–4), Woodcock (0–5), Robson (0–6), Anderson (0–7),
   J. Barnes (0–8)
Turkey: Yasar; Ismail; Yusuf; Kemal; Cem; Rasit; Mujdat; Ridvan; Ahmet; Ilyas
   (Hasan); Erdal.
England: Shilton; Anderson; Sansom; Williams (G. A. Stevens); M. Wright;
   Butcher; Robson; Wilkins; Withe; Woodcock (T. Francis); J. Barnes.

27 February 1985 – NORTHERN IRELAND v ENGLAND at Belfast
Half-time – 0–0
Full-time – 0–1: Hateley (0–1)
Northern Ireland: Jennings; J. Nicholl; Donaghy; O'Neill; McClelland; Ramsey;
   Armstrong; McIlroy; Quinn; Whiteside; Stewart.
England: Shilton; Anderson; Sansom; Wilkins; Martin; Butcher; Steven; G. A.
   Stevens; Hateley; Woodcock (T. Francis); J. Barnes.

1 May 1985 – ROMANIA v ENGLAND at Bucharest
Half-time – 0–0
Full-time – 0–0
Romania: Lung; Negrila; Iorgulescu (Iovan); Stefanescu; Ungureanu; Rednic;
   Hagi; Coras (Lacatus); Boloni; Klein; Camataru.
England: Shilton; Anderson; Sansom; Steven; M. Wright; Butcher; Robson;
   Wilkins; Mariner (Lineker); T. Francis; J. Barnes (Waddle).

22 May 1985 – FINLAND v ENGLAND at Helsinki
Half-time – 1–0: Rantanen (1–0)
Full-time – 1–1: Hateley (1–1)
Finland: Huttunen; Lahtinen (Petaja); Kymalainen; Ikalainen; Nieminen;
   Turunen; Houtsonen; Ukkonen (Hjelm); Lipponen; Rautiainen; Rantanen.
England: Shilton; Anderson; Sansom; Steven (Waddle); Fenwick; Butcher;
   Robson; Wilkins; Hateley; T. Francis; J. Barnes.

11 September 1985 – ENGLAND v ROMANIA at Wembley
Half-time – 1–0: Hoddle (1–0)
Full-time – 1–1: Camataru (1–1)
England: Shilton; M. G. Stevens; Sansom; Reid; M. Wright; Fenwick; Robson;
   Hoddle; Hateley; Lineker (Woodcock); Waddle (J. Barnes).
Romania: Lung; Negrila; Stefanescu; Ungureanu; Rednic; Iovan; Coras (Gabor);
   Klein (Mateut); Camataru; Boloni; Hagi.

16 October 1985 – ENGLAND v TURKEY at Wembley
Half-time – 4–0: Waddle (1–0), Lineker (2–0), Robson (3–0), Lineker (4–0)
Full-time – 5–0: Lineker (5–0)
England: Shilton; M. G. Stevens; Sansom; Hoddle; M. Wright; Fenwick; Robson
   (Steven); Wilkins; Hateley (Woodcock); Lineker; Waddle.
Turkey: Yasar; Ismail; Yusuf; Rasit; Sedat; Abdulkerim; Mujdat; Unal; Senol
   (S. Hasan); V. Hasan; Selcuk.

13 November 1985 – ENGLAND v NORTHERN IRELAND at Wembley
Half-time – 0–0
Full-time – 0–0
England: Shilton; M. G. Stevens; Sansom; Wilkins; M. Wright; Fenwick;
  Bracewell; Lineker; Dixon; Hoddle; Waddle.
Northern Ireland: Jennings; Nicholl; O'Neill; McDonald; Donaghy; Penney
  (Armstrong); McIlroy; McCreery; Stewart (Worthington); Whiteside; Quinn.

Other group results:
Finland 1 Northern Ireland 0; Northern Ireland 3 Romania 2; Turkey 1 Finland 2;
Northern Ireland 2 Finland 1; Romania 3 Turkey 0; Northern Ireland 2 Turkey 0;
Finland 1 Romania 1; Romania 2 Finland 0; Turkey 0 Northern Ireland 0;
Finland 1 Turkey 0; Romania 0 Northern Ireland 1; Turkey 1 Romania 3.

World Cup Qualifying Group 3

	P	W	D	L	F	A	Pts
ENGLAND	8	4	4	0	21	2	12
Northern Ireland	8	4	2	2	8	5	10
Romania	8	3	3	2	12	7	9
Finland	8	3	2	3	7	12	8
Turkey	8	0	1	7	2	24	1

1986 WORLD CUP FINALS

Hosts   Mexico
Holders Italy

England Squad

Goalkeepers		Age	Caps
Peter Shilton	Southampton	35	82
Gary Bailey	Manchester United	27	2
Chris Woods	Norwich City	26	3
Fullbacks			
M. Gary Stevens	Everton	23	9
Kenny Sansom	Arsenal	27	65
Viv Anderson	Arsenal	29	21
Central defence			
Alvin Martin	West Ham United	27	15
Terry Butcher	Ipswich Town	27	40
Terry Fenwick	Queen's Park Rangers	26	15
Midfield			
Glenn Hoddle	Tottenham Hotspur	28	33
Bryan Robson	Manchester United	29	50
Ray Wilkins	AC Milan	29	82
Gary A. Stevens	Tottenham Hotspur	24	5
Peter Reid	Everton	29	6
Trevor Steven	Everton	22	10
Steve Hodge	Aston Villa	23	3
Forwards			
Kerry Dixon	Chelsea	24	6
Mark Hateley	AC Milan	24	18

Gary Lineker	Everton	25	13
Chris Waddle	Tottenham Hotspur	25	16
John Barnes	Watford	22	27
Peter Beardsley	Newcastle United	25	5

Manager	Bobby Robson
Average age	26.2 years
Average experience	23.9 caps

Group F

3 June 1986 – ENGLAND v PORTUGAL at Monterrey
Half-time – 0–0
Full-time – 0–1: Manuel (0–1)
England: Shilton; M. G. Stevens; Sansom; Hoddle; Fenwick; Butcher; Robson
(Hodge); Wilkins; Hateley; Lineker; Waddle (Beardsley).
Portugal: Bento; Alvaro; Frederico; Oliveira; Inacio; Diamantino (Antonio);
Andre; Manuel; Pacheco; Sousa; Gomes (Futre).

6 June 1986 – ENGLAND v MOROCCO at Monterrey
Half-time – 0–0
Full-time – 0–0
England: Shilton; M. G. Stevens; Sansom; Hoddle; Fenwick; Butcher; Robson
(Hodge); Wilkins; Hateley (G. A. Stevens); Lineker; Waddle.
Morocco: Zaki; Khalifa; Lamris (Ouadini); El Biaz; Bouyahyaoui; Dolmy;
Bouderbala; Krimau; Timoumi; Merry Mustapha (Souleymani); Khairi.

11 June 1986 – ENGLAND v POLAND at Monterrey
Half-time – 3–0: Lineker (1–0), Lineker (2–0), Lineker (3–0)
Full-time – 3–0
England: Shilton; M. G. Stevens; Fenwick; Butcher; Sansom; Steven; Hoddle;
Reid; Hodge; Beardsley (Waddle); Lineker (Dixon).
Poland: Mlynarczyk; Pawlak; Ostrowski; Wojcicki; Matysik (Buncol); Urban;
Majewski; Smolarek; Komornicki (Karas); Dziekanowski; Boniek.

Other group results:
Poland 0 Morocco 0; Portugal 0 Poland 1; Portugal 1 Morocco 3.

Group F final table

	P	W	D	L	F	A	Pts
Morocco	3	1	2	0	3	1	4
ENGLAND	3	1	1	1	3	1	3
Poland	3	1	1	1	1	3	3
Portugal	3	1	0	2	2	4	2

SECOND ROUND

18 June 1986 – ENGLAND v PARAGUAY at the Azteca Stadium
Half-time – 1–0: Lineker (1–0)
Full-time – 3–0: Beardsley (2–0), Lineker (3–0)
England: Shilton; M. G. Stevens; Sansom; Hoddle; Martin; Butcher; Steven;
Reid (G. A. Stevens); Hodge; Lineker; Beardsley (Hateley).
Paraguay: Fernandez; Torales (Guasch); Zabala; Schettina; Delgado; Nunez;
Ferreira; Romero; Cabanas; Canete; Mendoza.

QUARTER-FINAL

22 June 1986 – ENGLAND v ARGENTINA at the Azteca Stadium
Half-time – 0–0
Full-time – 1–2: Maradona (0–1), Maradona (0–2), Lineker (1–2)
England: Shilton; M. G. Stevens; Sansom; Hoddle; Fenwick; Butcher; Steven
   (J. Barnes); Reid (Waddle); Hodge; Lineker; Beardsley.
Argentina: Pumpido; Cuciuffo; Brown; Ruggeri; Olarticoechea; Giusti; Batista;
   Enrique; Burruchaga (Tapia); Maradona; Valdano.

WORLD CUP 1990

QUALIFYING ROUND

19 October 1988 – ENGLAND v SWEDEN at Wembley
Half-time – 0–0
Full-time – 0–0
England: Shilton; M. G. Stevens; Pearce; Webb; Adams (Walker); Butcher;
   Robson; Beardsley; Waddle; Lineker; J. Barnes (Cottee).
Sweden: Ravelli; R. Nilsson (Schiller); Hysen; P. Larsson; Ljung; Thern;
   Stromberg; Prytz; J. Nilsson; Holmqvist (Ekstrom); Pettersson.

8 March 1989 – ALBANIA v ENGLAND at Tirana
Half-time – 0–1: J. Barnes (0–1)
Full-time – 0–2: Robson (0–2)
Albania: Mersini; Zmijani; Josa; Hodja; Gega; Jera; Shehu; Lekbello; Millo
   (Majaci); Minga; Demollari.
England: Shilton; M. G. Stevens; Pearce; Webb; Walker; Butcher; Robson;
   Rocastle; Waddle (Beardsley); Lineker (Smith); J. Barnes.

26 April 1989 – ENGLAND v ALBANIA at Wembley
Half-time – 2–0: Lineker (1–0), Beardsley (2–0)
Full-time – 5–0: Beardsley (3–0), Waddle (4–0), Gascoigne (5–0)
England: Shilton; M. G. Stevens (Parker); Pearce; Webb; Walker; Butcher;
   Robson; Rocastle (Gascoigne); Beardsley; Lineker; Waddle.
Albania: Nallbani; Zmijani; Bubeqi; Hodja; Gega; Jera; Shehu; Lekbello; Millo;
   Hasanpapa (Noga); Demollari.

3 June 1989 – ENGLAND v POLAND at Wembley
Half-time – 1–0: Lineker (1–0)
Full-time – 3–0: J. Barnes (2–0), Webb (3–0)
England: Shilton; M. G. Stevens; Pearce; Webb; Walker; Butcher; Robson;
   Waddle (Rocastle); Beardsley (Smith); Lineker; J. Barnes.
Poland: Bako; Wijas; Wojcicki; Wdowczyk; Lukasik; Matysik; Prusik; Urban
   (Tarasiewicz); Furtok; K. Warzycha; Lesniak (Kosecki).

6 September 1989 – SWEDEN v ENGLAND at Solna
Half-time – 0–0
Full-time – 0–0
Sweden: T. Ravelli; R Nilsson; Hysen; P. Larsson; Ljung; Enqvist; Thern;
   Ingesson (Stromberg); J. Nilsson (Limpar); Ekstrom; Magnusson.

England: Shilton; M. G. Stevens; Pearce; Walker; Butcher; McMahon; Waddle; Webb (Gascoigne); Beardsley; Lineker; J. Barnes (Rocastle).

11 October 1989 – POLAND v ENGLAND at Chorzów
Half-time – 0–0
Full-time – 0–0
Poland: Bako; Czachowski; Kaczmarek; Wdowczyk; R. Warzycha; Nawrocki; Tarasiewicz; Ziober; Kosecki; Dziekanowski; K. Warzycha (Furtok).
England: Shilton; M. G. Stevens; Pearce; Walker; Butcher; McMahon; Robson; Rocastle; Beardsley; Lineker; Waddle.

Other group results:
Poland 1 Albania 0; Albania 1 Sweden 2; Sweden 2 Poland 1;
Sweden 3 Albania 1; Poland 0 Sweden 2; Albania 1 Poland 2.

World Cup Qualifying Group 2

	P	W	D	L	F	A	Pts
Sweden	6	4	2	0	9	3	10
ENGLAND	6	3	3	0	10	0	9
Poland	6	2	1	3	4	8	5
Albania	6	0	0	6	3	15	0

1990 WORLD CUP FINALS

Hosts   Italy
Holders Argentina

England Squad

Goalkeepers		*Age*	*Caps*
Peter Shilton	Derby County	39	118
Chris Woods	Glasgow Rangers	30	16
David Seaman	Queen's Park Rangers	26	3
Fullbacks			
Paul Parker	Queen's Park Rangers	26	5
M. Gary Stevens	Glasgow Rangers	27	39
Stuart Pearce	Nottingham Forest	28	24
Tony Dorigo	Chelsea	24	3
Central defence			
Des Walker	Nottingham Forest	24	18
Terry Butcher	Glasgow Rangers	31	72
Mark Wright	Derby County	26	24
Midfield			
Steve Hodge	Nottingham Forest	27	22
Bryan Robson	Manchester United	33	85
Paul Gascoigne	Tottenham Hotspur	23	11
David Platt	Aston Villa	24	5
Steve McMahon	Liverpool	28	12
Trevor Steven	Glasgow Rangers	26	26
Neil Webb	Manchester United	26	19
Forwards			
Chris Waddle	Marseille	29	52

John Barnes	Liverpool	26	53
Gary Lineker	Tottenham Hotspur	29	51
Steve Bull	Wolverhampton Wanderers	25	7
Peter Beardsley	Liverpool	29	40

Manager	Bobby Robson
Average age	27.5 years
Average experience	32 caps

Group F

11 June 1990 – ENGLAND v REPUBLIC OF IRELAND at Cagliari
Half-time – 1–0: Lineker (1–0)
Full-time – 1–1: Sheedy (1–1)
England: Shilton; M. G. Stevens; Walker; Butcher; Pearce; Robson; Beardsley (McMahon); Gascoigne; Waddle; J. Barnes; Lineker (Bull).
Republic of Ireland: Bonner; Morris; McCarthy; Moran; Staunton; McGrath; Houghton; Sheedy; Aldridge (McLoughlin); Townsend; Cascarino.

16 June 1990 – ENGLAND v HOLLAND at Cagliari
Half-time – 0–0
Full-time – 0–0
England: Shilton; Parker; Walker; M. Wright; Butcher; Pearce; Robson (Platt); Waddle (Bull); Gascoigne; J. Barnes; Lineker.
Holland: Van Breukelen; Van Aerle; Rijkaard; R. Koeman; Van Tiggelen; Wouters; Gullit; Witschge; van't Schip (Kieft); Gillhaus; Van Basten.

21 June 1990 – ENGLAND v EGYPT at Cagliari
Half-time – 0–0
Full-time – 1–0: M. Wright (1–0)
England: Shilton; Parker; M. Wright; Walker; Pearce; Waddle (Platt); McMahon; Gascoigne; J. Barnes; Lineker; Bull (Beardsley).
Egypt: Shobeir; I. Hassan; Yakan; H. Ramzy; Yassein; Youssef; Abdelghani; El Kass (Soliman); A. Ramzy; Abdelhamid (Abdelrahman); H. Hassan.

Other group results:
Egypt 1 Holland 1; Egypt 0 Republic of Ireland 0;
Republic of Ireland 1 Holland 1.

Group F final table
	P	W	D	L	F	A	Pts
ENGLAND	3	1	2	0	2	1	4
Republic of Ireland	3	0	3	0	2	2	3
Holland	3	0	3	0	2	2	3
Egypt	3	0	2	1	1	2	2

SECOND ROUND

26 June 1990 – ENGLAND v BELGIUM at Bologna
Half-time – 0–0
Full-time – 0–0
Extra-time – 1–0: Platt (1–0)
England: Shilton; Parker; Butcher; M. Wright; Walker; Pearce; Waddle; Gascoigne; McMahon (Platt); J. Barnes (Bull); Lineker.

Belgium: Preud'homme; Gerets; Grun; Demol; Clijsters; De Wolf; van der Elst; Scifo; Versavel (Vervoort); Ceulemans; Degryse (Claesen).

QUARTER-FINALS

1 July 1990 – CAMEROON v ENGLAND at Naples
Half-time – 0–1: Platt (0–1)
Full-time – 2–2: Kunde pen. (1–1), Ekeke (2–1), Lineker pen. (2–2)
Extra-time – 2–3: Lineker pen. (2–3)
Cameroon: N'Kono; Tataw; Massing; Kunde; Ebwelle; Maboang (Milla); Libiih; Pagal; Makanaky; Mfede (Ekeke); Omam-Biyik.
England: Shilton; Parker; Butcher (Steven); M. Wright; Walker; Pearce; Waddle; Platt; Gascoigne; J. Barnes (Beardsley); Lineker.

SEMI-FINALS

4 July 1990 – WEST GERMANY v ENGLAND at Turin
Half-time – 0–0
Full-time – 1–1: Brehme (1–0), Lineker (1–1)
After extra time – 1–1: Germany won 4–3 on penalties
West Germany: Illgner; Berthold; Augenthaler; Buchwald; Kohler; Hässler (Reuter); Matthäus: Thon; Brehme; Klinsmann; Voller (Riedle).
England: Shilton; Parker; Butcher (Steven); M. Wright; Walker; Pearce; Platt; Gascoigne; Waddle; Beardsley; Lineker.

THIRD PLACE PLAY-OFF

7 July 1990 – ITALY v ENGLAND at Bari
Half-time – 0–0
Full-time – 2–1: R. Baggio (1–0), Platt (1–1), Schillaci pen. (2–1)
Italy: Zenga; Bergomi; Baresi; Ferrara; Maldini; Vierchowod; De Agostini (Berti); Ancelotti; Giannini (Ferri); R. Baggio; Schillaci.
England: Shilton; G. M. Stevens; M. Wright (Waddle); Parker; Walker; Dorigo; Steven; Platt; McMahon (Webb); Beardsley; Lineker.

WORLD CUP 1994

QUALIFYING ROUNDS

14 October 1992 – ENGLAND v NORWAY at Wembley
Half-time – 0–0
Full-time – 1–1: Platt (1–0), Rekdal (1–1)
England: Woods; Dixon (Palmer); Walker; Adams; Pearce; Batty; Ince; Platt; Gascoigne; I. Wright (Merson); Shearer.
Norway: Thorstvedt; R. Nilsen; Bratseth; T. Pedersen (Berg); Bjornebye; Halle; J. I. Jakobsen; Ingebrigtsen; Mykland (Flo); Rekdal; Sorloth.

18 November 1992 – ENGLAND v TURKEY at Wembley
Half-time – 2–0: Gascoigne (1–0), Shearer (2–0)
Full-time – 4–0: Pearce (3–0), Gascoigne (4–0)

England: Woods; Dixon; Pearce; Palmer; Walker; Adams; Platt; Gascoigne; Shearer; I. Wright; Ince.
Turkey: Hayrettin; Recep; Bulent; Gokhan; Ogun; Orhan; Hami (Riza); Unal; Mehmet (Ugur); Oguz; Hakan.

17 February 1993 – ENGLAND v SAN MARINO at Wembley
Half-time – 2–0: Platt (1–0), Platt (2–0)
Full-time– 6–0: Platt (3–0), Palmer (4–0), Platt (5–0), L. Ferdinand (6–0)
England: Woods; Dixon; Walker; Adams; Dorigo; Gascoigne; Batty; Platt; Palmer; L. Ferdinand; J. Barnes.
San Marino: Benedettini; B. Muccioli; Zanotti; M. Mazza; Gennari; Canti; Guerra; Manzaroli; Bacciocchi (P. Mazza); Bonini; Francini (Matteoni).

31 March 1993 – TURKEY v ENGLAND at Izmir
Half-time – 0–2: Platt (0–1), Gascoigne (0–2)
Full-time – 0–2
Turkey: Engin (Hayrettin); Recep (Hami); Ogun; Ali Guncar; Tugay; Bulent; Feyyaz; Unal; Mehmet; Oguz; Orhan.
England: Woods; Dixon (Clough); Sinton; Palmer; Walker; Adams; Platt; Gascoigne; J. Barnes; I. Wright (Sharpe); Ince.

28 April 1993 – ENGLAND v HOLLAND at Wembley
Half-time – 2–1: J. Barnes (1–0), Platt (2–0), Bergkamp (2–1)
Full-time – 2–2: Van Vossen pen. (2–2)
England: Woods; Dixon; Walker; Adams; Keown; Ince; Gascoigne (Merson); Palmer; J. Barnes; Platt; Ferdinand.
Holland: De Goey; Blind; F. De Boer; Rijkaard; Winter; Wouters; Witschge; Gullit (Van Vossen); Bergkamp; Bosman (De Wolf); Overmars.

29 May 1993 – POLAND v ENGLAND at Chorzów
Half-time – 1–0: Adamczuk (1–0)
Full-time – 1–1: I. Wright (1–1)
Poland: Bako; Czachowski; Szewczyk; Kozminski; Lesiak; Brzeczek (Jalocha); Swierczewski; Adamczuk; Furtok; Kosecki; Lesniak (Wegrzyn).
England: Woods; Bardsley; Dorigo; Palmer (I. Wright); Walker; Adams; Platt; Gascoigne (Clough); Sheringham; J. Barnes; Ince.

2 June 1993 – NORWAY v ENGLAND at Oslo
Half-time – 1–0: Leonhardsen (1–0)
Full-time – 2–0: Bohinen (2–0)
Norway: Thorstvedt; Halle; T. Pedersen; Bratseth (R. Nilsen); Bjornebye; Flo; Mykland; Leonhardsen; Fjortoft (Sorloth); Rekdal; Bohinen.
England: Woods; Dixon; Pallister; Palmer; Walker (Clough); Adams; Platt; Gascoigne; L. Ferdinand; Sheringham (I. Wright); Sharpe.

8 September 1993 – ENGLAND v POLAND at Wembley
Half-time – 1–0: L. Ferdinand (1–0)
Full-time – 3–0: Gascoigne (2–0), Pearce (3–0)
England: Seaman; Jones; Pearce; Ince; Pallister; Adams; Platt; Gascoigne; L. Ferdinand; I. Wright; Sharpe.
Poland: Bako; Czachowski; Brzeczek; Kozminski; Lesiak; R. Warzycha; Swierczewski; Adamczuk (Bak); Kosecki; Furtok (Ziober); Lesniak.

13 October 1993 – HOLLAND v ENGLAND at Rotterdam
Half-time – 0–0
Full-time – 2–0: R. Koeman (1–0), Bergkamp (2–0)
   Holland: De Goey; De Wolf; R. Koeman; F. De Boer; Rijkaard; Wouters;
   Bergkamp; E. Koeman; Overmars (Winter); R. De Boer (Van Gobbel);
   Roy.
England: Seaman; Parker; Dorigo; Palmer (Sinton); Adams; Pallister; Platt;
   Ince; Shearer; Merson (I. Wright); Sharpe.

17 November 1993 – SAN MARINO v ENGLAND at Bologna
Half-time – 1–3: Gualtieri (1–0), Ince (1–1), I. Wright (1–2), L. Ferdinand (1–3)
Full-time – 1–7: I. Wright (1–4), Ince (1–5), I. Wright (1–6), I. Wright (1–7)
San Marino: Benedettini; Valentini (Gobbi); Zanotti; Canti; Gennari; Guerra;
   Manzaroli; Della Valle; Bacciocchi (P. Mazza); Bonini; Gualtieri.
England: Seaman; Dixon; Pearce; Ince; Walker; Pallister; Ripley; I. Wright;
   L. Ferdinand; Platt; Sinton.

Other group results:
Norway 10 San Marino 0; Norway 2 Holland 1; Poland 1 Turkey 0;
San Marino 0 Norway 2; Holland 2 Poland 2; Turkey 4 San Marino 1;
Turkey 1 Holland 3; Holland 3 Turkey 1; San Marino 0 Turkey 0;
Holland 6 San Marino 0; Norway 3 Turkey 1; Poland 1 San Marino 0;
San Marino 0 Poland 3; Holland 0 Norway 0; Norway 1 Poland 0;
San Marino 0 Holland 7; Poland 0 Norway 3; Turkey 2 Poland 1;
Turkey 2 Norway 1; Poland 1 Holland 3.

World Cup Qualifying Group 2

	P	W	D	L	F	A	Pts
Norway	10	7	2	1	25	5	16
Holland	10	6	3	1	29	9	15
ENGLAND	10	5	3	2	26	9	13
Poland	10	3	2	5	10	15	8
Turkey	10	3	1	6	11	19	7
San Marino	10	0	1	9	2	46	1

WORLD CUP 1998

QUALIFYING ROUNDS

1 September 1996 – MOLDOVA v ENGLAND at Kishinev
Half-time – 0–2: Barmby (0–1), Gascoigne (0–2)
Full-time – 0–3: Shearer (0–3)
Moldova: Romanenco; Secu; Nani; Testimitanu; Gaidamsciuc; Belous (Sischin);
   Epureanu; Curtianu; Clescenco; Miterev (Rebeja); Popovici.
England: Seaman; G. Neville; Pearce; Southgate; Pallister; Hinchcliffe; Barmby
   (Le Tissier); Ince; Shearer; Gascoigne (Batty); Beckham.

9 October 1996 – ENGLAND v POLAND at Wembley
Half-time – 2–1: Citko (0–1), Shearer (1–1), Shearer (2–1)
Full-time – 2–1
England: Seaman; G. Neville; Pearce; Southgate (Pallister); Ince; Hinchcliffe;
   McManaman; Gascoigne; Shearer; L. Ferdinand; Beckham.

Poland: Wozniak; Waldoch; Zielinski; Juskowiak; Hajto; Michalski; Baluszynski; Wojtala; Nowak; Citko; K. Warzycha (Saganowski).

9 November 1996 – GEORGIA v ENGLAND at Tbilisi

Half-time – 0–2: Sheringham (0–1), L. Ferdinand (0–2)
Full-time – 0–2

Georgia: Zoidze; Lobjanidze; Tskhadadze; Shelia; Gogichaishvili (Gudushauri); Nemsadze; Kinkladze; Jamarauli; Kobiashvili; Ketsbaia; Aveladze (Gogrichiani).

England: Seaman; Campbell; Hinchcliffe; Batty; Southgate; Adams; Beckham; Gascoigne; L. Ferdinand (I. Wright); Sheringham; Ince.

12 February 1997 – ENGLAND v ITALY at Wembley

Half-time – 0–1: Zola (0–1)
Full-time – 0–1

England: Walker; G. Neville; Pearce; Ince; Campbell; Batty (I. Wright); McManaman (Merson); Le Tissier (L. Ferdinand); Shearer; Beckham; Le Saux.

Italy: Peruzzi; Ferrara; Costacurta; Cannavaro; Di Livio; D. Baggio; Albertini; Di Matteo; Maldini; Zola (Fuser); Casiraghi (Ravanelli).

30 April 1997 – ENGLAND v GEORGIA at Wembley

Half-time – 1–0: Sheringham (1–0)
Full-time – 2–0: Shearer (2–0)

England: Seaman; G. Neville; Le Saux; Batty; Campbell; Adams (Southgate); Lee; Ince (Redknapp); Shearer; Sheringham; Beckham.

Georgia: Zoidze; Chikhradze; Shekiladze; Tskhadadze; Shelia; Machavariani (Gogrichiani) (A. Arveladze); Nemsadze; Jamarauli; Ketsbaia; Kinkladze (Gakhokidze); S. Arveladze.

31 May 1997 – POLAND v ENGLAND at Chorzów

Half-time – 0–1: Shearer (0–1)
Full-time – 0–2: Sheringham (0–2)

Poland: Wozniak; Jozwiak; Waldoch; Zielinski; Kaluzny; Ledwon; Bukalski (Swierczewski); Nowak (Kucharski); Majak; Juskowiak (Adamczyk); Dembinski.

England: Seaman; G. Neville; Le Saux; Southgate; Campbell; Ince; Lee; Gascoigne (Batty); Shearer; Sheringham; Beckham (P. Neville).

10 September 1997 – ENGLAND v MOLDOVA at Wembley

Half-time – 1–0: Scholes (1–0)
Full-time – 4–0: I. Wright (2–0), Gascoigne (3–0), I. Wright (4–0)

England: Seaman; G. Neville; P. Neville; Batty; Campbell; Southgate; Beckham (Ripley) (Butt); Gascoigne; I. Wright; L. Ferdinand (Collymore); Scholes.

Moldova: Romanenko; Fistican; Testimitanu; Stroenco; Kulibaba (Suharev); Rebeja; Spanu; Sischin (Popovici); Curtianu; Miterev; Rogaciov (Cebotari).

11 October 1997 – ITALY v ENGLAND at Rome

Half-time – 0–0
Full-time – 0–0

Italy: Peruzzi; Nesta; Costacurta; Cannavaro; Di Livio; Albertini; D. Baggio; Maldini (Benarrivo); Zola (Del Piero); Vieri; Inzaghi (Chiesa).

England: Seaman; Campbell; Le Saux; Southgate; Adams; Batty; Beckham; Gascoigne (Butt); I. Wright; Sheringham; Ince.

Other group results:
Moldova 1 Italy 3; Italy 1 Georgia 0; Poland 2 Moldova 1; Italy 3 Moldova 0;
Poland 0 Italy 0; Italy 3 Poland 0; Georgia 2 Moldova 0; Poland 4 Georgia 1;
Georgia 0 Italy 0; Moldova 0 Georgia 1; Moldova 0 Poland 3; Georgia 3 Poland 0.

World Cup Qualifying Group 2

	P	W	D	L	F	A	Pts
ENGLAND	8	6	1	1	15	2	19
Italy	8	5	3	0	11	1	18
Poland	8	3	1	4	10	12	10
Georgia	8	3	1	4	7	9	10
Moldova	8	0	0	8	2	21	0

1998 WORLD CUP FINALS

Hosts France
Holders Brazil

England Squad

Goalkeepers		*Age*	*Caps*
David Seaman	Arsenal	34	40
Tim Flowers	Blackburn Rovers	31	11
Nigel Martyn	Leeds United	31	7
Fullbacks			
Gary Neville	Manchester United	23	27
Graham Le Saux	Chelsea	29	25
Phil Neville	Manchester United	21	12
Central defence			
Tony Adams	Arsenal	31	51
Gareth Southgate	Aston Villa	27	25
Sol Campbell	Tottenham Hotspur	23	16
Martin Keown	Arsenal	31	18
Rio Ferdinand	West Ham United	19	3
Midfield			
Darren Anderton	Tottenham Hotspur	26	18
David Batty	Leeds United	29	31
Paul Scholes	Manchester United	23	7
Paul Ince	Liverpool	30	39
David Beckham	Manchester United	23	15
Robert Lee	Newcastle United	32	17
Steve McManaman	Liverpool	26	21
Forwards			
Teddy Sheringham	Manchester United	32	33
Michael Owen	Liverpool	19	5
Alan Shearer	Newcastle United	27	39
Paul Merson	Middlesbrough	30	18

Manager	Glenn Hoddle
Average age	27.1 years
Average experience	21.7 caps

Group G

15 June 1998 – ENGLAND v TUNISIA at Marseilles
Half-time – 1–0: Shearer (1–0)
Full-time – 2–0: Scholes (2–0)
England: Seaman; Southgate; Adams; Campbell; Anderton; Batty; Scholes; Ince; Le Saux; Sheringham (Owen); Shearer.
Tunisia: El Ouaer; Boukadida; Badra; S. Trabelsi; H. Trabelsi (Thabet); Ghodbane; Souayah (Baya); Chihi; Clayton; Sellimi; Ben Slimane (Ben Younes).

22 June 1998 – ROMANIA v ENGLAND at Toulouse
Half-time 0–0
Full-time 2–1: Moldovan (1–0), Owen (1–1), Petrescu (2–1)
Romania: Stelea; Petrescu; Ciobotariu; Gheorghe Popescu; Filipescu; Munteanu; Hagi (Stanga) (Marinescu); Galca; Gabriel Popescu; Moldovan (Lacatus); Ilie.
England: Seaman; G. Neville; Adams; Campbell; Anderton; Ince (Beckham); Scholes; Batty; Le Saux; Sheringham (Owen); Shearer.

26 June 1998 – COLOMBIA v ENGLAND at Lens
Half-time – 0–2: Anderton (0–1), Beckham (0–2)
Full-time – 0–2
Colombia: Mondragon; Cabrera; Bermudez; Palacios; Moreno; Rincon; Serna (Aristizabal); Lozano; Valderrama; Preciado (Valencia); De Avila (Ricard).
England: Seaman; G. Neville; Adams; Campbell; Anderton (Lee); Beckham; Ince (Batty); Le Saux; Scholes (McManaman); Owen; Shearer.

Other group results:
Romania 1 Colombia 0; Colombia 1 Tunisia 0; Romania 1 Tunisia 1.

Group G final table
	P	W	D	L	F	A	Pts
Romania	3	2	1	0	4	2	7
ENGLAND	3	2	0	1	5	2	6
Colombia	3	1	0	2	1	3	3
Tunisia	3	0	1	2	1	4	1

SECOND ROUND

30 June 1998 – ARGENTINA v ENGLAND at St Etienne
Half-time – 2–2: Batistuta pen. (1–0), Shearer pen. (1–1), Owen (1–2), Zanetti (2–2)
Full-time – 2–2
After extra time – 2–2: Argentina won 4–3 on penalties
Argentina: Roa; Vivas; Ayala; Chamot; Zanetti; Almeyda; Simeone (Berti); Ortega; Verón; Batistuta (Crespo); Lopez (Gallardo).
England: Seaman; G. Neville; Adams; Campbell; Anderton (Batty); Beckham; Ince; Le Saux (Southgate); Scholes (Merson); Owen; Shearer.

WORLD CUP 2002

QUALIFYING ROUNDS

7 October 2000 – ENGLAND v GERMANY at Wembley
Half-time – 0–1: Hamann (0–1)
Full-time – 0–1
England: Seaman; G. Neville (Dyer); Le Saux (Barry); Southgate; Keown;
   Adams; Beckham (Parlour); Barmby; Andy Cole; Owen; Scholes.
Germany: Kahn; Rehmer; Nowotny; Linke; Deisler; Ramelow; Hamann;
   Ballack; Bode (Ziege); Scholl; Bierhoff.

11 October 2000 – FINLAND v ENGLAND at Helsinki
Half-time – 0–0
Full-time – 0–0
Finland: Niemi; Helin (Reini); Tihinen; Hyypia; Saarinen (Salli); Nurmela;
   Wiss; Valakari; Johansson; Litmanen; Forssell (Kuqi).
England: Seaman; P. Neville; Barry (Brown); Southgate; Keown; Wise; Parlour;
   Scholes; Andy Cole; Sheringham (McManaman); Heskey.

24 March 2001 – ENGLAND v FINLAND at Anfield
Half-time – 1–1: G. Neville o.g. (0–1), Owen (1–1)
Full-time – 2–1: Beckham (2–1)
England: Seaman; G. Neville; Powell; R. Ferdinand; Campbell; Scholes;
   Beckham; Gerrard; Andy Cole (Fowler); Owen (Butt); McManaman (Heskey).
Finland: Niemi; Pasanen; Hyypia, Tihinen; Ylonen (Helin); Wiss; Nurmela
   (Forssell); Riihilahti; Litmanen; Kolkka (Kuqi); Johansson.

28 March 2001 – ALBANIA v ENGLAND at Tirana
Half-time 0–0
Full-time 1–3: Owen (0–1), Scholes (0–2), Rraklli (1–2), Andy Cole (1–3)
Albania: Strakosha; Cipi; Fakaj; Lala; Xhumba; Hasi; F. Vata (Rraklli); Kola
   (Mukaj); Bellai; Tare (Skela); Bushi.
England: Seaman; G. Neville; Ashley Cole; R. Ferdinand; Campbell (Brown); Butt;
   Beckham; Scholes; Andy Cole; Owen (Sheringham); McManaman (Heskey).

6 June 2001 – GREECE v ENGLAND at Athens
Half-time – 0–0
Full-time – 2–0: Scholes (0–1), Beckham (0–2)
Greece: Nikopolidis; Goumas; Ouzounidis; Dabizas; Mavrogenidis
   (Giannakopoulos); Basinas; Zagorakis; Fyssas; Karagounis (Liberopoulos);
   Machlas (Alexandris); Vryzas.
England: Seaman; P. Neville; Ashley Cole; Gerrard; Keown; R. Ferdinand;
   Beckham; Scholes (Butt); Fowler (Smith); Owen; Heskey (McManaman).

1 September 2001 – GERMANY v ENGLAND at Munich
Half-time – 1–2: Jancker (1–0), Owen (1–1), Gerrard (1–2)
Full-time – 1–5: Owen (1–3), Owen (1–4), Heskey (1–5)
Germany: Kahn; Wörns (Asamoah); Nowotny; Linke; Rehmer; Hamann;
   Ballack (Klose); Böhme; Deisler; Jancker; Neuville (Kehl).
England: Seaman; G. Neville; Ashley Cole; Gerrard (Hargreaves); R. Ferdinand;
   Campbell; Beckham; Scholes (Carragher); Heskey; Owen; Barmby
   (McManaman).

5 September 2001 – ENGLAND v ALBANIA at St James' Park
Half-time – 1–0: Owen (1–0)
Full-time – 2–0: Fowler (2–0)
England: Seaman; G. Neville; Ashley Cole; Gerrard (Carragher); R. Ferdinand; Campbell; Beckham; Scholes; Heskey (Fowler); Owen; Barmby (McManaman).
Albania: Strakosha; Dede; Fakaj; Cipi; Xhumba; Murati; F. Vata; Bellai; Hasi (Bushi); Bogdani (Tare); Rraklli (Mukaj).

6 October 2001 – ENGLAND v GREECE at Old Trafford
Half-time – 0–1: Haristeas (0–1)
Full-time – 2–2: Sheringham (1–1), Nikolaidis (1–2), Beckham (2–2)
England: Martyn; G. Neville; Ashley Cole (McManaman); Gerrard; R. Ferdinand; Keown; Beckham; Scholes; Fowler (Sheringham); Heskey; Barmby (Andy Cole).
Greece: Nikopolidis; Patsatzoglou; Dabizas; Konstantinidis; Vokolos; Fyssas; Charisteas (Lakis); Zagorakis (Basinas); Karagounis; Kassapis; Nikolaidis (Machlas).

Other group results:
Finland 2 Albania 1; Germany 2 Greece 0; Greece 1 Finland 0;
Albania 2 Greece 0; Germany 2 Albania 1; Greece 2 Germany 4;
Finland 2 Germany 2; Greece 1 Albania 0; Albania 0 Germany 2;
Albania 0 Finland 2; Finland 5 Greece 1; Germany 0 Finland 0.

World Cup Qualifying Group 9

	P	W	D	L	F	A	Pts
ENGLAND	8	5	2	1	16	6	17
Germany	8	5	2	1	14	10	17
Finland	8	3	3	2	12	7	12
Greece	8	2	1	5	7	17	7
Albania	8	1	0	7	5	14	3

2002 WORLD CUP FINALS

Hosts   South Korea and Japan
Holders   France

England Squad

Goalkeepers

		Age	*Caps*
David Seaman	Arsenal	38	68
Nigel Martyn	Leeds United	31	23
David James	West Ham United	31	9

Fullbacks

Danny Mills	Leeds United	25	7
Ashley Cole	Arsenal	21	8
Wayne Bridge	Southampton	21	5

Central defence

Martin Keown	Arsenal	35	43
Sol Campbell	Arsenal	27	46
Gareth Southgate	Middlesbrough	31	49
Rio Ferdinand	Leeds United	23	22

Midfield

Paul Scholes	Manchester United	27	44
David Beckham	Manchester United	27	49
Kieron Dyer	Newcastle United	23	9
Owen Hargreaves	Bayern Munich	21	6
Joe Cole	West Ham United	20	6
Nicky Butt	Manchester United	27	24
Trevor Sinclair	West Ham United	29	5

Forwards

Darius Vassell	Aston Villa	22	5
Michael Owen	Liverpool	23	36
Emile Heskey	Liverpool	24	24
Teddy Sheringham	Tottenham Hotspur	36	47
Robbie Fowler	Leeds United	27	25

Manager	Sven-Göran Eriksson
Average age	26.8 years
Average experience	25.5 caps

Group F

2 June 2002 – ENGLAND v SWEDEN at Saitama
Half-time – 1–0: Campbell (1–0)
Full-time – 1–1: Alexandersson (1–1)
England: Seaman; Mills; Ashley Cole; Hargreaves; Campbell; R. Ferdinand; Beckham (Dyer); Scholes; Vassell (J. Cole); Owen; Heskey.
Sweden: Hedman; Mellberg; Lucic; Linderoth; Mjallby; Jakobsson; Alexandersson; Ljungberg; Allback (A. Andersson); Larsson; M. Svensson (A. Svensson).

7 June 2002 – ARGENTINA v ENGLAND at Sapporo
Half-time – 0–1: Beckham pen. (0–1)
Full-time – 0–1
Argentina: Cavellero; Zanetti; Kily; Gonzalez (C. Lopez); Pochettino; Samuel; Placente; Simeone; Verón (Aimar); Batistuta (Crespo); Ortega; Sorin.
England: Seaman; Mills; Ashley Cole; Hargreaves (Sinclair); Butt; Campbell; R. Ferdinand; Beckham; Scholes; Owen (Bridge); Heskey (Sheringham).

12 June 2002 – NIGERIA v ENGLAND at Osaka
Half-time – 0–0
Full-time – 0–0
Nigeria: Enyeama; Sodje; Udeze; Christopher; Yobo; Okoronkwo; Okocha; Obiorah; Aghahowa; Akwuegbu; Opabunmi (Ikedia).
England: Seaman; Mills; Ashley Cole (Bridge); Butt; Campbell; R. Ferdinand; Beckham; Scholes; Heskey (Sheringham); Owen (Vassell); Sinclair.

Other group results:
Argentina 1 Nigeria 0; Sweden 2 Nigeria 1; Argentina 1 Sweden 1.

Group F final table

	P	W	D	L	F	A	Pts
Sweden	3	1	2	0	4	3	5
ENGLAND	3	1	2	0	2	1	5
Argentina	3	1	1	1	2	2	4
Nigeria	3	0	1	2	1	3	1

SECOND ROUND

15 June 2002 – DENMARK v ENGLAND at Niigata
Half-time – 0–3: R. Ferdinand (0–1), Owen (0–2), Heskey (0–3)
Full-time – 0–3
Denmark: Sorensen; Helveg (Bogelund); N. Jensen; Gravesen; Laursen;
   Henriksen; Rommedahl; Tofting (C. Jensen); Sand; Tomasson; Gronkjaer.
England: Seaman; Mills; Ashley Cole; Butt; Campbell; R. Ferdinand; Beckham;
   Scholes (Dyer); Heskey (Sheringham); Owen (Fowler); Sinclair.

QUARTER-FINALS

21 June 2002 – ENGLAND v BRAZIL at Shizuoka
Half-time – 1–1: Owen (1–0), Rivaldo (1–1)
Full-time – 1–2: Ronaldinho (1–2)
England: Seaman; Mills; Ashley Cole (Sheringham); Butt; Campbell;
   R. Ferdinand; Beckham; Scholes; Heskey; Owen (Vassell); Sinclair (Dyer).
Brazil: Marcos; Cafu; Roberto Carlos; Lucio; Roque Junior; Edmilson;
   Kleberson; Gilberto Silva; Ronaldo (Edilson); Rivaldo; Ronaldinho.

WORLD CUP 2006

QUALIFYING ROUNDS

4 September 2004 – AUSTRIA v ENGLAND at Vienna
Half-time – 0–1: Lampard (0–1)
Full-time – 2–2: Gerrard (0–2), Kollmann (1–2), Ivanschitz (2–2)
Austria: Manninger; Standfest; Stranzl; Hiden; Pogatetz; Sick; Kuhbauer;
   Aufhauser (Kiesenebner); Ivanschitz; Glieder (Kollmann); Haas (Hieblinger).
England: James; G. Neville; Ashley Cole; Gerrard (Carragher); Terry; King;
   Beckham; Lampard; Smith (Defoe); Owen; Bridge (J. Cole).

8 September 2004 – POLAND v ENGLAND at Chorzów
Half-time – 0–1: Defoe (0–1)
Full-time – 1–2: Zurawski (1–1), Glowacki o.g. (1–2)
Poland: Dudek; Michal Zewlakow; Bak; Glowacki; Krzynowek; Rzasa; M.
   Lewandowski; Mila (Kukielka); Kosowski (Gorawski); Zurawski; Rasiak
   (Niedzielan).
England: Robinson; G. Neville (Carragher); Ashley Cole; Gerrard; Terry; King;
   Beckham (Hargreaves); Lampard; Defoe (Dyer); Owen; Bridge.

9 October 2004 – ENGLAND v WALES at Old Trafford
Half-time – 1–0: Lampard (1–0)
Full-time – 2–0: Beckham (2–0)
England: Robinson; G. Neville; Ashley Cole; Butt; Campbell; R. Ferdinand;
   Beckham (Hargreaves); Rooney (King); Owen; Defoe (Smith); Lampard.
Wales: P. Jones; Delaney; Thatcher; Pembridge (C. Robinson); Gabbidon;
   Speed; Koumas (Earnshaw); Bellamy; Hartson; Giggs; Davies.

13 October 2004 – AZERBAIJAN v ENGLAND at Baku
Half-time – 0–1: Owen (0–1)
Full-time – 0–1

Azerbaijan: Hasanzade; Hajiyev; Shukurov; E. Guliyev (I. Gurbanov); Sadygov; Amirbekov; Kerimov; Ponomarev; K. Guliyev; Nabiev (Abdullayev); Aliyev (G. Gurbanov).

England: Robinson; G. Neville; Ashley Cole; Butt; Campbell; R. Ferdinand; Jenas (Wright-Phillips); Rooney (J. Cole); Owen; Defoe (Smith): Lampard.

26 March 2005 – ENGLAND v NORTHERN IRELAND at Old Trafford

Half-time – 0–0

Full-time – 4–0: J. Cole (1–0), Owen (2–0), Baird o.g. (3–0), Lampard (4–0)

England: Robinson; G. Neville; Ashley Cole; Gerrard (Hargreaves); R. Ferdinand; Terry; Beckham (Dyer); Lampard; Owen; Rooney (Defoe); J. Cole.

Northern Ireland: Taylor; Baird; Capaldi; Doherty (Davis); A. Hughes; Murdock; Gillespie; Johnson; Healy (Kirk); Elliott; Whitley (S. Jones).

30 March 2005 – ENGLAND v AZERBAIJAN at St James' Park

Half-time – 0–0

Full-time – 2–0: Gerrard (1–0), Beckham (2–0)

England: Robinson; G. Neville; Ashley Cole; R. Ferdinand (King); Terry; Gerrard; Beckham (Defoe); Lampard; Owen; Rooney (Dyer); J. Cole.

Azerbaijan: Kramarenko; Abdurahmanov; Amirbekov (V. Guliyev); Sadygov; Hajiyev; Hashimov; Bahshiev; Melikov; Kerimov; G. Gurbanov (Ponomarev); Nabiev (Ahtyamov).

3 September 2005 – WALES v ENGLAND at the Millennium Stadium

Half-time – 0–0

Full-time – 1–0: J. Cole (1–0)

Wales: Coyne; Page (Collins); Gabbidon; Partridge, Duffy; Davies (Earnshaw); Fletcher; C. Robinson (Koumas); Ricketts; Giggs; Hartson.

England: Robinson; Young; Carragher; R. Ferdinand; Ashley Cole; Gerrard (Richardson); Beckham; Lampard; Rooney; Wright-Phillips (Defoe); J. Cole (Hargreaves).

7 September 2005 – NORTHERN IRELAND v ENGLAND at Belfast

Half-time – 0–0

Full-time – 1–0: Healy (1–0)

Northern Ireland: Taylor; Baird; Capaldi; Hughes; Craigan; Davis; Gillespie; Johnson; Healy (Sproule); Quinn (Feeney); Elliott (Duff).

England: Robinson; Young; R. Ferdinand; Carragher; Ashley Cole; Lampard (Hargreaves); Beckham; Gerrard (Defoe); Rooney; Owen; Wright-Phillips (J. Cole).

8 October 2005 – ENGLAND v AUSTRIA at Old Trafford

Half-time – 1–0: Lampard pen. (1–0)

Full-time – 1–0

England: Robinson; Young; Terry; Campbell (R. Ferdinand); Carragher; Beckham; Gerrard; Lampard; J. Cole (King); Crouch; Owen (Richardson).

Austria: Macho; Dober; Stranzl; Scharner; Ibertsberger (Lasnik); Aufhauser; Schopp (Kuljic); Kiesenebner; Ivanschitz; Weissenberger (Sariyar); Linz.

12 October 2005 – ENGLAND v POLAND at Old Trafford

Half-time – 1–1: Owen (1–0), Frankowski (1–1)

Full-time – 2–1: Lampard (2–1)

England: Robinson; Young; Terry; R. Ferdinand; Carragher; Wright-Phillips (Crouch); Lampard; J. Cole (Smith); King; Rooney; Owen (Jenas).

Poland: Boruc; Jop; Baszcyznski; Bak; Zewlakow; Sobolewski (Radomski); Smolarek (Krzynowek); Lewandowski; Kosowski; Zurawski (Frankowski); Rasiak.

Other group results:
Northern Ireland 0 Poland 3; Azerbaijan 1 Wales 1; Wales 2 Northern Ireland 2; Austria 2 Azerbaijan 0; Austria 1 Poland 3; Azerbaijan 0 Northern Ireland 0; Northern Ireland 3 Austria 3; Wales 2 Poland 3; Poland 8 Azerbaijan 0; Wales 0 Austria 2; Austria 1 Wales 0; Poland 1 Northern Ireland 0; Azerbaijan 0 Poland 3; Northern Ireland 2 Azerbaijan 0; Poland 3 Austria 2; Poland 1 Wales 0; Azerbaijan 0 Austria 0; Northern Ireland 2 Wales 3; Austria 1 Northern Ireland 0; Wales 2 Azerbaijan 0.

World Cup Qualifying Group 6

	P	W	D	L	F	A	Pts
ENGLAND	10	8	1	1	17	5	25
Poland	10	8	0	2	27	9	24
Austria	10	4	3	3	14	12	15
Northern Ireland	10	2	3	5	10	17	9
Wales	10	2	2	6	10	15	8
Azerbaijan	10	0	3	7	1	21	3

6 TAKING ON EUROPE

England's European Championship Record

1964 EUROPEAN NATIONS CUP

First round, 1st leg
England 1 France 1

First round, 2nd leg
France 5 England 2 (aggregate: England 3 France 6)

1968 EUROPEAN NATIONS CUP

Group 8 qualifier results
Northern Ireland 0 England 2
England 5 Wales 1
England 2 Scotland 3
Wales 0 England 3
England 2 Northern Ireland 0
Scotland 1 England 1

Final qualifier group placings

	P	W	D	L	F	A	Pts
ENGLAND	6	4	1	1	15	5	9
Scotland	6	3	2	1	10	8	8
Wales	6	1	2	3	6	12	5
Northern Ireland	6	1	1	4	2	8	3

Quarter-finals, 1st leg
England 1 Spain 0

Quarter-finals, 2nd leg
Spain 1 England 2 (aggregate: England 3 Spain 1)

Semi-final
England 0 Yugoslavia 1

Third-place play-off
England 2 Soviet Union 0

1972 EUROPEAN NATIONS CUP

Group 3 qualifier results
Malta 0 England 1
England 3 Greece 0
England 5 Malta 0

Switzerland 2 England 3
England 1 Switzerland 1
Greece 0 England 2

Final qualifier group placings

	P	W	D	L	F	A	Pts
ENGLAND	6	5	1	0	15	3	11
Switzerland	6	4	1	1	12	5	9
Greece	6	1	1	4	3	8	3
Malta	6	0	1	5	2	16	1

Quarter-finals, 1st leg
England 1 West Germany 3

Quarter-finals, 2nd leg
West Germany 0 England 0 (aggregate: England 1 West Germany 3)

1976 EUROPEAN CHAMPIONSHIPS

Group 1 qualifier results
England 3 Czechoslovakia 0
England 0 Portugal 0
England 5 Cyprus 0
Cyprus 0 England 1
Czechoslovakia 2 England 1
Portugal 1 England 1

Final qualifier group placings

	P	W	D	L	F	A	Pts
Czechoslovakia	6	4	1	1	15	5	9
ENGLAND	6	3	2	1	11	3	8
Portugal	6	2	3	1	5	7	7
Cyprus	6	0	0	6	0	16	0

1980 EUROPEAN CHAMPIONSHIPS

Group 1 qualifier results
Denmark 3 England 4
Eire 1 England 1
England 4 Northern Ireland 0
Bulgaria 0 England 3
England 1 Denmark 0
Northern Ireland 1 England 5
England 2 Bulgaria 0
England 2 Eire 0

Final qualifier group placings

	P	W	D	L	F	A	Pts
ENGLAND	8	7	1	0	22	5	15
Northern Ireland	8	4	1	3	8	14	9
Eire	8	2	3	3	9	8	7
Bulgaria	8	2	1	5	6	14	5
Denmark	8	1	2	5	13	17	4

Group 2 final results
Belgium 1 England 1
Italy 1 England 0
England 2 Spain 1

Final table

	P	W	D	L	F	A	Pts
Belgium	3	1	2	0	3	2	4
Italy	3	1	2	0	1	0	4
ENGLAND	3	1	1	1	3	3	3
Spain	3	0	1	2	2	4	1

1984 EUROPEAN CHAMPIONSHIPS

Group 3 qualifier results
Denmark 2 England 2
Greece 0 England 3
England 9 Luxembourg 0
England 0 Greece 0
England 2 Hungary 0
England 0 Denmark 1
Hungary 0 England 3
Luxembourg 0 England 4

Final qualifier group placings

	P	W	D	L	F	A	Pts
Denmark	8	6	1	1	17	5	13
ENGLAND	8	5	2	1	23	3	12
Greece	8	3	2	3	8	10	8
Hungary	8	3	1	4	18	17	7
Luxembourg	8	0	0	8	5	36	0

1988 EUROPEAN CHAMPIONSHIPS

Group 4 qualifier results
England 3 Northern Ireland 0
England 2 Yugoslavia 0
Northern Ireland 0 England 2
Turkey 0 England 0
England 8 Turkey 0
Yugoslavia 1 England 4

Final qualifier group placings

	P	W	D	L	F	A	Pts
ENGLAND	6	5	1	0	19	1	11
Yugoslavia	6	4	0	2	13	9	8
Northern Ireland	6	1	1	4	2	10	3
Turkey	6	0	2	4	2	16	2

Group 2 final results
England 0 Eire 1
England 1 Holland 3
England 1 Soviet Union 3

Final table

	P	W	D	L	F	A	Pts
Soviet Union	3	2	1	0	5	2	5
Holland	3	2	0	1	4	2	4
Eire	3	1	1	1	2	2	1
ENGLAND	3	0	0	3	2	7	0

1992 EUROPEAN CHAMPIONSHIPS

Group 7 qualifier results
England 2 Poland 0
Eire 1 England 1
England 1 Eire 1
Turkey 0 England 1
England 1 Turkey 0
Poland 1 England 1

Final qualifier group placings

	P	W	D	L	F	A	Pts
ENGLAND	6	3	3	0	7	3	9
Eire	6	2	4	0	11	6	8
Poland	6	2	3	1	8	6	7
Turkey	6	0	0	6	1	14	0

Group 1 final results
Denmark 0 England 0
France 0 England 0
Sweden 2 England 1

Final table

	P	W	D	L	F	A	Pts
Sweden	3	2	1	0	4	2	5
Denmark	3	1	1	1	2	2	3
France	3	0	2	1	2	2	2
ENGLAND	3	0	2	1	1	2	2

1996 EUROPEAN CHAMPIONSHIPS

Group A final results
England 1 Switzerland 1
England 2 Scotland 0
England 4 Holland 1

Final table

	P	W	D	L	F	A	Pts
ENGLAND	3	2	1	0	7	2	7
Holland	3	1	1	1	3	4	4
Scotland	3	1	1	1	1	2	4
Switzerland	3	0	1	2	1	4	1

Quarter-finals
Spain 0 England 0
England won 4–2 on penalties

Semi-finals
Germany 1 England 1
Germany won 6–5 on penalties

2000 EUROPEAN CHAMPIONSHIPS

Group 5 qualifier results
Sweden 2 England 1
England 0 Bulgaria 0
Luxembourg 0 England 3
England 3 Poland 1
England 0 Sweden 0
Bulgaria 1 England 1
England 6 Luxembourg 0
Poland 0 England 0

Final qualifier group placings

	P	W	D	L	F	A	Pts
Sweden	8	7	1	0	10	1	22
ENGLAND	8	3	4	1	14	4	13
Poland	8	4	1	3	12	8	13
Bulgaria	8	2	2	4	6	8	8
Luxembourg	8	0	0	8	2	23	0

Play-offs, 1st leg
Scotland 0 England 2

Play-offs, 2nd leg
England 0 Scotland 1 (aggregate: England 2 Scotland 1)

Group A final results
Portugal 3 England 2
England 1 Germany 0
England 2 Romania 3

Final table

	P	W	D	L	F	A	Pts
Portugal	3	3	0	0	7	2	9
Romania	3	1	1	1	4	4	4
ENGLAND	3	1	0	2	5	6	3
Germany	3	0	1	2	1	5	1

2004 EUROPEAN CHAMPIONSHIPS

Group 7 qualifier results
Slovakia 1 England 2
England 2 Macedonia 2
Liechtenstein 0 England 2

England 2 Turkey 0
England 2 Slovakia 1
Macedonia 1 England 2
England 2 Liechtenstein 0
Turkey 0 England 0

Final qualifier group placings

	P	W	D	L	F	A	Pts
ENGLAND	8	6	2	0	14	5	20
Turkey	8	6	1	1	17	5	19
Slovakia	8	3	1	4	11	9	10
Macedonia	8	1	3	4	11	14	6
Luxembourg	8	0	1	7	2	22	1

Group B final results
France 2 England 1
England 3 Switzerland 0
Croatia 2 England 4

Final table

	P	W	D	L	F	A	Pts
France	3	2	1	0	7	4	7
ENGLAND	3	2	0	1	8	4	6
Croatia	3	0	2	1	4	6	2
Switzerland	3	0	1	2	1	6	1

Quarter-finals
Portugal 2 England 2
Portugal won 6–5 on penalties

APPENDIX

ENGLAND'S RECORD AGAINST THE HOME NATIONS

ENGLAND v SCOTLAND

P	W	D	L	F	A
110	45	24	41	192	169

Year	Venue	E	S
1872	Glasgow	0	0
1873	Kennington Oval	4	2
1874	Glasgow	1	2
1875	Kennington Oval	2	2
1876	Glasgow	0	3
1877	Kennington Oval	1	3
1878	Glasgow	2	7
1879	Kennington Oval	5	4
1880	Glasgow	4	5
1881	Kennington Oval	1	6
1882	Glasgow	1	5
1883	Sheffield	2	3
1884	Glasgow	0	1
1885	Kennington Oval	1	1
1886	Glasgow	1	1
1887	Blackburn	2	3
1888	Glasgow	5	0
1889	Kennington Oval	2	3
1890	Glasgow	1	1
1891	Blackburn	2	1
1892	Glasgow	4	1
1893	Richmond	5	2
1894	Glasgow	2	2
1895	Everton	3	0
1896	Glasgow	1	2
1897	Crystal Palace	1	2
1898	Glasgow	3	1
1899	Birmingham	2	1
1900	Glasgow	1	4
1901	Crystal Palace	2	2
1902	Birmingham	2	2
1903	Sheffield	1	2
1904	Glasgow	1	0
1905	Crystal Palace	1	0
1906	Glasgow	1	2
1907	Newcastle	1	1
1908	Glasgow	1	1
1909	Crystal Palace	2	0
1910	Glasgow	0	2
1911	Everton	1	1
1912	Glasgow	1	1
1913	Chelsea	1	0
1914	Glasgow	1	3
1920	Sheffield	5	4
1921	Glasgow	0	3
1922	Aston Villa	0	1
1923	Glasgow	2	2
1924	Wembley	1	1
1925	Glasgow	0	2
1926	Manchester	0	1
1927	Glasgow	2	1
1928	Wembley	1	5
1929	Glasgow	0	1
1930	Wembley	5	2
1931	Glasgow	0	2
1932	Wembley	3	0
1933	Glasgow	1	2
1934	Wembley	3	0
1935	Glasgow	0	2
1936	Wembley	1	1
1937	Glasgow	1	3
1938	Wembley	0	1
1939	Glasgow	2	1
1947	Wembley	1	1
1948	Glasgow	2	0
1949	Wembley	1	3
1950	Glasgow	1	0
1951	Wembley	2	3
1952	Glasgow	2	1
1953	Wembley	2	2
1954	Glasgow	4	2
1955	Wembley	7	2
1956	Glasgow	1	1
1957	Wembley	2	1
1958	Glasgow	4	0
1959	Wembley	1	0

1960	Glasgow	1	1
1961	Wembley	9	3
1962	Glasgow	0	2
1963	Wembley	1	2
1964	Glasgow	0	1
1965	Wembley	2	2
1966	Glasgow	4	3
1967	Wembley	2	3
1968	Glasgow	1	1
1969	Wembley	4	1
1970	Glasgow	0	0
1971	Wembley	3	1
1972	Glasgow	1	0
1973	Glasgow	5	0
1973	Wembley	1	0
1974	Glasgow	0	2
1975	Wembley	5	1
1976	Glasgow	1	2
1977	Wembley	1	2
1978	Glasgow	1	0
1979	Wembley	3	1
1980	Glasgow	2	0
1981	Wembley	0	1
1982	Glasgow	1	0
1983	Wembley	2	0
1984	Glasgow	1	1
1985	Glasgow	0	1
1986	Wembley	2	1
1987	Glasgow	0	0
1988	Wembley	1	0
1989	Glasgow	2	0
1996	Wembley	2	0
1999	Glasgow	2	0
1999	Wembley	0	1

ENGLAND v WALES

P	W	D	L	F	A
99	64	21	14	242	90

		E	W
1879	Kennington Oval	2	1
1880	Wrexham	3	2
1881	Blackburn	0	1
1882	Wrexham	3	5
1883	Kennington Oval	5	0
1884	Wrexham	4	0
1885	Blackburn	1	1
1886	Wrexham	3	1
1887	Kennington Oval	4	0

1888	Crewe	5	1
1889	Stoke	4	1
1890	Wrexham	3	1
1891	Sunderland	4	1
1892	Wrexham	2	0
1893	Stoke	6	0
1894	Wrexham	5	1
1895	Queen's Club	1	1
1896	Cardiff	9	1
1897	Sheffield	4	0
1898	Wrexham	3	0
1899	Bristol	4	0
1900	Cardiff	1	1
1901	Newcastle	6	0
1902	Wrexham	0	0
1903	Portsmouth	2	1
1904	Wrexham	2	2
1905	Liverpool	3	1
1906	Cardiff	1	0
1907	Fulham	1	1
1908	Wrexham	7	1
1909	Nottingham	2	0
1910	Cardiff	1	0
1911	Millwall	3	0
1912	Wrexham	2	0
1913	Bristol	4	3
1914	Cardiff	2	0
1920	Highbury	1	2
1921	Cardiff	0	0
1922	Liverpool	1	0
1923	Cardiff	2	2
1924	Blackburn	1	2
1925	Swansea	2	1
1926	Crystal Palace	1	3
1927	Wrexham	3	3
1927	Burnley	1	2
1928	Swansea	3	2
1929	Chelsea	6	0
1930	Wrexham	4	0
1931	Liverpool	3	1
1932	Wrexham	0	0
1933	Newcastle	1	2
1934	Cardiff	4	0
1936	Wolverhampton	1	2
1936	Cardiff	1	2
1937	Middlesbrough	2	1
1938	Cardiff	2	4
1946	Manchester	3	0
1947	Cardiff	3	0
1948	Aston Villa	1	0
1949	Cardiff	4	1

1950	Sunderland	4	2
1951	Cardiff	1	1
1952	Wembley	5	2
1953	Cardiff	4	1
1954	Wembley	3	2
1955	Cardiff	1	2
1956	Wembley	3	1
1957	Cardiff	4	0
1958	Aston Villa	2	2
1959	Cardiff	1	1
1960	Wembley	5	1
1961	Cardiff	1	1
1962	Wembley	4	0
1963	Cardiff	4	0
1964	Wembley	2	1
1965	Cardiff	0	0
1966	Wembley	5	1
1967	Cardiff	3	0
1969	Wembley	2	1
1970	Cardiff	1	1
1971	Wembley	0	0
1972	Cardiff	3	0
1972	Cardiff	1	0
1973	Wembley	1	1
1973	Wembley	3	0
1974	Cardiff	2	0
1975	Wembley	2	2
1976	Wrexham	2	1
1976	Cardiff	1	0
1977	Wembley	0	1
1978	Cardiff	3	1
1979	Wembley	0	0
1980	Wrexham	1	4
1981	Wembley	0	0
1982	Cardiff	1	0
1983	Wembley	2	1
1984	Wrexham	0	1
2004	Old Trafford	2	0
2005	Millennium Stadium	1	0

ENGLAND v N. IRELAND
(INC. IRELAND UP TO 1922)

P	W	D	L	F	A
98	75	16	7	323	81

		E	I
1882	Belfast	13	0
1883	Liverpool	7	0
1884	Belfast	8	1
1885	Manchester	4	0
1886	Belfast	6	1
1887	Sheffield	7	0
1888	Belfast	5	1
1889	Everton	6	1
1890	Belfast	9	1
1891	Wolverhampton	6	1
1892	Belfast	2	0
1893	Birmingham	6	1
1894	Belfast	2	2
1895	Derby	9	0
1896	Belfast	2	0
1897	Nottingham	6	0
1898	Belfast	3	2
1899	Sunderland	13	2
1900	Dublin	2	0
1901	Southampton	3	0
1902	Belfast	1	0
1903	Wolverhampton	4	0
1904	Belfast	3	1
1905	Middlesbrough	1	1
1906	Belfast	5	0
1907	Everton	1	0
1908	Belfast	3	1
1909	Bradford	4	0
1910	Belfast	1	1
1911	Derby	2	1
1912	Dublin	6	1
1913	Belfast	1	2
1914	Middlesbrough	0	3
1919	Belfast	1	1
1920	Sunderland	2	0
1921	Belfast	1	1
1922	West Bromwich	2	0
1923	Belfast	1	2
1924	Everton	3	1
1925	Belfast	0	0
1926	Liverpool	3	3
1927	Belfast	0	2
1928	Everton	2	1
1929	Belfast	3	0
1930	Sheffield	5	1
1931	Belfast	6	2
1932	Blackpool	1	0
1933	Belfast	3	0
1935	Everton	2	1
1935	Belfast	3	1
1936	Stoke	3	1
1937	Belfast	5	1
1938	Manchester	7	0
1946	Belfast	7	2

1947	Everton	2	2	1970	Wembley	3	1
1948	Belfast	6	2	1971	Belfast	1	0
1949	Manchester	9	2	1972	Wembley	0	1
1950	Belfast	4	1	1973	Everton	2	1
1951	Aston Villa	2	0	1974	Wembley	1	0
1952	Belfast	2	2	1975	Belfast	0	0
1953	Everton	3	1	1976	Wembley	4	0
1954	Belfast	2	0	1977	Belfast	2	1
1955	Wembley	3	0	1978	Wembley	1	0
1956	Belfast	1	1	1979	Wembley	4	0
1957	Wembley	2	3	1979	Belfast	2	0
1958	Belfast	3	3	1979	Belfast	5	1
1959	Wembley	2	1	1980	Wembley	1	1
1960	Belfast	5	2	1982	Wembley	4	0
1961	Wembley	1	1	1983	Belfast	0	0
1962	Belfast	3	1	1984	Wembley	1	0
1963	Wembley	8	3	1985	Belfast	1	0
1964	Belfast	4	3	1985	Wembley	0	0
1965	Wembley	2	1	1986	Wembley	3	0
1966	Belfast	2	0	1987	Belfast	2	0
1967	Wembley	2	0	2005	Old Trafford	4	0
1969	Belfast	3	1	2005	Belfast	0	1

ENGLAND'S RECORD AGAINST ALL NATIONS

	P	W	D	L	F	A
Albania	4	4	0	0	12	1
Argentina*	14	6	4	3	21	15
Australia	6	3	2	1	6	5
Austria	17	9	4	4	57	27
Azerbaijan	2	2	0	0	3	0
Belgium	20	14	5	1	69	25
Bohemia	1	1	0	0	4	0
Brazil	21	3	8	10	18	29
Bulgaria	8	4	4	0	9	2
Cameroon	4	3	1	0	9	4
Canada	1	1	0	0	1	0
Chile	5	2	2	1	4	3
China	1	1	0	0	3	0
CIS	1	0	1	0	2	2
Colombia	5	3	2	0	10	3
Croatia	3	2	1	0	7	3
Cyprus	2	2	0	0	6	0
Czechoslovakia	12	7	3	2	25	15
Czech Republic	1	1	0	0	2	0
Denmark	17	10	4	3	33	18
East Germany	4	3	1	0	7	3
Ecuador	1	1	0	0	2	0
Egypt	2	2	0	0	5	0
Eire*	14	5	6	2	19	12

* one match was abandoned – no result

	P	W	D	L	F	A
FIFA	1	1	0	0	3	0
Finland	11	9	2	0	36	7
France	26	16	4	6	65	32
Georgia	2	2	0	0	4	0
Germany	9	4	2	3	20	12
Greece	8	6	2	0	19	3
Holland	16	5	7	4	23	18
Hungary	20	13	2	5	51	28
Iceland	2	1	1	0	7	2
Ireland (pre-1923)	37	30	5	2	157	26
Israel	2	1	1	0	2	1
Italy	22	7	6	9	28	26
Japan	2	1	1	0	3	2
Kuwait	1	1	0	0	1	0
Liechtenstein	2	2	0	0	4	0
Luxembourg	9	9	0	0	47	3
Macedonia	2	1	1	0	4	3
Malaysia	1	1	0	0	4	2
Malta	3	3	0	0	8	1
Mexico	8	5	1	2	20	3
Moldova	2	2	0	0	7	0
Morocco	2	1	1	0	1	0
New Zealand	2	2	0	0	3	0
Nigeria	2	1	1	0	1	0
Northern Ireland	61	45	11	5	166	55
Norway	10	5	3	2	26	7
Paraguay	2	2	0	0	7	0
Peru	2	1	0	1	5	4
Poland	17	10	6	1	27	10
Portugal	21	9	9	3	45	25
Rest of Europe	1	0	1	0	4	4
Rest of the World	1	1	0	0	2	1
Romania	11	2	6	3	10	10
San Marino	2	2	0	0	13	1
Saudi Arabia	2	0	2	0	1	1
Scotland	110	45	24	41	192	169
Serbia & Montenegro	1	1	0	0	2	1
Slovakia	2	2	0	0	4	2
South Africa	2	2	0	0	4	2
South Korea	1	0	1	0	1	1
Soviet Union	11	5	3	3	19	13
Spain	20	11	3	6	38	21
Sweden	20	6	8	6	30	24
Switzerland	19	12	4	3	45	15
Tunisia	2	1	1	0	3	1
Turkey	10	8	2	0	31	0
Ukraine	2	2	0	0	5	0
Uruguay	9	2	3	4	8	12
USA	8	6	0	2	33	8

Wales	99	64	21	14	242	90
West Germany	16	7	3	6	24	19
Yugoslavia	14	5	5	4	23	20

Complete Record

Played	834
Won	469
Drawn	201
Lost	162
Abandoned	2
Goals Scored	1862
Goals Conceded	852

Correct to end of November 2005

TOP 50 APPEARANCES

As with League football, Peter Shilton takes the top spot - though a rivalry with Ray Clemence, who gained 61 caps between 1972 and 1983, cost Shilton the chance to stake an even more commanding lead. He was twenty-one years old when awarded his first cap against East Germany, and forty when he won his last.

Though Shilton's tenure will undoubtedly last a little longer, both David Beckham (86) and Michael Owen (75) are hot on his heels.

	Player	Career Dates	Total Appearances
1	Peter Shilton	1970–90	125
2	Bobby Moore	1962–73	108
3	Bobby Charlton	1958–70	106
4	Billy Wright	1946–59	105
5	Bryan Robson	1980–91	90
6=	Kenny Sansom	1979–88	86
	David Beckham	1996–	86
8	Ray Wilkins	1976–86	84
9	Gary Lineker	1984–92	80
10	John Barnes	1983–95	79
11	Stuart Pearce	1987–99	78
12=	Terry Butcher	1980–90	77
	Gary Neville	1995–	77
14	Tom Finney	1946–58	76
15=	David Seaman	1989–2002	75
	Michael Owen	1998–	75
17	Gordon Banks	1963–72	73
18	Alan Ball	1965–75	72
19	Martin Peters	1966–74	67
20=	Tony Adams	1987–2000	66
	Sol Campbell	1996–	66
	Paul Scholes	1997–	66

23	Dave V. Watson	1974–82	65
24=	Ray Wilson	1960–68	63
	Kevin Keegan	1972–82	63
	Alan Shearer	1992–2000	63
27=	Emlyn Hughes	1969–80	62
	Chris Waddle	1985–91	62
	David Platt	1989–96	62
30	Ray Clemence	1972–83	61
31=	Peter Beardsley	1986–96	59
	Des Walker	1988–93	59
33=	Jimmy Greaves	1959–67	57
	Paul Gascoigne	1988–98	57
	Gareth Southgate	1995–	57
36	Johnny Haynes	1954–62	56
37	Stanley Matthews	1934–57	54
38=	Glenn Hoddle	1979–88	53
	Paul Ince	1992–2000	53
40=	Trevor Francis	1977–86	52
	Phil Neville	1996–	52
42	Teddy Sheringham	1993–2002	51
43	Phil Neal	1976–83	50
44=	Ron Flowers	1955–66	49
	Geoff Hurst	1966–72	49
46=	Jimmy Dickinson	1949–56	48
	Colin Bell	1968–75	48
48	Trevor Brooking	1974–82	47
49=	Mick Channon	1972–77	46
	M. Gary Stevens	1985–92	46

TOP 50 GOALSCORERS

No one player has yet scored a half-century of goals for England, and, given the intensity of the modern game, it looks less likely as time passes – though Michael Owen and Wayne Rooney may think otherwise.

Gary Lineker was still in with a shout of at least equalling Bobby Charlton's record before manager Graham Taylor controversially withdrew him from his final match against Sweden.

In terms of strike rate, dividing goals scored by games played, the leaders of the pack are George Camsell, Vivian Woodward, George Hilsdon, Steve Bloomer and Fred Dewhurst. It should be remembered, though, that substitute appearances are included as full games in these totals.

	Player	**Career Dates**	**Total**	**Games Played**	**Strike Rate**
1	Bobby Charlton	1958–70	49	106	0.46
2	Gary Lineker	1984–92	48	80	0.60
3	Jimmy Greaves	1959–67	44	57	0.77
4	Michael Owen	1998–	35	75	0.47
5=	Tom Finney	1946–58	30	76	0.39

	Nat Lofthouse	1950–58	30	33	0.91
	Alan Shearer	1992–2000	30	63	0.48
8	Vivian Woodward	1903–11	29	23	1.26
9	Steve Bloomer	1895–1907	28	23	1.22
10	David Platt	1989–96	27	62	0.44
11	Bryan Robson	1980–91	26	90	0.29
12	Geoff Hurst	1966–72	24	49	0.49
13	Stan Mortensen	1947–53	23	25	0.92
14	Tommy Lawton	1938–48	22	23	0.96
15=	Mick Channon	1972–77	21	46	0.46
	Kevin Keegan	1972–82	21	63	0.33
17	Martin Peters	1966–74	20	67	0.30
18=	Dixie Dean	1927–32	18	16	1.13
	George Camsell	1929–36	18	9	2.00
	Johnny Haynes	1954–62	18	56	0.32
	Roger Hunt	1962–69	18	34	0.53
22=	Tommy Taylor	1953–57	16	19	0.84
	Tony Woodcock	1978–86	16	42	0.38
	David Beckham	1996–	16	86	0.19
25	Tinsley Lindley	1886–91	15	13	1.15
26=	George Hilsdon	1907–09	14	8	1.75
	Paul Scholes	1997–	14	66	0.21
28=	Bobby Smith	1960–63	13	15	0.87
	Martin Chivers	1971–73	13	24	0.54
	Paul Mariner	1977–85	13	35	0.37
31=	Charles Bambridge	1879–87	12	18	0.67
	John Goodall	1888–98	12	14	0.86
	Gilbert Smith	1893–1901	12	20	0.60
	Cliff Bastin	1931–38	12	21	0.57
	Trevor Francis	1977–86	12	52	0.23
36=	Fred Dewhurst	1886–89	11	9	1.22
	Stanley Matthews	1934–57	11	54	0.20
	Wilf Mannion	1946–51	11	26	0.42
	Bryan Douglas	1957–63	11	36	0.31
	John Barnes	1983–95	11	79	0.14
	Teddy Sheringham	1993–2002	11	51	0.22
	Wayne Rooney	2003–	11	28	0.39
43=	Eric Brook	1929–37	10	18	0.56
	Jackie Milburn	1948–55	10	13	0.76
	Dennis Wilshaw	1953–56	10	12	0.83
	Ron Flowers	1955–66	10	49	0.20
	Francis Lee	1968–72	10	27	0.37
	Allan Clarke	1970–75	10	19	0.52
	Paul Gascoigne	1988–98	10	57	0.18
	Frank Lampard Jnr	1999–	10	38	0.26

INDEX OF PLAYERS

On pages 19–144 the players are listed chronologically, in order of appearance. This index provides an alphabetical list of players, and should prove useful when searching for individual players by surname.